Cover art: *Kitchen Ball at White Sulphur Springs in Virginia,* by Christian Mayr, 1838 / De Agostini Picture Library / Bridgeman Images

About the Cover Image

Kitchen Ball at White Sulphur Springs in Virginia, by Christian Mayr, 1838

In the nineteenth century, wealthy white southerners often spent summer months in mountain areas to avoid the heat and humidity of the lowlands. They socialized with friends and family and received medical treatments at mineral spas. The hotel and cottages at White Sulphur Springs, Virginia, housed slave-owning families as well as their enslaved and free black domestic workers. German artist Christian Friedrich Mayr visited the spa in 1838, five years after migrating to the United States. He had spent time in South Carolina painting portraits of elite Southerners, but in "Kitchen Ball," he captures a rare moment of African Americans socializing away from white supervision. Avoiding the crude caricatures of blacks prominent in this period, Mayr portrays his subjects as dignified and graceful. He also depicts the diverse skin colors and facial features that illuminate the complex history of sexual abuse and miscegenation in early American history.

American River College Library
4700 College Oak Drive
Sacramento, CA 95841

VALUE EDITION

Exploring American Histories

A SURVEY

Third Edition

Volume I: To 1877

Nancy A. Hewitt
Rutgers University

Steven F. Lawson
Rutgers University

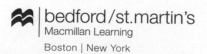 bedford/st.martin's
Macmillan Learning

Boston | New York

To Mary and Charles Takacs, Florence and Hiram Hewitt,
Sarah and Abraham Parker, Lena and Ben Lawson,
who made our American histories possible.

For Bedford/St. Martin's

Vice President, Editorial, Macmillan Learning Humanities: Edwin Hill
Publisher for History: Michael Rosenberg
Senior Executive Editor for History: William J. Lombardo
Executive Development Managers: Laura Arcari, Maura Shea
Senior Content Project Manager: Kerri A. Cardone
Editorial Assistant: Stephanie Sosa
Media Editors: Tess Fletcher, Mollie Chandler
Senior Workflow Content Manager: Lisa McDowell
Senior Production Supervisor: Robert Cherry
Marketing Manager: Melissa Rodriguez
Copy Editor: Harold Johnson
Cartography: Mapping Specialists, Ltd.
Photo Researchers: Naomi Kornhauser, Christine Buese
Permissions Editor: Kalina Ingham
Art Director: Diana Blume
Text Design: Jerilyn Bockorick, Cenveo Publisher Services
Cover Design: William Boardman
Cover Art/Cover Photo: Kitchen Ball at White Sulphur Springs in Virginia, by Christian Mayr,
    1838 / De Agostini Picture Library / Bridgeman Images
Composition: Lumina Datamatics, Inc.
Printing and Binding: LSC Communications, Crawfordsville

Copyright © 2019, 2017, 2013 by Bedford/St. Martin's.

All rights reserved. No part of this book may be reproduced, stored in a retrieval system, or transmitted
in any form or by any means, electronic, mechanical, photocopying, recording, or otherwise, except as
may be expressly permitted by the applicable copyright statutes or in writing by the Publisher.

Manufactured in the United States of America.

1   2   3   4   5   6   23   22   21   20   19   18

For information, write: Bedford/St. Martin's, 75 Arlington Street, Boston, MA 02116
    (617-399-4000)

ISBN-13: 978-1-3191-0649-2 (Combined Edition, Value)
ISBN-13: 978-1-3191-0652-2 (Volume 1, Value)
ISBN-13: 978-1-3191-0655-3 (Volume 2, Value)

Acknowledgments
Art acknowledgments and copyrights appear on the same page as the art selections they cover.

Preface
Why This Book This Way?

We are delighted to publish the third Value Edition of *Exploring American Histories*. The Value Edition provides our signature emphasis on the diverse histories of the United States in a two-color, trade-sized format at a low price. Featuring pedagogical tools, the Value Edition continues to make a broad and diverse American history accessible to a new generation of students and instructors interested in a more engaged learning and teaching style. In this third edition, we have updated the narrative, expanded the map program, placed a greater emphasis throughout the book on interpretation and analysis, and offer new ways to engage students in active learning and assess their progress with affordable and easy-to-use digital tools.

Narrative Approach: Diverse Stories

Recent historical scholarship has transformed our vision of the past, most notably by dramatically increasing the range of people historians study, and thus deepening and complicating traditional understandings of change over time. The new research has focused particularly on gender, race, ethnicity, class, and region and historians have produced landmark work in women's history, African American history, American Indian history, Latino history, Asian American history, labor history, and histories of the West and the South.

Throughout the narrative we acknowledge recent scholarship by highlighting the theme of diversity and recognizing the American past as a series of interwoven stories made by a great variety of historical actors. We do this within a strong national framework that allows our readers to see how the numerous stories fit together and to understand why they matter. Our approach to diversity also allows us to balance the role of individual agency with larger structural forces as we push readers to consider the many forces that create historical change. Each chapter opens with **Comparing American Histories**, a pair of biographies that showcase individuals who experienced and influenced events in a particular period, and then returns to them throughout the chapter to strengthen the connections and highlight their place in the larger picture. These biographies cover both well-known Americans—such as Daniel Shays, Frederick Douglass, Andrew Carnegie, and Eleanor Roosevelt—and those who never gained fame or fortune—such as the Cherokee chief John Ross, activist Amy Post, labor organizer Luisa Moreno, and World War II internee Fred Korematsu. Introducing such a broad range of biographical subjects illuminates the many ways that individuals shaped and were shaped by historical events. This strategy also makes visible throughout the text the intersections where history from the top down meets history from the bottom up, and the relationships between social and political histories and economic, cultural, and diplomatic developments.

Helping Students Understand the Narrative

We know that students need help making sense of their reading. As instructors, we have had students complain that they cannot figure out what's important in the textbooks we assign. For many of our students, especially those just out of high school, their college history survey textbook is likely the most difficult book they have ever encountered. Students come to the U.S. history survey with different levels of preparation. We understand the challenges our students face, so in addition to the extensive sources program, we have included the following pedagogical features designed to help students get the most from the narrative:

♦ **Learning Objectives** in the chapter openers prepare students to read the chapter with clear goals in mind.

♦ Clear **chapter overview** and **conclusions** preview and summarize the chapters to help students identify main developments.

♦ **Review and Relate** questions help students focus on main themes and concepts presented in each major section of the chapter.

♦ **Key terms** in boldface highlight important content. All terms are explained in the narrative as well as defined in a glossary at the end of the book.

♦ A full-page **Chapter Review** lets students review key terms, important concepts, and notable events.

New Coverage and Updates to the Narrative

As a consequence of the constructive feedback we have received from many reviewers, in this third edition we present an even more rounded view of the history of the United States.

Enriched Diversity and Increased Focus on the West. We continue to pay significant attention to African Americans and women throughout the text and to expand coverage on the histories of American Indians, Hispanic and Latino Americans, and Asian Americans. We have not confined our discussion of these subjects to a few chapters, but we have placed them throughout the book and integrated them into the narrative. For the third edition, in Volume 1, there is updated information on the peopling of the Americas in chapter 1 as well as greater coverage of native peoples' response to the Spanish conquest; additional attention to Indian-French encounters in chapters 3 and 4; expanded discussion of the roles of native peoples in the late colonial and revolutionary eras in chapters 5 and 6 and in the early nineteenth century in chapter 11. In Volume 2, we have updated the struggles of American Indians in chapter 15, which covers Westward expansion. We have also added new material on Mexican Americans and immigration in the 1920s (chapter 21) and Native Americans in relationship to World War II (chapter 23) and the 1960s (chapter 26). In addition, the impact of the closing of the western frontier in the 1890s on U.S. imperialism is explored in chapter 20, and the political influence of the modern West is discussed in chapter 28 with respect to rising conservatism. With these additions, the American West appears in nearly every chapter.

Updated and Expanded Coverage. We have also absorbed the most recent scholarship to ensure that the most useful and accurate textbook is placed in the hands of students. In addition to more expansive attention to regional, racial, and ethnic diversity, we revised our approach to a number of other historical developments. Chapter 1 once again incorporates the most recent research on the settlement of the Americas while chapter 2 adds coverage of the experiences of a black indentured servant. Chapter 4 addresses transatlantic print culture and the complex ways that both Enlightenment thought and religious revivals shaped popular protests and politics, while chapter 5 discusses more fully the tensions among colonists over British versus American identities and loyalties. The sources of anti-authoritarian and anti-British ideas are explored in more detail in chapter 6 while the discussion of Romanticism as well as religious revitalization is expanded in chapter 8. The environment is given greater coverage in chapters 9 and 10. Chapter 10 also adds new material on the market revolution and its effects on middle-class and working-class families as well as a new Guided Analysis based on the 1850 federal census. Chapter 16 on industrial America shows how the growth of large-scale business organizations fostered the expansion of a managerial class as well as the creation of new middle-class clerical jobs for both men and women. There is new material in chapter 23 on the role played by female codebreakers during World War II as well as on the innovative military strategy of "island-hopping" in the Pacific theater. The brutal treatment of Allied prisoners of war by the Japanese military also has been added to this chapter. One story rarely told appears in chapter 25 on the 1950s. The courageous efforts of an African American family to integrate suburban Levittown, Pennsylvania, are described and placed in the context of racial conflicts in the North. Likewise, chapter 26 on the 1960s makes an often overlooked connection between the moderate Republican President Dwight Eisenhower and the young radicals of the Students for a Democratic Society in challenging the military-industrial complex.

New Maps and Visuals. We have placed additional maps throughout the text to give students even more opportunity to learn how to read and think about these important historical tools. In Volume 1, we have added maps on the West Indies and Carolina in the Seventeenth Century (chapter 2), Religious Diversity in 1750 (chapter 4), and the Underground Railroad (chapter 10). In Volume 2, we have added maps on the Great Railroad Strike of 1877 (chapter 17), the immigrant population as of 1910 (chapter 18), the location of national parks during the Progressive era (chapter 19), European alliances during World War I (chapter 20), the shift from rural to urban population in the 1920s (chapter 21), the Dust Bowl during the Great Depression (chapter 22), and conflict between the U.S. and Cuba in the early 1960s (chapter 26). We have also changed about one-third of the illustrations accompanying the text from the previous edition.

Modification to Learning Objectives. We have reviewed the **Learning Objectives** for each chapter in order to strengthen them. In doing so, we have focused more on stimulating student thinking about the key issues around which each chapter is organized. We are attempting to get students to practice some of the skills used by historians: description, identification, explanation, analysis, and evaluation. To promote interpretation and analysis, we have added questions to all figure captions throughout the book.

Adjustments to Chapter Organization and Focus. Based on reviewers' comments, we also reframed and re-organized several chapters. In Volume 1, chapters 10 and 11 have been flipped. Students are now introduced to the market revolution and social movements, including abolition, in the North in chapter 10, **(Social and**

Cultural Ferment in the North, 1820–1850). Chapter 11 (Slavery Expands South and West) then focuses on the expansion of slavery and its effects on regional development, the national economy and politics, and the daily lives of southern blacks and whites. Chapter 27 (The Swing toward Conservatism, 1968–1980) and chapter 28 (The Triumph of Conservatism, the End of the Cold War, and the Rise of the New World Order, 1980–1992) have been reorganized along chronological lines to reduce the overlap in time periods that previously existed. Chapter 27 now traces domestic and foreign affairs primarily during the 1970s. In reorganizing this chapter, we have replaced the opening Comparing American Histories biography of Anita Hill, who gained public attention in the 1980s, with that of Louise Day Hicks, the Boston antibusing leader who reached national prominence in the 1970s. We have rearranged chapter 28 to cover domestic and global events through the 1980s. In this way, we are offering students a sharper understanding of the interplay of events inside the U.S. with those on the world stage.

The final chapter of a history textbook is necessarily and continuously evolving, and for this edition we have added material on the extremely divisive 2016 presidential election and Donald Trump's victory over Hillary Clinton. This chapter now covers President Trump's first year in office and his efforts to roll back the accomplishments of his predecessor, Barack Obama. The new material traces the rise of the reactionary alt-right and its appeal, to racial, ethnic, and gender grievances as well as the manipulation of digital social media in shaping the results. This updated chapter further explores revelations about Russian efforts to interfere in the election and U.S. responses to them. Also covered is the rise of the #MeToo movement consisting of an extraordinary number of women coming forward to voice widespread experience with sexual harassment in the workplace and elsewhere. While revelations during the campaign of Trump's inappropriate sexual behavior in the past stunned some Americans, it was testimonies about similar behavior among movie moguls, actors, television personalities, and other politicians that sparked a social movement. These events are still unfolding and the new additions are intended to provide students a framework for understanding these controversial issues as they evolve.

Promoting Active Learning in the Digital Age

As all instructors know, students can often "do the assignment" or read the required chapter and yet have little understanding of it when they come to class. The problem, frequently, is passive studying—a quick once-over, perhaps some highlighting of the text—but little sustained involvement with the material. A central pedagogical problem in all teaching is how to encourage more active, engaged styles of learning. We want to enable students to manipulate the information of the book, using its ideas and data to answer questions, to make comparisons, to draw conclusions, to criticize assumptions, and to infer implications that are not explicitly disclosed in the text itself.

Exploring American Histories seeks to promote active learning in various ways. Most obviously, the primary and secondary sources in the companion reader **Thinking through Sources for Exploring American Histories** (also available on LaunchPad) invite students to engage actively with documents and images alike, assisted by abundant questions to guide that engagement.

In addition, whenever an instructor assigns the **LaunchPad e-Book** (which can be bundled for free with the print book), students have at their disposal all the resources of the comprehensive print text (*Exploring American Histories: A Survey with Sources*), including its special features and its primary and secondary sources. But they also gain access to **LearningCurve**, an online adaptive learning tool that helps students actively rehearse what they have read and foster a deeper understanding and retention of the material. With this adaptive quizzing, students accumulate points toward a target score as they go, giving the interaction a game-like feel. Feedback for incorrect responses explains why the answer is incorrect and directs students back to the text to review before they attempt to answer the question again. The end result is a better understanding of the key elements of the text. Instructors who actively assign LearningCurve report that their students come to class prepared for discussion and their students enjoy using it. In addition, LearningCurve's reporting feature allows instructors to quickly diagnose which concepts students are struggling with so they can adjust lectures and activities accordingly.

Further opportunities for active learning are available with the special online activities accompanying *Thinking through Sources for Exploring American Histories* in **LaunchPad**. When required by instructors, the wrap-around pedagogy that accompanies the sources virtually ensures active learning. These activities supply a distinctive and sophisticated pedagogy of self-grading exercises that help students not only understand the sources but also think critically about them. More specifically, a short **quiz after each source** offers students the opportunity to check their understanding of materials that often derive from quite distant times and places. Some questions focus on audience, purpose, point of view, limitations, or context, while others challenge students to draw conclusions about the source or to compare one source with another. And a **Draw Conclusions from the Evidence activity** challenges students to assess whether a specific piece of evidence drawn from the sources supports or challenges a stated conclusion. Collectively these assignments create an active learning environment where reading with a purpose is reinforced by immediate feedback and support. This feedback for each rejoinder creates an active learning environment where students are rewarded for reaching the correct answer through their own process of investigation. LaunchPad is thus a rich asset for instructors who want to support students in all settings, from traditional lectures to "flipped" classrooms.

For instructors who need a mobile and accessible option for delivering adaptive quizzing with the narrative alone, Macmillan's new **Achieve Read & Practice** e-Book platform offers an exceptionally easy-to-use and affordable option. This simple product pairs the Value Edition with the power of LearningCurve's quizzing, all in a format that students can use wherever they go. Available for the first time with this edition, Achieve Read & Practice's interactive e-Book, adaptive quizzing, and gradebook are built with an intuitive interface that can be read on mobile devices and are fully accessible and available at an affordable price.

To learn more about the benefits of LearningCurve, LaunchPad, Achieve Read & Practice, and the different versions to package with these digital tools, see the Versions and Supplements section on page xv.

Acknowledgments

We wish to thank the talented scholars and teachers who were kind enough to give their time and knowledge to help us with our revision, as well as those who provided advice in preparation for previous editions. Historians who provided special insight for the third edition include the following:

Rob Alderson, *Perimeter College at Georgia State University*

Chad Gregory, *Tri-County Technical College*

Larry Grubbs, *Georgia State University*

Don Knox, *Wayland Baptist University*

Leslie Leighton, *Georgia State University*

Amani Marshall, *Georgia State University*

Ricky Moser, *Kilgore College*

David Soll, *University of Wisconsin, Eau Claire*

Ramon Veloso, *Palomar College*

We are also grateful to those who provided ideas and suggestions previous editions:

Benjamin Allen, *South Texas College*; Daniel Allen, *Trinity Valley Community College*; Leann Almquist, *Middle Georgia State University*; Christine Anderson, *Xavier University*; Uzoamaka Melissa C. Anyiwo, *Curry College*; Rebecca Arnfeld, *California State University, Sacramento*; David Arnold, *Columbia Basin College*; Brian Alnutt, *Northampton Community College*; Anthony A. Ball, *Housatonic Community College*; Terry A. Barnhart, *Eastern Illinois University*; John Belohlavek, *University of South Florida*; Edwin Benson, *North Harford High School*; Paul Berk, *Christian Brothers University*; Deborah L. Blackwell, *Texas A&M International University*; Jeff Bloodworth, *Gannon University*; Carl Bon Tempo, *University at Albany–SUNY*; Thomas Born, *Blinn College*; Margaret Bramlett, *St. Andrews Episcopal High School*; Martha Jane Brazy, *University of South Alabama*; Lauren K. Bristow, *Collin College*; Tsekani Browne, *Duquesne University*; Jon L. Brudvig, *Dickinson State University*; Richard Buckelew, *Bethune-Cookman University*; Timothy Buckner, *Troy University*; Dave Bush, *Shasta College*; Monica Butler, *Seminole State College of Florida*; Barbara Calluori, *Montclair State University*; Julia Schiavone Camacho, *The University of Texas at El Paso*; Jacqueline Campbell, *Francis Marion University*; Amy Canfield, *Lewis-Clark State College*; Michael Cangemi, *Binghamton University*; Roger Carpenter, *University of Louisiana, Monroe*; Dominic Carrillo, *Grossmont College*; Mark R. Cheathem, *Cumberland University*; Keith Chu, *Bergen Community College*; Laurel A. Clark, *University of Hartford*; Myles L. Clowers, *San Diego City College*; Remalian Cocar, *Georgia Gwinnett College*; Lori Coleman, *Tunxis Community College*; Wilbert E. Corprew, *SUNY Broome*; Hamilton Cravens, *Iowa State University*; Audrey Crawford, *Houston Community College*; Vanessa Crispin-Peralta, *Moorpark College*; John Crum, *University of Delaware*; David Cullen, *Collin College*; Gregory K. Culver, *Austin Peay State University*; Alex G. Cummins, *St. Johns River State College*; Robert Chris Davis, *Lone Star College – Kingwood*; Susanne Deberry-Cole, *Morgan State University*; Julian J. DelGaudio, *Long Beach City College*; Patricia Norred Derr, *Kutztown University*; Thomas Devine *California State University, Northridge*; Tom Dicke, *Missouri State University*; Andy Digh, *Mercer University*; Gary Donato, *Massachusetts Bay Community College*; John Donoghue, *Loyola University Chicago*; Timothy Draper, *Waubonsee Community College*; David Dzurec, *University of Scranton*; Susan Eckelmann, *University of Tennessee, Chattanooga*; George Edgar, *Modesto Junior College*; Keith Edgerton, *Montana State University Billings*; Taulby Edmondson, *Virginia Tech*; Ashton Ellett, *University of Georgia*;

Blake Ellis, *Lone Star College*; Christine Erickson, *Indiana University–Purdue University Fort Wayne*; Keona K. Ervin, *University of Missouri*; Todd Estes, *Oakland University*; Gabrielle Everett, *Jefferson College*; Julie Fairchild, *Sinclair Community College*; Robert Glen Findley, *Odessa College*; Randy Finley, *Georgia Perimeter College*; Tiffany Fink, *Hardin-Simmons University*; Kirsten Fischer, *University of Minnesota*; Michelle Fishman-Cross, *College of Staten Island*; Roger Flynn, *TriCounty Technical College*; Jeffrey Forret, *Lamar University*; Jonathan Foster, *Great Basin College*; Kristen Foster, *Marquette University*; Sarah Franklin, *University of North Alabama*; Michael Frawley, *University of Texas of the Permian Basin*; Susan Freeman, *Western Michigan University*; Nancy Gabin, *Purdue University*; Kevin Gannon, *Grand View University*; Benton Gates, *Indiana University–Purdue University Fort Wayne*; Bruce Geelhoed, *Ball State University*; Mark Gelfand, *Boston College*; Robert Genter, *Nassau Community College*; Jason George, *The Bryn Mawr School*; Judith A. Giesberg, *Villanova University*; Dana Goodrich, *Northwest Vista College*; Sherry Ann Gray, *Mid-South Community College*; Patrick Griffin, *University of Notre Dame*; Audrey Grounds, *University of South Florida*; Abbie Grubb, *San Jacinto College - South*; Kenneth Grubb, *Wharton County Junior College*; Aaron Gulyas, *Mott Community College*; Scott Gurman, *Northern Illinois University*; Melanie Gustafson, *University of Vermont*; Ashley Haines, *Mt. San Antonio College*; Dennis Halpin, *Virginia Tech*; Hunter Hampton, *University of Missouri*; Tona Hangen, *Worcester State University*; Brian Hart, *Del Mar College*; Paul Hart, *Texas State University*; Paul Harvey, *University of Colorado Colorado Springs*; Stephen Henderson, *William Penn University*; Kimberly Hernandez, *University of Wisconsin-Milwaukee*; Lacey A. Holley-McCann, *Columbia State Community College*; Woody Holton, *University of Richmond*; Vilja Hulden, *University of Arizona*; Creed Hyatt, *Lehigh Carbon Community College*; Colette A. Hyman, *Winona State University*; Brenda Jackson-Abernathy, *Belmont University*; Joe Jaynes, *Collin College*; Troy R. Johnson, *California State University, Long Beach*; Shelli Jordan-Zirkle, *Shoreline Community College*; Stephen Katz, *Community College of Philadelphia*; Lesley Kauffman, *San Jacinto College-Central*; Jennifer Kelly, *The University of Texas at Austin*; Kelly Kennington, *Auburn University*; Andrew E. Kersten, *University of Wisconsin–Green Bay*; Tina M. Kibbe, *Lamar University*; Melanie Kiechle, *Virginia Tech*; Janilyn M. Kocher, *Richland Community College*; Max Krochmal, *Duke University*; Peggy Lambert, *Lone Star College*; Stephanie Lamphere, *Sierra College*; Jennifer R. Lang, *Delgado Community College*; Todd Laugen, *Metropolitan State University of Denver*; Carolyn J. Lawes, *Old Dominion University*; John Leazer, *Carthage College*; Marianne Leeper, *Trinity Valley Community College*; Alan Lehmann, *Blinn College – Brenham*; John S. Leiby, *Paradise Valley Community College*; Mitchell Lerner, *The Ohio State University*; Carole N. Lester, *University of Texas at Dallas*; Amanda Littauer, *Northern Illinois University*; Matthew Loayza, *Minnesota State University, Mankato*; Gabriel J. Loiacono, *University of Wisconsin Oshkosh*; Carmen Lopez, *Miami Dade College*; Robert Lyle, *University of North Georgia*; John F. Lyons, *Joliet Junior College*; Lorie Maltby, *Henderson Community College*; Christopher Manning, *Loyola University Chicago*; Amani Marshall, *Georgia State University*; Phil Martin, *San Jacinto College - South*; David Mason, *Georgia Gwinnett College*; Marty D. Matthews, *North Carolina State University*; Eric Mayer, *Victor Valley College*; Suzanne K. McCormack, *Community College of Rhode Island*; David McDaniel, *Marquette University*; J. Kent McGaughy, *Houston Community College, Northwest*; Alan McPherson, *Howard University*; Sarah Hand Meacham, *Virginia Commonwealth University*; Jason Mead, *Johnson University*; Brian Craig Miller, *Emporia State University*; Robert Miller, *California State University, San Marcos*; Brett Mizelle, *California State University, Long Beach*; Mark Moser, *The University of North Carolina at Greensboro*; Ricky Moser, *Kilgore College*; Jennifer Murray, *Coastal Carolina University*; Peter

C. Murray, *Methodist University*; Steven E. Nash, *East Tennessee State University*; Chris New-man, *Elgin Community College*; David Noon, *University of Alaska Southeast*; Richard H. Owens, *West Liberty University*; Alison Parker, *College at Brockport, SUNY*; Craig Pascoe, *Georgia College*; David J. Peavler, *Towson University*; Linda Pelon, *McLennan Community College*; Laura A. Perry, *University of Memphis*; Wesley Phelps, *University of St. Thomas*; Jamie Pietruska, *Rutgers University*; Sandra Piseno, *Clayton State University*; Merline Pitre, *Texas Southern University*; Eunice G. Pollack, *University of North Texas*; Kimberly Porter, *University of North Dakota*; Cynthia Prescott, *University of North Dakota*; Gene Preuss, *University of Houston*; Sandra Pryor, *Old Dominion University*; Rhonda Ragsdale, *Lone Star College*; Ray Rast, *Gonzaga University*; Michaela Reaves, *California Lutheran University*; Peggy Renner, *Glendale Community College*; Steven D. Reschly, *Truman State University*; Barney J. Rickman, *Valdosta State University*; Pamela Riney-Kehrberg, *Iowa State University*; Paul Ringel, *High Point University*; Jason Ripper, *Everett Community College*; Timothy Roberts, *Western Illinois University*; Glenn Robins, *Georgia Southwestern State University*; Alicia E. Rodriquez, *California State University, Bakersfield*; Mark Roehrs, *Lincoln Land Community College*; Patricia Roessner, *Marple Newtown High School*; John G. Roush, *St. Petersburg College*; James Russell, *St. Thomas Aquinas College*; Eric Schlereth, *The University of Texas at Dallas*; Gregory L. Schneider, *Emporia State University*; Debra Schultz, *Kingsborough Community College, CUNY*; Ronald Schultz, *University of Wyoming*; Stanley K. Schultz, *University of Wisconsin–Madison*; Scott Seagle, *University of Tennessee at Chattanooga*; Donald Seals, *Kilgore College*; Sharon Shackelford, *Erie Community College*; Donald R. Shaffer, *American Public University System*; Gregory Shealy, *Saint John's River State College*; Cathy Hoult Shewring, *Montgomery County Community College*; Jill Silos-Rooney, *Massachusetts Bay Community College*; David J. Silverman, *The George Washington University*; Beth Slutsky, *California State University, Sacramento*; Andrea Smalley, *Northern Illinois University*; Karen Smith, *Emporia State University*; Molly Smith, *Friends School of Baltimore*; Suzie Smith, *Trinity Valley Community College*; Troy Smith, *Tennessee Tech University*; David L. Snead, *Liberty University*; David Snyder, *Delaware Valley College*; David Soll, *University of Wisconsin - Eau Claire*; Gary Sprayberry, *Columbus State University*; Jodie Steeley, *Merced College*; Bethany Stollar, *Tennessee State University*; Bryan E. Stone, *Del Mar College*; Jason Stratton, *Bakersfield College*; Emily Straus, *SUNY Fredonia*; Kristen Streater, *Collin College*; Joseph Stromberg, *San Jacinto College - Central*; Jean Stuntz, *West Texas A&M University*; Sarah Swedberg, *Colorado Mesa University*; Nikki M. Taylor, *University of Cincinnati*; Heather Ann Thompson, *Temple University*; Timothy Thurber, *Virginia Commonwealth University*; Christopher Thrasher, *Calhoun Community College*; T. J. Tomlin, *University of Northern Colorado*; Jeffrey Trask, *Georgia State University*; Laura Trauth, *Community College of Baltimore County–Essex*; Russell M. Tremayne, *College of Southern Idaho*; Laura Tuennerman-Kaplan, *California University of Pennsylvania*; Linda Upham-Bornstein, *Plymouth State University*; Mark VanDriel, *University of South Carolina*; Kevin Vanzant, *Tennessee State University*; Ramon C. Veloso, *Palomar College*; Morgan Veraluz, *Tennessee State University*; Vincent Vinikas, *The University of Arkansas at Little Rock*; David Voelker, *University of Wisconsin–Green Bay*; Melissa Walker, *Converse College*; William Wantland, *Mount Vernon Nazarene University*; Ed Wehrle, *Eastern Illinois University*; David Weiland, *Collin College*; Eddie Weller, *San Jacinto College-South*; Shane West, *Lone Star College-Greenspoint Center*; Geoffrey West, *San Diego Mesa College*; Kenneth B. White, *Modesto Junior College*; Matt White, *Paris Junior College*; Anne Will, *Skagit Valley College*; John P. Williams, *Collin College*; Zachery R. Williams, *University of Akron*; Gregory Wilson, *University of Akron*; Kurt Windisch, *University of Georgia*; Jonathan Wlasiuk, *The Ohio State University*; Timothy Wright *Shoreline Community College*; Timothy L.

Wood, *Southwest Baptist University*; Nancy Beck Young, *University of Houston*; Maria Cristina Zaccarini, *Adelphi University*; Nancy Zens, *Central Oregon Community College*; Jean Hansen Zuckweiler, *University of Northern Colorado*

We especially want to thank Julia Bowes, our research assistant for the third edition, who left no library shelf untouched in her quest to locate the secondary sources that we have excerpted. We also appreciate the help the following scholars, archivists, and students gave us in providing the information we needed at critical points in the writing of this text: Lori Birrell, Leslie Brown, Andrew Buchanan, Gillian Carroll, Susan J. Carroll, Jacqueline Castledine, Derek Chang, Paul Clemens, Dorothy Sue Cobble, Jane Coleman-Harbison, Alison Cronk, Kayo Denda, Elisabeth Eittreim, David Foglesong, Phyllis Hunter, Tera Hunter, Molly Inabinett, Kenneth Kvamme, William Link, James Livingston, Julia Livingston, Justin Lorts, Melissa Mead, Gilda Morales, Andrew Preston, Vicki L. Ruiz, Julia Sandy-Bailey, Susan Schrepfer, Bonnie Smith, Melissa Stein, Margaret Sumner, Camilla Townsend, Jessica Unger, Anne Valk, and Melinda Wallington.

We want to thank Rob Heinrich and Julia Sandy for compiling the primary source projects for the original companion source reader, *Thinking through Sources: Exploring American Histories*. Stephanie Sosa at Bedford/St. Martin's deftly orchestrated the development of the new edition of the reader collaborating with us to locate interesting and varied sources that aptly fit with the themes of the third edition, and we owe her our thanks.

We would particularly like to applaud the many hardworking and creative people at Bedford/St. Martin's who guided us through the labyrinthine process of writing this third edition. No one was more important to us than Laura Arcari and Maura Shea, our editors. We could not have had a better team than Edwin Hill, Michael Rosenberg, William Lombardo, Stephanie Sosa, Tess Fletcher, Kerri Cardone, Melissa Rodriguez, Christine Buese, and Kalina Ingham. The team at Bedford/St. Martin's also enlisted help from Naomi Kornhauser and Elaine Kosta, for which we are grateful. We will always remain thankful to Sara Wise and Patricia Rossi for their advice about and enthusiasm for a primary source-based American History textbook and to Joan Feinberg, who had the vision that guided us through every page of this book. Finally, we would like to express our gratitude to our friends and family who have encouraged us through all three editions and have even read the book without it being assigned.

Nancy A. Hewitt and Steven F. Lawson

Versions and Supplements

Adopters of *Exploring American Histories* and their students have access to abundant print and digital resources and tools, the acclaimed *Bedford Series in History and Culture* volumes, and much more. The LaunchPad course space for *Exploring American Histories* provides access to the narrative as well as a wealth of primary sources and other features, along with assignment and assessment opportunities at the ready. Achieve Read & Practice supplies adaptive quizzing and our mobile, accessible Value Edition e-Book, in one easy-to-use, affordable product. See below for more information, visit the book's catalog site at **macmillanlearning.com**, or contact your local Bedford/St. Martin's sales representative.

Get the Right Version for Your Class

To accommodate different course lengths and course budgets, *Exploring American Histories* is available in several different versions and formats to best suit your course needs. The comprehensive *Exploring American Histories* includes a full-color art program and a robust set of features. The Value Edition offers a trade-sized two-color option with the full narrative and selected art and maps (without the primary documents) at a steep discount. The Value Edition is also offered at the lowest price point in loose-leaf format, and both versions of the book are available as e-Books. For the best value of all, package a new print book with LaunchPad or Achieve Read & Practice at no additional charge to get the best each format offers. LaunchPad users get a print version for easy portability with an interactive e-Book for the full-feature text and course space, along with LearningCurve and loads of additional assignment and assessment options. Achieve Read & Practice users get a print version with a mobile, interactive Value Edition e-Book plus LearningCurve adaptive quizzing in one exceptionally affordable, easy-to-use product.

- ◆ **Combined Volume** (Chapters 1–29): available in paperback, Value Edition, loose-leaf, and e-Book formats and in LaunchPad and Achieve Read & Practice.
- ◆ **Volume 1: To 1877** (Chapters 1–14): available in paperback, Value Edition, loose-leaf, and e-Book formats and in LaunchPad and Achieve Read & Practice.
- ◆ **Volume 2: Since 1865** (Chapters 14–29): available in paperback, Value Edition, loose-leaf, and e-Book formats and in LaunchPad and Achieve Read & Practice.

As noted below, any of these volumes can be packaged with additional titles for a discount. To get ISBNs for discount packages, visit **macmillanlearning.com** for the comprehensive version or Value Edition or contact your Bedford/St. Martin's representative.

LaunchPad macmillan learning **Assign LaunchPad—an Assessment-Ready Interactive e-Book and Course Space** Available for discount purchase on its own or for packaging with new books at no additional charge, LaunchPad is a breakthrough solution for history courses. Intuitive and easy-to-use for students and instructors alike, LaunchPad is ready to use as is, and can be edited, customized with your own material, and assigned quickly. *LaunchPad for Exploring American Histories* includes Bedford/St. Martin's high-quality content all in one place, including the full interactive e-Book and the companion reader *Thinking through Sources for Exploring American Histories*, plus LearningCurve adaptive quizzing, guided reading activities designed to help students read actively for key concepts, auto-graded quizzes for each primary source, Thinking through Sources activities that use the document projects in the companion source reader to prompt students to build arguments and practice historical reasoning, and chapter summative quizzes. Through a wealth of formative and summative assessments, including the adaptive learning program of LearningCurve (see the full description ahead), students gain confidence and get into their reading before class. These features, plus additional primary source documents, video sources and tools for making video assignments, map activities, flashcards, and customizable test banks, make LaunchPad an invaluable asset for any instructor.

LaunchPad easily integrates with course management systems, and with fast ways to build assignments, rearrange chapters, and add new pages, sections, or links, it lets teachers build the courses they want to teach and hold students accountable. For more information, visit **launchpadworks.com** or to arrange a demo, contact us at **historymktg@macmillan.com**.

☑ **Assign LearningCurve So Your Students Come to Class Prepared.** Students using LaunchPad or Achieve Read & Practice receive access to LearningCurve for *Exploring American Histories*. Assigning LearningCurve in place of reading quizzes is easy for instructors, and the reporting features help instructors track overall class trends and spot topics that are giving students trouble so they can adjust their lectures and class activities. This online learning tool is popular with students because it was designed to help them rehearse content at their own pace in a nonthreatening, game-like environment. The feedback for wrong answers provides instructional coaching and sends students back to the book for review. Students answer as many questions as necessary to reach a target score, with repeated chances to revisit material they haven't mastered. When LearningCurve is assigned, students come to class better prepared.

Achieve READ & PRACTICE **Assign Achieve Read & Practice So Your Students Can Read and Study Wherever They Go.** Available for discount purchase on its own or for packaging with new books at no additional charge, Achieve Read & Practice is Bedford/St. Martin's most affordable digital solution for history courses. Intuitive and easy-to-use for students and instructors alike, Achieve Read & Practice is ready to use as is, and can be assigned quickly. *Achieve Read & Practice for Exploring American Histories* includes the Value Edition interactive e-Book, LearningCurve formative quizzing, assignment tools, and a gradebook. All this is built with an intuitive interface that can be read on mobile devices, and is fully accessible and available at a discounted price so anyone can use it. Instructors can set due dates for reading assignments and LearningCurve quizzes in just a few clicks, making it a simple and affordable way to engage students with the narrative and hold students accountable for course reading so they will come to class better prepared. For more information, visit **macmillanlearning.com/ReadandPractice**.

▷ iClicker iClicker, Active Learning Simplified

iClicker offers simple, flexible tools to help you give students a voice and facilitate active learning in the classroom. Students can participate with the devices they already bring to class using our iClicker Reef mobile apps (which work with smart phones, tablets, or laptops) or iClicker remotes. We've now integrated iClicker with Macmillan's LaunchPad to make it easier than ever to synchronize grades and promote engagement—both in and out of class. iClicker Reef access cards can also be packaged with LaunchPad or your textbook at a significant savings for your students. To learn more, talk to your Macmillan Learning representative or visit us at **www.iclicker.com**.

Take Advantage of Instructor Resources

Bedford/St. Martin's has developed a rich array of teaching resources for this book and for this course. They range from lecture and presentation materials and assessment tools to course management options. Most can be found in LaunchPad or can be downloaded or ordered from the Instructor's Resources tab of the book's catalog site at **macmillanlearning.com**.

Bedford Coursepack for Blackboard, Canvas, Brightspace by D2L, or Moodle. We can help you integrate our rich content into your course management system. Registered instructors can download coursepacks that include our popular free resources and book-specific content for *Exploring American Histories*. Visit **macmillanlearning.com** to find your version or download your coursepack.

Instructor's Resource Manual. The instructor's manual offers both experienced and first-time instructors tools for presenting textbook material in engaging ways. It includes content learning objectives, annotated chapter outlines, and strategies for teaching with the textbook, plus suggestions on how to get the most out of Learning-Curve, and a survival guide for first-time teaching assistants. In addition, a guide for teaching with documents, written by the textbook authors, provides detailed advice for getting the most out of the book's sources in the classroom.

Guide to Changing Editions. Designed to facilitate an instructor's transition from the previous edition of *Exploring American Histories* to this new edition, this guide presents an overview of major changes as well as of changes in each chapter.

Online Test Bank. The test bank includes a mix of fresh, carefully crafted multiple-choice, matching, short-answer, and essay questions for each chapter. Many of the multiple-choice questions feature a map, an image, or a primary-source excerpt as the prompt. All questions appear in Microsoft Word format and in easy-to-use test bank software that allows instructors to add, edit, re-sequence, filter by question type or learning objective, and print questions and answers. Instructors can also export questions into a variety of course management systems.

The Bedford Lecture Kit: Lecture Outlines, Maps, and Images. Look good and save time with **The Bedford Lecture Kit**. These presentation materials include fully customizable multimedia presentations built around chapter outlines that are embedded with maps, figures, and images from the textbook and are supplemented by more detailed instructor notes on key points and concepts.

Print, Digital, and Custom Options for More Choice and Value

For information on free packages and discounts up to 50%, visit **macmillanlearning .com**, or contact your local Bedford/St. Martin's sales representative.

Thinking through Sources for Exploring American Histories, Third Edition. This companion reader provides an additional primary source project with four to five written and visual sources focused on a central topic to accompany each chapter of *Exploring American Histories*. To aid students in approaching and interpreting the sources, the project for each chapter contains an introduction, document headnotes, and questions for discussion. Available free when packaged with the print book and included in the LaunchPad e-Book. Also available on its own as a downloadable e-Book.

Bedford Tutorials for History. Designed to customize textbooks with resources relevant to individual courses, this collection of brief units, each 16 pages long and loaded with examples, guides students through basic skills such as using historical evidence effectively, working with primary sources, taking effective notes, avoiding plagiarism and citing sources, and more. Up to two tutorials can be added to a Bedford/St. Martin's history survey title at no additional charge, freeing you to spend your class time focusing on content and interpretation. For more information, visit **macmillanlearning.com/ historytutorials**.

Bedford Document Collections. This source collection provides a flexible and affordable online repository of discovery-oriented primary-source projects ready to assign. Each curated project—written by a historian about a favorite topic—poses a historical question and guides students step by step through analysis of primary sources. Examples include What Caused the Civil War?; The California Gold Rush: A Trans-Pacific Phenomenon; and, War Stories: Black Soldiers and the Long Civil Rights Movement. For more information, visit **macmillanlearning.com/bdc/ushistory/catalog**. You can also select up to two document projects from the collection to add in print for free to customize your Bedford/St. Martin's textbook. Additional document projects can be added for a reasonable cost. For more information, visit **macmillanlearning.com/ custombdc/ushistory** or contact your Bedford/St. Martin's representative.

Bedford Select for History. This custom option allows you to create the ideal text-book for your course with only the chapters you need. Starting from the Value Edition of *Exploring American Histories*, you can rearrange chapters, delete unnecessary chapters, select chapters of primary sources from *Thinking through Sources for Exploring American Histories* and add document projects from the Bedford Document Collections, or choose to improve your students' historical thinking skills with the Bedford Tutorials for History. In addition, you can add your own original content to create just the book you're looking for. With Bedford Select, students pay only for material that will be assigned in the course, and nothing more. Order your textbook every semester, or modify from one term to the next. It is easy to build your customized textbook, without compromising the quality and affordability you've come to expect from Bedford/St. Martin's.

The Bedford Series in History and Culture. More than 100 titles in this highly praised series combine first-rate scholarship, historical narrative, and important primary documents for undergraduate courses. Each book is brief, inexpensive, and focused on a specific topic or period. Recently published titles include: *The Chinese Exclusion Act and Angel Island: A Brief History with Documents*, by Judy Yung; *The Life of P.T. Barnum, Written by Himself, With Related Documents*, edited with an introduction by Stephen Mihm; and *The California Gold Rush: A Brief History with Documents*, by Andrew C. Isenberg. For a complete list of titles, visit **macmillanlearning.com**. Package discounts are available.

Rand McNally Atlas of American History. This collection of more than eighty full-color maps illustrates key events and eras from early exploration, settlement, expansion, and immigration to U.S. involvement in wars abroad and on U.S. soil. Introductory pages for each section include a brief overview, timelines, graphs, and photos to quickly establish a historical context. Free when packaged.

The Bedford Glossary for U.S. History. This handy supplement for the survey course gives students historically contextualized definitions for hundreds of terms—from *abolitionism* to *zoot suit*—that they will encounter in lectures, reading, and exams. Free when packaged.

Trade Books. Titles published by sister companies Hill and Wang; Farrar, Straus and Giroux; Henry Holt and Company; St. Martin's Press; Picador; and Palgrave Macmillan are available at a 50% discount when packaged with Bedford/St. Martin's textbooks. For more information, visit **macmillanlearning.com/tradeup**.

A Pocket Guide to Writing in History. This portable and affordable reference tool by Mary Lynn Rampolla provides reading, writing, and research advice useful to students in all history courses. Concise yet comprehensive advice on approaching typical history assignments, developing critical reading skills, writing effective history papers, conducting research, using and documenting sources, and avoiding plagiarism—enhanced with practical tips and examples throughout—have made this slim reference a best-seller. Package discounts are available.

A Student's Guide to History. This complete guide to success in any history course provides the practical help students need to be successful. In addition to introducing students to the nature of the discipline, author Jules Benjamin teaches a wide range of skills from preparing for exams to approaching common writing assignments, and explains the research and documentation process with plentiful examples. Package discounts are available.

Going to the Source: The Bedford Reader in American History. Developed by Victoria Bissell Brown and Timothy J. Shannon, this reader combines a rich diversity of primary and secondary sources with in-depth instructions for how to use each type of source. Mirroring the chronology of the U.S. history survey, each of the main chapters familiarizes students with a single type of source—from personal letters to political cartoons—while focusing on an intriguing historical episode such as the Cherokee Removal or the 1894 Pullman Strike. The reader's wide variety of chapter topics and sources provoke students' interest as it teaches them the skills they need to successfully interrogate historical sources. Package discounts are available.

America Firsthand. With its distinctive focus on first person accounts from ordinary people, this primary documents reader by Anthony Marcus, John M. Giggie, and David Burner, offers a remarkable range of perspectives on America's history from those who lived it. Popular Points of View sections expose students to different perspectives on a specific event or topic. Package discounts are available.

Brief Contents

Contents

CHAPTER 9
Defending and Redefining the Nation 1809–1832 205

CHAPTER 10
Social and Cultural Ferment in the North 1820–1850 232

CHAPTER 11
Slavery Expands South and West 1830–1850   259

Maps, Figures, and Tables

1

Mapping Global Frontiers

to 1590

LEARNING OBJECTIVES

After reading this chapter you should be able to:

- Describe the diverse societies that populated the Americas prior to European exploration.
- Explain the reasons for European exploration and expansion, and compare the impact of this expansion on Europe and Africa.
- Evaluate the reasons for Europeans' success in reaching the Americas, and compare the impact of the Columbian Exchange on American Indians, Africans, and Europeans.
- Analyze how the Spanish created an empire in the Americas, and describe the impact of Spain's empire building on Indian empires and European nations.

COMPARING AMERICAN HISTORIES

In 1519 a young Indian woman named Malintzin was thrust into the center of dramatic events that transformed not only her world but also the world at large. As a young girl, Malintzin, whose birth name is lost to history, lived in the rural area of Coatzacoalcos on the frontier between the expanding kingdom of the Mexica and the declining Mayan states of the Yucatán peninsula. Raised in a noble household, Malintzin was fluent in Nahuatl, the language of the Mexica.

In 1515 or 1516, when she was between the ages of eight and twelve, Malintzin was taken by or given to Mexica merchants, perhaps as a peace offering to stave off military attacks. She then entered a well-established trade in slaves, consisting mostly of women and girls, who were sent

1

eastward to work in the expanding cotton fields or the households of their owners. She may also have been forced into a sexual relationship with a landowner. Whatever her situation, Malintzin learned the Mayan language during her captivity.

In 1517 Mayan villagers sighted Spanish adventurers along local rivers and drove them off. But in 1519 the Spaniards returned. The Maya's lightweight armor made of dense layers of cotton, cloth, and leather and their wooden arrows were no match for the invaders' steel swords, guns, and horses. Forced to surrender, the Maya offered the Spaniards food, gold, and twenty enslaved women, including Malintzin. The Spanish leader, Hernán Cortés, baptized the enslaved women and assigned each of them Christian names, although the women did not consent to this ritual. Cortés then divided the women among his senior officers, giving Malintzin to the highest-ranking noble.

Already fluent in Nahuatl and Mayan, Malintzin soon learned Spanish. Within a matter of months, she became the Spaniards' chief translator. As Cortés moved into territories ruled by the Mexica (whom the Spaniards called Aztecs), his success depended on his ability to understand Aztec ways of thinking and to convince subjugated groups to fight against their despotic rulers. Malintzin thus accompanied Cortés at every step, including his triumphant conquest of the Aztec capital in the fall of 1521.

At the same time that Malintzin played a key role in the conquest of the Aztecs, Martin Waldseemüller sought to map the frontiers along which these conflicts erupted. Born in present-day Germany in the early 1470s, Waldseemüller enrolled at the University of Fribourg in 1490, where he probably studied theology. He would gain fame, however, as a cartographer, or mapmaker.

In 1507 Waldseemüller and Mathias Ringmann, working at a scholarly religious institute in St. Dié in northern France, produced a map of the world, a small globe, and a Latin translation of the four voyages of the Italian explorer Amerigo Vespucci. The map and the globe, entitled *Universalis Cosmographia*, depict the "known" world as well as the "new" worlds recently discovered by European explorers. The latter include an elongated territory labeled *America*, in honor of Amerigo, who first recognized that the lands Columbus reached were part of a separate continent. It was set between the continents of Africa and Asia. The map, covering some 36 square feet, offered a view of the world never before attempted.

In 1516 Waldseemüller produced an updated map of the world, the *Carta Marina*. Apparently in response to challenges regarding Vespucci's role in discovering new territories, he substituted the term *Terra Incognita* ("unknown land") for the region he had earlier labeled America. But the 1507 map had already circulated widely, and *America* became part of the European lexicon.

A COMPARISON OF THE PERSONAL HISTORIES of Malintzin and Martin Waldseemüller highlights the profound consequences of contact between the peoples of Europe and those of the Americas. The Mexica, or Aztec, and the Spanish were most affected during this period, but France and England would soon also seek footholds in the Americas. For millennia, travel and communication between the two sides of the Atlantic had been extremely limited. Then, in the sixteenth century—and despite significant obstacles—animals, plants, goods, ideas, and people began circulating between Europe and what became known as America. Malintzin and Waldseemüller, in their very different ways, helped map the frontiers of this global society and contributed to the dramatic transformations that followed.

Native Peoples in the Americas

The first people in the Americas almost certainly arrived as migrants from northeast Asia, but the timing of such migrations remains in doubt. They likely began at least 25,000 years ago. It is also difficult to estimate the population of the Americas before contact with Europeans. Estimates range from 37 million to 100 million. It is clear, however, that the vast majority of people lived within a few hundred miles of the equator, and the smallest number—perhaps 4 to 7 million—lived in present-day North America. By the fifteenth century, like other regions of the world, the Americas were home to diverse societies, ranging from coastal fishing villages to nomadic hunter-gatherers to settled horticulturalists to large city-centered empires.

Native Peoples Develop Diverse Cultures

The settlement of the Americas was encouraged by the growth of glaciers on the North American continent between about 38,000 and 14,000 B.C.E. This development led to a dramatic drop in sea levels and created a land bridge in the Bering Strait, between present-day Siberia and Alaska, called **Beringia**. The first migrations may have occurred about 20,000 to 25,000 years ago, during a warming trend when melting glaciers retreated from large areas of land. During the warming trend, some settlers probably traveled from the northeastern region of the Asian Steppe (southern Siberia) to Beringia, following herds of mammoths, musk oxen, and woolly rhinoceroses. Then, 15,000 to 20,000 years ago, descendants of some of these settlers followed coastal pathways and the Pacific shore line, taking advantage of the rich maritime resources. These coastal journeys may help explain how Asiatic migrants peopled vast areas of South America in just a few thousand years. As immense expanses of ice returned to many regions some 13,000 years ago, the routes that migrants could follow shifted and forced many groups to push inland as well as further south.

Whether over land or sea, most early groups traveled southward. Those moving inland had to skirt melting glaciers to find better hunting grounds and more abundant plant life. When the mammoths and other large game disappeared from large areas about 10,000 years ago, people became more dependent on smaller game, fish, roots, berries, and other plant foods to survive. At the same time, new groups of migrants headed east from Beringia. These included Inuit and Aleut peoples who arrived in present-day Alaska thousands of years after more southern areas had been settled (Map 1.1).

Between 8000 and 2000 B.C.E., some communities in the Americas began establishing agricultural systems that encouraged more stable settlements and population

MAP 1.1
The Settling of the Americas   Beginning about 25,000 B.C.E., Asian peoples likely migrated to America across a land bridge after expanding glaciers lowered sea levels. Others probably followed the coastline in boats. As glaciers retreated over several centuries, they opened corridors along which people migrated, leaving traces in archaeological sites in present-day Wisconsin, New Mexico, Florida, Central America, and Chile.

growth. **Horticulture**—a form of agriculture in which people work small plots of land with simple tools—became highly developed in the area of present-day Mexico. There men and women developed improved strains of maize (or Indian corn). They also cultivated protein-rich beans, squash, tomatoes, potatoes, and manioc (a root vegetable, also known as cassava or yucca root). The combination of beans, squash, and corn offered an especially nutritious diet while maintaining the fertility of the soil. Moreover, high yields produced surplus food that could be stored or traded to neighboring communities.

By 500 C.E., complex societies, rooted in intensive agriculture, began to thrive in the equatorial region. Between 500 and 1500 C.E., the spread of maize cultivation northward into the present-day American Southwest and beyond fostered economic developments that necessitated irrigation and led to the diversification of native societies. Small bands of hunters and gatherers continued to thrive in deserts and forests while impressive civilizations arose on swamplands and grasslands, and in the mountains.

The Aztecs, the Maya, and the Incas

Three significant civilizations had emerged by the early sixteenth century: Aztec and Mayan societies in the equatorial region and the Inca society along the Pacific coast in present-day Peru. Technologically advanced and with knowledge of mathematics and astronomy, these societies were characterized by vast mineral wealth, large urban centers, highly ritualized religions, and complex political systems. Unlike their counterparts in Europe, Asia, and Africa, they did not develop the wheel to aid in transportation, nor did they have steel tools and weapons. Since most of their commerce was carried out over land or along rivers and coastlines, they did not build large boats. They also lacked horses, which had disappeared from the region thousands of years earlier. Still, the Aztecs, Maya, and Incas established grand cities and civilizations.

Around 1325 C.E., the **Aztecs**, who called themselves Mexica, built their capital, Tenochtitlán, on the site of present-day Mexico City. As seminomadic warriors who had invaded and then settled in the region, the Aztecs drew on local residents' knowledge of irrigation and cultivation and adopted their written language. Aztec commoners, who tilled communally owned lands, were ruled over by priests and nobles. The nobles formed a warrior class and owned vast estates on which they employed both serfs and slaves captured from non-Aztec communities in the region. Priests promised fertility—for the land and its people—but demanded human sacrifices, including thousands of men and women from captured tribes. To sustain their society, Aztecs extended their trade networks, offering pottery, cloth, and leather goods in exchange for textiles and obsidian to make sharp-edged tools and weapons. As Malintzin's story illustrates, slaves made up an important component of this trade.

When Malintzin was sold to a Mayan village by Aztec merchants, she was being traded from one grand civilization to another. The **Maya** had slowly settled the Yucatán peninsula and the rain forests of present-day Guatemala between roughly 900 B.C.E. and 300 C.E. They established large cities that were home to skilled artisans and developed elaborate systems for irrigation and water storage. Farmers worked the fields and labored to build huge stone temples and palaces for rulers who claimed to be descended from the gods. Learned men developed mathematical calculations, astronomical systems, hieroglyphic writing, and a calendar.

Yet the Mayan civilization began to decline around 800 C.E. An economic crisis, likely the result of drought and exacerbated by heavy taxation, probably drove peasant families into the interior. Many towns and religious sites were abandoned. Yet some communities survived the crisis and reemerged as thriving city-states. By the early sixteenth century, they were trading with the Aztecs.

The **Incas** developed an equally impressive civilization in the Andes Mountains along the Pacific coast. The Inca empire, like the Aztec empire, was built on the accomplishments of earlier societies. At the height of their power, in the fifteenth century, the Incas controlled some 16 million people spread over 350,000 square miles. They constructed an expansive system of roads and garrisons to ensure the flow of food, trade goods, and soldiers from their capital at Cuzco through the surrounding mountains and valleys.

The key to Inca success was the cultivation of fertile mountain valleys. Cuzco, some eleven thousand feet above sea level, lay in the center of the Inca empire, with the Huaylas and Titicaca valleys on either side. Here residents cultivated potatoes and other crops on terraces watered by an elaborate irrigation system. Miners dug gold and silver from the mountains, and artisans crafted the metals into jewelry and decorative items. Thousands of laborers constructed elaborate palaces and temples. And like the Aztec priests, Inca priests sacrificed humans to the gods to stave off natural disasters and military defeat.

Native Cultures to the North

To the north of these grand civilizations, smaller societies with less elaborate cultures thrived. In present-day Arizona and New Mexico, the Mogollon and Hohokam established communities around 500 C.E. The Mogollon were expert potters, while the Hohokam, migrating north from Mexico, developed extensive irrigation systems. Farther north, in present-day Utah and Colorado, the ancient Pueblo people built adobe and masonry homes cut into cliffs around 750 C.E. After migrating south and constructing large buildings that included administrative offices, religious centers, and craft shops, the Pueblo returned to their cliff dwellings in the 1100s for protection from invaders. There, drought eventually caused them to disperse into smaller groups.

Farther north on the plains that stretched from present-day Colorado into Canada, hunting societies developed around herds of bison. A weighted spear-throwing device, called an *atlatl*, allowed hunters to capture smaller game, while nets, hooks, and snares allowed them to catch birds, fish, and small animals. Societies in the Great Plains as well as the Great Basin (between the Rockies and the Sierra Nevada) generally remained small and widely scattered. Given the arid conditions in these regions, communities needed a large expanse of territory to ensure their survival as they followed migrating animals or seasonal plant sources. Here the adoption of the bow and arrow, in about 500 C.E., proved the most significant technological development.

Other native societies, like the Mandan, settled along rivers in the heart of the continent (present-day North and South Dakota). The rich soil along the banks fostered farming, while forests and plains attracted diverse animals for hunting. Around 1250 C.E., however, an extended drought forced these settlements to contract, and competition for resources increased among Mandan villages and with other native groups in the region.

Hunting-gathering societies also emerged along the Pacific coast, where the abundance of fish, small game, and plant life provided the resources to develop permanent settlements. The Chumash Indians, near present-day Santa Barbara, California, harvested resources from the land and the ocean. Women gathered acorns and pine nuts, while men fished and hunted. The Chumash, whose villages sometimes held a thousand inhabitants, participated in regional exchange networks up and down the coast.

Even larger societies with more elaborate social, religious, and political systems developed near the Mississippi River. A group that came to be called the **Hopewell people** established a thriving culture there in the early centuries C.E. The river and its surrounding lands provided fertile fields and easy access to distant communities. Centered in present-day southern Ohio and western Illinois, the Hopewell constructed

Serpent Mound Memorial   This mound, located in Locust Grove, Ohio, was likely constructed sometime between 950 and 1200 c.e. by the Mississippian society. A sun-worshipping culture, the Mississippians aligned the head of the serpent with the sunset of the summer solstice (June 20 or 21). Goods found at such sites indicate that Hopewell networks were further extended by the Mississippians.   Tony Linck/SuperStock

towns of four to six thousand people. Artifacts from their burial sites reflect extensive trading networks that stretched from the Missouri River to Lake Superior, and from the Rocky Mountains to the Appalachian region and Florida.

Beginning around 500 c.e., the Hopewell culture gave birth to larger and more complex societies that flourished in the Mississippi River valley and to the south and east. As bows and arrows spread into the region, people hunted more game in the thick forests. But Mississippian groups also learned to cultivate corn. The development of corn as a staple crop allowed the population to expand dramatically, and more complex political and religious systems developed in which elite rulers gained greater control over the labor of farmers and hunters. Mississippian peoples created massive earthworks sculpted in the shape of serpents, birds, and other creatures. Some earthen sculptures stood higher than 70 feet and stretched longer than 1,300 feet. Mississippians also constructed huge temple mounds that could cover nearly 16 acres.

By about 1100 c.e., the Cahokia people established the largest Mississippian settlement, which may have housed ten to thirty thousand inhabitants (Map 1.2). Powerful chieftains extended their trade networks from the Great Lakes to the Gulf of Mexico, conquered smaller villages, and created a centralized government. But in the 1200s environmental factors affected the Cahokian people, too. Deforestation, drought, and perhaps disease as well as overhunting diminished their strength, and many settlements dispersed. After 1400, increased warfare and political turmoil joined with environmental changes to cause Mississippian culture as a whole to decline.

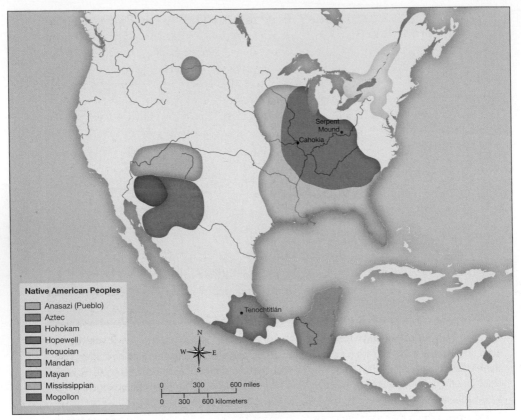

Native American Peoples
- Anasazi (Pueblo)
- Aztec
- Hohokam
- Hopewell
- Iroquoian
- Mandan
- Mayan
- Mississippian
- Mogollon

MAP 1.2
Native American Peoples, c. 500–1500 C.E.   Many distinct cultures developed in the Americas in the ten centuries before 1500. Some societies, like the Mississippians, developed extensive trade networks over land or along rivers and coastlines. Societies in the same region often learned from those who preceded them, such as the Aztec from the Maya, but other groups battled over scarce resources.

REVIEW & RELATE
- Compare and contrast the Aztecs, Incas, and Maya. What similarities and differences do you note?
- How did the societies of North America differ from those of the equatorial zone and the Andes?

Europe Expands Its Reach

The complex societies that emerged in the Americas were made possible by an agricultural revolution that included the establishment of crop systems, the domestication of animals, and the development of tools. These developments had occurred between 4000 and 3000 B.C.E. in the Fertile Crescent of the Middle East and in China. The increased productivity in these areas ensured population growth and allowed attention to science, trade, politics, religion, and the arts. Over millennia, knowledge from these civilizations made its way into Europe. At the height of the Roman empire in the early centuries C.E., dense global trade networks connected the peoples of Europe, Africa, and Asia. With the decline of Roman power in western Europe, those connections broke down, but commercial ties continued to thrive among diverse peoples surrounding the Mediterranean Sea. Portuguese explorers, denied access to that rich Mediterranean world by the politics of the period, instead sought trade routes along the coast of Africa. Increased trade with African kingdoms by Portugal and other European societies included the purchase of slaves. This lucrative and devastating form of commerce would expand dramatically as European nations colonized the Americas.

The Mediterranean World

Beginning in the seventh century Islam proved one of the most dynamic cultural, political, and military forces in the world. By the ninth century, Islamic (also known as Muslim) regimes created an Arab empire that controlled most of southwest Asia and North Africa and conquered parts of the Iberian peninsula in Europe. In the eleventh and twelfth centuries, Catholic leaders launched several military and religious campaigns to reclaim Jerusalem and other sites associated with Jesus for the Church. Later known as the **Crusades**, these campaigns largely failed, but they enhanced the roles of Italian merchants, who profited from both outfitting Crusaders and opening new trade routes to the East. Moreover, these campaigns inspired explorers and adventurers throughout Europe.

Europeans also learned of successful civilizations in the Middle East, where inhabitants had managed to survive droughts and other ecological crises, largely because of their productive economic systems. In the Mediterranean world, this productivity depended on technological advances in irrigation and navigation and a vast network of slave-trading centers and enslaved laborers. It was the productivity of agriculture—developed centuries earlier than in Europe or America—that allowed societies along the southern Mediterranean, in northern Africa, and in southwest Asia to excel in astronomy, mathematics, architecture, and the arts.

Medieval European states proved far less adept at staving off human and environmental disasters than their counterparts to the south. Besieged by drought and disease as well as wars and peasant rebellions, rulers across the continent expended most of their resources on trying to sustain their population and protect their borders. In the 1340s, as Europeans began to trade with various regions of Asia, fleas on rats carried the bubonic plague and similar epidemic diseases on board ships and into European seaports. From the 1340s to the early fifteenth century, the bubonic plague—later called the **Black Death**—periodically ravaged European cities and towns. During the initial outbreak between 1346 and 1350, about 36 million people—half of Europe's population—perished. At the same time, France and England engaged in a century-long war that added to the death and destruction.

By the early fifteenth century, the plague had retreated from much of Europe, and the climate had improved. Only then were European peoples able to benefit significantly from the riches of the East. Smaller populations led to an improved standard of living. Then rising birthrates and increased productivity, beginning in Italian city-states, fueled a resurgence of trade with other parts of the world. The profits from agriculture and commerce allowed the wealthy and powerful to begin investing in the arts and luxury goods. Indeed, a cultural **Renaissance** (from the French word for "rebirth") flourished in the Italian city-states and then spread to France, Spain, the Low Countries, and central Europe.

The cultural rebirth went hand in hand with political unification as more powerful rulers extended their control over smaller city-states and principalities. A vibrant and religiously tolerant culture had existed in Muslim Spain from the eighth to the tenth century, but that was followed by a long period of persecution of Christians. When Christians began reconquering Spain after 1200, Muslims and Jews alike became targets. Then in 1469, the marriage of Isabella of Castile and Ferdinand II of Aragon sealed the unification of Christian Spain. By 1492 their combined forces expelled the last Muslim conquerors from the Iberian peninsula. Promoting Catholicism to create a more unified national identity, Isabella and Ferdinand launched an Inquisition against supposed heretics and executed or expelled some 200,000 Jews as well. Despite the brutality of the reconquest and the Inquisition, Catholic Spain had the wealth and military power to forge its own trade networks with North Africa, India, and other Asian lands.

Yet Italy controlled the most important routes through the Mediterranean, so leaders in Spain and neighboring Portugal sought alternate paths to riches. Their efforts were aided by explorers, missionaries, and merchants who traveled to Morocco, Turkey, India, and other distant lands. They brought back trade goods and knowledge of astronomy, shipbuilding, mapmaking, and navigation that allowed Iberians to venture farther south along the Atlantic coast of Africa and, eventually, west into the uncharted Atlantic Ocean.

Portugal Pursues Long-Distance Trade

Cut off from the Mediterranean by Italian city-states and Muslim rulers in North Africa, Portugal looked toward the Atlantic. Although a tiny nation, Portugal benefited from the leadership of its young prince, Henry, who launched explorations of the African coast in the 1420s, hoping to find a passage to India via the Atlantic Ocean. Prince Henry—known as Henry the Navigator—gathered information from astronomers, geographers, mapmakers, and craftsmen in the Arab world and recruited Italian cartographers and navigators along with Portuguese scholars, sailors, and captains. He then launched a systematic campaign of exploration, observation, shipbuilding, and long-distance trade that revolutionized Europe and shaped developments in Africa and the Americas.

Prince Henry and his colleagues developed ships known as caravels—vessels with narrow hulls and triangular sails that were especially effective for navigating the coast of West Africa. His staff also created state-of-the-art maritime charts, maps, and astronomical tables; perfected navigational instruments; and mastered the complex wind and sea currents along the African coast. Soon Portugal was trading in gold, ivory, and slaves from West Africa.

In 1482 Portugal built Elmina Castle, a trading post and fort on the Gold Coast (present-day Ghana). Further expeditions were launched from the castle; five years later, a fleet led by Bartolomeu Dias rounded the Cape of Good Hope, on the southernmost tip of Africa. This feat demonstrated the possibility of sailing directly from the Atlantic to the Indian Ocean. Vasco da Gama followed this route to India in 1497, returning to Portugal in 1499, his ships laden with valuable cinnamon and pepper.

By the early sixteenth century, Portuguese traders had wrested control of the India trade from Arab fleets. They established fortified trading posts at key locations on the Indian Ocean and extended their expeditions to Indonesia, China, and Japan. Within a decade, the Portuguese had become the leaders in international trade. Spain, England, France, and the Netherlands competed for a share of this newfound wealth by developing long-distance markets that brought spices, ivory, silks, cotton cloth, and other luxury goods to Europe.

With expanding populations and greater agricultural productivity, European nations developed more efficient systems of taxation, built larger military forces, and adapted gunpowder to new kinds of weapons. The surge in population provided the men to labor on merchant vessels, staff forts, and protect trade routes. More people began to settle in cities, which grew into important commercial centers. Slowly, a form of capitalism based on market exchange, private ownership, and capital accumulation and reinvestment developed across much of Europe.

European Encounters with West Africa

African slaves were among the most lucrative goods traded by European merchants. Slavery had been practiced in Europe, America, Africa, and other parts of the world for centuries. But in most times and places, slaves were captives of war or individuals sold in payment for deaths or injuries to conquering enemies. Under such circumstances, slaves generally retained some legal rights, and bondage was rarely permanent and almost never inheritable. With the advent of large-scale European participation in the African slave trade, however, the system of bondage began to change, transforming Europe and Africa and eventually the Americas.

In the fifteenth century, Europeans were most familiar with North Africa, a region deeply influenced by Islam and characterized by large kingdoms, well-developed cities, and an extensive network of trading centers. In northeast Africa, including Egypt, city-states flourished, with ties to India, the Middle East, and China. In northwest Africa, Timbuktu linked North Africa to empires south of the Great Desert as well as to Europe. Here African slaves labored for wealthier Africans in a system of bound labor long familiar to Europeans.

As trade with western Africa increased, however, Europeans learned more about communities that lived by hunting and subsistence agriculture. By the mid-sixteenth century, European nations established competing forts along the African coast from the Gold Coast and Senegambia in the north to the Bight of Biafra and West Central Africa farther south. The men and women shipped from these forts to Europe generally came from communities that had been raided or conquered by more powerful groups. They arrived at the coast exhausted, hungry, dirty, and with few clothes. They worshipped gods unfamiliar to Europeans, and their cultural customs and social practices seemed strange and primitive. Over time, it was the image of the West African slave that came to dominate European visions of the entire continent.

African Salt Cellar This ivory salt cellar was carved in the fifteenth or sixteenth century in Sierra Leone, on the West African coast and was made for sale to Portuguese traders. The artisan depicted traditional geometric designs and African reptiles but clothed the four male and four female African figures in items of European dress. Werner Forman Archive/Bridgeman Images

As traders from Portugal, Spain, Holland, and England brought back more stories and more African slaves, these negative portraits took deeper hold. Woodcuts and prints circulated in Europe showing half-naked Africans who were portrayed more like apes than humans. Biblical stories also reinforced notions of Africans as naturally inferior to Europeans. In the Bible, Ham had sinned against his father, Noah. Noah then cursed Ham's son Canaan to a life of slavery. Increasingly, European Christians considered Africans the "sons of Ham," infidels rightly assigned by God to a life of bondage. This self-serving idea was used to justify the enslavement of black men, women, and children.

Of course, these images of West Africa failed to reflect the diverse peoples who lived in and the diverse societies that developed in the area's tropical rain forests, plains, and savannas. As the slave trade expanded in the sixteenth and seventeenth centuries, it destabilized large areas of western and central Africa, with smaller societies decimated by raids and even larger kingdoms damaged by the extensive commerce in human beings.

Still, rulers of the most powerful African societies helped shape the slave trade. For instance, because women were more highly valued by Muslim traders in North Africa and Asia, African traders steered women to these profitable markets. At the same time, African societies organized along matrilineal lines—where goods and political power passed through the mother's line—often tried to protect women against enslavement. Other groups sought to limit the sale of men.

Ultimately, men, women, and children were captured by African as well as Portuguese, Spanish, Dutch, and English traders. Still, Europeans did not institute a system of perpetual slavery, in which enslavement was inherited from one generation to the next. Instead, Africans formed another class of bound labor, alongside peasants, indentured servants, criminals, and apprentices. Crucially, distinctions among bound laborers on   and Irish laborers as ignorant and unruly heathens. However, as Europeans began to conquer and colonize the Americas and demands for labor increased dramatically, ideas about race and slavery would change significantly.

REVIEW & RELATE	• How and why did Europeans expand their connections with Africa and the Middle East in the fifteenth century? • How did early European encounters with West Africans influence Europeans' ideas about African peoples and reshape existing systems of slavery?

Worlds Collide

In the 1520s and 1530s, Spain and Portugal chartered traders to ship enslaved Africans to the Caribbean, Brazil, Mexico, and Peru. The success of this trade relied heavily on the efforts of European cartographers, who used information from explorers and adventurers to map these areas. The maps illustrate the growing connections among Europe, Africa, and the Americas even as they also reflect the continued dominance of the Mediterranean region, the Middle East, India, and China in European visions of the world. Yet that world was changing rapidly as Europeans introduced guns, horses, and new diseases to the Americas and came in contact with previously unknown flora and fauna. The resulting exchange of plants, animals, and germs transformed the two continents as well as the wider world.

Europeans Cross the Atlantic

The first Europeans to discover lands in the western Atlantic were Norsemen. In the late tenth century, Scandinavian seafarers led by Erik the Red reached Greenland. Sailing still farther west, Erik's son Leif led a party that discovered an area in North America that they called Vinland, near the Gulf of St. Lawrence. The Norse established a small settlement there around 1000 C.E., and people from Greenland continued to visit Vinland for centuries. By 1450, however, the Greenland settlements had disappeared.

Nearly a half century after Norse settlers abandoned Greenland, a Genoese navigator named Christopher Columbus visited the Spanish court of Ferdinand and Isabella and proposed an **Enterprise of the Indies**. Portuguese explorers used this name for the region that included present-day South Asia and Southeast Asia and surrounding islands. Because Italian city-states controlled the Mediterranean and Portugal dominated the routes around Africa, Spain sought a third path to the rich Eastern trade. Columbus claimed he could find it by sailing west across the Atlantic to Japan, China, or the Indies themselves.

Columbus's 1492 proposal was timely. Having just expelled the last Muslims and Jews from Granada and imposed Catholic orthodoxy on a now-unified nation, the Spanish monarchs sought to expand their empire. After winning Queen Isabella's support, the Genoese captain headed off in three small ships with ninety men. They stopped briefly at the Canary Islands and then headed due west on September 6, 1492.

Columbus had calculated the distance to Japan, which he judged the nearest island, based on Ptolemy's division of the world into 360 degrees of north-south lines of longitude. But in making his calculations, Columbus made a number of errors that led him to believe that it was possible to sail from Spain to Asia in about a month. The miscalculations nearly led to mutiny, but disaster was averted when a lookout finally spotted a small island on October 12. Columbus named the island San Salvador and made contact with local residents, whom he named Indians in the belief that he had found East Indies islands near Japan or China. Columbus was impressed with their warm welcome and considered the gold jewelry Indians wore as a sign of great riches in the region.

Columbus and his crew were welcomed as heroes when they returned to Spain in March 1493. Their discovery of islands seemingly unclaimed by any known power led the pope to confer Spanish sovereignty over all lands already claimed or to be claimed 100 leagues west of the Cape Verde Islands. A protest by Portugal soon led to a treaty that moved the line 270 leagues farther west, granting Portugal control of territory that became Brazil and Spain control of the rest of what became known as South America.

Europeans Explore the Americas

Columbus made three more voyages to the Caribbean to claim land for Spain and sought to convince those who accompanied him to build houses, plant crops, and cut logs for forts. But the men had come for gold, and when the Indians stopped trading willingly, the Spaniards used force to claim their riches. Columbus sought to impose a more rigid discipline but failed. On his final voyage, he introduced a system of **encomienda**, by which leading men received land and the labor of all Indians residing on it. By the time of Columbus's death in 1506, the islands he had discovered were dissolving into chaos as traders and adventurers fought with Indians and one another over the spoils of conquest. By then, no one believed that Columbus had discovered a route to China, but few people understood the revolutionary importance of the lands he had found.

Nonetheless, Columbus's voyages inspired others to head across the Atlantic (Map 1.3). In 1497 another Genoese navigator, John Cabot (or Caboto), sailing under the English flag, reached an island off Cape Breton in the North Atlantic, where he discovered good cod fishing but met no local inhabitants. Over the next several years, Cabot and his son Sebastian made more trips to North America, but England failed to follow up on their discoveries.

More important at the time, Portuguese and Spanish mariners continued to explore the western edges of the Caribbean. Amerigo Vespucci, a Florentine merchant, joined one such voyage in 1499. It was Vespucci's account of his journey that led Martin Waldseemüller to identify the new continent he charted on his 1507 *Universalis Cosmographia* as "America." Meanwhile, Spanish explorers subdued tribes like the Arawak and Taino in the Caribbean and headed toward the mainland. In 1513 Vasco Nuñez de Balboa traveled across the Isthmus of Darien (now Panama) and became the first known European to see the Pacific Ocean. That same year, the Spanish explorer

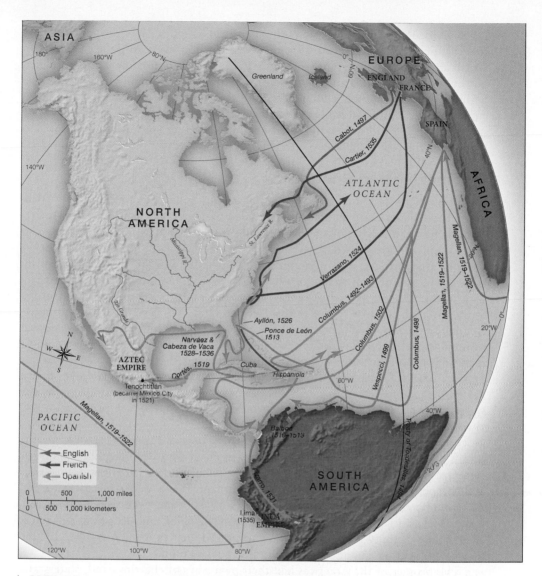

MAP 1.3

European Explorations in the Americas, 1492–1536   Early explorers, funded by Spain, sought trade routes to Asia or gold, silver, and other riches in the Americas. The success of these voyages encouraged adventurous Spaniards to travel throughout the West Indies, South America, and regions immediately to the north. It also inspired the first expeditions by the French and the English in North America.

Juan Ponce de León launched a search for gold and slaves along a peninsula he named Florida and claimed for Spain.

Ferdinand Magellan launched an even more impressive expedition in August 1519 when he, with the support of Charles V of Spain, sought a passageway through South America to Asia. In October 1520, after fifteen months of struggle and travail,

his crew discovered a strait at the southernmost tip of South America that connected
the Atlantic and Pacific Oceans. Ill with scurvy and near starvation, the crew reached
Guam and then the Philippines in March 1521. Magellan died there a month later,
but one of his five ships and eighteen of the original crew finally made it back to
Seville in September 1522, having successfully circumnavigated the globe. Despite the
enormous loss of life and equipment, Magellan's lone ship was loaded with valuable
spices and detailed information for cartographers, and his venture allowed Spain to
claim the Philippine Islands.

Mapmaking and Printing

Waldseemüller's 1507 map reflected the expanding contacts among Europe, Africa,
and the Americas. Over the following decades, cartographers charted newly discovered islands, traced coastlines and bays, and situated each new piece of data in relation to lands already known.

   The dissemination of geographical knowledge was greatly facilitated by
advances in information technology. The Chinese had developed a form of printing
with wood blocks in the tenth century, and woodcut pictures appeared in Europe
in the fifteenth century. In the 1440s, German craftsmen invented a form of movable metal type in which each letter was created in a separate mold. This allowed
printers to rearrange the type for each page and create multiple copies of a single
manuscript more quickly and more cheaply than ever before. Between 1452 and
1455, Johannes Gutenberg, a German goldsmith, printed some 180 copies of the
Bible with movable type. Although this was not the first book printed using the new
system, Gutenberg's Bible marked a revolutionary change in the production and
circulation of written texts.

   Innovations in printing helped publicize Portuguese and Spanish explorations, the
travels of European adventurers, and the atlases created by Waldseemüller and other
cartographers. Italian craftsmen contributed by manufacturing paper that was thinner
and cheaper than traditional vellum and parchment. Books were still expensive, and
they could be read only by the small minority of Europeans who were literate. Still,
mechanical printing rapidly increased the speed with which knowledge was circulated.
The enhanced ability to exchange ideas encouraged their expression and ensured the
flow of information among scholars and rulers across Europe.

   The peoples of the Americas had their own ways of charting land, waterways,
and boundary lines and of circulating information. The Maya, for instance, developed a system of glyphs—images that represented prefixes, suffixes, numbers, people, or words. Scribes carved glyphs into large flat stones, or *stela*, providing local
residents with histories of important events. In settled farming villages, this system
communicated information to a large portion of the population. But it could not
serve, as printed pages did, to disseminate ideas more widely. Similarly, the extant
maps created by the Maya, Aztecs, and other native groups tended to focus on specific locales. Still, we know that these groups traded across long distances, so they
must have had some means of tracing rivers, mountains, and villages beyond their
own communities.

The Columbian Exchange

The Spaniards were aided in their conquest of the Americas as much by germs as by maps, guns, or horses. Because native peoples in the Western Hemisphere had had almost no contact with the rest of the world for millennia, they lacked immunity to most germs carried by Europeans. Disease along with warfare first eradicated the Arawak and Taino on Hispaniola, wiping out some 300,000 people. In the Inca empire, the population plummeted from about 9 million in 1530 to less than half a million by 1630. Among the Aztecs, the Maya, and their neighbors, the population collapsed from some 40 million people around 1500 to about 3 million a century and a half later. The germs spread northward as well, leading to catastrophic epidemics among the Pueblo peoples of the Southwest and the Mississippian cultures of the Southeast.

These demographic disasters—far more devastating even than the bubonic plague in Europe—were part of what historians call the **Columbian exchange**. But this exchange also involved animals, plants, and seeds and affected Africa and Asia as well as Europe and the Americas. The transfer of flora and fauna and the spread of diseases transformed the economies and environments of all four continents. Initially, the catastrophic decline in Indian populations ensured the victory of Spain and other European powers over American populations. Africans' partial immunity to malaria and yellow fever then made them attractive to Europeans seeking laborers for Caribbean islands after the native population was decimated. At the same time, African coconuts and bananas were traded to Europe, while European traders provided their African counterparts with iron and pigs. Asia also participated in the exchange, introducing both Europe and Africa not only to the bubonic plague but also to sugar, rice, tea, and highly coveted spices.

America provided Europeans with high-yielding, nutrient-rich foods like maize and potatoes, as well as new indulgences like tobacco and cacao. The conquered Inca and Aztec empires also provided vast quantities of gold and silver, making Spain the treasure-house of Europe and ensuring its dominance on the continent for several decades. Sugar was first developed in the East Indies, but it also became a source of enormous profits once it took root on Caribbean islands, which became known as the West Indies. Moreover, when mixed with cacao, sugar created an addictive drink known as chocolate.

In exchange for products that America offered to Europe and Africa, these continents sent rice, wheat, rye, lemons, and oranges as well as horses, cattle, pigs, chickens, and honeybees to the Western Hemisphere (Map 1.4). The grain crops transformed the American landscape, particularly in North America, where wheat became a major food source. Cattle and pigs, meanwhile, changed native diets, while horses inspired new methods of farming, transportation, and warfare throughout the Americas.

The Columbian exchange benefited Europe far more than the Americas. Initially, it also benefited Africa, providing new crops with high yields and rich nutrients. Ultimately, however, the spread of sugar and rice to the West Indies and European cravings for tobacco and cacao increased the demand for labor, which could not be met by the declining population of Indians. This situation ensured the expansion of the African slave trade to the Americas. The consequences of the Columbian exchange were thus monumental for the peoples of all three continents.

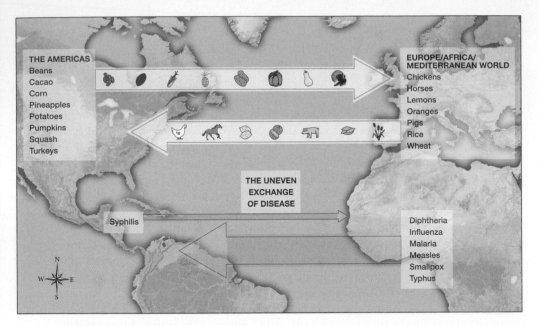

THE AMERICAS
Beans
Cacao
Corn
Pineapples
Potatoes
Pumpkins
Squash
Turkeys

EUROPE/AFRICA/
MEDITERRANEAN WORLD
Chickens
Horses
Lemons
Oranges
Pigs
Rice
Wheat

THE UNEVEN
EXCHANGE
OF DISEASE

Syphilis

Diphtheria
Influenza
Malaria
Measles
Smallpox
Typhus

MAP 1.4
The Columbian Exchange, Sixteenth Century   When Europeans made contact with Africa
and the Americas, they initiated an exchange of plants, animals, and germs that transformed
all three continents. The contact among these previously isolated ecosystems caused dramatic
transformations in food, labor, and mortality. American crops changed eating habits across Europe,
while diseases devastated native populations even as foreign grains and domesticated animals
thrived in the Americas.

REVIEW & RELATE	• What were the short-term consequences in both Europe and the Americas of Columbus's voyages? • How did the Columbian exchange transform both the Americas and Europe?

Europeans Make Claims to North America

With the help of native translators, warriors, and laborers, Spanish soldiers called
conquistadors conquered some of the richest and most populous lands in South
America in the early sixteenth century. Others then headed north, hoping to find gold
in the southern regions of North America or develop new routes to Asia. At the same
time, rulers of other European nations began to fund expeditions to North America.
France and England both launched efforts to claim colonies in the Americas, though
they failed to find the riches Spain had acquired. By the late sixteenth century,
Spanish supremacy in the Americas and the wealth acquired there transformed the
European economy. But conquest also raised critical questions about Spanish responsibilities to God and humanity.

Spaniards Conquer Indian Empires

Although rulers in Spain supposedly set the agenda for American ventures, it was difficult to control the campaigns of their emissaries at such a distance. The Spanish crown held the power to grant successful leaders vast amounts of land and Indian labor via the encomienda system. But the leaders themselves then divided up their prizes to reward those who served under them, giving them in effect an authority that they sometimes lacked in law. This dynamic helped make Cortés's conquest of the Aztecs possible.

Diego de Velásquez, the Spanish governor of Cuba, granted Cortés the right to explore and trade along the coast of South America. He gave him no authority, however, to attack native peoples in the region or claim land for himself. But seeing the possibility for gaining great riches, Cortés forged alliances with local rulers willing to join the attack against the Aztec chief, Montezuma. From the perspective of local Indian communities, Cortés's presence offered an opportunity to strike back against the brutal Aztec regime.

Despite their assumption of cultural superiority, many Spaniards who accompanied Cortés were astonished by Aztec cities, canals, and temples, which rivaled those in Europe. Seeing these architectural wonders may have given some soldiers pause about trying to conquer the Indian kingdom. But when Montezuma presented Cortés with large quantities of precious objects, including gold-encrusted jewelry, as a peace offering, he alerted Spaniards to the vast wealth awaiting them in the Aztec capital.

When Cortés and his men marched to Tenochtitlán in 1519, Montezuma was indecisive in his response. After an early effort to ambush the Spaniards failed, the Aztec leader allowed Cortés to march his men into the capital city, where they took Montezuma hostage. In response, Aztec warriors attacked the Spaniards, but Cortés and his men managed to fight their way out of Tenochtitlán. They suffered heavy losses and might have been crushed by their Aztec foes but for the alliances forged with native groups in the surrounding area. Given time to regroup, the remaining Spanish soldiers and their allies attacked the Aztecs with superior steel weapons, horses, and trained dogs and gained a final victory.

The Spanish victory was also aided by the germs that soldiers carried with them. Smallpox swept through Tenochtitlán in 1521, killing thousands and leaving Montezuma's army dramatically weakened. This human catastrophe as much as military resources and strategies allowed Cortés to conquer the capital that year. He then claimed the entire region as New Spain, assigned soldiers to construct the new capital of Mexico City, and asserted Spanish authority over the native groups that had allied with him.

As news of Cortés's victory spread, other Spanish conquistadors sought gold and glory in the Americas. Most important, in 1524 Francisco Pizarro conquered the vast Inca empire in present-day Peru. Once again, the Spaniards were aided by the spread of European diseases and conflicts among peoples subjected to Inca rule. This victory ensured Spanish access to vast supplies of silver in Potosí (in present-day Bolivia) and the surrounding mountains. It also ensured the spread of enslaved African labor from plantation agriculture to mining. Spain was now in control of the most densely populated regions of South America, which also contained the greatest mineral wealth. Still, the diversity of populations in these regions—wealthy Spanish *encomenderos*, much poorer Spanish soldiers, Indians, and Africans—concerned authorities. In response,

An Aztec with Smallpox Smallpox followed the Spanish conquest, killing thousands of native peoples. In the sixteenth century, Bernardino de Sahagún, a missionary and educator, learned Nahuatl and wrote an illustrated history of New Spain with the aid of indigenous students. This illustration shows a woman with smallpox aided by a native healer. But the incurable disease ultimately led to death or disfigurement.   Granger, NYC

the Spanish developed a caste system the defined the status of these diverse populations and ensured that Spaniards remained at the top of the hierarchy even as wealthy landowners distinguished themselves from their poorer countrymen. In one decade, life for Aztecs and other Indians as well as the Spanish changed dramatically.

Spanish Adventurers Head North

In 1526, a company of Spanish women and men traveled from the West Indies as far north as the Santee River in present-day South Carolina. They planned to settle in the region and then search for gold and other valuables. The effort failed, but two years later Pánfilo de Narváez—one of the survivors—led four hundred soldiers from Cuba to Florida's Tampa Bay. Seeking precious metals, the party instead confronted hunger, disease, and hostile Indians. The ragtag group continued to journey along the Gulf coast, until only four men, led by Álvar Nuñez Cabeza de Vaca, made their way from Galveston Bay back to Mexico City. In both cases, native peoples effectively defended their political sovereignty, economic prosperity, and religious beliefs.

A decade later, in 1539, a survivor of Narváez's ill-fated venture—a North African named Esteban—led a party of Spaniards from Mexico back north. Lured by tales of Seven Golden Cities, the party instead encountered Zuñi Indians, who attacked the Spaniards and killed Esteban. Still, the men who returned to Mexico passed on stories of large and wealthy cities. Hoping to find fame and fortune, Francisco Vásquez de Coronado launched a grand expedition northward in 1540. Angered when they failed to discover fabulous wealth, Coronado and his men terrorized the region, burning towns, killing residents, and stealing goods before returning to Mexico.

Hernando de Soto headed another effort to find wealth in North America. An experienced conquistador, de Soto received royal authority in 1539 to explore Florida. That spring he established a village near Tampa Bay with more than six hundred Spanish, Indian, and African men, and a few women. A few months later, de Soto and the bulk of his company traveled up the west Florida coast with Juan Ortiz, a member of the Narváez expedition and an especially useful guide and interpreter. That winter, the expedition traveled into present-day Georgia and the Carolinas in an unsuccessful search for riches (Map 1.5).

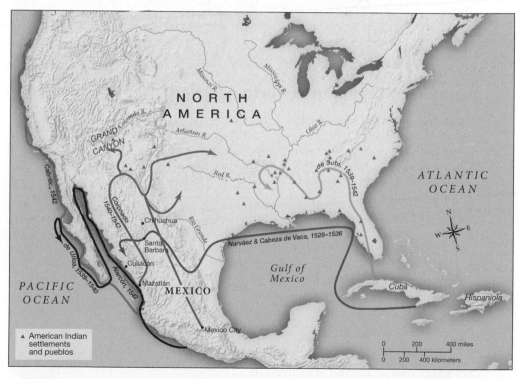

MAP 1.5

Spanish Explorations in North America, 1528–1542   Spanish explorers in North America hoped to find gold and other treasures. Instead, they encountered difficult terrain and native peoples hostile to Spanish intruders. Many Spaniards died on these expeditions, and they failed to discover new sources of wealth. But they laid the foundations for Spanish settlements in Florida, northern Mexico, and California while devastating local Indian populations.

On their return trip, de Soto's men engaged in a brutal battle with local Indians led by Chief Tuskaloosa. Although the Spaniards claimed victory, they lost a significant number of men and horses and most of their equipment. Fearing that word of the disaster would reach Spain, de Soto steered his men away from supply ships in the Gulf of Mexico and headed back north. The group traveled into present-day Tennessee, then turned west, and in May 1541 became the first Europeans to report seeing the vast Mississippi River. Crossing it, they journeyed on into Arkansas, Oklahoma, and Texas. By the winter of 1542, the expedition had lost more men and supplies to Indians, and de Soto had died. The remaining members finally returned to Spanish territory in the summer of 1543.

The lengthy journey of de Soto and his men brought European diseases into new areas, leading to epidemics and the depopulation of once-substantial native communities. At the same time, the Spaniards left horses and pigs behind, creating new sources of transportation and food for native peoples. Although most Spaniards considered de Soto's journey a failure, the Spanish crown claimed vast new territories. Two decades later, in 1565, Pedro Menéndez de Avilés established a mission settlement on the northeast coast of Florida, named St. Augustine. It became the first permanent European settlement in North America. Still, unlike the conquest of central and South America, the colonization of North America forced Spaniards to accept some of the native people's political and economic systems, religious beliefs, and even gender roles. When they refused to do so, open rebellions often resulted.

Europeans Compete in North America

Spain's early ventures in North America helped inspire French and English explorers to establish their own footholds on the continent. The French entered the race for empire in 1524, when an Italian navigator named Giovanni da Verrazano led a French company along the coast of North America. Landing initially near Cape Fear on the Carolina coast, the expedition headed north, sailing into what would become New York harbor. Verrazano then continued north, claiming lands all along the coast for France.

A decade later, in 1534, the Frenchman Jacques Cartier sailed to the Gulf of St. Lawrence. In two subsequent expeditions, Cartier pushed deeper into the territory known as Canada. Although he failed to discover precious metals or the elusive passage to the Pacific Ocean, he did trade for furs with local Indians. Cartier also inspired a French nobleman, the Sieur de Roberval, and several hundred followers to attempt a permanent settlement at Quebec in 1542. But the project was abandoned within a year because of harsh weather, disease, and high mortality.

English interest in North America was ignited by Spanish and French challenges to claims Cabot had made along the North Atlantic coast in the 1490s. To secure these rights, the English needed to colonize the disputed lands. Since the English crown did not have funds to support settlement, the earliest ventures were financed by minor noblemen who hoped to gain both wealth and the crown's favor. The earliest of these, in Newfoundland and Maine, failed.

The most promising effort to secure an English foothold was organized by Sir Walter Raleigh. Claiming all the land north of Florida for England, Raleigh called the vast territory Virginia (after Elizabeth I, "the Virgin Queen"). In 1585 Raleigh sent a group of soldiers to found a colony on Roanoke Island, off the coast of present-day

North Carolina. The colony would establish England's claims and allow English sailors stationed there to seize Spanish ships laden with valuables. This venture lasted less than a year. But in 1587 Raleigh tried again, sending a group of 117 men, women, and children to Roanoke. However, when supply ships came to fortify the settlement in 1590, the settlers had all disappeared, and their fate remains unknown.

By 1590, then, nearly a century after Columbus's initial voyage, only Spain had established permanent colonies in the Americas, mostly in the West Indies, Mexico, and South America. The French and the English, despite numerous efforts, had not sustained a single ongoing settlement by the end of the sixteenth century. Yet neither nation gave up hope of benefiting from the wealth of the Americas.

Spain Seeks Dominion in Europe and the Americas

The continued desire of European nations to gain colonies in the Americas resulted from the enormous wealth garnered by Spanish conquests. That wealth transformed economies throughout Europe. Between 1500 and 1650, Spanish ships carried home more than 180 tons of gold and 16,000 tons of silver from Mexico and Potosí. About one-fifth of this amount was taken by the Spanish crown for taxes; the rest was dispersed among supporters of the expeditions; family and friends of those who conquered lands, gained *encomiendas*, or participated in trade; and soldiers and sailors who returned from America. The money was spent mainly on luxury goods imported from the Americas, Asia, or other European nations. Very little of this wealth was invested in improving conditions at home. Indeed, the rapid infusion of gold and silver fueled inflation, making it harder for ordinary people to afford the necessities of life.

In one area, however, employment for the poor expanded rapidly. Spain's King Philip II (r. 1556–1598) used American gold and silver to fund a variety of military campaigns, ensuring an endless demand for soldiers and sailors. The king, a devout Catholic, claimed to be doing God's work as Spain conquered Italy and Portugal, including the latter's colonies in Africa, and tightened its grip on the Netherlands, which had been acquired by Spain through marriage in the early sixteenth century.

Despite the obvious material benefits, the Spaniards were not blind to the enormous human costs of colonization, and the conquest of the Americas inspired heated debates within Spain. Catholic leaders believed that the conversion of native peoples to Christianity was critical to Spanish success in the Americas. However, most royal officials and colonial agents viewed the extraction of precious metals as far more important. They argued that cheap labor was essential to creating wealth. Yet brutal conditions led to the death of huge numbers of Indians, which made it nearly impossible to convert others to Catholicism.

By 1550, tales of the widespread torture and enslavement of Indians convinced the Spanish king Carlos V (r. 1519–1556) to gather a group of theologians, jurists, and philosophers at Valladolid to discuss the moral and legal implications of conquest. Bartolomé de Las Casas took a leading role in defending the rights of Indians. A former conquistador and Dominican friar, Las Casas had spent many years preaching to Indians in America. He asked, "And so what man of sound mind will approve a war against men who are harmless, ignorant, gentle, temperate, unarmed, and destitute of every human defense?" Las Casas reasoned that even if Spain defeated the Indians, the souls of those killed would be lost to God, while among the survivors "hatred and loathing of the Christian religion" would prevail. He even suggested replacing Indian labor with African labor, apparently less concerned with the souls of black people.

Juan Ginés de Sepúlveda, the royal historian, attacked Las Casas's arguments. Although he had never set foot in America, he read reports of cannibalism and other violations of "natural law" among native peoples. Since the Indians were savages, the civilized Spaniards were obligated to "destroy barbarism and educate these people to a more humane and virtuous life." If they refused such help, Spanish rule "can be imposed upon them by force of arms." Although Ginés de Sepúlveda spoke for the majority at Valladolid, Las Casas and his supporters continued to press their case as Spain expanded its reach into North America.

At the same time, American riches increasingly flowed beyond Spain's borders. The Netherlands was a key beneficiary of this wealth, becoming a center for Spanish shipbuilding and trade. Still, the Dutch were never completely under Spanish control, and they traded gold, silver, and other items to France, England, and other European nations. Goods also followed older routes across the Mediterranean to the Ottoman empire, where traders could make huge profits on exotic items from the Americas. Thus, while some Europeans suffered under Spanish power, others benefited from the riches brought to the continent. By the late sixteenth century, the desire for a greater share of those riches revitalized imperial dreams among the French and English as well as the Dutch.

REVIEW & RELATE	• What motivated the Spanish to conquer and colonize the Americas?
	• What were the consequences in Europe of Spain's acquisition of an American empire?

Conclusion: A Transformed America

For centuries, Asian peoples migrated to the Americas by land and sea. They developed an astonishing array of cultures and societies, from small hunting-and-gathering bands to complex empires. In the fourteenth and fifteenth centuries, extensive commercial and political networks existed among the Mississippians, the Aztecs, and the Incas, although only the latter two continued to thrive by the late 1400s. In southern Europe, too, during the fifteenth century, economic, cultural, and political advances fueled interest in long-distance trade and exploration. Italy and Portugal led these efforts, but their monopoly of trade routes across the Mediterranean and around Africa to Asia forced Spain to look west in hopes of gaining access to China and the Indies. In doing so, the Spanish unexpectedly came into contact with the Americas.

When Spanish explorers happened upon Caribbean islands and the nearby mainland, they created contacts between populations that would be dramatically transformed in a matter of decades. While native residents of the Americas were sometimes eager to trade with the newcomers and to form alliances against their traditional enemies, they fought against those they considered invaders. Yet some of the most significant invaders—plants, pigs, and especially germs—were impossible to defend against. Even Europeans seeking peaceful relations with native inhabitants or bent on conversion rather than conquest brought diseases that devastated local populations, and plants and animals that transformed their landscape, diet, and traditional ways of life.

Waldseemüller died in 1521 or 1522, so he did not see the most dramatic changes that his remarkably accurate maps inspired. Malintzin, however, experienced those changes firsthand. She watched as disease ravaged not only rural villages but even the capital city of Tenochtitlán. She encountered horses, pigs, attack dogs, and other European animals. She ate the foods and wore the clothes that her Spanish captors provided. In 1522, Malintzin gave birth to Cortés's son; two years later, she served as interpreter when he ventured north to conquer more territory. In 1526 or 1527, however, she married a Spanish soldier, Juan Jaramillo, settled in Mexico City, and bore two more children. As more and more Spaniards, including the first women, settled in New Spain, Malintzin realized that her children would grow up in a world very different from the one in which she was raised.

From 1490 to 1590, the most dramatic and devastating changes for native peoples occurred in Mexico, the West Indies, Central America, and South America. But events there also presaged what would happen throughout the Americas. As Spanish conquistadors ventured into Florida and the Gulf Coast and French and English explorers sought to gain footholds along the Atlantic seaboard, they carried sufficient germs, seeds, and animals to transform native societies even before Europeans established permanent settlements in North America.

In the century to come, contacts and conflicts between native peoples and Europeans would escalate as France, England, and the Netherlands joined Spain in colonizing North America. Conflicts among European nations also multiplied as they struggled to control land, labor, and trade. Moreover, as Indian populations died out in some regions and fended off conquest in others, Europeans turned increasingly to the trade in Africans to provide the labor to produce enormously profitable items like sugar, coffee, and tobacco.

Chapter 1 Review

KEY TERMS

Beringia (p. 3)
Horticulture (p. 4)
Aztecs (p. 5)
Maya (p. 5)
Incas (p. 5)
Hopewell people (p. 6)
Crusades (p. 9)

Black Death (p. 9)
Renaissance (p. 10)
Enterprise of the Indies (p. 13)
encomienda (p. 14)
Columbian exchange (p. 17)
conquistadors (p. 18)

REVIEW & RELATE

1. Compare and contrast the Aztecs, Incas, and Maya. What similarities and differences do you note?
2. How did the societies of North America differ from those of the equatorial zone and the Andes?
3. How and why did Europeans expand their connections with Africa and the Middle East in the fifteenth century?
4. How did early European encounters with West Africans influence Europeans' ideas about African peoples and reshape existing systems of slavery?
5. What were the short-term consequences in both Europe and the Americas of Columbus's voyages?
6. How did the Columbian exchange transform both the Americas and Europe?
7. What motivated the Spanish to conquer and colonize the Americas?
8. What were the consequences in Europe of Spain's acquisition of an American empire?

TIMELINE OF EVENTS

25,000–13,000 B.C.E.	• First northeast Asians migrate to the Americas
900 B.C.E.–300 C.E.	• Maya settle Yucatán peninsula
500 C.E.	• Mogollon and Hohokam settle in southwestern North America; spread of maize cultivation northward begins
500–1400	• Mississippian peoples establish complex cultures
800	• Mayan civilization begins to decline
1000	• Norse settle in North America
1325	• Aztecs build Tenochtitlán
1340s	• Black Death (bubonic plague) in Europe
1400–1500	• Inca empire reaches its height
1440s	• Portuguese begin to trade along the coast of West Africa
1452–1455	• Johannes Gutenberg prints Bibles using movable type
1469	• Unification of Spain
1487	• Bartolomeu Dias rounds the Cape of Good Hope
1492	• Spain expels Muslim conquerors and Jews • Christopher Columbus's first voyage to the Americas
1497	• Vasco da Gama sails to India
1507	• Martin Waldseemüller and Mathias Ringmann publish *Universalis Cosmographia*
1519	• Malintzin captured by Spaniards
1519–1521	• Hernán Cortés conquers the Aztecs
1519–1522	• Ferdinand Magellan's fleet circumnavigates the globe
1524	• Francisco Pizarro conquers the Incas
1587	• English settle Roanoke Island

2

Colonization and Conflicts

1580–1680

LEARNING OBJECTIVES

After reading this chapter you should be able to:

- Discuss the impact of the Reformation and Counter-Reformation on European nations and their imperial goals in the American colonies.
- Evaluate the ways that England's hopes for its North American colonies were transformed by relations with Indians, upheavals among indentured servants, the development of tobacco, and the emergence of slavery.
- Analyze the influence of Puritanism on New England's development and how religious and political upheavals in England fueled Puritan expansion and conflicts with Indians in the colonies.

COMPARING AMERICAN HISTORIES

Born in 1580 to a yeoman farm family in Lincolnshire, John Smith left England as a young man "to learne the life of a Souldier." After fighting and traveling in Europe, the Mediterranean, and North Africa for several years, Captain Smith returned to England around 1605. There he joined the Virginia Company, whose wealthy investors planned to establish a private settlement on mainland North America. In April 1607, Captain Smith and 104 men arrived in Chesapeake Bay, where they founded Jamestown, named in honor of King James I, and claimed the land for themselves and their country. However, the area was already controlled by a powerful Indian leader, Chief Powhatan.

   In December 1607, when Powhatan's younger brother discovered Smith and two of his Jamestown comrades in the chief's territory, the Indians executed the two comrades but eventually released Smith. It is likely that before sending him back to Jamestown, Powhatan performed an adoption ceremony in an effort to bring Smith and the English under his authority. A typical ceremony would have involved Powhatan sending out one of his daughters—in this case, Pocahontas, who was about twelve years old—to indicate that the captive was spared. Refusing to accept his new status, if he understood it, Smith returned to Jamestown and urged residents to build fortifications for security.

The following fall, the colonists elected Smith president of the Jamestown council. Smith insisted that intimidating the Indians was the way to win Powhatan's respect. He also demanded that the English labor on farms and fortifications six hours a day. Many colonists resisted. Those who claimed the status of gentlemen considered manual labor beneath them, and the many who were adventurers sought wealth and glory, not hard work. The Virginia Company soon replaced Smith with a new set of leaders. In October 1609, angry and bitter, he returned to England.

Captain Smith published his criticisms of Virginia Company policies in 1612, which brought him widespread attention. He then set out to map the Atlantic coast farther north. In 1616 Smith published a tract that emphasized the similarity of the area's climate and terrain to the British Isles, calling it New England. He argued that colonies there could be made commercially viable but that success depended on recruiting settlers with the necessary skills and offering them land and a say in the colony's management.

English men and women did settle New England in the 1620s, but they sought religious sanctuary, not commercial success or military dominance. Yet they, too, suffered schisms in their ranks. Anne Hutchinson, a forty-five-year-old wife and mother, was at the center of one such division. Born in Lincolnshire in 1591, Anne was well educated when she married William Hutchinson, a merchant, in 1612. The Hutchinsons and their children began attending Puritan sermons and by 1630 embraced the new faith. Four years later, they followed the Reverend John Cotton to Massachusetts Bay.

The Reverend Cotton soon urged Anne Hutchinson to use her exceptional knowledge of the Bible to hold prayer meetings in her home on Sundays for pregnant and nursing women who could not attend regular services. Hutchinson, like Cotton, preached that individuals must rely solely on God's grace rather than a saintly life or good works to ensure salvation.

Hutchinson began challenging Puritan ministers who opposed this position, charging that they posed a threat to their congregations. She soon attracted a loyal and growing following that included men as well as women. Puritan leaders met in August 1637 to denounce Hutchinson's views and condemn her meetings. In November 1637, after she refused to recant, she was put on trial. Hutchinson mounted a vigorous defense. Unmoved, the

Puritan judges convicted her of heresy and banished her from Massachusetts Bay. Hutchinson and her family, along with dozens of followers, then settled in the recently established colony of Rhode Island.

COMPARING THE AMERICAN HISTORIES of John Smith and Anne Hutchinson illustrates the diversity of motives that drew English men and women to North America in the seventeenth century. Smith led a group of artisans, gentlemen, and adventurers whose efforts to colonize Virginia were in many ways an extension of a larger competition between European states. Hutchinson's journey to North America was rooted in the Protestant Reformation, which divided Europe into rival factions. Yet as different as these two people were, both furthered English settlement in North America even as they generated conflict within their own communities. Communities like theirs also confronted the expectations of diverse native peoples and the colonial aspirations of other Europeans while reshaping North America between 1550 and 1680.

Religious and Imperial Transformations

The Puritans were part of a relatively new religious movement known as **Protestantism** that had emerged around 1520. Protestants challenged Catholic policies and practices but did not form a single church of their own. Instead, a number of theologians formed distinct denominations in various regions of Europe. Catholics sought to counter their claims by revitalizing their faith and reasserting control. These religious conflicts shaped developments in North America as the Spanish, French, Dutch, and English competed for lands and sometimes souls.

The Protestant Reformation

Critiques of the Catholic Church multiplied in the early sixteenth century, driven by papal involvement in conflicts among monarchs and corruption among church officials. But the most vocal critics focused on immorality, ignorance, and absenteeism among clergy. These anticlerical views appeared in popular songs and printed images as well as in learned texts by theologians such as Martin Luther.

Luther, a professor of theology in Germany, believed that faith alone led to salvation, which could be granted only by God. He challenged the Catholic Church's claim that individuals could achieve salvation by buying indulgences, which were documents that absolved the buyer of sin. The church profited enormously from these sales, but they suggested that God's grace could be purchased. In 1517 Luther wrote an extended argument against indulgences and sent it to the local bishop. Although intended for learned clerics and academics, his writings soon gained a wider audience.

Luther's followers, who protested Catholic practices, became known as Protestants. His teachings circulated widely through sermons and printed texts, and his claim that ordinary people should read and reflect on the Scriptures appealed to the literate middle classes. Meanwhile his attacks on indulgences and corruption attracted those who resented the church's wealth and priests' lack of attention to their flocks. In

Switzerland, John Calvin developed a version of Protestantism in which civil magistrates and reformed ministers ruled over a Christian society. Calvin argued that God had decided at the beginning of time who was saved and who was damned. Calvin's idea, known as predestination, energized Protestants who understood salvation as a gift from an all-knowing God in which the "works" of sinful humans played no part.

The Protestant Reformation quickly spread through central and northern Europe. England, too, came under the influence of Protestantism in the 1530s, although for different reasons. When the pope refused to annul the marriage of King Henry VIII (r. 1509–1547) and Catherine of Aragon, Henry denounced papal authority and established the **Church of England**, or Anglicanism, with himself as "defender of the faith." Despite the king's conversion to Protestantism, the Church of England retained many Catholic practices.

In countries like Spain and France with strong central governments and powerful ties to the Catholic Church, a strong Catholic Counter-Reformation largely quashed Protestantism. At the same time, Catholic leaders initiated reforms to counter their critics. In 1545 Pope Paul II called together a commission of cardinals, known as the Council of Trent (1545–1563), which initiated a number of reforms, such as the founding of seminaries to train priests and the return of monastic orders to their spiritual foundations.

Religious upheavals in Europe turned many eyes toward North America. Protestant and Catholic leaders urged followers to spread their faith across the Atlantic, while religious minorities sought a safe haven free from persecution. Just as important, political struggles erupted between Catholic and Protestant rulers in Europe following the Reformation. The resulting economic and military crises pushed (or forced) people to seek new opportunities in the Americas. Thus, in a variety of ways, religious transformations in Europe fueled the construction of empires in America.

Spain's Global Empire Declines

As religious conflicts escalated in Europe, the Spaniards in America continued to push north from Florida and Mexico in hopes of expanding their empire. The nature of Spanish expansion, however, changed. As a result of the Council of Trent and the Catholic Counter-Reformation, Spain increasingly emphasized its religious mission. Thus Spanish authorities decided in 1573 that missionaries rather than soldiers should direct all new settlements. Franciscan priests began founding missions on the margins of Pueblo villages north of Mexico. They named the area Nuevo México (New Mexico), and many learned Indian languages. Over the following decades, as many as twenty thousand Pueblos officially converted to Catholicism, although many still retained traditional beliefs and practices. Missionaries made a considerable effort to eradicate such beliefs and practices, including flogging ceremonial leaders, but to no avail.

At the same time, the Franciscans tried to force the Pueblo people to adopt European ways. They insisted that men rather than women farm the land and that the Pueblos speak, cook, and dress like the Spaniards. Yet the missionaries largely ignored Spanish laws intended to protect Indians from coerced labor, demanding that the Pueblos build churches, provide the missions with food, and carry their goods

San Esteban del Rey Mission   Opened in 1644 after fourteen years of construction, this Spanish mission in present-day New Mexico provided instruction in Christianity and Hispanic customs for the Acoma (Pueblo) people. To this end, Spanish missionaries prohibited traditional Pueblo practices such as performing dances and wearing masks. The mission was one of the few to survive Pueblo revolts in the late seventeenth century.   © age fotostock/SuperStock

to market. Wealthy landowners who followed the missionaries into New Mexico also demanded tribute in the form of goods and labor.

Then in 1598 Juan de Oñate, a member of a wealthy mining family, established a trading post and fort in the upper Rio Grande valley. The 500 soldiers who accompanied him seized corn and clothing from Pueblo villages and murdered or raped those who resisted. When the Spanish force was confronted by Indians at the Acoma pueblo, 11 soldiers were killed. The Spanish retaliated, slaughtering 500 men and 300 women and children. Fearing reprisals from outraged Indians, most Spanish settlers withdrew from the region.

In 1610 the Spanish returned, founded Santa Fe, and established a network of missions and estates owned by *encomenderos*, Spanish elites granted land and the right to exploit local Indian labor. This time the Pueblo people largely accepted the new situation. In part, they feared military reprisals if they challenged Spanish authorities. But they were also facing drought, disease, and raids by hostile Apache and Navajo tribes. The Pueblos hoped to gain protection from Spanish soldiers and priests. Yet their faith in the Franciscans' spiritual power soon began to fade when conditions did not improve. Although Spain maintained a firm hold on Florida and its colonies in the West Indies, it began focusing most of its efforts on staving off growing resistance among the Pueblo people. Thus as other European powers expanded their reach into North America, the Spaniards were left with few resources to protect their eastern frontier.

France Enters the Race for Empire

In the late sixteenth century, French, Dutch, and English investors became increasingly interested in gaining a foothold in North America. But until Catholic Spain's grip on the Atlantic world was broken, other nations could not hope to compete for an American empire. It was the Protestant Reformation that helped shape the alliances that shattered Spain's American monopoly. As head of the Church of England, Queen Elizabeth I (King Henry VIII's daughter, r. 1558–1603) sought closer political and commercial ties with Protestant nations like the Netherlands. The queen also assented to, and benefited from, Francis Drake's raids on Spanish ships. In 1588 King Philip II of Spain (r. 1556–1598) decided to punish England for its attacks against Spanish shipping and intervention in the Netherlands and sent a massive armada to spearhead the invasion of England. Instead, the English, aided by Dutch ships, defeated the armada and ensured that other nations could compete for riches and colonies in North America.

Although French rulers shared Spain's Catholic faith, the two nations were rivals, and the defeat of the armada provided them as well as the Dutch and English with greater access to North American colonies. Moreover, once in North America, the French adopted attitudes and policies that were significantly different from those of Spain. This was due in part to their greater interest in trade than in conquest. The French had fished the North Atlantic since the mid-sixteenth century, but in the 1580s they built stations along the Newfoundland coast for drying codfish. French traders then established relations with local Indians, exchanging iron kettles and other European goods for valuable beaver skins.

By the early seventeenth century, France's King Henry IV (r. 1589–1610) sought to profit more directly from the resources in North America. With the Edict of Nantes (1598), the king ended decades of religious wars by granting political rights and limited toleration to French Protestants, known as Huguenots, many of whom had earlier sought refuge in North America. Now he could focus on developing the increasingly lucrative trade in American fish and furs. Samuel de Champlain founded the first permanent French settlement in North America in 1608 at Quebec. Accompanied by several dozen men, Champlain joined a Huron raid on the Iroquois, who resided south of the Great Lakes. By using guns, the French helped ensure a Huron victory and a powerful ally for the French. But the battle also fueled lasting bitterness among the Iroquois.

Trade relations flourished between the French and their Indian allies, but relatively few French men and even fewer French women settled in North America in the seventeenth century. Government policies discouraged mass migration, and peasants were also concerned by reports of short growing seasons and severe winters in Canada. Cardinal Richelieu, the king's chief minister, urged priests and nuns to migrate to New France, but he barred continued emigration by Huguenots, which further limited colonization. Thus into the 1630s, French settlements in North America consisted largely of fishermen, fur traders, and Catholic missionaries.

Fur traders were critical to sustaining the French presence and warding off encroachment by the English. They journeyed throughout eastern Canada, aided by the Huron tribe. Some Frenchmen took Indian wives, who provided them with both domestic labor and kinship ties to powerful trading partners. Despite Catholic criticism of these marriages, they enhanced French traders' success and fostered alliances among the Ojibwe and Dakota nations to the west. These alliances, in turn, created a middle ground in which economic and cultural exchanges led to a remarkable degree of mutual adaptation. French traders benefited from Indian women's skills in preparing beaver skins for market as well as from Indian canoes, while natives adopted iron cooking pots and European cloth.

In their ongoing search for new sources of furs, the French established a fortified trading post at Montreal in 1643, and over the next three decades they continued to push farther west. However, as they extended the fur trade beyond the St. Lawrence River valley, the French left their Huron allies behind. The Iroquois wanted to keep the Huron tribe from trading their high-quality furs to the Dutch. With guns supplied by Dutch merchants, the Iroquois could fend off economic competition and secure captives to restore their population, which was decimated by disease. The result was a series of devastating assaults on Huron villages.

The ongoing wars among native rivals limited the ability of France to capitalize on its North American colonies. Indeed, the only hope of maintaining profits from the fur trade was to continue to move westward. But in doing so, the French carried European diseases into new areas, ignited warfare among more native groups, and stretched their always small population of settlers ever thinner. Still, French explorers, traders, and priests extended their reach across Canada and by 1681 had moved southward along the Mississippi to a territory they named Louisiana in honor of King Louis XIV (r. 1643–1715).

The conflicts between commerce and conversion so evident in Spanish America were far less severe in New France. French traders relied on Indian allies, and some French Jesuit priests also sought to build on native beliefs and to learn the Indians' language and customs. Although Catholics assumed that their own religious beliefs and cultural values were superior to those of the Indians, many sought to engage Indians on their own terms. Thus one French Jesuit employed the Huron belief that "our souls have desires which are inborn and concealed" to explain Christian doctrines of sin and salvation to potential converts. Still, French traders and missionaries carried deadly germs, and Catholics sought conversion, not mutual adaptation. Thus while Indians clearly benefited from their alliances with the French in the short term, the long-term costs would prove devastating.

The Dutch Expand into North America

The Protestant Dutch made no pretense of bringing religion to Indians in America. From the beginning, their goals were primarily economic. As Spain's shipbuilding center, the Netherlands benefited from the wealth pouring in from South America, and an affluent merchant class emerged. But the Dutch also embraced Calvinism and sought to separate themselves from Catholic Spain. In 1581 the Netherlands declared its independence from King Philip II (r. 1556–1598), although Spain refused to recognize the new status for several decades. Still, by 1600 the Netherlands was both a

Protestant haven and the trading hub of Europe. Indeed, the Dutch East India Company controlled trade routes to much of Asia and parts of Africa.

With the technology and skills developed under Spanish control, the Dutch decided to acquire their own American colonies. In 1609 the Dutch established a fur-trading center on the Hudson River in present-day New York. The small number of Dutch traders developed especially friendly relations with the powerful Mohawk nation, and in 1614 the trading post was relocated to Fort Orange, near present-day Albany.

In 1624, to fend off French and English raids on ships sent downriver from Fort Orange, the Dutch established New Amsterdam on Manhattan Island, which they purchased from the Lenape Indians. The new settlement was organized by the Dutch West India Company, which had been chartered three years earlier. New Amsterdam was the centerpiece of the larger New Netherland colony and attracted a diverse community of traders, fishermen, and farmers. It was noted for its representative government and religious toleration.

The European settlers of New Netherland, which became part of the Middle Colonies, may have gotten along with one another, but the same could not be said for settlers and local Indians. Tensions increased as Dutch colonists carved out farms north of New Amsterdam where large communities of Algonquian Indians lived. In 1639 conflict escalated when Governor William Kieft demanded an annual tribute in wampum or grain. Local Algonquians resisted, raiding Dutch farms on the frontier and killing at least two colonists. Then in 1643 Kieft launched a surprise attack on an Indian encampment on Manhattan Island, murdering eighty people, mostly women and children. Outraged Algonquians burned and looted homes north of the city, killed livestock, and murdered settlers. For two decades, sporadic warfare continued, but eventually the Algonquians were defeated.

At the same time, the Dutch eagerly traded for furs with Mohawk Indians along the upper Hudson River. The Mohawks were a powerful tribe that had the backing of the even more powerful Iroquois Confederacy. Their ties to Indian nations farther west allowed them to provide beaver skins to Dutch traders long after beavers had died out in the Hudson valley. Still, the Mohawk people did not deceive themselves. As one chief proclaimed in 1659, "The Dutch say we are brothers and that we are joined together with chains, but that lasts only so long as we have beavers."

Meanwhile reports of atrocities by both Indians and the Dutch circulated in the Netherlands. These damaged New Amsterdam's reputation and slowed migration dramatically. A series of wars with their former ally England further weakened Dutch power in America. In 1664, the England sent a naval convoy to take New Amsterdam. Exhausted by decades of unrelenting conflict, the Dutch surrendered New Amsterdam to the English without a fight.

| REVIEW & RELATE | • How did the Protestant Reformation shape the course of European expansion in the Americas? |
| | • How did the French and Dutch colonies in North America differ from the Spanish empire to the south? |

The English Seek an Empire

The English, like the French and the Dutch, entered the race for an American empire well after the Spanish. England did not have a permanent settlement in the Americas until the founding of **Jamestown** at the mouth of Chesapeake Bay in 1607. In the 1620s, the English also established settlements in the West Indies, which quickly became the economic engine of English colonization. Expansion into these areas demanded new modes of labor to ensure a return on investment. Large numbers of indentured servants crossed the Atlantic, while growing numbers of Africans were forced onto ships for sale in the Americas. meanwhile, the rapid expansion of English settlement fostered conflicts with Indian nations and also fueled tensions among settlers themselves.

The English Establish Jamestown

England's success in colonizing North America depended in part on a new economic model in which investors purchased shares in joint-stock companies that could raise large amounts of money quickly. If the venture succeeded, investors shared the profits. If they failed, no investor suffered the whole loss. In 1606 a group of London merchants formed the Virginia Company, and King James I granted them the right to settle a vast area of North America, from present-day New York to North Carolina.

A Susquehannock Warrior
John Smith published a remarkably accurate map of Virginia in 1612. It included major geographical features and the names of some 200 Indian towns. Smith placed a sketch of a Susquehannock warrior in the upper right-hand corner; at his feet, Smith noted that the Susquehannock were "a Gyant-like people." This map was widely used for seven decades.   Beinecke Rare Book and Manuscripts Library, Yale University

Some of the men that the Virginia Company recruited as colonists were gentlemen who hoped to get rich through the discovery of precious metals. They also recruited skilled artisans and laborers to launch the settlement, many of whom hoped to gain wealth and status. Some men who planned to stay for an extended period even brought their wives, which was almost unheard of among Spanish and French explorers and missionaries. Arriving on the coast of North America in April 1607, the colonists established Jamestown on a site they chose mainly for its easy defense since it lay within territory controlled by a large confederation of Indians. Although bothered by the settlement's mosquito-infested environment, the colonists variously focused their energies on constructing buildings, producing food, and searching for gold and silver.

The Englishmen quickly made contact with the Indian chief Powhatan. He presided over the confederation of some 14,000 Algonquian-speaking Indians from twenty-five to thirty tribes, which surrounded the small Jamestown settlement. The **Powhatan Confederacy** was far more powerful than the English settlers, and, indeed, for the first two years the settlers depended on the Indians to survive. A shortage of food, caused by a severe drought between 1606 and 1612, affected both Indians and the English. It was exacerbated in Jamestown by some colonists' refusal to engage in manual labor. Moreover, the nearby water was tainted by salt from the ocean, and diseases that festered in the low-lying area killed more than half of the original settlers.

Despite the Englishmen's aggressive posture, Powhatan assisted the new settlers in hopes they could provide him with English cloth, iron hatchets, and even guns. His capture and subsequent release of John Smith in 1607 suggests his interest in developing trade relations with the newcomers even as he sought to subordinate them. But leaders like Captain Smith considered Powhatan and his warriors a threat rather than an asset. When unable to feed themselves that first year, Jamestown residents raided Indian villages for corn and other food, making Powhatan increasingly wary. The settlers' decision to construct a fort under Smith's direction only bolstered the Indians' concern.

Meanwhile the Virginia Company devised a new plan to stave off the collapse of its colony. It started selling seven-year joint-stock options to raise funds and recruited new settlers to produce staple crops, glassware, or other items for export. Interested individuals who could not afford to invest cash could sign an indenture for service in Virginia. After seven years, these indentured servants would gain their freedom and receive a hundred acres of land. In June 1609, a new contingent of colonists attracted by this plan—five hundred men and a hundred women—sailed for Jamestown.

The new arrivals, however, had not brought enough supplies to sustain the colony through the winter. Powhatan did offer some aid, but Indians, too, suffered from shortages in the winter of 1609–1610. A "starving time" settled on Jamestown. By the spring of 1610, seven of every eight settlers who had arrived in Jamestown since 1607 were dead.

That June, the sixty survivors decided to abandon Jamestown and sail for home. But they changed their minds when they met three English ships in the harbor loaded with supplies and three hundred more settlers. Emboldened by fresh supplies and an enlarged population, Jamestown's new leaders adopted an aggressive military posture, attacking native villages, burning crops, killing many Indians, and taking others captive. They believed that such brutality would convince neighboring tribes to obey English demands for food and labor.

Tobacco Fuels Growth in Virginia

It was not military aggression, however, but the discovery of a viable cash crop that saved the colony. Orinoco tobacco, grown in the West Indies and South America, sold well in England and Europe. Virginia colonist John Rolfe began to experiment with its growth in 1612, just as the drought lifted. Production of the leaf soared as eager investors poured seeds, supplies, and labor into Jamestown. Exports multiplied rapidly, from 2,000 pounds in 1615 to 40,000 pounds five years later and an incredible 1.5 million pounds by 1629.

Tobacco cultivation exacerbated tensions between the English and the Indians. As production increased and prices declined, farmers could increase their profits only by obtaining more land and more laborers. That is why the Virginia Company was willing to offer land to indentured laborers who spent seven years clearing new fields and creating more plantations. Yet in most cases, the land the Virginia Company offered these would-be colonists was already settled by members of the Powhatan Confederacy. Thus the rapid increase in tobacco cultivation intensified competition between colonists and Indians.

Nonetheless, Powhatan tried one last time to create an alliance between his confederacy and the English settlers. Perhaps he was encouraged by the return of rain, assuming that increased productivity would ensure better trade relations with the English. In 1614 he agreed to allow his daughter Pocahontas to marry John Rolfe. Pocahontas converted to Christianity and two years later traveled to England with Rolfe and their infant son. While there, she fell ill and died in 1617. Rolfe returned to Virginia just as relations with the Powhatan Confederacy began to change. In 1618 Powhatan died, and his younger brother Opechancanough took over as chief.

A year later, in 1619, the English crown granted Virginia the right to establish a local governing body, the **House of Burgesses**. Its members could make laws and levy taxes, although the English governor or the company council in London held veto power. The Virginia Company also resolved to recruit more female settlers as a way to increase the colony's population. More young women and men arrived as **indentured servants**, working in the fields and homes of more affluent Englishmen for a set period of time in exchange for passage to America. A Dutch ship carried the first boatload of twenty Africans to Jamestown that same year, bound as indentured servants to farmers desperate for labor.

Although the English colony still hugged the Atlantic coast, its expansion increased conflict with native inhabitants. In March 1622, after repeated English incursions on land cleared and farmed by Indians, Chief Opechancanough and his allies launched a surprise attack that killed nearly a third of the colonists. In retaliation, Englishmen assaulted native villages, killed inhabitants, burned cornfields, and sold captives into slavery.

The English proclaimed victory in 1623, but hostilities continued for nearly a decade. In 1624, in the midst of the crisis, King James annulled the Virginia Company charter and took control of the colony. He appointed the governor and a small advisory council, required that legislation passed by the House of Burgesses be ratified by the Privy Council, and demanded that property owners pay taxes to support the Church of England. These regulations became the model for royal colonies throughout North America.

Still, royal proclamations could not halt Indian opposition. In 1644 Opechancanough launched a second uprising against the English, killing hundreds of colonists. After two years of bitter warfare, Chief Opechancanough was finally captured and then killed. With the English population now too large to eradicate, the Chesapeake Indians finally submitted to English authority in 1646.

Expansion, Rebellion, and the Emergence of Slavery

By the 1630s, despite continued conflicts with Indians, Virginia was well on its way to commercial success. The most successful tobacco planters used indentured servants, including some Africans as well as thousands of English and Irish immigrants. Between 1640 and 1670, some 40,000 to 50,000 of these migrants settled in Virginia and neighboring Maryland (Map 2.1). Maryland was founded in 1632 when King Charles I, the successor to James I, granted most of the territory north of Chesapeake Bay to Cecilius Calvert and appointed him Lord Baltimore. Calvert was among the minority of English who remained a Catholic, and he planned to create Maryland as a refuge for his persecuted co-worshippers. Appointing his brother Leonard Calvert as governor, he carefully prepared for the first settlement. The Calverts recruited artisans and farmers (mainly Protestant) as well as wealthy merchants and aristocrats

MAP 2.1

The Growth of English Settlement in the Chesapeake, c. 1650   With the success of tobacco, English plantations and forts spread along the James River and north to St. Mary's. By 1650 most Chesapeake Indian tribes had been vanquished or forced to move north and west. The fall line, which marked the limit of navigable waterways, kept English settlements close to the Atlantic coast but also ensured easy shipment of goods.

(mostly Catholic) to settle the colony. Although conflict continued to fester between the Catholic elite and the Protestant majority, Governor Calvert convinced the Maryland assembly to pass the Act of Religious Toleration in 1649, granting religious freedom to all Christians.

Taken together, Maryland and Virginia formed the Chesapeake region of the English empire. Both colonies relied on tobacco to produce the wealth that fueled their growth, and both introduced African labor to complement the supply of white indentured servants. Still, neither colony had yet developed a legal code of slavery. From 1650 on, however, improved economic conditions in England meant fewer English men and women were willing to gamble on a better life in North America. Thus even though the number of African laborers remained small until late in the century, colonial leaders considered measures to increase their control over the African population. Thus in 1660 the House of Burgesses passed an act that allowed black laborers to be enslaved and in 1662 defined slavery as an inherited status passed on from mothers to children. In 1664 Maryland followed suit. The slow march toward full-blown racial slavery had begun. In legalizing human bondage, Virginia legislators followed a model established in Barbados, where the booming sugar industry spurred the development of plantation slavery. By 1660 Barbados had become the first English colony with a black majority population. Twenty years later, there were seventeen slaves for every white indentured servant on Barbados. The growth of slavery on the island depended almost wholly on imports from Africa since slaves there died faster than they could reproduce themselves. In the context of high death rates, brutal working conditions, and massive imports, Barbados systematized its slave code, defining enslaved Africans as chattel—that is, as mere property more akin to livestock than to human beings.

While African slaves would become, in time, a crucial component of the Chesapeake labor force, indentured servants made up the majority of bound workers in Virginia and Maryland for most of the seventeenth century. They labored under harsh conditions, and punishment for even minor infractions could be severe. They were beaten, whipped, and branded for a variety of behaviors. Some white servants made common cause with black laborers who worked side by side with them on tobacco plantations. They ran away together, stole goods from their masters, and planned uprisings and rebellions.

By the 1660s and 1670s, the population of former servants who had become free formed a growing and increasingly unhappy class. Most were struggling economically, working as common laborers or tenants on large estates. Those who managed to move west and claim land on the frontier were confronted by hostile Indians like the Susquehannock. Virginia governor Sir William Berkeley, who levied taxes to support nine forts on the frontier, had little patience with the complaints of these colonists. The labor demands of wealthy tobacco planters needed to be met, and frontier settlers' call for an aggressive Indian policy would hurt the profitable deerskin trade with the Algonquian Indians.

In late 1675, conflict erupted when frontier settlers attacked Indians in the region. Unlike colonial leaders back east, men on the frontier generally considered all Indians hostile. Rather than attacking only the Susquehannock nation, they also assaulted Indian communities allied with the English. When a large force of local Virginia militiamen did surround a Susquehannock village, they ignored pleas for peace and murdered five chiefs. Susquehannock warriors retaliated with raids on frontier farms.

Despite the outbreak of open warfare, Governor Berkeley still refused to send troops, so disgruntled farmers turned to Nathaniel Bacon. Bacon came from a wealthy family and was related to Berkeley by marriage. But he defied the governor's authority and called up an army to attack Indians across the colony. **Bacon's Rebellion** had begun. Frontier farmers formed an important part of Bacon's coalition. But affluent planters who had been left out of Berkeley's inner circle also joined Bacon in hopes of gaining access to power and profits. And bound laborers, black and white, assumed that any-one who opposed the governor was on their side.

In the summer of 1676, Governor Berkeley declared Bacon guilty of treason. Rather than waiting to be captured, Bacon led his army toward Jamestown. Berkeley then arranged a hastily called election to undercut the rebellion. Even though Berkeley had rescinded the right of men without property to vote, Bacon's supporters won control of the House of Burgesses, and Bacon won new adherents. These included "news wives," lower-class women who spread information (and rumors) about oppres-sive conditions to aid the rebels. As Bacon and his followers marched across Virginia, his men plundered the plantations of Berkeley and his supporters. In September they reached Jamestown after the governor and his administration fled across Chesapeake Bay. The rebels burned the capital to the ground, victory seemingly theirs.

Only a month later, however, Bacon died of dysentery, and the movement he formed unraveled. Governor Berkeley quickly reclaimed power. He hanged twenty-three rebel leaders and incited his followers to plunder the estates of planters who had supported Bacon. But he could not undo the damage to Indian relations on the Virginia frontier. Bacon's army had killed or enslaved hundreds of once-friendly Indians and left behind a tragic and bitter legacy.

An even more important consequence of the rebellion was that wealthy planters and investors realized the depth of frustration among poor whites who were willing to make common cause with their black counterparts. Having regained power, the planter elite worked to crush any such interracial alliance. Virginia legislators began to improve the conditions and rights of poor white settlers while imposing new restric-tions on blacks. At nearly the same time, in an effort to meet the growing demand for labor in the West Indies and the Chesapeake, King Charles II chartered the Royal African Company in 1672 to carry enslaved Africans to North America.

The English Compete for West Indies Possessions

While tobacco held great promise in Virginia, investors were eager to find other lucra-tive exports. Some turned their sights on the West Indies. In the 1620s, the English developed more permanent settlements on St. Christopher, Barbados, and Nevis (Map 2.2). Barbados quickly became the most attractive of these West Indies colonies. English migrants settled Barbados in growing numbers, bringing in white indentured servants, many Irish and Scotch, to cultivate tobacco and cotton and raise livestock.

In the 1630s, falling tobacco prices resulted in economic stagnation on Barbados. By that time, however, a few forward-looking planters were already considering another avenue to wealth: sugarcane. English and European consumers absorbed as much sugar as the market could provide, but producing sugar was difficult, expensive, and labor-intensive. In addition, the sugar that was sent from America needed further refinement in Europe before being sold to consumers. The Dutch had built the best

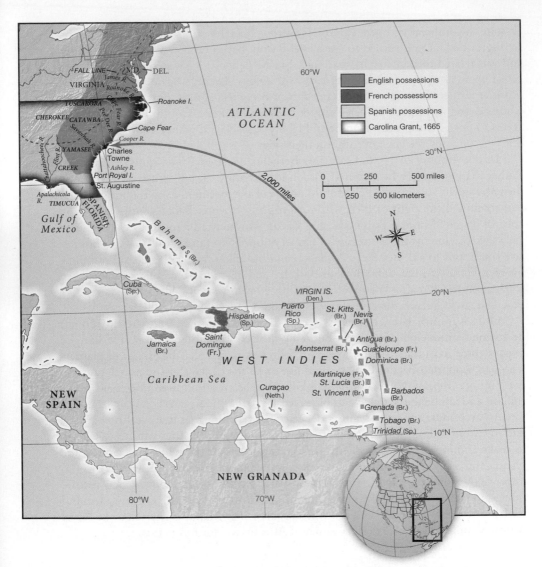

MAP 2.2
West Indies and Carolina in the Seventeenth Century   Beginning in the 1630s, sugar
cultivation transformed West Indies colonies. The British consumed sugar in large quantities,
ensuring the economic success of Barbados and its neighbors and a vast increase in the enslaved
population. In the 1660s, Barbados planters obtained a charter for Carolina and sent many early
settlers—white planters and merchants as well as enslaved laborers—to this mainland colony.

refineries in Europe, but their small West Indies colonies could not supply sufficient
raw material. By 1640 they formed a partnership with English planters, offering them
the knowledge and financing to cultivate sugar on Barbados, which then would be
refined in the Netherlands. That decision reshaped the economic and political landscape of North America and intensified competition for both land and labor.

Sugar Manufacturing in the West Indies This seventeenth-century engraving, which was later colorized, depicts the use of enslaved labor in the production of sugar in the West Indies. The Dutch, English, and French used slaves to plant sugarcane and then cut, press, and boil it to produce molasses. The molasses was turned into rum and refined sugar, both highly profitable exports. Sarin Images, Granger, NYC

REVIEW & RELATE	• How did the Virginia colony change and evolve between 1607 and the 1670s? • How did the growth of the English colonies on the mainland and in the West Indies shape conflicts in Virginia and demands for labor throughout North America?

Pilgrims and Puritans Settle New England

Along with merchants, planters, and indentured servants, religious dissenters also traveled to North America. Critics of the Church of England formed a number of congregations in the early seventeenth century, and some sought refuge in New England. One such group, the **Pilgrims** (also known as Separatists), landed on the Massachusetts coast in 1620 and established a permanent settlement at Plymouth. Their goal was to establish a religious community wholly separate from the Anglican Church. The Puritans, who hoped to purify rather than separate from the Church of England, arrived a decade later with plans to develop their own colony. Over the next two decades, New England colonists prospered, but they also confronted internal dissent and conflicts with local Indians.

Pilgrims Arrive in Massachusetts

In the 1610s, to raise capital, the Virginia Company began offering legal charters to groups of private investors, who were promised their own tract of land in the Virginia colony with minimal company oversight. One such charter was purchased by a group of English Pilgrims who wanted to form a separate church and community in a land untainted by Catholicism, Anglicanism, or European cosmopolitanism. Thirty-five Pilgrims from Leiden in the Dutch Republic and several dozen from England set sail on the *Mayflower* from Plymouth, England, in September 1620.

Battered by storms, the ship veered off course, landing at Cape Cod in present-day Massachusetts in early December. Before leaving the ship, the settlers, led by William Bradford, signed a pact to form a "civill body politick," which they considered necessary because they were settling in a region where they had no legal authority. The pact, known as the **Mayflower Compact**, was the first written constitution adopted in North America. It followed the Separatist model of a self-governing religious congregation.

After several forays along the coast, the Pilgrims located an uninhabited village surrounded by cornfields where they established their new home, Plymouth. Uncertain of native intentions, the Pilgrims were unsettled by sightings of Indians. They did not realize that a smallpox epidemic in the area only two years earlier had killed nearly 90 percent of the local Wampanoag population. Indeed, fevers and other diseases proved far more deadly to the settlers than did Indians. By the spring of 1621, only half of the 102 Pilgrims remained alive.

Desperate to find food, the survivors were stunned when two English-speaking Indians—Samoset and Squanto—appeared at Plymouth that March. Both had been captured as young boys by English explorers, and they now negotiated a fragile peace between the Pilgrims and Massasoit, chief of the Wampanoag tribe. Although concerned by the power of English guns, Massasoit hoped to create an alliance that would assist him against his traditional native enemies. With Wampanoag assistance, the surviving Pilgrims soon regained their health.

In the summer of 1621, reinforcements arrived from England, and the next year the Pilgrims received a charter granting them rights to Plymouth Plantation and a degree of self-government. Although some Pilgrims hoped to convert the Indians, other leaders favored a more aggressive stance toward hostile Indians. One Indian nation, the Massachusetts, posed an especially serious threat. So in 1623 Captain Miles Standish led an attack on a Massachusetts tribal village after kidnapping and killing the chief and his younger brother. Standish's strategy, though controversial, ensured that Massasoit, the colonists' Wampanoag ally, was now the most powerful chief in the region.

The Puritan Migration

As the Pilgrims gradually expanded their colony during the 1620s, a new group of English dissenters, the **Puritans**, made plans to develop their own settlement. Puritans believed that their country's church and government had grown corrupt and was being chastened by an all-powerful God. During the early seventeenth century, the English population boomed but harvests failed, leading to famine, crime, unemployment, and inflation. The enclosure movement, in which landlords fenced in fields and hired a few laborers and tenants to replace a large number of peasant farmers, increased the number of landless vagrants. At the same time, the English cloth industry nearly collapsed under the weight of competition from abroad. In the Puritans' view, all of these problems were divine punishments for the nation's sins.

The Puritans envisioned New England as a safe haven from God's wrath. Under Puritan lawyer John Winthrop's leadership, a group of affluent Puritans obtained a royal charter for the Massachusetts Bay Company, established in 1623 by English investors hoping to gain wealth through the establishment of North American colonies. However, New England was more than just a place of safety to the Puritans. Unlike the Pilgrims, they believed that England and the Anglican Church could be redeemed. By prospering spiritually and materially in America, they could establish a model "City upon a Hill" that would then inspire reform among residents of the mother country.

About one-third of English Puritans chose to leave their homeland for North America. They were better supplied, more prosperous, and more numerous than either their Pilgrim or Jamestown predecessors. Following John Smith's recommendations, the settlers, arriving on seventeen ships, included ministers, merchants, craftsmen, and farmers. Many Puritans sailed with entire families. The community benefited from being well supplied, including women who traditionally nursed their families, and settling in a cold climate that reduced the spread of disease. These factors ensured the rapid growth of the colony.

The first Puritan settlers arrived on the coast north of Plymouth in 1630 and named their community Boston, after the port city in England from which they had departed. Once established, they relocated the Massachusetts Bay Company's capital and records to New England, thereby converting their commercial charter into the founding document of a self-governing colony. They instituted a new kind of polity in which adult male church members participated in the election of a governor, deputy governor, and legislature. Although the Puritans suffered a difficult first winter, they quickly recovered and soon cultivated sufficient crops to feed themselves and a steady stream of new migrants. During the 1630s, some eighteen thousand Puritans migrated to New England. Even without a cash crop like tobacco or sugar, the Puritan colony flourished.

Eager to take advantage of the abundant land, the close-knit community spread quickly beyond its original boundaries. The legislature was thus forced early on to develop policies for establishing townships with governing bodies that supported a local church and school. By the time the migration of Puritans slowed around 1640, the settlers had turned their colony into a thriving commercial center. They shipped codfish, lumber, grain, pork, and cheese to England in exchange for manufactured goods and to the West Indies for rum and molasses. This trade, along with the healthy climate, relatively egalitarian distribution of property, and more equal ratio of women to men, ensured a stable and prosperous colony.

Puritans also sought friendly relations with some local natives, particularly the neighboring Massachusetts tribe, who were longtime enemies of the Pilgrims' allies, the Wampanoags. Many Puritans hoped that their Indian neighbors might be converted to Christianity. Puritan missionaries taught their pupils how to read the Bible, and a few students attended Harvard College, founded in 1636. In an effort to wean converts from their traditional customs and beliefs, missionary John Eliot created "praying towns." There Christian Indians could live among others who shared their faith while being protected from English settlers seeking to exploit them. Yet most "praying Indians" continued to embrace traditional rituals and beliefs alongside Christian practices.

The Puritan Worldview

Opposed to the lavish rituals and hierarchy of the Church of England and believing that few Anglicans truly felt the grace of God, Puritans set out to establish a simpler form of worship. They focused on their inner lives and on the purity of their church and community. Puritans followed Calvin, believing in an all-knowing God whose true Word was presented in the Bible. The biblically sanctioned church was a congregation formed by a group of believers who made a covenant with God. Only a small minority of people, known as Saints, were granted God's grace.

Whether one was a Saint and thereby saved was predetermined by and known only to God. Still, some Puritans believed that the chosen were likely to lead a saintly life. Visible signs included individuals' passionate response to the preaching of God's Word, their sense of doubt and despair over their own soul, and that wonderful sense of reassurance that came with God's "saving grace." God's hand in the world appeared in nature as well. Comets and eclipses were considered "remarkable providences." But so, too was a smallpox epidemic that killed several thousand Massachusetts Indians in 1633–1634 and thereby opened up land for Puritan settlers.

Shared religious beliefs helped forge a unified community where faith guided civil as well as spiritual decisions. While ministers were discouraged from holding political office, political leaders were devout Puritans who were expected to promote a godly society. Such leaders determined who got land, how much, and where; they also served as judge and jury for those accused of crimes or sins. Their leadership was largely successful. Even if colonists differed over who should get the most fertile strip of land, they agreed on basic principles. Still, almost from the beginning, certain Puritans challenged some of the community's fundamental beliefs and, in the process, the community itself.

Dissenters Challenge Puritan Authority

In the early 1630s, Roger Williams, a Salem minister, criticized Puritan leaders for not being sufficiently pure in their rejection of the Church of England and the English monarchy. He preached that not all the Puritan leaders were Saints and that some were bound for damnation. By 1635 Williams was forced out of Salem and moved south with his followers to found Providence in the area that became Rhode Island. Believing that there were very few Saints in the world, Williams and his followers accepted that one must live among those who were not saved. Thus unlike Massachusetts Bay, Providence welcomed Quakers, Baptists, and Jews to the community, and Williams's followers insisted on a strict separation of church and state. Williams also forged alliances with the Narragansetts, the most powerful Indian nation in the region.

A year after Williams's departure, Anne Hutchinson was accused of sedition, or trying to overthrow the government by challenging colonial leaders. She was put on trial in November 1637. An eloquent orator, Hutchinson ultimately claimed that her authority to challenge the Puritan leadership came from "an immediate revelation" from God, "the voice of his own spirit to my soul." Since Puritans believed that God spoke only through the intermediary of properly appointed male ministers, her claim was condemned as heretical.

Hutchinson was seen as a threat not only because of her religious beliefs but also because she was a woman. The Reverend Hugh Peter, for example, reprimanded her at trial: "You have stept out of your place, you have rather bine a Husband than a Wife and a preacher than a Hearer; and a Magistrate than a Subject." Many considered her challenge to Puritan authority especially serious because she also challenged traditional gender hierarchies. After being banished from Massachusetts Bay, Hutchinson and her followers joined Williams's Rhode Island colony.

Wars in Old and New England

As Anne Hutchinson and Roger Williams confronted religious leaders, Puritans and Pilgrims faced serious threats from their Indian neighbors as well. The Pequot nation, which was among the most powerful tribes in New England, had been allies of the English for several years. Yet some Puritans feared that the Pequots, who opposed the colonists' continued expansion, "would cause all the Indians in the country to join to root out all the English." Using the death of two Englishmen in 1636 to justify a military expedition against the Pequots, the colonists went on the attack. The Narragansetts, whom Roger Williams had befriended, allied with the English in the **Pequot War**. After months of bloody conflict, the English and their Indian allies launched a brutal attack on a Pequot fort in May 1637 that left some four hundred men, women, and children dead.

Puritans in England were soon engaged in armed conflict as well, but this time against other Englishmen. Differences over issues of religion, taxation, and royal authority had strained relations between Parliament and the crown for decades, as James I (r. 1603–1625) and his son Charles I (r. 1625–1649) sought to consolidate their own power at Parliament's expense. In 1642 the relationship between Parliament and King Charles I broke down completely, and the country descended into civil war. Oliver Cromwell, a Puritan, emerged as the leader of the Protestant parliamentary forces, and after several years of fighting, he claimed victory. Charles I was executed, Parliament established a republican commonwealth, and bishops and elaborate rituals were banished from the Church of England. Cromwell ruled England as a military dictator until his death in 1658. By then, much of England had tired of religious conflict and Puritan rule, so Charles I's son, Charles II (r. 1660–1685), was invited to return from exile on the continent and restore the monarchy and the Church of England. In 1660, when Charles II acceded to the throne, the Puritans recognized that their only hope for building a godly republic lay in North America.

During the civil war of the 1640s, English settlements had quickly spread as a result of both natural increase and migration. English communities stretched from Connecticut through Massachusetts and Rhode Island and into Maine and what became New Hampshire. The English king and Parliament, embroiled in war, paid little attention to events in North America, allowing these New England colonies to develop with little oversight. In 1664, after the restoration of the monarchy, the English wrested control of New Amsterdam from the Dutch and renamed it New York. By 1674 the English could claim dominance—in population, trade, and politics—over the other European powers vying for empires along the northern Atlantic coast.

The spread of English control was still contested, however, by diverse Indian groups. In New England, only 15,000 to 16,000 native people remained by 1670, a loss of about 80 percent over fifty years. Meanwhile the English population reached more than 50,000, with settlers claiming ever more land. In 1671 the English demanded that the Wampanoags, who had been their allies since the 1620s, surrender their guns and be ruled by English law. Instead, many Indians hid their weapons and, over the next several years, raided frontier farms and killed several settlers. English authorities responded by hanging three Wampanoag men.

By 1675 the Wampanoag chief Metacom, called King Philip by the English, came to believe that Europeans had to be forced out of New England if Indians were going to survive. As conflict escalated between the English and the Wampanoags, Metacom gained the support of the Narragansett and Nipmuck Indians. Together warriors from the three tribes attacked white settlements throughout the region, burning fields, killing male settlers, and taking wives and children captive.

Initially, the English were convinced they could win an easy victory over their Indian foes and insisted on calling the conflict King Philip's War, using the local chief's English name. There was no easy victory, however, and the war, called **Metacom's War** by Wampanoags, dragged on and became increasingly brutal on both sides. Some 1,000 English settlers were killed and dozens were taken captive during the war. Metacom's forces attacked Plymouth and Providence and marched within twenty miles of Boston. The English meanwhile made an alliance with Mohawks, Pequots, Mohegans, and praying Indians (mostly Christian Wampanoags) in the region, who ambushed Narragansett forces. The English attacked enemy villages, killing hundreds of Indians and selling hundreds more into slavery in the West Indies, including Metacom's wife and son. Indian losses were catastrophic on both sides of the conflict, as food shortages and disease combined with military deaths to kill as many as 4,500 men, women, and children. About a quarter of the remaining Indian population of New England died in 1675–1676.

The war finally ended when Wampanoag, Narragansett, and Nipmuck forces ran short of guns and powder and the Mohawks ambushed and killed Metacom. The remaining Algonquian-speaking Indians moved north and gradually intermarried with tribes allied with the French. As the carnage of the war spilled into New York, Iroquois leaders and colonists met at Albany in 1677 in hopes of salvaging their lucrative fur trade. There they formed an alliance, the Covenant Chain, to forestall future conflict. In the following decades, furs and land would continue to define the complex relations between Indians and Europeans across the northern regions of North America.

| REVIEW & RELATE | • How did Puritan religious views shape New England's development?
• Why did conflict between New England settlers and the region's Indians escalate over the course of the seventeenth century? |

Conclusion: European Empires in North America

When John Smith died in 1631, the English were just beginning to establish colonies in North America. Smith realized early on that a successful empire in Virginia required a different approach than the Spanish had taken in Mexico and Peru. North American colonies demanded permanent settlement, long-term investment, and hard work. Liberal land policies, self-government, and trade formed the touchstones of colonies along the north Atlantic coast. Colonies in New England, established by Pilgrims and Puritans, were especially successful. These religious dissenters benefited from liberal land policies, self-government, and trade. In addition, their large families, diverse skills, and settlement in relatively healthy northern climes aided their success.

European colonists found ways to prosper in Virginia, Quebec, and New Amsterdam as well as Massachusetts Bay, but they still faced daunting choices. Most important, should they create alliances with local Indians for sustenance and trade, or should they seek to dominate them and take what they needed? Smith, Miles Standish, and many others supported an aggressive policy, much like that of Spain. In Virginia this policy ended the most serious threats from the Powhatan Confederacy by the 1640s. But many Europeans, especially in New England, New Amsterdam, and Canada, advocated a less violent approach. A few French Jesuit priests and Puritans like Roger Williams focused on the spiritual and material benefits of conversion. Far more argued that building alliances was the most effective means of advancing trade and gaining land, furs, and other goods valued by Europeans.

Throughout the early and mid-seventeenth century, English, Dutch, and French colonists profited from trade relations and military alliances with Indian nations. Nonetheless, European demands for land fueled repeated conflicts with tribes like the Pequot in the 1630s and the Wampanoag and Narragansett in the 1670s. The exhaustion of furs along the Atlantic coast only increased the vulnerability of those Indians who could no longer provide this valuable trade item. Already devastated by European-borne diseases, their very survival was at stake. Indians in New Amsterdam as well as New England resisted the loss of their land and livelihood, often with violence. Such violence led to the death of Anne Hutchinson. In 1642 she and her six youngest children moved to the outskirts of New Netherland after the death of her husband. A year later, Anne and all but one of her children were massacred by Indians outraged by Dutch governor William Kieft's 1643 slaughter of peaceful Indians on Manhattan Island.

Still, as European settlements reached deeper into North America in the late seventeenth century and early eighteenth century, their prosperity continued to depend on trade goods and land that were often in Indian hands. At the same time, a growing demand for labor led wealthier settlers to seek an increased supply of indentured servants from Europe and enslaved workers from Africa. Over the next half century, relations between wealthy and poor settlers, between whites and blacks, between settlers and Indians, and among the European nations that vied for empire would grow only more complicated.

Chapter 2 Review

KEY TERMS

Protestantism (p. 30)
Church of England (p. 31)
Jamestown (p. 36)
Powhatan Confederacy (p. 37)
House of Burgesses (p. 38)
indentured servants (p. 38)

Bacon's Rebellion (p. 41)
Pilgrims (p. 43)
Mayflower Compact (p. 44)
Puritans (p. 44)
Pequot War (p. 47)
Metacom's War (p. 48)

REVIEW & RELATE

1. How did the Protestant Reformation shape the course of European expansion in the Americas?
2. How did the French and Dutch colonies in North America differ from the Spanish empire to the south?
3. How did the Virginia colony change and evolve between 1607 and the 1670s?
4. How did the growth of the English colonies on the mainland and in the West Indies shape conflicts in Virginia and demands for labor throughout North America?
5. How did Puritan religious views shape New England's development?
6. Why did conflict between New England settlers and the region's Indians escalate over the course of the seventeenth century?

TIMELINE OF EVENTS

1517	• Protestant Reformation begins
1530s	• England breaks with the Roman Catholic Church
1545–1563	• Council of Trent
1598	• Acoma pueblo uprising, Edict of Nantes
1607	• Jamestown founded
1608	• French settle in Quebec
1609	• Dutch settle on the Hudson River
1612–1614	• Tobacco cultivation begins in Virginia
1619	• First Africans arrive in Virginia
1620	• Pilgrims found Plymouth settlement
1624	• Dutch establish New Amsterdam

1630	• Puritans found Massachusetts Bay colony
1632	• Maryland founded
1635	• Roger Williams moves to Rhode Island
1636–1637	• Pequot War
1637	• Anne Hutchinson banished from Massachusetts Bay colony
1642–1649	• English civil war
1660	• Monarchy restored in England
1660–1664	• Virginia and Maryland establish lifelong, inherited slavery
1664	• Dutch surrender New Amsterdam to the English
1675–1676	• Metacom's War
1676	• Bacon's Rebellion

3

Colonial America amid Global Change

1680–1754

LEARNING OBJECTIVES

After reading this chapter you should be able to:

- Compare the development of Spanish, French, and English colonies from the late sixteenth to the mid-seventeenth century.
- Analyze the effects of European wars on relations among different groups of European colonists and between colonists and diverse Indian nations in North America.
- Examine how the American colonies became part of a global trading network.
- Describe the changing character of labor in the English colonies and the rise of slavery.

COMPARING AMERICAN HISTORIES

In 1729, at age thirty, William Moraley Jr. signed an indenture to serve a five-year term as a "bound servant" in the "American Plantations." This was not what his parents had imagined for him. The son of a journeyman watchmaker, Moraley received a good education and was offered a clerk-ship with a London lawyer. But Moraley preferred London's pleasures to legal training. At age nineteen, out of money, he was forced to return home and become an apprentice watchmaker for his father. Moraley made a poor apprentice, and in 1725, fed up with his son's lack of enterprise, Moraley's father rewrote his will, leaving him just 20 shillings. When Moraley's father died unexpectedly, his wife gave her son 20 pounds, and in 1728 Moraley headed back to London.

But times were hard in London, and Moraley failed to find work. After being imprisoned for debt, he sold his labor for five years in return for passage to America. Arriving in the colonies in December 1729, Moraley was indentured to Isaac Pearson, a Quaker clockmaker and goldsmith in Burlington, New Jersey. Preferring to live in a large city like Philadelphia, Moraley ran away but was soon captured. Most runaway servants had their contracts extended, but Moraley did not. For the next three years, he worked for Pearson alongside another indentured servant and an enslaved boy. Pearson allowed Moraley to travel the countryside fixing clocks and watches, and the servant observed the far worse conditions of enslaved workers. Perhaps having recouped his investment, Pearson released Moraley from his contract two years early.

Moraley spent the next twenty months traveling the northern colonies, but found no steady employment. Hounded by creditors, he returned to England, penniless and unemployed. In 1743, hoping to cash in on popular interest in adventure tales, he published an account of his travels. In the book, entitled *The Infortunate, the Voyage and Adventures of William Moraley, an Indentured Servant*, he offered a poor man's view of eighteenth-century North America. Like so much else in Moraley's life, the book was not a success.

In 1738, while Moraley was back in England trying to carve out a career as a writer, sixteen-year-old Eliza Lucas, the eldest daughter of Colonel George Lucas, arrived at Wappoo, her father's estate near Charleston, South Carolina. Eliza had been born on Antigua, where her father served with the British army and owned a sugar plantation. The move north, made necessary by her mother's ill health, created an unusual opportunity for Eliza, who was left in charge of the estate when Colonel Lucas was called back to Antigua in May 1739.

For the next five years, Eliza Lucas managed Wappoo and two other Carolina plantations owned by her father. Rising each day at 5 a.m., she checked on the fields and the enslaved laborers who worked them, balanced the books, nursed her mother, taught her younger sister to read, and wrote to her younger brothers at school in England. She also befriended neighboring planters, including Charles Pinckney, whom she would later marry, adding her landholdings to his.

While still single, Eliza improved the value of her family's estates by experimenting with new crops. With her father's enthusiastic support, she cultivated indigo, a plant used for making textile dyes. When her experiments proved successful, Eliza Lucas encouraged other planters to follow her lead, and with financial aid from the colonial legislature and Parliament, indigo became a profitable export from South Carolina, second only to rice.

COMPARING THE AMERICAN HISTORIES of William Moraley and Eliza Lucas illuminates profound shifts in global trading patterns that resulted in the circulation of labor and goods among Asia, Africa, Europe, and the Americas. Between 1680 and 1750, indentured servants, enslaved Africans, planters, soldiers, merchants, and artisans traveled along these new trade networks. So, too, did sugar, rum, tobacco, indigo, cloth, and a host of other items. As England, France, and Spain expanded their empires, colonists developed new crops for export and increased the demand for manufactured goods from home. Yet the vibrant, increasingly global economy was fraught with peril. Economic crises, the uncertainties of maritime navigation, and outbreaks of war caused constant disruptions. For some, the opportunities offered by colonization outweighed the dangers; for others, fortune was less kind, and the results were disappointing, even disastrous.

Europeans Expand Their Claims

Beginning with the restoration of the monarchy in 1660, English kings began granting North American land and commercial rights to men who were loyal to the crown. France and Spain also expanded their empires in North America, and all three would frequently come into conflict with each other in the late seventeenth and early eighteenth centuries. At the same time, American Indians challenged various European efforts to displace them from their homelands.

English Colonies Grow and Multiply

Shortly after Charles II (r. 1660–1685) was restored to the English throne, Connecticut and Rhode Island requested and received royal charters that granted them some local authority. Because the charters could be changed only with the agreement of both parties, Connecticut and Rhode Island maintained this local autonomy throughout the colonial period. In other colonies, however, Charles II asserted his authority by rewarding loyal supporters with land grants and commercial rights, which could more easily be changed or revoked than royal charters could. He also appointed his supporters to the newly formed Councils for Trade and Plantations, and provided them other privileges. He gave his brother James, the Duke of York, control over all the lands between the Delaware and Connecticut Rivers, once known as New Netherland, but now known as New York. He then conveyed the adjacent lands to investors who established the colonies of East and West Jersey. Finally, Charles II repaid debts to Admiral Sir William Penn by granting his son huge tracts of land in the Middle Atlantic region. Six years later, William Penn Jr. left the Church of England and joined the Society of Friends, or Quakers. This radical Protestant sect was severely persecuted in England, so the twenty-two-year-old Penn turned his holdings into a Quaker refuge named Pennsylvania.

Between 1660 and 1685, York, Penn, and other English gentlemen were established as the proprietors of a string of **proprietary colonies** from Carolina to New York. Although Charles II could have intruded into the government of these colonies, he rarely did. Instead, local conditions largely dictated what was possible. Most proprietors envisioned the creation of a manorial system in their colony, one in which they and other gentry presided over workers producing goods for export. In practice, however, a range of relationships emerged between property owners and workers. For instance, small farmers and laborers in northern Carolina rose up and forced proprietors there to offer land at reasonable prices and a semblance of self-government. In the southern part of Carolina, however, English planters with West Indies connections dominated. They created a mainland version of Barbados by introducing enslaved Africans as laborers, carving out plantations, and trading with the West Indies.

William Penn provided a more progressive model of colonial rule. He established friendly relations with the local Lenni-Lenape Indians and drew up a Frame of Government in 1681 that recognized religious freedom for all Christians. It also allowed all property-owning men to vote and hold office. Under Penn's leadership, Pennsylvania attracted thousands of middling farm families, most of them Quakers, as well as artisans and merchants.

Charles's death in 1685 marked an abrupt shift in crown-colony relations. Charles's successor, James II (r. 1685–1688), instituted a more authoritarian regime both at home and abroad. He consolidated the colonies in the Northeast and established tighter controls. His royal officials banned town meetings, challenged land titles granted under the original colonial charters, and imposed new taxes. Fortunately for the colonists, the Catholic James II alienated his subjects in England as well as in the colonies, inspiring a bloodless coup in 1688, the so-called **Glorious Revolution**. His Protestant daughter Mary and her husband, William of Orange (r. 1689–1702), then ascended the throne, introducing more democratic systems of governance in England and the colonies. Two years later, John Locke, a physician and philosopher, wrote a widely circulated treatise supporting the initiatives of William and Mary by insisting that government depended on the consent of the governed.

Eager to restore political order and create a commercially profitable empire, William and Mary established the new colony of Massachusetts (which included Plymouth, Massachusetts Bay, and Maine) and restored town meetings and an elected assembly. But the 1692 charter also granted the English crown the right to appoint a royal governor and officials to enforce customs regulations. It ensured religious freedom to members of the Church of England and allowed all male property owners (not just Puritans) to be elected to the assembly. In Maryland, too, the crown imposed a royal governor and replaced the Catholic Church with the Church of England as the established religion. And in New York, wealthy English merchants won the backing of the newly appointed royal governor, who instituted a representative assembly and supported a merchant-dominated Board of Aldermen. Thus, taken as a whole, William and Mary's policies instituted a partnership between England and colonial elites by allowing colonists to retain long-standing local governmental institutions but also asserting royal authority to appoint governors and ensure the influence of the Church of England (Table 3.1).

In the early eighteenth century, England's North American colonies took the form that they would retain until the revolution in 1776. In 1702 East and West Jersey united into the colony of New Jersey. Delaware separated from Pennsylvania in 1704. By 1710 North Carolina became fully independent of South Carolina. Finally, in 1732, the colony of Georgia was chartered as a buffer between Spanish Florida and the plantations of South Carolina. At the same time, settlers pushed back the frontier in all directions.

TABLE 3.1 English Colonies Established in North America, 1607–1750

Colony	Date	Original Colony Type	Religion	Status in 1750
Virginia	1624	Royal	Church of England	Royal
Massachusetts	1630	Charter	Congregationalist	Royal with charter
Maryland	1632	Proprietary	Catholic	Royal
Connecticut	1662	Charter	Congregationalist	Charter
Rhode Island	1663	Charter	No established church	Charter
Carolina	1663	Proprietary	Church of England	
North	1691	Proprietary		Royal
South	1691	Proprietary		Royal
New Jersey	1664	Proprietary	Church of England	Royal
New York	1664	Proprietary	Church of England	Royal
Pennsylvania	1681	Proprietary	Quaker	Proprietary
Delaware	1704	Proprietary	Lutheran/Quaker	Proprietary
Georgia	1732	Charter	Church of England	(Royal 1752)
New Hampshire (separated from Massachusetts)	1691	Royal	Congregationalist	Royal

The Pueblo Revolt and Spain's Fragile Empire

Spain's empire was spread dangerously thin on its northern reaches. In Florida, Indians resisted the spread of cattle ranching in the 1670s. Some moved their settlements north to the Carolina border, wooed by the English who eagerly exchanged European goods for deerskins. The efforts of the English to interfere with Spanish-Indian trade networks fueled growing tensions along this Anglo-Spanish border. Those tensions would erupt into violence when war erupted in Europe in 1702. In New Mexico, tensions between Spanish missionaries and *encomenderos* and the Pueblo nation had simmered for decades (see "Spain's Global Empire Declines" in chapter 2). Relations worsened in the 1670s when a drought led to famine among many area Indians and brought a revival of Indian rituals that the Spaniards considered threatening. Meanwhile, Spanish forces were failing to protect the Pueblos against devastating raids by Apache and Navajo warriors, while Catholic prayers proved unable to stop Pueblo deaths in a 1671 epidemic.

When some Pueblos returned to their traditional priests, Spanish officials hanged three Indian leaders for idolatry and whipped and incarcerated forty-three others. Among those punished was Popé, a militant Pueblo who upon his release began planning a broad-based revolt. On August 10, 1680, seventeen thousand Pueblo Indians initiated a coordinated assault on numerous Spanish missions and forts. They destroyed buildings and farms, burned crops and houses, and smeared excrement on Christian altars. The Spaniards retreated to Mexico without launching any significant counterattack.

Still, the Spaniards returned in the 1690s and reconquered parts of New Mexico, aided by growing internal conflict among the Pueblos and raids by the Apache. The governor general of New Spain worked hard to subdue the province and in 1696 crushed the rebels and opened new lands for settlement. Meanwhile Franciscan missionaries improved relations with the Pueblos by allowing them to retain more indigenous practices.

Yet despite the Spanish reconquest, in the long run the **Pueblo revolt** limited Spanish expansion by strengthening other indigenous peoples in the region. In the aftermath of the revolt, some Pueblo refugees moved north and taught the Navajo how to grow corn, raise sheep, and ride horses. Through the Navajo, the Ute, Shoshone, and Comanche peoples also gained access to horses. By the 1730s, the Comanches launched mounted bison hunts as well as raids on other Indian nations. At Taos, they traded Indian captives into slavery for more horses and guns. Thus the Pueblos provided other Indian nations with the means to support larger populations, wider commercial networks, and more warriors, allowing them to continue to contest Spanish rule.

At the same time, Spain sought to reinforce its claims to Texas (named after the Tejas Indians) in response to French settlements in the lower Mississippi valley. In the early eighteenth century, Spanish missions and forts appeared along the route from San Juan Batista to the border of present-day Louisiana. Although small and scattered, these outposts were meant to ensure Spain's claim to Texas. But the presence of large and powerful Indian nations, including the Caddo and the Apache, forced Spanish residents to accept many native customs in order to maintain their presence in the region.

France Seeks Land and Control

Louis XIV of France (r. 1643–1715) claimed absolute power derived from what he believed was his divine right to rule. One of his missions was to extend the boundaries of France's North American colonies. However, French efforts were focused more on exploration and trade than on settlement. In 1682 French adventurers and their Indian allies journeyed from the *Pays d'en Haut,* the Upper Country surrounding the Great Lakes, down the Mississippi River. Led by the French explorer René-Robert Cavelier, Sieur de La Salle, the party traveled to the Gulf of Mexico and claimed all the land drained by the river's tributaries for France. The new territory of Louisiana promised great wealth, but its development stalled when La Salle failed in his attempt to establish a colony.

Still eager for a southern outlet for furs, the French did not give up. After several more attempts at colonization in the early eighteenth century, French settlers maintained a toehold along Louisiana's Gulf coast. Most important, Pierre LeMoyne d'Iberville and his brother established forts at Biloxi and Mobile bays, where they traded with local Choctaw Indians. They recruited settlers from Canada and France, and these two small outposts survived despite conflicts among settlers, pressure from

Ambush of the Villasur Expedition, c. 1720   An unknown artist painted this battle scene on buffalo hide. In 1720, Spanish soldiers and Pueblo warriors tried to expel the French from the lower Mississippi River valley. Instead, French soldiers and their Indian allies ambushed the expedition and killed forty-five men. Two of the dead, Spanish Father Juan Minguez and Pueblo leader Joseph Naranjo, are shown here in the center.   Palace of the Governors Photo Archive (NMHM/DCA), negative 149804

the English and the Spanish, a wave of epidemics, and a lack of supplies from France. Nevertheless, Louisiana counted only three hundred French settlers by 1715.

Continuing to promote commercial relations with diverse Indian nations, the French built a string of missions and forts along the upper Mississippi and Illinois Rivers. The most important of these, Kaskaskia (just south of Cahokia), became a multicultural community of diverse Indian groups, French fur traders, and Jesuit missionaries. These outposts in the continent's interior allowed France to challenge both English and Spanish claims to North America. In addition, extensive trade with a range of Indian nations ensured that French power was far greater than the small number of French settlers suggests.

REVIEW & RELATE

- What role did the crown play in the expansion of the English North American colonies in the second half of the seventeenth century?
- How did the development of the Spanish and French colonies in the late seventeenth century differ from that of the English colonies?

European Wars and American Consequences

Developments in North America in the late seventeenth and early eighteenth centuries were driven as much by events in Europe as by those in the colonies. From 1689 until 1713, Europe was in an almost constant state of war, with continental conflicts spilling over into colonial possessions in North America. The result was increased tensions between colonists of different nationalities, Indians and colonists, and colonists and their home countries.

Colonial Conflicts and Indian Alliances

France was at the center of much of the European warfare of the period. Louis XIV hoped to expand France's borders and gain supremacy in Europe. To this end, he built a powerful professional army under state authority. Having gained victories in the Spanish Netherlands, Flanders, Strasbourg, and Lorraine, the French army seemed invincible.

Between 1689 and 1697, France and England fought their first sustained war in North America, **King William's War**. The war began over conflicting French and English interests on the European continent, but it soon spread to the American frontier when English and Iroquois forces attacked French and Huron settlements around Montreal and northern New York.

Although neither side had gained significant territory when peace was declared in 1697, the war had important consequences. Many colonists serving in the English army died of battle wounds, smallpox, and inadequate rations. Those who survived resented their treatment and the unnecessary deaths of so many comrades. The Iroquois fared even worse. Their fur trade was devastated, and hundreds of Mohawks and Oneidas were forced to flee from France's Indian allies along the eastern Great Lakes. "French Indians" and Iroquois continued to attack each other after the peace settlement, but in 1701 the Iroquois agreed to end the raids and remain neutral in all future European conflicts. Wary of further European entanglements, Iroquois leaders focused on rebuilding their tattered confederacy.

A second protracted conflict, known as the **War of the Spanish Succession** (1702–1713) or Queen Anne's War, had even more devastating effects on North America. The conflict erupted in Europe when Charles II of Spain (r. 1665–1700) died without an heir, launching a contest for the Spanish kingdom and its colonies. France and Spain squared off against England, the Netherlands, Austria, and Prussia. In North America, however, it was England alone that faced France and Spain, with each nation hoping to gain additional territory. Both sides recruited Indian allies.

After more than a decade of savage fighting, Queen Anne's War ended in 1713 with the Treaty of Utrecht, which sought to secure a prolonged peace by balancing the interests of the great powers in Europe and their colonial possessions. Yet England benefited the most in North America. At the same time, it consolidated power at home by incorporating Scotland into Great Britain through the 1707 Act of Union. Just six years later, France surrendered Newfoundland, Nova Scotia, and the Hudson Bay Territory to England, while Spain granted England control of St. Kitts in the West Indies, Gibraltar, and Minorca as well as the right to sell African slaves in its American colonies. Yet neither the treaty nor Britain's consolidation forestalled further conflict.

MAP 3.1

European Empires in North America, 1715–1750   European nations competed with one
another and with numerous Indian nations for control of vast areas of North America. Although wars
continually reshaped areas under European and Indian control, this map shows the general outlines
of the empires claimed by each European nation, the key forts established to maintain those claims,
and the major Indian nations in each area.

Indeed, Spain, France, and Britain all strengthened fortifications along their North
American borders (Map 3.1).

Indians Resist European Encroachment

The European conflicts in North America put incredible pressure on Indian peoples
to choose sides. It was increasingly difficult for native peoples in colonized areas to
remain autonomous, yet Indian nations were not simply pawns of European powers.
Some actively sought European allies against their native enemies, and nearly all
desired European trade goods like cloth, guns, and horses. As colonial expansion and

trade led to war, however, the power of young male warriors increased in many tribes. In societies like the Cherokee and Iroquois, in which older women had long held significant economic and political authority, this change threatened traditional gender and generational relations. Moreover, struggles among English, French, and Spanish forces both reinforced conflicts among Indian peoples that existed before European settlement and created new ones.

The trade in guns was especially significant in escalating conflicts among tribes in the Southeast during the late seventeenth century. By that period, the most precious commodity Indians had to trade was Indian captives sold as slaves. Indians had always taken captives in war, but some of those captives had been adopted into the victorious nation. Now, however, war was almost constant in some areas, and captives were more valuable when sold as slaves to Europeans. The English in Carolina encouraged the Westo and later the Savannah nation to raid tribes in Spanish Florida, exchanging the captives for guns. As slave raiding spread across the Anglo-Spanish borders, more peaceful tribes were forced to acquire guns for self-protection. In addition, many Indian nations were forced off traditional lands by slave-raiding Indian foes. Some of these displaced groups merged to form new tribes, like the Yamasee in the Southeast.

By the 1710s, the vicious cycle of guns and slaves convinced some southern Indians to develop a pan-Indian alliance similar to that forged by New England Indians in the 1670s (see "Wars in Old and New England" in chapter 2). First, a group of Tuscarora warriors, hoping to gain support from other tribes, launched an attack on North Carolina settlements in September 1711. In the **Tuscarora War** that followed, South Carolina colonists came to the aid of their North Carolina countrymen and persuaded the Yamasee, Catawba, and Cherokee nations to join forces against the Tuscarora. Meanwhile political leaders in North Carolina convinced a competing group of Tuscarora to ally with the colonists. By 1713 the war was largely over, and in 1715 the Tuscarora signed a peace treaty and forfeited their lands. Many then migrated north and were accepted as the sixth nation of the Iroquois Confederacy.

The end of the Tuscarora War did not mean peace, however. For the next two years, a Yamasee-led coalition attacked the South Carolina militia. The Yamasee people remained deeply in debt to British merchants as the trade in deerskins and slaves moved west. They thus secured allies among the Creeks and in 1715 launched an all-out effort to force the British out. The British gained victory in the **Yamasee War** only after the Cherokee switched their allegiance to the colonists in early 1716. The final Indian nations withdrew from the conflict in 1717, and a fragile peace followed.

The Yamasee War did not oust the British, but it did transform the political landscape of native North America. In its aftermath, the Creek and Catawba tribes emerged as powerful new confederations, the Cherokee became the major trading partner of the British, and the Yamasee nation was seriously weakened. Moreover, as the Cherokees allied with the British, the Creek and the Caddo tribes strengthened their alliance with the French.

Despite the British victory, colonists on the Carolina frontier faced raids on their settlements for decades to come. In the 1720s and 1730s, settlers in the Middle Atlantic colonies also experienced fierce resistance to their westward expansion. And attacks on New Englanders along the Canadian frontier periodically disrupted settlement there. Still, many Indian tribes were pushed out of their homelands. As they resettled in new regions, they alternately allied and fought with native peoples already living there. At the same time, the trade in Indian slaves expanded in the west as the French and the Spanish competed for economic partners and military allies.

Conflicts on the Southern Frontier

Indians were not the only people to have their world shaken by war. By 1720 years of warfare and upheaval had transformed the mind-set of many colonists. Although most considered themselves loyal British subjects, many believed that British proprietors remained largely unconcerned with the colonies' welfare. Others resented the British army's treatment of colonial militia and Parliament's unwillingness to aid settlers against Indian attacks. Moreover, the growing numbers of settlers who arrived from other parts of Europe had little investment in British authority.

The impact of Britain's ongoing conflicts with Spain during the 1730s and 1740s illustrates this development. Following the Yamasee War, South Carolina became a royal colony, and its profitable rice and indigo plantations spread southward. Then, in 1732, Parliament established Georgia (named after King George II, r. 1727–1760) on lands north of Florida as a buffer between Carolina colonists and their longtime Spanish foes.

Spanish authorities were furious at this expansion of British territorial claims. Thus in August 1739, a Spanish naval ship captured an English ship captain who was trading illegally in the Spanish West Indies and severed his ear. In response, Great Britain attacked St. Augustine and Cartagena (in present-day Colombia), but its troops were repulsed. In 1742 Spain sent troops into Georgia, but the colonial militia pushed back the attack. By then, the American war had become part of a more general European conflict. Once again France and Spain joined forces while Great Britain supported Germany in Europe. When the war ended in 1748, Britain had ensured the future of Georgia and reaffirmed its military superiority. Once again, however, victory cost the lives of many colonial settlers and soldiers, and some colonists began to wonder whether their interests and those of the British government were truly the same.

Southern Indians were also caught up in ongoing disputes among Europeans. While both French and Spanish forces attacked the British along the Atlantic coast, they sought to outflank each other in the lower Mississippi River valley and Texas. With the French relying on Caddo, Choctaw, and other Indian allies for trade goods and defense, the Spaniards needed to expand their alliances beyond those with the Tejas. In 1749, when Spaniards agreed to stop kidnapping and enslaving Apache women and children, they were able to negotiate peace with that powerful Indian nation.

The British meanwhile became increasingly dependent on a variety of European immigrants to defend colonial frontiers against the French, Spaniards, and Indians. Certainly many Anglo-Americans moved westward as coastal areas became overcrowded, but frontier regions also attracted immigrants from Scotland and Germany who sought refuge and economic opportunity in the colonies. Many headed to the western regions of Virginia and Carolina and to Georgia in the 1730s and 1740s. Meanwhile, South Carolina officials recruited Swiss, German, and French Huguenot as well as Scots-Irish immigrants in the 1740s. Small communities of Jews settled in Charleston as well. Gradually many of these immigrants moved south into Georgia, seeking more and cheaper land. Thus when Spanish, French, or Indian forces attacked the British colonial frontier, they were as likely to face Scots-Irish and German immigrants as Englishmen.

| REVIEW & RELATE | • How did the European wars of the late seventeenth and early eighteenth centuries impact relations between colonists and England? |
| | • How were Indian alliances, with other Indians and with European nations, shaped by the trade in slaves and guns and by wars between European powers? |

The Benefits and Costs of Empire

The combined forces of global trade and international warfare altered the political and economic calculations of imperial powers. This was especially true for British North America, where colonists settled as families and created towns that provided key markets for Britain's commercial expansion. Over the course of the eighteenth century, British colonists became increasingly avid consumers of products from around the world. Meanwhile the king and Parliament sought greater control over these far-flung commercial networks.

Colonial Traders Join Global Networks

In the late seventeenth and early eighteenth centuries, trade became truly global. Not only did goods from China, India, the Middle East, Africa, and North America gain currency in England and the rest of Europe, but the tastes of European consumers also helped shape goods produced in other parts of the world. For instance, by the early eighteenth century the Chinese were making porcelain teapots and bowls specifically for the English market. The trade in cloth, tea, tobacco, and sugar was similarly influenced by European tastes. The exploitation of African laborers contributed significantly to this global commerce. They were a crucial item of trade in their own right, and their labor in the Americas ensured steady supplies of sugar, rice, tobacco, and indigo for the world market.

By the early eighteenth century, both the volume and the diversity of goods multiplied. Silk, calico, porcelain, olive oil, wine, and other items were carried from the East to Europe and the American colonies, while cod, mackerel, shingles, pine boards, barrel staves, rum, sugar, rice, and tobacco filled ships returning west. A healthy trade also grew up within North America as New England fishermen, New York and Charleston merchants, and Caribbean planters met one another's needs. Salted cod and mackerel flowed to the Caribbean, and rum, molasses, and slaves flowed back to the mainland. This commerce required ships, barrels, docks, warehouses, and wharves, all of which ensured a lively trade in lumber, tar, pitch, and rosin (Map 3.2).

The flow of information was critical to the flow of goods and credit. By the early eighteenth century, coffeehouses flourished in port cities around the Atlantic, providing access to the latest news. Merchants, ship captains, and traders met in person to discuss new ventures and to keep apprised of recent developments. British and American periodicals reported on parliamentary legislation, commodity prices in India and Great Britain, the state of trading houses in China, the outbreak of disease in foreign ports, and stock ventures in London. Still, these markets were volatile. In 1720

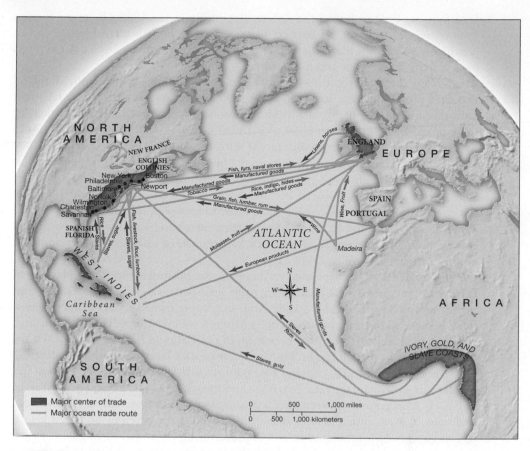

MAP 3.2

North Atlantic Trade in the Eighteenth Century   North Atlantic trade provided various parts of the British empire with raw materials, manufactured goods, and labor. Many ships traveled between only two regions because they were equipped to carry particular kinds of goods—slaves, grains, or manufactured goods. Ultimately, however, people and goods were exchanged among four key points: the West Indies, mainland North America, West Africa, and Great Britain.

shares in the British South Seas Company, which had risen to astronomical heights, collapsed. Thousands of investors, including William Moraley's father, lost a great deal of money.

Imperial Policies Focus on Profits

European sovereigns worked to ensure that this international trade and their colonial possessions benefited their own European treasuries. In the late seventeenth century, both Louis XIV and his English rivals embraced a system known as **mercantilism**, which centered on the maintenance of a favorable balance of trade, with more gold and silver flowing into the home country than flowed out. In France, finance minister

Jean-Baptiste Colbert honed the system. Beginning in the 1660s, he taxed foreign imports while removing all barriers to trade within French territories. Colonies provided valuable raw materials that could be used to produce manufactured items for sale to foreign nations and to colonists.

While France's mercantile system was limited by the size of its empire, England benefited more fully from such policies. The English crown had access to a far wider array of natural resources from which to manufacture goods and a larger market for these products. Beginning in 1660, Parliament passed a series of **Navigation Acts** that required merchants to conduct trade with the colonies only in English-owned ships. In addition, certain items imported from foreign ports had to be carried in English ships or in ships with predominantly English crews. Finally, a list of "enumerated articles"—including tobacco, cotton, sugar, and indigo—had to be shipped from the colonies to England before being reexported to foreign ports. Thus the crown benefited directly or indirectly from nearly all commerce conducted by its colonies. But colonies, too, often benefited, as when Parliament helped subsidize the development of indigo in South Carolina.

In 1663 Parliament expanded its imperial reach through additional Navigation Acts, which required that goods sent from Europe to English colonies also pass through British ports. And a decade later, ship captains had to pay a duty or post bond before carrying enumerated articles between colonial ports. These acts ensured not only greater British control over shipping but also additional revenue for the crown as captains paid duties in West Indies, mainland North American, and British ports. Beginning in 1673, England sent customs officials to the colonies to enforce the various parliamentary acts. By 1680, London, Bristol, and Liverpool all thrived as barrels of sugar and tobacco and stacks of deer and beaver skins were unloaded and bolts of dyed cloth and cases of metal tools and guns were put on board for the return voyage. As mechanization and manufacturing expanded in England, Parliament sought to keep the profits at home by quashing nascent industries in the colonies. It thus prohibited the sale of products such as American-made textiles (1699), hats (1732), and iron goods (1750). In addition, Parliament worked to restrict trade among the North American colonies, especially between those on the mainland and in the West Indies.

Despite the increasing regulation, American colonists could own British ships and transport goods produced in the colonies. Indeed, by the mid-eighteenth century, North American merchants oversaw 75 percent of the trade in manufactures sent from Bristol and London to the colonies and 95 percent of the trade with the West Indies. Ironically, then, a system established to benefit Great Britain ended up creating a mercantile elite in British North America. Most of those merchants traded in goods, but some traded in human cargo.

The Atlantic Slave Trade

Parliament chartered the Royal African Company in 1672 as it expanded its role in the Atlantic slave trade. Between 1700 and 1808, some 3 million captive Africans were carried on British and Anglo-American ships, about 40 percent of the total of those sold in the Americas in this period (Figure 3.1). Half a million Africans died on the voyage across the Atlantic. Huge numbers also died in Africa, while being

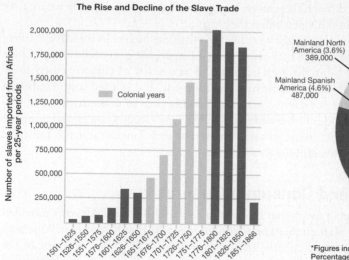

The Rise and Decline of the Slave Trade

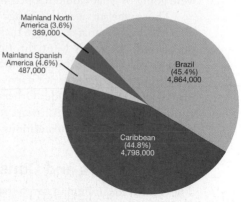

The Destinations of Slaves*

Mainland North America (3.6%) 389,000

Mainland Spanish America (4.6%) 487,000

Brazil (45.4%) 4,864,000

Caribbean (44.8%) 4,798,000

*Figures indicate numbers of slaves disembarked. Percentages are approximate and do not add up to 100%.

FIGURE 3.1

The Slave Trade in Numbers, 1501–1866   Extraordinary numbers of Africans were shipped as slaves to other parts of the world from the sixteenth to the nineteenth century. The slave trade transformed mainland North America, Brazil, and the West Indies. What broad patterns about the African slave trade can you infer from this data?

Source: Estimates Database. 2009. Voyages: Trans-Atlantic Slave Trade Database, http://www.slavevoyages.org/tast /assessment/estimates.faces. Accessed June 15, 2010.

marched to the coast or held in forts waiting to be forced aboard ships. Yet despite this astounding death rate, the slave trade yielded enormous profits and had far reaching consequences: The Africans whom British traders bought and sold transformed labor systems in the colonies, fueled international trade, and enriched merchants, planters, and their families and communities.

European traders worked closely with African merchants to gain their human cargo, trading muskets, metalware, and linen for men, women, and children. Originally many of those sold into slavery were war captives. But by the time British and Anglo-American merchants became central to this notorious trade, their contacts in Africa were procuring labor in any way they could. Over time, African traders moved farther inland to fill the demand, devastating large areas of West Africa, particularly the Congo-Angola region, which supplied some 40 percent of all Atlantic slaves.

The trip across the Atlantic, known as the **Middle Passage**, was a brutal and often deadly experience for Africans. Exhausted and undernourished by the time they boarded the large oceangoing vessels, the captives were placed in dark and crowded holds. Most had been poked and prodded by slave traders, and some had been branded to ensure that a trader received the exact individuals he had purchased. Once in the hold, they might wait for weeks before the ship finally set sail. By that time, the foul-smelling and crowded hold became a nightmare of disease and despair. There was never sufficient food or fresh water for the captives, and women especially were subject to sexual abuse by crew members. Many captives could not communicate with each other since they spoke different languages, and none of them knew exactly where they were going or what would happen when they arrived.

Those who survived the voyage were likely to find themselves in the slave markets of Barbados or Jamaica, where they were put on display for potential buyers. Once purchased, the slaves went through a period of seasoning as they regained their strength, became accustomed to their new environment, and learned commands in a new language. Some did not survive seasoning, falling prey to malnutrition and disease or committing suicide. Others adapted to the new circumstances and adopted enough European or British ways to carry on even as they sought means to resist the shocking and oppressive conditions.

Seaport Cities and Consumer Cultures

The same trade in human cargo that brought misery to millions of Africans provided traders, investors, and plantation owners with huge profits that helped turn America's seaport cities into centers of culture and consumption. Charleston was one of the main ports receiving African slaves in the early 1700s, and Eliza Lucas was impressed with its prosperous character. Arriving in 1738, she noted that "the Metropolis is a neat pretty place. The inhabitants [are] polite and live in a very gentile [genteel] manner." North American seaports, with their elegant homes, fine shops, and lively social seasons, did capture the most dynamic aspects of colonial life. Although cities like New York, Boston, Philadelphia, Baltimore, and Charleston contained less than 10 percent of the colonial population, they served as focal points of economic, political, social, and cultural activity.

Affluent urban families created a consumer revolution in North America. Changing patterns of consumption challenged traditional definitions of status. Less tied to birth and family pedigree, status in the colonies became more closely linked to financial success and a genteel lifestyle. Successful men of humble origins and even those of Dutch, Scottish, French, and Jewish heritage might join the British-dominated colonial gentry.

Of those who made this leap in the early eighteenth century, Benjamin Franklin was the most notable. Franklin was apprenticed to his brother, a printer, an occupation that matched his interest in books, reading, and politics. At age sixteen, Benjamin published (anonymously) his first essays in his brother's paper, the *New England Courant*. Two years later, a family dispute led Benjamin to try his luck in New York and then Philadelphia. His fortunes were fragile, but unlike William Moraley Jr., he combined hard work with a quick wit, good luck, and political connections, which together led to success. In 1729 Franklin purchased the *Pennsylvania Gazette* and became the colony's official printer.

While Franklin worried about the concentration of wealth in too few hands, most colonial elites in the early eighteenth century happily displayed their profits. Leading merchants in Boston, Salem, New York, and Philadelphia emulated British styles and built fine homes that had separate rooms for sleeping, eating, and entertaining guests. Mercantile elites also redesigned the urban landscape, donating money for brick churches and stately town halls. They constructed new roads, wharves, and warehouses to facilitate trade, and they invested in bowling greens and public gardens.

The spread of international commerce created a lively cultural life and great affluence in colonial cities. The colonial elite replicated British fashions, including

A View of Charleston, South Carolina, c. 1760s   This eighteenth-century oil painting by English artist Thomas Mellish offers a view of Charleston harbor c. 1760s. A ship flying an English flag looms in the foreground. The other ships and small boats along with the substantial buildings surrounding the harbor reflect Charleston's stature as one of the main commercial centers of the North American colonies.   Ferens Art Gallery, Hull Museums, UK/Bridgeman Images

elaborate tea rituals. In Boston, the wives of merchants served fine teas imported from East Asia in cups and saucers from China while decorated bowls held sugar from the West Indies. However, the emergence of a colonial aristocracy also revealed growing inequality. Wealthy urban merchants and professionals lived alongside a middling group of artisans and shopkeepers and a growing class of unskilled laborers, widows, orphans, the elderly, the disabled, and the unemployed. In seaport cities, enslaved laborers might live in their owners' homes or be relegated to separate and impover-ished communities. In New York City, which boasted the second largest slave market in the mainland colonies in the 1710s, blacks were regularly buried outside the city limits. The frequent wars of the late seventeenth and early eighteenth centuries con-tributed to these economic and social divisions by boosting the profits of merchants, shipbuilders, and artisans. They temporarily improved the wages of seamen as well. But in their aftermath, rising prices, falling wages, and a lack of jobs led to the concen-tration of wealth in fewer hands.

REVIEW & RELATE

- What place did North American colonists occupy in the eighteenth-century global trade network?
- How and with what success did the British government maintain control over the colonial economy and ensure that it served Britain's economic and political interests?

Labor in North America

What brought the poor and the wealthy together was the demand for labor. Labor was sorely needed in the colonies, but this did not mean that it was easy to find steady, high-paying employment. Many would-be laborers had few skills and faced fierce competition from other workers for limited, seasonal manual labor. Moreover, a majority of European immigrants and nearly all Africans arrived in America with significant limits on their freedom.

Finding Work in the Colonies

The demand for labor did not necessarily help free laborers find work. Many employers preferred indentured servants, apprentices, or others who came cheap and were bound by contract. Others employed criminals or purchased slaves, who would provide years of service for a set price. Free laborers who sought a decent wage and steady employment needed to match their desire to work with skills that were in demand.

When William Moraley ended his indenture and sought work, he discovered that far fewer colonists than Englishmen owned timepieces, leaving him without a useful trade. So he tramped the countryside, selling his labor when he could, but found no consistent employment. Thousands of other men and women, most without Moraley's education or skills, also found themselves at the mercy of unrelenting economic forces.

Many poor men and women found jobs building homes, loading ships, or spinning yarn. But they were usually employed for only a few months a year. The rest of the time they scrounged for bread and beer, begged in the streets, or stole what they needed. Most lived in ramshackle buildings filled with cramped and unsanitary rooms. Children born into such squalid circumstances were lucky to survive their first year. Those raised in seaport cities might earn a few pence running errands for captains or sailors, but they would never have access to the bounteous goods unloaded at the docks.

By the mid-eighteenth century, older systems of labor, like indentured servitude, began to decline in many areas. In some parts of the North and across the South, white servants were gradually replaced by African slaves (Figure 3.2). At the same time, farm families who could not usefully employ all their children began to bind out sons and daughters to more prosperous neighbors. Apprentices, too, competed for positions. Unlike most servants, apprentices contracted to learn a trade. They trained under the supervision of a craftsman, who gained cheap labor by promising to teach a young man (and most apprentices were men) his trade. But master craftsmen limited the number of apprentices they accepted to maintain the value of their skills.

Another category of laborers emerged in the 1720s. A population explosion in Europe and the rising price of wheat and other items convinced many people to seek passage to America. Shipping agents offered them loans for their passage that were

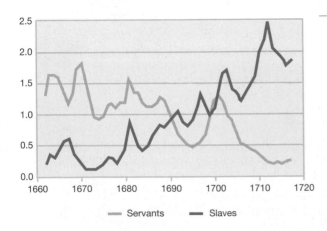

FIGURE 3.2
Indentured Servants and Slaves in Six Maryland Counties, 1662–1717   This chart illustrates a dramatic shift in the Chesapeake labor force between 1662 and 1717. Although based on a study of estate inventories from six Maryland counties, what does the trend shown here suggest about the larger transition in the use of white indentured servants and black slaves on Chesapeake farms?   Based on Gloria L. Main, *Tobacco Colony: Life in Early Maryland, 1650–1720* (Princeton: Princeton University Press, 1982), 26.

repaid when the immigrants found a colonial employer who would redeem (that is, repay) the agents. In turn, these **redemptioners**, who often traveled with families, labored for the employer for a set number of years. The redemption system was popular in the Middle Atlantic colonies, especially among German immigrants who hoped to establish farms on the Pennsylvania frontier. While many succeeded, their circumstances could be extremely difficult.

Large numbers of convicts, too, entered the British colonies in the eighteenth century. Jailers in charge of Britain's overcrowded prisons offered inmates the option of transportation to the colonies. Hundreds were thus bound out each year to American employers. The combination of indentured servants, redemptioners, apprentices, and convicts ensured that as late as 1750 the majority of white workers—men and women—in the British colonies were bound to some sort of contract.

Sometimes white urban workers also competed with slaves, especially in the northern colonies. Africans and African Americans formed only a small percentage of the northern population, just 5 percent from Pennsylvania to New Hampshire in 1750. In the colony of New York, however, blacks formed about 14 percent of inhabitants. While some enslaved blacks worked on agricultural estates in the Hudson River valley and New Jersey, even more labored as household servants, dockworkers, seamen, and blacksmiths in New York City alongside British colonists and European immigrants.

Coping with Economic Distress

Some white workers who were bound by contracts felt common cause with their black counterparts. But whites had a far greater chance of gaining their freedom even before slavery was fully entrenched in colonial law. Still, several challenges confronted white servants, apprentices, redemptioners, and convicts looking to purchase land, open a shop, or earn a decent wage. First, white women and men who gained their freedom from indentures or other contracts had to compete for jobs with a steady supply of redemptioners, convicts, and apprentices as well as other free laborers. Second, by the early eighteenth century, many areas along the Atlantic coast faced a land shortage that threatened the fortunes even of long-settled families. Finally, a population boom in Britain's North American colonies produced growing numbers of young people seeking land and employment. Thus many free laborers migrated from town to town and from country to city seeking work. They hoped to find farmers who needed extra hands for planting and harvesting, ship captains and contractors who would hire them to load or unload cargo or assist in the construction of homes and churches, or wealthy families who needed cooks, laundresses, or nursemaids.

Seasonal and temporary demands for labor created a corps of transient workers. Many New England towns developed systems to "warn out" those who were not official residents. Modeled after the British system, warning-out was meant to ensure that strangers did not become public dependents. Still, being warned did not mean immediate removal. Sometimes transients were simply warned that they were not eligible for poor relief. At other times, constables returned them to an earlier place of residence. In many ways, warning-out served as an early registration system, allowing authorities to encourage the flow of labor, keep residents under surveillance, and protect the town's coffers. But it rarely aided those in need of work.

Residents who were eligible for public assistance might be given food and clothing or boarded with a local family. Many towns began appointing Overseers of the Poor to deal with the growing problem of poverty. By 1750 every seaport city had constructed an almshouse that sheltered residents without other means of support. In 1723 the Bridewell prison was added to Boston Almshouse, built in 1696. Then in 1739 a workhouse was opened on the same site to employ the "able-bodied" poor in hopes that profits from it would help fund the almshouse and prison. Still, these efforts at relief fell far short of the need, especially in hard economic times.

Rural Americans Face Changing Conditions

While seaport cities and larger towns fostered a growing cohort of individuals who lived outside traditional households, families remained the central unit of economic organization in rural areas, where the vast majority of Americans lived. Yet even farms were affected by the transatlantic circulation of goods and people.

In areas along the Atlantic coast, rural families were drawn into commercial networks in a variety of ways. Towns and cities needed large supplies of vegetables, meat, butter, barley, wheat, and yarn. Farm families sold these goods to residents and bought sugar, tea, and other imported items that diversified their diet. Few rural families purchased ornamental or luxury items, but cloth or cheese bought in town saved hours of labor at home. Just as important, coastal communities like Salem, Massachusetts and Wilmington, Delaware that were once largely rural became thriving commercial centers in the late seventeenth century.

In New England, the land available for farming shrank as the population soared. In the original Puritan colonies, the population rose from 100,000 in 1700 to 400,000 in 1750, and many parents were unable to provide their children with sufficient land for profitable farms. The result was increased migration to the frontier, where families were more dependent on their own labor and a small circle of neighbors. And even this option was not accessible to all. Before 1700, servants who survived their indenture had a good chance of securing land, but by the mid-eighteenth century only two of every ten were likely to become landowners.

In the Middle Atlantic region, the population surged from 50,000 in 1700 to 250,000 in 1750. The increase was due in part to the rapid rise in wheat prices, which leaped by more than 50 percent in Europe. Hoping to take advantage of this boon, Anglo-Americans, Germans, Scots-Irish, and other non-English groups flooded into the region in the early eighteenth century. By the 1740s, German families had created self-contained communities in western Pennsylvania, New York's Mohawk River valley, and the Shenandoah Valley of Virginia. They worshipped in German churches, read German newspapers, and preserved German traditions. Meanwhile Scots-Irish immigrants established churches and communities in New Jersey, central Pennsylvania, and western Maryland and Virginia (Map 3.3).

In the South, immigrants could acquire land more easily, but their chances for economic autonomy were increasingly influenced by the spread of slavery. As hundreds and then thousands of Africans were imported into the Carolinas in the 1720s and 1730s, economic and political power became more entrenched in the hands of planters and merchants. Increasingly, they controlled the markets, wrote the laws, and set the terms by which white as well as black families lived. Farms along inland

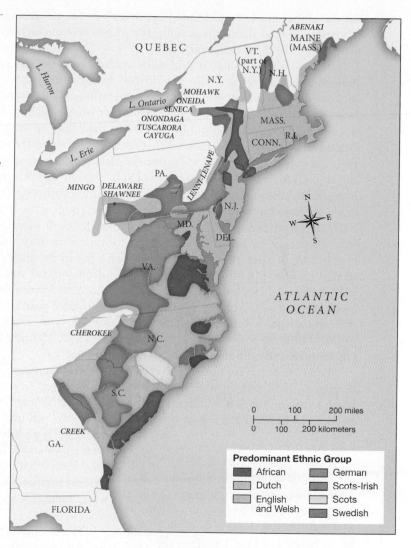

MAP 3.3 Ethnic and Racial Diversity in British North America, 1750 By 1750 British North America was a far more diverse region than it had been fifty years earlier. In 1700 the English dominated most regions, while the Dutch controlled towns and estates in the Hudson River valley. By 1750, however, growing numbers of African Americans, German and Scots-Irish immigrants, and smaller communities of other ethnic groups predominated in various regions.

waterways and on the frontier were crucial in providing food and other items for urban residents and for planters with large labor forces. But farm families depended on commercial and planter elites to market their goods and help defend their communities against hostile Indians or Spaniards.

Slavery Takes Hold in the South

The rise of slavery reshaped the South in numerous ways. A major shift from white indentured servants to black slaves began in Virginia after 1676 and soon spread across the Chesapeake (see Figure 3.2). The Carolinas, meanwhile, developed as a slave society from the start. Slavery in turn allowed for the expanded cultivation of cash crops like tobacco, rice, and indigo, which promised high profits for planters as well as merchants. But these developments also made southern elites more dependent on the global market and limited opportunities for poorer whites and all blacks. They also ensured that Indians and many whites were pushed farther west as planters sought more land for their ventures.

In the 1660s, as tobacco cultivation spread across the Chesapeake, the Virginia Assembly passed a series of laws that defined slavery as a distinct status based on racial identity and passed on through future generations. The enactment of these **slave laws** was driven largely by the growing need for labor, which neither enslaved Indians nor indentured servants could fill. Modeling their laws on statutes passed earlier in Barbados, political leaders ensured that Africans and their descendants would spend their entire lives laboring for white owners. Slavery became a status inherited through the mother; the status could not be changed by converting to Christianity; and masters were granted the right to kill slaves who resisted their authority. In 1680 the Assembly made it illegal for "any negro or other slave to carry or arme himself with any club, staffe, gunn, sword, or any other weapon of defence or offence." Nor could slaves leave their master's premises without a certificate of permission. Increasingly harsh laws in Virginia and Maryland coincided with a rise in the number of slaves imported to the colonies. The statutes also ensured the decline of the free black population in the Chesapeake. In 1668 one-third of all Africans and African Americans in Virginia and Maryland were still free, but the numbers dwindled year by year. Once the Royal African Company started supplying the Chesapeake with slaves directly from Africa in the 1680s, the pace of change quickened. By 1750, 150,000 blacks resided in the Chesapeake, and only about 5 percent remained free.

Direct importation from Africa had other negative consequences on slave life. Far more men than women were imported, skewing the sex ratio in a population that was just beginning to form families and communities. Women, like men, performed heavy field work, and few bore more than one or two children. When these conditions, along with brutal work regimens, sparked resistance by the enslaved, fearful whites imposed even stricter regulations, further distinguishing between white indentured servants and enslaved blacks.

While slavery in the Carolinas was influenced by developments in the

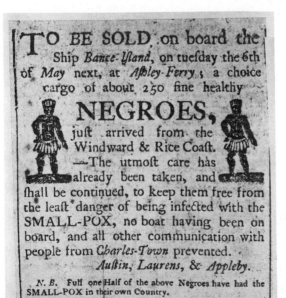

Sale of Slaves in Charleston, South Carolina   Henry Laurens, one of the major slave traders in Charleston, formed a partnership with two other men to import enslaved Africans to North America. This ad focuses on the health of the 250 Africans they are offering for sale, half of whom have developed immunity to smallpox. Being from the Rice Coast, they were also likely skilled in cultivating rice.   Library of Congress, 3a52072 Peter Newark American Pictures/Bridgeman Images

Chesapeake, it was shaped even more directly by practices in the British West Indies. Many wealthy families from Barbados, Antigua, and other sugar islands—including that of Colonel Lucas—established plantations in the Carolinas. At first, they brought slaves from the West Indies to oversee cattle and pigs and assist in the slaughter of livestock and curing of meat for shipment back to the West Indies. Some of the slaves grew rice, using techniques learned in West Africa, to supplement their diet. Owners soon realized that rice might prove very profitable. Although not widely eaten in Europe, rice could provide cheap and nutritious food for sailors, orphans, convicts, and peasants. Relying initially on Africans' knowledge, planters began cultivating rice for export. (See Map 2.2 in chapter 2.)

The need for African rice-growing skills and the fear of attacks by Spaniards and Indians led Carolina owners to grant slaves rights unheard of in the Chesapeake or the West Indies. Initially slaves were allowed to carry guns and serve in the militia. For those who nonetheless ran for freedom, Spanish and Indian territories offered refuge. Still, most stayed, depending for support on bonds they had developed in the West Indies. The frequent absence of owners also offered Carolina slaves greater autonomy.

Yet as rice cultivation expanded from the 1690s through the early 1700s, slavery in the Carolinas turned more brutal. The Assembly enacted harsher and harsher slave codes to ensure control of the growing labor force. No longer could slaves carry guns, join militias, meet in groups, or travel without a pass. At the same time, the increase in the direct import of slaves skewed gender balances and disrupted older community networks. New military patrols by whites enforced laws and labor practices. Some plantations along the Carolina coast turned into virtual labor camps, where thousands of mostly male slaves worked under harsh conditions with no hope of improvement.

By 1720 blacks outnumbered whites in the Carolinas, and fears of slave rebellions inspired South Carolina officials to impose even harsher laws and more brutal enforcement measures. When indigo joined rice as a cash crop in the 1740s, the demand for slave labor increased further. Although far fewer slaves—about 40,000 by 1750—resided in South Carolina than in the Chesapeake, they constituted more than 60 percent of the colony's total population.

Africans Resist Their Enslavement

Enslaved laborers in British North America resisted their subjugation in a variety of ways. They sought to retain customs, foods, belief systems, and languages from their homelands. They tried to incorporate work patterns passed down from one generation to the next into new environments. They challenged masters and overseers by refusing to work, breaking tools, feigning illness, and other means of disputing whites' authority. Some ran for freedom, others fought back in the face of punishment, and still others used arson, poison, or other means to defy owners. A few planned revolts.

The consequences for resisting were severe, from whipping, mutilation, and branding to summary execution. Fearful of rebellion, whites often punished people falsely accused of planning revolts. Yet some slaves did plot insurrections against their owners or whites in general, and both southern and northern colonies lived with the threat of slave rebellion. In New York City in 1712, several dozen enslaved Africans and Indians set fire to a building. When whites rushed to the scene, the insurgents attacked them with clubs, pistols, axes, and staves, killing 8 and injuring many more. The rebels were soon defeated by the militia, however. Authorities executed 18 insurgents, burning several at the stake as a warning to others, while 6 of those imprisoned committed suicide. In 1741 a series of suspicious fires in the city led to accusations against a white couple who owned an alehouse where blacks gathered to drink. To protect herself from prosecution, an Irish indentured servant testified that she had overheard discussions of an elaborate plot involving black and white conspirators. Frightened of any hint that poor whites and blacks might make common cause, authorities immediately arrested suspects and eventually executed 34 people, including 4 whites. They also banished 72 blacks from the city. Among those executed was Cuffee, a slave who claimed that "a great many people have too much, and others too little."

The most serious slave revolt, however, erupted in South Carolina, just a few miles from Wappoo, the Lucas plantation. A group of recently imported Africans led the **Stono rebellion** in 1739. On Sunday, September 9, a group of enslaved men stole weapons from a country store and killed the owners. They then marched south, along the Stono River, beating drums and recruiting others to join them. Torching plantations and killing whites along the route, they had gathered more than fifty insurgents when armed whites overtook them. In the ensuing battle, dozens of rebels died. The militia, along with Indians hired to assist them, killed another twenty over the next two days and then captured a group of forty, who were executed without trial.

This revolt reverberated widely in a colony where blacks outnumbered whites nearly two to one, direct importation from Africa was at an all-time high, and Spanish authorities in Florida promised freedom to runaway slaves. In 1738 the Spanish governor formed a black militia company, and he allowed thirty-eight fugitive families to settle north of St. Augustine and build Fort Mose for their protection. When warfare erupted between Spain and Britain over commercial rivalries in 1739, the Carolina slaves may have seen their chance to gain freedom en masse. But as with other rebellions, this one failed, and the price of failure was death.

REVIEW & RELATE	• What were the sources of economic inequality in North America in the early eighteenth century? • How did the laws and conditions under which poor black and white workers lived during the late seventeenth and early eighteenth centuries differ?

Conclusion: Changing Fortunes in British North America

Global commerce, international wars, and immigration reshaped the economy and geography of North America between 1680 and 1750. Many colonists and some Indians thrived as international trade boomed. In seaport cites, a consumer revolution transformed daily life, fueling the emergence of a colonial elite and the demand for skilled artisans. Others found greater opportunities by pushing inland and establishing farms and communities along new frontiers. But many people failed to benefit from these changes. Indians were often dispossessed of their land as white settlers pushed west. Many indentured servants found it impossible to obtain land or decent wages after they gained their independence. Still, even if white servants and unskilled workers struggled amid periodic economic upheavals, they had the benefit of freedom. Black workers were increasingly forced into slavery, with the shrinking percentage of free blacks suffering from intensifying discrimination against the race as a whole. The consequences of international trade and imperial conflicts only widened the gap between economically successful and impoverished or enslaved Americans.

Increased mechanization and the growth of manufacturing in England shaped the lives of working people on both sides of the Atlantic Ocean. William Moraley Jr., for example, lived out his life in Newcastle-upon-Tyne, making and repairing watches at a time when cheap watches were being turned out in large numbers. Yet these economic changes had far more positive effects for some colonists. The mechanization of cloth production in England demanded vast amounts of raw material from the English countryside and the colonies. It ensured, for example, the profitability of indigo. This crop benefited South Carolina planters like Eliza Lucas and—after her marriage in 1744—her husband, Charles Pinckney, a successful planter himself. Still, profits from indigo could be gained only through the labor of hundreds of slaves.

Eliza Pinckney's sons became important leaders in South Carolina, and despite their English education and the benefits they gained through British trade, both developed a strong belief in the rights of the colonies to control their own destinies. Like many American colonists, they were spurred by the consumer revolution, geographical expansion, growing ethnic diversity, and conflicts with Indian and European enemies to develop a mind-set that differed significantly from their counterparts in England. Yet this turn away from the religious and political beliefs that had sustained them for generations soon spurred a series of revivals that initially reinforced the importance of faith but ultimately challenged the authority of traditional institutions.

Chapter 3 Review

KEY TERMS

proprietary colonies (p. 53)
Glorious Revolution (p. 54)
Pueblo revolt (p. 56)
King William's War (p. 58)
War of the Spanish Succession (p. 58)
Tuscarora War (p. 60)
Yamasee War (p. 60)

mercantilism (p. 63)
Navigation Acts (p. 64)
Middle Passage (p. 65)
redemptioners (p. 69)
slave laws (p. 72)
Stono rebellion (p. 74)

REVIEW & RELATE

1. What role did the crown play in the expansion of the English North American colonies in the second half of the seventeenth century?

2. How did the development of the Spanish and French colonies in the late seventeenth century differ from that of the English colonies?

3. How did the European wars of the late seventeenth and early eighteenth centuries impact relations between colonists and England?

4. How were Indian alliances, with other Indians and with European nations, shaped by the trade in slaves and guns and by wars between European powers?

5. What place did North American colonists occupy in the eighteenth-century global trade network?

6. How and with what success did the British government maintain control over the colonial economy and ensure that it served Britain's economic and political interests?

7. What were the sources of economic inequality in North America in the early eighteenth century?

8. How did the laws and conditions under which poor black and white workers lived during the late seventeenth and early eighteenth centuries differ?

TIMELINE OF EVENTS

1660
- Monarchy restored in England

1660–1673
- Navigation Acts

1660–1685
- Charles II grants North American proprietorships

1672
- Royal African Company chartered

1680
- Pueblo Revolt

1688
- Glorious Revolution

1689–1697
- King William's War

1691–1710
- North Carolina separates from South Carolina

1692
- Colony of Massachusetts established

1700–1750
- New England colonial population quadruples
- Middle Atlantic colonial population quintuples

1700–1808
- British ships carry 3 million African slaves to the Americas

1702
- East and West Jersey unite into New Jersey

1702–1713
- War of the Spanish Succession

1704
- Delaware separates from Pennsylvania

1711–1713
- Tuscarora War

1715–1717
- Yamasee War

1732
- Colony of Georgia established

1739
- Stono rebellion

1749
- Spanish settlers in Texas make peace with the Apache

Religious Strife and Social Upheavals

1680–1754

LEARNING OBJECTIVES

After reading this chapter you should be able to:

- Explain the relationships among religious, economic, and political tensions and accusations of witchcraft.
- Describe family dynamics, particularly between husbands and wives, and how they changed over time and differed by class and region.
- Understand the ways that economic developments and increasing diversity fueled conflicts in early eighteenth-century colonial society.
- Explain the emergence of the Great Awakening and identify its critics and legacies.
- Describe how the Great Awakening shaped political developments in the 1730s and 1740s.

COMPARING AMERICAN HISTORIES

The son of a Scots-Irish clergyman, Gilbert Tennent was born in Vinecash, Ireland, in 1703 and at age fifteen moved with his family to Philadelphia. After receiving an M.A. from Yale College in 1725, Gilbert was ordained a Presbyterian minister in New Brunswick, New Jersey, with little indication of the role he would play in a major denominational schism.

Tennent entered the ministry at a critical moment, when leaders of a number of denominations had become convinced that the colonies were descending into spiritual apathy. Tennent dedicated himself to sparking a rebirth of Christian commitment, and by the mid-1730s the pastor had gained fame as a revival preacher. At the end of the decade, he journeyed through the middle colonies with Englishman George Whitefield, an Anglican preacher known for igniting powerful revivals. Then in the fall of 1740, following the death of his wife, Tennent launched his own evangelical "awakenings."

Revivals inspired thousands of religious conversions across denominations, but they also fueled conflicts within established churches. Presbyterians in Britain and America disagreed about whether only those who had had a powerful, personal conversion experience were qualified to be ministers. Tennent made his opinion clear by denouncing unconverted ministers in his sermons, a position that led to his expulsion from the Presbyterian Church in 1741. But many local churches sought converted preachers, and four years later a group of ejected pastors formed a rival synod that trained its own evangelical ministers.

While ministers debated the proper means of saving sinners, ordinary women and men searched their souls. In Pomfret, Connecticut, Sarah Grosvenor certainly feared for hers in the summer of 1742 when the unmarried nineteen-year-old realized she was pregnant. Her situation was complicated by her status in the community. She was the daughter of Leicester Grosvenor, an important landowner, town official, and member of the Congregational Church.

The pew next to Sarah and her family was occupied by Nathaniel Sessions and his sons, including the twenty-six-year-old Amasa, who had impregnated Sarah. Many other young women became pregnant out of wedlock in the 1740s, but families accepted the fact as long as the couple married before the child was born. In Sarah's case, however, Amasa refused to marry her and suggested instead that she have an abortion.

Although Sarah was reluctant to follow this path, Amasa insisted. When herbs traditionally used to induce a miscarriage failed, Amasa introduced Sarah to John Hallowell, a doctor who claimed he could remove the fetus with forceps. After admitting her agonizing situation to her older sister Zerviah and her cousin Hannah, Sarah allowed Hallowell to proceed. He finally induced a miscarriage, but Sarah soon grew feverish, suffered convulsions, and died ten days later.

Apparently Sarah's and Amasa's parents were unaware of the events leading to her demise. Then in 1745, a powerful religious revival swept through the region, and Zerviah and Hannah suffered great spiritual anguish. It is likely they finally confessed their part in the affair since that year officials brought charges against Amasa Sessions and John Hallowell for Sarah's death. At the men's trial, Zerviah and Hannah testified about their roles and those of Sessions and Hallowell. Still, their spiritual anguish did not lead to earthly justice. Hallowell was found guilty but escaped punishment by fleeing to Rhode Island. Sessions was acquitted and remained in Pomfret, where he married and became a prosperous farmer.

COMPARING THE AMERICAN HISTORIES of Gilbert Tennent and Sarah Grosvenor reveals the power of the religious forces—later called the Great Awakening—that swept through the colonies in the early eighteenth century. Those forces are best understood in the context of larger social, economic, and political changes. Many young people became more independent of their parents and developed tighter bonds with siblings, cousins, and neighbors their own age. Towns and cities developed clearer hierarchies by class and status, which could protect wealthier individuals from being punished for their misdeeds. A double standard of sexual behavior became more entrenched as well, with women subject to greater scrutiny than men for their sexual behavior. Of course, most young women did not meet the fate of Sarah Grosvenor. Still, pastors like Gilbert Tennent feared precisely such consequences if the colonies—growing ever larger and more diverse—did not reclaim their religious foundations.

An Ungodly Society?

As American colonists became more engaged in international and domestic commerce, spiritual commitments appeared to wane. In New England, Congregational ministers condemned the apparent triumph of worldly ambition over religiosity. Nonetheless, some ministers saw economic success as a reward for godly behavior even as they worried that wealth and power opened the door to sin. In the late seventeenth century, these anxieties deepened when accusations of witchcraft erupted across southern New England.

The Rise of Religious Anxieties

In 1686 the Puritan minister Samuel Sewell railed against the behavior of Boston mercantile elites. Citing examples of their depravity in his diary, including drunkenness and cursing, he claimed that such "high-handed wickedness has hardly been heard of before." Sewell was outraged as well by popular practices such as donning powdered wigs in place of God-given hair, wearing scarlet and gold jackets rather than simple black cloth, and offering toasts rather than prayers.

While Sewell spoke for many Puritans concerned with the consequences of commercial success, other religious leaders tried to meld old and new. The Reverend Cotton Mather complained that many colonists showed greater interest in the latest fashions than in the state of their souls. Yet he was attracted by the luxuries available to colonists and hoped to make his own son "a more finished Gentleman." Mather was also fascinated by new scientific endeavors and supported inoculations for smallpox, which others viewed as challenging God's power.

Certainly news of the Glorious Revolution in England (1688) offered Puritans hope of regaining their customary authority (see "English Colonies Grow and Multiply" in chapter 3). But the outbreak of King William's War in 1689 quickly ended any notion of an easy return to peace and prosperity. Instead, continued conflicts and renewed fears of Indian attacks on rural settlements heightened the sense that Satan was at work in the region. Soon, accusations of witchcraft joined outcries against other forms of ungodly behavior.

Cries of Witchcraft

Belief in witchcraft had been widespread in Europe and England for centuries. It was part of a general belief in supernatural causes for events that could not otherwise be explained—severe storms, a suspicious fire, a rash of deaths among livestock. When a community began to suspect witchcraft, they often pointed to individuals who challenged cultural norms. Women who were quarrelsome, eccentric, poor, or simply too independent were easy to imagine as cavorting with evil spirits and invisible demons.

Witchcraft accusations tended to be most common in times of change and uncertainty. Over the course of the seventeenth century, colonists had begun to spread into new areas seeking more land and greater economic opportunities. But expansion brought with it confrontations with Indians, exposure to new dangers, and greater vulnerability to a harsh environment. As the stress of expansion mounted, witchcraft accusations emerged. Some 160 individuals, mostly women, were accused of witchcraft in Massachusetts and Connecticut and 15 were put to death between 1647 and 1691. Many of the accused were poor, childless, or disgruntled women, but widows who inherited property also came under suspicion, especially if they fought for control against male relatives and neighbors.

The social and economic complexities of witchcraft accusations are well illustrated by the most famous American witch-hunt, the Salem witch trials of the early 1690s. In 1692 residents of Salem, Massachusetts confronted conflicts between long-settled farmers and newer mercantile families, political uncertainties following the Glorious Revolution, ongoing threats from Indians, and quarrels over the choice of a new minister. These tensions were brought to a head when the Reverend Samuel Parris's daughter and niece learned voodoo lore and exotic dances from the household's West Indian slave, Tituba. The daughters and servants of neighboring families also became entranced by Tituba's tales and began to tell fortunes, speak in gibberish, and contort their bodies into painful positions. When the girls were questioned about their strange behavior, they pointed not only to Tituba but also to other people in the community. They first accused an elderly female pauper and a homeless widow of bewitching them, but later singled out respectable churchwomen as well as a minister, a wealthy merchant, and a four-year-old child.

Within weeks, more than one hundred individuals, 80 percent of them women, stood accused of witchcraft. Governor William Phips established a special court to handle the cases, over which the Reverend Samuel Sewell presided. Twenty-seven of the accused came to trial, and twenty were found guilty based on testimony from the girls and on **spectral evidence**, that is, evidence that came to the girls in dreams or visions. In court, the young accusers were seen writhing, shaking, and crying out in pain as spirits of the accused, invisible to everyone else, came to them in visions and pinched, choked, and bit them. Based on such evidence, nineteen people were hanged, and one was pressed to death with stones.

But when accusations reached into prominent Salem and Boston families, Governor Phips ended the proceedings and released the remaining suspects. In the following months, leading ministers and colonial officials condemned the use of spectral evidence, and some of the young accusers recanted their testimony.

The Salem trials illuminate far more than beliefs in witchcraft. The trials pitted the daughters and servants of prosperous farmers against the wives and widows of recently arrived merchants. The accusers included young women like nineteen-year-old Mercy Lewis, who was bound out as a servant when her parents were killed by Indians. Fear of attack from hostile Indians, hostile officials in England, or hostile neighbors fostered anxieties in Salem, as it did in many colonial communities. Other anxieties also haunted the accusers. A shortage of land led many New England men to seek their fortune farther west, leaving young women with few eligible bachelors to choose from. Marriage prospects were affected as well by battles over inheritance. Thomas Putnam Jr., who housed three of the accusers, was in the midst of one such battle, which left his three sisters—the accusers' aunts—in limbo as they awaited legacies that could enhance their marriage prospects. As young women in Salem forged tight bonds in the face of such uncertainties, they turned their anger not against men, but instead against older women, including respectable "goodwives" like Abigail Faulkner.

REVIEW & RELATE

- What factors led to a rise in tensions within colonial communities in the early 1700s?
- How did social, economic, and political tensions contribute to an increase in accusations of witchcraft?

Family and Household Dynamics

Concerns about marriage, property, and inheritance were not limited to Salem or to New England. As the American colonies became more populous and the numbers of women and men more balanced, husbands gained greater control over the behavior of household members, and the legal and economic rewards available to most women declined. Yet some women improved their situation by wielding their skills as midwives, brewers, or even plantation managers to benefit their families.

Women's Changing Status

In most early American colonies, the scarcity of women and workers ensured that many white women gained economic and legal leverage. In the first decades of settlement in the Chesapeake, where women were in especially short supply and mortality was high, young women who arrived as indentured servants and completed their term might marry older men of property. If the husbands died first, widows often took control of the estate and passed on the property to their children. Even in New England, where the numbers of men and women were more balanced from the beginning, the crucial labor of wives in the early years of settlement was sometimes recognized by their control of family property after a husband's death.

By the late seventeenth century, however, as the sex ratio in the Chesapeake evened out, women lost the opportunity to marry "above their class" (see Table 4.1). And across the colonies, widows lost control of family estates. Even though women still performed vital labor, the spread of indentured servitude and slavery lessened the recognition of their contributions, while in urban areas the rise of commerce highlighted their role as consumers rather than as producers. As a result, most wives and daughters of white settlers were assigned primarily domestic roles. They also found

TABLE 4.1   **Sex Ratios in the White Population for Selected Colonies, 1624–1755**

Date	Colony	White Male Population	White Female Population	Females per 100 Males
1624–1625	Virginia	873	222	25
1660	Maryland	c. 600	c. 190	32
1704	Maryland	11,026	7,136	65
1698	New York	5,066	4,677	92
1726	New Jersey	15,737	14,124	90
1755	Rhode Island	17,860	17,979	101

their legal and economic rights restricted to those accorded their female counterparts in Great Britain.

According to English common law, a wife's status was defined as *feme covert*, which meant that she was legally covered over by (or hidden behind) her husband. The husband controlled his wife's labor, the house in which she lived, the property she brought into the marriage, and any wages she earned. He was also the legal guardian of their children, and through the instrument of a will he could continue to control the household after his death.

With the growth and diversity of colonial towns and cities, the **patriarchal family**—a model in which fathers held absolute authority over wives, children, and servants—came to be seen as a crucial bulwark against disorder. Families with wealth were especially eager to control the behavior of their sons and daughters as the parents sought to build social, commercial, and political alliances. The refusal of Amasa Sessions to marry Sarah Grosvenor, for instance, may have resulted from his father's expectation of a better match.

Working Families

Still, for most colonial women and men, daily rounds of labor shaped their lives more powerfully than legal statutes or inheritance rights. Husbands and wives depended on each other to support the family. By the early eighteenth century, many colonial writers promoted the idea of marriage as a partnership, even if the wife remained the junior partner.

This concept of marriage as a partnership took practical form in communities across the colonies. In towns, the wives of artisans often learned aspects of their husband's craft and assisted their husbands in a variety of ways. Given the overlap between homes and workplaces in the eighteenth century, women often cared for apprentices, journeymen, and laborers as well as their own children. Husbands meanwhile labored alongside their subordinates and represented their families' interests to the larger community. Both spouses were expected to provide models of godliness and to encourage prayer and regular church attendance among household members.

On farms, where the vast majority of colonists lived, women and men played crucial if distinct roles. In general, wives and daughters labored inside the home as well as

Harvest Scene   Mary Woodhull was born on Long Island in 1743 and created this colorful needlepoint sampler sometime before her marriage to Amos Underhill. Such decorative samplers were often hung in the family parlor to illustrate the young woman's ideals and skills to prospective husbands. Interestingly here, both the woman and the man are holding scythes used to cut the grain.   Granger Collection, NYC

in the surrounding yard with its kitchen garden, milk house, chicken coop, dairy, or washhouse. Husbands and sons worked the fields, kept the livestock, and managed the orchards. Many families supplemented their own labor with that of servants, slaves, or hired field hands. And surplus crops and manufactured goods such as cloth or sausage were exchanged with neighbors or sold at market, creating an economic network of small producers.

Indeed, in the late seventeenth and early eighteenth centuries, many farm families in long-settled areas participated in a household mode of production. Men lent each other tools and draft animals and shared grazing land, while women gathered to spin, sew, and quilt. Individuals with special skills like midwifery or blacksmithing assisted neighbors, adding farm produce or credit to the family ledger. One woman's cheese might be bartered for another woman's jam. A family that owned the necessary equipment might brew barley and malt into beer, while a neighbor with a loom would turn yarn into cloth. The system of exchange, managed largely through barter, allowed individual households to function even as they became more specialized in what they produced. Whatever cash was obtained could be used to buy sugar, tea, and other imported goods.

Reproduction and Women's Roles

Maintaining a farm required the work of both women and men, which made marriage an economic as well as a social and religious institution. In the early eighteenth century, more than 90 percent of white women married. By 1700 a New England wife who married at age twenty and survived to forty-five bore an average of eight children, most of whom lived to adulthood. In the Chesapeake, mortality rates remained higher and the sex ratio still favored men. It took another generation for southern white women to come close to the reproductive rates of their northern counterparts.

Fertility rates among enslaved Africans and African Americans were much lower than those among whites in the early eighteenth century, and fewer infants survived to adulthood. It was not until the 1740s that the majority of slaves were born in the colonies rather than imported as some southern slave owners began to realize that encouraging reproduction made good economic sense. Still, enslaved women, most of whom worked in the fields, gained only minimal relief from their labors during pregnancy.

Colonial mothers combined childbearing and child rearing with a great deal of other work. While some affluent families could afford wet nurses and nannies, most women fended for themselves or hired temporary help for particular tasks. In rural areas, mothers with babies on hip and children under foot hauled water, fed chickens, collected eggs, picked vegetables, prepared meals, spun thread, and manufactured soap and candles. Children were at constant risk of disease and injury, but were spared the overcrowding, the raw sewage, and the foul water that marked most cities in this period.

Infants were the most vulnerable to disease, and parents were relieved when their children passed their first birthdays. Colonists feared the deaths of mothers as well. In 1700 roughly one out of thirty births ended in the mother's death. Women who bore six to eight children thus faced death on a regular basis. One minister urged pregnant women to prepare their souls, "For ought you know your Death has entered into you."

When a mother died while her children were still young, her husband was likely to remarry soon afterward in order to maintain the family and his farm or business. Even though fathers held legal guardianship over their children, there was little doubt that child rearing, especially for young children, was women's work. Many husbands acknowledged this role, prayed for their wife while in labor, and sought to ease her domestic burdens near the end of a pregnancy. But some women drew little help or protection from their husbands.

The Limits of Patriarchal Order

While most families accepted the idea of female subordination in return for patriarchal protection, there were signs of change in the early eighteenth century. Sermons against fornication; ads for runaway spouses, servants, and slaves; reports of domestic violence; poems about domineering wives; petitions for divorce; and legal suits charging rape, seduction, or breach of contract make clear that ideals of patriarchal authority did not always match the reality. It is impossible to quantify the frequency with which women contested their subordination, but a variety of evidence points to increasing tensions around issues of control—by husbands over wives, fathers over children, and men over women.

Women's claims about men's misbehavior were often demeaned as gossip, but gossip could be an important weapon for those who had little chance of legal redress. In colonial communities, credit and trust were central to networks of exchange, so damaging a man's reputation could be a serious matter. Still, gossip was not as powerful as legal sanctions. Thus some women who bore illegitimate children, suffered physical and sexual abuse, or were left penniless by a husband who drank might seek assistance from the courts.

Divorce was as rare in the colonies as it was in England. In New England, colonial law allowed for divorce, but few were granted and almost none to women before 1750. In other colonies, divorce could be obtained only by an act of the colonial assembly and was therefore confined to the wealthy and powerful. If a divorce was granted, the wife usually received an allowance for food and clothing. Yet without independent financial resources, she nearly always had to live with relatives. Custody of any children was awarded to fathers who had the economic means to support them, although infants or young girls might be assigned to live with the mother. A quicker and cheaper means of ending an unsatisfactory marriage was to abandon one's spouse. Again wives were at a disadvantage since they had few means to support themselves or their children. Colonial divorce petitions citing desertion and newspaper ads for runaway spouses suggest that husbands fled in at least two-thirds of such cases.

In the rare instances when women did obtain a divorce, they had to bring multiple charges against their husbands. Domestic violence, adultery, or abandonment alone was insufficient to gain redress. Indeed, ministers and relatives were likely to counsel abused wives to change their behavior or suffer in silence. Even evidence of brutal assaults on a wife rarely led to legal redress because husbands had the legal right to "correct" their wives and children and because physical punishment was widely accepted.

Single women also faced barriers in seeking legal redress. By the late seventeenth century, church and civil courts in New England gave up on coercing sexually active couples to marry. Judges, however, continued to hear complaints of seduction or breach of contract brought by the fathers of single women who were pregnant but unmarried. Had Sarah Grosvenor survived the abortion, her family could have sued Amasa Sessions on the grounds that he gained "carnal knowledge" of her through "promises of marriage." If the plaintiffs won, the result was no longer marriage, however, but financial support for the child. In 1730 in Concord, Massachusetts, Susanna Holding sued a farmer, Joseph Bright, whom she accused of fathering her illegitimate child. When Bright protested his innocence, Holding found townsmen to testify that the farmer, "in his courting of her . . . had designed to make her his Wife." In this case, the abandoned mother mobilized members of the community, including men, to uphold popular understandings of patriarchal responsibilities. Without such support, women were less likely to win their cases.

Women who were raped faced even greater legal obstacles than those who were seduced and abandoned. In most colonies, rape was a capital crime, punishable by death, and all-male juries were reluctant to find men guilty. Unlikely to win and fearing humiliation in court, few women charged men with rape. Yet more did so than the records might show since judges and justices of the peace sometimes downgraded rape charges to simple assault or fornication, that is, sex outside of marriage (Table 4.2).

Young white women had the best chance of gaining support and redress for seduction or rape if they confided in their parents or other elders. But by the mid-eighteenth century, young people were seeking more control over their sexual behavior and marriage prospects, and certain behaviors—for example, sons settling in towns distant from the parental home, younger daughters marrying before their older sisters, and single women finding themselves pregnant—increased noticeably. In part, these trends were natural consequences of colonial growth and mobility. The bonds that once held families and communities together began to loosen. But in the process, young women's chances of protecting themselves against errant and abusive men diminished. Just as important, even when they faced desperate situations, young women like Sarah Grosvenor increasingly turned to sisters and friends rather than fathers or ministers.

TABLE 4.2   Sexual Coercion Cases Downgraded in Chester County, Pennsylvania, 1731–1739

Date	Defendant/Victim	Charge on Indictment in Testimony	Charge in Docket
1731	Lawrence MacGinnis/Alice Yarnal	Assault with attempt to rape	None
1731	Thomas Culling/Martha Claypool	Assault with attempt to rape	Assault
1734	Abraham Richardson/Mary Smith	Attempted rape	Assault
1734	Thomas Beckett/Mindwell Fulfourd	Theft (testimony of attempted rape)	Theft
1734	Unknown/Christeen Pauper	(Fornication charge against Christeen)	None
1735	Daniel Patterson/Hannah Tanner	Violent assault to ravish	Assault
1736	James White/Hannah McCradle	Attempted rape/adultery	Assault
1737	Robert Mills/Catherine Parry	Rape	None
1738	John West/Isabella Gibson	Attempt to ravish/assault	Fornication
1739	Thomas Halladay/Mary Mouks	Assault with intent to ravish	None

Source: Sharon Block, *Rape and Sexual Power in Early America* (Chapel Hill: University of North Carolina Press). Data from Chester County Quarter Sessions Docket Books and File Papers, 1730–1739.

Poor women, especially those who labored as servants, had even fewer options. Servants faced tremendous obstacles in obtaining legal independence from masters or mistresses who beat or sexually assaulted them. Colonial judges and juries generally refused to declare a man who was wealthy enough to support servants guilty of criminal acts against them. Moreover, poor women generally and servants in particular were regularly depicted as lusty and immoral, making it unlikely that they would gain the sympathy of white judges or juries. Slaves faced many of the same obstacles and had even less hope of prevailing against brutal owners. Thus for most servants and slaves, running away was their sole hope for escaping abuse; however, if they were caught, their situation would likely worsen. Even poor whites who lived independently had little chance of addressing issues of domestic violence, seduction, or rape through the courts.

REVIEW & RELATE

- Why and how did the legal and economic status of colonial women decline between 1650 and 1750?
- How did patriarchal ideals of family and community shape life and work in colonial America? What happened when men failed to live up to those ideals?

Diversity and Competition in Colonial Society

As the English colonies in North America expanded, divisions increased between established families living in long-settled regions—whether on rural farmsteads or in urban homesteads—and the growing population of women and men with few resources. Although most colonists still hoped to own their own land and establish themselves as farmers, artisans, or shopkeepers, fewer were likely to succeed than in the past. By 1760 half of all white men in North America were propertyless. This growing class cleavage was accompanied by increasing racial, national, and religious diversity, which also fostered economic competition and conflict.

Population Growth and Economic Competition

After 1700, the population grew rapidly across the colonies. In 1700 about 250,000 people lived in England's North American colonies. By 1725 that number had doubled, and fifty years later it had reached 2.5 million. Much of the increase was due to natural reproduction, but in addition nearly 250,000 immigrants and Africans arrived in the colonies between 1700 and 1750.

Because more women and children arrived than in earlier decades, higher birthrates and a more youthful population resulted. At the same time, most North American colonists enjoyed a better diet than their counterparts in Europe and had access to more abundant natural resources. Thus colonists in the eighteenth century began living longer, with more adults surviving to watch their children and grandchildren grow up.

However, as the population soared, the chance for individuals to obtain land or start a business of their own diminished. Those who had established businesses early generally expanded to meet new needs, making it more difficult for others to compete. Those bent on making their living from the land often found the soil exhausted in long-settled regions. On the frontier, settlers might have to carve out farms amid forests, swamps, or areas already claimed by Indian, French, or Spanish residents. While owning land did not automatically lead to prosperity, those who were landless had to find work as tenant farmers, laborers, or in other unskilled occupations. In the South Carolina backcountry, a visitor in the mid-eighteenth century noted that many residents "have nought but a Gourd to drink out of, nor a Plate, Knive or Spoon, a Glass, Cup, or anything."

In prosperous parts of the Middle Atlantic colonies like Pennsylvania, many landless laborers abandoned rural life and searched for urban opportunities. They moved to Philadelphia or other towns and cities in the region, seeking jobs as dockworkers, street vendors, or servants, or as apprentices in one of the skilled trades. But newcomers found the job market flooded and the chances for advancement growing slim (Figure 4.1).

In the South, too, divisions between rich and poor became more pronounced in the early decades of the eighteenth century. Tobacco was the most valuable product in the Chesapeake, and the largest tobacco planters lived in relative luxury. They developed mercantile contacts in seaport cities on the Atlantic coast and in the Caribbean and imported luxury goods from Europe. They also began training some of their slaves as domestic workers to relieve wives and daughters of the strain of household labor.

Small farmers could also purchase and maintain a farm based on the profits from tobacco. In 1750 two-thirds of white families farmed their own land in Virginia, a larger percentage than in northern colonies. An even higher percentage did so in the Carolinas. Yet small farmers became increasingly dependent on large landowners, who controlled markets, political authority, and the courts. Many artisans, too, depended on wealthy planters for their livelihood, either working for them directly or for the

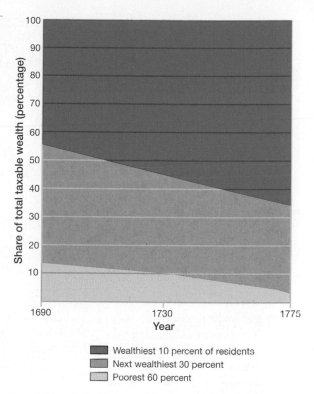

FIGURE 4.1
Wealth Inequality in Northern Cities, 1690–1775   During the eighteenth century, the wealth of merchants rose much faster than that of artisans and laborers. This table tracks the percent of wealth held by three groups of taxable residents in major northern cities from the late seventeenth century to the eve of the American Revolution. Over this period, how did the wealth of the top 10 percent of this population change in relation to the next wealthiest 30 percent and the poorest 60 percent?
Data from Gary B. Nash, *The Urban Crucible: Social Change, Political Consciousness, and the Origins of the American Revolution* (Cambridge, MA: Harvard University Press, 1979).

■ Wealthiest 10 percent of residents
■ Next wealthiest 30 percent
□ Poorest 60 percent

shipping companies and merchants that relied on plantation orders. And the growing number of tenant farmers relied completely on large landowners for their sustenance.

Some southerners fared far worse. One-fifth of all white southerners owned little more than the clothes on their backs in the mid-eighteenth century. At the same time, free blacks in the South found their opportunities for landownership and economic independence increasingly curtailed, while enslaved blacks had little hope of gaining their freedom and held no property of their own.

Increasing Diversity

Population growth and economic divisions were accompanied by increased diversity in the North American colonies. Indentured servants arrived from Ireland, Scotland, and Germany as well as England. Africans were imported in growing numbers and entered a more highly structured system of slavery, whether laboring on southern farms, on northern estates, or in seaport cities. In addition, free families and redemptioners from Ireland, Scotland, the German states, and Sweden came in ever-larger numbers and developed their own communities and cultural institutions. There were also more colonists who had spent time in the Caribbean before settling on the mainland, and the frontiers of British North America were filled with American Indians and French and Spanish settlers as well.

As the booming population demanded more land, colonists pushed westward to find territory that either was not claimed by others or could be purchased. At the beginning of the eighteenth century, German and Scots-Irish immigrants joined Anglo-American settlers in rural areas of New Jersey, Pennsylvania, and Delaware. Many immigrants to Pennsylvania settled in areas like Shamokin that were dotted with Iroquois, Algonquian, and Siouan towns and negotiated with Indians to obtain

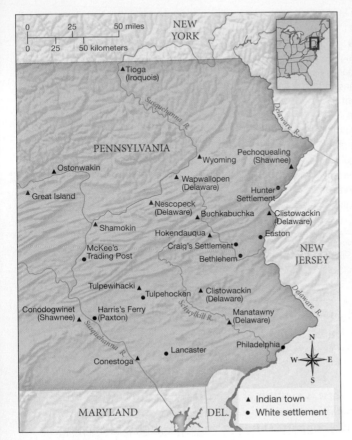

MAP 4.1
Frontier Settlements and Indian Towns in Pennsylvania, 1700–1740 German and Scots-Irish immigrants to Pennsylvania mingled with Indian settlements in the early eighteenth century as Delaware and Shawnee groups were pushed west from New Jersey. In the 1720s and 1730s, however, European migration escalated dramatically in the fertile river valleys. In response, once-independent Indian tribes joined the Delaware and Shawnee nations to strengthen their position against the influx of colonists. From *At the Crossroads: Indians & Empires on a Mid-Atlantic Frontier, 1700–1763* by Jane T. Merritt, Published for the Omohundro Institute of Early American History and Culture. Copyright © 2003 by the University of North Carolina Press. Used by permission of the publisher. www.uncpress.unc.edu.

farmland. At the same time, Delaware and Shawnee groups, who were pushed out of New Jersey and the Ohio Valley by pressure from settlers, also moved into Pennsylvania. They negotiated with colonists, the colonial government, and other Indian groups to establish communities for themselves. All along the Pennsylvania frontier, the lines between Indian and immigrant settlements blurred. Still, many communities prospered in the region, with white settlers exchanging European and colonial trade goods for access to Indian-controlled orchards, waterways, and lands (Map 4.1).

In the 1720s and 1730s, however, Scots-Irish settlers flooded into Pennsylvania when bad harvests and high rents caused them to flee oppressive conditions back home. The new immigrants overwhelmed native communities that had welcomed earlier settlers. The death of William Penn in 1718 exacerbated the situation as his sons and closest advisers struggled to gain control over the colony. Indians were increasingly pushed to the margins as growing numbers of European settlers moved into frontier territories.

Expansion and Conflict

As more and more colonists sought economic opportunities on the frontier, conflicts erupted regularly between earlier British and newer immigrant settlers as well as among immigrant groups. In Pennsylvania, Dutch, Scots-Irish, and German colonists took each other to court, sued land surveyors, and even burned down cabins built by their immigrant foes. For longtime British settlers, such acts only reinforced their sense that recent immigrants were a threat to their society. In 1728 James Logan, William Penn's longtime secretary, complained that the "Palatines [Germans] crowd in upon us and the Irish yet faster." For Logan, these difficulties were exacerbated by what he considered the "idle," "worthless," and "indigent" habits of Scots-Irish and other recent arrivals.

Anglo-Americans hardly set high standards themselves, especially when negotiating with Indians. Even in Pennsylvania, where William Penn had established a reputation for (relatively) fair dealing, the desire for Indian land led to dishonesty and trickery. Conflicts among Indian nations aided colonial leaders in prying territory from the Indians. Hoping to assert their authority over the independent-minded Delaware Indians, Iroquois chiefs insisted that they held rights to much of the Pennsylvania territory and therefore must be the ones to negotiate with colonial officials. Those colonial authorities, however, produced a questionable treaty supposedly drafted by Penn in 1686 that allowed them to claim large portions of the contested territory. James Logan "discovered" a copy of this treaty, which allowed the English to control an area that could be walked off in a day and a half. Seeking to maintain control of at least some territory, the Iroquois finally agreed to this **Walking Purchase**. The Delaware tribe, far smaller, was then pressured into letting Pennsylvania officials walk off the boundaries. By the time the Delaware acquiesced in the fall of 1737, Pennsylvania surveyors had already marked off the "shortest and best course," which allowed them to extend the boundaries by at least thirty miles beyond those set in the original, and questionable, treaty.

The rapid expansion of the colonial population ensured that conflicts between Indian and colonial leaders over land rights would continue to erupt. Meanwhile migrants and immigrants on the Anglo-American frontier claimed land simply by taking control of it, building houses, and planting crops. This led to conflicts with Indian communities that considered the territory their own, with English officials who demanded legal contracts and deeds, and among immigrants who settled in the same area.

These conflicts contrasted with developments around the Great Lakes where French traders and Algonquian inhabitants forged military and economic alliances. In this region, called *Pays d'en Haut* (upper country) by the French, colonists and Indians sought diplomatic solutions to problems to protect mutually beneficial trade relations and fend off challenges from other European and indigenous groups.

Some religiously minded immigrants also worked to improve relations with Indians in Pennsylvania, at least temporarily. The tone had been set by William Penn's Quakers, who generally accepted Indian land claims and tried to pursue honest and fair negotiations. German Moravians who settled in eastern Pennsylvania in the 1740s also developed good relations with area tribes. On Pennsylvania's western frontier, Scots-Irish Presbyterians established alliances with Delaware and Shawnee groups. These alliances, however, were rooted less in religious principles than in the hope of profiting from the fur trade as Indians sought new commercial partners when their French allies became too demanding.

Still, as tensions escalated between English and French officials in the region, conflicts intensified among the various immigrant and religious communities and with Indians. The distinct religious traditions and the dramatically different visions of

Bethlehem, Pennsylvania, 1757   This painting by Nicholas Garrison shows Bethlehem sixteen years after its settlement by German Moravians. The Moravians fled religious persecution in
Germany in the early 1700s and established communal societies in Pennsylvania and New Jersey.
Moravians pooled their labor and resources so they could sustain farms and shops, establish
separate schools for their children, and missionize among local Indians.   Art Resource, NY

Indian-settler relations drawn from these traditions also sharpened boundaries within
and between colonial communities. German Moravians and Scots-Irish Presbyterians
in Pennsylvania established churches and schools separate from their Quaker neighbors, while Puritan New Englanders remained suspicious of Quakers as well as other
Protestant sects. Moravians and other German sects also flourished in Georgia and
the Carolinas, and nearly all sought to isolate themselves from the influences of other
religious and ethnic groups.

Some religious groups were isolated as much by force as by choice. While most
early Irish immigrants were Protestant, by the early eighteenth century more Irish
Catholics began to arrive. Then in 1745 some forty thousand Scots who had supported the Catholic monarchs in England prior to the Glorious Revolution were
shipped to the Carolinas after a failed rebellion. Even long-settled Catholics, like those
in Maryland, were looked on with suspicion by many Protestants. Although only a few
hundred Jewish families resided in the colonies by 1750, they formed small but endur-
ing communities in a number of seaport cities, where they established synagogues and
developed a variety of mercantile ventures.

Africans, too, brought new ideas and practices to North America. Transported by
force to an unknown land, they may have found religious faith particularly important.
Enslaved blacks included some Catholics from regions long held by the Portuguese

and a few thousand Muslims, but many Africans embraced religions that were largely unknown to their Anglo-American masters.

As religious affiliations in the colonies multiplied, they reinforced existing concerns about spiritual decline. Moreover, spiritual differences often exacerbated cleavages rooted in nationality and class. And they heightened concerns among many well-established families over the future of British culture and institutions in North America.

REVIEW & RELATE	• How and why did economic inequality in the colonies increase in the first half of the eighteenth century?
	• How did population growth and increasing diversity contribute to conflict among and anxieties about the various groups inhabiting British North America?

Religious Awakenings

Whether rooted in fears that worldly concerns were overshadowing spiritual devotion or that growing religious diversity was undermining the power of the church, many Protestant ministers lamented the state of faith in eighteenth-century America. Church leaders in Britain and the rest of Europe shared their fears. Ministers eager to address this crisis of faith—identified in the colonies as **New Light clergy**—worked together to reenergize the faithful and were initially welcomed, or at least tolerated, by more traditional **Old Light clergy**. But by the 1740s, fears that the passionate New Light clergy had gone too far led to a backlash.

The Roots of the Great Awakening

By the eighteenth century, the **Enlightenment**, a European cultural movement that emphasized rational and scientific thinking over traditional religion and superstition, had taken root in the colonies, particularly among elites. The development of a lively print culture spread the ideas of Enlightenment thinkers like the English philosopher John Locke, the German intellectual Immanuel Kant, and the French writer Voltaire across the Atlantic. These thinkers argued that through reason humans could discover the laws that governed the universe and thereby improve society. Benjamin Franklin, a leading printer in Philadelphia, was one of the foremost advocates of Enlightenment ideas in the colonies. His experiments with electricity reflected his faith in rational thought, and his publication of the *Pennsylvania Gazette* and *Poor Richard's Almanac* spread such ideas throughout the colonies in the 1720s and 1730s.

As more colonists were influenced by Enlightenment thought, they became more accepting of religious diversity, which had spread as settlers from diverse countries and denominations arrived in the English colonies. At the same time, Enlightenment ideas could undermine the religious vitality of the colonies. Many Enlightenment thinkers believed in a Christian God but rejected the revelations and rituals that defined traditional church practices and challenged ministerial claims that God was directly engaged in the daily workings of the world.

There were, however, countervailing forces. The German **Pietists** in particular challenged Enlightenment ideas that had influenced many Congregational and

Anglican leaders in Europe. Pietists decried the power of established churches and urged individuals to follow their hearts rather than their heads in spiritual matters. Persecuted in Germany, Pietists migrated to Great Britain and North America, where their ideas influenced Scots-Irish Presbyterians and members of the Church of England. John Wesley, the founder of Methodism and a professor of theology at Oxford University, taught Pietist ideas to his students, including George Whitefield. Like the German Pietists, Whitefield considered the North American colonies a perfect venue for restoring intensity and emotion to religious worship.

Some colonists had begun rethinking their religious commitments before Whitefield or the Pietists arrived. By 1700 both laymen and ministers voiced growing concern with the state of colonial religion. Preachers educated in England or at colonial colleges like Harvard and William and Mary often emphasized learned discourse over passion. At the same time, there were too few clergy to meet the demands of the rapidly growing population in North America. In many rural areas, residents grew discouraged at the lack of ministerial attention. Meanwhile urban churches increasingly reflected the class divisions of the larger society, with wealthier members paying substantial rents to seat their families in the front pews. Farmers and shopkeepers rented the cheaper pews in the middle of the church, while the poorest congregants sat on free benches at the very back or in the gallery. Educated clergy might impress the richest parishioners with their learned sermons, but they did little to move the spirits of the congregation at large.

In 1719 the Reverend Theodorus Frelinghuysen, a Dutch Reformed minister in New Jersey, began emphasizing parishioners' emotional investment in Christ. The Reverend William Tennent, the father of Gilbert Tennent, arrived in neighboring Pennsylvania with his family about the same time. He despaired that Presbyterian ministers were too few in number to reach the growing population and, like Frelinghuysen, feared that their approach was too didactic. Tennent soon established his own one-room academy to train his sons and other young men for the ministry. Though disparaged by Presbyterian authorities, the school attracted devout students.

Jonathan Edwards, a Congregational minister in Northampton, Massachusetts, joined Enlightenment ideas with religious fervor. A brilliant scholar who studied natural philosophy and science as well as theology, Edwards viewed the natural world as powerful evidence of God's design. He came to view the idea that God elected some individuals for salvation and others for damnation as a source of mystical joy. Although Edwards wrote erudite books and essays, he proclaimed that "our people do not so much need to have their heads stored [with knowledge] as to have their hearts touched." From 1733 to 1735, his sermons on God's absolute sovereignty over man initiated a revival in Northampton that reached hundreds of parishioners.

A few years earlier, Gilbert Tennent had begun urging his flock in New Brunswick, New Jersey to embrace "a true living faith in Jesus Christ." He took his lead from Frelinghuysen, who viewed conversion as a three-step process: Individuals must be convinced of their sinful nature, experience a spiritual rebirth, and then behave piously as evidence of their conversion. Tennent embraced these measures, believing they could lance the "boil" of an unsaved heart and apply the "balsam" of grace and righteousness. Then in 1739 Tennent met Whitefield, who launched a wave of revivals that revitalized and transformed religion across the colonies.

An Outburst of Revivals

Whitefield was perfectly situated to extend the series of revivals that scholars later called the **Great Awakening**. Gifted with a powerful voice, he understood that the expanding networks of communication and travel—developed to promote commerce—could also be used to promote religion. Advertising in newspapers and broadsides and traveling by ship, coach, and horseback, Whitefield made seven trips to the North American colonies beginning in 1738. He reached audiences from Georgia to New England to the Pennsylvania backcountry and inspired ministers in the colonies to expand upon his efforts.

In 1739 Whitefield launched a fifteen-month preaching tour that reached tens of thousands of colonists. Like Edwards, Frelinghuysen, and Tennent, he asked individuals to invest less in material goods and more in spiritual devotion. If they admitted their depraved and sinful state and truly repented, God would hear their prayers. Whitefield danced across the platform, shouted and raged, and gestured dramatically, drawing huge crowds everywhere he went. He attracted 20,000 people to individual events, at a time when the entire city of Boston counted just 17,000 residents.

New Light ministers carried on Whitefield's work throughout the 1740s, honing their methods and appeal. Less concerned with denominational affiliation than with core beliefs, they denounced urbane and educated clergy, used extemporaneous oratorical styles and outdoor venues to attract crowds, and invited colonists from all walks of life to build a common Christian community. Some became itinerant preachers, preferring to carry their message throughout the colonies than be constrained by a single church. [Map 4.2]

New Light clergy brought young people to religion by the thousands. In addition, thousands of colonists who were already church members were "born again," recommitting themselves to their faith. Poor women and men who felt little connection to preaching when they sat on the back benches eagerly joined the crowds at outdoor revivals, where they could stand as close to the pulpit as a rich merchant.

Religious Dissension

Initially, the Great Awakening drew support from large numbers of ministers because it increased religious enthusiasm and church attendance throughout the colonies. After decades of decline, religion once again took center stage. But the early embrace by Old Light clergy diminished as revivals spread farther afield, as critiques of educated clergy became more pointed, and as worshippers left established congregations for new churches. A growing number of ministers and other colonial leaders began to fear that revivalists were providing lower-class whites, free blacks, women, and even slaves with compelling critiques of those in power. As the Great Awakening peaked in 1742, a backlash developed among more settled ministers and their congregations.

Itinerant preachers traveling across the South seemed especially threatening as they invited blacks and whites to attend revivals together and proclaimed their equality before God. Although New Light clergy rarely attacked slavery directly, they implicitly challenged racial hierarchies. Revivalists also attracted African Americans and Indians by emphasizing communal singing and emotional expressions of the spirit, which echoed traditional African and Indian practices.

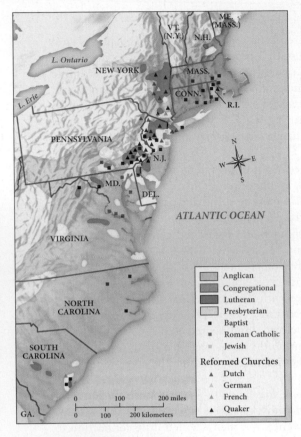

MAP 4.2

Religious Diversity in 1750 Despite the universal appeal of Whitefield and other New Light ministers, religious diversity had increased by 1750. Baptist churches multiplied in New England, where Congregationalists long held sway, while Presbyterian and Lutheran churches spread across the South where Anglicanism was the established church. Non-evangelical houses of worship, such as Quaker meeting houses and Jewish synagogues, also gradually increased in number.

In the North, too, Old Light ministers and local officials began to question New Light techniques and influences. One of the most radical New Light preachers, James Davenport, attracted huge crowds when he preached in Boston in the early 1740s. Drawing thousands of colonists to Boston Common day after day, Davenport declared that the people "should drink rat poison rather than listen to corrupt, unconverted clergy." Boston officials finally called a grand jury into session to silence him "on the charge of having said that Boston's ministers were leading the people blindfold to hell."

Even some New Light ministers, including Tennent, considered Davenport extreme. Yet revivals continued throughout the 1740s. Still, over time they lessened in intensity as churches and parishioners settled back into a more ordered religious life. Moreover, the central tenets of revivalist preaching—criticisms of educated clergy, itinerancy, and extemporaneous preaching—worked against the movement's institutionalization. The Great Awakening echoed across the colonies for at least another generation, but its influence was felt more often in attitudes and practices than in institutions.

For example, when, in 1750, King George II (r. 1727–1760) threatened to appoint an Anglican bishop for the North American colonies, many North American ministers, both Old Light and New, resisted the appointment. Most colonists had become used to religious diversity and toleration, at least for Protestants, and had little desire to add church officials to the existing hierarchies of colonial authorities. In various ways, revivalists also highlighted the democratic tendencies in the Bible, particularly in the New Testament. Even as they proclaimed God's wrath against sinners, they also preached that a lack of wealth and power did not diminish a person in God's eyes. And revivalists honed a style of passionate and popular preaching that would shape American religion as well as politics for centuries to come. This mode of communication had immediate application as colonists mobilized to resist what they saw as tyrannical actions by colonial officials and others in authority.

REVIEW & RELATE

- What was the relationship between the Enlightenment and the religious revivals of the early eighteenth century?
- What was the immediate impact of the Great Awakening, and what were its legacies for American religious and social life?

Political Awakenings

The effects of eighteenth-century religious awakenings rippled out from churches and revivals to influence social and political relations. New Light clergy allowed colonists to view their resistance to traditional authorities as part of their effort to create a better and more just world. Experiences of self-government, Enlightenment ideas, and protests against perceived corruption in the imperial system also led some colonists to question the right of those in power to impose their will on the community as a whole.

Changing Political Relations

The settlements of the seventeenth century could be regulated with a small number of officials, and in most colonies male settlers agreed on who should rule. However, with geographical expansion, population growth, and commercial development, colonial officials—whether appointed by the crown or selected by local residents—found themselves confronted with a more complex, and more contentious, situation. In New England, most colonies developed participatory town meetings that elected members to their colonial legislatures. In the South, wealthy planters exercised greater authority locally and colony-wide, but they still embraced ideals of self-governance and political liberty.

Throughout the British American colonies, officials were usually educated men who held property and had family ties to other colonial elites. Although ultimate political authority—or sovereignty—rested with the king and Parliament, many decisions were made by local officials because the king and Parliament were too distant to have a hand in daily colonial life. Another factor that weakened the power of royal officials was the tradition of town meetings and representative bodies, like the Virginia House of Burgesses, that gave colonists a stake in their own governance. Officials in England and the colonies assumed that most people would defer to those in authority, and they minimized resistance by holding public elections in which freemen cast ballots by voice vote. Not surprisingly, those with wealth and power continued to win office.

Still, evidence from throughout the colonial period indicates that deference to authority was not always sufficient to maintain order. Roger Williams and Anne Hutchinson, Bacon's Rebellion, the Stono rebellion, the Salem witchcraft trials, and the radical preaching of James Davenport make clear that not everyone willingly supported their supposed superiors. These episodes of dissent and protest were widely scattered across time and place. But as the ideas disseminated by New Light clergy and Enlightenment thinkers converged with changing political relations, resistance to established authority became more frequent and more collective.

Boston Town Hall   Boston's Town Hall and the broad avenue on which it sat was engraved by the German artist Franz Xavier Habermann, who specialized in scenes of urban North America. The buildings reflect a European view of the city's affluence in the mid-eighteenth century, as do the clothes worn by the two gentlemen talking over their walking sticks.   Bibliotheque Nationale, Paris, France/Bridgeman Images Private Collection/Bridgeman Images

Dissent and Protest

Protests against colonial elites multiplied from the 1730s on. The issues and methods varied, but they indicate a growing sense of political and economic autonomy among North American colonists. Some protests focused on royal officials like governors and Royal Navy captains; others focused on local authorities, merchants, or large landowners. Whatever the target of resistance, protests demonstrated colonists' belief that they had rights that were worth protecting, even against those who held legitimate authority. Just as importantly, dissenters included the poor, women, and African Americans as well as property-owning white men.

Access to reasonably priced food, especially bread, inspired regular protests in the eighteenth century. During the 1730s, the price of bread—a critical staple in colonial diets—rose despite falling wheat prices and a recession in seaport cities. Bread rioters attacked grain warehouses, bakeries, and shops, demanding more bread at lower prices. In New England, such uprisings were often led by women, who were responsible for putting bread on the table. When grievances involved domestic or consumer issues, women felt they had the right to make their voices heard, a right reinforced by evangelical clergy's insistence on their moral obligations to society.

Public markets were another site where struggles over food led to collective protests. In 1737, for instance, Boston officials decided to construct a public market and charge fees to farmers who sold their goods there. Small farmers, who were used to selling produce from the roadside for free, clashed with officials and with larger merchants over the venture. Many Boston residents supported the protesters because the market fees would lessen competition and raise prices for consumers. Adopting a rational approach to voice their concerns, residents petitioned city officials. When that had no effect, however, opponents demolished the market building and stalls in the middle of the night. Local authorities could find no witnesses to the crime.

Access to land was also a critical issue in the colonies. Beginning in the 1740s, protests erupted on estates in New Jersey and along the Hudson River in New York over the leasing policies of landlords as well as the amount of land controlled by speculators. Here, again, when tenants and squatters petitioned colonial officials and received no response, they took collective action. They formed associations, targeted specific landlords, and then burned barns, attacked livestock, and emptied houses and farm buildings of furniture and tools. Embracing Enlightenment ideas of "natural law," they also established regional committees to hear grievances and formed "popular" militia companies and courts to mete out justice to recalcitrant land owners. When landlords and colonial officials called out local militia to arrest the perpetrators, they failed to consider that militia members were often the same poor men whose protests they ignored.

In seaport cities, a frequent source of conflict was the **impressment** of colonial men who were seized and forcibly drafted into service in the Royal Navy. Viewed as a sign of the corrupt practices of imperial authorities, the challenge to impressment energized diverse groups of colonists. Sailors, dockworkers, and men drinking at taverns along the shore feared being pressed into military service, while colonial officials worried about labor shortages. Those officials petitioned the British government to stop impressment, but working men who faced the navy's high mortality rates, bad food, rampant disease, and harsh discipline took action on their own behalf. Asserting their growing sense of political liberty, they fought back against both colonial and British authorities. In 1747 in Boston, a general impressment led to three days of rioting. An observer noted that "Negros, servants, and hundreds of seamen seized a naval lieutenant, assaulted a sheriff, and put his deputy in stocks, surrounded the governor's house, and stormed the Town House (city hall)." Such riots did not end the system of impressment, but they showed that many colonists now refused to be deprived of what they considered their natural rights.

The religious upheavals and economic uncertainties of the 1730s and 1740s led colonists to challenge colonial and British officials with greater frequency than in earlier decades and to justify their actions in evangelical or Enlightenment terms. Still, most protests also accentuated class lines as, small farmers, craftsmen, and the poor fought against merchants, landowners, and local officials. However, the resistance to impressment proved that colonists could mobilize across economic differences when British policies affected diverse groups of colonial subjects.

Transforming Urban Politics

The development of cross-class alliances in the 1730s and 1740s was also visible in the more formal arena of colonial politics. Beginning in the 1730s, some affluent political leaders in cities like New York and Philadelphia began to seek support from a wider constituency. In most cases, it was conflicts among the elite that led to these appeals to the "popular" will. In 1731, for instance, a new royal charter confirmed New York City's existence as a "corporation" and stipulated the rights of freemen (residents who could vote in local elections after paying a small fee) and freeholders (individuals, whether residents or not, who held property worth £40 and could vote on that basis). A large number of artisans, shopkeepers, and laborers acquired the necessary means to vote, and shopkeepers and master craftsmen now sat alongside wealthier men on the Common Council. Yet most laboring men did not participate actively in elections until 1733, when local elites led by Lewis Morris sought to mobilize the mass of voters against royal officials, like Governor William Cosby, appointed in London.

Morris, a wealthy man and a judge, joined other colonial elites in believing that the royal officials recently appointed to govern New York were tied to ministerial corruption in England. Morris, as chief justice of the provincial court, ruled against Governor Cosby in a suit the new governor brought against his predecessor. Cosby then suspended Morris from office. In the aftermath, Morris and his supporters—the Morrisites—took his case to the people, who were suffering from a serious economic depression. Morrisites launched an opposition newspaper, published by apprentice printer John Peter Zenger, to mobilize artisans, shopkeepers, and laborers around an agenda to stimulate the economy and elect men supportive of workers to the city's common council.

In his *New-York Weekly Journal,* Zenger leaped into the political fray, accusing Governor Cosby and his cronies of corruption, incompetence, election fraud, and tyranny. The vitriolic attacks led to Zenger's indictment for seditious libel and his imprisonment in November 1734. At the time, libel related only to whether published material undermined government authority, not whether it was true or false. But Zenger's lead attorney, Andrew Hamilton of Philadelphia, argued that truth must be recognized as a defense against charges of libel. Appealing to a jury of Zenger's peers, Hamilton proclaimed, "It is not the cause of a poor printer, nor of New York alone, which you are now trying. . . . It is the best cause. It is the cause of liberty." In response, jurors ignored the law as written and acquitted Zenger.

Although the decision in the Zenger case did not lead to a change in British libel laws, it did signal the willingness of colonial juries to side with fellow colonists against king and Parliament in at least some situations. Building on their success, Morris and his followers continued to gain popular support. In 1737 his son, Lewis Morris Jr., was appointed speaker of the new Assembly, and the Assembly appointed Zenger as its official printer. But soon the group fell into disarray when royal officials offered political prizes to a few of their leaders. Indeed, the elder Morris accepted appointment as royal governor of New Jersey, after which he switched allegiances and became an advocate of executive authority. Nonetheless, the political movement he led had aroused ordinary freemen to participate in elections, and newspapers and pamphlets now readily attacked corrupt officials and threats to the rightful liberties of British colonists.

Even as freemen gained a greater voice in urban politics, they could challenge the power of economic and political leaders only when the elite were divided. Moreover, the rewards they gained sometimes served to reinforce class divisions. Thus many city workers had benefited when the elder Morris used his influence to ensure the building of the city's first permanent almshouse in 1736. The two-year project employed large numbers of artisans and laborers in a period of economic contraction. Once built, however, the almshouse became a symbol of the growing gap between rich and poor. Its existence was also used by future city councils as a justification to eliminate other forms of relief, leaving the poor in worse shape than before.

The rising inequality of wealth was especially apparent in the largest cities of British North America—New York, Philadelphia, Boston, and Charleston—but economic distinctions were also growing in smaller cities and towns. As the price of some goods, such as sugar and tobacco, fell in the 1750s, more colonists were able to afford them. At the same time, the expansion of transatlantic trade ensured that wealthier colonists had growing access to silver plates, clocks, tea services, bed and table linens, and other luxury goods. With British exporters extending more credit to colonial merchants and affluent white consumers, the division between rich and poor became increasingly visible to colonists of all backgrounds.

REVIEW & RELATE	• How did ordinary colonists, both men and women, black and white, express their political opinions and preferences in the first half of the eighteenth century? • How did politics bring colonists together across economic lines in the first half of the eighteenth century? How did politics highlight and reinforce class divisions?

Conclusion: A Divided Society

By 1754 religious and political awakenings had transformed colonists' sense of their relation to spiritual and secular authorities. Both Gilbert Tennent and Sarah Grosvenor were caught up in these transitions. As a man and a minister, however, Tennent had far more power to control his destiny than did Grosvenor. While wives and daughters in elite families benefited from their wealth and position, they were also constrained by the strictures of the patriarchal family. Women who were poor, indentured, or enslaved were forced into the greatest dependency on male employers and civic officials. But even women in farm and artisanal families depended on loving husbands and fathers to offset the strictures of patriarchal authority. While few colonists conceived of themselves as part of a united body politic, women probably identified most deeply with their family, town, or church. Yet men, too, thought of themselves as English, or Scots-Irish, or German, rather than more broadly American. At best, they claimed identity as residents of Massachusetts, New Jersey, or South Carolina rather than British North America.

Between the 1680s and the 1750s, the diversity and divisions among colonists increased as class, racial, religious, and regional differences multiplied across the colonies. Immigrants from Germany, Ireland, and Scotland created their own communities; religious awakenings led to cleavages among Protestants and between them and other religious groups; and economic inequality deepened in seacoast cities. At the same time, conflicts between Indians and settlers intensified along the frontier as growing numbers of enslaved Africans reshaped economic and social relations in the urban North and the rural South.

By midcentury, the colonies as a whole had been transformed in significant ways. Religious leaders had gained renewed respect, colonial assemblies had wrested more autonomy from royal hands, freemen participated more avidly in political contests and debates, printers and lawyers insisted on the rights and liberties of colonists, and local communities defended those rights in a variety of ways. When military conflicts brought British officials into more direct contact with their colonial subjects in the following decade, they sought to check these trends, with dramatic consequences.

American River College Library

Chapter 4 Review

KEY TERMS

spectral evidence (p. 81)
patriarchal family (p. 83)
Walking Purchase (p. 91)
New Light clergy (p. 93)
Old Light clergy (p. 93)

Enlightenment (p. 93)
Pietists (p. 93)
Great Awakening (p. 95)
impressment (p. 99)

REVIEW & RELATE

1. What factors led to a rise in tensions within colonial communities in the early 1700s?

2. How did social, economic, and political tensions contribute to an increase in accusations of witchcraft?

3. Why and how did the legal and economic status of colonial women decline between 1650 and 1750?

4. How did patriarchal ideals of family and community shape life and work in colonial America? What happened when men failed to live up to those ideals?

5. How and why did economic inequality in the colonies increase in the first half of the eighteenth century?

6. How did population growth and increasing diversity contribute to conflict among and anxieties about the various groups inhabiting British North America?

7. What was the relationship between the Enlightenment and the religious revivals of the early eighteenth century?

8. What was the immediate impact of the Great Awakening, and what were its legacies for American religious and social life?

9. How did ordinary colonists, both men and women, black and white, express their political opinions and preferences in the first half of the eighteenth century?

10. How did politics bring colonists together across economic lines in the first half of the eighteenth century? How did politics highlight and reinforce class divisions?

TIMELINE OF EVENTS

1688
- Glorious Revolution

1692
- Salem witch trials

1700–1750
- 250,000 immigrants and Africans arrive in the colonies

1700–1775
- Population of British North America grows from 250,000 to 2.5 million

1720–1740
- Influx of Scots-Irish to Pennsylvania

1734
- John Peter Zenger acquitted of libel

1737
- Iroquois and Delaware acquiesce to Walking Purchase
- Protest against public market in Boston

1739
- George Whitefield launches preaching tour of the colonies

1745
- 40,000 Scottish Catholics shipped to the Carolinas after failed rebellion

1747
- Rioting in Boston against impressment

1750
- Colonists resist appointment of an Anglican bishop for North America

5

War and Empire
1754–1774

LEARNING OBJECTIVES

After reading this chapter you should be able to:

- Describe the causes and consequences of the French and Indian War.
- Explain how British policies following the French and Indian War fostered colonial grievances.
- Analyze the major British policies from 1764 to 1774 and how colonial responses to them became more unified.

COMPARING AMERICAN HISTORIES

Praised as the father of the United States, George Washington remained a loyal British subject for forty-three years. He was born in 1732 to a prosperous farm family in eastern Virginia. When his father died in 1743, George became the ward of his half-brother Lawrence, who took control of the family's Mount Vernon estate. Lawrence's father-in-law, William Fairfax, was an agent for Lord Fairfax, one of the chief proprietors of the colony. When George was sixteen, William hired him to help survey Lord Fairfax's land on Virginia's western frontier.

As a surveyor, George journeyed west, coming into contact with Indians, both friendly and hostile, as well as other colonists seeking land. George began investing in western properties, but when Lawrence Washington died in 1752, George suddenly became head of a large estate. He gradually expanded Mount Vernon's boundaries and its enslaved workforce, increasing its profitability.

George was soon appointed Lieutenant Colonel in the Virginia militia, and in the fall of 1753 Virginia's governor sent him to warn the French against encroaching on British territory in the Ohio River valley. The French commander rebuffed Washington and, within six months, gained control of a British post near present-day Pittsburgh, Pennsylvania and named it Fort Duquesne. With help from Indians hostile to the French, Washington's surprise attack on Fort Duquesne in May 1754 led the governors of Virginia and North Carolina to provide the newly promoted Colonel Washington with more troops. The French then responded with a much larger force that compelled Washington to surrender.

Washington's fortunes and his family increased when he married the wealthy widow Martha Dandridge Custis in 1759. With more land to defend, Washington supported efforts to extend Britain's North American empire westward to create a protective buffer against European and Indian foes.

Like Washington, Hermon Husband hoped to improve his lot through hard work and new opportunities on the frontier. Born to a modest farm family in Maryland in 1724, he was swept up by George Whitefield's preaching in 1739, but eventually joined the Society of Friends, or Quakers. Although his farm in Maryland was thriving, Husband explored prospects on the North Carolina frontier. In 1762 he settled with his family at Sandy Creek.

There Husband again proved a successful farmer, but he began to speak against wealthy landowners and speculators who made it difficult for small farmers to obtain sufficient land. He also challenged established leaders in the local Quaker community, or meeting, and was among a number of worshippers disowned from the Cane Creek Friends Meeting in 1764. Disputes within radical Protestant congregations were not unusual in this period, as members with deep religious convictions chose the liberty of their individual conscience over church authority.

In 1766 local farmers joined Husband in organizing the Sandy Creek Association, through which they sought to increase their political clout in order to combat corruption among local officials. The association disbanded after two years, but its ideas lived on in a group called the Regulation, which brought together frontier farmers to "regulate" government abuse. The Regulators petitioned the North Carolina Assembly and Royal Governor William Tryon, demanding legislative reforms and suing local officials for extorting labor, land, and money from poorer residents.

Husband quickly emerged as one of the organization's chief pamphleteers, articulating the demands of the Regulators and echoing other colonial pro-testers of the period. Governor Tryon viewed the Regulators as threatening the colony's peace and order and, in 1768 and 1771, had Husband and other Regulators arrested. This confirmed the group's belief that they could not receive fair treatment at the hands of colonial officials. They then turned to extralegal methods to assert their rights, such as taking over courthouses so that legal proceedings against debt-ridden farmers could not proceed.

COMPARING THE AMERICAN HISTORIES of Washington and Husband demonstrates how colonists' lives were shaped by both opportunities and conflicts. Mid-eighteenth-century colonial America offered greater opportunities for social advancement and personal expression than anywhere in Europe, but collective efforts to take advantage of these opportunities often led to tension and discord. Frontier conflicts foreshadowed a broader struggle for land and power within the American colonies. Religious and economic as well as political discord intensified in the mid-eighteenth century as upheavals among colonists increasingly occurred alongside challenges to British authority. Whatever their grievances, most colonists worked hard to reform systems they considered unfair or abusive before resorting to more radical means of instituting change.

Imperial Conflicts and Indian Wars, 1754–1763

The war that erupted in the Ohio valley in 1754 sparked an enormous shift in political and economic relations in colonial North America. What began as a small-scale, regional conflict expanded into a brutal and lengthy war around the world. Known as the French and Indian War in North America and as the Seven Years' War in Great Britain and Europe, the extended conflict led to a dramatic expansion of British territory in North America and to increasing demands from American colonists for more control over their own lives.

The Opening Battles

Even before Washington and his troops were defeated in July 1754, the British sought to protect the colonies against threats from the French and the Indians. To limit such threats, the British were especially interested in cementing an alliance with the powerful Iroquois Confederacy, composed of six northeastern tribes. Thus the British invited an official delegation from the Iroquois to a meeting in June 1754 in Albany, New York with representatives from several colonies. Benjamin Franklin of Philadelphia had drawn up a Plan of Union that would establish a council of representatives from the various colonial assemblies to debate issues of frontier defense, trade, and territorial expansion and to recommend terms mutually agreeable to colonists and Indians. Their deliberations were to be overseen by a president-general appointed and supported by the British crown. Despite the proposed council's mandate, Franklin excluded Iroquois or other Indian representatives from participation.

The **Albany Congress** created new bonds among a small circle of colonial leaders, but it failed to establish a firmer alliance with the Iroquois or resolve problems of colonial governance. The Mohawk warrior and sachem Hendrick Peters Theyanoguin urged British representatives at the Congress to take more forceful action, including military action, against its enemies. His views were reported in the British and colonial press. By July, Iroquois delegates, angered by Franklin's plan, left the Congress and broke off talks with the British. The Plan of Union was also rejected by the individual colonies because they were unwilling to give up any of their autonomy in military, trade, and political matters to some centralized body. Meanwhile officials in the royal

Join or Die   Benjamin Franklin created the first political cartoon in American history to accompany an editorial he wrote in the *Pennsylvania Gazette* in 1754. Franklin's cartoon urged the mainland British colonies to unite politically during the French and Indian War. Legend had it that a snake could come back to life if its severed sections were attached before dusk.   Library of Congress, 3g05315

government worried that the debates might force its hand in dealing with the French and their Indian allies.

If war was going to erupt between the British and the French, the Iroquois and other Indian tribes could not afford to have the outcome decided by imperial powers alone. For most Indians, contests among European nations for land and power offered them the best chance of survival in the eighteenth century. They gained leverage as long as various imperial powers needed their trade items, military support, and political alliances. This leverage would be far more limited if one European nation controlled most of North America.

Still, Indian tribes adopted different strategies. The Delaware, Huron, Miami, and Shawnee nations, for example, allied themselves with the French, hoping that a French victory would stop the far more numerous British colonists from invading their settlements in the Ohio River valley. Members of the Iroquois Confederacy, on the other hand, tried to play one power against the other, hoping to win concessions from the British in return for their military support. The Creek, Choctaw, and Cherokee nations also sought to perpetuate the existing stalemate among European powers by bargaining alternately with the British in Georgia and the Carolinas, the French in Louisiana, and the Spaniards in Florida. Faced with incursions into their lands, some Indian tribes, like the Abenaki in northern New England, launched preemptive attacks on colonial settlements.

The British government soon decided it had to send additional troops to defend its American colonies against attacks from Indians and intrusions from the French. General Edward Braddock and two regiments arrived in 1755 to expel the French from Fort Duquesne. At the same time, colonial militia units were sent to battle the French and their Indian allies along the New York and New England frontiers. Colonel Washington joined Braddock as his personal aide-de-camp. Within months, however, Braddock's forces were ambushed, bludgeoned by French and Indian forces, and Braddock was killed.

Other British forces fared little better during the next three years. Despite having far fewer colonists in North America than the British, the French had established extensive trade networks that helped them sustain a protracted war with support from numerous Indian nations. Alternating guerrilla tactics with conventional warfare, the

French captured several important forts, built a new one on Lake Champlain, and moved troops deep into British territory. The ineffectiveness of the British and colonial armies also encouraged Indian tribes along the New England and Appalachian frontiers to reclaim land from colonists. Bloody raids devastated many outlying settlements, leading to the death and capture of hundreds of Britain's colonial subjects.

A Shift to Global War

As the British faced defeat after defeat in North America, European nations began to contest imperial claims elsewhere in the world. In 1756 France and Great Britain officially declared war against each other. Eventually Austria, Russia, Sweden, most of the German states, and Spain allied with France, while Portugal and Prussia sided with Great Britain. Naval warfare erupted in the Mediterranean Sea and the Atlantic and Indian Oceans. Battles were also fought in Europe, the West Indies, India, and the Philippines. By the end of 1757, Britain and its allies had been defeated in nearly every part of the globe. The war appeared to be nearing its end, with France in control.

Then in the summer of 1757, William Pitt took charge of the British war effort. He transformed the political and military landscape in the American colonies, while Prussian forces held the line in Europe. Pouring more soldiers and arms into the North American campaign along with young and ambitious officers like Colonel Henry Bouquet, Pitt energized colonial and British troops.

By the summer of 1758, the tide began to turn. In July, British generals recaptured the fort at Louisburg on Cape Breton Island, a key to France's defense of Canada. Then British troops with Bouquet and Washington's aid seized Fort Duquesne, which was renamed Fort Pitt. Other British forces captured Fort Frontenac along the St. Lawrence River, while Prussia defeated France and its allies in Europe and Britain gained key victories in India (Map 5.1). In 1759 General Jeffrey Amherst captured Forts Ticonderoga and Crown Point on Lake Champlain while General James Wolfe attacked a much larger French force in Quebec. Despite heavy casualties, including Wolfe himself, the British won Quebec and control of Canada.

The Costs of Victory

Despite Wolfe's dramatic victory, the war dragged on in North America, Europe, India, and the West Indies for three more years. By then, however, King George III had tired of Pitt's grand, and expensive, strategy and dismissed him. He then opened peace negotiations with France and agreed to give up a number of conquered territories in order to finalize the **Peace of Paris** in 1763. Other countries were ready to negotiate as well. To regain control of Cuba and the Philippines, Spain ceded Florida to Great Britain. While France was expelled from North America, it rewarded Spanish support by granting Spain Louisiana and all French lands west of the Mississippi River. Despite these concessions, the British empire reigned supreme, regaining control of India as well as North America east of the Mississippi, all of Canada, and a number of Caribbean islands.

The wars that erupted between 1754 and 1763 reshaped European empires, transformed patterns of global trade, and initially seemed to tighten bonds between North American residents and the mother country. Yet the Peace of Paris did not resolve

MAP 5.1

The French and Indian War, 1754–1763   Clashes between colonial militia units and French and Indian forces erupted in North America in 1754. The conflict helped launch a wider war that engulfed Europe as well as the West Indies and India. In the aftermath of this first global war, Britain gained control of present-day Canada and India, but France retained its West Indies colonies.

many of the problems that had plagued the colonies before the war, and it created new ones as well.

The incredible cost of the war raised particularly difficult problems. Over the course of the war, the national debt of Great Britain had more than doubled. At the same time, as the North American colonies grew and conflicts erupted along their frontiers, the costs of administering these colonies increased fivefold. With an empire that stretched around the globe, the British crown and Parliament were forced to consider how to pay off war debts, raise funds to administer their far-flung territories, and keep sufficient currency in circulation for expanding international trade. Just as important, the Peace of Paris ignored the claims of Indian tribes to the territories that France and Spain turned over to Great Britain. Nor did the treaty settle contested claims among the colonies themselves over lands in the Ohio River valley and elsewhere along British North America's new frontiers.

Battles and Boundaries on the Frontier

The sweeping character of the British victory encouraged thousands of colonists to move farther west, into lands once controlled by France. This exacerbated tensions that were already rising on the southern and western frontiers of British North America.

In late 1759, for example, the Cherokee nation, reacting to repeated incursions on its hunting grounds, dissolved its long-term trade agreement with South Carolina. Cherokee warriors attacked backcountry farms and homes, leading to counterattacks by British troops. The fighting continued into 1761, when Cherokees on the Virginia frontier launched raids on colonists there. General Jeffrey Amherst then sent 2,800 troops to invade Cherokee territory and end the conflict. The soldiers sacked fifteen villages; killed men, women, and children; and burned acres of fields.

Although British raids diminished the Cherokees' ability to mount a substantial attack, sporadic assaults on frontier settlements continued for years. These conflicts fueled resentments among backcountry settlers not only against Indians but also against political leaders in eastern parts of the colonies who rarely provided sufficient resources for frontier defense.

A more serious conflict erupted in the Ohio River valley when Indians realized the consequences of British victories. When the British captured French forts along the Great Lakes and in the Ohio valley in 1760, they immediately antagonized local Indian groups by hunting and fishing on tribal lands and depriving villages of much-needed food. British traders also defrauded Indians on numerous occasions and ignored traditional obligations of gift giving.

The harsh realities of the British regime led some Indians to seek a return to ways of life that preceded the arrival of white men. An Indian visionary named Neolin preached that Indians had been corrupted by contact with Europeans and urged them to purify themselves by returning to their ancient traditions, abandoning white ways, and reclaiming their lands. Neolin was a prophet, not a warrior, but his message inspired others, including an Ottawa leader named Pontiac.

When news arrived in early 1763 that France was about to cede all of its North American lands to Britain and Spain, Pontiac convened a council of more than four hundred Ottawa, Potawatomi, and Huron leaders near Fort Detroit. Drawing on Neolin's vision, he proclaimed, "It is important my brothers, that we should exterminate from our land this nation [Britain], whose only object is our death. You must all be sensible," he continued, "that we can no longer supply our wants the way we were accustomed to do with our Fathers the French." Pontiac then mobilized support to drive out the British. In May 1763, Pontiac's forces laid siege to Detroit and soon gained the support of eighteen Indian nations. They then attacked Fort Pitt and other British frontier outposts as well as white settlements along the Virginia and Pennsylvania frontier (Map 5.2).

Accounts of violent encounters with Indians on the frontier circulated throughout the colonies and sparked resentment among settlers as well as British troops. Many colonists did not distinguish between friendly and hostile Indians. In December 1763, a group of men from Paxton Creek, Pennsylvania raided families of peaceful, Christian Conestoga Indians near Lancaster, killing thirty. Protests from eastern colonists infuriated the Paxton Boys, who then marched on Philadelphia demanding protection from "savages" on the frontier.

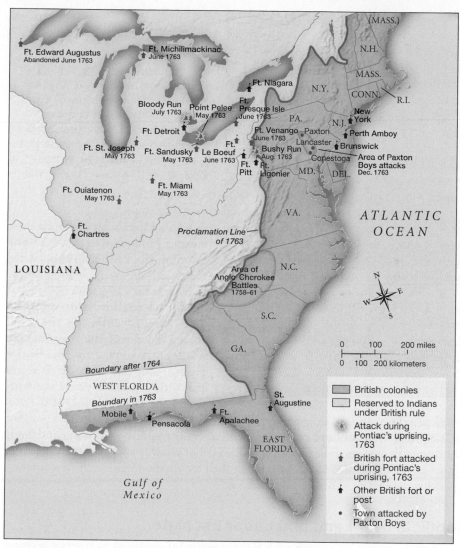

MAP 5.2

British Conflicts with Indians, 1758–1763, and the Proclamation Line   The entrance of British troops into former French territory in the Ohio River valley following the French and Indian War fueled conflicts with Indian nations. Colonists in Pennsylvania and the Carolinas also battled with Indians, including tribes who were allies or remained neutral during the war. Parliament established the Proclamation Line to limit westward expansion and thereby diminish such hostilities.

Although violence on the frontier slowly subsided, neither side had achieved victory. Without French support, Pontiac and his followers had to retreat. Meanwhile, Benjamin Franklin negotiated a truce between the Paxton Boys and the Pennsylvania authorities, but it did not settle the fundamental issues over protection of western settlers. Convinced that it could not endure further costly frontier clashes, the British crown issued a proclamation in October 1763 forbidding colonial settlement west of a line running

The Indians Delivering Up English Captives, 1766   This hand-colored engraving was based on a Benjamin West sketch made in 1764 when Colonel Henry Bouquet led an army of 1,500 men into the Ohio territory. His mission was to force the Shawnee and Delaware to accept the Peace of Paris and release all English captives. The image suggests that not all captives wanted to leave their Indian families.   Library of Congress 3b49465

down the Appalachian Mountains to create a buffer between Indians and colonists. But Parliament also ordered Colonel Bouquet to subdue hostile Indians in the Ohio region.

The **Proclamation Line of 1763** denied colonists the right to settle west of the Appalachian Mountains. Imposed by the British government following the Peace of Paris, the Proclamation Line frustrated colonists who sought the economic benefits won by a long and bloody war. Small farmers, backcountry settlers, and squatters who had hoped to improve their lot by acquiring rich farmlands were told to stay put. Meanwhile Washington and other wealthy speculators managed to acquire additional western lands, certain that the Proclamation was merely "a temporary expedient to quiet the Minds of the Indians."

Conflicts over Land and Labor Escalate

Conflicts among colonists and with Britain were not confined to frontier regions. Land riots directed against the leasing policies of landlords and the greed of speculators had plagued New York's Hudson valley and New Jersey before the war, and these struggles continued into the 1760s. New clashes also occurred in the Carolinas as settlers like Hermon Husband stood up to landlords and government officials.

Even before the French and Indian War ended, the owners of large estates along the Hudson River in New York State raised rents and reduced the rights of tenants. In the early eighteenth century, the titles to some of these estates were challenged by small landowners and tenants, but even where legitimate titles existed, tenants declared a moral right to own the land they had long farmed. The manors and estates of the Hudson valley, they claimed, were more appropriate to a feudal government than to an enlightened empire.

Farmers in neighboring New Hampshire were drawn into battles over land when the king's Privy Council in London decided in 1764 that the Green Mountains belonged to New York rather than New Hampshire. Landlords along the Hudson River hoped to expand eastward into this region, but the farmers already living there claimed they had bought the land in good faith and deserved to keep it. These farmers launched guerrilla warfare against New York authorities and large landowners as well as against New York farmers who claimed land that New Hampshire families had cleared and settled. These Green Mountain Boys, led by Ethan Allen, refused to recognize New York authorities as legitimate and established their own local governments and popular courts.

Inspired by the Green Mountain Boys and uprisings in New Jersey, tenants in the Hudson valley banded together in 1765 and 1766. Under the leadership of Irish immigrant William Prendergast, a group of tenants calling themselves Levellers refused to pay rent and instead claimed freehold title to the land they farmed. New York tenants petitioned the colonial assembly and sought redress in a variety of ways. But landowners refused to negotiate, and Prendergast concluded that "there was no law for poor men."

In many ways, the beliefs of Allen, Prendergast, and their followers echoed those of Hermon Husband and the North Carolina **Regulators**. All of these groups developed visible, well-organized networks of supporters, targeted specific landlords, sought redress first through colonial courts and assemblies, and then established popular militias and other institutions to govern themselves and to challenge those in authority.

REVIEW & RELATE

- How did the French and Indian War and the subsequent peace treaty affect relations among Britain, American Indian nations, and American colonies?
- How did the French and Indian War and the increasing power of large landowners contribute to conflict between average colonists and colonial elites?

Postwar British Policies and Colonial Unity

Even as ordinary colonists challenged the authority of economic and political elites, colonial leaders tried to persuade the disaffected to turn their anger against royal authorities in Britain. By highlighting colonists' rights as British subjects, local traditions of self-rule, and Enlightenment ideas, these leaders slowly gained support. Some of them even joined earlier opponents like Hermon Husband in arguing for the rights of the individual. The imposition of new British policies in the decade following the French and Indian War, from 1764 to 1774, was equally important in nurturing common grievances and uniting colonists across regional and economic differences. For instance, the Proclamation Line of 1763 inspired widespread dissent as poor farmers, large landowners, and speculators sought to expand westward. A second policy, impressment, by which the Royal Navy forced young colonial men into military service, also aroused anger across regions and classes. At the same time, the Great Awakening provided colonists with shared ideas about moral principles and new techniques for mass communication. Finally, Britain's efforts to repay its war debts by taxing colonists and its plan to continue quartering troops in North America led colonists to forge intercolonial protest movements.

Common Grievances

Like the Proclamation Line, which denied all colonists the right to settle beyond the Appalachian Mountains, the policy of impressment affected port city residents of all classes. Impressment had been employed by the British during the extended wars of the eighteenth century to procure seamen. While plucking poor men from ports throughout the British empire, the Royal Navy faced growing resistance to this practice in the American colonies from merchants and common folk alike.

Seamen and dockworkers had good reason to fight off impressment agents. Men in the Royal Navy faced low wages, bad food, harsh punishment, rampant disease, and high mortality. As the practice escalated with each new war, the efforts of British naval officers and impressment agents to capture new "recruits" met violent resistance, especially in the North American colonies where several hundred men might be impressed at one time. In such circumstances, whole communities joined in the battle.

In the aftermath of the French and Indian War, serious impressment riots erupted in Boston, New York City, and Newport, Rhode Island. Increasingly, poor colonial seamen and dockworkers made common cause with owners of merchant ships and mercantile houses in protesting British policy. Colonial officials—mayors, governors, and customs agents—were caught in the middle. Some insisted on upholding the Royal Navy's right of impressment; others tried to placate both naval officers and local residents; and still others resisted what they saw as an oppressive imposition on the rights of colonists. Both those who resisted British authority and those who sought a compromise had to gain the support of the lower and middling classes to succeed.

Employers and politicians who opposed impressment gained an important advantage if they could direct the anger of colonists away from themselves and toward British policies. The decision of British officials to continue quartering troops in the colonies gave local leaders another opportunity to join forces with ordinary colonists. Colonial towns and cities were required to quarter (that is, house and support) British troops even after the Peace of Paris was signed. While the troops were intended to protect the colonies, they also provided reinforcements for impressment agents and surveillance over other illegal activities like smuggling and domestic manufacturing. Thus a range of issues and policies began to bind colonists together through common grievances against the British Parliament.

Forging Ties across the Colonies

The ties forged between poorer and wealthier colonists over issues of westward expansion, impressment, and quartering grew stronger in the 1760s, but they tended to be localized in seaport cities or in specific areas of the frontier. Creating bonds across the colonies required considerably more effort in a period when communication and transportation beyond local areas were limited. Means had to be found to disseminate information and create a sense of common purpose if the colonists were going to persuade Parliament to take their complaints seriously. One important model for such intercolonial communication was the Great Awakening.

By the 1750s, the Great Awakening seemed to be marked more by dissension than by unity as new denominations continued to split from traditional churches. For example, in the Sandy Creek region of North Carolina, home to Hermon Husband, radical Protestants formed the Separate Baptists, who proclaimed a message of absolute spiritual equality. From the late 1750s through the 1770s, Separate Baptists converted thousands of small farmers, poor whites, and enslaved women and men and established churches throughout Virginia, Georgia, and the Carolinas.

Like Separate Baptists, Methodists, Dunkards, Moravians, and Quakers also offered southern residents religious experiences that highlighted spiritual equality. Some dissenting preachers invited slaves and free blacks to attend their services alongside local white farmers, farmwives, and laborers. Slaveholders and other elite southerners considered such practices outrageous and a challenge to the political as well as the social order.

Most women and men who converted to Separate Baptism, Methodism, or other forms of radical Protestantism did not link their religious conversion directly to politics. But as more and more ordinary colonists and colonial leaders voiced their anger at offensive British policies, evangelical techniques used to rouse the masses to salvation became important for mobilizing colonists to protest.

Thus even though the Great Awakening had spent its religious passion in most parts of North America by the 1760s, the techniques of mass communication and critiques of opulence and corruption it initiated provided emotional and practical ways of forging ties among widely dispersed colonists. Many evangelical preachers had condemned the lavish lifestyles of colonial elites and the spiritual corruption of local officials. Now in the context of conflicts with Great Britain, colonial leaders used such rhetoric to paint Parliament and British officials as aristocrats with little faith and less compassion.

The public sermons and mass gatherings used during the Great Awakening to inspire loyalty to a greater moral cause could now be translated into forms applicable to political protest. The efforts of Great Britain to assert greater control over its North American colonies provided colonial dissidents an opportunity to test out these new ways to forge inter-colonial ties.

Great Britain Seeks Greater Control

Until the French and Indian War, British officials and their colonial subjects coexisted in relative harmony. Economic growth led Britain to ignore much of the smuggling and domestic manufacturing that took place in the colonies, since such activities did not significantly disrupt Britain's mercantile policies (see "Imperial Policies Focus on Profits" in chapter 3). Similarly, although the king and Parliament held ultimate political sovereignty, or final authority, over the American colonies, it was easier to allow some local control over political decisions, given the communication challenges created by distance.

This pattern of **benign** (or "salutary") **neglect** led some American colonists to view themselves as more independent of British control than they really were. Many colonists came to see smuggling, domestic manufacturing, and local self-governance as rights rather than privileges. Thus when British officials decided to assert greater control, many colonists protested.

To King George III and to Parliament, asserting control over the colonies was both right and necessary. In 1763 King George appointed George Grenville to lead the British government. As Prime Minister and Chancellor of the Exchequer, Grenville faced an economic depression in England, rebellious farmers opposed to a new tax on domestic cider, and growing numbers of unemployed soldiers returning from the war.

He believed that regaining political and economic control in the colonies could help resolve these crises at home.

Eighteenth-century wars, especially the French and Indian War, cost a fortune. British subjects in England paid taxes to help offset the nation's debts, even though few of them benefited as directly from the British victory as did their counterparts in the American colonies. The colonies would cost the British treasury more if the crown could not control colonists' movement into Indian territories, limit smuggling and domestic manufacturing, and house British troops in the colonies cheaply.

To reassert control, Parliament launched a three-pronged program. First, it sought stricter enforcement of existing laws and established a Board of Trade to centralize policies and ensure their implementation. The **Navigation Acts**, which prohibited smuggling, established guidelines for legal commerce, and set duties on trade items, were the most important laws to be enforced. Second, Parliament extended wartime policies into peacetime. For example, the Quartering Act of 1765 ensured that British troops would remain in the colonies to enforce imperial policy. Colonial governments were expected to support them by allowing them to use vacant buildings and providing them with food and supplies.

The third part of Grenville's colonial program was the most important. It called for the passage of new laws to raise funds and reestablish the sovereignty of British rule. The first revenue act passed by Parliament was the American Duties Act of 1764, known as the **Sugar Act**. It imposed an **import duty**, or tax, on sugar, coffee, wines, and other luxury items. The act actually reduced the import tax on foreign molasses, which was regularly smuggled into the colonies from the West Indies, but insisted that the duty be collected. The crackdown on smuggling increased the power of customs officers and established the first vice-admiralty courts in North America to ensure that the Sugar Act raised money for the crown. That same year, Parliament passed the Currency Act, which prohibited colonial assemblies from printing paper money or bills of credit. Taken together, these provisions meant that colonists would pay more money into the British treasury even as the supply of money (and illegal goods) diminished in the colonies.

Some colonial leaders protested the Sugar Act through speeches, pamphlets, and petitions, and Massachusetts established a **committee of correspondence** to circulate concerns to leaders in other colonies. However, dissent remained disorganized and ineffective. Nonetheless, the passage of the Sugar and Currency Acts caused anxiety among many colonists, which was heightened by passage of the Quartering Act the next year. Colonial responses to these developments marked the first steps in an escalating conflict between British officials and their colonial subjects.

| **REVIEW & RELATE** | • How did Britain's postwar policies lead to the emergence of unified colonial protests? |
| | • Why did British policymakers believe they were justified in seeking to gain greater control over Britain's North American colonies? |

Resistance to Britain Intensifies

Over the next decade, between 1764 and 1774, the British Parliament sought to extend its political and economic control over the American colonies, and the colonists periodically resisted. With each instance of resistance, Parliament demanded further submission to royal authority. With each demand for submission, colonists responded with greater assertions of their rights and autonomy. Still, no one imagined that a revolution was in the making.

The Stamp Act Inspires Coordinated Resistance

Grenville decided next to impose a stamp tax on the colonies similar to that long used in England. The stamp tax required that a revenue stamp be affixed to all transactions involving paper items, from newspapers and contracts to playing cards and diplomas. Grenville announced his plans in 1764, a full year before Parliament enacted the **Stamp Act** in the spring of 1765. The tax was to be collected by colonists appointed for the purpose, and the money was to be spent within the colonies at the direction of Parliament for "defending, protecting and securing the colonies." To the British government, the Stamp Act seemed completely fair. After all, Englishmen paid on average 26 shillings in tax annually, while Bostonians averaged just 1 shilling. Moreover, the act was purposely written to benefit the American colonies.

The colonists viewed it in a more threatening light. The Stamp Act differed from earlier parliamentary laws in three important ways. First, by the time of its passage, the colonies were experiencing rising unemployment, falling wages, and a downturn in trade. All of these developments were exacerbated by the Sugar, Currency, and Quartering Acts passed by Parliament the previous year. Second, critics viewed the Stamp Act as an attempt to control the *internal* affairs of the colonies. It was not an indirect tax on trade, paid by importers and exporters, but a direct tax on daily business. Third, such a direct intervention in the economic affairs of the colonies unleashed the concerns of both local officials and ordinary residents that Parliament was taxing colonists who had no representation in its debates and decisions.

By announcing the Stamp Act a year before its passage, Grenville allowed colonists plenty of time to organize their opposition. In New York City, Boston, and other cities, merchants, traders, and artisans formed groups dedicated to the repeal of the Stamp Act. Soon Sons of Liberty, Daughters of Liberty, Sons of Neptune, Vox Populi, and similar organizations emerged to challenge the imposition of the Stamp Act. Even before the act was implemented, angry mobs throughout the colonies attacked stamp distributors. Some were beaten, others tarred and feathered, and all were forced to take an oath never to sell stamps again.

Colonists lodged more formal protests with the British government as well. The Virginia House of Burgesses, led by Patrick Henry, acted first. It passed five resolutions, which it sent to Parliament, denouncing taxation without representation. The Virginia Resolves were reprinted in many colonial newspapers and repeated by orators to eager audiences in Massachusetts and elsewhere. At the same time, the Massachusetts House adopted a circular letter—a written protest circulated to the other colonial assemblies—calling for a congress to be held in New York City in October 1765 to consider the threat posed by the Stamp Act.

In the meantime, popular protests multiplied. The protests turned violent in Boston, where **Sons of Liberty** leaders like Samuel Adams, a Harvard graduate and town official, organized mass demonstrations. Adams modeled his oratory on that of itinerant preachers, but with a political twist. Other activists used more visual means of inspiring their audiences. At dawn on August 14, 1765, the Boston Sons of Liberty hung an effigy of stamp distributor Andrew Oliver on a tree and called for his resignation. A mock funeral procession, joined by farmers, artisans, apprentices, and the poor, marched to Boston Common. The crowd, led by shoemaker and French and Indian War veteran Ebenezer Mackintosh, carried the fake corpse to the Boston stamp office and destroyed the building. Demonstrators saved pieces of lumber, "stamped" them, and set them on fire outside Oliver's house. Oliver, wisely, had already left town.

Oliver's brother-in-law, Lieutenant Governor Thomas Hutchinson, arrived at the scene and tried to quiet the crowd, but he only angered them further. They soon destroyed Oliver's stable house, coach, and carriage, which the crowd saw as signs of aristocratic opulence.

The battle against the Stamp Act unfolded across the colonies with riots, beatings, and resignations reported from Newport, Rhode Island, to New Brunswick, New Jersey, to Charles Town (later Charleston), South Carolina. On November 1, 1765, when the Stamp Act officially took effect, not a single stamp agent remained in his post in the colonies.

Protesters carefully chose their targets: stamp agents, sheriffs, judges, and colonial officials. Even when violence erupted, it remained focused, with most crowds destroying stamps and stamp offices first and then turning to the private property of Stamp Act supporters. These protests made a mockery of notions of deference toward British rule. But they also revealed growing autonomy on the part of middling- and working-class colonists who attacked men of wealth and power, sometimes choosing artisans rather than wealthier men as their leaders. However, this was not primarily a class conflict because many wealthier colonists made common cause with artisans, small farmers, and the poor. Indeed, colonial elites considered themselves the leaders, inspiring popular uprisings through the power of their political arguments and oratorical skills. Still, they refused to support actions they considered too radical.

It was these more affluent protesters who dominated the Stamp Act Congress that met in New York City in October 1765. It brought together twenty-seven delegates from nine colonies. The delegates petitioned Parliament to repeal the Stamp Act, arguing that taxation without representation was tyranny. Delegates then urged colonists to boycott British goods and refuse to pay the stamp tax. Yet they still proclaimed their loyalty to king and country.

The question of representation became a mainstay of colonial protests. Whereas the British accepted the notion of "virtual representation," by which members of Parliament gave voice to the views of particular classes and interests, the North American colonies had developed a system of representation based on locality. According to colonial leaders, only members of Parliament elected by colonists could represent their interests.

Even as delegates at the Stamp Act Congress declared themselves loyal, if disaffected, British subjects, they participated in the process of developing a common identity in the American colonies. Christopher Gadsden of South Carolina expressed the feeling most directly. "We should stand upon the broad common ground of natural rights," he argued. "There should be no New England man, no New-Yorker, known on the continent, but all of us Americans."

Eventually the British Parliament was forced to respond to colonial protests and even more to rising complaints from English merchants and traders whose business had been damaged by the colonists' boycott. Parliament repealed the Stamp Act in March 1766, and King George III granted his approval a month later. Victorious colonists looked forward to a new and better relationship between themselves and the British government.

From the colonists' perspective, the crisis triggered by the Stamp Act demonstrated the limits of parliamentary control. Colonists had organized effectively and forced Parliament to repeal the hated legislation. Protests had raged across the colonies and attracted support from a wide range of colonists. Individual leaders, like Patrick Henry of Virginia and Samuel Adams of Massachusetts, became more widely known through their fiery oratory and their success in appealing to the masses. The Stamp Act agitation also demonstrated the growing influence of ordinary citizens who led parades and demonstrations and joined in attacks on stamp agents and the homes of British officials. And the protests revealed the growing power of the written word and printed images in disseminating ideas among colonists. Broadsides, political cartoons, handbills, newspapers, and pamphlets circulated widely, reinforcing discussions and proclamations at taverns, rallies, demonstrations, and more formal political assemblies.

For all the success of the Stamp Act protests, American colonists still could not imagine in 1765 that protest would ever lead to open revolt against British sovereignty. More well-to-do colonists were concerned that a revolution against British authority might fuel a dual revolution in which small farmers, tenants, servants, slaves, and laborers would rise up against their political and economic superiors in the colonies. Even most middling- and working-class protesters believed that the best solution to the colonies' problems was to gain greater economic and political rights within the British empire, not to break from it.

The Townshend Act

The repeal of the Stamp Act in March 1766 led directly to Parliament's passage of the Declaratory Act. That act declared that Parliament had the authority to pass any law "to bind the colonies and peoples of North America" closer to Britain. No new tax or policy was established; Parliament simply wanted to proclaim Great Britain's political supremacy in the aftermath of the successful stamp tax protests.

Following this direct assertion of British sovereignty, relative harmony prevailed in the colonies for more than a year. Then in June 1767, a new chancellor of the Exchequer, Charles Townshend, rose to power in England. He persuaded Parliament to return to the model offered by the earlier Sugar Act. The **Townshend Act**, like the Sugar Act, instituted an import tax on a range of items sent to the colonies, including glass, lead, paint, paper, and tea.

Now, however, even an indirect tax led to immediate protests and calls for a boycott of taxed items. In February 1768, Samuel Adams wrote a circular letter reminding colonists of the importance of the boycott, and the Massachusetts Assembly disseminated it to other colonial assemblies. In response, Parliament posted two more British army regiments in Boston and New York City to enforce the law. Angry colonists did not retreat when confronted by this show of military force. Instead, a group of outspoken colonial leaders demanded that colonists refuse to import goods of any kind from Britain.

In 1767 and 1768, John Dickinson, a prominent Pennsylvania attorney and Quaker, published a series of letters attacking the Townshend Act. He presented himself as an ordinary colonist by using the pen name "A Farmer." Arguing that any duty on goods was a tax, he insisted, "Those who are taxed without their own consent, given by themselves, or their representatives, are slaves. We are taxed without our own consent given by ourselves, or our representatives. We are therefore—I speak it with grief—I speak it with indignation—we are slaves." Clearly, a boycott was necessary to demonstrate colonists' rights as British subjects.

This boycott depended especially on the support of women, who were often in charge of the day-to-day purchase of household items. Wives and mothers were expected to boycott a wide array of British goods, and even single women and widows who supported themselves as shopkeepers were expected not to sell British goods. Women were called upon as well to provide substitutes for boycotted goods. Many wives and mothers produced homespun shirts and dresses and brewed herbal teas to replace British products.

Despite the hardships, many colonial women, including twenty-two-year-old Charity Clarke, embraced the boycott. She wrote to a friend in England, "If you English folks won't give us the liberty we ask . . . I will try to gather a number of ladies armed with spinning wheels [along with men] who shall learn to weave & keep sheep, and will retire beyond the reach of arbitrary power." Other women also organized spinning bees in which dozens of participants produced yards of homespun cloth, the wearing of which symbolized female commitment to the cause.

Refusing to drink tea offered another way for women to protest parliamentary taxation. In February 1770, more than "300 Mistresses of Families, in which number the Ladies of the Highest Rank and Influence," signed a petition in Boston and pledged to abstain from drinking tea. Dozens of women from less prosperous families signed their own boycott agreement.

The Boston Massacre

Boston women's refusal to drink tea and their participation in spinning bees were part of a highly publicized effort to make their city the center of opposition to the Townshend Act. Printed propaganda, demonstrations, rallies, and broadsides announced to the world that Bostonians rejected Parliament's right to impose its will, or at least its taxes, on the American colonies. Angry over Parliament's taxation policies, Boston men also considered the soldiers, who moonlighted for extra pay, as economic competitors. Throughout the winter of 1769–1770, boys and young men reacted by harassing the growing number of British soldiers stationed in the city.

On the evening of March 5, 1770, young men began throwing snowballs at the lone soldier guarding the Boston Customs House. An angry crowd began milling about, now joined by a group of sailors led by Crispus Attucks, an ex-slave of mixed African and Indian ancestry. The guard called for help, and Captain Thomas Preston arrived at the scene with seven British soldiers. He appealed to the "gentlemen" present to disperse the crowd. Instead, the harangues of the crowd continued, and snowballs, stones, and other projectiles flew in greater numbers. Then a gun fired, and soon more shooting erupted. Eleven men in the crowd were hit, and four were "killed on the Spot," including Attucks.

Despite confusion about who, if anyone, gave the order to fire, colonists expressed outrage at the shooting of ordinary men on the streets of Boston. Samuel Adams and other Sons of Liberty recognized the incredible potential for anti-British propaganda. Adams organized a mass funeral for those killed, and thousands watched the caskets being paraded through the city. Newspaper editors and broadsides printed by the Sons of Liberty labeled the shooting a "massacre." But when the accused soldiers were tried in Boston for the so-called **Boston Massacre**, the jury acquitted six of the eight of any crime. Still, ordinary colonists as well as colonial leaders were growing more convinced that British rule had become tyrannical and that such tyranny must be opposed.

To ensure that colonists throughout North America learned about the Boston Massacre, committees of correspondence formed once again to spread the news. These committees became important pipelines for sending information about plans and protests across the colonies. They also circulated an engraving by Bostonian Paul Revere that suggested the soldiers purposely shot at a peaceful crowd.

Parliament was already considering the repeal of the Townshend duties, and in the aftermath of the shootings, public pressure increased to do so. Merchants in England and North America insisted that parliamentary policies had resulted in economic losses on both sides of the Atlantic. In response, Parliament repealed all of the Townshend duties except the import tax on tea, which it retained to demonstrate its political authority to tax the colonies.

Continuing Conflicts at Home

As colonists in Boston and other seaport cities rallied to protest British taxation, other residents of the thirteen colonies continued to challenge authorities closer to home. In the same years as the Stamp Act and Townshend Act protests, tenants in New Jersey and the Hudson valley continued their campaign for economic justice. So, too, did Hermon Husband and the Regulators. Conflicts escalated when the North Carolina Assembly, dominated by the eastern slaveholding elite, approved a measure in 1768 to build a stately mansion for Governor Tryon with public funds. Outraged frontier farmers withheld their taxes, took over courthouses, and harassed corrupt local officials. While Governor Tryon claimed that Parliament abused its power in taxing the colonies, he did not recognize such abuses in his own colony. Instead, he increasingly viewed the Regulators as traitors. In spring 1771, he recruited a thousand militiamen to quell what he considered open rebellion on the Carolina frontier. The Regulators amassed two thousand farmers to defend themselves, although Husband, a pacifist, was not among them. But when twenty Regulators were killed and more than a hundred wounded at the Battle of Alamance Creek in May 1771, he surely knew many of the fallen. Six of the defeated Regulators were hanged a month later. Many local residents harbored deep resentments against colonial officials for what they viewed as the slaughter of honest, hardworking men. Hermon Husband fled the Carolina frontier and headed north.

Resentments against colonial leaders were not confined to North Carolina. An independent Regulator movement had emerged in South Carolina in 1767. Far more effective than their North Carolina counterparts, South Carolina Regulators seized control of the western regions of the colony, took up arms, and established their own system of frontier justice. In 1769 the South Carolina Assembly negotiated a settlement with the Regulators, establishing new parishes in the colony's interior that ensured greater representation for frontier areas and extending colonial political institutions, such as courts and sheriffs, to the region.

Tea and Widening Resistance

For a brief period after the Boston Massacre, conflicts within the colonies generally overshadowed protests against British policies. During this period, the tea tax was collected, the increased funds ensured that British officials in the colonies were less dependent on local assemblies to carry out their duties, and general prosperity seemed to lessen the antagonism between colonists and royal authorities. In May 1773, however, all that changed. That month Parliament passed a new act that granted the revered but financially struggling East India Company a monopoly on shipping and selling tea in the colonies. Although this did not add any new tax or raise the price of tea, it did fuel a new round of protests.

Samuel Adams, Patrick Henry, Christopher Gadsden, and other radicals had continued to view the tea tax as an illegal imposition on colonists and refused to pay it as a matter of principle. They had established committees of correspondence to keep up the pressure for a colony-wide boycott, and Adams published and circulated "Rights of the Colonies," a pamphlet that listed a range of grievances against British policies. Their concerns became the basis for a new round of protests when Parliament, many of whose members invested in the East India Company, granted its monopoly. By eliminating colonial merchants from the profits to be made on tea and implementing a monopoly for a single favored company, Parliament pushed merchants into joining with radicals to demand redress.

Committees of correspondence quickly organized another colony-wide boycott. In some cities, like Charleston, South Carolina, tea was unloaded from East India Company ships but never sold. In others, like New York, the ships were turned back at the port. Only in Boston, however, did violence erupt as ships loaded with tea sat anchored in the harbor. On the night of December 16, 1773, the Sons of Liberty organized a "tea party." After a massive rally against British policy, a group of about fifty men disguised as Indians boarded the British ships and dumped forty-five tons of tea into the sea.

Although hundreds of spectators knew who had boarded the ship, witnesses refused to provide names or other information to British investigators. The Boston Tea Party was a direct challenge to British authority and resulted in large-scale destruction of valuable property.

Parliament responded immediately with a show of force. The **Coercive Acts**, passed in 1774, closed the port of Boston until residents paid for the tea, moved Massachusetts court cases against royal officials back to England, and revoked the colony's charter in order to strengthen the authority of royal officials and weaken that of the colonial assembly. The British government also approved a new Quartering Act, which forced Boston residents to accommodate more soldiers in their own homes or build more barracks.

The royal government passed the Coercive Acts to punish Massachusetts and to discourage similar protests in other colonies. Instead, the legislation, which colonists called the **Intolerable Acts**, spurred a militant reaction. Committees of correspondence spread news of the fate of Boston and of Massachusetts. Colonial leaders, who increasingly identified themselves as patriots, soon formed committees of safety—armed groups of colonists who gathered weapons and munitions and vowed to protect themselves against British encroachments on their rights and institutions. Other colonies sent

The Edenton Proclamation, 1774 In Edenton, North Carolina, a group of women published a proclamation in 1774 stating their allegiance to the cause of liberty by refusing to serve or drink British tea. Their public statement received much attention in the American and the British press. This political cartoon, which satirizes the women who signed the declaration, appeared in several London newspapers.   Library of Congress, LC-DIG-ppmsca-19468

support, both political and material, to Massachusetts and instituted a boycott of British goods. All ranks of people throughout the colonies joined the boycott.

At the same time, a group of patriots meeting in Williamsburg, Virginia in the spring of 1774 called for colonies to send representatives to a **Continental Congress** to meet in Philadelphia the following September to discuss relations between the North American colonies and Great Britain.

By passing the Coercive Acts, Parliament had hoped to dampen the long-smoldering conflict with the colonies. Instead, it flared even brighter, with radical leaders committing themselves to the use of violence, moderate merchants and shopkeepers making common cause with radicals, and ordinary women and men embracing a boycott of all British goods.

The Continental Congress and Colonial Unity

When the Continental Congress convened in Philadelphia in September 1774, fifty-six delegates represented every colony but Georgia. Many of these men—and they were all men—had met before. Some had worked together in the Stamp Act Congress in 1765; others had joined forces in the intervening years on committees of correspondence or in petitions to Parliament. Still, the representatives disagreed on many fronts. Some were radicals like Samuel Adams, Patrick Henry, and Christopher Gadsden. Others held moderate views, including George Washington and John Dickinson of Pennsylvania. And a few, like John Jay of New York, voiced more conservative positions.

Despite their differences, all the delegates agreed that the colonies must resist further parliamentary encroachments on their liberties. They talked not of independence but rather of reestablishing the freedoms that colonists had enjoyed in an earlier period. Washington voiced the sentiments of many. Although opposed to the idea of independence, he echoed John Locke by refusing to submit "to the loss of those valuable rights and privileges, which are essential to the happiness of every free State, and without which life, liberty, and property are rendered totally insecure."

To demonstrate their unified resistance to the Coercive Acts, delegates called on colonists to continue the boycott of British goods and to end all colonial exports to Great Britain. Committees were established in all of the colonies to coordinate and enforce these actions. Delegates also insisted that Americans were "entitled to a free and exclusive power of legislation in their several provincial legislatures." By 1774 a growing number of colonists supported these measures and the ideas on which they were based.

The delegates at the Continental Congress could not address all the colonists' grievances, and most had no interest in challenging race and class relations within the colonies themselves. Nonetheless, it was a significant event because the congress drew power away from individual colonies and local organizations and placed the emphasis instead on colony-wide plans and actions. To some extent, the delegates also shifted leadership of the protests away from more radical artisans, like Ebenezer Mackintosh, and put planning back in the hands of men of wealth and standing. Moreover, even as they denounced Parliament, many representatives felt a special loyalty to the king and sought his intervention to rectify relations between the mother country and the colonies.

REVIEW & RELATE	• How and why did colonial resistance to British policies escalate in the decade following the conclusion of the French and Indian War? • How did internal social and economic divisions shape the colonial response to British policies?

Conclusion: Liberty within Empire

From the Sugar Act in 1764 to the Continental Congress in 1774, colonists reacted strongly to parliamentary efforts to impose greater control over the colonies. Their protests grew increasingly effective as colonists developed organizations, systems of communication, and arguments to buttress their position. Residents of seacoast cities like Boston and New York City developed especially visible and effective challenges, in large part because they generally had the most to lose if Britain implemented new economic, military, and legislative policies.

In frontier areas, such as the southern backcountry, the Hudson valley, and northern New England, complaints against British tyranny vied with those against colonial land speculators and officials throughout the 1760s and 1770s. Still, few of these agitators questioned the right of white colonists to claim Indian lands or enslave African labor. In this sense, at least, most frontier settlers made common cause with more elite colonists, including the many planters and large landowners who attended the Continental Congress.

One other tie bound the colonists together in 1774. No matter how radical the rhetoric, the aim continued to be resistance to particular policies, not independence from the British empire. Colonists sought greater liberty within the empire. Only on rare occasions did a colonist question the fundamental framework of imperial governance. And despite some colonists' opposition to certain parliamentary acts, many others supported British policies. Indeed, the majority of colonists did not participate in protest activities. Most small farmers and backcountry settlers were far removed from centers of protest activity, while poor families in seaport cities who purchased few items to begin with had little interest in boycotts of British goods. Finally, some colonists hesitated to consider open revolt against British rule for fear of a revolution from below. The activities of land rioters, Regulators, evangelical preachers, female petitioners, and African American converts to Christianity reminded more well-established settlers that the colonies harbored their own tensions and conflicts.

The fates of George Washington and Hermon Husband suggest the uncertainties that plagued the colonies and individual colonists in 1774. As Washington returned to his Virginia estate from the Continental Congress, he began to devote more time to military affairs. He took command of the volunteer militia companies in the colonies and chaired the committee on safety in his home county. Although still opposed to rebellion, he was nonetheless preparing for it. Hermon Husband, on the other hand, had watched his rebellion against oppressive government fail at the Battle of Alamance Creek. When the Continental Congress met in Philadelphia, he was working to reestablish his farm and family on the Pennsylvania frontier. Whether ruled by Great Britain or eastern colonial elites, Husband was most concerned with the rights of poor farmers and working people. Yet he and Washington would have agreed with the great British parliamentarian Edmund Burke, who, on hearing of events in the American colonies in 1774, lamented, "Clouds, indeed, and darkness, rest upon the future."

Chapter 5 Review

KEY TERMS

Albany Congress (p. 106)
Peace of Paris (p. 108)
Proclamation Line of 1763 (p. 112)
Regulators (p. 113)
benign neglect (p. 115)
Navigation Acts (p. 116)
Sugar Act (p. 116)
import duty (p. 116)

committee of correspondence (p. 116)
Stamp Act (p. 117)
Sons of Liberty (p. 117)
Townshend Act (p. 119)
Boston Massacre (p. 121)
Coercive Acts (Intolerable
    Acts) (p. 122)
Continental Congress (p. 123)

REVIEW & RELATE

1. How did the French and Indian War and the subsequent peace treaty affect relations among Britain, American Indian nations, and American colonies?

2. How did the French and Indian War and the increasing power of large landowners contribute to conflict between average colonists and colonial elites?

3. How did Britain's postwar policies lead to the emergence of unified colonial protests?

4. Why did British policymakers believe they were justified in seeking to gain greater control over Britain's North American colonies?

5. How and why did colonial resistance to British policies escalate in the decade following the conclusion of the French and Indian War?

6. How did internal social and economic divisions shape the colonial response to British policies?

TIMELINE OF EVENTS

1754–1763	• French and Indian War (Seven Year's War)	**1765**	• Stamp Act passed • Stamp Act Congress convenes
1754	• George Washington attacks Fort Duquesne • Albany Congress convenes	**1766**	• Sandy Creek Association formed • Stamp Act repealed and Declaratory Act passed
1757	• William Pitt takes charge of British war effort	**1767**	• Townshend Act passed
May 1763	• Pontiac launches pan-Indian revolt	**1770**	• Boston Massacre
		1771	• Battle of Alamance Creek, North Carolina
June 1763	• Peace of Paris		
October 1763	• Proclamation Line of 1763 established	**1773**	• Boston Tea Party
December 1763	• Paxton Boys attack Conestoga Indians	**1774**	• Coercive Acts passed • Continental Congress convenes
1764	• Green Mountain Boys resist New York authorities • Sugar Act passed		

6

The American Revolution

1775–1783

LEARNING OBJECTIVES

After reading this chapter you should be able to:

- Explain the relationship between the beginning of armed conflict and patriots' decision to declare independence.

- Understand the choices of colonists, American Indians, and African Americans to support or oppose independence.

- Analyze the military strategies of the British and the Americans in 1776–1777, the roles that various allies played, and the importance of women and other groups on the home front.

- Explain the major accomplishments of and conflicts within the new state and federal governments during the Revolution.

- Analyze the shift of warfare to the South and West from 1778 to 1781; the importance of American Indians, foreign allies, and colonial soldiers in patriot victories there; and the challenges Americans faced once they defeated the British.

COMPARING AMERICAN HISTORIES

One of the foremost pamphleteers of the patriot cause, Thomas Paine was born in 1737 in England, where his parents trained him as a corset maker. Eventually he left home and found work as a seaman, a teacher, and a tax collector. He drank heavily and beat both his wives. Yet he also taught working-class children to read and pushed the British government to improve the working conditions and pay of tax collectors. In 1772 Paine was fired from his government job, but a pamphlet he wrote had caught the eye of Benjamin Franklin, who persuaded him to try his luck in the colonies.

127

Arriving in Philadelphia in November 1774 at age thirty-seven, Paine secured a job on the *Pennsylvania Magazine*. The newcomer quickly gained in-depth political knowledge of the intensifying conflicts between the colonies and Great Britain. He also gained patrons for his political tracts among Philadelphia's economic and political elite. When armed conflict with British troops erupted in April 1775, colonial debates over whether to declare independence intensified. Pamphlets were a popular means of influencing these debates, and Paine wrote one entitled *Common Sense* to tip the balance in favor of independence.

Published in January 1776, *Common Sense* proved an instant success. It provided a rationale for independence and an emotional plea for creating a new democratic republic. Paine urged colonists to separate from England and establish a political structure that would ensure liberty and equality for all Americans. "A government of our own is our natural right," he concluded. "'Tis time to part."

When *Common Sense* was published, sixteen-year-old Deborah Sampson was working as an indentured servant to Jeremiah and Susanna Thomas in Marlborough, Massachusetts. Jeremiah Thomas thought education was above the lot of servant girls, but Sampson insisted on reading whatever books she could find. However, her commitment to American independence likely developed less from reading and more from the fighting that raged in Massachusetts and drew male servants and the Thomases' five sons into the Continental Army.

When Deborah Sampson's term of service ended in 1778, she sought work as a weaver and then a teacher. In March 1782 she disguised herself as a man and enlisted in the Continental Army. Her height and muscular frame allowed her to fool local recruiters, and she accepted the bounty paid to those who enlisted. But Deborah never reported for duty, and when her charade was discovered, she was forced to return the money.

In May 1782 Sampson enlisted a second time under the name Robert Shurtliff. For the next year, Sampson, disguised as Shurtliff, marched, fought, and lived with her Massachusetts regiment. Her ability to carry off the deception was helped by lax standards of hygiene: Soldiers rarely undressed fully to bathe, and most slept in their uniforms.

Even after the formal end of the war in March 1783, Sampson/Shurtliff continued to serve in the Continental Army. That fall, she was sent to Philadelphia to help quash a mutiny by Continental soldiers angered over the army's failure to provide back pay. While there, Sampson/Shurtliff fell ill with a raging fever, and a doctor at the army hospital discovered that "he" was a woman. The doctor reported the news to General John Paterson, and Sampson was honorably discharged, having served the army faithfully for more than a year.

COMPARING THE AMERICAN HISTORIES of Thomas Paine and Deborah Sampson demonstrates how the American Revolution transformed individual lives as well as the life of the nation. Paine had failed financially and personally in England but gained fame in the colonies through his skills as a patriot pamphleteer. Sampson, who was forced into an early independence by her impoverished family, excelled as a soldier. Still, while the American Revolution offered opportunities for some colonists, it promised hardship for others. Most Americans had to choose sides long before it was clear whether the colonists could defeat Great Britain, and the long years of conflict (1775–1783) took a toll on families and communities across the thirteen colonies. Moreover, even with English converts like Paine and homegrown supporters like Sampson, the patriots would need foreign allies to achieve victory. And even battlefield victory could not ensure political stability in the new nation.

The Question of Independence

The Continental Congress that met to protest the Coercive Acts adjourned in October 1774, but delegates reconvened in May 1775. During the intervening months, patriot leaders honed their arguments for resisting British tyranny, and committees of correspondence circulated the latest news. While some patriots began advocating resistance in the strongest terms, the eruption of armed clashes between British soldiers and local farmers created the greatest push for independence. It also led the Continental Congress to establish the Continental Army in June 1775. A year later, in July 1776, the congress declared independence.

Armed Conflict Erupts

As debates over independence intensified, patriots along the Atlantic coast expanded their efforts. The Sons of Liberty and other patriot groups spread propaganda against the British, gathered and stored weapons, and organized and trained local militia companies. In addition to boycotting British goods, female patriots manufactured bandages and bullets. Some northern colonists freed enslaved African Americans who agreed to enlist in the militia. Others kept close watch on the movements of British troops.

On April 18, 1775, Boston patriots observed British movement in the harbor. British soldiers were headed to Lexington, intending to confiscate guns and ammunition hidden there and in neighboring Concord and perhaps arrest patriot leaders. To warn his fellow patriots, Paul Revere raced to Lexington on horseback but was stopped on the road to Concord by the British. By that time, however, a network of riders was spreading the alarm and alerted Concord residents of the impending danger.

Early in the morning of April 19, the first shots rang out on the village green of Lexington. After a brief exchange between British soldiers and local militiamen— known as minutemen for the speed with which they assembled—eight colonists lay dead. The British troops then marched on Concord, where they burned colonial supplies. However, patriots in nearby towns had now been alerted. Borrowing guerrilla tactics from American Indians, colonists hid behind trees, walls, and barns and battered the British soldiers as they marched back to Boston, killing 73 and wounding 200.

Word of the conflict traveled quickly. Outraged Bostonians attacked British troops and forced them to retreat to ships in the harbor. The victory was short-lived, however, and the British soon regained control of Boston. But colonial forces entrenched themselves on hills just north of the city. Then in May, Ethan Allen and his Green Mountain Boys joined militias from Connecticut and Massachusetts to capture the British garrison at Fort Ticonderoga, New York. The battle for North America had begun.

When the **Second Continental Congress** convened in Philadelphia on May 10, 1775, the most critical question for delegates like Pennsylvania patriot John Dickinson was how to ensure time for discussion and negotiation. Armed conflict had erupted, but should, or must, revolution follow? Other delegates, including Patrick Henry, insisted that independence was the only appropriate response to armed attacks on colonial residents.

Just over a month later, on June 16, British forces under General Sir William Howe attacked patriot fortifications on Breed's Hill and Bunker Hill, north of Boston. The British won the **Battle of Bunker Hill** when patriots ran out of ammunition. But the redcoats—so called because of their bright red uniforms—suffered twice as many casualties as the patriots. The victory allowed the British to maintain control of Boston for nine more months, but the heavy losses emboldened patriot militiamen.

Building a Continental Army

The Battle of Bunker Hill convinced the Continental Congress to establish an army for the defense of the colonies. They appointed forty-three-year-old George

The Battle of Bunker Hill   On June 16, 1775, 2,500 British infantry sought to dislodge 1,500 patriot volunteers from Breeds Hill, 600 yards below Charlestown's strategic Bunker Hill. Although the British managed to root out the patriots during a third assault, more than a thousand British soldiers were wounded or killed. British General Thomas Gage lost his command, and the Royal Army no longer seemed invincible.   akg-images

Washington as commander in chief, and he headed to Massachusetts to take command of militia companies already engaged in battle. Since the congress had not yet proclaimed itself a national government, Washington depended largely on the willingness of local militias to accept his command and of individual colonies to supply soldiers, arms, and ammunition. Throughout the summer of 1775, Washington wrote numerous letters to patriot political leaders detailing the army's urgent need for men and supplies. He also sought to remove incompetent officers and improve order among the troops, who spent too much time carousing.

As he worked to forge a disciplined army, Washington and his officers developed a twofold military strategy. They sought to drive the British out of Boston and to secure the colonies from attack by British forces and their Indian allies in New York and Canada. In November 1775, American troops under General Richard Montgomery captured Montreal. However, the difficult trek in cold weather and the spread of smallpox decimated the patriot reinforcements led by General Benedict Arnold, and American troops failed to dislodge the British from Quebec.

Despite the disastrous outcome of the Canadian invasion, the Continental Army secured important victories in the winter of 1775–1776. To improve Washington's position in Massachusetts, General Henry Knox retrieved weapons captured at Fort Ticonderoga. In March, Washington positioned the forty-three cannons on Dorchester Heights and surprised the British with a bombardment that drove them from Boston and forced them to retreat to Nova Scotia.

Reasons for Caution and for Action

When the British retreated from Boston, the war had already spread into Virginia. In spring 1775, local militias forced Lord Dunmore, Virginia's royal governor, to take refuge on British ships in Norfolk harbor. Dunmore encouraged white servants and black slaves to join him there, and hundreds of black men fought with British troops when the governor led his army back into Virginia in November 1775. After the Battle of Great Bridge, Dunmore reclaimed the governor's mansion and issued an official proclamation that declared "all indent[ur]ed Servants, Negroes or others (appertaining to Rebels)" to be free if they were "able and willing to bear Arms" for the British.

Dunmore's Proclamation, offering freedom to slaves who fought for the crown, reinforced other challenges to social hierarchies. During the 1760s, Baptist preachers had repudiated class and racial distinctions, and even in the South, they invited poor whites and enslaved blacks to their services. By 1775, 15 percent of whites in Virginia and hundreds of African Americans had joined Baptist churches. In England itself, a group of radicals drew on anti-authoritarian ideas developed during the English Civil War (1642–1651) to criticize British rule over its expanding empire. Through pamphlets and newspapers, their ideas circulated widely in the colonies. In addition, Enlightenment thinkers generally emphasized individual talent over inherited privilege, a view reinforced by the success of a man like Thomas Paine.

Still, many delegates at the Continental Congress, which included large planters, successful merchants, and professional men, hesitated to act. They held out hope for a negotiated settlement that would increase the colonies' political liberty without disrupting social and economic hierarchies. However, the king and Parliament refused to compromise in any way with colonies they considered in rebellion. Instead, in December 1775, the king prohibited any negotiation or trade with the colonies, increasing the leverage of radicals who argued independence was a necessity. The January 1776 publication of Thomas Paine's **Common Sense** bolstered their case. Paine wielded both biblical references and Enlightenment ideas in his best-selling pamphlet. It impressed patriot leaders as well as ordinary farmers and artisans, who debated his ideas at taverns and coffeehouses.

By the spring of 1776, a growing number of patriots believed that independence was necessary. Colonies began to take control of their legislatures and instruct their delegates to the Continental Congress to support independence. Meanwhile, the congress requested economic and military assistance from France. And in May, the congress advised colonies that had not yet done so to establish independent governments.

Still, many colonists opposed the idea of breaking free from Britain. Charles Inglis, the rector at Trinity Church in New York City, insisted that "limited monarchy is the form of government which is most favorable to liberty."

Declaring Independence

As colonists argued back and forth, Richard Henry Lee of Virginia introduced a motion to the Continental Congress in early June 1776 resolving that "these United Colonies are, and of right ought to be, Free and Independent States." A heated debate followed in which Lee and John Adams argued passionately for independence. Eventually, even more cautious delegates, like Robert Livingston of New York, were convinced. Livingston concluded that "they should yield to the torrent if they hoped to direct it." He then joined Adams, Thomas Jefferson, Benjamin Franklin, and Roger Sherman on a committee to draft a formal statement justifying independence.

The thirty-three-year-old Jefferson took the lead in preparing the declaration, building on ideas expressed by Paine, Adams, and Lee. He also drew on language used in dozens of "declarations" written by town meetings, county officials, and colonial assemblies, particularly the Virginia Declaration of Rights drafted by George Mason in May 1776. Several of these documents insisted on religious freedom since the power of faith strengthened the view of many Americans that they were uniquely blessed with liberty. Another principle central to these documents was the contract theory of government, proposed by the seventeenth-century British philosopher John Locke. Locke argued that sovereignty resided in the people, who submitted voluntarily to laws and authorities in exchange for protection of their life, liberty, and property. The people could therefore reconstitute or overthrow a government that abused its powers. Jefferson summarized this argument and then listed the abuses and crimes perpetrated by King George III against the colonies, which justified the patriots' decision to break their contract with British authorities.

Once prepared, the **Declaration of Independence** was debated and revised. In the final version, all references to slavery were removed. But delegates agreed to list among the abuses suffered by the colonies the fact that the king "excited domestic insurrections amongst us," referring to the threat posed by Dunmore's Proclamation. On July 2, 1776, delegates from twelve colonies approved the Declaration, with only New York abstaining. Independence was publicly proclaimed on July 4 when the Declaration was published as a broadside to be circulated throughout the colonies.

**REVIEW &
RELATE**

- What challenges did Washington face when he was given command of the Continental Army?
- How and why did proponents of independence prevail in the debates that led to the Declaration of Independence?

Choosing Sides

Probably no more than half of American colonists actively supported the patriots. Perhaps a fifth actively supported the British. The rest tried to stay neutral or were largely indifferent unless the war came to their doorstep. Both patriots and loyalists included men and women from all classes and races and from both rural and urban areas.

Recruiting Supporters

Men who took up arms against the British before independence was declared and the women who supported them clearly demonstrated their commitment to the patriot cause. In some colonies, patriots organized local committees, courts, and assemblies to assume governance should British officials lose their authority. At the same time, white servants and enslaved blacks in Virginia who fled to British ships or marched with Lord Dunmore made their loyalties known as well. Some Indians, too, declared their allegiance early in the conflict. In May 1775, Colonel Guy Johnson, the British superintendent for Indian affairs, left Albany, New York and sought refuge in Canada. He was accompanied by 120 British loyalists and 90 Mohawk warriors led by their mission-educated chief, Joseph Brant (Thayendanegea).

The Continental Congress, like Johnson, recognized the importance of Indians to the outcome of any colonial war. It appointed commissioners from the "United Colonies" to meet with representatives of the Iroquois Confederacy in August 1775. While Brant's group of Mohawk warriors were already committed to the British, some Oneida Indians, influenced by missionaries and patriot sympathizers, wanted to support the colonies. Others, however, urged neutrality, at least for the moment.

Once independence was declared, there was far more pressure to choose sides. The stance of political and military leaders and soldiers was clear. But to win against Great Britain required the support of a large portion of the civilian population as well. As battle lines shifted back and forth across New England, the Middle Atlantic region, and the South, civilians caught up in the fighting were faced with difficult decisions.

Many colonists who remained loyal to the king found safe haven in cities like New York, Newport, and Charleston, which remained under British control throughout much of the war. **Loyalist** men were welcomed by the British army. Still, those who made their loyalist sympathies clear risked a good deal. When British troops were forced out of cities or towns they had temporarily occupied, many loyalists faced harsh reprisals. Patriots had no qualms about invading the homes of loyalists, punishing women and children, and destroying or confiscating property.

Many loyalists were members of the economic and political elite. Others came from ordinary backgrounds. Tenants, small farmers, and slaves joined the loyalist cause in defiance of their landlords, large property owners, and wealthy planters. Many poorer loyalists lived in the Hudson valley, their sympathy for the British heightened by the patriot commitments of the powerful men who controlled the region. When the fighting moved south, many former Regulators also supported the British, who challenged the domination of patriot leaders among North Carolina's eastern elite.

Perhaps most important, the majority of Indian nations ultimately sided with the British. The Mohawk, Seneca, and Cayuga nations in the North and the Cherokee and Creek nations in the South were among Great Britain's leading allies. Although British efforts to limit colonial migration, such as the Proclamation Line of 1763, had failed, most Indian nations still believed that a British victory offered the only hope of ending further encroachments on their territory.

Choosing Neutrality

Early in the war, many Indian nations proclaimed their neutrality. This included the Delaware and Shawnee in the Ohio River valley and the Oneida in Connecticut. The Oneida's chief warriors declared that the English and patriots were *"two brothers of one blood. We are unwilling to join on either side in such a contest."* But patriots often refused to accept Indian neutrality. Indeed, colonial troops killed the Shawnee chief Cornstalk under a flag of truce in 1777, leading that nation to ally, finally, with the British.

Colonists who sought to remain neutral during the war also faced hostility. Some 80,000 Quakers, Mennonites, Amish, Shakers, and Moravians considered war immoral and embraced neutrality. These men refused to bear arms, hire substitutes, or pay taxes to new state governments. The largest number of religious pacifists lived in Pennsylvania. Despite Quakerism's deep roots there, pacifists were treated as suspect by both patriots and loyalists.

In June 1778, Pennsylvania authorities jailed nine Mennonite farmers who refused to take an oath of allegiance to the revolutionary government. Their worldly goods were sold by the state, leaving their wives and children destitute. Quakers were routinely fined and imprisoned for refusing to support the patriot cause and harassed by British authorities in the areas they controlled. At the same time, Quaker meetings regularly disciplined members who offered aid to either side. Betsy Ross was among those disowned Quakers. Her husband joined the patriot forces, and she sewed flags for the Continental Army and Navy.

Committing to Independence

After July 4, 1776, the decision to support independence took on new meaning. If the United States failed to win the war, all those who actively supported the cause could be considered traitors. The families of Continental soldiers faced especially difficult decisions as the conflict spread and soldiers moved farther and farther from home. Men too old or too young to fight proved their patriotism by gathering arms and ammunition and patrolling local communities.

Some female patriots accompanied their husbands or fiancés as camp followers, cooking, washing clothes, nursing, and providing other services for soldiers. Most patriot women remained at home, however, and demonstrated their commitment by raising funds, gathering information, and sending clothes, bedding, and other goods to soldiers at the front. The Continental Army was desperately short of supplies from the beginning of the war. Northern women were urged to increase cloth production,

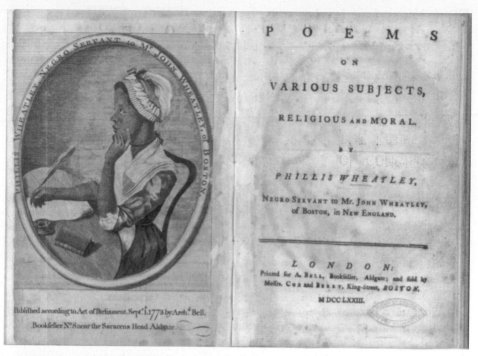

Phillis Wheatley   This portrait of Phillis Wheatley appears facing the title page of her book of poems, printed in London in 1773. It was painted by another Boston slave, Scipio Moorhead. Phillis Wheatley converted to Christianity and sided with the patriots in the Revolution. She won her freedom but never gained sufficient support to publish another book of poems.   Library of Congress, 3b04682

while southern women were asked to harvest crops for hungry troops. The response was overwhelming. Women in Hartford, Connecticut produced 1,000 coats and vests and 1,600 shirts in 1776 alone. Across the colonies, women collected clothing door-to-door and opened their homes to sick and wounded soldiers.

Some African American women also became ardent patriots. Phillis Wheatley of Boston, whose owners taught her to read and write, published a collection of poems in 1776 and sent a copy to General Washington. She urged readers to recognize Africans as children of God. Rewarded with freedom by her master, Wheatley was among a small number of blacks who actively supported the patriot cause. Still, the vast majority of blacks labored as slaves. While some escaped and joined the British in hopes of gaining their freedom, most were not free to choose sides.

REVIEW & RELATE
- How did colonists choose sides during the Revolutionary War? What factors influenced their decisions?
- Why would some Indian tribes try to stay neutral during the conflict? Why did most of those who chose sides support the British?

Fighting for Independence, 1776–1777

After July 4, 1776, battles between British and colonial troops intensified, but it was not until December that the patriots celebrated a major military victory. The rebellion faced a formidable set of challenges. Over the course of the eighteenth century, Great Britain had developed the world's most powerful military force, including a huge navy. Moreover, once independence was declared, the colonists lost their main trading partner and had to find ways to sustain their economy while funding a war. To succeed, the patriots needed support from men and women on the home front as well as the battlefront and assistance from Europeans experienced in fighting the British. It took two years for the patriots and the Continental Army to gain traction against British forces.

British Troops Gain Early Victories

In the summer of 1776, when General Washington tried to lead his army out of Boston to confront British troops set to invade New York City, many soldiers deserted and returned home. They believed that New York men should defend New York. Among the soldiers who remained with Washington, many were landless laborers whose wives and sisters followed the troops as their only means of support. Although Washington considered these camp followers undesirable, the few hundred women provided critical services to ordinary soldiers. Ultimately, Washington arrived in New York with 19,000 men, many of whom were poorly armed and poorly trained and some of whom were coerced into service by local committees of safety.

Meanwhile, throughout the summer British ships sailed into New York harbor or anchored off the coast of Long Island. General Howe, hoping to overwhelm the colonists, ordered 10,000 troops to march into the city in the weeks immediately after the Declaration of Independence was signed. Still, the Continental Congress rejected Howe's offer of peace and a royal pardon.

So Howe prepared to take control of New York City by force and then march up the Hudson valley, isolating New York and New England from the rest of the rebellious colonies. He was aided by some 8,000 Hessian mercenaries (Germans being paid to fight for the British). On August 27, 1776, British forces clashed with a far smaller contingent of Continentals on Long Island. More than 1,500 patriots were killed or wounded in the fierce fighting.

By November, the British had captured Fort Lee in New Jersey and attacked the Continental Army at Fort Washington, north of New York City. Meanwhile Washington led his weary troops and camp followers into Pennsylvania, while the Continental Congress, fearing a British attack on Philadelphia, fled to Baltimore.

Although General Howe might have ended the patriot threat right then by an aggressive campaign, he wanted to wear down the Continental Army and force the colonies to sue for peace. Washington did not have the troops or arms to launch a major assault, and he hoped that the British would accept American independence once they saw the enormous effort it would take to defeat the colonies. So the war continued.

Patriots Prevail in New Jersey

The Continental Army did not gain a single military victory between July and December 1776. Fortunately for Washington, Howe followed the European tradition of waiting out the winter months and returning to combat after the spring thaw. This gave the patriots the opportunity to regroup, repair weapons and wagons, and recruit soldiers. Yet Washington was reluctant to face the cold and discomfort of winter with troops discouraged by repeated defeats and retreats.

Camped in eastern Pennsylvania, Washington learned that Hessian troops had been sent to occupy the city of Trenton, New Jersey, just across the Delaware River. On Christmas Eve, Washington attacked Trenton in an icy rain, and the Continentals quickly routed the surprised Hessians. They then marched on Princeton and defeated regular British troops on January 3, 1777. The British army soon retreated from New Jersey, settling back into New York City, and the Continental Congress returned to Philadelphia. By mid-January 1777, it seemed clear to both sides that the conflict would be harder, more costly, and more deadly than anyone had imagined.

A Critical Year of Warfare

The British army emerged from winter camp in spring 1777. Its regular army units, American loyalists, Indian allies, Hessians, and naval men-of-war were concentrated largely in New York City and Canada. The Continental forces, numbering fewer than 5,000 men, were then entrenched near Morristown, New Jersey. With his troops ravaged by smallpox over the winter, Washington feared that an aggressive British assault might succeed.

Meanwhile, the Continental Congress had returned to Philadelphia, but members feared that the British would seek to capture the city and split the United States in two. General Howe did indeed plan on capturing Philadelphia, hoping to force a patriot surrender. Although Washington's force was too small to defeat Howe's army, it delayed his advance by guerrilla attacks and skirmishes. En route, Howe learned that he was expected to reinforce General John Burgoyne's soldiers, who were advancing south from Canada. Instead he continued to Philadelphia and captured it in September 1777. Meanwhile Burgoyne and his 7,200 troops regained control of Fort Ticonderoga on July 7. He continued south, but by late July his forces had to stop until supplies from Canada and reinforcements from Howe and General Barry St. Leger reached them.

St. Leger was marching his troops east through New York State, and Joseph Brant and his sister Molly Brant were gathering a force of Mohawk, Seneca, and Cayuga warriors to support them. But on August 6, they suffered a stunning defeat. In the **Battle of Oriskany** in New York, a band of German American farmers led by General Nicholas Herkimer held off the British advance, allowing General Arnold to reach nearby Fort Stanwix with reinforcements. On August 23, the British and Indian troops retreated to Canada (Map 6.1).

When General Howe's reinforcements also did not materialize, Burgoyne faced a brutal onslaught from patriot forces. In September patriots defeated the British at Freeman's Farm, with the British suffering twice the casualties of the Continentals. Fighting intensified in early October, when Burgoyne lost a second battle at Freeman's Farm. Ten days later, he surrendered his remaining army of 5,800 men to General Gates at nearby Saratoga, New York.

The Continental Army's victory in the **Battle of Saratoga** stunned the British. It undercut the significance of Howe's victory at Philadelphia and indicated the general's

MAP 6.1
The War in the North, 1775–1778   After early battles in Massachusetts, patriots invaded Canada but failed to capture Quebec. The British army captured New York City in 1776 and Philadelphia in 1777, but New Jersey remained a battle zone through 1778. Meanwhile General Burgoyne secured Canada for Britain and then headed south, but his forces were defeated by patriots at the crucial Battle of Saratoga.

misunderstanding of the nature of the war he was fighting. Meanwhile, the patriot victory energized Washington and his troops as they dug in at Valley Forge for another long winter. It also gave Benjamin Franklin, the Continental Congress envoy to Paris, greater leverage for convincing French officials to support American independence.

Patriots Gain Critical Assistance

Despite significant Continental victories in the fall of 1777, the following winter proved especially difficult. The quarters at **Valley Forge** were again marked by bitter cold, poor food, inadequate clothing, and scarce supplies. A French volunteer arrived to see "a few militia men, poorly clad, and for the most part without shoes; many of them badly armed." Many recent recruits were also poorly trained. Critical assistance arrived with Baron Friedrich von Steuben, a Prussian officer recruited by Benjamin Franklin, who took charge of drilling soldiers. Other officers experienced in European warfare also joined the patriot cause that winter: the Marquis de Lafayette of France, Johann Baron de Kalb of Bavaria, and Thaddeus Kosciusko and Casimir Count Pulaski, both of Poland. The Continental Army continued to be plagued by problems of recruitment, discipline, wages, and supplies. But the contributions of foreign volunteers, along with the leadership of Washington and his officers, sustained the military effort.

Patriots on the home front were also plagued by problems in 1777–1778. Families living in battlefield areas were especially vulnerable to the shifting fortunes of war. When British troops captured Philadelphia in fall 1777, a British officer commandeered the home of Elizabeth Drinker, a Quaker matron. An angry Drinker reported that the officer moved in with "3 Horses 2 Cows 2 Sheep and 3 Turkeys." Women who lived far from the conflict were isolated from such intrusions but were forced to fend for themselves with husbands at the front. Meanwhile, wives of patriot leaders, anxious to end the conflict, formed voluntary associations, like the Ladies Association of Philadelphia, to provide critical resources for the army.

While most women worked tirelessly on the home front, some cast their fate with the army. Camp followers continued to provide critical services to the military and suffered, as the troops did, from scarce supplies and harsh weather. Some women also served as spies and couriers for British or Continental forces. Lydia Darragh, a wealthy Philadelphian, eavesdropped on conversations among the British officers who occupied her house and carried detailed reports to Washington hidden in the folds of her dress. Others, like Nancy Hart Morgan of Georgia, took more direct action. Morgan lulled half a dozen British soldiers into a sense of security at dinner, hid their guns, and shot two before neighbors came to hang the rest.

Some patriot women took up arms on the battlefield. A few, such as Margaret Corbin, accompanied their husbands to the front lines. When her husband was killed at Fort Washington in November 1776, Corbin took his place loading and firing cannons. In addition, a small number of women, like Deborah Sampson, disguised themselves as men and enlisted as soldiers.

Surviving on the Home Front

Whether black or white, enslaved or free, women and children faced hardship, uncertainty, loneliness, and fear as a result of the war. Even those who did not directly engage enemy troops took on enormous burdens during the conflict. Farm wives plowed and planted and carried on their domestic duties as well. In cities, women worked ceaselessly to find sufficient food, wood, candles, and cloth to maintain themselves and their children.

As the war intensified, Continental and British forces slaughtered cattle and hogs for food, stole corn and other crops or burned them to keep the enemy from obtaining supplies, looted houses and shops, and kidnapped or liberated slaves and servants. Some home invasions turned savage. Both patriot and loyalist papers in New York, Philadelphia, and Charleston reported cases of rape.

In these desperate circumstances, many women asserted themselves in order to survive. When merchants hoarded goods in order to make greater profits from rising prices, housewives raided stores and warehouses and took the supplies they needed. Others learned as much as they could about family finances and submitted reports to local officials when their houses, farms, or businesses were damaged or looted. Growing numbers of women banded together to assist one another, help more impoverished families, and supply troops with badly needed clothes, food, bandages, and bullets.

REVIEW & RELATE	• How did the patriot forces fare in 1776? How and why did the tide of war turn in 1777?
	• What role did colonial women and foreign men play in the conflict in the early years of the war?

Governing in Revolutionary Times

Amid the constant upheavals of war, patriot leaders established new governments. At the national level, responsibilities ranged from coordinating and funding military operations to developing diplomatic relations with foreign countries and Indian nations. At the state level, constitutions had to be drafted and approved, laws enforced, and military needs assessed and met. Whether state or national, new governments had to assure their followers that they were not simply replacing old forms of oppression with new ones. Yet few states moved to eliminate the most oppressive institution in the nation, slavery.

Colonies Become States

For most of the war, the Continental Congress acted in lieu of a national government while the delegates worked to devise a more permanent structure. But the congress had depended mainly on states for funds and manpower. Delegates did draft the **Articles of Confederation** in 1777, creating a central government with limited powers. They submitted them to the states for approval, and eight of the thirteen states ratified the plan for a national government by mid-1778. But nearly three more years passed before the last state, Maryland, approved the Articles.

Without a formal central government, state governments played crucial roles throughout the war. Even before the Continental Congress declared American independence, some colonies had forced royal officials to flee and established new state governments. Some states abided by the regulations in their colonial charters or by English common law. Others created new governments based on a written constitution.

These constitutions reflected the opposition to centralized power fueled by the struggle against British tyranny. In Pennsylvania, patriots developed one of the most democratic constitutions. The governor was replaced by an executive council. The legislature consisted of a single house elected by popular vote. Legislators could only serve for four in any seven years to discourage the formation of a political aristocracy. Although Pennsylvania's constitution was among the most radical, all states limited centralized power in some way.

Thus, most states, adopting Virginia's model, included in their constitutions a bill of rights that ensured citizens freedom of the press, freedom of elections, speedy trials by one's peers, humane punishments, and the right to form militias. Some states also insisted on people's freedom of speech and assembly, the right to petition and to bear arms, and equal protection of the laws. The New Jersey constitution of 1776 enfranchised all free inhabitants who met the property qualifications, thereby allowing some single and widowed women and free blacks to vote. However, most new state constitutions allowed only white men with property to vote, and nearly all granted significant power to the legislative branch, where white men of property dominated.

Patriots Divide over Slavery

Although state constitutions were revolutionary in many respects, few of them addressed the issue of slavery. Only Vermont abolished slavery in its 1777 constitution. Legislators in Pennsylvania approved a gradual abolition law by which slaves born after 1780 could claim their freedom at age twenty-eight. In Massachusetts, two slaves sued for their freedom in county courts in 1780–1781. Quock Walker, who had been promised his emancipation by a former master, sued his current master to gain his freedom. About the same time, an enslaved woman, Mum Bett, who was the widow of a Revolutionary soldier, initiated a similar case. Mum Bett won her case and changed her name to Elizabeth Freeman. When Walker's owner appealed the local court's decision to free his slave, the Massachusetts Supreme Court cited Mum Bett's case and ruled that slavery conflicted with the state constitution.

In southern states like Virginia, the Carolinas, and Georgia, however, life for slaves grew increasingly harsh during the war. Because British forces promised freedom to blacks who fought with them, slave owners and patriot armies in the South did everything possible to ensure that African Americans did not make it behind British lines. When the British retreated, some generals, like Lord Dunmore and Sir Henry Clinton, took black volunteers with them. But thousands more were left behind to fend for themselves.

Nonetheless, the American Revolution dealt a blow to human bondage. For many blacks, Revolutionary ideals required the end of slavery. Northern free black communities grew rapidly during the war, especially in seaport cities. In the South, too, thousands of slaves gained freedom, either by joining the British army or by fleeing in the midst of battlefield chaos. As many as one-quarter of South Carolina's slaves had emancipated themselves by the end of the Revolution. Yet as the Continental Congress worked toward developing a framework for a national government, few delegates considered the abolition of slavery a significant issue.

France Allies with the Patriots

The Continental Congress considered an alliance with France far more critical to patriot success than the issue of slavery. France's long rivalry with Britain made it a likely ally, and the French government had secretly provided funds to the patriots early in the war. In December 1776, the Continental Congress sent Benjamin Franklin to Paris to serve as its unofficial liaison. Franklin was enormously successful, securing supplies and becoming a favorite among the French aristocracy and ordinary citizens alike.

But the French were initially unwilling to forge a formal compact with the upstart patriots. Only after the patriot victory at Saratoga in October 1777 did King Louis XVI agree to an alliance. In February 1778, Franklin secured an agreement that approved trading rights between the United States and all French possessions. France then recognized the United States as an independent nation, relinquished French territorial claims on mainland North America, and sent troops to reinforce the Continental Army. In return, the United States promised to defend French holdings in the Caribbean. A year later, Spain allied itself with France to protect its own North American holdings.

British leaders responded by declaring war on France. Yet doing so ensured that military conflicts would spread well beyond North America and military expenditures would skyrocket. French forces attacked British outposts in Gibraltar, the Bay of Bengal, Senegal in West Africa, and Grenada in the West Indies. At the same time, the French supplied the United States with military officers, weapons, funds, and critical naval support.

Faced with this new alliance, Britain's prime minister, Lord North (1771–1782), decided to concentrate British forces in New York City. This tactic forced the British army to abandon Philadelphia in summer 1778. For the remainder of the war, New York City provided the sole British stronghold in the North, serving as a supply center and prisoner-of-war camp.

Raising Armies and Funds

The French alliance did create one unintended problem for the Continental Army. When Americans heard that France was sending troops, fewer men volunteered for military service. Local officials had the authority to draft men into the army or to accept substitutes for draftees. In the late 1770s, some draftees forced enslaved men to take their place; others hired landless laborers, the handicapped, or the mentally unfit as substitutes.

As the war spread south and west in 1778–1779, Continental forces were stretched thin, and enlistments faltered further. Soldiers faced injuries, disease, and shortages of food and ammunition. They also risked capture by the British, one of the worst fates to befall a Continental. Considered traitors by the British, most captives were held on ships in New York harbor. They faced filthy accommodations, a horrid stench, inadequate water, and widespread disease and abuse. Altogether, between 8,000 and 11,500 patriots died in British prisons in New York—more than died in battle.

Even if the British had allowed the Continental Congress to aid prisoners, it could do little, given the financial problems it faced. With no authority to impose taxes on American citizens, the congress had to borrow money from wealthy patriots, accept loans from France and the Netherlands, and print money of its own—some $200 million by 1780. However, money printed by the states was used far more widely than were Continental dollars. "Continentals" depreciated so quickly that by late 1780 it took one hundred continentals to buy one silver dollar's worth of goods. In 1779, with the cost of goods skyrocketing, housewives, sailors, and artisans in Philadelphia and other cities attacked merchants who were hoarding goods, forcing officials to distribute food to the poor.

The congress finally improved its financial standing slightly by using a $6 million loan from France to back certificates issued to wealthy patriots. Meanwhile states raised money through taxes to provide funds for government operations, backing for its paper money, and other expenses. Most residents found such taxes incredibly burdensome given wartime inflation, and even the most patriotic began to protest increased taxation. Thus the financial status of the new nation remained precarious.

Indian Affairs and Land Claims

The congress also sought to settle land claims in the western regions of the nation and build alliances with additional Indian nations. The two issues were intertwined, and both were difficult to resolve. Most Indian nations had long-standing complaints against colonists who intruded on their lands, and many patriot leaders made it clear that independence would mean further expansion.

In the late 1770s, British forces and their Indian allies fought bitter battles against patriot militias and Continental forces all along the frontier. Each side destroyed property, ruined crops, and killed civilians. In the summer and fall of 1778, Indian and American civilians suffered through a series of brutal attacks in Wyoming, Pennsylvania; Onoquaga, New York; and Cherry Valley, New York. Patriots and Indians also battled along the Virginia frontier after pioneer and militia leader Daniel Boone established a fort there in 1775. In the South, 6,000 patriot troops laid waste to Cherokee villages in the Appalachian Mountains in retaliation for the killing of white intruders along the Watauga River by a renegade Cherokee warrior, Dragging Canoe.

Regardless of Indian rights, much western land had already been claimed by individual states like Connecticut, Georgia, New York, Massachusetts, and Virginia. These states hoped to use western lands to reward soldiers and expand their settlements. However, states without such claims, like Maryland, argued that if such lands were "wrested from the common enemy by the blood and treasure of the thirteen States," they should be considered "common property, subject to be parcelled out by Congress into free and independent governments." In 1780 New York State finally ceded its western claims to the Continental Congress, and Connecticut and Massachusetts followed suit.

With land disputes settled, Maryland ratified the Articles of Confederation in March 1781. A new national government was finally formed, unifying the rebellious states just as it appeared they would gain their independence. Still, the congress's guarantee that western lands would be "disposed of for the common benefit of the United States" ensured continued conflicts with Indians as the Confederation government took charge.

REVIEW & RELATE	• What values and concerns shaped state governments during the Revolutionary War? • What issues and challenges did the Continental Congress face even after the French joined the patriot side?

Winning the War and the Peace, 1778–1783

From 1778 to 1781, the battlefront in the Revolution moved south and west. The king, who believed that southern colonists' sympathies were more loyalist than patriot, insisted on pursuing a southern strategy. At the same time, patriot conflicts with Britain and its Indian allies intensified along the western frontier. The patriots' eventual victory rested on a combination of superb strategy, their French and Spanish allies, and the continued support of affluent men and women. Still, even after Britain's surrender in October 1781, the war dragged on while peace terms were negotiated. The celebrations following the signing of a peace treaty were themselves tempered by protests among Continental soldiers demanding back pay and by the realization of the new nation's looming problems.

Fighting in the West

While the congress debated the fate of western land claims, battles continued in the Ohio and Mississippi River valleys. The British commander at Fort Michilimackinac on Lake Huron recruited Sioux, Chippewa, and Sauk warriors to attack Spanish forces along the Mississippi, while soldiers at Fort Detroit armed Ottawa, Fox, and Miami warriors to assault American settlers flooding into the Ohio River valley. British forces also moved deeper into this region, establishing a post at Vincennes on the Wabash River.

The response to these British forays was effective, if not well coordinated. In 1778 a patriot surveyor, George Rogers Clark of Virginia, organized an expedition to counter Indian raids in the West and to reinforce Spanish and French allies in the upper Mississippi valley. He fought successfully against British and Indian forces at Kaskaskia and Cahokia on the Mississippi River. Then Clark launched a surprise attack on British forces at Vincennes. Although Detroit remained in British hands, Spanish troops defeated British-allied Indian forces at St. Louis, giving the patriots greater control in the Ohio River valley (Map 6.2).

Patriot General John Sullivan employed the same tactic in central New York, leading a 1779 campaign to wipe out British allies by destroying Mohawk, Seneca, Cayuga, and Onondaga villages. As Mary Jemison, an Irish immigrant captured by Indians in 1755, recalled, "they destroyed every article of the food kind that they could lay their hands on. A part of our corn they burnt, and threw the remainder into the river. They burnt our houses, killed what few cattle and horses they could find, destroyed our fruit trees, and left nothing but the bare soil and timber." Sullivan temporarily ended attacks by Britain's Iroquois allies and disrupted supplies sent out by British forces at Fort Niagara. However, over the next two years, Iroquois warriors and British troops attacked several white settlements in central and eastern New York, killing or capturing dozens of American colonists. In 1782, such retaliatory violence in Ohio led to an atrocity at a Moravian mission. There Pennsylvania militiamen massacred 160 Delaware men, women, and children. They had refused to fight on either side but had assisted patriots as guides and spies.

Battles between Indian nations and American settlers did not end with the American Revolution. For the moment, however, the patriots and their allies had defeated British and Indian efforts to control the Mississippi and Ohio River valleys.

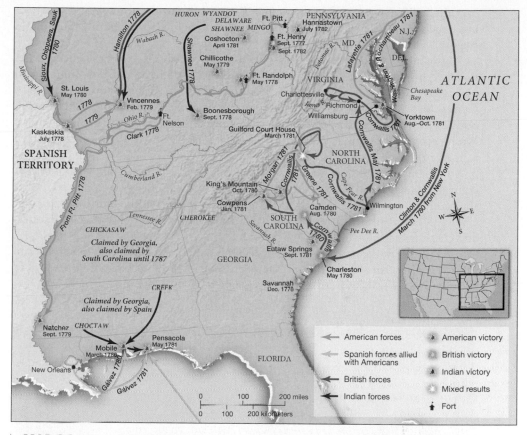

MAP 6.2

The War in the West and the South, 1777–1782 Between 1780 and 1781, major battles between Continental and British troops took place in Virginia and the Carolinas, and the British general Cornwallis finally surrendered at Yorktown, Virginia in October 1781. But patriot forces also battled British troops and their Indian allies from 1777 to 1782 in the Ohio River valley, the lower Mississippi River, and the Gulf coast.

War Rages in the South

Meanwhile British troops sought to regain control of southern states from Georgia to Virginia. British troops captured Savannah, Georgia in 1778 and soon extended their control over the entire state. When General Clinton was called north later that year, he left the southern campaign in the hands of Lord Charles Cornwallis.

In May 1780, General Cornwallis reclaimed Charleston, South Carolina. He then evicted patriots from the city, purged them from the state government, gained military control of the state, and imposed loyalty oaths on all Carolinians able to fight. To aid his efforts, local loyalists organized militias to battle patriots in the interior. Banastre Tarleton led one especially vicious company of loyalists who slaughtered civilians and murdered many who surrendered. In retaliation, patriot planter Thomas Sumter organized 800 men who showed a similar disregard for regular army procedures, raiding largely defenseless loyalist settlements near Hanging Rock, South Carolina in August 1780.

As retaliatory violence erupted in the interior of South Carolina, General Gates marched his Continental troops south to join 2,000 militiamen from Virginia and North Carolina. But his troops were exhausted and short of food, and on August 16 Cornwallis won a smashing victory against the combined patriot forces at Camden, South Carolina (see Map 6.2). Soon after news of Gates's defeat reached General Washington, he heard that Benedict Arnold, commander at West Point, had defected to the British.

Suddenly, British chances for victory seemed more hopeful. Cornwallis was in control of Georgia and South Carolina, and local loyalists were eager to gain control of the southern countryside. Meanwhile Continental soldiers in the North mutinied in early 1780 over enlistment terms and pay. Patriot morale was low, funds were scarce, and civilians were growing weary of the war.

Yet somehow the patriots prevailed. A combination of luck, strong leadership, and French support turned the tide. In October 1780, when Continental hopes looked

"Crossing the Peedee River"   Francis Marion, known as "the Swamp Fox," and his militia waged guerilla war against the British in South Carolina. They wreaked havoc by conducting quick surprise attacks. In this 1850 painting, Marion, a Patriot icon, is crossing the river with horses, soldiers, equipment, and enslaved laborers. He sits on the reddish-brown horse with his uniform visible under his brown cloak.   William T. Raney, Amon Carter Museum, Fort Worth, Texas; 1983126 especially bleak, a group of 800 frontier sharpshooters routed loyalist troops at King's Mountain in South Carolina. The victory kept Cornwallis from advancing into North Carolina and gave the Continentals a chance to regroup.

Shortly after the battle at King's Mountain, Washington sent General Nathanael Greene to replace Gates as head of southern operations. Taking advice from local militia leaders like Daniel Morgan and Francis Marion, Greene divided his limited force into even smaller units. Marion and Morgan each led 300 Continental soldiers into the South Carolina backcountry, picking up hundreds of local militiamen along the way. At the village of Cowpens, Morgan inflicted a devastating defeat on Tarleton's much larger force.

Despite their victory, Continental forces were spread thin and retreated in order to regroup. Cornwallis, enraged at the patriot victory, pursued these Continental forces, but his troops had outrun their cannons, and Greene circled back and attacked them at Guilford Court House. Although Cornwallis eventually forced the far smaller Continental company to withdraw from the battlefield, British troops suffered enormous losses. In August 1781, frustrated at the ease with which patriot forces still found local support in the South, he hunkered down in Yorktown on the Virginia coast and waited for reinforcements from New York.

Washington now coordinated strategy with his French allies. Comte de Rochambeau marched 5,000 troops south from Rhode Island to Virginia as General Lafayette led his troops south along Virginia's eastern shore. At the same time, French naval ships headed north from the West Indies. One unit cut off a British fleet trying to resupply Cornwallis by sea. Another joined up with American privateers to bombard Cornwallis's forces. By mid-October, British supplies had run out, and it was clear that reinforcements would not be forthcoming. On October 19, 1781, the British army admitted defeat.

An Uncertain Peace

The Continental Army had managed the impossible. It had defeated the British army and won the colonies' independence. Yet even with the surrender after the **Battle of Yorktown**, the war continued in fits and starts. Peace negotiations in Paris dragged on as French, Spanish, British, and American representatives sought to settle a host of issues. Meanwhile, British forces challenged Continental troops in and around New York City.

Some Continental soldiers continued to fight, but others focused on the long-festering issue of overdue wages. When the congress decided in June 1783 to discharge the remaining troops without providing back pay, a near mutiny erupted in Pennsylvania. Nearly three hundred soldiers marched on the congress in Philadelphia. Washington sent troops, including Deborah Sampson/Robert Shurtliff, to put down the mutiny. Bloodshed was avoided when the Pennsylvania soldiers agreed to accept half pay and certificates for the remainder. Despite this compromise, the issue of back pay would continue to plague the nation.

Meanwhile patriot representatives in Paris—Benjamin Franklin, John Adams, and John Jay—continued to negotiate peace terms. Rising antiwar sentiment on the British home front forced the government's hand. But the Comte de Vergennes, the French foreign minister, opposed the Americans' republican principles and refused to consider the American delegates as his political equals. Given the importance of the French to the American victory, the congress had instructed its delegates to defer to French wishes. This blocked the American representatives from signing a separate peace with the British.

Eventually, however, U.S. delegates finalized a treaty that secured substantial benefits for the young nation. The United States gained control of all lands south of Canada and north of Louisiana and Florida stretching to the Mississippi River. In addition, the treaty recognized the United States to be "free Sovereign and independent states." Spain signed a separate treaty with Great Britain in which it regained control of Florida. Despite their role in the war, none of the Indian nations that occupied the lands under negotiation were consulted.

When the **Treaty (Peace) of Paris** was finally signed on September 2, 1783, thousands of British troops and their supporters left the colonies for Canada, the West Indies, or England. British soldiers on the western frontier were supposed to be withdrawn at the same time, but they remained for many years and continued to foment hostilities between Indians in the region and U.S. settlers along the frontier.

The evacuation of the British also entailed the exodus of thousands of African Americans who had fought against the patriots. At the end of the war, British officials granted certificates of manumission (freedom) to more than 1,300 men, 900 women, and 700 children. Most of these freed blacks settled in Nova Scotia, where they received small allotments of land from the British, but they generally lacked the resources to make such homesteads profitable. Despite these obstacles, some created a small Afro-Canadian community in Nova Scotia, while others migrated to areas considered more hospitable to black residents, such as Sierra Leone.

A Surprising Victory

Americans had managed to defeat one of the most powerful military forces in the world. That victory resulted from the convergence of many circumstances. Certainly Americans benefited from fighting on their own soil. Their knowledge of the land and its resources as well as earlier experiences fighting against Indians and the French helped prepare them for battles against the British.

Just as important, British troops and officers were far removed from centers of decision making and supplies. Even supplies housed in Canada could not be easily transported the relatively short distance into New York. British commanders were often hesitant to make decisions independently, but awaiting instructions from England proved costly on several occasions, especially since strategists in London often had little sense of conditions in America.

Both sides depended on outsiders for assistance, but here, too, Americans gained the advantage. The British army relied heavily on German mercenaries, Indian allies, and freed blacks to bolster its regular troops. In victory, such "foreign" forces were relatively reliable, but in defeat, many of them chose to look out for their own interests. The patriots meanwhile marched with French and Spanish armies well prepared to challenge British troops and motivated to gain advantages for France and Spain if Britain was defeated.

Perhaps most important, a British victory was nearly impossible without conquering the American colonies one by one. Because a large percentage of colonists supported the patriot cause, British troops had to contend not only with Continental soldiers but also with an aroused citizenry fighting for its independence.

REVIEW & RELATE	• How and why did the Americans win the Revolutionary War? • What uncertainties and challenges did the new nation face in the immediate aftermath of victory?

Conclusion: Legacies of the Revolution

After the approval of the Declaration of Independence, Thomas Hutchinson, the British official who had gained fame during the Stamp Act upheavals in Boston, charged that patriot leaders had "sought independence from the beginning." But the gradual and almost reluctant move from resistance to revolution in the American colonies suggests otherwise. When faced with threats from British troops, a sufficient number of colonists took up arms to create the reality of war, and this surge of hostilities finally gave the advantage to those political leaders urging independence.

The victory over Great Britain won that independence but left the United States confronting difficult problems. Most soldiers simply wanted to return home and reestablish their former lives. But the government's inability to pay back wages and the huge debt the nation owed to private citizens and state and foreign governments hinted at difficult economic times ahead. And these problems affected American Indians and African Americans as well as whites. Using western lands to reward officers and soldiers who had not received full pay intensified conflicts along the new nation's western frontier. Warfare between settlers and Indians west of the Appalachian Mountains, from the Ohio River valley to Georgia, continued for decades. At the same time, slaveowners seeking more fertile fields also expanded into the trans-Appalachian region. By 1800 they had carried tens of thousands of enslaved blacks into Kentucky, Tennessee, and the Mississippi Territory. Separated from families back east, slaves on the frontier engaged in backbreaking labor without the support or camaraderie of the communities left behind.

Although faced with far better opportunities than enslaved laborers, many white soldiers still found the adjustment to postwar life difficult. Like many other soldiers, Deborah Sampson embraced a conventional life after the war. She married a farmer, Benjamin Gannett, and had three children. But times were hard. A decade after she was discharged, Massachusetts finally granted her a small pension for her wartime service. Deborah Gannett earned some money by lecturing on her wartime adventures and received a small federal pension in 1804. Many men waited at least as long to receive any compensation for their wartime service while they struggled to reestablish farms and businesses and pay off debts accrued while fighting for independence.

Political leaders tried to address the concerns of former soldiers and ordinary citizens while they developed a new government. Within a few years of achieving independence, financial distress among small farmers and tensions with Indians on the western frontier intensified concerns about the ability of the confederation government to secure order and prosperity. While some patriots demanded a new political compact to strengthen the national government, others feared replicating British tyranny.

In the decade following the Revolution, leading patriots engaged in heated disagreements over the best means to unify and stabilize the United States. However, key leaders like Thomas Jefferson, Benjamin Franklin, and John Adams were living abroad as ambassadors, strengthening U.S. ties to Britain and France. In 1787 Thomas Paine, too, left for England, where he wrote pamphlets supporting the French Revolution. He eventually moved to France, but his radical political ideas led to his imprisonment there, and he returned to the United States upon his release. Even here, however, Paine was maligned for his attacks on organized religion and private property. Thus he played no part in the intense debates about how to secure the political future of the United States while holding on to the republican impulses that drove Americans to revolution.

Chapter 6 Review

KEY TERMS

Second Continental Congress (p. 130)
Battle of Bunker Hill (p. 130)
Dunmore's Proclamation (p. 131)
Common Sense (p. 132)
Declaration of Independence (p. 132)
loyalist (p. 133)

Battle of Oriskany (p. 137)
Battle of Saratoga (p. 137)
Valley Forge (p. 139)
Articles of Confederation (p. 140)
Battle of Yorktown (p. 147)
Treaty (Peace) of Paris (p. 148)

REVIEW & RELATE

1. What challenges did Washington face when he was given command of the Continental Army?

2. How and why did proponents of independence prevail in the debates that led to the Declaration of Independence?

3. How did colonists choose sides during the Revolutionary War? What factors influenced their decisions?

4. Why would some Indian tribes try to stay neutral during the conflict? Why did most of those who chose sides support the British?

5. How did the patriot forces fare in 1776? How and why did the tide of war turn in 1777?

6. What role did colonial women and foreign men play in the conflict in the early years of the war?

7. What values and concerns shaped state governments during the Revolutionary War?

8. What issues and challenges did the Continental Congress face even after the French joined the patriot side?

9. How and why did the Americans win the Revolutionary War?

10. What uncertainties and challenges did the new nation face in the immediate aftermath of victory?

TIMELINE OF EVENTS

April 19, 1775 • Battles of Lexington and Concord

June 1775 • Continental Congress establishes Continental Army

June 16, 1775 • Battle of Bunker Hill

August 1775 • Representatives of Continental Congress and Iroquois Confederacy meet

November 1775 • Lord Dunmore issues his proclamation

January 1776 • Thomas Paine publishes *Common Sense*

July 4, 1776 • Continental Congress publicly declares independence

July to mid-December 1776 • British forces defeat Continental Army

December 1776–January 1777 • Patriot victories at Trenton and Princeton

October 1777 • Patriot victory at Saratoga

Winter 1777–1778 • Continental Army encamps at Valley Forge

1778 • Articles of Confederation ratified by eight states

February 1778 • France declares alliance with the United States

Summer 1779 • Patriot forces destroy Iroquois villages

1780 • Elizabeth "Mum Bett" Freeman sues for freedom

1780–1781 • Iroquois warriors and British troops attack New York settlements

March 1781 • Articles of Confederation ratified

October 19, 1781 • British surrender at Yorktown, Virginia

September 2, 1783 • Treaty (Peace) of Paris

7

Forging a New Nation
1783–1800

LEARNING OBJECTIVES

After reading this chapter you should be able to:

- Analyze the major threats to the new nation after the Revolution.
- Explain which groups of Americans were marginalized in this period and how they responded to the changes that occurred.
- Describe the chief debates over the Constitution and its ratification.
- Evaluate the ways that the young nation's economic policies affected its relations with European nations abroad and on the U.S. frontier and fostered competing political views.
- Describe how the presidency of John Adams exacerbated differences between Federalists and Democratic-Republicans and led to Thomas Jefferson's election in 1800.

COMPARING AMERICAN HISTORIES

One of six children born to Irish parents in Hopkinton, Massachusetts, Daniel Shays received little formal education. In 1772, age twenty-five, he married, had a child, and settled into farming. But in April 1775, he, his father, and his brother raced toward Concord to meet the British forces. By June, he was among the patriots defending Bunker Hill.

After distinguished service in the Continental Army, Shays purchased a farm in Pelham, Massachusetts in 1780 and hoped to return to a normal life. Instead, economic turmoil roiled the region and the nation. Many farmers had fallen into debt while fighting for independence. They returned to an economic recession and increased taxes as state governments labored to repay wealthy creditors and fund their portion of the federal budget. In western Massachusetts, many farmers faced eviction. Shays kept his farm and represented his town at county conventions that petitioned the state government for economic relief. However, the legislature largely ignored the farmers' concerns.

In 1786, angered by the state's failure to act, armed groups of farmers attacked courthouses throughout western Massachusetts. Although a reluctant leader, Shays headed the largest band of more than a thousand farmer-soldiers. In January 1787, this group headed to the federal arsenal at Springfield, Massachusetts to seize guns and ammunition. The farmers were routed by state militia and pursued by governor James Bowdoin's army. Many rebel leaders were captured; others, including Shays, escaped to Vermont and New York. Four were convicted and two were hanged before Bowdoin granted amnesty to the others in hopes of avoiding further conflict.

This uprising, known as Shays's Rebellion, alarmed many state and national leaders who feared such insurgencies might emerge elsewhere. Among those outraged by the rebels was Alexander Hamilton, a young New York politician. Hamilton was born illegitimate and impoverished in the British West Indies. Orphaned at eleven, he was apprenticed to a firm of merchants that sent him to the American colonies. There Hamilton was drawn into the activities of radical patriots and joined the Continental Army in 1776.

During the war, Hamilton fell in love with Elizabeth Schuyler, who came from a wealthy New York family. They married in December 1780. After the war, Hamilton used military and marital contacts to establish himself as a lawyer and financier in New York City. In 1786, Hamilton was elected to the New York State legislature, where he focused on improving the state's finances, and served as a delegate to a convention on interstate commerce held in Annapolis, Maryland. Hamilton and several other delegates advocated a stronger central government. They pushed through a resolution calling for a second convention "to render the constitution of the Federal Government adequate to the exigencies of the Union."

Although the initial response to the call was lukewarm, the eruption of Shays's Rebellion and the government's financial problems soon convinced many political leaders that change was necessary. Although Hamilton played only a small role in the 1787 convention in Philadelphia, he worked tirelessly for ratification of the Constitution drafted there. When the new federal government was established in 1789, Hamilton became the nation's first secretary of the treasury.

COMPARING THE HISTORIES of Daniel Shays and Alexander Hamilton demonstrates that the patriots may have come together to win the Revolutionary War but that they did not share a common vision of the new nation. Despite the suppression of Shays's Rebellion, the grievances that fueled the uprising persisted and Americans differed significantly over how best to resolve them. By 1787, demand for a stronger central government led to the ratification of a new U.S. Constitution. Hamilton played a leading role in advocating and establishing the new government, particularly by seeking to stabilize and strengthen the national economy. While many political and economic elites applauded his efforts, other national leaders and many ordinary citizens opposed them. These differences, exacerbated by foreign and frontier crises, eventually led to the development of competing political parties and the first contested presidential election in American history.

Financial, Frontier, and Foreign Problems

The United States faced serious financial instability in its formative years. The situation was so desperate that Continental Army officers threatened to march on the confederation congress if they did not receive their pay. Other issues also threatened the emerging nation. Conflicts between settlers and Indians in western areas forced the confederation government to attend more closely to its frontier territories. Meanwhile, Spain closed the port of New Orleans to U.S. trade as individual states struggled to regulate domestic and foreign commerce. Off the coast of North Africa, Barbary pirates attacked U.S. merchant ships. Clearly, diplomatic relations with European powers were crucial but difficult, given America's outstanding war debts and the relative weakness of the confederation government.

Continental Officers Threaten Confederation

As the American Revolution ground to an end, issues of military pay sparked conflict. Uprisings by ordinary soldiers were common but successfully put down. Complaints from Continental officers, however, posed a greater problem. In 1780 they had extracted a promise from the Continental Congress for half pay for life but had received no compensation since. Officers encamped at Newburgh, New York, awaiting a peace treaty, petitioned the confederation government in December 1782 for back pay for themselves and their soldiers, again with no success. By March 1783, most soldiers had returned home without pay, but some five hundred officers remained at Newburgh. Many confederation leaders were sympathetic to the officers' plight and hoped to use pressure from this formidable group to enhance the powers of the congress.

Alexander Hamilton had been pressing state governments to grant the confederation congress a new duty of 5 percent on imported goods, thereby providing the federal government with an independent source of revenue. Perhaps threats of an uprising by officers could convince states like New York to agree to the collection of this import duty. Quietly encouraged by political supporters, dissident officers circulated veiled threats of a military takeover. However, on March 15 the officers were confronted by General George Washington. In an emotional speech, he urged them to respect civilian control of the government. Most officers quickly retreated from their "infamous propositions." At the same time, congressional leaders promised the officers full pay for five years. However, lacking sufficient funds, they could provide only "commutation certificates," promising future payment.

Indians, Land, and the Northwest Ordinance

One anonymous petitioner at Newburgh suggested that the officers move as a group to "some unsettled country" and let the confederation fend for itself. In reality, no such unsettled country existed beyond the thirteen states. Numerous Indian nations and growing numbers of American settlers claimed control of western lands. In 1784 some two hundred Indian leaders from the Iroquois, Shawnee, Creek, Cherokee, and other nations gathered in St. Louis, where they complained to the Spanish governor that the Americans were "extending themselves like a plague of locusts."

Despite the continued presence of British and Spanish troops in the Ohio River valley, the United States hoped to convince Indian nations that it controlled the territory. In October 1784, U.S. commissioners met with Iroquois delegates at Fort Stanwix, New York and demanded land cessions in western New York and the Ohio valley. When the Seneca chief Cornplanter and other leaders refused, the commissioners insisted that "you are a subdued people" and must submit. An exchange of gifts and captives taken during the Revolution finally ensured the deal. Indian leaders not at the meeting disavowed the **Treaty of Fort Stanwix**. But the confederation government insisted it was legal, and New York State began surveying and selling the land. With a similar mix of negotiation and coercion, U.S. commissioners signed treaties at Fort McIntosh, Pennsylvania (1785), and Fort Finney, Ohio (1786), claiming lands held by the Wyandots, Delawares, Shawnees, and others.

As eastern Indians were increasingly pushed into the Ohio River valley, they crowded onto lands already claimed by other nations. Initially, these migrations increased conflict among Indians, but eventually some leaders used this forced intimacy to launch pan-Indian movements against further American encroachment on their land.

Indians and U.S. political leaders did share one concern: the vast numbers of squatters, mainly white men and women, living on land to which they had no legal claim. In fall 1784 George Washington traveled west to survey nearly thirty thousand acres of territory he had been granted as a reward for military service. He found much of it occupied by squatters who refused to acknowledge his ownership. Such flaunting of property rights deepened his concerns about the weaknesses of the confederation government.

The confederation congress was less concerned about individual property rights and more with the refusal of some states to cede the western lands they claimed to federal control. Slowly, between 1783 and 1785, the congress finally persuaded the two remaining states with the largest claims, Virginia and Massachusetts, to relinquish all territory north of the Ohio River (Map 7.1).

To regulate this vast territory, Thomas Jefferson drafted the **Northwest Ordinance** in 1785. It provided that the territory be surveyed and divided into adjoining townships. He hoped to carve nine small states out of the region to enhance the representation of western farmers and to ensure the continued dominance of agrarian views in the national government. The congress revised his proposal, however, stipulating that only three to five states be created from the vast territory and thereby limiting the future clout of western settlers in the federal government.

The population of the territory grew rapidly, with speculators buying up huge tracts of land and selling smaller parcels to eager settlers. In response, congressional leaders modified the Northwest Ordinance in 1787, clarifying the process by which

MAP 7.1

Cessions of Western Land, 1782–1802   Beginning under the Articles of Confederation, political leaders sought to resolve competing state claims to western territory based on colonial charters. The confederation congress and, after ratification of the Constitution, the U.S. Congress gradually persuaded states to cede their claims and create a "national domain," part of which was then organized as the Northwest Territory.

territories could become states. The congress appointed territorial officials and guaranteed residents the basic rights of U.S. citizens. After a territory's population reached 5,000, residents could choose an assembly, but the territorial governor retained the power to veto legislation. When a prospective state reached a population of 60,000, it could apply for admission to the United States. Thus the congress established an orderly system by which territories became states in the Union.

The 1787 ordinance also tried to address concerns about race relations in the region. It encouraged fair treatment of Indian nations but did not include any means of enforcing such treatment and failed to resolve Indian land claims. It also abolished slavery throughout the Northwest Territory but mandated the return of fugitive slaves to their owners to forestall a flood of fugitives.

The 1787 legislation did not address territory south of the Ohio River. As American settlers streamed into areas that became Kentucky and Tennessee, they confronted Creek, Choctaw, and Chickasaw tribes, well supplied with weapons by Spanish traders, as well as Cherokee who had sided with the British during the Revolution. Conflicts there were largely ignored by the national government for the next quarter century.

Depression and Debt

Disputes over western lands were deeply intertwined with the economic difficulties that plagued the new nation. Victory in the Revolution was followed by years of economic depression and mushrooming debt. While the war fueled the demand for domestic goods and ensured high employment, both the demand and the jobs declined in peacetime. International trade was also slow to recover from a decade of disruption. Meanwhile the nation was saddled with a huge war debt. Individuals, the states, and the federal government all viewed western lands as a solution to their problems. Farm families could start over on "unclaimed" land; states could distribute land in lieu of cash to veterans or creditors; and congress could sell land to fund its debts. Yet there was never enough land to meet these conflicting needs, nor did the United States hold secure title to the territory.

Some national leaders, including Hamilton, focused on other ways of repaying the war debt. Fearing that wealthy creditors would lose faith in a nation that could not repay its debts, they urged states to grant the federal government a percentage of import duties as a way to increase its revenue. But states had their own problems. Legislators in Massachusetts and other states passed hard-money laws that required debts to be repaid in gold or silver rather than in paper currency. Affluent creditors favored these measures to ensure repayment in full. But small farmers, including veterans, who had borrowed paper money during the war, now had to repay those loans in hard currency as the money supply shrank. Taxes, too, were rising as states sought to cover the interest on wartime bonds held by wealthy investors.

Failures of American diplomacy weakened the nation's economy further. In 1783 the British Parliament denied the United States the right to trade with the British West Indies. The following year, Spain, seeking leverage over disputed western territories, prohibited U.S. ships from accessing the port of New Orleans. Spain and Great Britain also threatened U.S. sovereignty by conspiring with American citizens on the frontier and promising them protection from Indians. At the same time, British troops remained in forts on America's western frontier and urged Indians to harass settlers there.

REVIEW & RELATE

- What challenges did the new nation face in the immediate aftermath of the Revolutionary War?
- How did farmers, financial leaders, foreign nations, and Indians react to government efforts to address challenges after the Revolution?

On the Political Margins

A young nation, the United States was forced to the political margins in international affairs. At the same time, some groups within the nation were marginalized as well. Small farmers suffered in the postwar period, but they were not alone. Church leaders who had enjoyed government support in the colonial period now had to compete for members and funds. African Americans, whose hopes for freedom had been raised by the Revolution, continued to fight for full-fledged citizenship and an end to slavery. Women, too, faced challenges as they sought to enhance their role in the nation.

Separating Church and State

Government support of churches ended in most states with the establishment of the United States. Anglican churches had long benefited from British support and taxed residents to support their ministry during the Revolution. But in 1786, the Virginia Assembly approved the Statute of Religious Freedom, which made church attendance and support voluntary. Many other states followed Virginia's lead and removed government support for established churches.

Churches that had dominated the various colonies now faced greater competition. Especially in frontier areas, Baptists and Methodists, the latter of which broke off from the Anglican Church in 1784, gained thousands of converts. The Society of Friends, or Quakers, and the Presbyterians also gained new adherents, while Catholics and Jews experienced greater tolerance than in the colonial era. This diversity ensured that no single religious voice or perspective dominated the new nation. Instead, all denominations competed for members, money, and political influence.

Some Protestant churches were also challenged from within by free blacks who sought a greater role in church governance. In 1794 Richard Allen, who had been born a slave, led a small group of Philadelphia blacks in founding the first African American church in the United States. Initially, this African Methodist Episcopal Church remained within the larger Methodist fold. By the early 1800s, however, Allen's church served as the basis for the first independent black denomination.

African Americans Struggle for Rights

It was no accident that the first independent black church was founded in Philadelphia, which attracted large numbers of free blacks after Pennsylvania adopted a gradual emancipation law in 1780. Although the northern states with the largest enslaved populations—New York and New Jersey—did not pass such laws until 1799 and 1804, the free black population increased throughout the region.

Many free blacks were migrants from the South, where tens of thousands of enslaved women and men gained their freedom during or immediately following the Revolution. A few slave owners took Revolutionary ideals to heart and emancipated their slaves following the war. Many others emancipated slaves in their wills. In addition, several states prohibited the importation of slaves from Africa during or immediately following the Revolution. At the same time, however, the enslaved population continued to grow rapidly, and southern legislators soon made it difficult for owners to free their slaves and for free blacks to remain in the region.

The limits on emancipation in the South only nurtured the growth of free black communities in the North, especially in seaport cities like Philadelphia, New York, and New Bedford. Most African Americans focused on finding jobs, supporting families, and securing the freedom of enslaved relatives. Others, like Richard Allen, sought to establish churches, schools, and voluntary societies and claim a political voice. Some northern states, such as New Jersey, granted property-owning blacks the right to vote. Others, such as Pennsylvania, did not specifically exclude them.

Some whites aided blacks in their struggles. The Society of Friends, the only religious denomination to oppose slavery in the colonial period, became more outspoken. By the 1790s, many Friends, also known as Quakers, had freed their slaves and withdrawn from the slave trade. Anthony Benezet, a writer and educator, advocated tirelessly for the abolition of slavery and directed one of several schools for blacks founded by the Society of Friends.

Women Seek Wider Roles

Quaker women as well as men testified against slavery in the 1780s, writing statements on the topic in separate women's meetings. Although few other women experienced such spiritual autonomy, many gained a greater sense of economic and political independence during the Revolution.

Abigail Adams had written her husband John in 1776, "[I]f perticuliar care and attention is not paid to the Laidies we are determined to foment a Rebelion" (see Source 6.8 in chapter 6). While she and other elite women sought a more public voice, only New Jersey granted women—widowed or single and property-owning—the right to vote. The vast majority of women could shape political decisions only by influencing their male relatives and friends. Fortunately, many leaders of the early Republic viewed wives and mothers as necessary to the development of a strong nation. In 1787 Benjamin Rush, in his *Essay on Female Education*, developed a notion of **republican motherhood**. He claimed that women could best shape political ideas and relations by "instructing their sons in principles of liberty and government." To prepare young women for this role, Rush suggested educating them in literature, music, composition, geography, history, and bookkeeping.

Judith Sargent Murray offered a more radical approach to women's education, arguing that "girls should be enabled to procure for themselves the necessaries of life; independence should be placed within their grasp" (see Source 7.2). A few American women in the late eighteenth century did receive broad educations, and some ran successful businesses; wrote plays, poems, and histories; and established urban salons where women and men discussed the issues of the day. In 1789 Massachusetts became the first state to institute free elementary education for all children, and female academies also multiplied in this period. While schooling for affluent girls was often focused on preparing them for domesticity, the daughters of artisans and farmers learned practical skills so they could assist in the family enterprise.

While women's influence was praised in the post-Revolutionary era, state laws rarely expanded women's rights. All states limited women's economic autonomy, although a few allowed married women to enter into business. Divorce was also legalized in many states but was still available only to the wealthy and well connected. Meanwhile women were excluded from juries, legal training, and, with rare exceptions, voting rights.

African American and Indian women lived under even more severe constraints than white women. Most black women were enslaved, and those who were free could

Judith Sargent Stevens, later Murray, c. 1772 Born into a wealthy Massachusetts family, Judith Sargent was allowed to study alongside her brother until she married John Stevens at age 18. In the 1770s, she wrote well-received essays on social and political topics and later promoted women's education and independence. Widowed at 35, she soon married Universalist minister John Murray and continued to publish into her sixties. Terra Foundation for American Art, Chicago/Art Resource, NY

usually find jobs only as domestic servants or agricultural workers. Among Indian nations, years of warfare enhanced men's role as warriors and diplomats while restricting women's political influence. U.S. government officials and Protestant missionaries encouraged Indians to embrace gender roles that mirrored those of Anglo-American culture, further diminishing women's roles. Indian women forced to move west also lost authority tied to their traditional control of land, crops, and households.

Indebted Farmers Fuel Political Crises

Unlike blacks, Indians, and women, many farmers and workingmen could hope to expand their political role in the new nation. Under constitutions written during the Revolution, most state governments broadened the electorate, allowing men with less property (or in some cases no property) to vote and hold office. They also increased representation from western areas.

Still, the economic interests of small farmers and workers diverged sharply from those of wealthy merchants and large landowners. As conflicts between debtors and creditors escalated between 1783 and 1787, state governments came down firmly on the side of the wealthy. But indebted farmers did not give up. They voted, petitioned, and protested to gain more favorable policies. When that failed, debt-ridden farmers in New Hampshire marched on the state capital in September 1786, demanding reform. But they were confronted by cavalry units, who quickly seized and imprisoned their leaders.

Assaults on national authority worried many political leaders far more than farmers' uprisings. The continued efforts of Great Britain and Spain to undercut U.S. sovereignty and ongoing struggles with Indian nations posed especially serious threats. When James Madison and Alexander Hamilton attended the 1785 convention in Annapolis to address problems related to interstate commerce, they discovered that their concerns about the weakness of the confederation were shared by many large landowners, planters, and merchants. Despite these concerns, state legislatures were reluctant to give up the powers conferred on them under the Articles of Confederation.

Still, it was **Shays's Rebellion**, the armed uprising of indebted farmers in western Massachusetts in 1786 to 1787, that crystallized fears among prominent patriots about the limits of the confederation model. On December 26, 1786, Washington wrote Henry Knox to express his concerns about the rebellion and upheavals along the frontier: "If the powers [of the central government] are inadequate, amend or alter them; but do not let us sink into the lowest states of humiliation and contempt." Hamilton agreed, claiming that Shays's Rebellion "marked almost the last stage of national humiliation."

REVIEW & RELATE	• How did America's experience of the Revolutionary War change the lives of African Americans and women? • What do uprisings by farmers and debtors tell us about social and economic divisions in the early Republic?

Reframing the American Government

The delegates who met in Philadelphia in May 1787 did not agree on the best way to reform the government. Some delegates, like James Monroe of Virginia, hoped to strengthen the existing government by amending the Articles of Confederation. Others joined with Madison and Hamilton, who argued for a new governmental structure. Once representatives agreed to draft a new constitution, they still disagreed over questions of representation, the powers of state and national governments, and the limits of popular democracy. Significant compromises had to be reached on these issues to frame a new Constitution.

Other issues arose once the Constitution was ratified and George Washington was inaugurated as president. The government needed to be organized and staffed. A system for levying, collecting, and distributing funds had to be put in place. Diplomatic relations with foreign powers and Indian nations needed to be reestablished. A bill of rights, demanded by many state ratifying conventions, had to be drafted and approved. Finally, both proponents and opponents of the Constitution had to be convinced that this new government could respond to the varied needs of its citizens.

The Constitutional Convention of 1787

The fifty-five delegates who attended the Philadelphia convention were composed of white, educated men of property, mainly lawyers, merchants, and planters.

Only eight had signed the Declaration of Independence eleven years earlier. The elite status of the delegates and the absence of many leading patriots raised concern among those who saw the convention as a threat to the rights of states and of citizens. Not wanting to alarm the public, delegates agreed to meet in secret until they had hammered out a new framework of government.

On May 25, the convention opened, and delegates quickly turned to the key question: Revise the Articles of Confederation or draft an entirely new document? The majority of men came to Philadelphia with the intention of amending the Articles. However, a core group who sought a more powerful central government had met before the convention and drafted a plan to replace the Articles. This **Virginia Plan** proposed a strong centralized state, including a bicameral (two-house) legislature in which representation was to be based on population. Members of the two houses would select the national executive and the national judiciary, and would settle disputes between states. Although most delegates opposed the Virginia Plan, it launched discussions in which strengthening the central government was assumed to be the goal.

Discussions of the Virginia Plan raised another issue that nearly paralyzed the convention: the question of representation. Heated debates pitted large states against small states, even though political interests were not necessarily determined by size. Yet delegates held on to size as the critical issue in determining representation. In mid-June, William Patterson introduced the **New Jersey Plan**, which highlighted the needs of smaller states. In this plan, Congress would consist of only one house, with each state having equal representation.

With few signs of compromise, the convention finally appointed a special committee to hammer out the problem of representation. Their report broke the logjam. Members of the House of Representatives were to be elected by voters in each state; members of the Senate would be appointed by state legislatures. Representation in the House would be determined by population—counted every ten years in a national census—while in the Senate, each state, regardless of size, would have equal representation. While the Senate had more authority than the House in many areas, only the House could introduce funding bills.

Included within this compromise was one of the few direct considerations of slavery at the Philadelphia convention. With little apparent debate, the committee decided that representation in the House of Representatives was to be based on an enumeration of the entire free population and three-fifths of "all other persons," that is, slaves. If delegates had moral scruples about this **three-fifths compromise**, most found them outweighed by the urgency of settling the troublesome question of representation.

Still, slavery was on the minds of delegates. In the same week that the Philadelphia convention tacitly accepted the institution of slavery, the confederation congress in New York City outlawed slavery in the Northwest Territory. News of that decision likely inspired representatives from Georgia and South Carolina to insist that the Constitution protect the slave trade. Delegates in Philadelphia agreed that the importation of slaves would not be interfered with for twenty years. Another provision guaranteed the return of fugitive slaves to their owners. At the same time, northern delegates insisted that the three-fifths formula be used in assessing taxation as well as representation, ensuring that the South paid for the increased size of its congressional delegation with increased taxes.

Two other issues provoked considerable debate in the following weeks. All delegates supported federalism, a system in which states and the central government shared power, but they disagreed over the balance of power between them. They also disagreed over the degree of popular participation in selecting national leaders. The new Constitution increased the powers of the central government significantly. For instance, Congress would now have the right to raise revenue by levying and collecting taxes and tariffs and coining money; raise armies; regulate interstate commerce; settle disputes between the states; establish uniform rules for the naturalization of immigrants; and make treaties with foreign nations and Indians. But Congress could veto state laws only when those laws challenged "the supreme law of the land," and states retained all rights that were not specifically granted to the federal government.

One of the important powers retained by the states was the right to determine who was eligible to vote, but the Constitution regulated the influence eligible voters would have in national elections. Members of the House of Representatives were to be elected directly by popular vote for two-year terms. Senators—two from each state—were to be selected by state legislatures for a term of six years. Selection of the president was even further removed from voters. The president would be selected by an electoral college, and state legislatures would decide how to choose its members. Finally, the federal judicial system was to be wholly removed from popular influence. Justices on the Supreme Court were to be appointed by the president and approved by the Senate. Once approved, they served for life to protect their judgments from the pressure of popular opinion. In addition, the Constitution created a separation of powers between these three branches—congressional, executive, and judicial—that limited the authority of each.

With the final debates concluded, delegates agreed that approval by nine states, rather than all thirteen, would make the Constitution the law of the land. Some delegates sought formal reassurance that the powers granted the federal government would not be abused and urged inclusion of a bill of rights, like the Virginia Declaration of Rights. But weary men eager to finish their business voted down the proposal. On September 17, 1787, the Constitution was approved and sent to the states for ratification.

Americans Battle over Ratification

The confederation congress sent the document to state legislatures and asked them to call conventions to consider ratification. These conventions could not modify the document, but only accept or reject it. Thousands of copies of the Constitution also circulated in newspapers and as broadsides. Pamphleteers, civic leaders, and ministers proclaimed their opinions publicly while ordinary citizens in homes, shops, and taverns debated the wisdom of establishing a stronger central government.

Fairly quickly, two sides emerged. The **Federalists**, who supported ratification, came mainly from urban and commercial backgrounds and lived in towns and cities along the Atlantic coast. They viewed a stronger central government as essential to the economic and political stability of the nation. Their opponents were generally more rural, less wealthy, and more likely to live in interior or frontier regions. Labeled **Antifederalists**, they opposed increasing the powers of the central government.

The pro-Constitution position was presented in a series of editorials that appeared in New York newspapers in 1787 to 1788 and published collectively as *The Federalist Papers*.

The authors James Madison, John Jay, and Alexander Hamilton articulated broad principles embraced by most supporters of the Constitution. Most notably, in *Federalist* No. 10, Madison countered the common wisdom that small units of government were most effective in representing the interests of their citizens and avoiding factionalism. He argued that in large units groups with competing interests had to collaborate and compromise, providing the surest check on the "tyranny of the majority."

Still, Antifederalists worried that a large and powerful central government could lead to tyranny. Small farmers claimed that a strong congress filled with merchants, lawyers, and planters was likely to place the interests of creditors above those of ordinary (and indebted) Americans. Even some wealthy patriots, like Mercy Otis Warren of Boston, feared that the Constitution would empower a few individuals who cared little for the "true interests of the people." And the absence of a bill of rights concerned many Americans.

Federalists worked in each state to soften their critics by persuasive arguments, flattering hospitality, and the promise of a bill of rights once the Constitution was ratified. They gained strength from the quick ratification of the Constitution by Delaware, Pennsylvania, New Jersey, Georgia, and Connecticut by January 1788. Federalists also gained the support of influential newspapers based in eastern cities and tied to commercial interests.

Still, the contest in many states was heated. In Massachusetts, Antifederalists, including leaders of Shays's Rebellion, gained the majority among convention delegates. Federalists worked hard to overcome the objections of their opponents, even drafting a preliminary bill of rights. On February 6, Massachusetts delegates voted 187 to 168 in favor of ratification. Maryland and South Carolina followed in April and May. A month later, New Hampshire Federalists won a close vote, making it the ninth state to ratify the Constitution.

However, two of the most populous and powerful states—New York and Virginia—had not yet ratified. Passionate debates erupted in both ratifying conventions, and Federalists decided it was prudent to wait until these states acted before declaring victory. After promising that a bill of rights would be added quickly, Virginia Federalists finally won the day by a few votes. A month later, New York approved the Constitution by a narrow margin. The divided nature of the votes, and the fact that two states (North Carolina and Rhode Island) had still not ratified, meant that the new government would have to prove itself quickly (Table 7.1).

Organizing the Federal Government

Most political leaders hoped that the partisanship of the ratification battle would fade away with the Constitution approved. The electoral college's unanimous decision to name George Washington the first president and John Adams as vice president helped calm the political turmoil. The two took office in April 1789, launching the new government.

To bring order to his administration, Washington appointed respected men to head three departments—State, War, and Treasury. Thomas Jefferson was named secretary of state; Henry Knox, secretary of war; and Alexander Hamilton, secretary of the treasury. He also appointed Edmund Randolph as attorney general, the first step toward establishing a Department of Justice.

TABLE 7.1   Votes of State-Ratifying Conventions

State	Date	For	Against
Delaware	December 1787	30	0
Pennsylvania	December 1787	46	23
New Jersey	December 1787	38	0
Georgia	January 1788	26	0
Connecticut	January 1788	128	40
Massachusetts	February 1788	187	168
Maryland	April 1788	63	11
South Carolina	May 1788	149	73
New Hampshire	June 1788	57	47
Virginia	June 1788	89	79
New York	July 1788	30	27
North Carolina	November 1788	194	77
Rhode Island	May 1790	34	32

Congress, meanwhile, worked to establish a judicial system. The Constitution called for a Supreme Court but provided no specific guidelines. The Judiciary Act of 1789 established a Supreme Court composed of six justices along with thirteen district courts and three circuit courts to hear cases appealed from the states. Congress also quickly produced a bill of rights. Representative James Madison gathered more than two hundred resolutions passed by state ratifying conventions and honed them down to twelve amendments, which Congress approved and submitted to the states for ratification. In 1791 ten of the amendments were ratified, and these became the **Bill of Rights**. It guaranteed the rights of individuals and states in the face of a powerful central government, including freedom of speech, the press, religion, and the right to petition.

Hamilton Forges an Economic Agenda

The new government's leaders recognized that without a stable economy, the best political structure could falter. Thus Hamilton's appointment as secretary of the treasury was especially significant. In formulating his economic policy, Hamilton's main goal was to establish the nation's credit. Paying down the debt and establishing a national bank would strengthen the United States in the eyes of the world and tie wealthy Americans more firmly to the federal government.

Hamilton advocated funding the national debt at face value and assuming the remaining state debts as part of the national debt. To pay for this policy, he planned to raise revenue through government bonds and new taxes. Hamilton also called for the establishment of a central bank to carry out the financial operations of the United States. In three major reports to Congress—on public credit and a national bank in 1790 and on manufactures in 1791—he laid out a system of state-assisted economic development.

Hamilton's proposal to repay at face value the millions of dollars in securities issued by the confederation was particularly controversial. Thousands of soldiers, farmers, and shopkeepers had been paid with these securities during the war; but needing money in its aftermath, most sold them to speculators for a fraction of their value. These speculators would make enormous profits if the securities were paid off at face value. One of the policy's most ardent critics, Patrick Henry, claimed that Hamilton's policy was intended "to erect, and concentrate, and perpetuate a large monied interest" that would prove "fatal to the existence of American liberty." Despite such passionate opponents, Hamilton gained the support of Washington and other key Federalists.

The federal government's assumption of the remaining state war debts also faced fierce opposition, especially from southern states like Virginia that had already paid off their debt. Hamilton again won his case, though this time only by agreeing to "redeem" (that is, reimburse) states that had repaid their debts. In addition, Hamilton and his supporters had to agree to move the nation's capital from Philadelphia to a more central location along the Potomac River.

Funding the national debt, assuming the remaining state debts, and redeeming state debts already paid would cost $75.6 million (about $1.5 billion today). But Hamilton believed maintaining some debt was useful. He thus proposed establishing a Bank of the United States, funded by $10 million in stock to be sold to private stockholders and the national government. The bank would serve as a repository for federal revenues and grant loans and sell bills of credit to merchants and investors, thereby creating a permanent national debt. This, he argued, would bind investors to the United States, turning the national debt into a "national blessing."

Not everyone agreed. Jefferson and Madison argued vehemently against the Bank of the United States, noting that there was no constitutional sanction for a federal bank. Hamilton fought back, arguing that Congress had the right to make "all Laws which shall be necessary and proper" for carrying out the provisions of the Constitution. Once again, he prevailed. Congress chartered the bank for a period of twenty years, and Washington signed the legislation into law.

The final piece of Hamilton's plan focused on raising revenue. Congress quickly agreed to pass tariffs on a range of imported goods, which generated some $4 million to $5 million annually. Some congressmen viewed these tariffs as a way to protect new industries in the United States, from furniture to shoes. Excise taxes placed on a variety of consumer goods, most notably whiskey, generated another $1 million each year.

Hamilton's financial policies proved enormously successful in stabilizing the American economy, repaying outstanding debts, and tying men of wealth to the new government. The federal bank effectively collected and distributed the nation's resources. Commerce flourished, revenues rose, and confidence revived among foreign and domestic investors. And while the United States remained an agricultural nation, Hamilton's 1791 "Report on the Subject of Manufactures" foreshadowed the growing significance of industry, which gradually lessened U.S. dependence on European nations.

| **REVIEW & RELATE** | • What issues attracted the most intense debate during the drafting and ratification of the Constitution? Why? |
| | • How did Hamilton's policies stabilize the national economy, and why did they nonetheless arouse opposition? |

Years of Crisis, 1792–1796

By 1792 Hamilton had succeeded in implementing his plan for U.S. economic development. Yet as Washington began his second term in the spring of 1793, signs of strain appeared throughout the nation. The French Revolution posed challenges to foreign trade and diplomacy. Migration to the frontier increased, which intensified conflicts between Indians and white settlers and increased hostilities between the United States and Great Britain. Yellow fever swept through Philadelphia and other cities, causing fear and disrupting political and economic life. Finally, the excise tax on whiskey fueled armed protests among frontier farmers. This cluster of crises split the Federalists into warring factions during Washington's second term.

Foreign Trade and Foreign Wars

Jefferson and Madison led the opposition to Hamilton's policies. Their supporters were mainly southern Federalists who envisioned the country's future rooted in agriculture, not the commerce and industry supported by Hamilton and his allies. Jefferson agreed with the Scottish economist Adam Smith that an international division of labor could best provide for the world's people. Americans could supply Europe with food and raw materials in exchange for manufactured goods. When wars in Europe, including a revolution in France, disrupted European agriculture in the 1790s, Jefferson's views were reinforced.

Although trade with Europe remained the most important source of goods and wealth for the United States, some merchants expanded into other parts of the globe. In the mid-1780s, the first American ships reached China, where they traded ginseng root and sea otter pelts for silk, tea, and chinaware. Still, events in Europe had a far greater impact on the United States at the time than those in the Pacific world.

The French Revolution (1789–1799) was especially significant for U.S. politics. The ideals of freedom of speech, assembly, and religion declared in the American Declaration of Independence resonated with French men and women who opposed the tyrannical rule of their King, Louis XVI. The resulting uprising disrupted French agriculture, increasing demand for American wheat, while the efforts of French revolutionaries to institute an egalitarian republic gained support from many Americans. The followers of Jefferson and Madison formed Republican societies, and members adopted the French term *citizen* when addressing each other. At the same time, the importance of workers and farmers among France's revolutionary forces reinforced critiques of the "monied power" that drove Federalist policies.

In late 1792, as French revolutionary leaders began executing thousands of their opponents in the Reign of Terror, wealthy Federalists grew more anxious. The beheading of King Louis XVI horrified them, as did the revolution's condemnation of Christianity. When France declared war against Prussia, Austria, and finally Great Britain, merchants worried about the impact on trade. In response, President Washington proclaimed U.S. neutrality in April 1793, prohibiting Americans from providing support or war materials to any belligerent nations—including France or Great Britain.

While the Neutrality Proclamation limited the shipment of certain items to Europe, Americans simultaneously increased trade with colonies in the British and French West Indies. Indeed, U.S. ships captured much of the lucrative sugar trade.

Americans Trade with China   This painting by a Chinese artist c. 1800 shows the Hongs at Canton, where ships from foreign countries arrived to unload and load goods. the foreign ships were limited to this small area outside Canton's city walls. There each nation established a trading post identified by its national flag and overseen by a Chinese merchant.   © Sotheby's/akg-images

At the same time, farmers in the Chesapeake and Middle Atlantic regions filled the growing demand for wheat in Europe, causing their profits to climb.

Yet these benefits did not bring about a political reconciliation. Although Jefferson condemned the French Reign of Terror, he protested the Neutrality Proclamation by resigning his cabinet post. Tensions escalated when the French envoy to the United States, Edmond Genêt, sought to enlist Americans in the European war. Republican clubs poured out to hear him speak and donated generously to the French cause. But the British also ignored U.S. neutrality. The Royal Navy stopped U.S. ships carrying French sugar and seized more than 250 vessels. The British also supplied Indians in the Ohio River valley with guns and encouraged them to raid U.S. settlements.

More concerned with addressing issues with Britain, President Washington sent John Jay to England to resolve concerns over trade with the British West Indies, compensation for seized American ships, the continued British occupation of frontier forts, and southerners' ongoing demands for reimbursement of slaves evacuated by the British during the Revolution. Jay returned from England in 1794 with a treaty, but it was widely criticized in Congress and the popular press. While securing limited U.S. trading rights in the West Indies, it failed to address British reimbursement for captured cargoes or slaves and granted Britain eighteen months to leave frontier forts. It also demanded that U.S. planters repay British firms for debts accrued during the Revolution. While the **Jay Treaty** was eventually ratified, it remained a source of contention among Federalists.

The Whiskey Rebellion

Despite these foreign crises, it was the effect of Federalist policies on the American frontier that crystallized opposing factions. In the early 1790s, Republican societies from Maine to Georgia demanded the removal of British and Spanish troops from frontier areas, while frontier farmers lashed out at enforcement of the so-called whiskey tax. Many farmers on the frontier grew corn and turned it into whiskey to make it easier to transport and more profitable to sell. The whiskey tax hurt these farmers, hundreds of whom petitioned the federal government for relief.

Western Pennsylvania farmers were particularly incensed and rallied in 1792 and 1793 to protest the tax and those who enforced it. Former North Carolina Regulator Hermon Husband was one of the most outspoken critics of the new excise tax (see American Histories in chapter 5). Adopting tactics from Stamp Act protests and Shays's Rebellion, farmers blocked roads, burned sheriffs in effigy, marched on courthouses, and assaulted tax collectors. Government operations in Philadelphia were largely paralyzed by a yellow fever epidemic from August to November 1793, but the lack of response only fueled the rebels' anger. By 1794 all-out rebellion had erupted.

Washington, Hamilton, and their supporters worried that the rebellion could spread and that it might encourage Indians to rise up as well. Since Spanish and British soldiers were eager to foment trouble along the frontier, the **Whiskey Rebellion** might spark their intervention as well. These Federalists also suspected that pro-French immigrants from Scotland and Ireland helped fuel the insurgency.

Unlike 1786, however, when the federal government had no power to intervene in Shays's Rebellion, Washington now federalized militias from four states, calling up nearly thirteen thousand soldiers to quash the uprising. The army that marched into western Pennsylvania in September 1794 vastly outnumbered the "whiskey rebels" and easily suppressed the uprising. Having gained victory, the federal government prosecuted only two of the leaders, who although convicted were later pardoned by Washington.

Washington proved that the Constitution provided the necessary powers to put down internal threats. Yet in doing so, the administration horrified many Americans who viewed the force used against the farmers as excessive. Jefferson and Madison voiced this outrage from within the Federalist government. The Revolutionary generation had managed to compromise on many issues, from representation and slavery to the balance between federal and state authority. But now Hamilton's economic policies had led to a frontier uprising, and Washington had used a federal army to destroy popular dissent. The Federalists were on the verge of open warfare themselves.

Further Conflicts on the Frontier

In one area, Federalists shared a common concern: the continued threats to U.S. sovereignty by Indian, British, and Spanish forces. In 1790 Congress had passed the Indian Trade and Intercourse Act to regulate Indian-white relations on the frontier and to ensure fair and equitable dealings. However, the act was widely ignored.

The government's failure to stem the flood of settlers into the Ohio and Mississippi River valleys proved costly. In 1790 Little Turtle, a war chief of the Miami nation, gathered a large force of Shawnee, Delaware, Ottawa, Chippewa, Sauk, Fox, and other Indians. This pan-Indian alliance successfully attacked federal troops in the Ohio valley that fall. A year later, the allied Indian warriors defeated a large force under General Arthur St. Clair (Map 7.2). The stunning defeat shocked Americans. In the meantime, Spanish authorities negotiated with Creeks and Cherokees to attack U.S. settlements on the southern frontier.

Washington decided to deal with problems in the Northwest Territory first, sending 2,000 men under the command of General Anthony Wayne into the Ohio frontier. In August 1794, Wayne's forces attacked 1,500 to 2,000 Indians gathered at a British fort. In the Battle of Fallen Timbers, the pan-Indian warriors, led by Little Turtle, suffered

MAP 7.2

American Indians in the Ohio River Valley, c. 1785–1795   Until the mid-eighteenth century, despite conflicts, Indian tribes in the Ohio River valley forged trade and diplomatic relations with various colonial powers. But once the United States established the Northwest Territory in 1785, conflicts between Indians and U.S. settlers and soldiers escalated dramatically. As tribes created pan-Indian alliances, the United States constructed numerous forts in the region.

a bitter defeat. A year later, the warring Indians in the Northwest Territory signed the **Treaty of Greenville**, granting the United States vast tracts of land.

Amid this turmoil, in November 1794, John Jay signed his controversial treaty with Great Britain. With Britain agreeing to withdraw its forces from the U.S. frontier by 1796, the treaty may have helped persuade Indian nations to accept U.S. peace terms at Greenville. Nonetheless, the Jay Treaty's requirement that Americans make "full and complete compensation" to British firms for Revolutionary War debts without the British compensating U.S. merchants or slave owners for their losses nearly led Congress to reject it. In June 1795, however, the Senate finally approved the treaty without a vote to spare. Before Jay's controversial treaty took effect, Spain agreed to negotiate an end to hostilities on the southern frontier of the United States. Envoy Thomas Pinckney negotiated that treaty, which recognized the thirty-first parallel as the boundary between U.S. and Spanish territory in the South and opened the Mississippi River and the port of New Orleans to U.S. shipping. Many Federalists, especially from the West and South, who opposed the Jay Treaty supported the **Pinckney Treaty**, which was ratified in 1796.

REVIEW & RELATE	• How did events overseas shape domestic American politics and frontier policy in the 1790s? • What common concerns underlay the Whiskey Rebellion and Shays's Rebellion? How did the U.S. government deal differently with each?

The First Party System

In September 1796, when President Washington decided not to run again, he offered a Farewell Address in which he warned against the "spirit of party." "It agitates the community with ill-founded jealousies and false alarms," he claimed, and "kindles the animosity of one part against another." By then, however, Jefferson, Madison, and other opponents of Hamilton's economic policies, Washington's assault on the whiskey rebels, and Jay's Treaty had already formed a distinct party. They called themselves **Democratic-Republicans** and supported Jefferson for president. The electoral college, hoping to bring the warring sides together, chose Federalist John Adams as president and Thomas Jefferson as vice president. The two disagreed fundamentally on a wide range of issues, and events soon heightened these divisions. Foreign crises once again fueled political antagonisms, and in this charged atmosphere, Federalists in Congress passed two acts in 1798 relating to aliens (immigrants) and to sedition (activities that promote civil disorder). Instead of resolving tensions, however, these laws exacerbated opposition to Federalist rule. By 1800, partisan differences had crystallized, and the Democratic-Republicans threatened to oust the Federalists from power.

The Adams Presidency

The election of 1796 was the first to be contested by candidates identified with opposing parties. Federalists supported John Adams for president and Thomas

Pinckney for vice president. The Democratic-Republicans chose Thomas Jefferson and Aaron Burr of New York to represent their interests. When the electoral college was established, political parties did not exist and, in fact, were seen as promoting conflict. Thus electors were asked to choose the best individuals to serve, regardless of their views. In 1796 they picked Adams for president and Jefferson for vice president, perhaps hoping to lessen partisan divisions by forcing men of different views to compromise. Instead, the effects of an administration divided against itself were nearly disastrous, and opposing interests became more thoroughly entrenched.

Adams and Jefferson had disagreed on almost every major policy issue during Washington's administration. Not surprisingly, the new president rarely took advice from his vice president. At the same time, Adams retained most of Washington's appointees, who often sought advice from Hamilton, undercutting Adams's authority. Worse still, the new president had poor political instincts and faced numerous challenges.

At first, foreign disputes enhanced the authority of the Adams administration. The Federalists remained pro-British, and French seizures of U.S. ships threatened to provoke war. In 1798 Adams tried to negotiate compensation for the losses suffered by merchants. When an American delegation arrived in Paris, however, three French agents demanded a bribe to initiate talks.

Adams made public secret correspondence from the French agents, whose names were listed only as X, Y, and Z. Americans, including Democratic-Republicans, expressed outrage at this French insult to U.S. integrity, which became known as the **XYZ affair**. Congress quickly approved an embargo act that prohibited trade with France and permitted privateering against French ships. For the next two years, the United States fought an undeclared war with France.

Despite praise for his handling of the XYZ affair, Adams feared dissent from opponents at home and abroad. Consequently, the Federalist majority in Congress passed a series of security acts in 1798. The Alien Act allowed the president to order the imprisonment or deportation of noncitizens and was directed primarily at Irish and Scottish dissenters who criticized the government's pro-British policies. Congress also approved the Naturalization Act, which raised the residency requirement for citizenship from five to fourteen years. Finally, Federalists pushed through the Sedition Act, which outlawed "false, scandalous, or malicious statements against President or Congress." In the following months, nearly two dozen Democratic-Republican editors and legislators were arrested for sedition, and some were fined and imprisoned.

Democratic-Republicans were understandably infuriated by the **Alien and Sedition Acts**. They considered the attack on immigrants an attempt to limit the votes of farmers, artisans, and frontiersmen, who formed the core of their supporters. The Sedition Act threatened Democratic-Republican critics of Federalist policies and the First Amendment's guarantee of free speech. Jefferson and Madison encouraged states to pass resolutions that would counter this violation of the Bill of Rights. Using language drafted by the two Democratic-Republican leaders, legislators passed the **Virginia and Kentucky Resolutions**, which declared the Alien and Sedition Acts "void and of no force." They protested against the "alarming infractions of the Constitution," particularly the freedom of speech that "has been justly deemed, the only effectual guardian of every other right." Virginia even claimed that states had a right to nullify any powers exercised by the federal government that were not explicitly granted to it.

Matthew Lyon and Roger Griswold   This political cartoon depicts a fight on the floor of the House of Representatives in February 1798 between Representatives Matthew Lyon of Vermont, a Democratic-Republican brandishing tongs, and Roger Griswold of Connecticut, a Federalist waving a cane. A newspaper editor and a critic of the Alien and Sedition Acts, Lyon was later convicted of sedition but won reelection while in jail.   Library of Congress, LC-DIG-ppmsca-19356

Although the Alien and Sedition Acts curbed dissent in the short run, they reinforced popular concerns about the power wielded by the Federalists. Combined with the ongoing war with France, continuing disputes over taxes, and relentless partisan denunciations in the press, these acts set the stage for the presidential election of 1800.

The Election of 1800

By 1800 Adams had negotiated a peaceful settlement of U.S. conflicts with France, considering it one of the greatest achievements of his administration. However, other Federalists, including Hamilton, disagreed and continued to seek open warfare and an all-out victory. Thus the Federalists faced the election of 1800 deeply divided. Democratic-Republicans meanwhile united behind Jefferson and portrayed the Federalists as the "new British" tyrants.

For the first time, congressional caucuses selected candidates for each party. The Federalists agreed on Adams and Charles Cotesworth Pinckney of South Carolina. The Democratic-Republicans again chose Jefferson and Burr as their candidates. The campaign was marked by bitter accusations and denunciations.

In the first highly contested presidential election, the different methods states used to record voters' preferences gained more attention. Only five states determined members of the electoral college by popular vote. In the rest, state legislatures appointed electors. Created at a time when political parties were considered injurious to good government, the electoral college was not prepared for the situation it faced in January 1801. Federalist and Democratic-Republican caucuses nominated one candidate for president and one for vice president on party tickets. As a result, Jefferson and Burr received exactly the same number of electoral college votes, and the House of Representatives then had to break the tie. There Burr sought to gain the presidency with the help of Federalist representatives ardently opposed to Jefferson. But Alexander Hamilton stepped in and warned against Burr's leadership. This helped Jefferson emerge victorious, but it also inflamed animosity between Burr and Hamilton that eventually led Burr to kill Hamilton in a duel in 1804.

President Jefferson labeled his election a revolution achieved not "by the sword" but by "the suffrage of the people." The election of 1800 was hardly a popular revolution, given the restrictions on suffrage and the methods of selecting the electoral college. Still, between 1796 and 1800, partisan factions had been transformed into opposing parties, and the United States had managed a peaceful transition from one party to another.

REVIEW & RELATE

- What were the main issues dividing the Federalists and the Democratic-Republicans?
- What do the Alien and Sedition Acts and the election of 1800 tell us about political partisanship in late-eighteenth-century America?

Conclusion: A Young Nation Comes of Age

In the 1780s and 1790s, the United States faced numerous obstacles to securing its place as a nation. Financial hardship, massive debts, hostile Indians, and European diplomacy had to be addressed by a federal government that, under the Articles of Confederation, was relatively weak. By 1787 concerns about national security, fueled by rebellious farmers and frontier conflicts, persuaded some political leaders to advocate a new governmental structure. While it required numerous compromises among groups with competing ideas and interests, the Constitution was drafted and, after a fierce battle in important states, ratified.

With the federal government's power strengthened, George Washington took office as the first American president. His administration sought to enhance U.S. power at home and abroad. Secretary of the treasury Alexander Hamilton proposed a series of measures to stabilize the American economy, pay off Revolutionary War debts, and promote trade and industry. However, these policies also aroused opposition, with leaders like Jefferson and Madison and ordinary farmers and frontiersmen questioning the benefits of Hamilton's economic priorities. Differences over the French Revolution also led to heated debates, while the imposition of an excise tax on whiskey fueled open rebellion on the Pennsylvania frontier. Although a majority of Federalists supported Hamilton and an alliance with Britain, they faced growing opposition from those who advocated agrarian ideals and supported the French Revolution.

While conflicts among Federalists drew many Americans into debates over government programs, large groups remained marginalized or excluded from the political system. Indians, African Americans, and women had little voice in policies that directly affected them. Even white workingmen and farmers found it difficult to influence political priorities and turned to petitions, protests, and even armed uprisings to demonstrate their views.

By 1796, Jefferson and Madison, who led the opposition among Federalists, had formed a separate political party, the Democratic-Republicans. They considered passage of the Alien and Sedition Acts as a direct attack on their supporters, and in 1800 wrested control of Congress and the presidency from the Federalists. Still, this peaceful transition in power boded well for the young United States.

Despite political setbacks, the Federalist legacy remained powerful. Hamilton's policies continued to shape national economic growth, and Federalists retained political power in the Northeast for decades. Meanwhile the benefits that small farmers and frontiersmen like Daniel Shays hoped to gain under Democratic-Republican rule proved largely elusive. Marginalized Americans such as Indians and African Americans also benefited little from the transition to Democratic-Republican leadership. Indeed, the growth of slavery and U.S. westward expansion created new burdens for these groups.

Yet the Democratic-Republican Party would not be seriously challenged for national power until 1824, giving it nearly a quarter century to implement its vision of the United States. Members of this heterogeneous party would now have to learn to compromise with each other if they were going to achieve their goal of limited federal power in an agrarian republic.

Chapter 7 Review

KEY TERMS

Treaty of Fort Stanwix (p. 156)
Northwest Ordinance (p. 156)
republican motherhood (p. 160)
Shays's Rebellion (p. 162)
Virginia Plan (p. 163)
New Jersey Plan (p. 163)
three-fifths compromise (p. 163)
Federalists (p. 164)
Antifederalists (p. 164)
Bill of Rights (p. 166)

Jay Treaty (p. 169)
Whiskey Rebellion (p. 170)
Treaty of Greenville (p. 172)
Pinckney Treaty (p. 172)
Democratic-Republicans (p. 172)
XYZ affair (p. 173)
Alien and Sedition Acts (p. 173)
Virginia and Kentucky Resolutions (p. 173)

REVIEW & RELATE

1. What challenges did the new nation face in the immediate aftermath of the Revolutionary War?

2. How did farmers, financial leaders, foreign nations, and Indians react to government efforts to address challenges after the Revolution?

3. How did America's experience of the Revolutionary War change the lives of African Americans and women?

4. What do uprisings by farmers and debtors tell us about social and economic divisions in the early Republic?

5. What issues attracted the most intense debate during the drafting and ratification of the Constitution? Why?

6. How did Hamilton's policies stabilize the national economy, and why did they nonetheless arouse opposition?

7. How did events overseas shape domestic American politics and frontier policy in the 1790s?

8. What common concerns underlay the Whiskey Rebellion and Shays's Rebellion? How did the U.S. government deal differently with each?

9. What were the main issues dividing the Federalists and the Democratic-Republicans?

10. What do the Alien and Sedition Acts and the election of 1800 tell us about political partisanship in late-eighteenth-century America?

TIMELINE OF EVENTS

1783	• Continental Army officers threaten to mutiny
1784	• Treaty of Fort Stanwix
1785	• Northwest Ordinance passed
	• Annapolis Convention
1786–1787	• Shays's Rebellion
1787	• Constitutional Convention in Philadelphia
	• Northwest Ordinance revised
1788	• U.S. Constitution ratified
1789	• Alexander Hamilton named secretary of the treasury
	• Judiciary Act of 1789 passed
1789–1799	• French Revolution
1790–1794	• Little Turtle leads pan-Indian alliance in the Ohio valley
1791	• Bill of Rights ratified
1793	• Neutrality Proclamation
	• Yellow fever epidemic paralyzes U.S. capital in Philadelphia
1794	• Whiskey Rebellion
	• African Methodist Episcopal Church founded
1796	• Jay Treaty and Pinckney Treaty ratified
	• Democratic-Republican Party established
1798	• Alien and Sedition Acts passed

The Early Republic

1790–1820

LEARNING OBJECTIVES

After reading this chapter you should be able to:

- Analyze the ways that social and cultural leaders worked to craft an American identity and how that was complicated by racial, ethnic, and class differences.
- Interpret how the Democratic-Republican ideal of limiting federal power was transformed by international events, westward expansion, and Supreme Court rulings between 1800 and 1808.
- Explain the ways that technology reshaped the American economy and the lives of distinct groups of Americans.

COMPARING AMERICAN HISTORIES

When Parker Cleaveland graduated from Harvard University in 1799, his parents expected him to pursue a career in medicine, law, or the ministry. Instead, he turned to teaching. In 1805 Cleaveland secured a position in Brunswick, Maine, as professor of mathematics and natural philosophy at Bowdoin College. A year later, he married Martha Bush. Over the next twenty years, the Cleavelands raised eight children on the Maine frontier, entertained visiting scholars, corresponded with families at other colleges, and boarded dozens of students. While Parker taught those students math and science, Martha trained them in manners and morals. The Cleavelands also served as a model of new ideals of companionate marriage, in which husbands and wives shared interests and affection.

Professor Cleaveland believed in using scientific research to benefit society. When Brunswick workers asked him to identify local rocks, Parker began studying geology and chemistry. In 1816 he published his *Elementary*

179

Treatise on Mineralogy and Geology, providing a basic text for students and interested adults. He also lectured throughout New England, displaying mineral samples and performing chemical experiments.

The Cleavelands viewed the Bowdoin College community as a laboratory in which distinctly American values and ideas could be developed and sustained. So, too, did the residents of other college towns. Although less than 1 percent of men in the United States attended universities at the time, frontier colleges were considered important vehicles for bringing virtue— especially the desire to act for the public good—to the far reaches of the early republic. Yet several of these colleges were constructed with the aid of slave labor, and all were built on land bought or confiscated from Indians.

The purchase of the Louisiana Territory by President Thomas Jefferson in 1803 marked a new American frontier and ensured further encroachments on native lands. The territory covered 828,000 square miles and stretched from the Mississippi River to the Rocky Mountains and from New Orleans to present-day Montana. The area was home to tens of thousands of Indian inhabitants.

In 1800 a Hidatsa raiding party swept into a Shoshone village and seized captives, including a girl about twelve years old. The girl, Sacagawea, and her fellow captives were marched hundreds of miles to a Hidatsa-Mandan village on the Missouri River. Eventually Sacagawea was sold to a French trader, Toussaint Charbonneau, along with another young Shoshone woman, and both became his wives.

In November 1804, an expedition led by Meriwether Lewis and William Clark set up winter camp near the Hidatsa village where Sacagawea lived. The U.S. government had sent Lewis and Clark to document flora and fauna in the Louisiana Territory, enhance trade, and explore routes to the Northwest. Charbonneau, who spoke French and Hidatsa, and Sacagawea, who spoke several Indian languages, joined the expedition as interpreters in April 1805.

The only woman in the party, Sacagawea traveled with her infant son strapped to her back. Although no portraits of her exist, her presence was crucial, as Clark noted in his journal: "The Wife of Chabono our interpreter we find reconsiles all the Indians, as to our friendly intentions." Sacagawea did help persuade Indian leaders to assist the expedition, but her extensive knowledge of the terrain and fluency in Indian languages were equally important.

COMPARING THE AMERICAN HISTORIES of Parker Cleaveland and Sacagawea highlights the distinct ways that individuals contributed to the development of the United States and of national identities. Cleaveland gained fame as part of a generation of intellectuals who symbolized Americans' ingenuity. Although Sacagawea was not considered learned, her understanding of Indian languages and western geography was crucial to Lewis and Clark's success. Like many other Americans, Sacagawea and Cleaveland forged new identities as the young nation developed. Still, racial, class, and gender differences made it impossible to create a single American identity. At the same time, Democratic-Republican leaders sought to shape a new national identity by promising to limit federal power and enhance state authority and individual rights. Instead, western expansion, international crises, and Supreme Court decisions all contributed to the growth of federal power.

The Dilemmas of National Identity

In his inaugural address in March 1801, President Thomas Jefferson argued that the vast distance between Europe and the United States was a blessing, allowing Americans to develop their own unique culture and institutions. For many Americans, education offered one means of ensuring a distinctive national identity. Public schools could train American children in republican values, while the wealthiest among them could attend private academies and colleges. Newspapers, sermons, books, magazines, and other printed works could also help forge a common identity among the nation's far-flung citizens. Even the presence of Indians and Africans contributed to art and literature that were uniquely American. In addition, the construction of a new capital city to house the federal government offered a potent symbol of nationhood.

Yet these developments also illuminated political and racial dilemmas in the young nation. The decision to move the U.S. capital south from Philadelphia was prompted by concerns among southern politicians about the power of northern economic and political elites. The very construction of the capital, in which enslaved and free workers labored side by side, highlighted racial and class differences. Educational opportunities differed by race and class as well as by sex. How could a singular notion of American identity be forged in a country where differences of race, class, and sex loomed so large?

Education for a New Nation

The desire to create a specifically American culture began as soon as the Revolution ended. In 1783 Noah Webster, a schoolmaster, declared that "America must be as independent in *literature as in Politics*, as famous for *arts* as for *arms*." To promote his vision, Webster published the *American Spelling Book* (1810) and the *American Dictionary of the English Language* (1828). Webster's books were widely used in the nation's expanding network of schools and academies and led to more standardized spelling and pronunciation of commonly used words.

Before the Revolution, public education for children was widely available in New England and the Middle Atlantic region. In the South, only those who could afford private schooling—perhaps 25 percent of the boys and 10 percent of the girls—received any formal instruction. Few young people enrolled in high school in any part of the colonies. Following the Revolution, state and national leaders proposed ambitious plans for public education, and in 1789 Massachusetts became the first state to demand that each town provide free schools for local children, though attendance policies were decided by the towns.

27

28

Four times 6 *are* 24.
I think I've seen your face before.

Four times 7 *are* 28.
Come with me and see me Skate.

Marmaduke Multiply's Merry Method of Making Minor Mathematics, c. 1815   After Noah Webster introduced his *American Spelling Book* in 1810, math instructors introduced books for young people like the one shown here. The book uses rhymes and colorful illustrations to teach students multiplication tables. More and more educational books for children were published as public schools multiplied in the decades following the Revolution.   Granger Collection, NY

The American colonies boasted nine colleges that provided higher education for young men, including Harvard, Yale, King's College (Columbia), Queen's College (Rutgers), and the College of William and Mary. After independence, many Americans worried that these institutions were tainted by British and aristocratic influences. New colleges based on republican ideals needed to be founded.

Frontier towns offered opportunities for colleges to enrich the community and benefit the nation. The relative isolation of these villages ensured that students would focus on education. And frontier colleges provided opportunities for ethnic and religious groups outside the Anglo-American mainstream—like Scots-Irish Presbyterians—to cement their place in American society. The young nation benefited as well, albeit at the expense of Indians and their lands. For example, the founding of Franklin College in Athens, Georgia encouraged white settlement in the state's interior, an area still largely populated by the Creek and Cherokee.

Frontier colleges were organized as community institutions composed of extended families, where administrators, faculty, and their wives guided students, hosted social events, and hired local workers, including servants and slaves. Women were viewed as exemplars of virtue in the new nation, and professors' wives served as maternal figures for young adults away from home. Families of modest means could send their sons to these less expensive colleges, depending on faculty couples to expand their intellect and provide moral guidance. In some towns, students at local female academies joined college men at chaperoned events to cultivate proper relations between the sexes.

Literary and Cultural Developments

Older universities also contributed to the development of a national identity. A group known as the Hartford Wits, most of them Yale graduates, gave birth to a new literary tradition. Its members identified mainly as Federalists and published paeans to democracy, satires about Shays's Rebellion, and plays about the proper role of the central government in a republican nation. Developments in Europe, particularly liberal social ideas and Romantic beliefs in human perfectibility, also shaped American art, literature, philosophy, and architecture in the early nineteenth century. European Romantics, like the English poet William Wordsworth, the German philosopher Immanuel Kant, and the French painter Eugène Delacroix, challenged Enlightenment ideas of rationality by insisting on the importance of human passion, the mysteries of nature, and the virtues of common folk.

American novelists in the early republic drew on these ideas as they sought to educate readers about virtue. Advances in printing and the manufacture of paper increased the circulation of novels, a literary genre developed in Britain and continental Europe at the turn of the eighteenth century. Improvements in girls' education then produced a growing audience for novels among women. American authors like Susanna Rowson and Charles Brockden Brown placed ordinary women and men in moments of high drama that tested their moral character. Novelists also emphasized new marital ideals, by which husbands and wives became affectionate partners and companions in creating a home and family.

Washington Irving was one of the most well-known literary figures in the early republic. He wrote a series of popular folktales, including "The Legend of Sleepy Hollow" and "Rip Van Winkle," that were published in his *Sketchbook* in 1820. They drew on the Dutch culture of the Hudson valley region and often poked fun at more celebratory tales of early American history. In one serious essay, Irving challenged popular accounts of colonial wars that ignored courageous actions by Indians while applauding white atrocities.

Still, books that glorified the nation's past were also enormously popular. Just as European Romantics emphasized individual, especially heroic, action, so too did America's earliest historical writers. Among the most influential were Mason Weems, author of the *Life of Washington* (1806), a celebratory if fanciful biography, and Mercy Otis Warren, who wrote a three-volume *History of the Revolution* (1805). The influence of American authors increased as residents in both urban and rural areas purchased growing numbers of books.

Artists, too, devoted considerable attention to historical themes, though in the late eighteenth century, they tended more to Enlightenment perspectives. Charles Willson Peale painted Revolutionary generals while serving in the Continental Army and became best known for his portraits of George Washington. Samuel Jennings offered a more radical perspective on the nation's character by incorporating women and African Americans into works like *Liberty Displaying the Arts and Sciences* (1792), but highlighted the importance of learning and rationality. So, too, did William

Bartram, the son of a botanist. He journeyed through the southeastern United States and Florida, and published beautiful, and scientifically accurate, engravings of plants and animals in his *Travels* (1791). Engravings were less expensive than paintings so circulated more widely, and many highlighted national symbols like flags, eagles, and Lady Liberty.

In 1780, the Massachusetts legislature established the American Academy of Arts and Sciences to promote American literature and science. Six years later, Philadelphia's American Philosophical Society created the first national prize for scientific endeavor. Philadelphia was also home to the nation's first medical college, founded at the University of Pennsylvania. Frontier colleges like Bowdoin also promoted new scientific discoveries. As in the arts, American scientists built on developments in continental Europe and Britain but prided themselves on contributing their own expertise.

Religious Renewal

Amid the wave of scientific discoveries, religious leaders sought to renew American spirituality. However, this spiritual renewal was rooted less in established churches and educated ministers than in new religious organizations and popular preachers. Methodist and Baptist churches were especially vital to this development. In 1780, only fifty Methodist churches existed in the United States. By 1820, it was the largest denomination in the nation, followed closely by Baptists. Believing that everyone could gain salvation, the two denominations appealed to small farmers, workers, and the poor as well to women and African Americans. In some cases, women and blacks joined this popular ministry, and a few attracted followings independent of any church. Jemima Wilkinson, a white woman who called herself "the Publick Universal Friend," developed a gender-neutral persona. Proclaiming herself the "Spirit of Light," she preached throughout the Northeast.

In rural and frontier areas, Baptists, Methodists, and Presbyterians organized camp meetings, where a dozen or more preachers, many without formal training, tapped into deep wells of spirituality. The first camp meeting, held in Cane Ridge, Kentucky in 1801, attracted some 10,000 men and women. Whites and blacks, enslaved and free, attended these meetings and were encouraged to dance, shout, sing, and pray. For the next two decades, camp meetings continued to attract large crowds across the South and West.

The Racial Limits of an American Culture

American Indians received significant attention from writers and scientists. White Americans in the early republic often wielded native names and symbols as they sought to create a distinct national identity. Some Americans, including whiskey rebels, followed in the tradition of the Boston Tea Party, dressing as Indians to protest economic and political tyranny (see "The Whiskey Rebellion" in Chapter 7). But more affluent whites also embraced Indian names and symbols. Tammany societies, which promoted patriotism and republicanism in the late eighteenth century, were named after a mythical Delaware chief called Tammend. They attracted large numbers of lawyers, merchants, and skilled artisans.

Poets, too, focused on American Indians. In his 1787 poem "Indian Burying Ground," Philip Freneau offered a sentimental portrait that highlighted the lost heritage of a nearly extinct native culture in New England. The theme of lost cultures and heroic (if still savage) Indians became even more pronounced in American poetry in the following decades. Such sentimental portraits of American Indians were decidedly less popular along the nation's frontier, where Indians continued to fight for their lands and rights.

Sympathetic depictions of Africans and African Americans by white artists and authors appeared less frequently. Most were produced in the North and were intended for the rare patrons who opposed slavery. Typical images of blacks, and of Indians as well, were far more demeaning. When describing Indians in frontier regions, white Americans generally focused on their savagery and their duplicity. Most images of Africans and African Americans exaggerated their perceived physical and intellectual differences from whites, to imply an innate inferiority.

Whether their depictions were realistic, sentimental, or derogatory, Africans, African Americans, and American Indians were almost always presented to the American public through the eyes of whites. Educated blacks like the Reverend Richard Allen of Philadelphia or the Reverend Thomas Paul of Boston wrote mainly for black audiences or corresponded privately with sympathetic whites. Similarly, cultural leaders among American Indians worked mainly within their own nations either to maintain traditional languages and customs or to introduce their people to Anglo-American ideas and beliefs.

The improved educational opportunities available to white Americans generally excluded blacks and Indians. Most southern planters had little desire to teach their slaves to read and write. Even in the North, states did not generally incorporate black children into their plans for public education. African Americans in cities with large free black populations established the most long-lived schools for their race. The Reverend Allen opened a Sunday school for children in 1795 at his African Methodist Episcopal Church, and other free blacks formed literary and debating societies. Still, only a small percentage of African Americans received an education equivalent to that available to whites in the early republic.

U.S. political leaders were more interested in the education of American Indians, but government officials left their schooling to religious groups. Several denominations sent missionaries to the Seneca, Cherokee, and other tribes, and a few successful students were then sent to American colleges to be trained as ministers or teachers for their own people. This was important since few whites bothered to learn Indian languages.

The divergent approaches that whites took to Indian and African American education demonstrated broader assumptions about the two groups. Most white Americans believed that Indians were untamed and uncivilized, but not innately different from Europeans. Africans and African Americans, on the other hand, were assumed to be inferior, and most whites believed that no amount of education could change that. As U.S. frontiers expanded, white Americans considered ways to "civilize" Indians and incorporate them into the nation. But the requirements of slavery made it much more difficult for whites to imagine African Americans as anything more than lowly laborers, despite free blacks who clearly demonstrated otherwise.

Aware of the limited opportunities available in the United States, some African Americans considered the benefits of moving elsewhere. In the late 1780s, the Newport African Union Society in Rhode Island developed a plan to establish a community for American blacks in Africa. Many whites, too, viewed the settlement of blacks in Africa as the only way to solve the nation's racial dilemma.

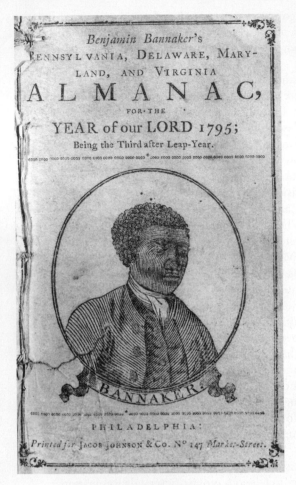

Benjamin Banneker's *Pennsylvania, Delaware, Maryland, and Virginia Almanac*, 1795   Benjamin Banneker (here spelled Bannaker) was a free black from Baltimore County, Maryland. Largely self-educated, he was a talented astronomer who compiled almanacs that included annual calendars, tide charts, lunar and solar observations, and statistical charts. Almanacs were widely used by farmers, sailors, and the general public. Banneker's almanac included his portrait to highlight his achievements as a black man.   Granger, NYC

Over the next three decades, the idea of emigration (as blacks viewed it) or colonization (as whites saw it) received widespread attention. Those who opposed slavery hoped to persuade slave owners to free or sell their human property on the condition that they be shipped to Africa. Others assumed that free blacks could find opportunities in Africa that were not available to them in the United States. Still others simply wanted to rid the nation of its race problem by ridding it of blacks. In 1817 a group of southern slave owners and northern merchants formed the **American Colonization Society (ACS)** to establish colonies of freed slaves and free-born American blacks in Africa. Although some African Americans supported this scheme, northern free blacks generally opposed it, viewing colonization as an effort originating "more immediately from prejudice than philanthropy." Ultimately the plans of the ACS proved impractical. Particularly as cotton production expanded from the 1790s on, few slave owners were willing to emancipate their workers.

A New Capital for a New Nation

The construction of Washington City, the new capital, provided an opportunity to highlight the nation's distinctive culture and identity. But here, again, slavery emerged as a crucial part of that identity. The capital was situated along the Potomac River between Virginia and Maryland, an area where more than 300,000 enslaved workers lived. Between 1792 and 1809, hundreds of enslaved men and a few women were hired out by their owners, who were paid $5 per month for each individual's labor. Enslaved men cleared trees and stumps, built roads, dug trenches, baked bricks, and cut and laid sandstone while enslaved women cooked, did laundry, and nursed the sick and injured. A small number performed skilled labor as carpenters or assistants to stonemasons and surveyors. Some four hundred slaves worked on the Capitol building alone, more than half the workforce.

Free blacks also participated in the development of Washington. Many worked alongside enslaved laborers, but a few held important positions. Benjamin Banneker, for example, a self-taught clock maker, astronomer, and surveyor, was hired as an assistant to the surveyor Major Andrew Ellicott. In 1791 Banneker helped to plot the 100-square-mile site on which the capital was to be built.

African Americans often worked alongside Irish immigrants, whose wages were kept in check by the availability of slave labor. Most workers, regardless of race, faced poor housing, sparse meals, malarial fevers, and limited medical care. Despite these obstacles, in less than a decade, a system of roads was laid out and cleared, the Executive Mansion was built, and the north wing of the Capitol was completed.

More prosperous immigrants and foreign professionals were also involved in creating the U.S. capital. Irish-born James Hoban designed the Executive Mansion. A French engineer developed the plan for the city's streets. A West Indian physician turned architect drew the blueprints for the Capitol building, the construction of which was directed by Englishman Benjamin Latrobe. Perhaps what was most "American" about the new capital was the diverse nationalities and races of those who designed and built it.

Washington's founders envisioned the city as a beacon to the world, proclaiming the advantages of the nation's republican principles. But its location on a slow-moving river and its clay soil left the area hot, humid, and dusty in the summer and muddy and damp in the winter and spring. When John Adams and his administration moved to Washington in June 1800, they considered themselves on the frontiers of civilization. The tree stumps that remained on the mile-long road from the Capitol to the Executive Mansion made it nearly impossible to navigate in a carriage. On rainy days, when roads proved impassable, officials walked or rode horses to work. Many early residents painted Washington in harsh tones. New Hampshire congressional representative Ebenezer Matroon wrote a friend, "If I wished to punish a culprit, I would send him to do penance in this place . . . this swamp—this lonesome dreary swamp, secluded from every delightful or pleasing thing."

Despite its critics, Washington was the seat of federal power and thus played an important role in the social and political worlds of American elites. From January through March, the height of the social season, the wives of congressmen, judges, and other officials created a lively schedule of teas, parties, and balls in the capital city. When Thomas Jefferson became president, he opened the White House to visitors on a regular basis. Yet for all his republican principles, Jefferson moved into the Executive Mansion with a retinue of slaves.

In decades to come, Washington City would become Washington, D.C., a city with broad boulevards decorated with beautiful monuments to the American political experiment. And the Executive Mansion would become the White House, a proud symbol of republican government. Yet Washington was always characterized by wide disparities in wealth, status, and power, which were especially visible when slaves labored in the Executive Mansion's kitchen, laundry, and yard. President Jefferson's efforts to incorporate new territories into the United States only exacerbated these divisions by providing more economic opportunities for planters, investors, and white farmers while ensuring the expansion of slavery and the decimation of American Indians.

**REVIEW &
RELATE**

• How did developments in education, literature, and the arts contribute to the emergence of a distinctly American identity?

• How did blacks and American Indians both contribute to and challenge the predominantly white view of American identity?

Extending Federal Power

Thomas Jefferson, like other Democratic-Republicans, envisioned the United States as a republic composed of small, independent farmers who had little need and less desire for expansive federal power. Despite Jefferson's early efforts to impose this vision on the government, developments in international affairs soon converged with Supreme Court rulings to expand federal power. But Jefferson, too, contributed to this expansion. Imagining the nation's extensive frontiers as a boon to its development, he purchased the Louisiana Territory from France in 1803. The purchase and development of this vast territory increased federal authority. It also raised new questions about the place of Indians and African Americans in a republican society.

A New Administration Faces Challenges

In 1801 Democratic-Republicans worked quickly to implement their vision of limited federal power. Holding the majority in Congress, they repealed the whiskey tax and let the Alien and Sedition Acts expire. Jefferson significantly reduced government expenditures, and immediately set about slashing the national debt, cutting it nearly in half by the end of his second term. Democratic-Republicans also worked to curb the powers granted to the Bank of the United States and the federal court system.

Soon, however, international upheavals forced Jefferson to make fuller use of his presidential powers. The U.S. government had paid tribute to the Barbary States of North Africa during the 1790s to gain protection for American merchant ships. The new president opposed this practice and in 1801 refused to continue the payments. The Barbary pirates quickly resumed their attacks, and Jefferson was forced to send the U.S. Navy and Marine Corps to retaliate. Although a combined American and Arab force did not achieve their objective of capturing Tripoli, the Ottoman viceroy agreed to negotiate a new agreement with the United States. Seeking to avoid all-out war, Congress accepted a treaty with the Barbary States that reduced the tribute payment.

Jefferson had also followed the developing crisis in the West Indies during the 1790s. In 1791 slaves on the sugar-rich island of Saint Domingue launched a revolt against French rule. Inspired in part by the American Declaration of Independence, the **Haitian Revolution** escalated into a complicated conflict in which free people of color, white slave owners, and slaves formed competing alliances with British and Spanish forces as well as with leaders of the French Revolution. Finally, in December 1799, Toussaint L'Ouverture, a military leader and former slave, claimed the presidency of the new Republic of Haiti. But Napoleon Bonaparte seized power in France that same year and sent thousands of troops to reclaim the island. Toussaint was shipped off to France, where he died in prison. Many Haitians fled to the United States, but other Haitian rebels continued the fight.

In the United States, reactions to the revolution were mixed, but southern whites feared that it might incite rebellions among their slaves. In 1800 Gabriel, an enslaved blacksmith in Richmond, Virginia, plotted such a rebellion. Inspired by both the American and Haitian revolutions, supporters rallied around the demand for "Death or Liberty." Gabriel's plan failed when informants betrayed him to authorities. Nonetheless, news of the plot traveled across the South and terrified white residents. Their anxieties were probably heightened when in November 1803, prolonged fighting, yellow fever, and the loss of sixty thousand soldiers forced Napoleon to admit defeat in Haiti. Haiti became the first independent black-led nation in the Americas.

Acquiring the Louisiana Territory

In France's defeat Jefferson saw an opportunity to gain navigation rights on the Mississippi River, which the French controlled. This was a matter of crucial concern to Americans living west of the Appalachian Mountains. Jefferson sent James Monroe to France to offer Napoleon $2 million to ensure Americans the right of navigation and deposit (i.e., offloading cargo from ships) on the Mississippi. To Jefferson's surprise, Napoleon offered instead to sell the entire Louisiana Territory for $15 million.

The president agonized over the constitutionality of this **Louisiana Purchase**. Since the Constitution contained no provisions for buying land from foreign nations, a strict interpretation would prohibit the purchase. In the end, though, the opportunity proved too tempting, and the president finally agreed to buy the Louisiana Territory. Jefferson justified his decision by arguing that the territory would allow for the removal of more Indians from east of the Mississippi River, end European influence in the region, and expand U.S. trade networks. Opponents viewed the purchase as benefiting mainly agrarian interests and suspected Jefferson of trying to offset Federalist power in the Northeast. Neither party seemed especially concerned about the French, Spanish, or native peoples living in the region. They came under U.S. control when the Senate approved the purchase in October 1803. And the acquisition proved popular among ordinary Americans, most of whom focused on the opportunities it offered rather than the expansion of federal power it ensured.

At Jefferson's request, Congress had already appropriated funds for an expedition known as the **Corps of Discovery** to explore territory along the Missouri River. That expedition could now explore much of the Louisiana Territory. The president's personal secretary, Meriwether Lewis, headed the venture and invited fellow Virginian William Clark to serve as co-captain. The two set off with about forty-five men on May 14, 1804. For two years, they traveled thousands of miles up the Missouri River, through the northern plains, over the Rocky Mountains, and beyond the Louisiana Territory to the Pacific coast. Sacagawea and her husband joined them in April 1805 as they headed into the Rocky Mountains. Throughout the expedition, members meticulously recorded observations about local plants and animals as well as Indian residents, providing valuable evidence for young scientists like Parker Cleaveland and fascinating information for ordinary Americans.

Sacagawea was the only Indian to travel as a permanent member of the expedition, but many other native women and men assisted the Corps when it journeyed near their villages. They provided food and lodging for the Corps, hauled baggage up steep mountain trails, and traded food, horses, and other items. The one African

American on the expedition, a slave named York, also helped negotiate trade with local Indians. York, who realized his value as a trader, hunter, and scout, asked Clark for his freedom when the expedition ended in 1806. York did eventually become a free man, but it is not clear whether it was by Clark's choice or York's escape.

Other expeditions followed Lewis and Clark's venture. In 1806 Lieutenant Zebulon Pike led a group to explore the southern portion of the Louisiana Territory (Map 8.1). After traveling from St. Louis to the Rocky Mountains, the expedition entered Mexican territory. In early 1807, Pike and his men were captured by Mexican forces. They were returned to the United States at the Louisiana border that July. Pike had learned a great deal about lands that would eventually become part of the United States and about Mexican desires to overthrow Spanish rule, information that proved valuable over the next two decades.

Early in this series of expeditions, in November 1804, Jefferson easily won reelection as president. His popularity among farmers, already high, increased when Congress reduced the minimum allotment for federal land sales from 320 to 160 acres. This act allowed more farmers to purchase land on their own rather than via

MAP 8.1
Lewis and Clark and Zebulon Pike Expeditions, 1804–1807   The expeditions led by Meriwether Lewis, William Clark, and Zebulon Pike illustrate the vast regions explored in just four years after the U.S. purchase of the Louisiana Territory. Journeying through and beyond the borders of that territory, the explorers gathered information about Indian nations, plants, animals, and the natural terrain even as Comanche and Shoshone nations, with access to horses, transformed the region.

speculators. Yet by the time of Jefferson's second inauguration in March 1805, the president's vision of limiting federal power had been shattered by his own actions and those of the Supreme Court.

The Supreme Court Extends Its Reach

In 1801, just before the Federalist-dominated Congress turned over power to the Democratic-Republicans, it passed a new **Judiciary Act**. The act created six additional circuit courts and sixteen new judgeships, which President Adams filled with Federalist "midnight appointments" before he left office. Jefferson accused the Federalists of having "retired into the judiciary" and worried that "from that battery all the works of Republicanism are to be beaten down and destroyed." Meanwhile John Marshall, chief justice of the United States (1801–1835), insisted that the powers of the Supreme Court must be equal to and balance those of the executive and legislative branches.

One of the first cases to test the Court's authority involved a dispute over President Adams's midnight appointments. Jefferson's secretary of state, James Madison, refused to deliver the appointment papers to several of the appointees, including William Marbury. Marbury and three others sued Madison to receive their commissions. In *Marbury v. Madison* (1803), the Supreme Court ruled that it was not empowered to force the executive branch to give Marbury his commission. But in his decision, Chief Justice Marshall declared that the Supreme Court did have the duty "to say what the law is." He thus asserted a fundamental constitutional power: that the Supreme Court had the authority to decide which federal laws were constitutional. The following year, the Court also claimed the right to rule on the constitutionality of state laws. In doing so, the justices rejected Democratic-Republicans' claim that state legislatures had the power to repudiate federal law. Instead, the Supreme Court declared that federal laws took precedence over state laws.

Over the next dozen years, the Supreme Court continued to assert Federalist principles. In 1810 it insisted that it was the proper and sole arena for determining matters of constitutional interpretation. Then in 1819, the highest court reinforced its loose interpretation of the Constitution's implied powers clause in *McCulloch v. Maryland*. This clause gave the federal government the right to "make all laws which shall be necessary and proper" for carrying out the explicit powers granted to it by the Constitution. Despite Democratic-Republicans' earlier opposition to a national bank, Congress chartered the Second Bank of the United States in 1816, and its branch banks issued notes that circulated widely in local communities. Legislators in Maryland, believing that branch banks had gained excessive power, approved a tax on their operations. Marshall's Court ruled that the establishment of the bank was "necessary and proper" for the functioning of the national government and rejected Maryland's right to tax the branch bank, claiming that "the power to tax involves the power to destroy."

By 1820 the Supreme Court, under the forceful direction of John Marshall, had established the power of judicial review—the authority of the nation's highest court to rule on cases involving states as well as the nation. From the Court's perspective, the judiciary was as important an institution in framing and preserving a national agenda as Congress or the president.

Democratic-Republicans Expand Federal Powers

Although Democratic-Republicans generally opposed Marshall's rulings, they, too, continued to expand federal power. Once again, international developments drove the Jefferson administration's political agenda. By 1805 the security of the United States was threatened by continued conflicts between France and Great Britain. Both sought alliances with the young nation, and both ignored U.S. claims of neutrality. Indeed, each nation sought to punish Americans for trading with the other. Britain's Royal Navy began stopping American ships carrying sugar and molasses from the French West Indies and, between 1802 and 1811, impressed more than eight thousand sailors from such ships, including many American citizens. France claimed a similar right to stop U.S. ships that continued to trade with Great Britain.

Unable to convince foreign powers to recognize U.S. neutrality, Jefferson and Madison pushed for congressional passage of an embargo that they hoped would, like colonial boycotts, force Great Britain's hand. In 1807 Congress passed the **Embargo Act**, which prohibited U.S. ships from leaving their home ports until Britain and France repealed their restrictions on American trade. Although the act kept the United States out of war, it had a devastating impact on national commerce.

New England merchants immediately voiced their outrage, and some began sending goods to Europe via Canada. In response, Congress passed the Force Act, granting extraordinary powers to customs officials to end such smuggling. The economic pain caused by the rapid decline in trade spread well beyond the merchant class. Parker Cleaveland was forced to sell his home to the Bowdoin trustees and become their tenant. Farmers and urban workers as well as southern planters suffered the embargo's effects more directly. Exports nearly stopped, and sailors and dockworkers faced escalating unemployment. With the recession deepening, American concerns about the expansion of federal power reemerged. Congress and the president had not simply regulated international trade; they had brought it to a halt.

Still, despite the failure of the Embargo Act, many Americans viewed Jefferson favorably. He had devoted his adult life to the creation of the United States. He had purchased the Louisiana Territory, opening up vast lands to American exploration and development. This geographical boon encouraged inventors and artisans to pursue ideas that would help the early republic take full advantage of its resources and recover from its current economic plight. Some must have wondered, however, how a Democratic-Republican president had so significantly expanded the power of the federal government.

REVIEW & RELATE	• How did the Federalist-dominated courts and the Democratic-Republican president and Congress each contribute to the expansion of the federal government?
	• How did the purchase of the Louisiana Territory from France and international conflicts with France and Britain shape domestic issues in the late eighteenth and early nineteenth centuries?

Remaking America's Economic Character

As the United States expanded geographically, technological ingenuity became a highly valued commodity. The spread of U.S. settlements into new territories necessitated improved forms of transportation and communication and increased demands for muskets and other weapons to protect the nation's frontier. The growing population also fueled improvements in agriculture and manufacturing to meet demands for clothing, food, and farm equipment. Continued conflicts with Great Britain and France also highlighted the need to develop the nation's natural resources and technological capabilities. Yet even though American ingenuity was widely praised, the daily lives of most Americans changed slowly. And for some, especially enslaved women and men, technological advances only added to their burdens.

U.S. Population Grows and Migrates

Although Democratic-Republicans initially hoped to limit the powers of the national government, the rapid growth of the United States pulled in the opposite direction. An increased population, combined with the exhaustion of farmland along the eastern seaboard, fueled migration to the West as well as the growth of cities. These developments heightened conflicts with Indians and over slavery, but they also encouraged innovations in transportation and communication and improvements in agriculture and manufacturing.

As white Americans encroached more deeply on lands long settled by native peoples, Indian tribes were forced ever westward. As early as 1800, groups like the Shoshone, who originally inhabited the Great Plains, had been forced into the Rocky Mountains by Indians moving into the plains from the Mississippi and Ohio valleys (Map 8.2). Sacagawea must have realized that the expedition she accompanied would only increase pressure on the Shoshone and other nations as white migration escalated.

Although the vast majority of Americans continued to live in rural areas, a growing number moved to cities as eastern farmland lost its fertility and young people sought job opportunities in manufacturing, skilled trades, and service work. Cities were defined at the time as places with 8,000 or more inhabitants, but New York City and Philadelphia both counted more than 100,000 residents by 1810. In New York, immigrants, most of them Irish, made up about 10 percent of the population in 1820 and twice that percentage five years later. At the same time, the number of African Americans in New York City increased to more than 10,000. Cities began to emerge along the nation's frontier as well. After the Louisiana Purchase, New Orleans became a key commercial center while western migration fueled cities like Cincinnati. Even smaller frontier towns, like Rock Island, Illinois, served important functions for migrants traveling west. Trading posts appeared across the Mississippi valley, which eased the migration of thousands headed farther west. They served as sites of exchange between Indians and white Americans and created the foundations for later cities (Table 8.1).

Most Americans who headed west hoped to benefit from the increasingly liberal terms for land offered by the federal government. Yeomen farmers sought sufficient acreage to feed their families and grow some crops for sale. They were eager to settle in western sections of the original thirteen states, in the Ohio River valley, or in newly opened territories along the Missouri and Kansas Rivers. In the South, small farmers had to compete with slave-owning planters who headed west in the early nineteenth century. Migrants to the Mississippi valley also had to contend with a sizable population of Spanish and French residents, as well as Chickasaw and Creek Indians in the South and Shawnee, Chippewa, Sauk, and Fox communities farther north.

MAP 8.2

Indian Land Cessions, 1790–1820   With the ratification of the Constitution, the federal government gained greater control over Indian relations, including land cessions. At the same time, large numbers of white settlers poured into regions west of the Appalachian Mountains. The U.S. government gained most Indian land by purchase or treaty, but these agreements were often the consequence of military victories by the U.S. Army.

   The development of roads and turnpikes hastened the movement of people and the transportation of goods. Frontier farmers wanted to get their produce to eastern markets quickly and cheaply. Before completion of the Lancaster Turnpike in Pennsylvania, it cost as much to carry wheat overland the sixty-two miles to Philadelphia as it did to ship it by sea from Philadelphia to London. Those who lived farther west faced even greater challenges. With the admission of Kentucky (1792), Tennessee (1796), and Ohio (1803) to the Union, demands for congressional support for building transportation routes grew louder. By 1819 five more states had been admitted along the Mississippi River, from Louisiana to Illinois.

TABLE 8.1 Prices at George Davenport's Trading Post, Rock Island, Illinois, c. 1820

Item	Price	Item	Price
Ax	$6.00	Large copper kettle	$30.00
Beaver trap	$8.00	Lead	$0.20 per pound
Black silk handkerchief	$2.00	Lead shot for guns	$1.00 per 5 pounds
Breechcloth	$3.00	Medium copper kettle	$10.00
Bridles	$2.00–$10.00	Muskrat spear	$2.00
Chain for staking down traps	$0.75 per 6 feet	Muskrat trap	$5.00
Combs	$1.00 per pair	Muslin or calico shirt	$3.00
File (for sharpening axes)	$2.00	Ordinary butcher knife	$0.50
Flannel	$1.00 per yard	Sheet iron kettle	$10.00
Flannel mantle	$3.00	Small copper kettle	$3.00
Gunflints	$1.00 per 15	Spurs	$6.00 per pair
Hand-size mirrors	$0.25	Tin kettle	$14.00
Heavy wool cloth	$10.00 per yard	Tomahawk	$1.50
Hoe	$2.00	Trade gun	$20.00–$25.00
Horn of gunpowder	$1.50	Wool blanket	$4.00
Horses	$35.00–$50.00	Wool mantle (short cloak or shawl)	$4.00

Source: Will Leinicke, Marion Lardner, and Ferrel Anderson, *Two Nations, One Land* (Rock Island, IL: Citizens to Preserve Black Hawk Park, 1981).

During Jefferson's administration, secretary of the treasury Albert Gallatin urged Congress to fund roads and canals to enhance the economic development of the nation. He advocated a "great turnpike road" along the Atlantic seaboard from Maine to Georgia as well as roads to connect the four main rivers that flowed from the Appalachians to the Atlantic Ocean. Although traditionally such projects were funded by the states, in 1815 Congress approved funds for a **National Road** from western Maryland through southwestern Pennsylvania to Wheeling, West Virginia. This so-called Cumberland Road was completed in 1818 and later extended into Ohio and Illinois.

Carrying people and goods by water remained faster and cheaper than transporting them over land, but rivers ran mainly north and south. In addition, although loads could be delivered quickly downstream, the return voyage was long and slow. While politicians advocated the construction of canals along east-west routes to link river systems, inventors and mechanics focused on building boats powered by steam to overcome the problems of sending goods upriver.

In 1804 Oliver Evans, a machinist in Philadelphia, invented a high-pressure steam engine attached to a dredge that cleaned the silt around the docks in Philadelphia harbor. He had insufficient funds, however, to pursue work on a steam-powered boat. Robert Fulton, a New Yorker, improved on Evans's efforts, using the low-pressure steam engine developed in England. In 1807 Fulton launched the first successful steamboat, the *Clermont*, which traveled some 150 miles up the Hudson River from New York City to Albany in only thirty-two hours. The powerful Mississippi River proved a greater challenge, but by combining Evans's high-pressure steam engine with a flat-bottom hull that avoided the river's sandbars, mechanics who worked along the frontier improved Fulton's design and launched the steamboat era in the West.

Technology Reshapes Agriculture and Industry

Advances in agricultural and industrial technology paralleled the development of roads and steamboats. And new inventions spurred others, inducing a **multiplier effect** that inspired additional dramatic changes. Two inventions in particular—the cotton gin and the spinning machine—transformed the deeply intertwined realms of southern agriculture and northern industry.

American developments were closely tied to the earlier rise of industry in Great Britain. By the 1770s, British manufacturers had built spinning mills in which steam-powered machines spun raw cotton into yarn. Eager to maintain their monopoly on industrial technology, the British made it illegal for engineers to emigrate. They could not stop everyone who worked in a cotton mill, however, from leaving. At age fourteen, Samuel Slater was hired as an apprentice in an English mill that used a yarn-spinning machine designed by Richard Arkwright. Slater was promoted to supervisor of the factory but in 1789, at age twenty-one, he emigrated to America, seeking greater opportunities. While working in New York City, he learned that Moses Brown, a wealthy Rhode Island merchant, was eager to develop a machine like Arkwright's. Funded by Rhode Island investors and assisted by local craftsmen, Slater designed and built a spinning mill in Pawtucket.

The mill opened in December 1790 and began producing yarn, which was then woven into cloth in private shops and homes. By 1815 a series of cotton mills dotted the Pawtucket River. These factories offered workers, most of whom were the wives and children of farmers, a steady income, and they ensured employment for weavers in the countryside. They also increased the demand for cotton in New England just as British manufacturers sought new sources of the crop as well.

Ensuring a steady supply of cotton required another technological innovation, this one created by Eli Whitney. After graduating from Yale, Whitney agreed to serve as a private tutor for a planter family in South Carolina. On the ship carrying him south, Whitney met the widow Catherine Greene, who invited him to stay at her Mulberry Plantation near Savannah, Georgia. There local planters complained to him about the difficulty of making a profit on cotton. Long-staple cotton, grown in the Sea Islands, yielded enormous profits, but the soil in most of the South could sustain only the short-staple variety, which required hours of intensive labor to separate its sticky green seeds from the cotton fiber.

In 1793, in as little as ten days, Eli Whitney built a machine that could speed the process of deseeding short-staple cotton. Using mesh screens, rollers, and wire brushes, Whitney's **cotton gin** could clean as much cotton fiber in one hour as several workers could clean in a day. Recognizing the gin's value, Whitney received a U.S. patent, but because the machine was easy to duplicate, he never profited from his invention.

Fortunately, Whitney had other ideas that proved more profitable. In June 1798, amid U.S. fears of a war with France, the U.S. government granted him an extraordinary contract to produce 4,000 rifles in eighteen months. Adapting the plan of Honoré Blanc, a French mechanic who devised a musket with interchangeable parts, Whitney demonstrated the potential for using machines to produce various parts of a musket, which could then be assembled in mass quantities. With Jefferson's enthusiastic support, the federal government extended Whitney's contract, and by 1809 his New Haven factory was turning out 7,500 guns annually. Whitney's factory became a model for the **American system of manufacturing**, in which water-powered machinery and the division of production into several small tasks allowed less skilled workers to produce mass quantities of a particular item. Moreover, the factories developed by Whitney and Slater became training grounds for younger mechanics and inventors who devised improvements in machinery or set out to solve new technological puzzles. Their efforts also transformed the lives of generations of workers—enslaved and free—who planted and picked the cotton, spun the yarn, wove the cloth, and sewed the clothes that cotton gins and spinning mills made possible.

Transforming Domestic Production

Slater and Whitney were among the most influential American inventors, but both required the assistance and collaboration of other inventors, machinists, and artisans to implement their ideas. The achievement of these enterprising individuals was seen by many Americans as part of a larger spirit of inventiveness and technological ingenuity that characterized U.S. identity. Although many Americans built on foreign ideas and models, a cascade of inventions did appear in the United States between 1790 and 1820.

Cotton gins and steam engines, steamboats and interchangeable parts, gristmills and spinning mills, clocks and woodworking lathes—each of these items and processes was improved over time and led to myriad other inventions. For instance, in 1811 Francis Cabot invented a power loom for weaving, a necessary step once spinning mills began producing more yarn than hand weavers could handle. Eventually clocks would be used to routinize the labor of workers in those mills so that they all arrived, ate lunch, and left at the same time.

Despite these rapid technological advances, the changes that occurred in the early nineteenth century were more evolutionary than revolutionary. Most political leaders and social commentators viewed gradual improvement as a blessing. For many Americans, the ideal situation consisted of either small mills scattered through the countryside or household enterprises that could supply neighbors with finer cloth, wool cards, sturdier chairs, or other items that improved household comfort and productivity.

The importance of domestic manufacturing increased after passage of the Embargo Act as imports of cloth and other items fell dramatically. Small factories, like those along the Pawtucket River, increased their output, and so did ordinary housewives. Blacksmiths, carpenters, and wheelwrights busily repaired and improved the spindles, looms, and other equipment that allowed family members to produce more and better cloth from wool, flax, and cotton. These developments allowed some Americans, especially in towns and cities, to achieve a middling status between poorer laborers and wealthier elites. In this middling sector of society, new ideas about companionate

The Cotton Gin, 1793
This colored lithograph by an anonymous American artist shows Eli Whitney's cotton gin at the center of complex transactions. Enslaved women and men haul and gin cotton. Meanwhile the planter appears to be bargaining with a cotton factor, or agent, who likely wants to purchase his crop for a northern manufacturer.
Private Collection/Peter Newark American Pictures/Bridgeman Images

marriage, which emphasized mutual obligations, may have encouraged husbands and wives to work more closely in domestic enterprises. While husbands generally carried out the heavier or more skilled parts of home manufacturing, like weaving, wives spun yarn and sewed together sections of cloth into finished goods.

At the same time, daughters, neighbors, and servants remained critical to the production of household items. In early nineteenth-century Hallowell, Maine, Martha Ballard labored alongside her daughters and a niece, producing cloth and food for domestic consumption, while she supplemented her husband's income as a surveyor by working as a midwife. Yet older forms of mutuality also continued, with neighbors sharing tools and equipment and those with specialized skills assisting neighbors in exchange for items they needed. Perhaps young couples imagined themselves embarking on more egalitarian marriages than those of their parents, but most still needed wider networks of support.

In wealthy households north and south, servants and slaves took on a greater share of domestic labor in the late eighteenth and early nineteenth centuries. Most female servants in the North were young and unmarried. Some arrived with children in tow or became pregnant while on the job, a mark of the rising rate of out-of-wedlock births following the Revolution. Meanwhile in the South, if household slaves became pregnant their children added to the owner's labor supply. Moreover, on larger plantations, owners increasingly assigned a few enslaved women to spin, cook, wash clothes, make candles, and wait on table. Plantation mistresses might also hire the wives of small farmers and landless laborers to spin cotton into yarn, weave yarn into cloth, and sew clothing for slaves and children. While mistresses in both regions still engaged in household production, they expanded their roles as domestic managers.

However, most Americans at the turn of the nineteenth century continued to live on family farms, to produce or trade locally to meet their needs, and to use techniques handed down for generations. Yet by 1820 their lives, like those of wealthier Americans, were transformed by the expanding market economy, which over the next twenty years would inspire a market revolution. Gradually, more and more families would sew clothes with machine-spun thread made from cotton ginned in the American South, work their fields with newly invented cast-iron plows, and vary their diet by adding items shipped from other regions by steamboat.

Technology, Cotton, and Slaves

Some of the most dramatic technological changes occurred in agriculture, and none was more significant than the cotton gin, which led to the vast expansion of agricultural production and slavery in the South. This in turn fueled regional specialization, ensuring that residents in one area of the nation—the North, South, or West—depended on those in other areas. Southern planters relied on a growing demand for cotton from northern merchants and manufacturers. At the same time, planters, merchants, manufacturers, and factory workers became more dependent on western farmers to produce grain and livestock to feed the nation.

As cotton gins spread across the South, cotton and slavery expanded into the interior of many southern states as well as into the lower Mississippi valley. While rice and sugar were also produced in the South, cotton quickly became the most important crop. In 1790 southern farms and plantations produced about 3,000 bales of cotton, each weighing about 300 pounds. By 1820, with the aid of the cotton gin, the South produced more than 330,000 bales annually (Table 8.2). For southern blacks, increased production meant increased burdens. Because seeds could be separated from raw cotton with much greater efficiency, farmers could plant vastly larger quantities of the crop. Although family members, neighbors, and hired hands performed this work on small farms with only a few or no slaves, wealthy planters, with perhaps a dozen slaves, took advantage of rising cotton prices in the early eighteenth century to purchase more slaves.

The dramatic increase in the amount of cotton planted and harvested each year was paralleled by a jump in the size of the slave population. Thus, even as northern states began to abolish the institution, southern planters significantly increased the number of slaves they held. In 1790 there were fewer than 700,000 slaves in the United States. By 1820 there were nearly 1.5 million. Despite this population increase, growing competition for field hands drove up the price of slaves, which roughly doubled between 1795 and 1805.

Although the international slave trade was banned in the United States in 1808, some planters smuggled in women and men from Africa and the Caribbean. Most planters, however, depended on enslaved women to bear more children, increasing the size of their labor force through natural reproduction. In addition, planters in the Deep

TABLE 8.2   Growth of Cotton Production in the United States, 1790–1830

Year	Production in Bales
1790	3,135
1795	16,719
1800	73,145
1805	146,290
1810	177,638
1815	208,986
1820	334,378
1825	532,915
1830	731,452

Source: Lewis Cecil Gray, *History of Agriculture in the Southern United States to 1860,* vol. 2 (Gloucester, MA: Peter Smith, 1958).

South—from Georgia and the Carolinas west to Louisiana—began buying slaves from farmers in Maryland and Virginia, where cotton and slavery were less profitable. Expanding slave markets in New Orleans and Charleston marked the continued importance of this domestic or internal slave trade as cotton moved west.

In the early nineteenth century, most white southerners believed that there was enough land to go around. And the rising price of cotton allowed small farmers to imagine they would someday be planters. Some southern Indians also placed their hopes in cotton. Cherokee and Creek Indians cultivated the crop, even purchasing black slaves to increase production. Some Indian villages now welcomed ministers to their communities, hoping that embracing white culture might allow them to retain their current lands. Yet other native residents foresaw the increased pressure for land that cotton cultivation produced and organized to defend themselves from whites' invasion. Regardless of the policies adopted by Indians, cotton and slavery expanded rapidly into Cherokee- and Creek-controlled lands in the interior of Georgia and South Carolina. And the admission of the states of Louisiana, Mississippi, and Alabama between 1812 and 1819 marked the rapid spread of southern agriculture farther west.

Enslaved men and women played critical roles in the South's geographical expansion. Without their labor, neither cotton nor sugar could have become mainstays of the South's economy. The heavy work of carving out new plantations led most planters to select young slave men and women to move west, breaking apart families in the process. Some slaves resisted their removal and, if forced to go, used their role in the labor process to limit owners' control. Slaves resisted by working slowly, breaking tools, and feigning illness or injury. Other enslaved women and men hid out temporarily as a respite from brutal work regimes or harsh punishments. Still others ran to areas controlled by Indians, hoping for better treatment, or to regions where slavery was no longer legal.

Yet given the power and resources wielded by whites, most slaves had to find ways to improve their lives within the system of bondage. The end of the international slave trade helped blacks in this regard since planters had to depend more on natural reproduction to increase their labor supply. To ensure that slaves lived longer and healthier lives, planters were forced to provide better food, shelter, and clothing. Some slaves gained leverage to fish, hunt, or maintain small gardens to improve their diet. With the birth of more children, southern blacks also developed more extensive kinship networks, which often allowed other family members to care for children if their parents were compelled to move west. Enslavement was still brutal, but slaves made small gains that improved their chances of survival.

To find release from the oppressive burdens of daily life, southern slaves not only joined the camp meetings and religious revivals that burned across the southern frontier in the late eighteenth and early nineteenth century but also established their own religious ceremonies. These were often held in the woods or swamps at night, away from the prying eyes of planters and overseers.

Evangelical religion, combined with revolutionary ideals promoted in the United States and Haiti, proved a potent mix, and planters rarely lost sight of the potential dangers this posed to the system of bondage. Outright rebellions occurred only rarely, yet victory in Haiti and Gabriel's conspiracy in Virginia reminded slaves and owners alike that uprisings were possible. Clearly, the power of new American identities could not be separated from the dangers embedded in the nation's oppressive racial history.

REVIEW & RELATE

- How did new inventions and infrastructure improvements contribute to the development of the American economy?
- Why did slavery expand and become more deeply entrenched in southern society in the early nineteenth century? What fears did this reinforce?

Conclusion: New Identities and New Challenges

The geographical and economic expansion that marked the period from 1790 to 1820 inspired scientific and technological advances as well as literary and artistic tributes to a distinctly American identity. For young ambitious men like Parker Cleaveland, Eli Whitney, Washington Irving, and Meriwether Lewis, the opportunities that opened in education, science, literature, and exploration offered possibilities for fame and financial success. While Whitney, Irving, and Lewis traveled widely, Cleaveland remained a professor of mathematics, mineralogy, and chemistry at Bowdoin, dying in Brunswick, Maine in 1858.

Lewis's efforts to open up the Louisiana Territory transformed the lives of many Americans. Along with the construction of roads, the invention of steamboats, and the introduction of iron plows, his Corps of Discovery opened up new lands for farming and also fueled the rise of western cities. Many white families sought fertile land, abundant wildlife, or opportunities for trade on the frontier. Yet these families often had to purchase land from speculators or compete with wealthy planters. And those who carved out farms might face Indians angered by the constant encroachment of white Americans on their lands.

New opportunities also appeared in eastern towns and cities as investors, inventors, and skilled artisans established factories and improved transportation. White women of middling or elite status could attend female academies, enter marriages based on ideals of companionship and mutual responsibilities, purchase rather than make cotton thread and cloth, and retain servants to perform the heaviest work. Yet these changes occurred gradually and unevenly. And while poorer white women might more easily find jobs in cotton mills or as servants, the pay was low and the hours long.

Transformations in white society introduced even more difficult challenges for African Americans. Despite the introduction of gradual emancipation in the North and the end of the international slave trade, slavery continued to grow. The invention of the cotton gin ensured the expansion of cotton cultivation into new areas, and many slaves were forced to move west and leave family and friends behind. Enslaved women and men honed means of survival and resistance, but few could imagine a revolution like the one that took place in Haiti.

At the same time, all along the expanding U.S. frontier, American Indians faced continued pressure to leave their lands, embrace white culture, or both. In 1810 Sacagawea, Charbonneau, and their son Baptiste apparently traveled to St. Louis at the invitation of William Clark, who offered to pay for Baptiste's schooling. Sacagawea left Baptiste in Clark's care, and it is not clear whether she ever saw her son again. William Clark wrote "Se car ja we au Dead" on the cover of his cash book for 1825–1828, suggesting that she died during those years. By then, the Shoshone and Hidatsa were facing the onslaught of white settlement. They, along with Indians living in areas like Georgia, the Carolinas, and Tennessee, continued to resist U.S. expansion and struggled to control the embattled frontier.

Indeed, the United States remained embattled throughout the early years of the republic. From 1790 to 1820, Great Britain, France, and the Barbary States of North Africa constantly challenged U.S. sovereignty from abroad while debates over slavery and conflicts over Indian lands multiplied at home. Moreover, as federal power expanded under Democratic-Republican rule, some Americans continued to worry about protecting the rights of states and of individuals. The American identities forged in the early republic would be continually tested as new challenges emerged and older conflicts intensified in the following decades.

Chapter 8 Review

KEY TERMS

American Colonization Society
   (ACS) (p. 186)
Haitian Revolution (p. 188)
Louisiana Purchase (p. 189)
Corps of Discovery (p. 189)
Judiciary Act (p. 191)
Marbury v. Madison (p. 191)

McCulloch v. Maryland (p. 191)
Embargo Act (p. 192)
National Road (p. 195)
multiplier effect (p. 196)
cotton gin (p. 196)
American system of
   manufacturing (p. 197)

REVIEW & RELATE

1. How did developments in education, literature, and the arts contribute to the emergence of a distinctly American identity?

2. How did blacks and American Indians both contribute to and challenge the predominantly white view of American identity?

3. How did the Federalist-dominated courts and the Democratic-Republican president and Congress each contribute to the expansion of the federal government?

4. How did the purchase of the Louisiana Territory from France and international conflicts with France and Britain shape domestic issues in the late eighteenth and early nineteenth centuries?

5. How did new inventions and infrastructure improvements contribute to the development of the American economy?

6. Why did slavery expand and become more deeply entrenched in southern society in the early nineteenth century? What fears did this reinforce?

TIMELINE OF EVENTS

1789
- Massachusetts institutes free public elementary education

1790
- Samuel Slater's spinning mill opens

1790–1820
- Cotton production in the South increases from 3,000 to 330,000 bales annually
- U.S. slave population rises from 700,000 to 1.5 million

1791–1803
- Haitian Revolution

1792–1809
- New capital of Washington City constructed

1793
- Eli Whitney invents cotton gin

1801
- Judiciary Act
- U.S. forces challenge Barbary pirates
- Thousands attend camp meeting in Cane Ridge, Kentucky

1803
- Louisiana Purchase
- *Marbury v. Madison*

1804–1806
- Corps of Discovery explores Louisiana Territory and Pacific Northwest

1807
- Robert Fulton launches first successful steamboat
- Embargo Act

1810
- Population of New York and Philadelphia each exceeds 100,000

1817
- American Colonization Society founded

1819
- *McCulloch v. Maryland*

1820
- Washington Irving publishes *Sketchbook*

1828
- Noah Webster publishes *American Dictionary of the English Language*

Defending and Redefining the Nation

1809–1832

LEARNING OBJECTIVES

After reading this chapter you should be able to:

- Analyze the intertwined effects of conflicts on the frontier and with Britain and on U.S. federal policies and the lives of white and Indian Americans.

- Describe the role of state and federal governments in the nation's expansion and how expansion affected relations among increasingly distinct regions.

- Evaluate how the panic of 1819 and the Missouri Compromise affected and were affected by the nation's economic expansion and political divisions.

- Discuss how expanded voting rights for white working men, new racial restrictions, and continued debates over federal power led to political realignment.

- Explain the challenges that President Jackson faced in implementing federal policies on the tariff, the national bank, and the removal of the Cherokee.

COMPARING AMERICAN HISTORIES

Dolley Payne was raised on a Virginia plantation. But her Quaker parents, moved by the Society of Friends' growing antislavery sentiment, decided to free their slaves. In 1783, when Dolley was fifteen, the Paynes moved to Philadelphia. There, Dolley's father suffered heavy economic losses, and Dolley lost her first husband and her younger son to yellow fever. In 1794 the young widow met and married Virginia congressman James Madison. When the newly elected president Thomas Jefferson appointed James secretary of state in 1801, the couple moved to the new capital city of Washington.

205

Since Jefferson and his vice president, Aaron Burr, were widowers, Dolley Madison served as hostess for White House affairs. When James Madison succeeded Jefferson as president in 1809, he, too, depended on his wife's social skills and networks. Dolley held lively informal receptions to which she invited politicians, diplomats, cabinet officers, and their wives. These social events helped bridge the ideological differences that continued to divide Congress and proved crucial in creating a unified front when Congress declared war on Great Britain in 1812.

During the War of 1812, British forces attacked Washington City and burned the Executive Mansion, now called the White House. With the president away, his wife was left to secure important state papers, emerging as a symbol of national courage at a critical moment in the conflict. When peace came the following year, Dolley Madison quickly reestablished a busy social calendar to help mend conflicts that had erupted during the war.

In 1817, at the end of the president's second term, the Madisons left Washington just as a young trader named John Ross entered the political arena. Born in 1790 in the Cherokee nation, John (also known as Guwisguwi) was the son of a Scottish trader and his wife, who was both Cherokee and Scottish. John Ross was raised in an Anglo-Indian world in eastern Tennessee, where he played with Cherokee children and attended tribal events but was educated by private tutors and in Protestant missionary schools. At age twenty, Ross was appointed as a U.S. Indian agent among the Cherokee and during the War of 1812 served as an adjutant (or administrative assistant) in a Cherokee regiment.

After the war, Ross focused on business ventures in Tennessee, including the establishment of a plantation. He also became increasingly involved in Cherokee political affairs, using his bilingual skills and Protestant training to represent Indian interests to government officials. In 1819 Ross was elected president of the Cherokee legislature. In the 1820s he moved to Georgia, where he served as president of the Cherokee constitutional convention in 1827. Having overseen the first written constitution produced by an Indian nation, Ross was then elected principal chief in 1828. Over the next decade, he battled to retain the Cherokee homeland against the pressures of white planters and politicians.

COMPARING THE AMERICAN HISTORIES of Dolley Madison and John Ross demonstrates that, while American politics was a white man's game, it was possible for those on the political margins to influence national developments. Both Madison and Ross sought to defend and expand the democratic ideals that defined the young nation. The First Lady helped to nurture a bipartisan political culture in Washington, which was particularly important following the War of 1812. Dolley Madison also struggled with the issue of slavery, an issue that fueled tensions among Democratic-Republicans when Missouri sought admission to statehood in 1819. Missouri's admission resulted from the nation's rapid geographical expansion. Its economic development proved more volatile, however, with the nation suffering its first major recession in 1819. Working men then demanded the right to vote to protect their economic interests. The Cherokee also asserted their rights. Ross encouraged Cherokees to embrace Anglo-American culture as a path to inclusion. But he could not overcome the power of planters and politicians to wrest valuable territory from his tribe. President Andrew Jackson, elected in 1828, ensured Cherokee removal and supported slavery. Yet he was lauded as a democratic hero for his frontier background and promotion of workingmen's rights. The United States successfully defended itself against British intervention, but still could not agree on which Americans truly belonged in the nation.

Conflicts at Home and Abroad

When Thomas Jefferson completed his second term as president in March 1809, he was succeeded by his friend and ally James Madison. Like Jefferson, Madison sought to end foreign interference in American affairs and to resolve conflicts between Indians and white residents on the nation's frontier. By 1815 the United States had weathered a series of domestic and foreign crises, including another war with Britain, but American sovereignty remained fragile. At the same time, even though Madison (like Jefferson) believed in a national government with limited powers, he, too, found himself expanding federal authority.

Tensions at Sea and on the Frontier

When President Madison took office, Great Britain and France remained embroiled in the Napoleonic Wars in Europe and refused to modify their policies toward American shipping or to recognize U.S. neutrality. American ships were subject to seizure by both nations, and British authorities continued to impress "deserters" into the Royal Navy. Just before Madison's inauguration in March 1809, Congress replaced the Embargo Act with the **Non-Intercourse Act**, which restricted trade only with France and Britain and their colonies. Although the continued embargo against Britain encouraged U.S. manufacturing and the act allowed trade with other European nations, many Americans still opposed Congress using its power to restrict their right to trade.

In the midst of these crises, Madison also faced difficulties in the Northwest Territory. In 1794 General Anthony Wayne had won a decisive victory against a multi-tribe coalition at the **Battle of Fallen Timbers**. But this victory inspired two forceful native leaders to create a pan-Indian alliance in the Ohio River valley. The Shawnee prophet Tenskwatawa and his half-brother Tecumseh, a warrior, encouraged native peoples to resist white encroachments on their territory and to give up all aspects of white society and culture, including liquor and other popular trade goods. They imagined an Indian nation that stretched from the Canadian border to the Gulf of Mexico.

Although powerful Creek and Choctaw nations in the lower Mississippi valley refused to join the alliance, Indians in the upper Midwest rallied around the brothers.

In 1808 Tenskwatawa and Tecumseh established Prophet Town along the Tippecanoe River in Indiana Territory. The next year, William Henry Harrison, the territorial governor, tricked several Indian leaders into signing a treaty selling three million acres of land to the United States for only $7,600. An enraged Tecumseh dismissed the treaty, claiming the land belonged to all the Indians together.

In November 1811, fearing the growing power of the Shawnee leaders, President Madison ordered Harrison to attack Prophet Town. With more troops and superior weapons, the U.S. army defeated the allied Indians forces and burned Prophet Town to the ground. The rout damaged Tenskwatawa's stature as a prophet, and he and his supporters fled to Canada, where skirmishes continued along the U.S.-Canadian border.

War Erupts with Britain

Convinced that British officials in Canada fueled Indian resistance, many Democratic-Republicans demanded an end to British intervention on the western frontier as well as British interference in transatlantic trade. Some called for the United States to declare war. Yet merchants in the Northeast, who hoped to renew trade with Great Britain and the British West Indies, feared the commercial disruptions that war entailed. Thus New England Federalists adamantly opposed a declaration of war.

For months, Madison avoided taking a clear stand on the issue. On June 1, 1812, however, with diplomatic efforts exhausted, Madison sent a secret message to Congress outlining U.S. grievances against Great Britain. Within weeks, Congress declared war by sharply divided votes in the House of Representatives and the Senate.

Supporters claimed that a victory over Great Britain would end threats to U.S. sovereignty and raise Americans' stature in Europe. However, the nation was ill prepared to launch a major offensive against such an imposing foe given cuts in federal spending, falling tax revenues, and diminished military resources. The U.S. navy, for example, established under President Adams, had been reduced to only six small gunboats by President Jefferson. Democratic-Republicans had also failed to recharter the Bank of the United States when it expired in 1811, so the nation lacked a vital source of credit. Nonetheless, many in Congress believed that Britain would be too engaged by the ongoing conflict with France to attack the United States.

Meanwhile U.S. commanders devised plans to attack Canada, but the U.S. army and navy proved no match for Great Britain and its Indian allies. Instead, Tecumseh, who was appointed a brigadier general in the British army, helped capture Detroit. Joint British and Indian forces also launched successful attacks on Fort Dearborn, Fort Mackinac, and other points along the U.S.-Canadian border.

Even as U.S. forces faced numerous defeats in the summer and fall of 1812, American voters reelected James Madison as president. While Madison won most western and southern states, where the war was most popular, he lost in New England and New York, where Federalist opponents held sway.

After a year of fighting, U.S. forces drove the British back into Canada in 1813 (Map 9.1). A naval victory on Lake Erie led by Commodore Oliver Perry proved crucial to U.S. success. Soon after, Tecumseh was killed in battle and U.S. forces burned York (present-day Toronto). Yet just as U.S. prospects in the war improved, New England Federalists demanded retreat. The war devastated the New England maritime trade, causing economic distress throughout the region. In 1813, state legislatures in

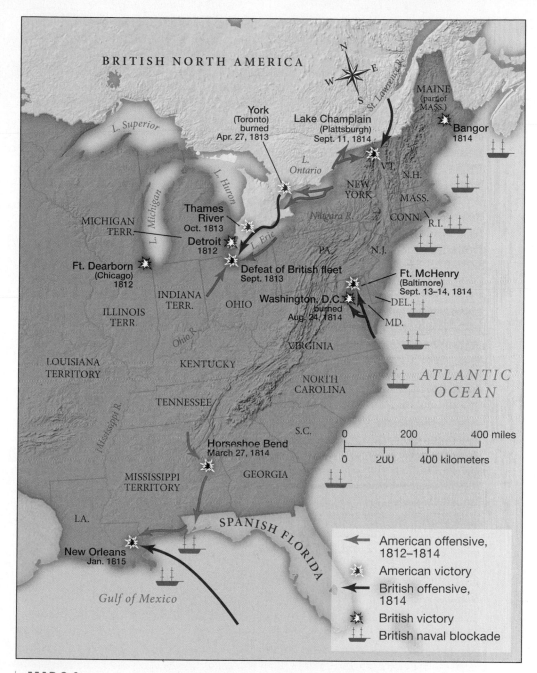

MAP 9.1

The War of 1812   Most conflicts in this war occurred in the Great Lakes region or around Washington, D.C. Yet two crucial victories occurred in the South. At Horseshoe Bend, troops under General Andrew Jackson and aided by Cherokee warriors defeated Creek allies of the British. At New Orleans, Jackson beat British forces shortly after a peace agreement was signed in Europe.

New England withdrew their support for any invasion of "foreign British soil," and Federalists in Congress sought to block war appropriations and the deployment of local militia units into the U.S. army.

New England Federalists were not powerful enough to change national policy, but they called a meeting at Hartford, Connecticut in 1814 to "deliberate upon the alarming state of public affairs." Some participants at the **Hartford Convention** called for New England's secession from the United States. Most supported amendments to the U.S. Constitution that would constrain federal power by limiting presidents to a single term and ensuring they were elected from diverse states (ending Virginia's domination of the office). Other amendments would require a two-thirds majority in Congress to declare war or prohibit trade.

The Hartford resolutions gained increased attention as British forces launched new attacks into the United States and British warships blockaded U.S. ports. In August 1814, the British sailed up the Chesapeake. As American troops retreated, Dolley Madison and a family slave, Peter Jennings, gathered up government papers and valuable belongings before fleeing the White House. The redcoats then burned

A CORRECT VIEW of the BATTLE Near the City of NEW ORLEANS, on the Eighth of January 1815, Under the Command of Genl. Andw. Jackson, Over 10,000 British Troops, in which 3 of their most distinguished Generals were killed & several wounded and upwards of 3,000 of their choicest Soldiers were killed wounded. and made Prisoners &c.

Battle of New Orleans   On January 8, 1815, General Andrew Jackson's troops launched grapeshot and canister bombs against British forces in New Orleans in this final battle of the War of 1812. Jackson's troops included Indian allies, backcountry immigrants, and French-speaking black soldiers. This engraving by Francisco Scacki shows the slain British commander, Major General Sir Edward Pakenham, in the center foreground.   Granger, NYC and sacked Washington City. U.S. troops quickly rallied, defeating the British in Maryland and expelling them from Washington and New York.

Meanwhile news arrived in March 1814 that Andrew Jackson and his Tennessee militiamen had defeated a force of Creek Indians, important British allies. Cherokee warriors (including John Ross), longtime foes of the Creek, joined the fight. At the **Battle of Horseshoe Bend**, in present-day Alabama, the combined U.S.-Cherokee forces slaughtered eight hundred Creek warriors. Although some Americans were appalled at the slaughter, in the resulting treaty the Creek nation lost two-thirds of its tribal domain.

Despite sporadic victories, the United States was no closer to winning the war when the British defeated Napoleon in June 1814. Six months later, the British fleet landed thousands of seasoned troops at New Orleans. Still, the British were losing steam as well, and representatives of the two countries met in Ghent, Belgium to negotiate a peace settlement. On Christmas Eve 1814, the **Treaty of Ghent** was signed, returning to each nation the lands it controlled before the war.

News of the treaty had not yet reached the United States in January 1815, when U.S. troops under General Andrew Jackson attacked and routed the British army at New Orleans. The victory cheered Americans, who, unaware that peace had already been achieved, made Jackson a national hero.

Although the War of 1812 achieved no formal territorial gains, it did represent an important defense of U.S. sovereignty and garnered international prestige for the young nation. In addition, Indians on the western frontier lost a powerful ally when British representatives at Ghent failed to act as advocates for their allies. Thus, in practical terms, the U.S. government gained greater control over vast expanses of land in the Ohio and Mississippi River valleys.

REVIEW & RELATE

- How were conflicts with Indians in the West connected to ongoing tensions between the United States and Great Britain on land and at sea?
- What were the long-term consequences of the War of 1812?

National Expansion and Regional Economies

By further expanding federal powers, the War of 1812 reinforced political changes that had been under way for more than a decade. At the Hartford Convention, Federalists who had once advocated broad national powers called for restrictions on federal authority. By contrast, Democratic-Republicans, who initially demanded restraints on federal power, now applauded its expansion. Indeed, Democratic-Republicans in Congress sought to use federal authority to settle boundary disputes in the West, make investments in transportation, and reestablish a national bank. Some state governments also invested in roads and canals. Federal power was again asserted to settle disputes with Britain and Spain over U.S. borders in the North and the South. At the same time, more secure borders and state and federal investments in transportation fueled overseas trade and the development of increasingly distinct regional economies.

Governments Fuel Economic Growth

In 1800 Thomas Jefferson captured the presidency by advocating a reduction in federal powers and a renewed emphasis on the needs of small farmers and working-men. Once in power, however, Jefferson and his Democratic-Republican supporters faced a series of economic and political developments that led many to embrace a loose interpretation of the U.S. Constitution and support federal efforts to aid economic growth.

Population growth and commercial expansion encouraged these federal efforts. In 1811 the first steamboat traveled down the Mississippi from the Ohio River to New Orleans; over the next decade, steamboat traffic expanded. This development helped western and southern residents but hurt trade on overland routes between northeastern seaports and the Ohio River valley. The federal government began construction of the Cumberland Road in 1811 to reestablish this regional connection by linking Maryland and Ohio. Congress passed additional bills to fund ambitious federal transportation projects, but President Madison vetoed much of this legislation, believing that it overstepped even a loose interpretation of the Constitution.

After the War of 1812, however, Democratic-Republican representative Henry Clay of Kentucky sketched out a plan to promote U.S. economic growth and advance commercial ties throughout the nation. Called the **American System**, it combined federally funded internal improvements, such as roads and canals, to aid farmers and

"Erie-Canal, Lockport," c. 1850   This steel engraving, based on an 1839 painting, depicts one of five locks that lifted boats sixty feet over a limestone ridge near the western end of the canal. The remarkable engineering feat required 1200 laborers to blast the ridge, clear the rocks, and build the locks. The village of Lockport, which emerged at the site, grew rapidly after 1825.   akg-images merchants with federal tariffs to protect U.S. manufacturing. Western expansion fueled demand for these internal improvements. The non-Indian population west of the Appalachian Mountains more than doubled between 1810 and 1820, from 1,080,000 to 2,234,000. Many veterans of the War of 1812 settled there after receiving 160-acre parcels of land in the region as payment for service. Congress admitted four new states to the Union in just four years: Indiana (1816), Mississippi (1817), Illinois (1818), and Alabama (1819).

Congress also negotiated with Indian nations to secure trade routes farther west. In the 1810s, Americans began trading along an ancient trail from Missouri to Santa Fe, a town in northern Mexico. But the trail cut across territory claimed by the Osage Indians. In 1825 Congress approved a treaty with the Osage to guarantee right of way for U.S. merchants. The Santa Fe Trail soon became a critical route for commerce between the United States and Mexico.

East of the Appalachian Mountains, state governments funded most internal improvement projects. The most significant of these was New York's **Erie Canal**, a 363-mile waterway stretching from the Mohawk River to Buffalo that was completed in 1825. Self-taught men directed this extraordinary engineering feat by which thousands of workers carved a swath forty feet wide and four feet deep through limestone cliffs, mountains, forests, and swamps. The canal, which rises 566 feet along its route, required the construction of 83 locks to lift and lower boats. The arduous and dangerous work was carried out mainly by Irish, Welsh, and German immigrants, many of whom settled along its route. Tolls on the Erie Canal quickly repaid the tremendous financial cost of its construction. Freight charges and shipping times plunged. And by linking western farmers to the Hudson River, the Erie Canal ensured that New York City became the nation's premier seaport (Map 9.2).

The Erie Canal's success inspired hundreds of similar projects in other states. Canals carried manufactured goods from New England and the Middle Atlantic states to rural households in the Ohio River valley. Western farmers, in turn, shipped agricultural products back east. Canals also linked smaller cities within Pennsylvania and Ohio, facilitating the rise of commercial and manufacturing centers like Harrisburg, Pittsburgh, and Cincinnati. Moreover, canals allowed vast quantities of coal to be transported out of the Allegheny Mountains, fueling industrial development throughout the Northeast.

Americans Expand the Nation's Borders

In 1816, in the midst of the nation's economic resurgence, James Monroe won an easy victory in the presidential election over Rufus King, a New York Federalist. To improve relations with Britain and resolve problems on the frontier, Monroe sent John Quincy Adams to London. He negotiated treaties that limited U.S. and British naval forces on the Great Lakes, set the U.S.-Canadian border at the forty-ninth parallel, and established joint British-U.S. occupation of the Oregon Territory. In 1817 and 1818, the Senate approved these treaties, which further restricted Indian rights and power.

President Monroe harbored grave concerns about the nation's southern boundary as well. He sought to limit Spain's power in North America and stop Seminole Indians in Florida and Alabama from claiming lands the defeated Creeks ceded to the United States. Shifting from diplomacy to military force, in 1817 the president sent General Andrew

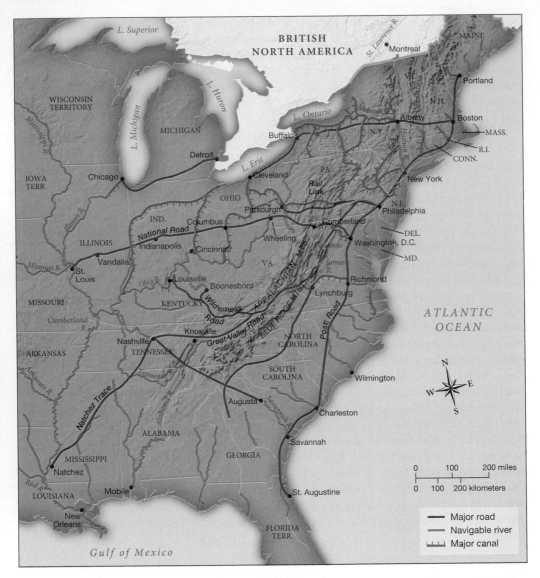

MAP 9.2
Roads and Canals to 1837   During the 1820s and 1830s, state and local governments as well as private companies built roads and canals to foster migration and commercial development. The Erie Canal, completed in 1825, was the most significant of these projects. Many other states, particularly in the Northeast and the old Northwest, sought to duplicate that canal's success over the following decade.

Jackson to force the Seminoles back into central Florida. But he ordered Jackson to avoid direct conflict with Spanish forces for fear of igniting another war. However, in spring 1818 Jackson attacked two Spanish forts, hanged two Seminole chiefs, and executed two British citizens.

Jackson's attacks spurred outrage among Spanish and British officials and many members of Congress. The threat of conflict with Britain, Spain, and the Seminole tribe prompted President Monroe to establish the nation's first peacetime army. In the end, the British chose to ignore the execution of citizens engaged in "unauthorized" activities, while Spain decided to sell the Florida Territory to the United States. Indeed, in the **Adams-Onís Treaty** (1819), negotiated by John Quincy Adams, Spain ceded all its lands east of the Mississippi to the United States.

Success in acquiring Florida encouraged the administration to look for other opportunities to limit European influence in the Western Hemisphere. By 1822 Argentina, Chile, Peru, Colombia, and Mexico had all overthrown Spanish rule. That March, President Monroe recognized the independence of these southern neighbors, and Congress quickly established diplomatic relations with the new nations. The following year, President Monroe added a codicil to a treaty with Russia that claimed that the Western Hemisphere was part of the U.S. sphere of influence. Although the United States did not have sufficient power to enforce what later became known as the **Monroe Doctrine**, it had declared its intention to challenge Europeans for authority in the Atlantic world.

By the late 1820s, U.S. residents were moving to and trading with newly independent Mexican territories. Southern whites began settling on Mexican lands in east Texas, while traders traveled the Santa Fe Trail. Meanwhile New England manufacturers and merchants began sending goods via clipper ships to another Mexican territory, Alta California.

Some Americans looked even farther afield. In the early nineteenth century, U.S. ships carried otter pelts and other merchandise across the Pacific, returning with Chinese porcelains and silks. In the early 1800s, the Alta California and China trades converged, expanding the reach of U.S. merchants and the demand for U.S. manufactured goods. Some Americans then set their sights on Pacific islands, especially Hawaii and Samoa.

Expanded trade routes along with wartime disruptions of European imports fueled the expansion of U.S. manufacturing, which improved opportunities for entrepreneurs and workers. By 1813 the area around Providence, Rhode Island boasted seventy-six spinning mills. Two years later, Philadelphia claimed pride of place as the nation's top industrial city, turning out glass, chemicals, metalwork, and leather goods.

Regional Economic Development

The roads, rivers, canals, and steamboats that connected a growing nation meant that people in one region could more easily exchange the goods they produced for those they needed. This development fostered the emergence of distinct, regional economies. In the South, for instance, vast Indian land cessions and the acquisition of Florida ensured the expansion of cotton cultivation. At the same time, overcultivation in older regions of the Southeast forced many planters to relocate further west and south. In the process, they extended slavery into new lands to produce cash crops like cotton, sugar, and rice. Small farmers often planted as much land in cotton as they could manage. Both groups used profits from these staple crops to buy grain and other food items from the West and manufactured shoes and cloth from the North.

When James and Dolley Madison returned to their plantation, Montpelier, in 1817, they experienced the new possibilities and problems of southern agriculture.

Plantation homes in long-settled areas like Montpelier in the Virginia piedmont became more fashionable as they incorporated luxury goods imported from China and Europe. But the soil in the region, depleted of nutrients, limited the profits from tobacco and made a shift to cotton impossible. As agricultural production declined, some Virginia planters made money by selling slaves to planters farther south and west. However, James Madison refused to break up slave families who had worked his plantation for decades and had no desire to relocate. Thus the Madisons were forced to reduce their standard of living.

However, many white Americans benefited from the expansion of southern agriculture west of the Appalachians. Southern farmers and planters who cultivated cotton made substantial profits in the 1810s. So did western farmers, who shipped vast quantities of agricultural produce to the South. Towns like Cincinnati, located across the Ohio River from Kentucky, sprang up as regional centers of commerce. Americans living in the Northeast increased their commercial connections with the South as well. Northern merchants became more deeply engaged in the southern cotton trade, opening warehouses in cities like Savannah and Charleston and sending agents into the countryside to bargain for cotton to be spun into thread in mills powered by water.

The southern cotton boom thus fueled northern industrial growth, the improvement of roads, the expansion of canals, and the building of larger and faster ships. Factory owners and merchants in New England could ship growing quantities of yarn, thread, and cloth along with shoes, tools, and leather goods to the South. Meanwhile, merchants in Philadelphia and Pittsburgh built ties to western farmers, exchanging manufactured goods for agricultural products. Over time America's regional economies became not only more distinctive but also increasingly interdependent.

REVIEW & RELATE	• What role did government play in early-nineteenth-century economic development?
	• How and why did economic development contribute to regional differences and shape regional ties?

Economic and Political Crises

Even as regional economies ensured economic interdependence, they highlighted political differences. For instance, the growth in trade between regions led to an increase in commercial institutions, such as banks, the largest of which were established in the North. When the nation's first severe recession hit in 1819, many southern planters and midwestern farmers blamed it on the banks. In reality, falling prices for cotton and wheat abroad as well as overextension of credit by U.S. banks contributed to the recession. Whatever the cause, the interdependence of regional economies ensured that everyone suffered. At the same time, these economies were built on distinct forms of labor, with the South becoming more dependent on slavery and the North less so. When Missouri, situated between the old Northwest Territory and expanding southern cotton lands, applied for statehood in 1819, these regional differences set off a furious national debate over slavery.

The Panic of 1819

The **panic of 1819** resulted primarily from irresponsible banking practices in the United States and was deepened by the declining overseas demand for American goods, especially cotton. Beginning in 1816, American banks, including the newly chartered Second Bank of the United States, loaned huge sums to settlers seeking land on the frontier and merchants and manufacturers expanding their businesses. Many loans were not backed by sufficient collateral because many banks assumed that continued economic growth would ensure repayment. Then, as agricultural production in Europe revived with the end of the Napoleonic Wars, the demand for American foodstuffs dropped sharply. Farm income plummeted by roughly one-third in the late 1810s.

In 1818 the directors of the Second Bank, fearing a continued expansion of the money supply, tightened the credit they provided to branch banks. This sudden effort to curtail credit led to economic panic. Some branch banks failed immediately. Others survived by calling in loans to companies and individuals, who in turn demanded repayment from those to whom they had extended credit. The chain of indebtedness pushed many people to the brink of economic ruin just as factory owners cut their workforce and merchants decreased orders for new goods. Individuals and businesses faced bankruptcy and foreclosure, and property values fell sharply.

Bankruptcies, foreclosures, unemployment, and poverty spread across the country. Cotton farmers were especially hard hit by declining exports and falling prices. Planters who had gone into debt to purchase land in Alabama and Mississippi were unable to pay their mortgages. Many western residents, who had invested all they had in new farms, lost their land or simply stopped paying their mortgages. This further strained state banks, some of which collapsed, leaving the national bank holding mortgages on vast amounts of western territory.

Many Americans viewed banks as the cause of the panic. Some states defied the Constitution and the Supreme Court by trying to tax Second Bank branches or printing state banknotes with no specie (gold or silver) to back them. Some Americans called for government relief, but there was no system to provide the kinds of assistance needed. When Congress debated how to reignite the nation's economy, regional differences quickly appeared. Northern manufacturers called for even higher tariffs to protect them from foreign competition, but southern planters argued that high tariffs raised the price of manufactured goods while agricultural profits declined. Meanwhile, workingmen and small farmers feared that their economic needs were being ignored by politicians tied to bankers, planters, manufacturers, and merchants.

By 1823 the panic had largely dissipated, but the prolonged economic crisis shook national confidence, and citizens became more skeptical of federal authority and more suspicious of banks. From 1819 until the Civil War, one of the greatest limitations on national growth remained the cycle of economic expansion and contraction.

Slavery in Missouri

A second national crisis highlighted regional systems of labor. In February 1819 the Missouri Territory applied for statehood. New York congressman James Tallmadge Jr. proposed that Missouri be admitted only if it banned further importation of slaves and passed a gradual emancipation law. Southern congressmen blocked Tallmadge's proposals, but the northern majority in the House of Representatives then rejected Missouri's admission.

MAP 9.3

The Missouri Compromise and Westward Expansion, 1820s   The debate over the Missouri
Compromise occurred as the United States began expanding farther westward. Within a few years
of its adoption, the growth of U.S. settlements in eastern Texas and increased trade with a newly
independent Mexico suggested the importance of drawing a clear boundary between slave and free
states.

Southern politicians were outraged, claiming that since the Missouri Territory
allowed slavery, so should the state of Missouri. With cotton production moving ever
westward, southern congressmen wanted to ensure the availability of new lands. They
also wanted to ensure the South's power in Congress. Because the northern population had grown more rapidly than that in the South, by 1819 northern politicians
controlled the House of Representatives. The Senate, however, was evenly divided. If
northerners could block the admission of slave states like Missouri while allowing the
admission of free states, the balance of power in the Senate would tip in the North's
favor.

For southern planters, the decision on Missouri defined the future of slavery.
With foreign trade in slaves outlawed, planters relied on natural increase and trading
slaves from older to newer areas of cultivation to meet the demand for labor. Moreover, free blacks packed the congressional galleries in Washington to listen to congressmen debate Missouri statehood, leading supporters of slavery to worry that any signs
of weakness would fuel resistance to slavery. Recent attacks on Georgia plantations by
a coalition of fugitive slaves and Seminole Indians lent power to such fears.

In 1820 Representative Henry Clay of Kentucky forged a compromise that resolved the immediate issues and promised a long-term solution. Maine was to be admitted as a free state and Missouri as a slave state, thereby maintaining the balance between North and South in the U.S. Senate (Map 9.3). At the same time, Congress agreed that the southern border of Missouri—latitude 36°30′—was to serve as the boundary between slave and free states throughout the Louisiana Territory.

The **Missouri Compromise** ended the crisis for the moment. Still, the debates made clear how quickly a disagreement over slavery could escalate into clashes that threatened the survival of the nation.

REVIEW & RELATE	• How did regional interdependency contribute to the panic of 1819?
	• What regional divisions did the conflict over slavery in Missouri reveal?

The Expansion and Limits of American Democracy

With the panic of 1819 and the debates over Missouri shaking many Americans' faith in their economic and political leaders and the frontier moving ever westward, the nation was ripe for change. Workingmen, small farmers, and frontier settlers, who had long been locked out of the electoral system by property qualifications and eastern elites, demanded the right to vote. The resulting political movement ensured voting rights for nearly all white men during the 1820s. Yet African Americans lost political and civil rights in the same period; and Indians fared poorly under the federal administrations brought to power by this expanded electorate. While some white women gained greater political influence as a result of the voting rights gained by fathers and husbands, they did not achieve independent political rights. Finally, as a wave of new voters entered the political fray, ongoing conflicts over slavery, tariffs, and the rights of Indian nations transformed party alignments.

Expanding Voting Rights

Between 1788 and 1820, the U.S. presidency was dominated by Virginia elites and after 1800 by Democratic-Republicans. With little serious political opposition at the national level, few people bothered to vote in presidential elections. Far more people engaged in political activities at the state and local levels. Many towns attracted large audiences to public celebrations on the Fourth of July and election days. Female participants sewed symbols of their partisan loyalties on their clothes and joined in parades and feasts organized by men.

The panic of 1819 stimulated even more political activity as laboring men, who were especially vulnerable to economic downturns, demanded the right to vote so they could hold politicians accountable. In New York State, Martin Van Buren, a rising star in the Democratic-Republican Party, led the fight to eliminate property qualifications for voting. At the state constitutional convention of 1821, the committee on suffrage argued that the only qualification for voting should be "the virtue and morality of the people." By the word people, Van Buren and the committee meant white men.

Despite opposition from powerful and wealthy men, by 1825 most states along the Atlantic seaboard had lowered or eliminated property qualifications on white male voters. Meanwhile states along the frontier that had joined the Union in the 1810s established universal white male suffrage from the beginning. And by 1824 three-quarters of the states (18 of 24) allowed voters, rather than state legislatures, to elect members of the electoral college.

Yet as white workingmen gained political rights in the 1820s, democracy did not spread to other groups. Indian nations were considered sovereign entities, so Indians voted in their own nations, not in U.S. elections. Women were excluded from voting because of their perceived dependence on men. And African American men faced increasing restrictions on their political rights. No southern legislature had ever granted blacks the right to vote, and northern states began disfranchising them as well in the 1820s. In many cases, expanded voting rights for white men went hand in hand with new restrictions on black men. In New York State, for example, the constitution of 1821, which eliminated property qualifications for white men, raised property qualifications for African American voters.

When African American men protested their disfranchisement, some whites spoke out on their behalf. They claimed that denying rights to men who had in no way abused the privilege of voting set "an ominous and dangerous precedent." In response, opponents of black suffrage offered explicitly racist justifications. Some argued that black voting would lead to interracial socializing, even marriage. Others feared that black voters might hold the balance of power in close elections, forcing white civic leaders to accede to their demands. Gradually, racist arguments won the day, and by 1840, 93 percent of free blacks in the North were excluded from voting.

Racial Restrictions and Antiblack Violence

Restrictions on voting followed other constraints on African American men and women. As early as 1790, Congress limited naturalization (the process of becoming a citizen) to white aliens, or immigrants. It also excluded blacks from enrolling in federal militias. In 1820 Congress authorized city officials in Washington, D.C. to adopt a separate legal code governing free blacks and slaves. This federal legislation encouraged states, in both the North and the South, to add their own restrictions, including the segregation of public schools, transportation, and accommodations. Some northern legislatures even denied African Americans the right to settle in their state.

In addition, blacks faced mob and state-sanctioned violence across the country. In 1822 officials in Charleston, South Carolina accused Denmark Vesey, a free black, of following the revolutionary leader Toussaint L'Ouverture's lead and plotting a conspiracy to free the city's slaves. Vesey had helped to organize churches, mutual aid societies, and other black institutions. His accomplishments were considered threatening to the future of slavery by challenging assumptions about black inferiority. Vesey may have organized a plan to free slaves in the city, but it is also possible that white officials concocted the plot to terrorize blacks. Despite scant evidence, Vesey and thirty-four of his alleged co-conspirators were found guilty and hanged. The

CLASS No. 1.

Comprises those prisoners who were found guilty and executed.

Prisoners Names.	Owners' Names.	Time of Commit.	How Disposed of.
Peter	James Poyas	June 18	Hanged on Tuesday the 2d July, 1822, on Blake's lands, near Charleston.
Ned	Gov. T. Bennett,	do.	
Rolla	do.	do	
Batteau	do.	do.	
Denmark Vesey	A free black man	22	
Jessy	Thos. Blackwood	23	
John	Elias Horry	July 5	Do. on the Lines near Ch.; Friday July 12.
Gullah Jack	Paul Pritchard	do.	
Mingo	Wm. Harth	June 21	Hanged on the Lines near Charleston, on Friday, 26th July.
Lot	Forrester	27	
Joe	P. L. Jore	July 6	
Julius	Thos. Forrest	8	
Tom	Mrs. Russell	10	
Smart	Robt. Anderson	do.	
John	John Robertson	11	
Robert	do.	do.	
Adam	do.	do.	
Polydore	Mrs. Faber	do.	
Bacchus	Benj. Hammet	do.	
Dick	Wm. Sims	13	
Pharaoh	— Thompson	do.	
Jemmy	Mrs. Clement	18	
Mauidore	Mordecai Cohen	19	
Dean	— Mitchell	do.	
Jack	Mrs. Purcell	12	
Bellisle	Est. of Jos. Yates	18	
Naphur	do.	do.	
Adam	do.	do.	
Jacob	John S. Glen	16	
Charles	John Billings	18	
Jack	N. McNeill	22	
Cæsar	Miss Smith	do.	
Jacob Stagg	Jacob Lankester	23	Do. Tues. July 30.
Tom	Wm. M. Scott	24	
William	Mrs. Garner	Aug. 2	Do. Friday, Aug. 9.

Record of Thirty-five Men Executed for Conspiring to Revolt against Their Masters
This official record of executions related to an alleged 1822 slave conspiracy lists the name of Denmark Vesey, the only free black man accused, fifth. The enslaved men are listed next to their owners' names, including the governor of South Carolina, twenty-one other men, and six women. There were no appeals of their convictions, and the hangings took place quickly. Granger, NYC

African Methodist Episcopal Church where they supposedly planned the insurrection was demolished. Northern blacks also suffered from violent attacks by whites. For example, in 1829 white residents of Cincinnati attacked black neighborhoods, and more than half of the city's black residents fled. Many of them resettled in Ontario, Canada. They were soon joined by Philadelphia blacks who had been attacked by groups of white residents in 1832. Such attacks continued in northern cities throughout the 1830s.

Political Realignments

Restrictions on black political and civil rights converged with the continued decline of the Federalists. Federalist majorities in New York State had approved the gradual abolition law of 1799. In 1821 New York Federalists advocated equal rights for black and white voters as long as property qualifications limited suffrage to respectable citizens. But Federalists were losing power, and the concerns of African Americans were low on the Democratic-Republican agenda.

Struggles within the Democratic-Republican Party now turned to a large extent on the limits of federal power. Many Democratic-Republicans had come to embrace a more expansive view of federal authority and a looser interpretation of the U.S. Constitution. Others argued forcefully for a return to limited federal power and a strict construction of the Constitution. At the same time, rising young politicians—like Martin Van Buren and Andrew Jackson—and newly enfranchised voters sought to seize control of the party from its longtime leaders.

The election of 1824 brought these conflicts to a head, splitting the Democratic-Republicans into rival factions that by 1828 coalesced into two distinct entities: the **Democrats** and the **National Republicans**. Unable to agree on a single presidential candidate in 1824, the Democratic-Republican congressional caucus fractured into four camps backing separate candidates: John Quincy Adams, Andrew Jackson, Henry Clay, and Secretary of the Treasury William Crawford.

As the race developed, Adams and Jackson emerged as the two strongest candidates. John Quincy Adams's stature rested on his diplomatic achievements and the reputation of his father, former president John Adams. He favored internal improvements and protective tariffs that would bolster northern industry and commerce. Jackson, on the other hand, relied largely on his fame as a war hero and Indian fighter to inspire popular support. He advocated limited federal power.

As a candidate who appealed to ordinary voters, Jackson held a decided edge. Outgoing and boisterous, Jackson took his case to the people. Emphasizing his humble origins, he appealed to small farmers and northern workers. Just as important, Jackson gained the support of Van Buren, who also wanted to expand the political clout of the "common [white] man" and limit the reach of a central government that was becoming too powerful.

The four presidential candidates created a truly competitive race, and turnout at the polls increased significantly. Jackson won the popular vote by carrying Pennsylvania, New Jersey, the Carolinas, and much of the West and led in the electoral college with 99 electors. But with no candidate gaining an absolute majority in the electoral college, the Constitution called for the House of Representatives to choose the president from the three leading contenders—Jackson, Adams, and Crawford.

Clay, who came in fourth, asked his supporters to back Adams, ensuring his election. Once in office, President Adams appointed Clay secretary of state. Jackson claimed that the two had engineered a "corrupt bargain," but Adams and Clay, who shared many ideas, formed a logical alliance.

Once in office, President Adams ran into vigorous opposition in Congress led by Van Buren. John C. Calhoun, a South Carolina Senator who had been elected vice president, also opposed Adams's policies. Van Buren argued against federal funding for internal improvements since New York State had financed the Erie Canal with its own monies. Calhoun, meanwhile, joined other southern politicians in opposing any expansion of federal power for fear it would then be used to restrict the spread of slavery.

The most serious battle in Congress, however, involved tariffs. The tariff of 1816 had excluded most cheap English cotton cloth from the United States to aid New England manufacturing. In 1824 the tariff was extended to more expensive cotton and woolen cloth and to iron goods. During the presidential campaign, Adams and Clay appealed to northern voters by advocating even higher duties on these items. When Adams introduced tariff legislation that extended duties to raw materials like wool, hemp, and molasses, he gained support from both Jackson and Van Buren, who considered these tariffs beneficial to farmers on the frontier. Despite the opposition of Vice President Calhoun and congressmen from southeastern states, the tariff of 1828 was approved, raising duties on imports to an average of 62 percent.

The tariff of 1828, however, was Adams's only notable legislative victory. His foreign policy was also stymied by a hostile Congress. Adams thus entered the 1828 election campaign with little to show in the way of domestic or foreign achievements, and Jackson and his supporters took full advantage of the president's political vulnerability.

The Presidential Election of 1828

The election of 1828 tested the power of the two major factions in the Democratic-Republican Party. President Adams followed the traditional approach of "standing" for office. He told supporters, "If my country wants my services, she must ask for them." Jackson and his supporters chose instead to "run" for office. They took their case directly to the voters, introducing innovative techniques to create enthusiasm among the electorate.

Van Buren managed the first truly national political campaign in U.S. history, seeking to re-create the original Democratic-Republican coalition among farmers, northern artisans, and southern planters while adding a sizable constituency of frontier voters. He was aided in the effort by Calhoun, who again ran for vice president and supported the Tennessee war hero despite their disagreement over tariffs. Jackson's supporters organized state nominating conventions rather than relying on the congressional caucus. They established local Jackson committees in critical states like Virginia and New York. They organized newspaper campaigns and developed a logo, the hickory leaf, based on the candidate's nickname, "Old Hickory."

Jackson traveled the country to build loyalty to himself as well as to his party. His Tennessee background, rise to great wealth, and reputation as an Indian fighter ensured his popularity among southern and western voters. He also reassured southerners that he advocated "judicious" duties on imports, suggesting that he might try to lower the

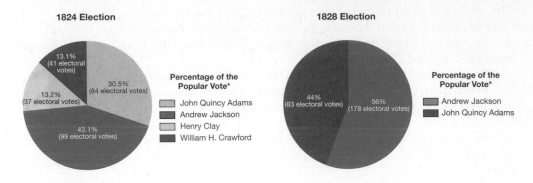

*Popular vote percentages are approximate.

FIGURE 9.1
The Elections of 1824 and 1828   Andrew Jackson lost the 1824 election to John Quincy Adams when the decision was thrown into the House of Representatives. In 1828 Jackson launched the first popular campaign for president, mobilizing working-class white men who were newly enfranchised. Three times as many men—more than one million voters—cast ballots in 1828 than in 1824, ensuring Jackson's election as president. How did the greater number of candidates running in 1824 complicate the Electoral College system of selecting a president?

1828 rates. At the same time, his support of the tariff of 1828 and his military credentials created enthusiasm among northern workingmen and frontier farmers.

President Adams's supporters demeaned the "dissolute" and "rowdy" men who attended Jackson rallies. They also launched personal attacks on the candidate and on his wife, Rachel. They questioned the timing of her divorce from her first husband and remarriage to Jackson. A Cincinnati newspaper headline asked: "Ought a convicted adulteress and her paramour husband be placed in the highest offices of this free and Christian land?"

Adams distanced himself from his own campaign. He sought to demonstrate his statesmanlike gentility by letting others speak for him. This strategy worked well when only men of wealth and property could vote. But with an enlarged electorate and an astonishing turnout of more than 50 percent of eligible voters, Adams's approach failed and Jackson became president (Figure 9.1).

The election of 1828 formalized a new party alignment. During the campaign Jackson and his supporters referred to themselves as "the Democracy" and forged a new national Democratic Party. In response Adams's supporters and the remaining diehard Federalists renamed themselves National Republicans. The competition between **Democrats and National Republicans** heightened interest in national politics among ordinary voters and ensured that the innovative techniques introduced by Jackson would be widely adopted in future campaigns.

REVIEW & RELATE
- How and why did the composition of the electorate change in the 1820s?
- How did Jackson's 1828 campaign represent a significant departure from earlier patterns in American politics?

Jacksonian Politics in Action

Jackson hoped to make government more responsive to the needs of white workers and frontier farmers. But the president's notion of democracy did not extend to Indians or African Americans. During his presidency, Indian nations actively resisted his efforts to take more of their land, and blacks continued to resist their enslavement. Of more immediate importance, once President Jackson had to take clear positions on tariffs and other controversial issues, he could not please all of his constituents. He also confronted experienced adversaries like Henry Clay, Daniel Webster, and John Quincy Adams, who was elected to the House of Representatives from Massachusetts in 1830. The president thus faced considerable difficulty in translating popular support into public policy.

A Democratic Spirit?

On March 4, 1829, crowds of ordinary citizens came to see Jackson's inauguration. Jackson's wife, Rachel, had died of heart failure shortly after his election, leaving her husband devastated. Now Jackson, dressed in a plain black suit, walked alone to the Capitol as vast throngs of supporters waved and cheered. A somber Jackson read a brief inaugural address, took the oath of office, and then rode his horse through the crowds to the White House.

The size and enthusiasm of the crowds soon shattered the decorum of the inauguration. Author Margaret Bayard Smith reported mobs "scrambling, fighting, [and] romping" through the White House reception. Jackson was nearly crushed to death by "rabble" eager to shake his hand. Tubs of punch laced with rum, brandy, and champagne were finally placed on the lawn to draw the crowds outdoors.

While Jackson and his supporters viewed the event as a symbol of a new democratic spirit, others were less optimistic. Bayard Smith and other conservative political leaders saw echoes of the French Revolution in the unruly behavior of the masses. Supreme Court justice Joseph Story, too, feared "the reign of King 'Mob.'"

Tensions between the president and the capital's traditional leaders intensified when Jackson appointed Tennessee senator John Eaton as secretary of war. Eaton had had an affair with a woman thought to be of questionable character and later married her. When Jackson announced his plans to appoint Eaton to his cabinet, congressional leaders urged him to reconsider. When the president appointed Eaton anyway, the wives of Washington's leading politicians snubbed Mrs. Eaton. This time Jackson was outmaneuvered in what became known as the **Petticoat Affair**, and Eaton was eventually forced from office.

In the aftermath of Eaton's resignation, Jackson asked his entire cabinet to resign so he could begin anew. Afterward, however, his legislative agenda stalled in Congress, and National Republicans regained the momentum they had lost with Adams's defeat. The Petticoat Affair reinforced concerns that the president used his authority to reward his friends, as did his reliance on an informal group of advisers, known as the Kitchen Cabinet. While his administration opened up government posts to a wider range of individuals, ensuring more democratic access, Jackson often selected appointees based on personal ties. He believed that "to the victor goes the spoils," and the resulting **spoils system**—continued by future administrations—assigned federal posts as gifts for partisan loyalty rather than as jobs that required experience or expertise.

Confrontations over Tariffs and the Bank

The Democratic Party that emerged in the late 1820s was built on an unstable foundation. The coalition that formed around Jackson included northern workers who benefited from high tariffs as well as southern farmers and planters who did not. It brought together western voters who sought federal support for internal improvements and strict constructionists who believed such expenditures were unconstitutional. In nearly every legislative battle, then, decisiveness aroused conflict. In 1830 Congress passed four internal improvement bills with strong support from National Republicans. Jackson vetoed each one, which pleased his southern constituency but not his frontier supporters.

Southern congressmen, however, were more interested in his stand on tariffs. The tariff of 1828 still enraged many southern planters and politicians, but most believed that once Jackson reached the White House, he would reverse course and reduce this **Tariff of Abominations**. Instead, he avoided the issue, and southern agriculture continued to suffer. Agricultural productivity in Virginia and other states of the Old South was declining from soil exhaustion, while prices for cotton and rice had not fully recovered after the panic of 1819. At the same time, higher duties on manufactured items raised prices for southerners on many goods.

Even as Calhoun campaigned with Jackson in 1828, the South Carolinian developed a philosophical argument to negate the effects of high tariffs on his state. In *The South Carolina Exposition and Protest*, published anonymously in 1828, Calhoun argued that states should have the ultimate power to determine the constitutionality of laws passed by Congress. When Jackson, after taking office, realized that his vice president advocated **nullification**—the right of individual states to declare individual laws void within their borders—it further damaged their relationship, which was already frayed by the Eaton affair.

When Congress debated the tariff issue in 1830, South Carolina senator Robert Hayne defended nullification. Claiming that the North intended to crush the South economically, he argued that only the right of states to nullify federal legislation could protect southern society. In response, Massachusetts Senator Daniel Webster denounced nullification and the states' rights doctrine on which it was built. Jackson further antagonized southern political leaders by supporting Webster's position.

Matters worsened in 1832 when Congress confirmed the high duties set four years earlier. In response South Carolina held a special convention that approved an Ordinance of Nullification. It stated that duties on imports would not be collected in the state after February 1, 1833, and threatened secession if federal authorities tried to collect them.

The tariff crisis thus escalated in the fall of 1832 just as Jackson faced reelection. The tariff debates had angered many southerners, and Calhoun refused to run again as his vice president. Fortunately for Jackson, opponents in Congress had provided him with another issue that could unite his supporters and highlight his commitment to ordinary citizens: the renewal of the charter of the Bank of the United States.

Clay and Webster persuaded Nicholas Biddle, head of the bank, to request an early recharter of the bank. Jackson's opponents in Congress knew they had the votes to pass a new charter in the summer of 1832, and they hoped Jackson would veto the bill and thereby split the Democratic Party just before the fall elections. The Second

Bank was a political quagmire. The bank had stabilized the economy during the 1820s by regularly demanding specie (gold or silver) payments from state-chartered banks. This kept those banks from issuing too much paper money and thereby prevented inflation and higher prices. This tight-money policy also kept banks from expanding too rapidly in the western states. Most financial elites applauded the bank's efforts, but its policies aroused hostility among the wider public. When state-chartered banks closed because of lack of specie, ordinary Americans were often stuck with worthless paper money. Tight-money policies also made it more difficult for individuals to get credit to purchase land, homes, or farm equipment.

As the president's opponents had hoped, Congress approved the new charter, and Jackson vetoed it. Yet rather than dividing the Democrats, Jackson's veto gained enormous support from voters across the country. In justifying his action, the president cast the Second Bank as a "monster" that was "dangerous to the liberties of the people"—particularly farmers, mechanics, and laborers—while promoting "the advancement of the few." Finally, Jackson noted that since wealthy Britons owned substantial shares of the bank's stock, national pride demanded ending the Second Bank's reign over the U.S. economy. Jackson rode the enthusiasm for his bank veto to reelection over National Republican candidate Henry Clay. Within a year, the Second Bank was dead, deprived of government deposits by Jackson.

Soon after his reelection, however, the president faced a grave political crisis related to the tariff issue. Jackson now supported lower tariffs, but he was adamant in his opposition to nullification. In early 1833, he persuaded Congress to pass a Force Bill, which gave him authority to use the military to enforce national laws in South Carolina. At the same time, Jackson made clear that he would work with Congress to reduce tariffs, allowing South Carolina to rescind its nullification ordinance without losing face. Open conflict was averted, but the question of nullification was not resolved.

Contesting Indian Removal

On another long-standing issue—the acquisition of Indian land—Jackson gained the support of white southerners and most frontier settlers. Yet not all Americans agreed with his effort to force Indians off their lands. In the 1820s nations like the Cherokee gained the support of Protestant missionaries who hoped to "civilize" Indians by converting them to Christianity and "American" ways. In 1819 Congress had granted these groups federal funds to advance these goals. Jackson, however, was unsupportive of such efforts and sided with political leaders who sought to force eastern Indians to accept homelands west of the Mississippi River.

In 1825, three years before Jackson was elected president, Creek Indians in Georgia and Alabama were forcibly removed to the Unorganized Territory (previously part of Arkansas Territory and later called Indian Territory) based on a fraudulent treaty. Jackson supported this policy. When he became president, politicians and settlers in Georgia, Florida, the Carolinas, and Illinois demanded federal assistance to force Indian communities out of their states.

The largest Indian nations vehemently protested their removal. The Cherokee, who had fought alongside Jackson at Horseshoe Bend, adopted a republican form of government in 1827 based on the U.S. Constitution. John Ross served as the president of the Cherokee constitutional convention and a year later was elected principal chief. He and the other chiefs then declared themselves a sovereign nation within the borders of the United States. The Georgia legislature rejected Cherokee claims of independence and argued that Indians were simply guests of the state, a position that gained added significance when gold was discovered in Cherokee territory in 1829. Ross appealed to Jackson to recognize Cherokee sovereignty, but the president was affronted by what he saw as a challenge to his authority. He urged Congress to pass the **Indian Removal Act** in 1830, by which the Cherokee and other Indian nations would be forced to exchange their lands in the Southeast for a "clear title forever" on territory west of the Mississippi River. The majority of Cherokees refused to accept these terms.

As the dispute between the Cherokee nation and Georgia unfolded, Jackson made clear his intention to implement the Indian Removal Act. In 1832 he sent federal troops into western Illinois to force Sauk and Fox peoples to move farther west. Instead, whole villages, led by Chief Black Hawk, fled to the Wisconsin Territory. Black Hawk and a thousand warriors confronted U.S. troops at Bad Axe, but the Sauk and Fox warriors were decimated in a brutal daylong battle. The survivors were forced to move west. Meanwhile the Seminole Indians prepared to go to war to protect their territory, while John Ross pursued legal means to resist removal through state and federal courts. The contest for Indian lands continued well past Jackson's presidency, but the president's desire to force indigenous nations westward would ultimately prevail.

REVIEW & RELATE	• What did President Jackson's response to the Eaton affair and Indian removal reveal about his vision of democracy? • Which of Jackson's policies benefited or antagonized which groups of southerners?

Conclusion: The Nation Faces New Challenges

From the 1810s through the early 1830s, the United States was buffeted by a series of crises. Although early in the period geographical expansion and economic growth led the federal government to invest in internal improvements, the War of 1812 soon threatened the nation's stability and revealed significant regional divisions. The panic of 1819 then threw the nation into economic turmoil and led to demands for expanded voting rights for white men, while African American men experienced increased restrictions on their political participation. Regional differences rooted in different natural resources and economic priorities—manufacturing in the North, cotton and rice cultivation in the South, and family agriculture in the Midwest— were increasing in the 1810s. They led to greater interdependence across regions, but distinct economic needs and uncertainties intensified political debates over issues like tariffs. The admission of Missouri similarly heightened debates over slavery as white southerners saw themselves losing out to the North in population growth and political representation. At the same time, continued western expansion escalated conflicts with a diverse array of Indian nations.

In navigating these difficult issues, some Americans sought to find a middle ground. Dolley Madison worked to overcome partisan divisions through social networking. After the death of her husband, James, in 1836, she returned to Washington and transformed her home into a center of elite social life. Although her son's mismanagement of Montpelier forced her to sell the beloved estate, Dolley secured her old age when Congress purchased President James Madison's papers from her. Similarly, John Ross wielded his biracial heritage to seek rights for Indians within a white-dominated world. He served as both a lobbyist for Cherokee interests in Washington and an advocate of acculturation to Anglo-American ways among the Cherokee. However, congressional passage of the Indian Removal Act challenged Ross's efforts to maintain his tribe's sovereignty and homeland. Henry Clay, too, was widely known for helping to forge compromises on issues like slavery and tariffs. In the 1820s, he brought a deeply divided Congress together, hoping that political leaders could eventually develop permanent solutions.

Despite the efforts of Madison, Ross, Clay, and others, differences often led to division in the 1820s and 1830s. Indeed, Clay's success in ensuring John Quincy Adams's selection as president in 1824 only furthered partisan divisions, leading to the emergence of two distinct political parties: the Democrats and the National Republicans. Andrew Jackson, who led the new Democratic Party, transformed the process of political campaigning. He gave voice to white workers and frontier farmers, but he also introduced the spoils system to government, smashed the Second Bank of the United States, and forced thousands of Indians off their lands. Indian removal, in turn, fostered the expansion of white settlement southward and westward, contributing to the growth of slavery.

Dolley Madison, who lived into the late 1840s, and John Ross, who survived the Civil War, observed the continuing conflicts created by geographical expansion and partisan agendas. Ross, however, faced much more difficult circumstances as the Cherokee nation divided over whether to accept removal and continued to face internal dissent and pressure from the federal government for years.

Despite the dramatically different backgrounds and careers of Madison and Ross, both worked to bridge differences in the young nation, and both defended it against attack. Ultimately, however, neither had the power to overcome the partisan rivalries and economic crises that shaped the young nation or to halt the rising social, economic, and political tensions that would plague Americans in the decades to come.

Chapter 9 Review

KEY TERMS

Non-Intercourse Act (p. 207)
Battle of Fallen Timbers (p. 207)
Hartford Convention (p. 210)
Battle of Horseshoe Bend (p. 211)
Treaty of Ghent (p. 211)
American System (p. 212)
Erie Canal (p. 213)
Adams-Onís Treaty (p. 215)
Monroe Doctrine (p. 215)

panic of 1819 (p. 217)
Missouri Compromise (p. 219)
Democrats and National
    Republicans (p. 224)
Petticoat Affair (p. 225)
spoils system (p. 225)
Tariff of Abominations (p. 226)
nullification (p. 226)
Indian Removal Act (p. 228)

REVIEW & RELATE

1. How were conflicts with Indians in the West connected to ongoing tensions between the United States and Great Britain on land and at sea?
2. What were the long-term consequences of the War of 1812?
3. What role did government play in early-nineteenth-century economic development?
4. How and why did economic development contribute to regional differences and shape regional ties?
5. How did regional interdependency contribute to the panic of 1819?
6. What regional divisions did the conflict over slavery in Missouri reveal?
7. How and why did the composition of the electorate change in the 1820s?
8. How did Jackson's 1828 campaign represent a significant departure from earlier patterns in American politics?
9. What did President Jackson's response to the Eaton affair and Indian removal reveal about his vision of democracy?
10. Which of Jackson's policies benefited or antagonized which groups of southerners?

TIMELINE OF EVENTS

1809
- Non-Intercourse Act

1811
- First steamboat travels down the Mississippi
- William Henry Harrison defeats Shawnees at Prophet Town

June 1812
- War of 1812 begins

1814
- Hartford Convention

March 1814
- Battle of Horseshoe Bend

August 1814
- British burn Washington City

December 1814
- Treaty of Ghent

1815
- Battle of New Orleans

1817–1818
- Andrew Jackson fights Spanish and Seminole forces in Florida

1818
- Great Britain and United States agree to joint occupation of Oregon Territory

1819
- Adams-Onís Treaty

1819–1823
- Panic of 1819

1820
- Missouri Compromise

1821
- White traders begin using Santa Fe Trail

1822
- Denmark Vesey accused of organizing a slave uprising

1823
- Monroe Doctrine articulated

1825
- Erie Canal completed

1828
- Tariff of 1828 (Tariff of Abominations)
- John Ross elected principal chief of the Cherokee nation

1829
- Petticoat Affair

1830
- Indian Removal Act

1832
- South Carolina passes Ordinance of Nullification

1833
- Force Bill

10

Social and Cultural Ferment in the North

1820–1850

LEARNING OBJECTIVES

After reading this chapter you should be able to:

- Explain the growth of and changes in northern cities, including issues of immigration, class stratification, and gender roles.
- Analyze how industrialization transformed workers' lives, was affected by the boom and bust economic cycle, and contributed to class and ethnic tensions.
- Describe the range and appeal of religious movements that emerged in the 1830s and 1840s.
- Evaluate the emergence of reform movements and the strategies they embraced.
- Explain the various forms of antislavery activism and their impact on other social and political changes.

COMPARING AMERICAN HISTORIES

The great revival preacher Charles Grandison Finney was born in 1792 and raised in rural New York State. As a young man, Finney studied the law. But in 1821, like many others of his generation, he experienced a powerful religious conversion. No longer interested in a legal career, he turned to the ministry instead.

After being ordained in the Presbyterian Church, Finney joined "New School" ministers who rejected the more conservative traditions of the Presbyterian Church and embraced a vigorous evangelicalism. In the early 1830s the Reverend Finney traveled throughout New York State preaching about Christ's place in a changing America. He held massive revivals in cities along the Erie Canal, most notably in Rochester, New York. He achieved his greatest success in places experiencing rapid economic development and an influx of migrants and immigrants, where the clash of cultures and classes fueled fears of moral decay.

Finney urged Christians to actively seek salvation. Once individuals reformed themselves, he said, they should work to abolish poverty, intemperance, prostitution, and slavery. He expected women to participate in revivals and good works but advised them to balance these efforts with their domestic responsibilities.

In many ways, Amy Kirby Post fit Finney's ideal. Born into a farm family in Jericho, New York, she found solace in spirituality and social reform. Like many other people in this period, Amy experienced the loss of loved ones. In 1825, at age twenty-three, Amy's fiancé died, and two years later she lost the sister to whom she was closest. The next year, Amy married a widower, Isaac Post. She mothered his two young children and bore five children of her own, two of whom died young. Yet Amy Post did not embrace evangelical revivals, but focused instead on the quiet piety preferred by her Quaker community.

Still, the personal upheavals Amy experienced in her twenties occurred amid heated controversies within the Society of Friends (Quakers). Elias Hicks claimed that the Society had abandoned its spiritual roots and become too much like a traditional church. His followers, called Hicksites, insisted that Quakers should reduce their dependence on disciplinary rules, elders, and preachers and rely instead on the "Inner Light"—the spirit of God dwelling within each individual. When the Society of Friends divided into Hicksite and Orthodox branches in 1827, Amy Kirby and Isaac Post joined the Hicksites.

In 1836 Amy Post moved with her husband and children to Rochester, New York. In a city marked by the spirit of Finney's revivals, Quakers emphasized quiet contemplation rather than emotional conversions, but the Society of Friends allowed members, including women, to preach when moved by the spirit. Quaker women also held separate meetings to discipline female congregants, evaluate marriage proposals, and write testimonies on important religious and social issues.

Amy Post's spiritual journey was increasingly shaped by the rising tide of abolition. Committed to ending slavery, she joined hundreds of local evangelical women in signing an 1837 antislavery petition. Five years later, she helped found the Western New York Anti-Slavery Society, which included Quakers and evangelicals, women and men, and blacks and whites. Post's growing commitment to abolition caused tensions in the Hicksite meeting since some members opposed working in "worldly" organizations alongside non-Quakers. In 1848 Post and other radical Friends formed a new, more activist-oriented Quaker meeting and embraced women's rights as well as abolition.

COMPARING THE AMERICAN HISTORIES of Charles Finney and Amy Post shows how individuals responded to and helped shape the dynamic religious, social, and economic developments of the early nineteenth century. Finney changed the face of American religion, aided by masses of evangelical Protestants. The transportation revolution, the expansion of the market economy, and the rise of cities, especially in the northern United States, benefitted many Americans. However, they also made problems like poverty, unemployment, alcohol abuse, crime, and prostitution more visible, drawing people to Finney's message. Like many Americans, Amy Post migrated with her family along improved roads and canals to seek better economic opportunities. But as the moral stain of slavery continued to grow, she joined other Quakers and some northern blacks in refusing to purchase any slave-produced goods. Bursting traditional religious bonds, she also reconsidered what it meant to do God's work. For both Finney and Post, Rochester—the fastest-growing city in the nation between 1825 and 1835—exemplified the possibilities and the problems created by the market revolution, urban expansion, and rapid social change.

The Market Revolution

Commercial and industrial development, immigration from Europe, and migration from rural areas led to the rapid growth of cities in the northern United States from 1820 on. Such growth both built on and furthered the expansion of roads and canals, which were funded by federal and state governments in the 1810s and 1820s. By linking northern industries with western farms and southern plantations, these innovations in transportation fueled a **market revolution** as the manufacture of goods became better organized and innovations in industry, agriculture, and communication increased efficiency and productivity. These changes fostered urbanization, which, in turn, reinforced economic growth and innovation. However, it also created social upheaval. Cultural divisions intensified in urban areas where Catholics and Protestants, workers and the well-to-do, immigrants, African Americans, and native-born whites lived side by side. Class dynamics also changed with the development of a clear middle class of shopkeepers, professionals, and clerks.

Creating an Urban Landscape

Across the North, urban populations boomed. As commercial centers, seaports like New York and Philadelphia were the most populous cities in the early nineteenth century. Between 1820 and 1850, the number of cities with 100,000 inhabitants increased from two to six; five were seaports. The sixth was the river port of Cincinnati, Ohio. Smaller boomtowns, like Rochester, New York, emerged along inland waterways as the completion of the Erie Canal in 1825 spurred agriculture and industry.

Development along the Erie Canal illustrates the ways that advancements in transportation transformed the surrounding landscape and ecology. As soon as the first stretch was completed in 1819, its economic benefits became clear. As the 40-foot-wide canal was extended across central and western New York State, settlers rushed to establish farms, mills, and ports. They chopped down millions of trees to construct homes and businesses and to open land for farms and orchards. Farmers shipped grain, cattle, and hogs to eastern markets or to emerging cities like Rochester. There millers and butchers turned them into flour, beef, and pork, products that were now easier and cheaper to ship further onward.

As the population in western New York and along the Great Lakes increased, residents demanded more and more manufactured goods. This demand fueled the growth of factories, especially in New England. Cotton, lumber, and flour mills were constructed near waterfalls for power, transforming isolated villages into mill towns while endangering the natural habitats of fish and wildlife. As thousands of newcomers cleared more and more land in Ohio and Michigan, they expanded trade between areas fueled by the Erie Canal and the Great Lakes and older towns from New England to New York City. Moreover, Midwesterners could ship food south via the Ohio and Mississippi Rivers in exchange for southern cotton, rice, and sugar.

Business and political leaders in Philadelphia and Baltimore, seeing the economic benefits created by the Erie Canal, demanded state funding for canals linking them to the Midwest. Where state funding proved insufficient, they persuaded English bankers and merchants to invest in American canals as well as railroads, which were just beginning to compete with waterways as a method to transport people and goods.

The Lure of Urban Life

As transportation improved and the economy expanded, cities across the North increased not only in size but also in diversity. During the 1820s, some 150,000 European immigrants entered the United States; during the 1830s, nearly 600,000; and during the 1840s, more than 1,700,000. This surge of immigrants included more Irish and German settlers than ever before as well as large numbers of Scandinavians. Many settled along the eastern seaboard. Others migrated west, including thousands of Irish immigrants who labored in difficult and dangerous conditions to build the Erie Canal. Many Irish workers quit these jobs and settled in local communities along the canal's route. Others added to the growth of frontier cities such as Cincinnati, St. Louis, and Chicago.

Late eighteenth-century Irish immigrants, many of whom were Protestants, were joined by hundreds of thousands more in the 1830s and 1840s, when Irish Catholics poured into the United States. The Irish countryside was then plagued by bad weather, a potato blight, and harsh economic policies imposed by the English government. In 1845 to 1846 a full-blown famine forced thousands more Irish Catholic families to emigrate. Young Irish women, who could easily find work as domestics or seamstresses, emigrated in especially large numbers. Poor harvests, droughts, failed revolutions, and repressive landlords convinced large numbers of Germans, including Catholics, Lutherans, and Jews, and Scandinavians to flee their homelands as well. By 1850 the Irish made up about 40 percent of immigrants to the United States, and Germans nearly a quarter (Figure 10.1).

These immigrants provided an expanding pool of cheap labor as well as skilled artisans who further fueled northern commerce and industry. Banks, mercantile houses, and dry-goods stores multiplied. Urban industrial enterprises included both traditional workshops and mechanized factories. Credit and insurance agencies emerged to aid entrepreneurs in their ventures. The increase in business also drove the demand for

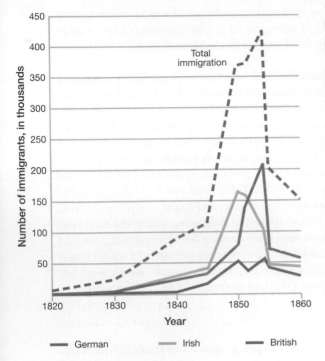

FIGURE 10.1
Immigration to the United States, 1820–1860 Famine, economic upheaval, and political persecution led masses of people from Ireland, Germany, and Britain to migrate to the United States from the 1820s through the 1850s. The vast majority settled in cities and factory towns in the North or on farms in the Midwest. An economic recession in the late 1850s finally slowed immigration, though only temporarily. What does this graph tell us about the growing diversity of the U.S. population?

ships, commercial newspapers, warehouses, and other commercial necessities, which created a surge in jobs for many urban residents.

Businesses focused on leisure also flourished. In the 1830s theater became afford-able to working-class families, who attended comedies, musical revues, and morality plays. They also joined middle- and upper-class audiences at productions of Shake-speare and contemporary dramas. Minstrel shows mocked self-important capitalists but also portrayed African Americans in crude caricatures. One of the most popular characters was Jim Crow, who appeared originally in an African American song. In the 1820s he was incorporated into a song-and-dance routine by Thomas Rice, a white performer who blacked his face with burnt cork.

The lures of urban life were especially attractive to the young. Single men and women and newly married couples flocked to cities. By 1850 half the residents of New York, Philadelphia, and other seaport cities were under sixteen years old. Young men sought work in factories, construction, and the maritime trades or in banks and com-mercial houses, while young women competed for jobs as seamstresses and domestic servants.

The Roots of Urban Disorder

While immigrant labor stimulated northern economic growth, immigrant families transformed the urban landscape. They crowded into houses and apartments and built ethnic institutions, including synagogues and convents—visible indicators of the growing diversity of northern cities. While most native-born Protestants applauded economic growth, cultural diversity aroused anxieties. Anti-Catholicism and anti-Semitism flourished in the 1830s and 1840s. Crude stereotypes portrayed Jews as manipulative moneylenders and Catholic nuns and priests as sexually depraved. Ethnic groups also battled stereotypes. Irishmen, for example, were often pictured as habitual drunkards.

Still, rising immigration did not deter rural Americans from seeking economic opportunities in the city. Native-born white men often set out on their own, but most white women settled in cities under the supervision of a husband, landlady, or employer. African Americans, too, sought greater opportunities in urban areas. In the 1830s, more blacks joined Philadelphia's vibrant African American community, attracted by its churches, schools, and mutual aid societies. New Bedford, Massachusetts, a thriving whaling center, recruited black workers and thus attracted fugitive slaves as well.

Yet even as cities welcomed many migrants and immigrants, newcomers also faced dangers. Racial and ethnic minorities regularly met discrimination and hostility. Physical battles erupted between immigrant and native-born residents, Protestant and Catholic gangs, and white and black workers. Criminal activity flourished as well, and disease spread quickly through densely populated neighborhoods. When innovations in transportation made it possible for more affluent residents to distance themselves from crowded inner cities, they moved to less congested neighborhoods on the urban periphery. Horse-drawn streetcar lines, first built in New York City in 1832, hastened this development.

By the 1840s, economic competition intensified, fueling violence among those driven to the margins. Native-born white employers and workers pushed Irish immigrants to the bottom of the economic ladder, where they competed with African Americans. Yet Irish workers insisted that their whiteness gave them a higher status than even the most skilled blacks. When black temperance reformers organized a parade in Philadelphia in August 1842, white onlookers—mostly Irish laborers— attacked the marchers, and the conflict escalated into a riot.

Americans who lived in small towns and rural areas regularly read news of urban violence and vice. Improvements in printing created vastly more and cheaper newspapers, while the construction of the first telegraph in 1844 ensured that news could travel more quickly from town to town. Tabloids wooed readers with sensational stories of crime, sex, and scandal. Even more respectable newspapers reported on urban mayhem, and religious periodicals warned parishioners against urban immorality. In response to both a real and a perceived increase in crime, cities replaced voluntary night watchmen with paid police forces.

The New Middle Class

Members of the emerging middle class, which developed first in the North, included ambitious businessmen, successful shopkeepers, doctors, and lawyers as well as teachers, journalists, ministers, and other salaried employees. At the top rungs, successful entrepreneurs and professionals adopted affluent lifestyles. At the lower rungs, a growing cohort of salaried clerks and managers hoped that their hard work, honesty, and thrift would be rewarded with upward mobility.

Education, religious affiliation, and sobriety were important indicators of middle-class status. A well-read man who attended a well-established church and drank in strict moderation was marked as belonging to this new rank. He was also expected to own a comfortable home, marry a pious woman, and raise well-behaved children. The rise of the middle class inspired a flood of advice books, ladies' magazines, religious periodicals, and novels advocating new ideals of womanhood. These publications emphasized the centrality of child rearing and homemaking to women's identities. This **cult of domesticity** ideally restricted wives to home and hearth, where they provided their husbands with respite from the cares and corruptions of the world.

In reality, however, entrance to the middle class required the efforts of wives as well as husbands. While upper middle-class men were expected to provide financial security, women helped cement social and economic bonds by entertaining the wives of business associates, serving in charitable and temperance societies, and organizing Sabbath schools. Families struggling to enter the middle class might take in boarders or extended family members to help secure their financial status. The adoption of new marital ideals of affection and companionship also made the boundaries between public and domestic life more fluid. In many middle-class families, husbands and wives both participated in church, civic, and reform activities, even if many did so through single-sex organizations. At the same time, husbands joined in domestic activities in the evening, presiding over dinner or reading to children.

Shoe Shopping from *Godey's Lady's Book*   In the 1830s and 1840s, women's magazines appeared to promote new ideals of middle-class womanhood and to guide them as consumers. This 1848 image of women shopping for shoes from *Godey's Lady's Book* encouraged female outings to elegant emporiums. The lavish engravings created by *Godey's* quickly made it the best-selling "ladies" magazine in the United States.   Archive Photos/Getty Images

The ideal of separate spheres of work and home had even less relevance to the millions of women who toiled on farms and factories or as domestic servants, providing goods and services for middle-class and elite families. In turn, those middle-class families played a crucial role in the growing market economy and the jobs it created. Wives and daughters were responsible for much of the family's consumption. They purchased cloth, rugs, chairs, clocks, and housewares, and, if wealthy enough, European crystal and Chinese porcelain figures. Middling housewives bought goods once made at home, such as butter and candles, and arranged music lessons and other educational opportunities for their children.

Although increasingly recognized for their ability to consume wisely, middle-class women also performed significant domestic labor. While many could afford servants, they often joined domestics and daughters in household tasks. Except for those in the upper middle class, most women still cut and sewed garments, cultivated gardens, canned fruits and vegetables, cooked at least some meals, and entertained guests. As houses expanded in size and clothes became fancier, domestic servants shouldered the most laborious and time-consuming chores, but many mothers and daughters still performed domestic labor as well. However, such work was increasingly invisible, focused inwardly on the family rather than outwardly as part of the market economy.

Middle-class men contributed to the consumer economy by creating and investing in industrial and commercial ventures. Moreover, in carrying out business and professional obligations, many enjoyed restaurants, the theater, or sporting events. Men attended plays and lectures with their wives and visited museums and circuses with their children. They also purchased hats, suits, mustache wax, and other accouterments of middle-class masculinity.

REVIEW & RELATE

- How did the market revolution, including improvements like the Erie Canal, reshape the landscape and lives of Americans in the North?
- As northern cities became larger and more diverse in the first half of the nineteenth century, what changes and challenges did urban residents face and what values and beliefs did the new middle class embrace?

The Rise of Industry

In the mid-nineteenth century, industrial enterprises in the Northeast transformed the nation's economy even though they employed less than 10 percent of the U.S. labor force. In the 1830s and 1840s, factories grew considerably in size, and some investors, especially in textiles, constructed factory towns. New England textile mills relied increasingly on the labor of girls and young women, while urban workshops hired children, young women and men, and older adults. Although men still dominated the skilled trades, making chairs, clocks, shoes, hats, and fine clothing, employment in these trades slowly declined as industrial jobs expanded. An economic panic in 1837 exacerbated this trend and increased tensions that made it more difficult for workers to organize across differences of skill, ethnicity, race, and sex.

Factory Towns and Women Workers

In the late 1820s investors and manufacturers joined forces to create factory towns in the New England countryside. The most famous mill town, Lowell, Massachusetts, was based on an earlier experiment in nearby Waltham. In the Waltham system, every step of the production process was mechanized; planned communities included factories, boardinghouses, government offices, and churches. Agents for the Waltham system recruited the daughters of New England farm families as workers, assuring parents that they would be watched over by managers and foremen as well as landladies. The young women were required to attend church and observe curfews, and their labor was regulated by clocks and bells to ensure discipline and productivity.

Farm families needed more cash because of the growing market economy, and daughters in the mills could contribute to family finances and save money for the clothes and linens required for married life. Factory jobs also provided an alternative to marriage as young New England men moved west and left a surplus of women behind. Boardinghouses provided a relatively safe, all-female environment for the young mill workers, and sisters and neighbors often lived together. Despite nearly constant supervision, many rural women viewed factory work as an adventure. They could set aside a bit of money for themselves, attend lectures and concerts, meet new people, and acquire a wider view of the world.

During the 1830s, however, working conditions began to deteriorate. Factory owners cut wages, lengthened hours, and sped up machines. Boardinghouses became overcrowded, and company officials regulated both rents and expenses so that higher prices for lodging did not necessarily mean better food or furnishings. Factory workers launched numerous strikes in the 1830s against longer hours, wage cuts, and speed-ups in factory production. The solidarity required to sustain these strikes was forged in boardinghouses and at church socials as well as on the factory floor. At age twelve, Harriet Robinson led a walkout at the Lowell Mills in 1836. In her memoir, written in 1898, she noted, "As I looked back at the long line that followed me, I was more proud than I have ever been since at any success I have achieved."

Despite mill workers' solidarity, it was difficult to overcome the economic power wielded by manufacturers. Working women's efforts at collective action were generally short-lived, lasting only until a strike was settled. Then employees returned to their jobs until the next crisis hit. And as competition increasingly cut into profits, owners resisted mill workers' demands more vehemently. When the panic of 1837 intensified fears of job loss, women's organizing activities were doomed until the economy recovered.

The Decline of Craft Work and Workingmen's Responses

While the construction of factory towns expanded economic opportunities for young women, the gradual decline of time-honored crafts narrowed the prospects for workingmen. Craft workshops gradually increased in size and hired fewer skilled workers and more men who performed single tasks, like attaching soles to shoes. Many tasks also became mechanized during the nineteenth century. The final product was less distinctive than an entire item crafted by a skilled artisan, but it was less expensive and available in mass quantities.

The shift from craft work to factory work threatened to undermine workingmen's skills, pay, and labor conditions. Masters began hiring foremen to regulate the workforce and installing bells and clocks to regulate the workday. As this process of **deskilling** transformed shoemaking, printing, tailoring, and other trades, laboring men fought to maintain their status.

Some workers formed mutual aid societies to provide assistance in times of illness, injury, or unemployment. Others participated in religious revivals or joined fraternal orders to find the camaraderie they once enjoyed at work. The expansion of voting rights in the 1820s offered another avenue for action. The first workingmen's political party was founded in Philadelphia in 1827, and working-class men in the North joined forces to support politicians sympathetic to their needs. Most workingmen's parties focused on practical proposals: government distribution of free land in the West, abolishing compulsory militia service and imprisonment for debt, public funding for education, and regulations on banks and corporations. Although the electoral success of these parties was modest, in the 1830s Democrats and Whigs adopted many of their proposals.

Workingmen also formed unions to demand better wages and working conditions. In the 1820s and 1830s, skilled journeymen held mass meetings to protest employers' efforts to lengthen the workday, merge smaller workshops into larger factories, and cut wages. In New York City in 1834, labor activists formed a citywide federation, the General Trades Union, which provided support for striking workers. The National Trades Union was established later that year, with delegates representing more than twenty-five thousand workers across the North. These organizations aided skilled workers but refused admission to women and unskilled men.

It proved difficult to establish broader labor organizations, however. Most skilled workers considered unskilled workers as competitors, not allies. Many workingmen feared women workers would undercut their wages and so refused to organize alongside them. And anti-immigrant and racist beliefs among many native-born Protestant workers interfered with organizing across racial and ethnic lines. With the onset of the panic of 1837, the common plight of workers became clearer. But the economic crisis made unified action nearly impossible as individuals sought to hold on to what little they had.

The Panic of 1837

The panic of 1837 began in the South but hit northern cotton merchants hard (see "Van Buren and the Panic of 1837" in Chapter 11). With cotton shipments sharply curtailed, textile factories drastically cut production, unemployment rose, and merchants and investors went broke. Those still employed saw their wages cut in half. In Rochester, the Posts temporarily moved in with family members and their oldest son left school to help save their pharmacy from foreclosure. Petty crime, prostitution, and violence also rose as men and women struggled to make ends meet.

In Lowell, hours increased and wages fell. Just as important, the process of deskilling intensified. Factory owners considered mechanization one way to improve their economic situation. A cascade of inventions, including power looms, steam boilers, and the steam press, transformed industrial occupations and led factory owners to invest more of their limited resources in machines. At the same time, the rising tide of immigrants provided a ready supply of relatively cheap labor. Artisans tried to maintain their traditional skills and status, but in many trades they were fighting a losing battle.

By the early 1840s, when the panic subsided, new technologies did spur new jobs. Factories demanded more workers to handle machines that ran at a faster pace. In printing, the steam press allowed publication of more newspapers and magazines, creating positions for editors, publishers, printers, engravers, reporters, and sales agents. Similarly, mechanical reapers sped the harvest of wheat and inspired changes in flour milling that required engineers to design machines and mechanics to build and repair them.

These changing circumstances fueled new labor organizations as well. Many of these unions comprised a particular trade or ethnic group, and almost all continued to address primarily the needs of skilled male workers. Textile operatives remained the one important group of organized female workers. In the 1840s, workingwomen joined with workingmen in New England to fight for a ten-hour day. Slowly, however, farmers' daughters left the mills as desperate Irish immigrants flooded in and accepted lower wages.

For most women in need, charitable organizations offered more support than unions. Organizations like Philadelphia's Female Association for the Relief of Women and Children in Reduced Circumstances provided a critical safety net for many poor families since public monies for such purposes were limited. Although most northern towns and cities now provided some form of public assistance, they never had sufficient resources to meet local needs in good times, much less the extraordinary demands posed by the panic.

REVIEW & RELATE	• How and why did American manufacturing change during the first half of the nineteenth century? • How did new technologies, immigration, and the panic of 1837 change the economic opportunities and organizing strategies for northern workers?

Saving the Nation from Sin

In the first half of the nineteenth century, men and women of all classes and races embraced the Protestant religious revival known as the **Second Great Awakening** to express deeply held beliefs and reclaim a sense of the nation's godly mission. Yet evangelical Protestantism was not the only religious tradition to thrive in this period. Catholic churches and Jewish synagogues multiplied with immigration, and in the North Quaker meetings and Unitarian congregations flourished as well. New religious groups also attracted thousands of followers while transcendentalists sought deeper engagements with nature as another path to spiritual renewal.

The Second Great Awakening

Although diverse religious traditions flourished in the United States, evangelical Protestantism proved the most powerful in the 1820s and 1830s. Evangelical churches hosted revivals, celebrated conversions, and organized prayer and missionary societies. This second wave of religious revivals began in Cane Ridge, Kentucky in 1801, and took root across the South. It then spread northward, transforming Protestant churches and the social fabric of northern life.

Ministers like Charles Grandison Finney adopted techniques first wielded by southern Methodists and Baptists: plain speaking, powerful images, and mass meetings. But Finney molded these techniques for a more affluent audience and held his "camp meetings" in established churches. By the late 1820s, boomtown growth along the Erie Canal aroused deep concerns among religious leaders about the rising tide of sin. In response, the Reverend Finney arrived in Rochester in September 1830. He began preaching in local Presbyterian churches, leading crowded prayer meetings that lasted late into the night. Individual supplicants walked to special benches designated for anxious sinners, who were prayed over in public. Female parishioners played crucial roles, encouraging their husbands, sons, friends, and neighbors to submit to God.

Thousands of Rochester residents joined in the evangelical experience as Finney's powerful message engulfed other denominations (Map 10.1). The significance of these revivals went far beyond an increase in church membership. Finney converted "the great mass of the most influential people" in the city: merchants, lawyers, doctors, master craftsmen, and shopkeepers. Equally important, he proclaimed that if Christians were "united all over the world the Millennium [Christ's Second Coming] might be brought about in three months." Preachers in Rochester and the surrounding towns took up his call, and converts committed themselves to preparing the world for Christ's arrival.

Developments in Rochester were replicated in cities across the North. Presbyterian, Congregational, and Episcopalian churches overflowed with middle-class and wealthy Americans, while Baptists and Methodists ministered to more laboring women and men. Black Baptists and Methodists evangelized in their own communities, combining powerful preaching with rousing spirituals. In Philadelphia, African Americans built fifteen churches between 1799 and 1830. A few black women joined men in evangelizing to their fellow African Americans.

MAP 10.1

Religious Movements in the Burned-Over District, 1831–1848 Western and central New York State was burned over by the fires of religious revivalism in the 1830s and 1840s. But numerous other religious groups also formed or flourished in the region in these decades, including Quakers, Mormons, and Millerites. In the 1840s, Fourierist phalanxes, the Oneida community, and other utopian experiments were established here.

Source: Whitney R. Cross, *The Burned-Over District: The Social and Intellectual History of Enthusiastic Religion in Western New York, 1800–1850* (Ithaca, NY: Cornell University Press, 1950).

Tens of thousands of black and white converts embraced evangelicals' message of moral outreach. No reform movement gained greater impetus from the revivals than **temperance**, whose advocates sought to moderate and then ban the sale and consumption of alcohol. In the 1820s Americans fifteen years and older consumed six to seven gallons of distilled alcohol per person per year (about double the amount consumed today). Middle-class evangelicals, who once accepted moderate drinking as healthful, now insisted on eliminating alcohol consumption altogether.

New Visions of Faith and Reform

Although enthusiasm for temperance and other reforms waned during the panic of 1837 and many churches lost members, the Second Great Awakening continued in its aftermath. But now evangelical ministers competed for souls with a variety of other religious groups, many of which supported good works and social reform. The Society of Friends, the first religious group to refuse fellowship to slaveholders, expanded throughout the early nineteenth century, but largely in the North and Midwest. Having divided in 1827 and again in 1848, the Society of Friends continued to grow. So, too, did its influence in reform movements as activists like Amy Post carried Quaker testimonies against alcohol, war, and slavery into the wider society. Unitarians also combined religious worship with social reform. They differed from other Christians by believing in a single unified higher spirit rather than the Trinity of the Father, the Son, and the Holy Spirit. Emerging mainly in New England in the early nineteenth century, Unitarian societies slowly spread west and south in the 1830s. Opposed to evangelical revivalism and dedicated to a rational approach to understanding the divine, Unitarians attracted prominent literary figures such as James Russell Lowell and Harvard luminaries like William Ellery Channing.

Other churches grew as a result of immigration. Dozens of Catholic churches were established to meet the needs of Irish and some German immigrants. With the rapid increase in Catholic churches, Irish priests multiplied in the 1840s and 1850s, and women's religious orders became increasingly Irish as well. At the same time, synagogues, Hebrew schools, and Hebrew aid societies signaled the growing presence of Jewish immigrants, chiefly from Germany, in the United States. These religious groups were less active in social reform and more focused on assisting their own congregants in securing a foothold in their new home.

Entirely new religious groups also flourished in the 1840s. One of the most important was the Church of Jesus Christ of Latter-Day Saints, or Mormons, founded by Joseph Smith. Smith began to receive visions from God at age fifteen and was directed to dig up gold plates inscribed with instructions for redeeming the Lost Tribes of Israel. *The Book of Mormon* (1830), supposedly based on these inscriptions, served, along with the Bible, as the scriptural foundation of the Church of Jesus Christ of Latter-Day Saints, which Smith led as the Prophet.

Smith founded not only a church but a theocracy (a community governed by religious leaders). In the mid-1830s Mormons established a settlement at Nauvoo, Illinois and recruited followers—black and white—from the eastern United States and England. When Smith voiced antislavery views, some local residents expressed outrage. But it was his claim to revelations sanctioning polygamy that led local authorities to arrest him and his brother. When a mob then lynched the Smith brothers, Brigham Young, a successful missionary, took over as Prophet. In 1846 he led 12,000 followers west, 5,000 of whom settled near the Great Salt Lake, in what would soon become the Utah Territory. Isolated from anti-Mormon mobs, Young established a thriving theocracy. In this settlement, leaders practiced polygamy and denied black members the right to become priests.

New religious groups also formed by separating from established denominations. William Miller, a prosperous farmer and Baptist preacher, claimed that the Bible proved that the Second Coming of Jesus Christ would occur in 1843. Thousands of Americans joined the Millerites. When various dates for Christ's Second Coming passed without incident, however, Millerites developed competing interpretations for the failure and divided into distinct groups. The most influential group formed the Seventh-Day Adventist Church in the 1840s.

Transcendentalism

Another important movement for spiritual renewal was rooted in the transcendent power of nature. The founder of this transcendentalist school of thought was Ralph

Thomas Cole, *View of the Round-Top in the Catskills Mountains*, 1827   Thomas Cole was born in England in 1801, migrated to America in 1818, and lived for many years in Catskill, New York with his wife and children until his death in 1848. Many of his paintings captured a romantic view of nature that combined a hint of wildness with the beauty of mountain mists and sunlit rivers shown here.   Bridgeman Images

Waldo Emerson. Raised a Unitarian, Emerson began challenging the church's ideas. His 1836 essay entitled "Nature" expounded his newfound belief in a Universal Being. This Being existed as an ideal reality beyond the material world and was accessible through nature. Emerson's natural world was distinctly American and suggested that moral perfection could be achieved in the United States. Emerson expressed his ideas in widely read essays and books and in popular lectures.

Emerson's hometown of Concord, Massachusetts served as a haven for writers, poets, intellectuals, and reformers who were drawn to **transcendentalism**. In 1840 Margaret Fuller, a close friend of Emerson, became the first editor of *The Dial*, a journal dedicated to transcendental thought. In 1844 she moved to New York City, where Horace Greeley hired her as a critic at the *New York Tribune*. She soon published a book, *Woman in the Nineteenth Century* (1845), which combined transcendental ideas with arguments for women's rights.

Henry David Thoreau also followed the transcendentalist path. He grew up in Concord and read "Nature" while a student at Harvard in the mid-1830s. In July 1845 Thoreau moved to a cabin near Walden Pond and launched an experiment in simple living. A year later he was imprisoned overnight for refusing to pay his taxes as a protest against slavery and the Mexican-American War. In the anonymous *Civil Disobedience* (1846), Thoreau argued that individuals of conscience had the right to resist government policies they believed to be immoral. Five years later, he published *Walden*, which highlighted the interplay among a simple lifestyle, natural harmony, and social justice.

Like Emerson, many American artists embraced the power of nature. Led by Thomas Cole, members of the Hudson River School painted romanticized landscapes from New York's Catskill and Adirondack Mountains. Some northern artists also traveled to the West, painting the region's grand vistas. Pennsylvanian George Catlin portrayed the dramatic scenery of western mountains, gorges, and waterfalls and also painted moving portraits of Plains Indians.

REVIEW & RELATE

- What impact did the Second Great Awakening have in the North?
- What new religious organizations and viewpoints emerged in the first half of the nineteenth century, *outside* of Protestant evangelical denominations?

Organizing for Change

Both religious commitments and secular problems spurred social activism in the 1830s and 1840s. In cities, small towns, and rural communities, Northerners founded organizations, launched campaigns, and established institutions to better the world around them. Yet even Americans who agreed that society needed to be reformed still often disagreed over priorities and solutions. Moreover, while some activists employed moral arguments to persuade Americans to follow their lead, others insisted that laws that imposed reform were the only effective means of change.

Varieties of Reform

Middle-class Protestants formed the core of many reform movements in the mid-nineteenth-century North. They had more time and money to devote to social reform than did their working-class counterparts and were less tied to traditional ways than their wealthy neighbors. Nonetheless, workers and farmers, African Americans and immigrants, Catholics and Jews also participated in efforts to improve society.

Reformers used different techniques to pursue their goals. Since women could not vote, for example, they were excluded from direct political participation. Instead, they established charitable associations, distributed food and medicine, constructed asylums, circulated petitions, organized boycotts, arranged meetings and lectures, and published newspapers and pamphlets. Other groups with limited political rights—African Americans and immigrants, for instance—embraced similar modes of action and also formed mutual aid societies. Native-born white men wielded these forms of activism and, in addition, organized political campaigns and lobbied legislators. The reform techniques chosen were also affected by the goals of a particular movement. Moral suasion worked best with families, churches, and local communities, while legislation was more likely to succeed if the goal involved transforming people's behavior across a whole state or region.

Reformers often used a variety of tactics to support a single cause, and many changed their approach over time. For instance, reformers who sought to eradicate prostitution in the 1830s prayed in front of urban brothels and attempted to rescue "fallen" women. They soon launched *The Advocate of Moral Reform*, a monthly journal filled with morality tales, advice to mothers, and lists of men who visited brothels. In small towns, moral reformers sought to alert young women and men to the dangers of city life. By the 1840s, urban reformers opened Homes for Virtuous and Friendless Females to provide safe havens for vulnerable women. And across the country, moral reformers began petitioning state legislators to make punishments for men who hired prostitutes as harsh as those for prostitutes themselves.

The Problem of Poverty

Poverty had existed since the colonial era, but the panic of 1837 aroused greater public concern. Leaders of both government and private charitable endeavors increasingly linked relief to the moral character of those in need. Affluent Americans had long debated whether the poor would learn habits of industry and thrift if they were simply given aid without working for it. The debate was deeply gendered. Women and children were considered the worthiest recipients of aid, and middle- and upper-class women the appropriate dispensers of charity. Successful men, meanwhile, often linked poverty to weakness and considered giving pennies to a beggar an unmanly act that indulged the worst traits of the poor.

While towns and cities had long relegated the poorest residents to almshouses or workhouses, charitable societies in the early nineteenth century sought to change the conditions that produced poverty. As the poor increased with urban growth, northern charitable ladies began visiting poor neighborhoods, offering blankets, clothing, food, and medicine to needy residents. But the problem seemed intractable, and many charitable organizations began building orphan asylums, hospitals, and homes for working women to provide deserving but vulnerable individuals with resources to improve their life chances.

The "undeserving" poor faced grimmer choices. They generally received assistance only through the workhouse or the local jail. By the 1830s images of rowdy men who drank or gambled away what little they earned, prostitutes who tempted respectable men into vice, and immigrants who preferred idle poverty to virtuous labor became stock figures in debates over the causes of and responses to poverty.

At the same time, young poor women—at least if they were white and Protestant—were increasingly portrayed as the victims of immoral men or unfortunate circumstance. In fictional tales, naive girls were seduced and abandoned by manipulative men. One of the first mass-produced books in the United States, Nathaniel Hawthorne's *The Scarlet Letter* (1850), was set in Puritan New England but addressed contemporary concerns about the seduction of innocents. It illustrated the social ostracism and poverty suffered by a woman who bore a child out of wedlock.

Other fictional tales placed the blame for fallen women on foreigners, especially Catholics. Such works drew vivid portraits of young nuns ravished by priests and then thrown out pregnant and penniless. These stories heightened anti-Catholic sentiment, which periodically boiled over into attacks on Catholic homes, schools, churches, and convents.

At the same time, economic competition intensified conflicts between immigrants and native-born Americans. By the 1840s Americans who opposed immigration took the name **nativists** and launched public political campaigns that blamed foreigners for poverty and crime. Samuel F. B. Morse, the inventor of the telegraph, was among the most popular anti-immigrant spokesmen. Irish Catholics were often targeted in attacks against immigrants. In May 1844 working-class nativists clashed with Irishmen in Philadelphia after shots were fired from a firehouse. A dozen nativists and one Irishman were killed the first day. The next night, nativists looted and burned Irish businesses and Catholic churches.

Many nativists blamed poverty among immigrants on their drinking habits. Others considered alcohol abuse, whether by native-born or immigrant Americans, the root cause not only of poverty but of many social evils.

The Temperance Movement

Temperance advocates first organized officially in 1826 with the founding of the American Temperance Society. This all-male organization was led by clergy and businessmen but focused on alcohol abuse among working-class men. Religious revivals inspired the establishment of some 5,000 local chapters, and black and white men founded other temperance organizations as well. Over time, the temperance movement changed its goal from moderation to total abstinence, targeted middle-class and elite as well as working-class men, and welcomed women's support. Wives and mothers were expected to persuade male kin to stop drinking and sign a temperance pledge. Women founded dozens of temperance societies in the 1830s, which funded the circulation of didactic tales, woodcuts, and etchings about the dangers of "demon rum."

Some workingmen viewed temperance as a way to gain dignity and respect. For Protestants, in particular, embracing temperance distinguished them from Irish Catholic workers. A few working-class temperance advocates criticized liquor dealers, whom they claimed directed "the vilest, meanest, most earth-cursing and hell-filling business ever followed." More turned to self-improvement. In the 1840s small groups of laboring men formed Washingtonian societies—named in honor of the nation's founder—to help each other stop excessive drinking. Martha Washington societies appeared shortly thereafter, composed of the wives, mothers, and sisters of male alcoholics.

Despite the rapid growth of temperance organizations, moral suasion failed to reduce alcohol consumption significantly. As a result, many temperance advocates turned to legal reform. In 1851 Maine was the first state to legally prohibit the sale of alcoholic beverages. By 1855 twelve more states had restricted the manufacture or sale of alcohol. Yet these stringent measures inspired a backlash. Hostile to the imposition of middle-class Protestant standards on the population at large, Irish workers in Maine organized the Portland Rum Riot in 1855. It led to the Maine law's repeal the next year. Still, the diverse strategies used by temperance advocates gradually reduced, but did not eliminate, the consumption of beer, wine, and spirits across the United States.

Utopian Communities

While most reformers reached out to the wider society to implement change, some activists established self-contained communities to serve as models for others. The architects of these **utopian societies**, most formed in the North and Midwest, gained inspiration from European intellectuals and reformers as well as American religious and republican ideals.

In the 1820s Scottish and Welsh labor radicals such as Frances Wright, Robert Owen, and his son Robert Dale Owen established several utopian communities in the United States. They perceived the young republic as open to experiments in communal labor, gender equality, and (in Wright's case) racial justice. Their efforts ultimately failed, but they did arouse impassioned debate.

Then in 1841, former Unitarian minister George Ripley established a transcendentalist community at Brook Farm in Massachusetts. Four years later, Brook Farm was reorganized according to the principles of the French socialist Charles Fourier. Fourier believed that cooperation across classes was necessary to temper the conflicts inherent in capitalist society. He developed a plan for communities, called phalanxes, where residents chose jobs based on individual interest but were paid according to the contribution of each job to the community's well-being. Fourier also advocated equality for women. More than forty Fourierist phalanxes were founded in the northern United States during the 1840s.

A more uniquely American experiment, the Oneida community, was established in central New York by John Humphrey Noyes in 1848. He and his followers believed that Christ's Second Coming had already occurred and embraced the communalism of the early Christian church. Noyes required members to relinquish their private property to the community and to embrace the notion of "complex marriage," in which women and men were free to have sexual intercourse with any consenting adult. He also introduced a form of birth control that sought to ensure women's freedom from constant childbearing and instituted communal child-rearing practices. Divorce and remarriage were also permitted. Despite the public outrage provoked by Oneida's economic and sexual practices, the community recruited several hundred residents and thrived for more than three decades.

"Women Drawing Water, Bishop Hill Colony," c. 1860   This painting by Olaf Kraus captures the collective labor that characterized communal life at Bishop Hill Colony, Illinois. This utopian community was founded in 1846 by Eric Jansen, a critic of the Lutheran Church in Sweden. Forced to emigrate, he recruited 1400 other dissidents to join him on the American prairie. Kraus painted several scenes while living at Bishop Hill.   Granger Collection, NYC

REVIEW & RELATE

- How did efforts to alleviate poverty and temper alcohol consumption reflect the range of reform tactics and participants during the 1830s and 1840s?
- What connections can you identify between utopian communities and mainstream reform movements in the first half of the nineteenth century?

Abolitionism Expands and Divides

For a small percentage of Northerners, slavery was the ultimate injustice. While most Northerners considered it sufficient to rid their own region of human bondage, antislavery advocates argued that the North remained complicit in the institution. After all, slaves labored under brutal conditions to provide cotton for New England factories, sugar and molasses for northern tables, and profits for urban traders. Free blacks were the earliest advocates of abolition, but their role in the movement generated conflict as more whites joined in the 1830s. The place of the church, of women, and of politics in antislavery efforts also stirred controversy. By the 1840s abolitionists disagreed over whether to focus on abolishing slavery in the South or simply preventing its extension into western territories. These debates often weakened individual organizations but expanded the range of antislavery associations and campaigns.

The Beginnings of the Antislavery Movement

In the 1820s African Americans and a few white Quakers led the fight to abolish slavery. They published pamphlets, lectured to small audiences, and helped runaway slaves reach freedom. In 1829 David Walker wrote the most militant antislavery statement, ***Appeal . . . to the Colored Citizens of the World***. The free son of an enslaved father, Walker left his North Carolina home for Boston in the 1820s and became a writer for *Freedom's Journal*, the country's first newspaper published by African Americans. In his *Appeal*, Walker warned that slaves would claim their freedom by force if whites did not agree to emancipate them. Some northern blacks feared Walker's radical *Appeal* would unleash a white backlash, while Quaker abolitionists like Benjamin Lundy, editor of the *Genius of Universal Emancipation*, admired Walker's courage but rejected his call for violence. Nonetheless the Appeal circulated widely among free and enslaved blacks, with copies spreading from northern cities to Charleston, Savannah, New Orleans, and Norfolk.

William Lloyd Garrison, a white Bostonian who worked on Lundy's newspaper, was inspired by Walker's radical stance. In 1831 he launched his own abolitionist newspaper, the ***Liberator***. He urged white antislavery activists to embrace the goal of immediate emancipation without compensation to slave owners, a position first advocated by the English Quaker Elizabeth Heyrick.

The *Liberator* demanded that whites take an absolute stand against slavery but use moral persuasion rather than armed force to halt its spread. With like-minded black and white activists in Boston, Philadelphia, and New York City, Garrison organized the **American Anti-Slavery Society (AASS)** in 1833. By the end of the decade, the AASS boasted branches in dozens of towns and cities across the North. Members supported lecturers and petition drives, criticized churches that refused to denounce slavery, and proclaimed the U.S. Constitution a proslavery document. Some Garrisonians also participated in the work of the **underground railroad**, a secret network of activists who assisted fugitives fleeing enslavement (Map 10.2).

In 1835 Sarah and Angelina Grimké joined the AASS and soon began lecturing for the organization. Daughters of a prominent South Carolina planter, they had moved to Philadelphia and converted to Quakerism. As white Southerners, their denunciations of slavery carried particular weight. Yet as women, their public presence aroused fierce opposition. In 1837 Congregationalist ministers in Massachusetts decried their presence in front of "promiscuous" audiences of men and women, but 1,500 female millworkers still turned out to hear them at Lowell's city hall.

Maria Stewart, a free black widow in Boston, spoke out against slavery even earlier. In 1831 to 1832, she lectured to mixed-sex and interracial audiences, demanding that northern blacks take more responsibility for ending slavery and fighting racial discrimination. In 1833 free black and white Quaker women formed an interracial organization, the Philadelphia Female Anti-Slavery Society, which advocated the boycott of cotton, sugar, and other slave-produced goods.

The abolitionist movement quickly expanded to the frontier, where debates over slave and free territory were especially intense. In 1836 Ohio claimed more antislavery

MAP 10.2

The Underground Railroad c. 1850   Free blacks and their white allies aided men and women who fled slavery from the 1790s on. By 1840, the system became more organized with individual conductors offering safe havens along well-worn routes. Former fugitives, most famously Harriet Tubman, joined the effort and provided advice to those deciding whether to stay in the states or continue on to Canada.

groups than any other state, and Ohio women initiated a petition drive to abolish slavery in the District of Columbia. The petition campaign, which spread across the North, inspired the first national meeting of women abolitionists in 1837. Other antislavery organizations, like the AASS, recruited male and female abolitionists, black and white. And still others remained all-white, all-black, and single-sex.

Abolition Gains Ground and Enemies

The growth of the abolitionist movement shocked many Northerners, and in the late 1830s violence often erupted in response to antislavery agitation. Northern manufacturers and merchants were generally hostile, fearing abolitionists' effect on the profitable trade in cotton, sugar, cloth, and rum. And white workingmen feared increased competition for jobs. In the 1830s mobs routinely attacked antislavery meetings, lecturers, and presses. At the 1838 Antislavery Convention of American Women at

Philadelphia's Pennsylvania Hall, mobs forced black and white women to flee and then burned the hall to the ground.

Massive antislavery petition campaigns in 1836 and 1837 generated opposition in and between the North and South. Thousands of abolitionists, including Amy Post and her husband, Isaac, signed petitions to ban slavery in the District of Columbia, end the internal slave trade, and oppose the annexation of Texas. Some evangelical women considered such efforts part of their Christian duty, but most ministers (including Finney) condemned antislavery work as outside women's sphere. Most female evangelicals retreated in the face of clerical disapproval, but others continued their efforts alongside their non-evangelical sisters. Meanwhile incensed Southern politicians persuaded Congress to pass the gag rule in 1836, which tabled all antislavery petitions without discussion.

But gag rules did not silence abolitionists. Indeed new groups of activists, especially fugitive slaves, offered potent personal tales of the horrors of bondage. The most famous fugitive abolitionist was Frederick Douglass, a Maryland-born slave who in 1838 fled to New Bedford, Massachusetts. He met Garrison in 1841, joined the AASS, and four years later published his life story, *Narrative of the Life of Frederick Douglass, as Told by Himself.* Having revealed his identity as a former slave, Douglass sailed for England, where he launched a successful two-year lecture tour. While he was abroad, British abolitionists purchased Douglass's freedom from his owner, and Douglass returned to the United States a free man. In 1847 he decided to launch his own antislavery newspaper, the *North Star*, a decision that Garrison and other white AASS leaders opposed. Douglass moved to Rochester, where he had earlier found free black and white Quaker allies, including Amy Post.

While eager to have fugitive slaves tell their dramatic stories, many white abolitionists did not match Post's vigorous support of African Americans who asserted an independent voice. Some abolitionists opposed slavery but still believed that blacks were racially inferior; others supported racial equality but assumed that black abolitionists would defer to white leaders. Thus several affiliates of the AASS refused to accept black members. Ultimately, the independent efforts of Douglass and other black activists expanded the antislavery movement even as they made clear the limits of white abolitionist ideals.

Conflicts also arose over the responsibility of churches to challenge slavery. The major Protestant denominations included southern as well as northern churches. If mainstream churches—Presbyterians, Baptists, Methodists—refused communion to slave owners, their southern branches would secede. Still, from the 1830s on, abolitionists pressured churches to take Christian obligations seriously and denounce human bondage. Individual congregations responded, but aside from the Society of Friends, larger denominations failed to follow suit.

In response, abolitionists urged parishioners to break with churches that admitted slaveholders as members. Antislavery preachers pushed the issue, and some worshippers "came out" from mainstream churches to form antislavery congregations. White Wesleyan Methodists and Free Will Baptists joined African American Methodists and Baptists in insisting that their members oppose slavery. Although these churches remained small, they served as a living challenge to mainstream denominations.

Abolitionism and Women's Rights

Women were increasingly active in the AASS and the "come outer" movement, but their growing participation aroused opposition even among abolitionists. By 1836 to 1837, female societies formed the backbone of many antislavery petition campaigns. More women also joined the lecture circuit, including Abby Kelley, a fiery orator who demanded that women be granted an equal role in the movement. But when Garrison and his supporters appointed Kelley to the AASS business committee in May 1839, angry debates erupted over the propriety of women participating "in closed meetings with men." Of the 1,000 abolitionists in attendance, some 300 walked out in protest. The dissidents, including many evangelical men, soon formed a new organization, the American and Foreign Anti-Slavery Society, which excluded women from public lecturing and office holding but encouraged them to support men's efforts.

Those who remained in the AASS then continued to expand the roles of women. In 1840 local chapters appointed a handful of female delegates, including Lucretia Mott of Philadelphia, to the World Anti-Slavery Convention in London. The majority of men at the meeting, however, rejected the female delegates' credentials. Women were then forced to watch the proceedings from a separate section of the hall, confirming for some that women could be effective in campaigns against slavery only if they gained more rights for themselves.

Finally, in July 1848, a small circle of women, including Lucretia Mott and a young American she met in London, Elizabeth Cady Stanton, organized the first convention focused explicitly on women's rights. Held in Stanton's hometown of Seneca Falls, New York, the convention attracted three hundred women and men. James Mott, husband of Lucretia, presided over the convention, and Frederick Douglass spoke, but women dominated the proceedings. One hundred participants, including Amy Post, signed the **Declaration of Sentiments**, which called for women's equality in everything from education and employment to legal rights and voting. Two weeks later, Post helped organize a second convention in Rochester, where participants took the radical action of electing a woman, Abigail Bush, to preside. Here, too, Douglass spoke alongside other black abolitionists and local working women.

Although abolitionism provided much of the impetus for the women's rights movement, other movements also contributed. Strikes by seamstresses and mill workers in the 1830s and 1840s highlighted women's economic needs. Utopian communities experimented with gender equality, and temperance reformers focused attention on domestic violence and sought changes in divorce laws. A diverse coalition also advocated for married women's property rights in the mid-1840s. Women's rights were debated among New York's Seneca Indians as well. Like the Cherokee, Seneca women had lost traditional rights over land and tribal policy as their nation adopted Anglo-American ways. In the summer of 1848, the creation of a written constitution threatened to enshrine these losses in writing. The Seneca constitution did strip women of their dominant role in selecting chiefs but protected their right to vote on the sale of tribal lands. Earlier in 1848, revolutions had erupted against repressive regimes in France and elsewhere in Europe. Antislavery newspapers like the *North Star* covered developments in detail, including European women's demands for political and civil recognition. The meetings in Seneca Falls and Rochester drew on these ideas and influences even as they focused primarily on the rights of white American women.

The Rise of Antislavery Parties

As women's rights advocates demanded female suffrage, debates over the role of partisan politics in the antislavery campaign intensified. Keeping slavery out of western territories depended on the actions of Congress, as did abolishing slavery in the nation's capital and ending the internal slave trade. Moral suasion had seemingly done little to change minds in Congress or in the South. To force abolition onto the national political agenda, the **Liberty Party** was formed in 1840. Many Garrisonians were appalled at the idea of participating in national elections when the federal government supported slavery in numerous ways, from the three-fifths compromise to allowing slavery in newly acquired territories. Still, the Liberty Party gained significant support among abolitionists in New York, the Middle Atlantic states, and the Midwest.

The Whigs and Democrats generally avoided the antislavery issue to keep their southern and northern wings intact, but that strategy became more difficult once the Liberty Party entered campaigns. In 1840 the party won less than 1 percent of the popular vote but organized rallies that attracted large crowds. In 1844 the party more than doubled its votes, which was sufficient to deny Henry Clay a victory in New York State and thus ensure the election of James K. Polk (see "Expanding to Oregon and Texas" in Chapter 11).

When President Polk led the United States into war with Mexico, interest in an antislavery political party surged. In 1848 the Liberty Party gained the support of antislavery Whigs, also called Conscience Whigs; northern Democrats who opposed the extension of slavery into the territories; and African American leaders like Frederick Douglass, who broke with Garrison on the utility of electoral politics. Seeing a political opportunity, more practically minded political abolitionists founded the **Free-Soil Party**, which quickly subsumed the Liberty Party. Free-Soilers focused less on the moral wrongs of slavery than on the benefits of keeping western territories free for northern whites seeking economic opportunity. The Free-Soil Party nominated Martin Van Buren, a former Democrat, for president in 1848 and won 10 percent of the popular vote. But once again, the result was to send a slaveholder to the White House— Zachary Taylor, a Mexican War hero. Nonetheless, the Free-Soil Party had expanded beyond the Liberty Party, raising fears in the South and in the two major parties that the battle over slavery could no longer be contained.

REVIEW & RELATE

- How did the American Anti-Slavery Society differ from earlier abolitionist organizations?
- How did conflicts over gender, race, and tactics shape the development of the abolitionist movement in the 1830s and 1840s?

Conclusion: From the North to the Nation

Charles Grandison Finney followed these political developments from Oberlin College, where he served as president in the 1840s. Skeptical that electoral politics could transform society, he continued to view individual conversions as the well-spring of change. As the nation expanded westward, he trained ministers to travel the frontier converting American Indians to Christianity and reminding pioneering families of their religious obligations. Amy Post took a more militant stand, rejecting any participation in a government that accepted slavery and fomented war. She disagreed with Frederick Douglass's decision to support the Liberty Party, but he argued that moral persuasion alone would never convince planters to end slavery.

The efforts of the tens of thousands of Northerners inspired by religious and reform movements between 1820 and 1850 had a greater impact because of the growth of cities and improvements in transportation and communication. It was far easier by the 1830s for evangelicals, Quakers, Mormons, transcendentalists, utopian communalists, and other activists to spread their ideas through sermons, lectures, newspapers, pamphlets, and conventions.

Urban development was driven by the migration of native-born Americans from rural areas and small towns as well as the increase in immigration from Ireland, Germany, and other European nations. The panic of 1837 fueled an economic crisis that lasted several years and temporarily stalled the market revolution. But the panic also inspired many Americans to organize against poverty, intemperance, prostitution, and other urban problems. At the same time, the concentration of workers, immigrants, and free blacks in cities allowed them to unite and claim rights for themselves. For workers, the need to organize was heightened by the growth of factories and factory towns even as the increasing diversity of the labor force aroused tensions among distinct racial and ethnic groups. Thus numerous attacks occurred against free blacks who competed for jobs with immigrants and poor whites even as the antislavery movement expanded across the North.

Of the numerous reform movements that emerged in this period, abolitionism carried the most powerful national implications by 1850. The growth of abolitionist sentiment was related in part to the rapid expansion of slavery. Yet the increase in the size of southern plantations and their spread westward also ensured a steady supply of raw materials, such as cotton, that drove commercial and industrial development across the North. Ultimately, however, the most significant transformations fueled by slavery occurred across the South.

Chapter 10 Review

KEY TERMS

market revolution (p. 234)
cult of domesticity (p. 238)
deskilling (p. 241)
Second Great Awakening (p. 242)
temperance (p. 244)
transcendentalism (p. 246)
nativists (p. 248)
utopian societies (p. 249)

Appeal . . . to the Colored Citizens of the World (p. 251)
Liberator (p. 251)
American Anti-Slavery Society (AASS) (p. 251)
underground railroad (p. 251)
Declaration of Sentiments (p. 254)
Liberty Party (p. 255)
Free-Soil Party (p. 255)

REVIEW & RELATE

1. How did the market revolution, including improvements like the Erie Canal, reshape the landscape and lives of Americans in the North?
2. As northern cities became larger and more diverse in the first half of the nineteenth century, what changes and challenges did urban residents face and what values and beliefs did the new middle class embrace?
3. How and why did American manufacturing change during the first half of the nineteenth century?
4. How did new technologies, immigration, and the panic of 1837 change the economic opportunities and organizing strategies for northern workers?
5. What impact did the Second Great Awakening have in the North?
6. What new religious organizations and viewpoints emerged in the first half of the nineteenth century, *outside* of Protestant evangelical denominations?
7. How did efforts to alleviate poverty and temper alcohol consumption reflect the range of reform tactics and participants during the 1830s and 1840s?
8. What connections can you identify between utopian communities and mainstream reform movements in the first half of the nineteenth century?
9. How did the American Anti-Slavery Society differ from earlier abolitionist organizations?
10. How did conflicts over gender, race, and tactics shape the development of the abolitionist movement in the 1830s and 1840s?

TIMELINE OF EVENTS

1820–1850
- Northern cities grow; immigration surges

1823
- Lowell mills built

1826
- American Temperance Society founded

1827
- First workingmen's political party founded

1829
- David Walker publishes *Appeal . . . to the Colored Citizens of the World*

1830
- Joseph Smith publishes *The Book of Mormon*

1830–1831
- Second Great Awakening in Rochester, New York

1833
- William Lloyd Garrison founds American Anti-Slavery Society (AASS)

1834
- National Trades Union founded

1837–1842
- Panic of 1837

1839
- American Anti-Slavery Society splits over the role of women

1840
- Liberty Party formed
- World Anti-Slavery Convention, London

1844
- Congress funds construction of the first telegraph line

May 1844
- Anti-immigrant violence in Philadelphia

1845
- Frederick Douglass publishes *Narrative of the Life of Frederick Douglass*
- Margaret Fuller publishes *Woman in the Nineteenth Century*

1845–1846
- Irish potato famine

1846
- Henry David Thoreau publishes *Civil Disobedience*

1848
- Free-Soil Party formed

July 1848
- Seneca Falls Woman's Rights Convention

1851
- Maine prohibits the sale of alcoholic beverages

11

Slavery Expands South and West

1830–1850

LEARNING OBJECTIVES

After reading this chapter you should be able to:

- Explain the development of a plantation society and the impact on planters and their families as well as slaves and their families.

- Discuss the importance of slave labor and the development of a distinctive slave culture, including forms of slave resistance.

- Analyze the differences among southern whites as slavery expanded and compare the techniques used by planters to control blacks and non-slaveholding whites.

- Evaluate the challenges that Indians, the panic of 1837, Texas independence, and the Whig Party posed for the Democratic Party.

- Evaluate the ways that the idea of manifest destiny shaped national elections and intensified debates over slavery.

COMPARING AMERICAN HISTORIES

Although James Henry Hammond became a wealthy plantation owner, he initially planned to pursue the law. Born in 1807 near Newberry, South Carolina, Hammond opened a law practice in Columbia, the state capital, in 1828. Two years later, bored by his profession, he established a newspaper, the *Southern Times*. Writing bold editorials that supported nullification of the "Tariff of Abominations," Hammond quickly gained attention. He soon married Catherine Fitzsimmons, the daughter of a wealthy, politically connected family. The marriage made Hammond the master of Silver Bluff, a 7,500-acre plantation worked by 147 slaves. A successful planter and agricultural reformer, Hammond was elected to the U.S. House of Representatives in 1834.

In 1836 Hammond campaigned successfully for congressional passage of the so-called gag rule, ensuring that antislavery petitions would be tabled rather than read on the floor of the House. Soon afterward, he took ill and resigned from Congress but returned to politics in 1842 as South Carolina's governor. His ambitions were stymied again, however, when Catherine discovered that her husband had made sexual advances on his four nieces, aged thirteen to sixteen. Fearing public exposure, Hammond withdrew from politics, but then joined southern intellectuals in arguing that slavery was a positive good rather than a necessary evil.

Solomon Northup was an African American who endured the ravages of slavery and held a distinctly different view of the institution than James Henry Hammond. His father, Mintus, was born into slavery but freed by his owner's will. He moved to Minerva, New York, married and had a son, Solomon, in 1808. At the age of twenty-one, the free-born Northup married Anne Hampton and worked transporting goods on the region's waterways. He was also hired as a fiddle player, while Anne worked as a cook. In 1834 the couple moved to Saratoga Springs, where they raised their three children until tragedy struck.

In March 1841 Northup met two white circus performers who hired him to play the fiddle for them on tour. They paid his wages up front and told him to obtain documents proving his free status. After reaching Washington, D.C., however, Northup was drugged, chained, and sold to James Birch, a notorious slave trader. Northup was resold in New Orleans to William Ford, who changed his name to Platt. Ford put him to work as a raftsman while Northup tried unsuccessfully to get word to his wife.

In 1842 Ford sold "Platt" to a neighbor, John Tibeats, who, unlike Ford, whipped and abused his workers. When Tibeats attacked Northup with an ax, he fought back and fled to Ford's house. His former owner shielded him from Tibeats's wrath and arranged his sale to the planter Edwin Epps. For the next ten years, Northup worked the cotton fields and played the fiddle at local dances.

Finally, in 1852 Samuel Bass, a Canadian carpenter who openly acknowledged his antislavery views, came to work on Epps's house. Northup persuaded Bass to send a letter to his wife in Saratoga Springs. Anne Northup, astonished to hear that her husband was still alive, took the letter to lawyer Henry Northup, the son of Mintus's former owner. After months of legal efforts, a local judge freed Solomon Northup in January 1853.

COMPARING THE AMERICAN HISTORIES of James Henry Hammond and Solomon Northup illuminates the struggle over slavery from two distinctive perspectives. Between 1820 and 1850 slave labor became central to the South's economic success and an important factor in fueling the market revolution across the nation. In this same period, however, slave ownership became concentrated in the hands of a small proportion of white families. These wealthy and powerful planter families gained increased authority over free blacks and non-slave-owning whites as well as slaves. The concentration of more slaves on each plantation did strengthen African American communities, although it did not negate the brutality they faced. At the same time, the volatility of the cotton market fueled economic instability, triggering the economic panic in 1837. Planters insisted that only expanding into new lands to cultivate more cotton could ensure economic growth. In response, Democratic administrations in Washington, D.C. forcibly removed Indians from the Southeast, supported independence for Texas, and proclaimed war on Mexico. However, these policies only intensified conflicts with Indian nations, heightened political tensions over slavery, and inspired the emergence of the Whig Party.

Planters Expand the Slave System

The cotton gin, developed in the 1790s, ensured the growth of southern agriculture into the 1840s. As the cotton kingdom spread west, **planters**, those who owned the largest plantations, forged a distinctive culture around the institution of slavery. But this slave-based agricultural economy limited the development of cities, technology, and educational institutions, leaving the South increasingly dependent on the North and West for many of its needs. In addition, westward expansion extended the trade in slaves within the South, shattering black families. Still, southern planters viewed themselves as national leaders, both the repository of traditional American values and the engine of economic progress.

A Plantation Society Develops in the South

Plantation slavery existed throughout the Americas in the early nineteenth century. Extensive plantations worked by large numbers of slaves existed in the West Indies and South America. In the U.S. South, however, the volatile cotton market and a scarcity of fertile land kept most plantations relatively small before 1830. But over the next two decades, territorial expansion and the profits from cotton, rice, and sugar allowed successful southern planters to build grand houses and purchase a variety of luxury goods.

As plantations grew, a wealthy aristocracy sought to ensure productivity by employing harsh methods of discipline. Although James Henry Hammond imagined himself a progressive master, he used the whip liberally, hoping thereby to ensure that his estate generated sufficient profits to support a lavish lifestyle.

Increased attention to comfort and luxury helped make the heavy workload of plantation mistresses tolerable. Mistresses were expected to manage their own families and the domestic slaves as well as the feeding, clothing, and medical care of the entire labor force. They also organized social events, hosted relatives and friends for extended stays, and sometimes directed the plantation in their husband's absence.

Still, plantation mistresses were relieved of the most arduous labor by enslaved women, who cooked, cleaned, and washed for the family, cared for the children, and even nursed the babies. Wealthy white women benefited from the best education, the greatest access to music and literature, and the finest clothes and furnishings. Yet the pedestal on which plantation mistresses stood was shaky, built on a patriarchal system in which husbands and fathers held substantial power. For example, most wives tried to ignore the sexual relations that husbands initiated with female slaves. Catherine Hammond did not. She moved to Charleston with her two youngest daughters when she discovered James's sexual abuse of an enslaved mother and daughter. Others, however, took out their anger and frustration on slave women already victimized by their husbands. Moreover, some mistresses owned slaves themselves, gave them as gifts or bequests to family members and friends, and traded them on the open market.

Not all slaveholders were wealthy planters like the Hammonds, with fifty or more slaves and extensive landholdings. Far more planters in the 1830s and 1840s owned between twenty and fifty slaves, and an even larger number of farmers owned just three to six slaves. As Hammond wrote a friend in 1847, "The planters here are essentially what the nobility are in other countries. They stand at the head of society & politics."

Urban Life in the Slave South

The insistence on the supremacy of slave owners had broad repercussions. The richest men in the South invested in slaves, land, and household goods, with little left to develop industry, technology, or urban institutions. The largest factory in the South, the Tredegar Iron Works in Richmond, Virginia, employed several hundred free and enslaved African Americans by 1850. Most southern industrialists, however, like South Carolina textile manufacturer William Gregg, employed poor white women and children. But neither Tredegar nor a scattering of textile mills fundamentally reshaped the region's economy.

The South also fell behind in urban development. The main exception was port cities. Yet even in Baltimore, Charleston, and Savannah, commerce was often directed by northern agents, especially cotton brokers. In addition, nearly one-third of southern whites had no access to cash and instead bartered goods and services, further restricting the urban economy.

Southern cities did attract many free blacks. The growing demand for cheap domestic labor in urban areas and planters' greater willingness to emancipate less valuable single female slaves meant that free black women generally outnumbered men in southern cities. These women worked mainly as washerwomen, cooks, and general domestics, while free black men labored as skilled artisans, dockworkers, or sailors. Free blacks competed for these jobs with slaves and growing numbers of European immigrants who flocked to southern cities in the 1840s and 1850s. The presence of immigrants and free blacks and the reputation of ports as escape hatches for runaway slaves ensured that cities remained suspect in the South.

The scarcity of cities and industry also curtailed the development of transportation. State governments invested little in roads, canals, and railroads. Most small farmers traded goods locally, and most planters used the South's extensive river system to ship goods to commercial hubs. Only Virginia and Maryland, with their proximity to the nation's capital, developed extensive road and rail networks.

The Consequences of Slavery's Expansion

Outside the South, industry and agriculture increasingly benefited from technological innovation. Planters, however, continued to rely on intensive manual labor. Even reform-minded planters focused on fertilizer and crop rotation rather than machines to enhance productivity. The limited use of new technologies—such as iron plows or seed drills—resulted from a lack of investment capital and planters' refusal to purchase expensive equipment that they feared might be broken or purposely sabotaged by slaves. Instead, they relied on continually expanding the acreage under cultivation.

One result of these practices was that a declining percentage of white Southerners came to control vast estates with large numbers of enslaved laborers. Between 1830 and 1850, the absolute number of both slaves and owners grew. But slave owners became a smaller proportion of all white Southerners because the white population grew faster than the number of slave owners. At the same time, distinctions among wealthy planters, small slaveholders, and whites who owned no slaves also increased.

The concern with productivity and profits and the concentration of more slaves on large plantations did have some benefits for black women and men. The end of the international slave trade in 1808 forced planters to rely more heavily on natural reproduction to increase their labor force. Thus many planters thought more carefully about how they treated their slaves, who were increasingly viewed as "valuable property." It was no longer good business to work slaves to death or cripple them by severe punishments.

Nonetheless, owners continued to whip slaves and made paltry investments in their diet and health care. Most slaves lived in small houses with dirt floors and little furniture and clothing. They ate a diet high in calories, especially fats and carbohydrates, but with little meat, fish, fresh vegetables, or fruits. The high mortality rate among slave infants and children—more than twice that of white children to age five—reflected this limited care.

The spread of slavery into Mississippi, Louisiana, Alabama, Missouri, and eventually Texas affected both white and black families, though again not equally. The younger sons of wealthy planters were often forced to move to the frontier, and their families generally lived in rough quarters on isolated plantations. A woman traveler noted that the men "think only of making money, and their houses are hardly fit to live in." A planter's wife complained, "Mississippi and Alabama are a dreary waste." Such moves were far more difficult for slaves, however. Between 1830 and 1850, more than 440,000 slaves were forced to move from the Upper South to the Lower South (Map 11.1), often tearing them away from their families. On the southern frontier, they endured especially harsh conditions as they cleared and cultivated new lands.

By the 1830s, slave markets blossomed in key cities across the South. Solomon Northup was held in one in Washington, D.C., where a woman named Eliza watched as her son Randall was "won" by a planter from Baton Rouge. She promised "to be the most faithful slave that ever lived" if he would also buy her and her daughter. The slave trader threatened the desperate mother with a hundred lashes, and her tears could not change the outcome. As slavery spread westward, such scenes were repeated thousands of times.

Slave Population, 1820
• One dot equals 200 slaves

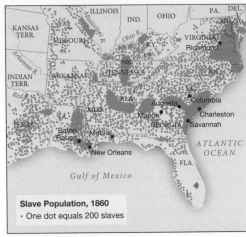

Slave Population, 1860
• One dot equals 200 slaves

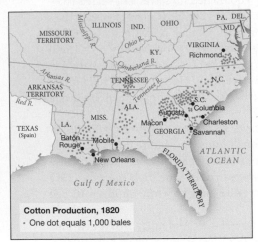

Cotton Production, 1820
• One dot equals 1,000 bales

Cotton Production, 1860
• One dot equals 1,000 bales

MAP 11.1
The Spread of Slavery and Cotton, 1820–1860   While tobacco, rice, and sugar remained important crops in a few states, cotton became the South's and the nation's major export. The need to find more fertile fields led planters to migrate to Alabama, Mississippi, and Louisiana. As a result of cotton's success, the number of enslaved people increased dramatically, the internal slave trade expanded, and labor demands intensified.

REVIEW & RELATE
• What role did the planter elite play in southern society and politics?
• What were the consequences of the dominant position of slave-based plantation agriculture for the southern economy?

Slave Society and Culture

Because slave labor formed the backbone of the southern economy, enslaved workers gained some leverage against owners and overseers. But blacks did not simply define themselves in relation to whites. They also developed relationships, identities, and cultural practices within the slave quarters. Many also found small ways to resist their enslavement on an everyday basis. Others resisted more openly, and a small number organized rebellions against their masters.

Slaves Fuel the Southern Economy

The labor of enslaved blacks drove the nation's economy as well as the South's. In 1820 the South produced some 500,000 bales of cotton, much of it exported to England. By 1850 the region produced nearly 3 million bales, feeding textile mills in New England and abroad. A decade later, cotton accounted for nearly two-thirds of the U.S. export trade and added nearly $200 million a year to the American economy.

Enslaved laborers, of course, saw little of this wealth. Carpenters, blacksmiths, and other skilled slaves were sometimes hired out and allowed to keep a small amount of the money they earned. They traveled to nearby households, compared their circumstances to those on other plantations, and sometimes made contact with free blacks. Some skilled slaves also learned to read and write and had access to tools and knowledge denied to field hands. Still, they were constantly hounded by whites who demanded travel passes and deference, and they were often suspected of involvement in rebellions.

Household slaves sometimes received old clothes and bedding or leftover food from their owners. Yet they were under the constant surveillance of whites, and women especially were vulnerable to sexual abuse. Moreover, the work they performed was physically demanding. Fugitive slave James Curry recalled that his mother, a cook in North Carolina, rose early each morning to milk cows, bake bread, and churn butter. She was responsible for meals for her owners and the slaves. In summer, she cooked her last meal around eight o'clock, after which she milked the cows again. Then she returned to her quarters, put her children to bed, and often fell asleep while mending clothes.

Once slaves reached the age of ten to twelve, they were put to work full-time, usually in the fields. Although field labor was defined by its relentless pace and drudgery, it also brought together large numbers of slaves for the entire day and thus helped forge bonds among laborers on the same plantation. Songs provided a rhythm for their work and offered slaves the chance to communicate their frustrations or hopes.

Field labor was generally organized by task or by gang. Under the task system, typical on rice plantations, slaves could return to their quarters once the day's task was completed. This left time for slaves to cultivate gardens, fish, or mend clothes. In the gang system, widely used on cotton plantations, men and women worked in groups under the supervision of a driver. Often working from sunup to sundown, they swept across fields hoeing, planting, or picking.

Developing an African American Culture

Amid hard work and harsh treatment, slaves created social bonds and a rich culture of their own. Thus African Americans continued for generations to employ African names, like Cuffee and Binah. Even if masters gave them English names, they might use African names in the slave quarters to sustain family memories and community networks. Elements of West African and Caribbean languages, agricultural techniques, medical practices, forms of dress, folktales, songs and musical instruments, dances, and courtship rituals demonstrated the continued importance of these cultures to African Americans. This hybrid culture was disseminated as slaves hauled cotton to market, forged families across plantation boundaries, or were sold farther south. It was also passed across generations through storytelling, music, rituals, and healthcare. Most slave births were attended by black midwives, and African American healers sought southern equivalents to herbal cures used in West Africa.

Religious practices offer an important example of this blended slave culture. Africans from Muslim communities often continued to pray to Allah even if they were also required to attend Protestant churches, while black Protestant preachers developed rituals that combined African and American elements. In the early nineteenth century, many slaves eagerly embraced the evangelical teachings offered by Baptist and Methodist preachers, which echoed some of the expressive spiritual forms in West Africa. On Sundays, slaves who listened in the morning to white ministers proclaim slavery as God's will might gather in the evening to hear their own preachers declare God's love and the possibilities of liberation, at least in the hereafter. Slaves often incorporated drums, dancing, or other West African elements into these worship services.

Although most black preachers were men, a few enslaved women gained a spiritual following. Many female slaves embraced religion enthusiastically, hoping that Christian baptism might substitute for West African rituals that protected newborn babies. Enslaved women sometimes called on church authorities to intervene when white owners, overseers, or even enslaved men abused them. They also considered the church one means of sanctifying slave marriages that were not recognized legally.

Resistance and Rebellion

Many slave owners worried that black preachers and West African folktales inspired blacks to resist enslavement. Fearing defiance, planters went to incredible lengths to control their slaves. Although they were largely successful in quelling open revolts, they were unable to eliminate more subtle forms of opposition, like slowing the pace of work, feigning illness, and damaging equipment. More overt forms of resistance— such as truancy and running away, which disrupted work and lowered profits—also proved impossible to stamp out.

The forms of everyday resistance slaves employed varied in part on their location and resources. Skilled artisans, mostly men, could do more substantial damage because they used more expensive tools, but they were less able to protect themselves through pleas of ignorance. Field laborers could often damage only hoes, but they could do so regularly without exciting suspicion. House slaves could burn dinners, scorch shirts, break china, and even poison owners. Often considered the most loyal slaves, they were also among the most feared because of their intimate contact with white families. Single male slaves were the most likely to run away, planning their escape to get as far away as

"A Slave Wedding," c. 1800   This rare water color painting of an African American wedding probably dates from the turn of the nineteenth century. The distance between the slave quarters and the plantation house suggests this may be a South Carolina scene. The enslaved women and men are dressed in their finest clothing and the musicians appear to be playing African-style instruments made from gourds.   Getty Images

possible before their absence was noticed. Women who fled plantations were more likely to hide out for short periods in the local area. Eventually, isolation, hunger, or concern for children led most of these truants to return if slave patrols did not find them first.

Despite their rarity, efforts to organize slave uprisings, such as the one supposedly hatched by Denmark Vesey in 1822, continued to haunt southern whites. Rebellions in the West Indies, especially the one in Saint Domingue (Haiti), also echoed through the early nineteenth century. Then in 1831 a seemingly obedient slave named Nat Turner organized a revolt in rural Virginia that stunned whites across the South. Turner was a religious visionary who believed that God had given him a mission. On the night of August 21, he and his followers killed his owners, the Travis family, and then headed to nearby plantations in Southampton County. The insurrection led to the deaths of 57 white men, women, and children and liberated more than 50 slaves. But on August 22, outraged white militiamen burst on the scene and eventually captured the black rebels. Turner managed to hide out for two months but was eventually caught, tried, and hung. Virginia executed 55 other African Americans suspected of assisting Turner.

Nat Turner's rebellion instilled panic among white Virginians, who beat and killed some 200 blacks with no connection to the uprising. White Southerners worried they might be killed in their sleep by seemingly submissive slaves. News of the rebellion traveled through slave communities as well, inspiring both pride and anxiety. The execution of Turner and his followers reminded African Americans how far whites would go to protect the institution of slavery.

A mutiny on the Spanish slave ship *Amistad* in 1839 reinforced white Southerners' fears of rebellion. When Africans being transported for sale in the West Indies seized control of the ship near Cuba, the U.S. navy captured the vessel and imprisoned the enslaved rebels. But international treaties outlawing the Atlantic slave trade and pressure applied by abolitionists led to a court case in which former president John Quincy Adams defended the right of the Africans to their freedom. The widely publicized case reached the U.S. Supreme Court in 1841, and the Court freed the rebels. While the ruling was cheered by abolitionists, white Southerners were shocked that the justices would liberate enslaved men.

REVIEW & RELATE	• How did enslaved African Americans create ties of family, community, and culture? • How did enslaved African Americans resist efforts to control and exploit their labor?

Planters Tighten Control

Fears of rebellion led to stricter regulations of black life, and actual uprisings temporarily reinforced white solidarity. Yet yeomen farmers, poor whites, and middle-class professionals all voiced some doubts about the ways in which slavery affected southern society. To ensure white unity, planters wielded their economic and political authority, highlighted bonds of kinship and religious fellowship, and promoted an ideology of white supremacy. Their efforts intensified as northern states and other nations began eradicating slavery.

Harsher Treatment for Southern Blacks

Slave revolts led many southern states to impose harsher controls; however, Nat Turner's rebellion led some white Virginians to question slavery itself. In December 1831, the state assembly established a special committee to consider the crisis. Representatives from western counties, where slavery was never profitable, argued for gradual abolition laws and the colonization of the state's black population in Africa. Hundreds of women in the region sent petitions to the Virginia legislature supporting these positions.

While advocates of colonization gained significant support, eastern planters vehemently opposed abolition or colonization, and leading intellectuals argued for the benefits of slavery. Professor Thomas Dew, president of the College of William and Mary, insisted that slaveholders performed godly work in raising Africans from the status of brute beast to civilized Christian. "Every one acquainted with southern slaves," he claimed, "knows that the slave rejoices in the elevation and prosperity of his master." In the fall of 1832 the Virginia legislature embraced Dew's proslavery argument, rejected gradual emancipation, and imposed new restrictions on slaves and free blacks.

From the 1820s to the 1840s, more stringent codes were passed across the South. Most southern legislatures prohibited owners from manumitting their slaves, made it illegal for whites to teach slaves to read or write, placed new limits on independent black churches, abolished slaves' limited access to courts, outlawed slave marriage, banned antislavery literature, defined rape as a crime only against white women, and outlawed assemblies of more than three blacks without a white person present.

States also regulated the lives of free blacks. Some prohibited free blacks from residing within their borders, others required large bonds to ensure good behavior, and most forbade free blacks who left the state from returning. The homes of free blacks could be raided at any time, and the children of free black women were subject to stringent apprenticeship laws that kept many in virtual slavery.

Such measures proved largely successful in controlling slaves, but there was a price to pay. Restricting education and mobility for blacks often hindered schooling and transportation for poor whites as well. Moreover, characterizing the region's primary labor force as savage and lazy discouraged investment in industry and other forms of economic development. And the regulations increased tensions between poorer whites, who were often responsible for enforcement, and wealthy whites, who benefited most clearly from their imposition.

White Southerners without Slaves

Yeomen farmers, independent owners of small plots who owned few or no slaves, had a complex relationship with the South's plantation economy. Many were related to slave owners, and they often depended on planters to ship their crops to market. Some made extra money by hiring themselves out to planters. Yet yeomen farmers also recognized that their economic interests and daily experiences often diverged from those of planters. This was particularly clear on slavery's frontier, where many yeoman farmers had to carve fields out of forests without the benefit of enslaved workers. They joined with friends and neighbors for barn raisings, corn shuckings, quilting bees, and other collective endeavors that combined labor with sociability. Church services and church socials also brought small farm families together.

While most yeomen farmers believed in slavery, they sometimes challenged planters' authority and assumptions. In the Virginia slavery debates, for example, small farmers from western districts advocated gradual abolition. As growing numbers gained the right to vote in the 1830s and 1840s, they voiced their concerns in county and state legislatures. They advocated more liberal policies toward debtors and demanded greater representation in state legislatures. They also protested planters' obstruction of common lands and waterways, such as building dams upriver that deprived farmers downriver of fishing rights. Yeomen farmers questioned certain ideals embraced by elites. Although plantation mistresses considered manual labor beneath them, the wives and daughters of many small farmers worked in the fields, hauled water, and chopped wood. Still, yeomen farmers' ability to diminish planter control was limited by the continued importance of cotton to the southern economy.

White Southerners who owned no property at all had fewer means of challenging planters' power. These poor whites depended on hunting and fishing in frontier areas, performing day labor on farms and plantations, or working on docks or as servants in southern cities. Poor whites competed with free blacks and slaves for employment and often harbored resentments as a result. Yet some, including poor immigrants from Ireland, Wales, and Scotland, built alliances with blacks based on their shared economic plight.

Some poor whites remained in the same community for decades, establishing themselves on the margins of society. They attended church regularly, performed day labor for affluent families, and taught their children to defer to those higher on the social ladder. Other poor whites moved frequently and survived by combining legal and illegal ventures. They might perform day labor while also stealing food from local farmers. These men and women often had few ties to local communities and little religious training or education. Although poor whites unnerved southern elites by flouting the law and sometimes befriending poor blacks, they could not mount any significant challenge to planter control.

The South's small but growing middle class distanced themselves from poorer whites in pursuit of stability and respectability. They worked as doctors, lawyers, teachers, and shopkeepers and often looked to the North for models to emulate. Many were educated in northern schools and developed ties with their commercial or professional counterparts in that region. They were avid readers of newspapers, religious tracts, and literary periodicals published in the North. And like middle-class Northerners, southern businessmen often depended on their wives' social and financial skills to succeed.

Nonetheless, middle-class southern men shared many of the social attitudes and political priorities of slave owners. They participated alongside planters in benevolent, literary, and temperance societies and agricultural reform organizations. Most middle-class Southerners also adamantly supported slavery. In fact, some suggested that bound labor might be useful to industry. Despite the emergence of a small middle class, however, the gap between rich and poor continued to expand in the South.

Planters Seek to Unify Southern Whites

Planters faced another challenge as nations in Europe and South America began to abolish slavery. Antislavery views, first widely expressed by Quakers, gained growing support among evangelical Protestants in Great Britain and the United States and among political radicals in Europe. Slave rebellions in Saint Domingue and the British West Indies in the early nineteenth century intensified these efforts. In 1807 the British Parliament forbade the sale of slaves within its empire and in 1834 emancipated all those who remained enslaved. France followed suit in 1848. As Spanish colonies such as Mexico and Nicaragua gained their independence in the 1820s and 1830s, they, too, eradicated the institution. Meanwhile gradual abolition laws in the northern United States slowly eliminated slavery there. Although slavery continued in Brazil and in Spanish colonies such as Cuba, and serfdom remained in Russia, international attitudes toward human bondage were shifting.

In response, planters wielded their political and economic power to forge tighter bonds among white Southerners. According to the three-fifths compromise in the U.S. Constitution, areas with large slave populations gained more representatives in Congress than those without. The policy also applied to state elections, giving such areas disproportionate power in state politics. In addition, planters used their resources to provide credit for those in need, offer seasonal employment for poorer whites, transport crops to market for yeomen farmers, and help out in times of crisis. Few whites could afford to antagonize these affluent benefactors.

Wealthy planters also emphasized ties of family and faith. James Henry Hammond, for example, regularly assisted his siblings and other family members financially. Many slave owners worshipped alongside their less well-to-do neighbors, and both the pastor and the congregation benefited from maintaining good relations with the wealthiest congregants. Most church members, like many relatives and neighbors, genuinely admired and respected planter elites who looked out for them.

While planters continued to insist that slavery and the right of states to enforce their own labor systems were protected by the U.S. Constitution, they did not take white solidarity for granted. From the 1830s on, they relied on the ideology of **white supremacy** to cement the belief that all whites, regardless of class or education, were superior to all blacks. Following on Thomas Dew, southern elites argued with growing vehemence that the moral and intellectual failings of blacks meant that slavery was not just a necessary evil but a positive good. At the same time, they insisted that blacks harbored deep animosity toward whites, which could be controlled only by regulating every aspect of their lives. Combining racial fear and racial pride, planters forged bonds with poor and middling whites to guarantee their continued dominance. They continued to seek support from state and national legislators as well.

REVIEW & RELATE

• What groups made up white southern society? How did their interests overlap or diverge?

• How and why did the planter elite seek to reinforce white solidarity?

Democrats Face Political and Economic Crises

Southern planters depended on federal power to expand and sustain the system of slavery. Despite differences on tariffs, both President Andrew Jackson and his successor, Martin Van Buren, stood with southern planters in support of Indian removal and independence for Texas from Mexico. But Van Buren faced a more well-organized opposition in the **Whig Party**, which formed in 1834. When later that decade U.S. rebels in Texas faced powerful resistance from Mexican and Comanche forces and a prolonged and severe economic panic gripped the nation, the Whigs found their opportunity to end Democratic control of the federal government. Over the next two decades, a **Second Party System** formed that pitted Whigs against Democrats on a wide range of economic, cultural, and political issues.

The Battle for Texas

As southern agriculture expanded westward, some whites looked toward Texas for fresh land. White Southerners had begun moving into eastern Texas in the early nineteenth century, but the Adams-Onís Treaty of 1819 guaranteed Spanish control of the territory. Then in 1821 Mexicans overthrew Spanish rule and claimed Texas as part of the new Republic of Mexico. But Mexicans faced serious competition from Comanche Indians, who controlled vast areas in northern Mexico and launched frequent raids into Texas.

Eager to increase settlement in the area and to create a buffer against the Comanches, the Mexican government granted U.S. migrants some of the best land in eastern Texas. It hoped these settlers would eventually spread into the interior, where Comanche raids had devastated Mexican communities. To entice more Southerners, the Mexican government negotiated a special exemption for U.S. planters when it outlawed slavery in 1829. But rather than spreading into the interior, American migrants stayed east of the Colorado River, out of reach of Comanche raids and close to U.S. markets in Louisiana.

Moreover, U.S. settlers resisted assimilation into Mexican society. Instead, they continued to worship as Protestants, speak English, send their children to separate schools, and trade mainly with the United States. By 1835 the 27,000 white Southerners and their 3,000 slaves far outnumbered the 3,000 Mexicans living in eastern Texas.

Forming a majority of the east Texas population and eager to expand their plantations and trade networks, growing numbers of U.S. settlers demanded independence. Then in 1836 Mexicans elected a strong nationalist leader, General Antonio López de Santa Anna, as president. He sought to calm **Tejanos** (Mexican Texans) angered by their vulnerability to Comanche attacks and to curb U.S. settlers seeking further concessions. However, when Santa Anna appointed a military commander to rule Texas, U.S. migrants organized a rebellion and, on March 2, declared their independence. Some elite Tejanos, long neglected by authorities in Mexico City, sided with the rebels. But the rebellion appeared to be short-lived. On March 6, 1836, General Santa Anna crushed settlers defending the **Alamo** in San Antonio. Soon thereafter, he captured the U.S. settlement at Goliad.

At this point, Santa Anna was convinced that the uprising was over. But the U.S. government, despite its claims of neutrality, aided the rebels with funds and army officers. American newspapers picked up the story of the Alamo and published accounts of the battle, describing the Mexican fighters as brutal butchers bent on saving Texas for the pope. These stories, though more fable than fact, increased popular support for the war at a time when many Americans were increasingly hostile to Catholic immigrants in the United States.

As hundreds of armed volunteers headed to Texas, General Sam Houston led rebel forces in a critical victory at San Jacinto in April 1836. While the Mexican government refused to recognize rebel claims, it did not try to regain the lost territory. Few of the U.S. volunteers arrived in time to participate in the fighting, but some settled in the newly liberated region. The Comanche nation quickly recognized the Republic of Texas and developed trade relations with residents to gain access to the vast U.S. market. Still, Santa Anna's failure to recognize Texas independence kept the U.S. government from granting the territory statehood for fear it would lead to war with Mexico.

President Jackson also worried that admitting a new slave state might split the national Democratic Party before the fall elections. To limit debate on the issue, Congress passed a **gag rule** in March 1836 that tabled all antislavery petitions without being read. Nevertheless, thousands of antislavery activists still flooded the House of Representatives with petitions opposing the annexation of Texas.

Indians Resist Removal

At the same time as the United States and Mexico battled over Texas, the United States also faced continued challenges from Indian nations. After passage of the Indian Removal Act in 1830, Congress hoped to settle the most powerful eastern

Indian tribes on land west of the Mississippi River. But some Indian peoples resisted. While federal authorities forcibly removed the majority of Florida Seminoles to Indian Territory between 1832 and 1835, a minority fought back. Jackson and his military commanders expected that this **Second Seminole War** would be short-lived. However, they misjudged the Seminoles' strength; the power of their charismatic leader, Osceola; and the resistance of black fugitives living among the Seminoles.

The conflict continued long after Jackson left the presidency. During the seven-year guerrilla war, 1,600 U.S. troops died. U.S. military forces defeated the Seminole in 1842 only by luring Osceola into an army camp with false promises of a peace settlement. Instead, officers took him captive, finally breaking the back of the resistance. Still, to end the conflict, the U.S. government had to allow fugitive slaves living among the Seminoles to accompany the tribe to Indian Territory.

Unlike the Seminole, members of the Cherokee nation challenged removal by peaceful means, believing that their prolonged efforts to coexist with white society would ensure their success. Indian leaders like John Ross had urged Cherokees to embrace Christianity, white gender roles, and a republican form of government as the best means to ensure control of their communities. Large numbers had done so, but in 1829 and 1830, Georgia officials sought to impose new regulations on the Cherokee living within the state's borders. Tribal leaders took them to court, demanding recognition as a separate nation and using evidence of their Americanization to claim their rights. In 1831 *Cherokee Nation v. Georgia* reached the Supreme Court, which denied a central part of the Cherokee claim. It ruled that all Indians were "domestic dependent nations" rather than fully sovereign governments. Yet the following year, in *Worcester v. Georgia*, the Court declared that the state of Georgia could not impose *state* laws on the Cherokee, for they had "territorial boundaries, within which their authority is exclusive," and that both their land and their rights were protected by the federal government.

President Jackson, who sought Cherokee removal, argued that only the tribe's removal west of the Mississippi River could ensure its "physical comfort," "political advancement," and "moral improvement." Most southern whites, seeking to mine gold and expand cotton production in Cherokee territory, agreed. But Protestant women and men in the North launched a massive petition campaign in 1830 supporting the Cherokees' right to their land. The Cherokee themselves forestalled action through Jackson's second term.

In December 1835, however, U.S. officials convinced a small group of Cherokee men—without tribal sanction—to sign the **Treaty of New Echota**. It proposed the exchange of 100 million acres of Cherokee land in the Southeast for $68 million and 32 million acres in Indian Territory. Outraged Cherokee leaders like John Ross lobbied Congress to reject the treaty. But in May 1836, Congress approved the treaty by a single vote and set the date for final removal two years later (Map 11.2).

In 1838, the U.S. army forcibly removed Cherokees who had not yet resettled in Indian Territory. That June, General Winfield Scott, assisted by 7,000 U.S. soldiers, forced some 15,000 Cherokees into forts and military camps. Indian families spent the next several months without sufficient food, water, sanitation, or medicine. In October, when the Cherokees finally began the march west, torrential rains were followed by snow. Although the U.S. army planned for a trip of less than three months, the journey actually took five months. As supplies ran short, many Indians died.

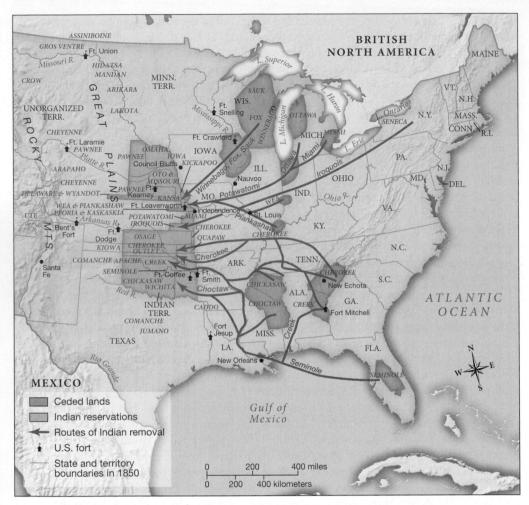

MAP 11.2
Indian Removals and Relocations, 1820s–1840s   In the 1820s and 1830s, the federal
government used a variety of tactics, including military force, to expel Indian nations residing east
of the Mississippi River. As these tribes resettled in the West, white migration along the Oregon and
other trails began to increase. The result, by 1850, was the forced relocation of many western Indian
nations as well.

The remaining Cherokees completed this **Trail of Tears**, as it became known, in
March 1839. But thousands remained near starvation a year later.

Following the Trail of Tears, Seneca Indians petitioned the federal government to
stop their removal from western New York. Federal agents had negotiated the Treaty of
Buffalo Creek with several Iroquois leaders in 1838. But some Seneca chiefs claimed
the negotiation was marred by bribery and fraud. With the aid of Quaker allies, the
Seneca petitioned Congress and the president for redress. Perhaps reluctant to repeat
the Cherokee and Seminole debacles, Congress approved a new treaty in 1842 that
allowed the Seneca to retain two of their four reservations in western New York.

Cherokee Removal, 1838 This woodcut appeared in a U.S. geography textbook about 1850. The title "Indian Emigrants" and the image of Cherokee disembarking from a steamboat falsely suggest that the emigration was voluntary and the means of travel relatively easy. The U.S. fort on the hill symbolizes the role of the federal government in forcing the Cherokee to move west of the Mississippi. Granger, NYC

Van Buren and the Panic of 1837

Although Jackson proposed the Indian Removal Act, it was President Martin Van Buren who confronted ongoing challenges from Indian nations. When Van Buren ran for president in 1836, the Whigs hoped to defeat him by bringing together diverse supporters: evangelical Protestants who objected to Jackson's Indian policy, financiers and commercial farmers who advocated internal improvements and protective tariffs, merchants and manufacturers who favored a national bank, and Southerners who were antagonized by the president's heavy-handed use of federal authority. But the Whigs could not agree on a single candidate, and this lack of unity allowed Democrats to prevail. Although Van Buren won the popular vote by only a small margin (50.9 percent), he secured an easy majority in the electoral college.

Inaugurated on March 4, 1837, President Van Buren soon faced a major financial crisis. The **panic of 1837** started in the South and was rooted in the changing fortunes of American cotton in Great Britain. During the 1820s and 1830s, British banks lent large sums to states such as New York to fund internal improvements, which drove the market revolution but also fueled inflation. The British also invested heavily in cotton plantations, and southern planters used the funds to expand production and improve shipping facilities.

In late 1836, the Bank of England, faced with bad harvests at home and a declining demand for textiles, tightened credit to limit the flow of money out of the country. This forced British investors to call in their loans, which drove up interest rates in the United States just as cotton prices started to fall. Some large American cotton merchants were forced to declare bankruptcy. The banks where they held accounts, many in the South, then failed—ninety-eight of them in March and April 1837 alone.

The economic crisis hit the South hard. Cotton prices continued to fall, cut by nearly half in less than a year. Land values declined dramatically, port cities came to a standstill, and cotton communities on the southern frontier collapsed. Because regional economies were increasingly intertwined, the panic radiated throughout the United States. Northern brokers, shippers, and merchants were devastated by losses in the cotton trade, and northern banks were hit by unpaid debts incurred for canals and other internal improvements. In turn, entrepreneurs who borrowed money to expand their businesses defaulted in large numbers, and shopkeepers, artisans, factory workers, and farmers in the North and Midwest suffered unemployment and foreclosures.

In the North and West, many Americans blamed Jackson's war against the Bank of the United States for precipitating the panic, and Americans everywhere were outraged at Van Buren's refusal to intervene in the crisis. While it is unlikely that any federal policy could have resolved the nation's economic problems, the president's apparent disinterest in the plight of the people inspired harsh criticisms from ordinary citizens as well as political opponents. Worse, despite brief signs of recovery in 1838, the depression deepened in 1839 and continued for four more years.

The Whigs Win the White House

Eager to exploit the weakness of Van Buren and the Democrats, the Whig Party organized its first national convention in fall 1840 and united behind military hero William Henry Harrison. Harrison was born to a wealthy planter family in Virginia, but he was portrayed as a self-made man who lived in a simple log cabin in Indiana. His running mate, John Tyler, another Virginia gentleman and a onetime Democrat, joined the Whigs because of his opposition to Jackson's stand on nullification. Whig leaders hoped he would attract southern votes. Taking their cue from the Democrats, the Whigs organized rallies, barbecues, parades, and mass meetings. They turned the tables on their foe by portraying Van Buren as an aristocrat and Harrison as a war hero and friend of the common man. The Whigs supported American innovation and the entrepreneurial spirit, proclaimed prosperous farmers and skilled workers the backbone of the country, and insisted on their moral and religious superiority to Democrats. At the same time, eager to remind voters that Harrison had defeated Tenskwatawa at the Battle of Tippecanoe, the Whigs adopted the slogan "Tippecanoe and Tyler Too."

The Whigs also welcomed women into the campaign. By 1840 thousands of women had circulated petitions against Cherokee removal, organized temperance and antislavery societies, promoted religious revivals, and joined charitable associations. They embodied the kind of moral force that the Whig Party claimed to represent. In October 1840, Whig senator Daniel Webster spoke to a gathering of 1,200 women, calling on them to encourage their brothers and husbands to vote for Harrison.

The Whig strategy paid off handsomely on election day. Harrison won easily, and the Whigs gained a majority in Congress. Yet the election's promise was shattered when Harrison died of pneumonia a month after his inauguration. Whigs in Congress now had to deal with John Tyler, whose sentiments were largely southern and Democratic. Vetoing many Whig efforts at reform, Tyler allowed the Democratic Party to regroup and set the stage for close elections in 1844 and 1848.

REVIEW & RELATE

- How did westward expansion affect white Southerners, white Northerners, enslaved blacks, and American Indians in the 1830s and 1840s?
- What economic and political developments led to a Whig victory in the election of 1840?

The National Government Looks to the West

Despite the Whig victory in 1840, planters wielded considerable clout in Washington, D.C., because of the importance of cotton to the U.S. economy. In turn, Southerners needed federal support to expand into more fertile areas. The presidential election of 1844 turned on this issue, with Democratic candidate James K. Polk demanding continued expansion into Oregon and Mexico. Once Polk was in office, his claims were contested not only by Britain and Mexico but also by the Comanche. After the United States won vast Mexican territories in 1848, conflicts with Indians and debates over slavery only intensified.

Expanding to Oregon and Texas

Southerners eager to expand the plantation economy were at the forefront of the push for territorial expansion. Yet expansion was not merely a southern strategy. Northerners demanded that the United States reject British claims to the Oregon Territory, and some northern politicians and businessmen advocated acquiring Hawaii and Samoa to benefit U.S. trade. In 1844 the Democratic Party built on these expansionist dreams to recapture the White House.

The Democrats nominated a Tennessee congressman and governor, James K. Polk. The Whigs, unwilling to nominate Tyler for president, chose Kentucky senator Henry Clay. Polk declared himself in favor of the annexation of Texas. Clay, meanwhile, waffled on the issue. This proved his undoing when the Liberty Party, a small antislavery party founded in 1840, denounced annexation. Liberty Party candidate James G. Birney captured just enough votes in New York State to throw the state and the election to Polk.

In February 1845, a month before Polk took office, Congress passed a joint resolution annexing the Republic of Texas. That summer, John L. O'Sullivan, editor of the *Democratic Review*, captured the American mood by declaring that nothing must interfere with "the fulfillment of our manifest destiny to overspread the continent allotted by Providence." This vision of **manifest destiny**—of the nation's God-given right to expand its borders—defined Polk's presidency.

With the Texas question seemingly resolved, President Polk turned his attention to Oregon, which stretched from the forty-second parallel to latitude 54°40' and was jointly occupied by Great Britain and the United States. In 1842, three years before Polk took office, glowing reports of the mild climate and fertile soil around Puget Sound had inspired thousands of farmers and traders to flood into Oregon's Willamette Valley. Alarmed by this "Oregon fever," the British tried to confine Americans to areas south of the Columbia River. But U.S. settlers demanded access to the entire territory. President Polk encouraged migration into Oregon but was unwilling to risk war with

Great Britain. Instead, diplomats negotiated a treaty in 1846 that extended the border with British Canada (the forty-ninth parallel) to the Pacific Ocean. Over the next two years, Congress admitted Iowa and Wisconsin to statehood, reassuring northern residents that expansion benefited all regions of the nation.

Some Americans hoped to gain even more territory by pushing Mexicans out of northern Mexico and California. Spanish missions and forts, built in the late eighteenth century, dotted the Pacific Coast from San Diego to San Francisco. When Mexico achieved independence in 1821, it took control of this missionary and military network. Diseases carried by the Spanish and forced labor in their missions and forts had decimated some Indian tribes in the region. As Mexican soldiers took control, some married into Indian families, gaining land and social status and nurturing compound cultures. More often, however, diseases, guns, thefts of food and animals, sexual assault, and forced labor continued to debilitate native peoples.

Indians in the lands newly claimed by the U.S. government faced some of these same dangers. In addition, as the U.S. government forced eastern tribes to move west of the Mississippi, tensions increased among Indian nations (see Map 11.2). When the Cherokee and other southeastern tribes were removed to Indian Territory, for example, they confronted tribes such as the Osage. Pushed into the Southwest, the Osage came into conflict with the Comanche, who had earlier fought the Apache for control of the southern plains. Other Indian nations were pushed onto the northern plains from the Old Northwest. When tribes like the Mandan were decimated by smallpox in the 1830s, the Sioux came to dominate the region.

The flood of U.S. migrants into Texas and the southern plains transformed relations among Indian nations as well as between Indians and Mexico. In the face of Spanish and then Mexican claims on their lands, for example, the Comanche forged alliances with former foes like the Wichita and the Osage. The Comanche also developed commercial ties with tribes in Indian Territory and with both Mexican and Anglo-American traders. They thereby hoped to benefit from the imperial ambitions of the United States and Mexico while strengthening bonds among Indians in the region.

Comanche expansion was especially problematic for Mexico. The young nation did not have sufficient resources to sustain the level of gift giving that Spanish authorities had used to maintain peace. As a result, Comanche warriors launched continual raids against Tejano settlements in Texas. But the Comanche also developed commercial relations with residents of New Mexico, who flaunted trade regulations promulgated in Mexico City. By 1846 Comanche trade and diplomatic relations with New Mexican settlements had seriously weakened the hold of Mexican authorities on their northern provinces.

Pursuing War with Mexico

At the same time, with Texas now a state, Mexico faced growing tensions with the United States. Conflicts centered on Texas's western border. Mexico insisted on the Nueces River as the boundary line, while Americans claimed all the land to the Rio Grande. In January 1846, Polk secretly sent emissary John Slidell to negotiate a border treaty with Mexico. But Polk also sent U.S. troops under General Zachary Taylor across the Nueces River. Mexican officials refused to see Slidell and instead sent their own troops across the Rio Grande. Meanwhile, U.S. naval commanders prepared to seize San Francisco Bay from the Mexicans if war was declared. The Mexican government responded by sending more troops into the disputed Texas territory.

When fighting erupted near the Rio Grande in May 1846 (Map 11.3), Polk claimed that "American blood had been shed on American soil" and declared a state of war. Many Whigs in Congress opposed the declaration, arguing that the president had provoked the conflict. However, antiwar Whigs failed to convince the Democratic majority, and Congress voted to finance the war. Although northern abolitionists protested the war, most Americans—North and South—considered westward expansion a boon.

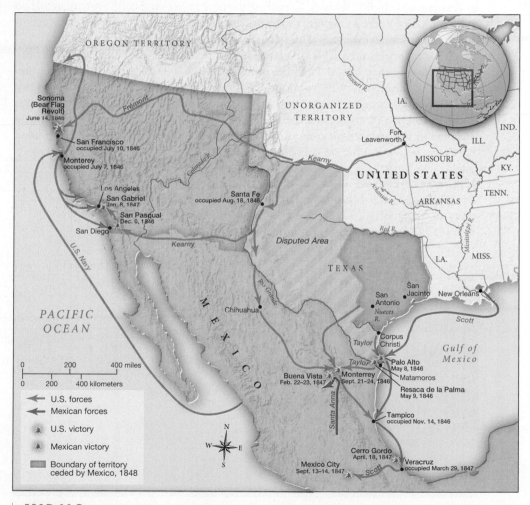

MAP 11.3

The Mexican-American War, 1846–1848   Although a dispute over territory between the Nueces River and the Rio Grande initiated the Mexican-American War, most of the fighting occurred between the Rio Grande and Mexico City. In addition, U.S. forces in California launched battles to claim independence for that region even before gold was discovered there.

Once the war began, battles erupted in a variety of locations. In May 1846, U.S. troops defeated Mexican forces in Palo Alto and Resaca de la Palma. A month later, the U.S. army captured Sonoma, California with the aid of local settlers. John Frémont then led U.S. forces to Monterey, where the navy launched a successful attack and declared the California territory part of the United States. That fall, U.S. troops gained important victories at Monterrey, Mexico, just west of the Rio Grande, and Tampico, along the Gulf coast.

Despite major U.S. victories, Santa Anna, who reclaimed the presidency of Mexico during the war, refused to give up. In February 1847, his troops attacked U.S. forces at Buena Vista and nearly secured a victory. Polk then agreed to send General Winfield Scott to Veracruz with 14,000 soldiers. Capturing the port in March, Scott's army marched on to Mexico City. After a crushing defeat of Santa Anna at Cerro Gordo, the president-general was removed from power and the new Mexican government sought peace.

With victory ensured, U.S. officials faced a difficult decision: How much Mexican territory should they claim? The U.S. army in central Mexico faced continued guerrilla attacks. Meanwhile Whigs and some northern Democrats denounced the war as a southern conspiracy to expand slavery. In this context, Polk agreed to limit U.S. claims to the northern regions of Mexico. The president signed the **Treaty of Guadalupe Hidalgo** in February 1848, committing the United States to pay Mexico $15 million

"Hanging of the San Patricios," 1847   In 1846–1847 more than two hundred immigrants, most of them Irish Catholics who defected from U.S. Army units, joined the Mexican Army. They formed the Batallón de San Patricios, which fought fiercely in many battles. When dozens were captured after the Battle of Chapultepec, the soldiers were convicted of desertion. Samuel Chamberlain painted one of two mass hangings that followed.   Herbert Orth/The LIFE Images Collection/Getty Images in return for control over Texas north and east of the Rio Grande plus California and the New Mexico territory.

Debates over Slavery Intensify

News of the U.S. victory traveled quickly across the United States. In the South, planters imagined slavery spreading into the lands acquired from Mexico. Northerners, too, applauded the expansion of U.S. territory but focused on California as a center for agriculture and commerce. Still, the acquisition of new territory heightened sectional conflicts. Debates over slavery had erupted during the war, fueled by abolitionist outrage, and a few northern Democrats joined Whigs in denouncing "the power of SLAVERY" to "govern the country, its Constitutions and laws." In August 1846, Democratic congressman David Wilmot of Pennsylvania proposed outlawing slavery in all territory acquired from Mexico so that the South could not profit from the war. While the **Wilmot Proviso** passed in the House, southern and proslavery northern Democrats defeated it in the Senate.

The presidential election of 1848 opened with the unresolved question of whether to allow slavery in the territories acquired from Mexico. With Polk declining to run for a second term, Democrats nominated Lewis Cass, a Michigan senator and ardent expansionist. Hoping to keep northern antislavery Democrats in the party, Cass argued that residents in each territory should decide whether to make the region free or slave. This strategy put the slavery question on hold but satisfied almost no one.

The Whigs, too, hoped to avoid the slavery issue for fear of losing southern votes. They nominated Mexican-American War hero General Zachary Taylor, a Louisiana slaveholder who had no declared position on slavery in the western territories. But they sought to reassure their northern wing by nominating Millard Fillmore of Buffalo, New York, for vice president. As a member of Congress in the 1830s, Fillmore had opposed the annexation of Texas.

The Liberty Party, disappointed in the Whig ticket, decided to run its own candidate for president. Its leaders hoped to expand their support by reconstituting themselves as the Free-Soil Party. This party focused more on excluding slaves from western territories than on the moral injustice of slavery. The party nominated former president Martin Van Buren and appealed to small farmers and urban workers who hoped to benefit from western expansion.

Once again, the presence of a third party affected the outcome of the election. While Whigs and Democrats tried to avoid the slavery issue, Free-Soilers demanded attention to it. By focusing on the exclusion of slavery in western territories rather than its abolition, the party won more adherents in northern states. Indeed, Van Buren won enough northern Democrats so that Cass lost New York State and the 1848 election. Zachary Taylor and the Whigs won, but only by placing a southern slaveholder in the White House.

REVIEW & RELATE	• How did the battle over Texas affect relations among Indian nations, among white Americans, and between Indians and whites? • How did the Mexican-American War reshape national politics and intensify debates over slavery?

Conclusion: Geographical Expansion and Political Division

By the mid-nineteenth century, the United States stood at a crossroads. Most Americans considered expansion advantageous and critical to revitalizing the economy. Planters certainly considered it critical to slavery's success. Yet as the number of slaves and the size of plantations grew, planters also sought to impose stricter controls over blacks, enslaved and free, and to bind non-slaveowning whites more firmly to their interests. Enslaved blacks, meanwhile, developed an increasingly rich culture by combining traditions and rituals from Africa and the Caribbean with U.S. customs and beliefs. This African American culture served as one form of resistance against slavery's brutality. Many enslaved laborers resisted in other ways as well: sabotaging tools, feigning illness, running away, or committing arson or theft. Smaller numbers engaged in outright rebellions.

While most white Northerners were willing to leave slavery alone where it already existed, many hoped to keep it out of newly acquired territories. In this sense, the removal of the Cherokee did not disturb Northerners since it was largely white yeoman farmers who would benefit from access to their land. Still many northern whites, including evangelical women, opposed removal on moral grounds. When it came to the Mexican-American War, more Northerners—black and white—feared victory would mainly benefit southern planters. The vast lands gained from Mexico in 1848 intensified debates over slavery and led small but growing numbers of white Northerners to join African Americans, American Indians, and Mexicans in protesting U.S. expansion. Even some yeomen farmers and middle-class professionals in the South questioned whether extending slavery benefited the region economically and politically.

It was the panic of 1837, however, that opened the way for a new political alignment. The extended depression allowed the newly formed Whig Party to gain support for its economic and reform agenda. In 1840 Whigs captured the White House and Congress, and a new antislavery force, the Liberty Party, emerged as well. But just four years later, James K. Polk's support of westward expansion and manifest destiny returned Democrats to power. The political volatility continued when the U.S. victory in the war with Mexico intensified debates over slavery in the territories, fracturing the Democratic Party and inspiring the founding of the Free-Soil Party.

Political realignments continued over the next decade, fueled by growing antislavery sentiment in the North and proslavery beliefs in the South. In 1853 Solomon Northup horrified thousands of antislavery readers with his book *Twelve Years a Slave*, which vividly described life in bondage. Such writings alarmed planters like James Henry Hammond, who continued to believe that slavery was a divine blessing. Yet in insisting on the benefits of slave labor, the planter elite inspired further conflict with Northerners, whose lives were increasingly shaped by commercial and industrial developments and the expansion of free labor.

Chapter 11 Review

KEY TERMS

planters (p. 261)
Nat Turner's rebellion (p. 267)
yeomen farmers (p. 269)
white supremacy (p. 271)
Whig Party (p. 271)
Second Party System (p. 271)
Tejanos (p. 272)
Alamo (p. 272)

gag rule (p. 272)
Second Seminole War (p. 273)
Treaty of New Echota (p. 273)
Trail of Tears (p. 274)
panic of 1837 (p. 275)
manifest destiny (p. 277)
Treaty of Guadalupe Hidalgo (p. 280)
Wilmot Proviso (p. 281)

REVIEW & RELATE

1. What role did the planter elite play in southern society and politics?

2. What were the consequences of the dominant position of slave-based plantation agriculture for the southern economy?

3. How did enslaved African Americans create ties of family, community, and culture?

4. How did enslaved African Americans resist efforts to control and exploit their labor?

5. What groups made up white southern society? How did their interests overlap or diverge?

6. How and why did the planter elite seek to reinforce white solidarity?

7. How did westward expansion affect white Southerners, white Northerners, enslaved blacks, and American Indians in the 1830s and 1840s?

8. What economic and political developments led to a Whig victory in the election of 1840?

9. How did the battle over Texas affect relations among Indian nations, among white Americans, and between Indians and whites?

10. How did the Mexican-American War reshape national politics and intensify debates over slavery?

TIMELINE OF EVENTS

1830	• Indian Removal Act	**1837–1843**	• Panic of 1837 triggers extended depression
1830–1850	• 440,000 slaves from Upper South sold to owners in Lower South	**1838–1839**	• Cherokee driven west on Trail of Tears
1831	• *Cherokee Nation v. Georgia* • Nat Turner leads slave uprising in Virginia • Virginia's Assembly establishes special committee on slavery	**1840**	• Whigs win the presidency and gain control of Congress
		1841	• Solomon Northup kidnapped and sold into slavery
1832	• *Worcester v. Georgia*	**1842**	• Seneca Indians win treaty to remain in New York
1834	• Britain abolishes slavery		
1835–1842	• Second Seminole War	**1845**	• U.S. annexes Texas
1836	• Treaty of New Echota	**1846**	• U.S. settles dispute with Great Britain over Oregon
March 2, 1836	• U.S. settlers declare eastern Texas an independent republic	**May 1846– February 1848**	• Mexican-American War
March 6, 1836	• General Santa Anna crushes U.S. rebels at the Alamo	**August 1846**	• David Wilmot proposes Wilmot Proviso
March 1836	• Congress passes gag rule	**March 1848**	• Treaty of Guadalupe Hidalgo

12

Imperial Ambitions and Sectional Crises
1842–1861

LEARNING OBJECTIVES

After reading this chapter you should be able to:

- Compare the experiences of different groups living in and migrating to the West.
- Explain how geographical expansion heightened sectional conflicts and how those conflicts shaped and were shaped by federal policies like the Compromise of 1850 and the Fugitive Slave Act.
- Analyze the ways that the spread of antislavery sentiments, partisan politics, and federal court decisions intensified sectional divisions.
- Evaluate the importance of John Brown's raid and the election of Abraham Lincoln as President in convincing southern states to secede from the Union.

COMPARING AMERICAN HISTORIES

John C. Frémont, a noted explorer and military leader, rose from humble beginnings. He was born out of wedlock to Anne Beverley Whiting Pryor of Savannah, Georgia, who abandoned her wealthy husband and ran off with a French immigrant. Frémont attended the College of Charleston, where he excelled at mathematics, but was eventually expelled for neglecting his studies. At age twenty, in 1833, he was hired to teach aboard a navy ship through the help of an influential South Carolina politician. He then obtained a surveying position to map new railroad lines and Cherokee lands in Georgia and was finally appointed a second lieutenant in the Corps of Topographical Engineers.

In 1840 Lieutenant Frémont moved to Washington, D.C., where he worked on maps and reports based on his surveys. The following year, he eloped with Jessie Benton, the daughter of Missouri senator Thomas Hart Benton. Despite the scandal, Senator Benton supported his son-in-law's selection for a federally funded expedition to the West. In 1842 Frémont and his guide, Kit Carson, led twenty-three men along the emerging Oregon Trail. Two years later, John returned to Washington, where Jessie helped him turn his notes into a vivid report on the Oregon Territory and California. Congress published the report, which inspired a wave of hopeful migrants to head west.

Frémont's success was tainted, however, by a quest for personal glory. On a federal mapping expedition in 1845, he left his post and headed to Sacramento, California. In the winter of 1846, he stirred support among U.S. settlers there for war with Mexico. His brash behavior nearly provoked a bloody battle. Frémont then fled to the Oregon Territory, where he and Kit Carson initiated conflicts with local Indians. As the United States moved closer to war with Mexico, Frémont returned to California to support Anglo-American settlers' efforts to declare the region an independent republic. After the war, Frémont worked tirelessly for California's admission to the Union and served as one of the state's first senators. With his wife's encouragement, he embraced abolition and in 1856 was nominated for president by the new Republican Party.

Dred Scott also traveled the frontier in the 1830s and 1840s, but not of his own free will. Born a slave in Southampton, Virginia around 1800, he and his master, Peter Blow, moved west to Alabama in 1818 and then to St. Louis, Missouri, in 1830. Three years later, Blow sold Scott to Dr. John Emerson, an assistant surgeon in the U.S. army. In 1836 Emerson took Scott to Fort Snelling in the Wisconsin Territory, a free territory. There Scott met Harriet Robinson, a young African American slave. Her master, an Indian agent, allowed the couple to marry in 1837 and transferred ownership of Harriet to Dr. Emerson. When Emerson moved back to St. Louis, the Scotts returned with him. After the doctor's death in 1843, the couple was hired out to local residents by Emerson's widow.

In April 1846, the Scotts initiated lawsuits to gain their freedom. The Missouri Supreme Court had ruled in earlier cases that slaves who resided for any time in free territory must be freed, and the Scotts had lived and married in Wisconsin. In 1850 the Missouri Circuit Court ruled in the Scotts' favor. However, the Emerson family appealed the decision to the state supreme court, with Harriet's case to follow the outcome of her husband's. Two years later, that court ruled against all precedent and overturned the lower court's decision. Dred Scott then appealed to the U.S. Supreme Court, but it, too, ultimately ruled against the Scotts, leaving them enslaved.

COMPARING THE AMERICAN HISTORIES of John Frémont and Dred Scott demonstrates how the explosive combination of westward expansion and growing regional divisions over the issue of slavery divided the nation by 1861. Whereas Frémont joined expeditions to map and conquer the West, Scott followed the migrations of slave owners and soldiers. Both Frémont and Scott were supported by strong women, and both men advocated government action to end slavery. Only Frémont, however, had the right to vote, run for office, and join the Republican Party. From their different positions, these two men reflected the dramatic changes that occurred as westward expansion pushed the issues of empire and slavery to the center of national debate.

Claiming the West

During the 1830s and 1840s, national debates over slavery intensified. The most important battles now centered on western territories gained through victory in the war with Mexico. Before 1848, government-sponsored expeditions had opened up vast new lands for American pioneers seeking opportunity, and migrants moved west in growing numbers. Then, following the Mexican-American War and the discovery of gold in California, tens of thousands of men rushed to the Pacific coast seeking riches. But the West was already home to a diverse population that included Indians, Mexicans, Mormons, and missionaries. Pioneers converged, and often clashed, with these groups.

Traveling the Overland Trail

In the 1830s a growing number of migrants followed overland trails to the far West. In 1836 Narcissa Whitman and Eliza Spaulding joined a group traveling to the Oregon Territory, the first white women to make the trip. They accompanied their husbands, both Presbyterian ministers, who hoped to convert the region's Indians. Their letters to friends and co-worshippers back east described the rich lands and needy souls in the Walla Walla valley. Such missives were widely shared and encouraged further migration.

The panic of 1837 also prompted families to head west. Thousands of U.S. migrants and European immigrants sought better economic prospects in Oregon, the Rocky Mountain region, and the eastern plains, while Mormons continued to settle in Salt Lake City. Some pioneers opened trading posts where Indians exchanged goods with Anglo-American settlers or with merchants back east. Small settlements developed around these posts and near the expanding system of U.S. forts that dotted the region.

For many pioneers, the journey on the **Oregon Trail** began at St. Louis. From there, they traveled by wagon train across the Great Plains and the Rocky Mountains to the Pacific coast. By 1860 some 350,000 Americans had made the journey, claimed land from the Mississippi River to the Pacific, and transformed the United States into an expanding empire.

Because the journey west required funds for wagons and supplies, most pioneers were of middling status. The majority of pioneers made the three- to six-month journey with family members, to help share the labor. Men, mainly farmers, comprised some 60 percent of these western migrants, but women and children traveled in significant numbers, often alongside relatives or neighbors from back east. Some courageous families headed west alone, but most traveled in wagon trains—from a few wagons to a few dozen—that provided support and security.

Traditional gender roles often broke down on the trail, and even conventional domestic tasks posed novel problems. Women had to cook unfamiliar food over open fires in all kinds of weather and with only a few pots and utensils. They washed laundry in rivers or streams and on the plains hauled water from great distances. Wood, too, was scarce on the plains, and women and children gathered buffalo dung (called "chips") for fuel. Men frequently had to gather food rather than hunt and fish, or they had to learn to catch strange (and sometimes dangerous) animals, such as jack rabbits and rattlesnakes. Few men were prepared for the dangerous work of floating wagons across rivers. Nor were many of them expert in shoeing horses or fixing wagon wheels, tasks that were performed by skilled artisans at home.

Expectations changed dramatically when men took ill or died. Then wives often drove the wagon, gathered or hunted for food, and learned to repair axles and other wagon parts. When large numbers of men were injured or ill, women might serve as scouts and guides or pick up guns to defend wagons under attack by Indians or wild animals. Yet despite their growing burdens, pioneer women gained little power over decision making. Moreover, the addition of men's jobs to women's responsibilities was rarely reciprocated. Few men cooked, did laundry, or cared for children on the trail.

In one area, however, relative equality reigned. Men and women were equally susceptible to disease, injury, and death during the journey. Accidents, gunshot wounds, drownings, broken bones, and infections affected people on every wagon train. Some groups were struck as well by deadly epidemics of measles or cholera. In addition, about 20 percent of women on the overland trail became pregnant, which posed even greater dangers than usual given the lack of medical services and sanitation. About the same percentage of women lost children or spouses on the trip west. Overall, about one in ten to fifteen migrants died on the western journey.

The Gold Rush

Despite the hazards, more and more Americans traveled overland to the Pacific coast, although only a few thousand Americans initially settled in California. Some were agents sent there by eastern merchants to purchase fine leather made from the hides of Spanish cattle. Several agents married into families of elite Mexican ranchers, known as Californios, and adopted their culture, even converting to Catholicism.

However, the Anglo-American presence in California changed dramatically after 1848 when gold was discovered at Sutter's Mill in northeastern California. Beginning in 1849 news of the discovery brought tens of thousands of settlers from the eastern United States, South America, Europe, and Asia. In the **gold rush**, "forty-niners" raced to claim riches in California, and men vastly outnumbered women.

The rapid influx of gold seekers heightened tensions between newly arrived whites, local Indians, and Californios. Forty-niners confiscated land owned by Californios, shattered the fragile ecosystem in the California mountains, and forced Mexican and Indian men to labor for low wages or a promised share in uncertain profits. New conflicts erupted when migrants from Asia and South America joined the search for wealth. Forty-niners from the United States regularly stole from and assaulted these foreign-born competitors.

Gold Rush Miners, 1849 These prospectors were two of some 80,000 who traveled to California after gold was discovered. While many Chinese miners were run off their claims, these two men, dressed in a mix of Chinese and American attire, panned for gold with the tools of their trade—pickax, hoe, and pan. A shed in the background may have served as their home. Granger Collection/NYC

The gold rush also led to the increased exploitation of women as thousands of male migrants demanded food, shelter, laundry, and medical care. While some California women earned a good living by renting rooms, cooking meals, washing clothes, or working as prostitutes, many faced exploitation and abuse. Indian and Mexican women were especially vulnerable to sexual harassment and rape, while Chinese women were imported specifically to provide sexual services for male miners.

Chinese men were also victims of abuse by whites, who ran them off their claims. Yet some Chinese men used the skills traditionally assigned them in their homeland—cooking and washing clothes—to earn a far steadier income than prospecting for gold could provide. Other men also took advantage of the demand for goods and services. Levi Strauss, a German Jewish immigrant, moved from New York to San Francisco to open a dry-goods store in 1853. He soon made his fortune producing canvas and then denim pants that could withstand harsh weather and long wear.

A Crowded Land

While U.S. promoters of migration continued to depict the West as open territory, it was in fact the site of competing national ambitions in the late 1840s. Despite granting statehood to Texas in 1845 and winning the war against Mexico in 1848, the United States had to battle for control of the Great Plains with powerful Indian nations, like the Sioux and Cheyenne (Map 12.1).

MAP 12.1
Western Trails and Indian Nations, c. 1850   As wagon trains and traders journeyed west in rapidly growing numbers during the 1830s and 1840s, the United States established forts along the most well-traveled routes. At the same time, Indians claimed or were forced into new areas through the pressure of Indian removals, white settlement, and the demands of hunting, trade, and agriculture.

Although attacks on wagon trains were rare, Indians did threaten frontier settlements throughout the 1840s and 1850s. Settlers often retaliated, and U.S. army troops joined them in efforts to push Indians back from areas newly claimed by whites. Yet in many parts of the West, Indians were as powerful as whites, and they did not cede territory without a fight. The Reverend Marcus Whitman and his wife, Narcissa, became victims of their success in promoting western settlement when pioneers brought a deadly measles epidemic to the region, killing thousands of Cayuse and Nez Percé Indians. In 1847, convinced that whites brought disease but no useful medicine, a group of Cayuse Indians killed the Whitmans and ten other white settlers.

Yet violence against whites could not stop the flood of migrants into the Oregon Territory. Indeed, attacks by one Indian tribe were often used to justify assaults on any Indian tribe. Thus John Frémont and Kit Carson, whose party was attacked by Modoc Indians in Oregon in 1846, retaliated by destroying a Klamath Indian village and killing its inhabitants. The defeat of Mexico and the discovery of gold in California only intensified such conflicts.

Although Indians and white Americans were the main players in many battles, Indian nations also competed with each other. In the southern plains, drought and disease exacerbated those conflicts in the late 1840s and dramatically changed the balance of power there. In 1845 the southern plains were struck by a dry spell, which lasted on and off until the mid-1860s. In 1848, smallpox ravaged Comanche villages, and a virulent strain of cholera was introduced into the region the next year by forty-niners traveling to California. In the late 1840s, the Comanche nation was the largest Indian group, with about twenty thousand members; by the mid-1850s, less than half that number remained.

Yet the collapse of the Comanche empire was not simply the result of outside forces. As the Comanche expanded their trade networks and incorporated smaller Indian nations into their orbit, they overextended their reach. Most important, they allowed too many bison to be killed to meet the needs of their Indian allies and the demand of Anglo-American and European traders. The Comanche also herded growing numbers of horses, which required expansive grazing lands and winter havens in the river valleys and forced the bison onto more marginal lands. Opening the Santa Fe Trail to commerce multiplied the problems by destroying vegetation and polluting springs, thereby diminishing resources in more of the region. The prolonged drought completed the depopulation of the bison on the southern plains. Without bison, the Comanche lost a trade item critical to sustaining their commercial and political control. As the Comanche empire collapsed, former Indian allies sought to advance their own interests. These developments reignited Indian wars on the southern plains as tens of thousands of pioneers poured through the region.

African Americans also participated in these western struggles. Many were held as slaves by southeastern tribes forced into Indian Territory, while others were freed and married Seminole or Cherokee spouses. The Creeks proved harsh masters, prompting some slaves to escape north to free states or south to Mexican or Comanche territory. Yet as southern officers in the U.S. army moved to frontier outposts, they carried more slaves into the region. Many, including Dr. John Emerson, changed posts frequently, taking slaves like Dred Scott into both slave and free territories. Still, it was white planters who brought the greatest numbers of African Americans into Texas, Missouri, and Kansas, pushing the frontier of slavery ever westward. At the same time, some free blacks joined the migration voluntarily in hopes of finding better economic opportunities and less overt racism in the West.

REVIEW & RELATE

- Why did Americans go west in the 1830s and 1840s, and what was the journey like?
- What groups competed for land and resources in the West? How did disease, drought, and violence shape this competition?

Expansion and the Politics of Slavery

The place of slavery in the West aroused intense political debates as territories in the region began to seek statehood. Debates over the eradication of slavery and limits on its expansion had shaped the highly contested presidential election of 1848. After the Mexican-American War, the debate intensified and focused more specifically on slavery's westward expansion. Each time a territory achieved the requirements for statehood, a new crisis erupted. To resolve these crises required strong political leadership, judicial moderation, and a spirit of compromise among the American people. None of these conditions prevailed. Instead, passage of the Fugitive Slave Act in 1850 aroused deeper hostilities, and President Franklin Pierce (1853–1857) encouraged further expansion but failed to address the crises that ensued.

California and the Compromise of 1850

In the winter of 1849, just before President Zachary Taylor's March inauguration, California applied for admission to the Union as a free state. Some California political leaders opposed slavery on principle. Others wanted to "save" the state for whites by outlawing slavery, discouraging free black migration, and restricting the rights of Mexican, Indian, and Chinese residents. Yet the internal debates among Californians were not uppermost in the minds of politicians. Southerners were concerned about the impact of California's free-state status on the sectional balance in Congress, while northern Whigs were shocked when President Taylor suggested that slavery should be allowed anywhere in the West.

Other debates percolated in Congress at the same time. Many Northerners were horrified by the spectacle of slavery and slave trading in the nation's capital and argued that it damaged America's international reputation. Southerners, meanwhile, complained that the Fugitive Slave Act of 1793 was being widely ignored in the North. A boundary dispute between Texas and New Mexico irritated western legislators, and Texas continued to claim that debts it accrued while an independent republic and during the Mexican-American War should be assumed by the federal government.

Senator Henry Clay of Kentucky, the Whig leader who had hammered out the Missouri Compromise in 1819 and 1820, again tried to resolve the many conflicts that stalled congressional action. He offered a compromise by which California would be admitted as a free state; the remaining land acquired from Mexico would be divided into two territories—New Mexico and Utah—and slavery there would be decided by popular sovereignty; the border dispute between New Mexico and Texas would be decided in favor of New Mexico, but the federal government would assume Texas's war debts; the slave trade (but not slavery) would be abolished in the District of Columbia; and a new and more effective fugitive slave law would be approved. Although Clay's compromise offered something to everyone, his colleagues did not immediately embrace it.

By March 1850, after months of passionate debate, the sides remained sharply divided, as did their most esteemed leaders. John C. Calhoun, a proslavery senator from South Carolina, refused to support any compromise that allowed Congress to decide the fate of slavery in the western territories. William H. Seward, an antislavery Whig senator from New York, proclaimed he could not support a compromise that forced Northerners to help hunt down fugitives from slavery. While Daniel Webster, a Massachusetts Whig, urged fellow senators to support the compromise to preserve the Union, Congress adjourned with the fate of California undecided.

Before the Senate reconvened in September 1850, however, the political landscape changed in unexpected ways. Henry Clay retired the previous spring, leaving the Capitol with his last great legislative effort unfinished. On March 31, 1850, Calhoun died; his absence from the Senate made compromise more likely. Then in July, President Taylor died unexpectedly, and his vice president, Millard Fillmore, became president. Fillmore then appointed Webster as secretary of state, removing him from the Senate as well.

In fall 1850, with President Fillmore's support, a younger cohort of senators and representatives steered the **Compromise of 1850** through Congress, one clause at a time. This tactic allowed legislators to support only those parts of the compromise they found palatable. In the end, all the provisions passed, and Fillmore quickly signed the bills into law.

The Compromise of 1850, like the Missouri Compromise thirty years earlier, fended off a sectional crisis but signaled future problems. Would popular sovereignty prevail when later territories sought admission to the Union, and would Northerners abide by a fugitive slave law that called on them to aid directly in the capture of runaway slaves?

The Fugitive Slave Act Inspires Northern Protest

The fugitive slave laws of 1793 and 1824 mandated that all states aid in apprehending and returning runaway slaves to their owners. The **Fugitive Slave Act of 1850** was different in two important respects. First, it eliminated jury trials for alleged fugitives. Second, the law required individual citizens, not just state officials, to help return runaways. The act angered many Northerners who believed that the federal government had gone too far in protecting the rights of slaveholders and thereby aroused sympathy for the abolitionist cause.

Before 1850, free blacks led the effort to aid fugitives, including David Ruggles in New York City; William Still in Philadelphia; and, after his own successful escape, Frederick Douglass. Among their staunchest allies were white Quakers such as Amy and Isaac Post in Rochester, Thomas Garrett in Chester County, Pennsylvania, and Levi and Catherine Coffin in Newport, Indiana. Political abolitionists, like wealthy reformer Gerrit Smith, of Peterboro, New York, also aided the cause.

Following passage of the Fugitive Slave Act, the number of slave owners and hired slave catchers pursuing fugitives increased dramatically. But so, too, did the number of northern abolitionists helping blacks escape. Once escaped slaves crossed into free territory, most contacted free blacks or sought out Quaker, Baptist, or Methodist meetinghouses whose members might be sympathetic to their cause. They then began the journey along the underground railroad, from house to house or barn to barn, until they found safe haven. A small number of fortunate slaves were led north by fugitives like Harriet Tubman, who returned south repeatedly to free dozens of family members and other enslaved men and women. Abolitionists purchased the freedom of a few others, including sisters Mary and Emily Edmondson who had been sold to slave traders after a failed escape attempt in 1848. Most fugitives followed disparate paths,

Anti-Fugitive Slave Law Convention, Cazenovia, New York, 1850 This rare daguerreotype captures abolitionists, outraged over the Fugitive Slave Law, at a massive protest meeting. Some 2,000 participants met in an apple orchard. Frederick Douglass sits at the left side of the table. The Edmondson sisters, in plaid shawls, stand behind him on either side of Gerrit Smith. The sisters were among fifty former slaves who attended the meeting.   Getty's Open Content Program/Getty Images

depending on "conductors" to get them from one stop to the next. Despite its limits, the underground railroad was an important resource for fugitives seeking refuge in Canada or hoping to blend into free black communities stateside.

Free blacks were endangered by the claim that slaves hid themselves in their midst. In Chester County, Pennsylvania, on the Maryland border, newspapers reported on at least a dozen free blacks who were kidnapped or arrested as runaways in the first three months of 1851. One provision of the Fugitive Slave Act encouraged such arrests: Commissioners were paid $10 for each slave sent back but only $5 if a slave was not returned. Without the right to a trial, a free black could easily be sent south as a fugitive.

At the same time, a growing number of Northerners challenged the federal government's right to enforce the law. Blacks and whites organized protest meetings throughout the free states. At a meeting in Boston in 1851, William Lloyd Garrison denounced the law: "We execrate it, we spit upon it, we trample it under our feet." On July 5, 1852, Frederick Douglass asked a mixed-race audience, "What to the American slave, is your 4th of July? I answer, a day that reveals to him . . . the gross injustice and cruelty to which he is the constant victim." He then declared, "There is not a nation on the earth guilty of practices more shocking and bloody than are the people of these United States at this very hour."

Some abolitionists established vigilance committees to rescue fugitives who had been arrested. In Syracuse in October 1851, Jermaine Loguen, Samuel Ward, and the Reverend Samuel J. May led a well-organized crowd that broke into a Syracuse courthouse and rescued a fugitive known as Jerry. They successfully hid him from authorities before spiriting him to Canada.

Meanwhile Americans continued to debate the law's effects. John Frémont, one of the first two senators from California, helped defeat a federal bill that would have imposed harsher penalties on those who assisted runaways. And Congress felt growing pressure to calm the situation, including from foreign officials who were horrified by the violence required to sustain slavery in the United States. Black abolitionists denounced the Fugitive Slave Act across Canada, Ireland, and England, intensifying foreign concern over the law. Great Britain and France had abolished slavery in their West Indian colonies and could not support what they saw as extreme policies to keep the institution alive in the United States. Yet southern slaveholders refused to compromise further, as did northern abolitionists.

Pierce Encourages U.S. Expansion

In the presidential election of 1852, the Whigs and the Democrats tried once again to appeal to voters across the North-South divide by running candidates who either skirted the slavery issue or voiced ambiguous views. The Democrats nominated Franklin Pierce of New Hampshire. A northern opponent of abolition, Pierce had served in Congress from 1833 to 1842 and in the U.S. army during the Mexican-American War. The Whigs rejected President Millard Fillmore, who had angered many by supporting popular sovereignty and vigorous enforcement of the Fugitive Slave Act. They turned instead to General Winfield Scott of Virginia. General Scott had never expressed any proslavery views and had served with distinction in the war against Mexico. The Whigs thus hoped to gain southern support while maintaining their northern base. The Free-Soil Party, too, hoped to expand its appeal by nominating John Hale, a New Hampshire Democrat.

Franklin Pierce's eventual victory left the Whigs and the Free Soilers in disarray. Seeking a truly proslavery party, a third of southern Whigs threw their support to the Democrats in the election. Many Democrats who had supported Free-Soilers in 1848 were driven to vote for Pierce by their enthusiasm over the admission of California as a free state. But despite the Democratic triumph, that party also remained fragile. The nation now faced some of its gravest challenges under a president with limited political experience and no firm base of support and a cabinet that included men of widely differing views. When confronted with difficult decisions, Pierce received contradictory advice and generally pursued his own expansionist vision.

Early in his administration, Pierce focused on expanding U.S. trade and extending the "civilizing" power of the nation to other parts of the world. Trade with China had declined in the 1840s, but the United States had begun commercial negotiations with Japan in 1846. These came to fruition in 1854, when U.S. emissary Commodore Matthew C. Perry, a renowned naval officer and founder of the Naval Engineer Corps, obtained the first formal mutual trade agreement with Japan. Within four years, the United States had expanded commercial ties and enhanced diplomatic relations with Japan, in large part by supporting the island nation against its traditional enemies in China, Russia, and Europe.

Pierce had rejected Commodore Perry's offer to take military possession of Formosa and other territories near Japan, but he was willing to consider conquests in the Caribbean and Central America. For decades, U.S. politicians, particularly Southerners, had looked to gain control of Cuba, Mexico, and Nicaragua. A "Young America" movement within the Democratic Party imagined manifest destiny reaching southward as well as westward. In hopes of stirring up rebellious Cubans against Spanish rule, some Democrats joined with private adventurers to send three unauthorized expeditions, known as **filibusters**, to invade Cuba. In 1854 the capture of one of the filibustering ships led to an international incident. Spanish officials confiscated the ship, and southern Democrats urged Pierce to seek an apology and redress from Spain. But many northern Democrats rejected any effort to obtain another slave state, and Pierce was forced to renounce the filibusters.

Other politicians still pressured Spain to sell Cuba to the United States. These included Pierce's secretary of state, William Marcy, and the U.S. ambassador to Great Britain, James Buchanan, as well as the ministers to France and Spain. In October 1854 these ministers met in Ostend, Belgium and sent a letter to Pierce urging the conquest of Cuba. When the **Ostend Manifesto** was leaked to the press, Northerners were outraged. They viewed the episode as "a dirty plot" to gain more slave territory and forced Pierce to give up plans to obtain Cuba. In 1855 a private adventurer named William Walker, who had organized four filibusters to Nicaragua, invaded that country and set himself up as ruler. He then invited southern planters to come to Nicaragua and establish plantations. Pierce and many Democrats endorsed his plan, but neighboring Hondurans forced Walker from power in 1857 and executed him three years later. Although Pierce's expansionist dreams failed, his efforts heightened sectional tensions.

REVIEW & RELATE	• What steps did legislators take in the 1840s and early 1850s to resolve the issue of the expansion of slavery? Were they successful? • How were slavery and American imperialist ambitions intertwined in the 1840s and 1850s?

Sectional Crises Intensify

The political crises of the early 1850s created a lively trade in antislavery literature. This cultural turmoil, combined with the weakness and fragmentation of the existing political parties, helped give rise to the Republican Party in 1854. The Republican Party soon absorbed enough Free-Soilers, Whigs, and northern Democrats to become a major political force. The events that drove these cultural and political developments included the publication of *Uncle Tom's Cabin*, continued challenges to the Fugitive Slave Act, a battle over the admission of Kansas to the Union, and a Supreme Court ruling in the *Dred Scott* case.

Popularizing Antislavery Sentiment

The Fugitive Slave Act forced Northerners to reconsider their role in sustaining the institution of slavery. In 1852, just months before Franklin Pierce was elected president, their concerns were heightened by the publication of the novel *Uncle Tom's Cabin* by Harriet Beecher Stowe. Stowe's father, Lyman Beecher, and brother Henry were among the nation's leading evangelical clergy, and her sister Catharine had opposed Cherokee removal and promoted women's education. Stowe was inspired to write *Uncle Tom's Cabin* by passage of the Fugitive Slave Act in 1850. Published in both serial and book forms, the novel created a national sensation.

Uncle Tom's Cabin built on accounts by former slaves as well as tales gathered by abolitionist lecturers and writers, which gained growing attention in the North. The autobiographies of Frederick Douglass (1845), Josiah Henson (1849), and Henry Bibb (1849) set the stage for Stowe's novel. So, too, did the expansion of the antislavery press, which by the 1850s included dozens of newspapers. Antislavery poems and songs also circulated widely and were performed at abolitionist conventions and fund-raising fairs.

Still, nothing captured the public's attention as did *Uncle Tom's Cabin*. Read by millions in the United States and England and translated into French and German, the book reached a mass audience. Its sentimental portrait of saintly slaves and its vivid depiction of cruel masters and overseers offered white Northerners a way to identify with enslaved blacks. Although some African Americans expressed frustration that a white woman's fictional account gained far more readers than their factual narratives, most recognized the book's important contribution to the antislavery cause.

Yet the real-life stories of fugitive slaves could often surpass their fictional counterparts for drama. In May 1854 abolitionists sought to free fugitive slave Anthony Burns from a Boston courthouse, where his master was attempting to reclaim him. They failed to secure his release, and Burns was soon marched to the docks to be shipped south. Twenty-two companies of state militia held back tens of thousands of angry Bostonians who lined the streets. A year later, supporters purchased Burns's freedom from his master, but the incident raised anguished questions among local residents. In a city that was home to so many intellectual, religious, and antislavery leaders, Bostonians wondered how they had come so far in aiding and abetting slavery.

The Kansas-Nebraska Act Stirs Dissent

Kansas provided the first test of the effects of *Uncle Tom's Cabin* on northern sentiments toward slavery's expansion. As white Americans displaced Indian nations from their homelands, diverse groups of Indians settled in the northern half of the Louisiana Territory. This unorganized region had once been considered beyond the reach of white settlement, but Democratic senator Stephen Douglas of Illinois was eager to have a transcontinental railroad run through his home state. He needed the federal government to gain control of land along the route he proposed and thus argued for the establishment of a vast Nebraska Territory. But to support his plan, Douglas also needed to convince southern congressmen, who sought a route through their own region. According to the Missouri Compromise, states lying above the southern border of Missouri were automatically free. To gain southern support, Douglas sought to reopen the question of slavery in the territories.

In January 1854 Douglas introduced the **Kansas-Nebraska Act** to Congress. The act extinguished Indians' long-held treaty rights in the region and repealed the Missouri Compromise. Two new territories—Kansas and Nebraska—would be carved out of the unorganized lands, and voters in each would determine whether to enter the nation as a slave or a free state (Map 12.2). The act spurred intense opposition from most Whigs and some northern Democrats who wanted to retain the Missouri Compromise line. Months of fierce debate followed, but the bill was ultimately voted into law.

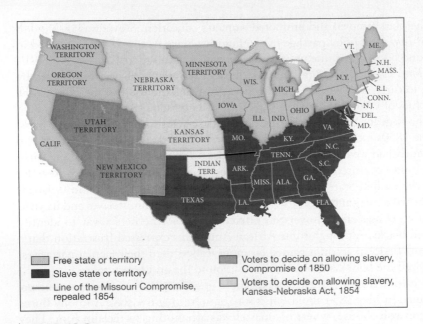

MAP 12.2

Kansas-Nebraska Territory   From 1820 on, Congress attempted to limit sectional conflict. But the Missouri Compromise (1820) and the Compromise of 1850 failed to resolve disagreements over slavery's expansion. The creation of the Kansas and Nebraska territories in 1854 heightened sectional conflict and ensured increased hostilities with Indians in the region.

Passage of the Kansas-Nebraska Act enraged many Northerners who considered the dismantling of the Missouri Compromise a sign of the rising power of the South. They were infuriated that the South—or what some now called the "Slave Power"—had again benefited from northern politicians' willingness to compromise. Although few of these opponents considered the impact of the law on Indians, the act also shattered treaty provisions that had protected the Arapaho, Cheyenne, Ponco, Pawnee, and Sioux nations. These Plains Indians lost half the land they had held by treaty as thousands of settlers swarmed into the newly organized territories. In the fall of 1855, conflicts between white settlers and Indians erupted across the Great Plains. The U.S. army then sent six hundred troops to retaliate against a Sioux village, killing eighty-five residents of Blue Water in the Nebraska Territory and triggering continued violence throughout the region.

As tensions escalated across the nation, Americans faced the 1854 congressional elections. The Democrats, increasingly viewed as supporting the priorities of slaveholders, lost badly in the North. But the Whig Party also proved weak, having failed to stop the Slave Power from extending its leverage over federal policies. A third party, the American Party, was founded in the early 1850s and attracted native-born workers and Protestant farmers who were drawn to its anti-immigrant and anti-Catholic message. They continued to seek limits on immigrants' political power and cultural influence. Responding to these political realignments, another new party, led by antislavery Whigs and Free-Soilers—the **Republican Party**—was founded in the spring of 1854. Among its early members was a Whig politician from Illinois, Abraham Lincoln.

Although established only months before the fall 1854 elections, the Republican Party gained significant support in the Midwest, particularly in state and local campaigns. Meanwhile the American Party gained control of the Massachusetts legislature and nearly captured New York. These victories marked the demise of the Whigs and the Second Party System. Unlike the Whig Party, however, with its national constituency, the Republican Party was rooted solely in the North. Like Free-Soilers, the Republicans argued that slavery should not be extended into new territories. But the Republicans also advocated a program of commercial and industrial development and internal improvements to attract a broader base than earlier antislavery parties. The Republican Party attracted both ardent abolitionists and men whose main concern was keeping western territories open to free white men. This latter group was more than willing to accept slavery where it already existed.

Bleeding Kansas and the Election of 1856

The 1854 congressional elections exacerbated sectional tensions by bringing representatives from a strictly northern party—the Republicans—into Congress. But the conflicts over slavery reached far beyond the nation's capital. After passage of the Kansas-Nebraska Act, advocates and opponents of slavery poured into Kansas in anticipation of a vote on whether the state would enter the Union slave or free.

John Doy and His Rescue Party, Kansas, 1859　John Doy and his son Charles were captured in Kansas in January 1859 while assisting thirteen slaves to escape their owners. Taken to Missouri, Charles was set free, but his father was sentenced to five years in prison for abducting slaves. Abolitionist friends freed him, and the group (with John Doy seated) posed for this picture when they reached Lawrence. Kansas State Historical Society

As Kansas prepared to hold its referendum, settlers continued to arrive daily, making it difficult to determine who was eligible to vote. In 1855 Southerners installed a proslavery government at Shawnee Mission, while abolitionists established a stronghold in Lawrence. Violence erupted when proslavery settlers invaded Lawrence, killing one resident, demolishing newspaper offices, and plundering shops and homes. Fearing that southern settlers in Kansas were better armed than antislavery Northerners in the territory, eastern abolitionists raised funds to ship rifles to Kansas.

In 1856 longtime abolitionist John Brown carried his own rifles to Kansas. Four of his sons already lived in the territory. To retaliate for proslavery attacks on Lawrence, the Browns and two friends kidnapped five proslavery advocates from their homes along Pottawatomie Creek and hacked them to death. The so-called Pottawatomie Massacre infuriated southern settlers, who then drew up the Lecompton Constitution, which declared Kansas a slave state. President Pierce made his support of the proslavery government clear, but Congress remained divided. While Congress deliberated, armed battles continued. In the first six months of 1856, more than fifty settlers—on both sides of the conflict—were killed in what became known as **Bleeding Kansas**.

Fighting also broke out on the floor of Congress. Republican senator Charles Sumner of Massachusetts delivered an impassioned speech against the continued expansion of the Slave Power. He launched scathing attacks on planter politicians like South Carolina senator Andrew Butler. Butler's nephew, Preston Brooks, a Democratic member of the House of Representatives, rushed to defend his family's honor. He assaulted Sumner in the Senate chamber, beating him senseless with a cane. Sumner, who never fully recovered from his injuries, was considered a martyr in the North. Meanwhile Brooks was celebrated throughout South Carolina.

The presidential election of 1856 began amid an atmosphere poisoned by violence and recrimination. The Democratic Party nominated James Buchanan of Pennsylvania, a proslavery advocate. Western hero John C. Frémont headed the Republican Party ticket. The American Party, in its final presidential contest, selected former president Millard Fillmore as its candidate. The strength of nativism in politics was waning, however, and Fillmore won only the state of Maryland. Meanwhile Frémont attracted cheering throngs as he traveled across the nation. Large numbers of women turned out to see Jessie Frémont, the first presidential candidate's wife to play a significant role in a campaign. Frémont carried most of the North and the West. Buchanan captured the South along with Pennsylvania, Indiana, and Illinois. Although Buchanan won only 45.2 percent of the popular vote, he received a comfortable majority in the electoral college, securing his victory. The nation was becoming increasingly divided along sectional lines, and President Buchanan would do little to resolve these differences.

The *Dred Scott* Decision

Just two days after Buchanan's inauguration, the Supreme Court finally announced its decision in the *Dred Scott* case (see "Comparing American Histories"). Led by Chief Justice Roger Taney, a proslavery Southerner, the majority ruled that a slave was not a citizen and therefore could not sue in court. Indeed, Taney claimed that black men had no rights that a white man was bound to respect. The ruling annulled Scott's suit and meant that he and his wife remained enslaved. But the ruling went further. The ***Dred Scott* decision** declared that Congress had no constitutional authority to exclude slavery from any territory, thereby nullifying the Missouri Compromise and any future effort to restrict slavery's expansion. The ruling outraged many Northerners, who were now convinced that a Slave Power conspiracy had taken hold of the federal government, including the judiciary.

In 1858, when Stephen Douglas faced reelection to the U.S. Senate, the Republican Party nominated Abraham Lincoln, a successful lawyer from Springfield, Illinois, to oppose him. The candidates participated in seven debates in which they explained their positions on slavery in the wake of the *Dred Scott* decision. Pointing to the landmark ruling, Lincoln asked Douglas how he could favor popular sovereignty, which allowed residents to keep slavery out of a territory, and yet support the *Dred Scott* decision, which protected slavery in all territories. Douglas claimed that if residents did not adopt local legislation to protect slaveholders' property, they could thereby exclude slavery for all practical purposes. At the same time, he accused Lincoln of advocating "negro equality," a position that went well beyond Lincoln's views. Lincoln did support economic opportunity for free blacks, but not political or social equality. Still, the Republican candidate did declare that "this government cannot endure permanently half slave and half free. . . . It will become all one thing or all the other."

The Lincoln-Douglas debates attracted national attention, but the Illinois legislature selected the state's senator. Narrowly controlled by Democrats, it returned Douglas to Washington. Although the senator retained his seat, he was concerned by how far the Democratic Party had tilted toward the South. So when President Buchanan tried to push the Lecompton Constitution through Congress, legitimating the proslavery government in Kansas, Douglas opposed him. The two struggled over control of the party, with Douglas winning a symbolic victory in January 1861 when Kansas was admitted as a free state. By then, however, the Democratic Party had split into southern and northern wings, and the nation was on the verge of civil war.

REVIEW & RELATE

- What factors contributed to the spread of antislavery sentiment in the North beyond committed abolitionists?
- How did the violence in Kansas and the *Dred Scott* decision reflect and intensify the growing sectional divide within the nation?

From Sectional Crisis to Southern Secession

During the 1850s, a profusion of abolitionist lectures, conventions, and literature swelled antislavery sentiment in the North. Mainstream newspapers regularly covered rescues of fugitives, the *Dred Scott* case, and the bloody crisis in Kansas. Republican candidates in state and local elections also kept concerns about slavery's expansion and southern power alive. Nothing, however, riveted the nation's attention as much as John Brown's raid on the federal arsenal at Harpers Ferry, Virginia in 1859. Less than a year later, Republican Abraham Lincoln captured the White House. In the wake of his election, South Carolina seceded from the Union.

John Brown's Raid

John Brown was committed not only to the abolition of slavery but also to complete equality between whites and blacks. A militant abolitionist and deeply religious man, Brown held views quite similar to those of David Walker, whose 1829 *Appeal* warned that slaves would eventually rise up and claim their freedom by force. Following the bloody battles in Kansas, Brown was convinced that direct action was the only answer. After the Pottawatomie killings, he went into hiding and reappeared back east, where he hoped to initiate an uprising to overthrow slavery.

Brown focused his efforts on the federal arsenal in **Harpers Ferry, Virginia**. With eighteen followers—five African Americans and thirteen whites, including three of his sons—Brown planned to capture the arsenal and distribute arms to slaves in the surrounding area. He hoped this action would ignite a rebellion that would destroy the plantation system. He tried to convince Frederick Douglass to join the venture, but Douglass considered it a foolhardy plan. However, Brown did manage to persuade a small circle of white abolitionists to bankroll the effort.

On the night of October 16, 1859, Brown and his men successfully kidnapped some leading townsmen and seized the arsenal. Local residents were stunned but managed to alert authorities, and state militia swarmed into Harpers Ferry. The next day, federal troops arrived, led by Colonel Robert E. Lee. With troops flooding into the town, Brown and his men were soon under siege, trapped in the arsenal. Fourteen rebels were killed, including two of Brown's sons. On October 18, Brown and three others were captured.

As word of the daring raid spread, Brown was hailed as a hero by many devoted abolitionists and depicted as a madman by southern planters. Southern whites were sure the raid was part of a widespread conspiracy led by power-hungry abolitionists. Federal authorities moved quickly to quell slaveholders' fears and end the episode. Brown rejected his lawyer's advice to plead insanity, and a local jury found him guilty of murder, criminal conspiracy, and treason. He was hanged on December 2, 1859.

John Brown's execution unleashed a massive outpouring of grief, anger, and uncertainty across the North. Abolitionists organized parades, demonstrations, bonfires, and tributes to the newest abolitionist martyr. Even many Quakers and other pacifists viewed John Brown as a hero for giving his life in the cause of emancipation. But most northern politicians and editors condemned the raid as a rash act that could only intensify sectional tensions.

Among southern whites, fear and panic greeted the raid on Harpers Ferry, and the execution of John Brown did little to quiet their outrage. By this time, southern intellectuals had developed a sophisticated proslavery argument that, to them, demonstrated the benefits of bondage for African Americans and its superiority to the northern system of wage labor. They argued that slave owners provided care and guidance for blacks from birth to death. Considering blacks too childlike to fend for themselves, proslavery advocates saw no problem with the enslaved providing labor and obedience in return for their care. Such arguments failed to convince abolitionists, who highlighted the brutality, sexual abuse, and shattered families that marked the system of bondage. In this context, Americans on both sides of the sectional divide considered the 1860 presidential election critical to the nation's future.

The Election of 1860

Brown's hanging set the tone for the 1860 presidential campaign. The Republicans met in Chicago five months after Brown's execution and distanced themselves from the more radical wing of the abolitionist movement. The party platform condemned both John Brown and southern "Border Ruffians," who initiated the violence in

Kansas. The platform accepted slavery where it already existed, but continued to advocate its exclusion from western territories. Finally, the platform insisted on the need for federally funded internal improvements and protective tariffs. The Republicans nominated Abraham Lincoln as their candidate for president. Recognizing the impossibility of gaining significant votes in the South, the party focused instead on winning large majorities in the Northeast and Midwest.

The Democrats met in Charleston, South Carolina. Although Stephen Douglas was the leading candidate, southern delegates were still angry with him over Kansas being admitted as a free state. When Mississippi senator Jefferson Davis introduced a resolution to protect slavery in the territories, Douglas's northern supporters rejected it. President Buchanan also came out against Douglas, and the Democratic convention ended without choosing a candidate. Instead, various factions met separately. A group of largely northern Democrats met in Baltimore and nominated Douglas. Southern Democrats selected John Breckinridge, the vice president, a slaveholder, and an advocate of annexing Cuba. The Constitutional Union Party, comprised mainly of former southern Whigs, advocated "no political principle other than the Constitution of the country, the union of the states, and the enforcement of the laws." Its members nominated Senator John Bell of Tennessee.

Although Lincoln won barely 40 percent of the popular vote, he carried a clear majority in the electoral college. With the admission of Minnesota and Oregon to the Union in 1858 and 1859, free states outnumbered slave states eighteen to fifteen, and Lincoln won all but one of them. Lincoln did not win a single Southern electoral vote. However, since free states were more populous than slave states, they therefore controlled a large number of electoral votes. Douglas ran second to Lincoln in the popular vote, but Bell and Breckinridge captured more electoral votes than Douglas did because of their success in the South. Despite a deeply divided electorate, Lincoln became president (Map 12.3).

Although many abolitionists were wary of the Republicans, who were willing to leave slavery alone where it existed, most were nonetheless relieved at Lincoln's

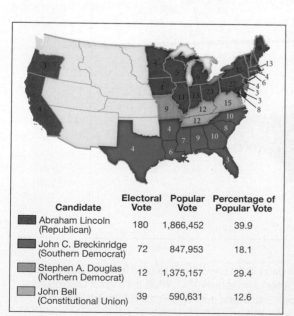

Candidate	Electoral Vote	Popular Vote	Percentage of Popular Vote
Abraham Lincoln (Republican)	180	1,866,452	39.9
John C. Breckinridge (Southern Democrat)	72	847,953	18.1
Stephen A. Douglas (Northern Democrat)	12	1,375,157	29.4
John Bell (Constitutional Union)	39	590,631	12.6

MAP 12.3

The Election of 1860 Four candidates vied for the presidency in 1860, and the voters split along clearly sectional lines. Although Stephen Douglas ran a vigorous campaign and gained votes in all regions of the country, he won a majority only in Missouri. Lincoln triumphed in the North and far West, and Breckinridge in most of the South.

victory and hoped he would become more sympathetic to their views once in office. Meanwhile, southern whites, especially those in the deep South, were furious that a Republican had won the White House without carrying a single southern state.

The Lower South Secedes

On December 20, 1860, six weeks after Lincoln's election, the legislature of South Carolina announced that because "a sectional party" had engineered "the election of a man to the high office of President of the United States whose opinions and purposes are hostile to slavery," the people of South Carolina dissolve their union with "the other states of North America." In early 1861, Mississippi, Florida, Alabama, Georgia, Louisiana, and Texas followed suit. Representatives from these states met on February 8 in Montgomery, Alabama, where they adopted a provisional constitution, elected Jefferson Davis as their president, and established the **Confederate States of America** (Map 12.4).

President Buchanan did nothing to stop the secession movement. His cabinet included three secessionists and two unionists, one of whom resigned in frustration over Buchanan's failure to act. But Washington, D.C. was filled with southern sympathizers, who urged caution on an already timid president. Although some Northerners were shocked by the decision of South Carolina and its allies, many others supported their right to leave or believed they would return to the Union when they realized they could not survive economically on their own. Moreover, with Virginia, Maryland, and other Upper South slave states still part of the nation, the secession movement seemed unlikely to succeed.

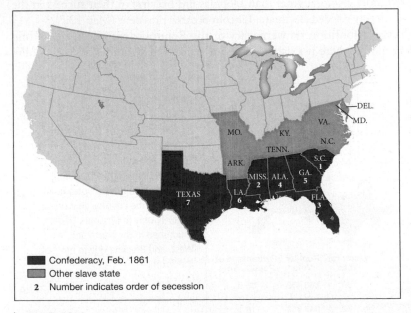

Confederacy, Feb. 1861
Other slave state
2   Number indicates order of secession

MAP 12.4
The Original Confederacy   Seven states in the Lower South seceded from the United States and formed the Confederate States of America in February 1861. While the original Confederacy was too limited in population and resources to defend itself against the U.S. government, its leaders hoped that other slave states would soon join them.

In the midst of the crisis, Kentucky senator John Crittenden proposed a compromise that gained significant support. Indeed, Congress approved the first part of his plan, which called for a constitutional amendment to protect slavery from federal interference in any state where it already existed. But the second part of the **Crittenden plan** failed to win Republican votes. It would have extended the Missouri Compromise line (latitude 36°30') to the California border and barred slavery north of that line. South of that line, however, slavery would be protected, including in any territories "acquired hereafter." Fearing that passage would encourage southern planters to again seek territory in Cuba, Mexico, or Central America, Republicans in Congress rejected the proposal. Despite the hopes of the Buchanan administration, it was becoming apparent that compromise was impossible.

REVIEW & RELATE

- How and why did John Brown's raid on Harpers Ferry move the country closer to civil war?
- Why did many in the South believe that the election of Abraham Lincoln was cause for secession?

Conclusion: A Nation Divided

Dred Scott did not live to see Abraham Lincoln take the oath of office in March 1861. Following the Supreme Court's 1857 ruling, Scott was returned to Irene Emerson, who had married abolitionist Calvin Chaffee. Unwilling to be the owner of the most well-known slave in America, Chaffee quickly returned Dred Scott and his family to his original owners, the Blow family. The Blows then freed the Scotts. For the next year and a half, before dying of tuberculosis, Dred Scott lived as a free man. Although Harriet and their daughters lived to see slavery abolished, in the spring of 1861 they could not imagine how that goal would be reached.

In 1860 John C. Frémont believed the nation was headed to war; and he was willing, once again, to serve a country he had helped expand. His work as a surveyor and soldier opened new territories to white settlement, and the gold rush then ensured California's admission to the Union. Yet what Frémont and other advocates of manifest destiny saw as U.S. victories had decimated many Indian nations as well as the property rights and livelihoods of many Mexicans. Despite the efforts of the Comanche and other tribes to fend off white encroachment, the U.S. government and white settlers claimed more and more territory. It was these western territories, moreover, that heightened conflicts over slavery and led the nation to the situation it faced in spring 1861.

While some Confederate planters imagined expanding the nation—and slavery—into Cuba, Nicaragua, and other southern regions, Northerners fought any such schemes. Outraged by the Fugitive Slave Act and appalled by Bleeding Kansas, militant activists applauded John Brown's raid at Harpers Ferry. Just as important, more moderate Northerners increasingly opposed slavery and voted for Lincoln in the fall of 1860. By the time Abraham Lincoln took office in March 1861, however, seven southern states had seceded, and the ever-widening political chasm brought the nation face-to-face with civil war.

Chapter 12 Review

KEY TERMS

Oregon Trail (p. 287)
gold rush (p. 288)
Compromise of 1850 (p. 293)
Fugitive Slave Act of 1850 (p. 293)
filibusters (p. 296)
Ostend Manifesto (p. 296)
Uncle Tom's Cabin (p. 296)

Kansas-Nebraska Act (p. 297)
Republican Party (p. 298)
Bleeding Kansas (p. 300)
Dred Scott decision (p. 300)
Harpers Ferry, Virginia (p. 302)
Confederate States of America (p. 304)
Crittenden plan (p. 305)

REVIEW & RELATE

1. Why did Americans go west in the 1830s and 1840s, and what was the journey like?

2. What groups competed for land and resources in the West? How did disease, drought, and violence shape this competition?

3. What steps did legislators take in the 1840s and early 1850s to resolve the issue of the expansion of slavery? Were they successful?

4. How were slavery and American imperialist ambitions intertwined in the 1840s and 1850s?

5. What factors contributed to the spread of antislavery sentiment in the North beyond committed abolitionists?

6. How did the violence in Kansas and the *Dred Scott* decision reflect and intensify the growing sectional divide within the nation?

7. How and why did John Brown's raid on Harpers Ferry move the country closer to civil war?

8. Why did many in the South believe that the election of Abraham Lincoln was cause for secession?

TIMELINE OF EVENTS

1842
- John C. Frémont leads expedition along the Oregon Trail

1848
- Gold discovered in California

1850
- Compromise of 1850
- Fugitive Slave Act

1852
- Harriet Beecher Stowe publishes *Uncle Tom's Cabin*

1854
- U.S.-Japanese treaty allows for mutual trading
- Republican Party founded
- Kansas-Nebraska Act

1854–1858
- Period of violence in Bleeding Kansas

1857
- *Dred Scott* case

1858
- Lincoln-Douglas debates

1859
- John Brown's raid on Harpers Ferry

November 1860
- Abraham Lincoln elected president

December 1860
- South Carolina secedes from the Union

January 1861
- Mississippi, Florida, Alabama, Georgia, Louisiana, and Texas secede

February 1861
- Confederate States of America established

March 1861
- Lincoln inaugurated as president

3

Civil War

1861–1865

LEARNING OBJECTIVES

After reading this chapter you should be able to:

• Explain why southern states seceded and describe the advantages and disadvantages that marked the Confederacy and the Union at the beginning of the Civil War.

• Describe the changing roles of African Americans, free and enslaved, in the war and the growing sentiment for emancipation in the North.

• Evaluate how the war changed northern and southern political priorities and the lives of soldiers and civilians.

• Identify turning points in the Civil War, including key battles in the eastern and western theaters of war, and explain the factors that led to Union victory and the abolition of slavery.

COMPARING AMERICAN HISTORIES

Born into slavery in 1818, Frederick Douglass became a celebrated orator, editor, and abolitionist in the 1840s. In 1845 Douglass published his autobiography, *Narrative of the Life of Frederick Douglass*, which described his enslavement in Maryland, his defiance against his masters, and his eventual escape to New York in 1838 with the help of Anna Murray, a free black servant.

After marrying in New York, Frederick and Anna moved to New Bedford, Massachusetts, and changed their last name to Douglass to avoid capture. In 1841 the American Anti-Slavery Society hired Frederick to present his vivid tale of slave life in public. Four years later, Douglass launched a British lecture tour that attracted enthusiastic audiences. Supporters in Britain purchased his freedom, and Douglass returned to Massachusetts a free man in 1847.

Late that year, Frederick moved to Rochester, New York with Anna and their children to launch his abolitionist paper, the *North Star.* Soon after, he broke with the Garrisonians and embraced the Liberty Party and eventually the Republicans. When war erupted in April 1861, Douglass lobbied President Lincoln relentlessly to make emancipation a war aim.

Initially Douglass feared that Lincoln was more committed to reconstituting the Union than abolishing slavery. But when the president issued the Emancipation Proclamation in January 1863, Douglass spoke enthusiastically on its behalf. He also argued that it was essential for black men to serve in the Union army. When African Americans were finally allowed to join in 1862 to 1863, Douglass helped recruit volunteers but also protested discrimination against black troops and the denial of black civil rights.

Like Douglass, Rose O'Neal was born on a Maryland plantation, but she was white and free. Her father was John O'Neal, a planter who was killed in 1817 when Rose was about four. In her teens, she and her sister moved to Washington, D.C., where their aunt ran a fashionable boardinghouse. Her boarders included John C. Calhoun, whose states' rights views Rose eagerly embraced. Rose was welcomed into elite social circles and in 1835 married Virginian Robert Greenhow, who worked for the State Department.

Rose O'Neal Greenhow quickly became a favorite Washington hostess, entertaining congressmen, cabinet ministers, and foreign diplomats. Ardent proslavery expansionists, the Greenhows supported efforts to acquire Cuba and expand slavery into western territories. When Robert died in 1854, Rose and their four children remained in D.C. and continued to entertain powerful political leaders.

In May 1861, as the Civil War commenced, a U.S. army captain about to join the Confederate cause recruited Greenhow to head an espionage ring in Washington, D.C. With her close ties to southern sympathizers in the capital, Greenhow gathered intelligence on Union plans. Although she initially avoided suspicion, by August 1861 Greenhow was investigated and placed under house arrest. After continuing to smuggle out letters, she was sent to the Old Capitol Prison in January 1862. When Greenhow again managed to transmit information, she was exiled to Richmond, where Confederate president Jefferson Davis hailed her as a hero.

COMPARING THE AMERICAN HISTORIES of Frederick Douglass and Rose O'Neal Greenhow illustrates the ways that Americans, black and white, northern and southern, men and women, were shaped by and shaped the war that followed secession. They were among hundreds of thousands of Americans who saw the war as a means to achieve their goals: a free nation, a haven for slavery, or a reunited country.

Once conflict erupted at Fort Sumter in April 1861, more southern states seceded although four slave states, reluctantly, remained in the Union. Even with the addition of more states, the Confederacy lagged behind the Union in population, industrial and agricultural production, and railroad lines. These differences became more important as the war unfolded. Initially, however, skilled officers and knowledge of the southern terrain benefited the Confederate army. On the home front, hundreds of thousands of Americans labored on farms and in factories, burgeoning government offices, and hospitals to support the Union or the Confederacy. After 1862, tens of thousands of African Americans joined the Union army, both free blacks and enslaved men freed by Union forces. The next year, the Emancipation Proclamation ensured that a Union victory would eradicate slavery. As the war dragged on, antiwar protests erupted North and South, fueled by inflation, conscription acts, and mounting casualties. Finally in 1865, the greater resources of the North, complemented by General Ulysses S. Grant's hard war strategy, led to Union victory and the final abolition of slavery.

The Nation Goes to War, 1861

When Abraham Lincoln took office, seven states in the Lower South had already formed the Confederate States of America, and more states threatened to secede. Lincoln had promised not to interfere with slavery where it existed, but many southern whites doubted such assurances. By seceding, southern slaveholders also proclaimed their unwillingness to become a permanent minority in the nation. Still, not all slave states were yet willing to cut their ties to the nation. Northerners, too, disagreed about the appropriate response to secession. Once fighting erupted, however, preparations for war became the primary focus in both the Union and the Confederacy.

The South Embraces Secession

Confederate president Jefferson Davis joined other planters in arguing that Lincoln's victory jeopardized the future of slavery and that secession was therefore a necessity. Advocates of secession contended that the federal government had failed to implement fully the Fugitive Slave Act and the *Dred Scott* decision. They were convinced that a Republican administration would do even less to support southern interests. White Southerners also feared that Republicans might inspire a massive uprising of slaves, and secession allowed whites to maintain control over the South's black population.

Still, when Lincoln was inaugurated, some legislators in the Upper South hoped a compromise could be reached, and the president hoped to bring the Confederates back into the Union without using military force. Most northern merchants, manufacturers, and bankers approved, wanting to maintain their economic ties to southern planters. Yet Lincoln also realized he must demonstrate Union strength to curtail further secessions. He focused on **Fort Sumter** in South Carolina's Charleston harbor, where a small Union garrison was running low on food and medicine. On April 8, 1861, Lincoln dispatched ships to the fort but promised to use force only if the Confederates blocked his peaceful effort to send supplies.

The Confederate government would now have to choose. It could attack the Union vessels and bear responsibility for starting a war or permit a "foreign power" to maintain a fort in its territory. President Davis and his advisers chose the aggressive course, demanding Fort Sumter's immediate and unconditional surrender.

The commanding officer refused, and on April 12 Confederate guns opened fire. Two days later, Fort Sumter surrendered. On April 15, Lincoln called for 75,000 volunteers to put down the southern insurrection.

The declaration of war led whites in the Upper South to reconsider secession. Some small farmers and landless whites were drawn to Republican promises of free labor and free soil and remained suspicious of the goals and power of secessionist planters. Yet the vast majority of southern whites, rich and poor, defined their liberty in relation to black bondage. They feared that Republicans would free the slaves and introduce racial amalgamation, the mixing of whites and blacks, in the South.

Fearing more secessions, Lincoln used the powers of his office to keep the border states that allowed slavery—Maryland, Delaware, Missouri, and Kentucky—in the Union. He waived the right of habeas corpus (which protects citizens against arbitrary arrest and detention), jailed secessionists, arrested state legislators, and limited freedom of the press. However, four other slave states—North Carolina, Virginia, Tennessee, and Arkansas—seceded. Virginia, with its strategic location near the nation's capital, was by far the most significant. Richmond, which would soon become the capital of the Confederacy, was also home to the South's largest iron manufacturer, which could produce weapons and munitions.

While Northerners differed over how to respond when the first seven states seceded, the firing on Fort Sumter prompted most to line up behind Lincoln's call for war. Manufacturers and merchants, once intent on maintaining commercial links with the South, now rushed to support the president, while northern workers, including immigrants, responded to Lincoln's call for volunteers. They assumed that the Union, with its greater resources and manpower, could quickly set the nation right. New York editor Horace Greeley proclaimed, "Jeff Davis and Co. will be swingin' from the battlements at Washington at least by the 4th of July."

FIGURE 13.1
Economies of the North and South, 1860 This figure provides graphic testimony to the enormous advantages in resources the North held on the eve of the Civil War. The North led the South in population, farm acreage, and railroad mileage as well as factories and commodity output. Over four years of war, how might the differences in each area affect the ability of the Union and the Confederacy to pursue their objectives? Source: Data from Stanley Engerman, "The Economic Impact of the Civil War," in *The Reinterpretation of American Economic History*, ed. Robert W. Fogel and Stanley Engerman (New York: Harper and Row, 1971).

Battle of Wilson's Creek
This lithograph depicts the First Iowa Regiment, led by General Nathaniel Lyon, charging Confederate forces at the Battle of Wilson's Creek, Missouri on August 10, 1861. The Confederates won the battle, and Lyon, on the ground here, became the first Union general to die in the war. The lithograph was created in 1893 based on a wartime sketch.   Library of Congress, 3g01767

Both Sides Prepare for War

At the onset of the war, the Union certainly held a decided advantage in resources and population. The Union states held more than 60 percent of the U.S. population, and the Confederate population included several million slaves who would not be armed for combat. The Union also far outstripped the Confederacy in manufacturing and even led the South in agricultural production. The North's many miles of railroad track ensured greater ease in moving troops and supplies. And the Union could launch far more ships to blockade southern ports (Figure 13.1).

Yet Union forces were less prepared for war than the Confederates, who had been organizing troops and gathering munitions for months. To match their efforts, Winfield Scott, general in chief of the U.S. army, told Lincoln he would need at least 300,000 men committed to serve for two or three years. Scott believed that massing such huge numbers of soldiers would force the Confederacy to negotiate a peace. But fearing to unnerve Northerners, the president asked for only 75,000 volunteers for three months. Moreover, rather than forming a powerful national army led by seasoned officers, Lincoln left recruitment, organization, and training largely to the states. The result was disorganization and the appointment of officers based more on political connections than military expertise.

Confederate leaders also initially relied on state militia units and volunteers, but they prepared for a prolonged war from the start. Before the firing on Fort Sumter,

President Davis signed up 100,000 volunteers for a year's service. The labor provided by slaves allowed a large proportion of white working-age men to volunteer for military service. And Southerners knew they were likely to be fighting mainly on home territory, where they had expert knowledge of the terrain. When the final four states joined the Confederacy, the southern army also gained important military leadership. It ultimately recruited 280 West Point graduates, including Robert E. Lee, Thomas "Stonewall" Jackson, James Longstreet, and others who had proved their mettle in the Mexican-American War.

The South's advantages were apparent in the first major battle of the war. And Confederate troops were also aided by information on Union plans sent by Rose Greenhow. When 30,000 Union troops marched on northern Virginia on July 21, 1861, Confederate forces were ready. At the **Battle of Bull Run** (or **Manassas**), later known as the First Battle of Bull Run, 22,000 Confederates repelled the Union attack. Civilians from Washington who traveled to the battle site to view the combat had to flee for their lives to escape Confederate artillery.

Despite Union defeats at Bull Run and then at Wilson's Creek, Missouri in August 1861, the Confederate army did not launch major strikes against Union forces. Meanwhile the Union navy began blockading the South's deepwater ports. By the time the armies settled into winter camps in 1861–1862, both sides had come to realize that the war was likely to be a long and costly struggle.

REVIEW & RELATE	• What led four more states to join the Confederacy in 1861 and four other slave states to remain in the Union? • What advantages and disadvantages did each side have at the onset of the war?

Military Conflict and Political Strife, 1861–1862

The Union and the Confederacy faced very different tasks in the war. The South had to defend its territory and force the federal government to halt military action. The North had a more complicated challenge. Initially, northern political leaders believed that secession was driven mainly by slave owners and that high death rates and destruction of property would only alienate southern whites who favored reconciliation. But a policy of conciliation depended on early Union victories. With early defeats, it was clear the North would have to invade the South and isolate it from potential allies abroad. At the same time, most northern politicians believed that the nation could be reunited without abolishing slavery while abolitionists argued that only emancipation could resolve the problems that led to war. Meanwhile, enslaved Southerners immediately looked for ways to loosen their bonds.

The Wartime Roles of African Americans and Indians

The outbreak of war intensified debates over abolition. Some 225,000 African Americans lived in the free states, and many offered their services in an effort to end slavery. African American leaders in Cleveland proclaimed, "Today, as in the times of '76, we are ready to go forth and do battle in the common cause of our country." But Secretary of War Simon Cameron had no intention of calling up black soldiers.

Northern optimism about a quick victory contributed to the rejection of African American volunteers. Union leaders feared that whites would not enlist if they had to serve alongside blacks. In addition, Lincoln and his advisers were initially wary of letting a war to preserve the Union become a war against slavery, and they feared that any further threat to slavery might drive the four slave states that remained in the Union into the Confederacy. This political strategy, however, depended on quick and overwhelming victories; and with U.S. soldiers posted mainly on the western frontier and a third of officers joining the Confederacy, victories were few. Nonetheless a rush of volunteers allowed Union troops to push into Virginia while the Union navy captured crucial islands along the Confederate coast.

Wherever Union forces appeared, southern slaves began considering freedom as a possibility. Enslaved workers living near battle sites circulated information on Union troop movements. Then, as planters in Virginia began sending male slaves to more distant plantations for fear of losing them, some managed to flee and headed to Union camps. Many slave owners tracked fugitives behind Union lines and demanded their return. Some Union commanders denied slaves entrance or returned them to their masters. However, a few Union officers recognized these fugitives' value: They knew the local geography well, could dig trenches and provide other services, and drained the Confederate labor supply. At the Union outpost at Fort Monroe, Virginia in May 1861, General Benjamin Butler offered fugitive slaves military protection. He claimed them as **contraband** of war: property forfeited by the act of rebellion.

Lincoln endorsed Butler's policy because it allowed the Union to strike at the institution of slavery without proclaiming a general emancipation that might prompt border states where slavery remained legal to secede. Congress expanded Butler's policy in August 1861 by passing a confiscation act. It proclaimed that any owner whose slaves were used by the Confederate army would lose all claim to those slaves. Although it was far from a clear-cut declaration of freedom, the act spurred the hopes of northern abolitionists and many southern slaves.

While Northerners continued to debate African Americans' role in the war effort, the Union army recruited a wide array of other ethnic and racial groups, including American Indians. Unlike blacks, however, Indians did not necessarily all support the Union. The Comanche negotiated with both Union and Confederate agents while raiding the Texas frontier for horses and cattle. The Confederacy gained significant support from slaveholding Indians who had earlier been removed from the Southeast. The Cherokee split over the war as they had over removal. General Stand Watie led a pan-Indian force into battle for the Confederates. Initially John Ross joined the Confederates as well, but later he led a group of Cherokee into Union army ranks alongside the Osage, Delaware, Seneca, and other Indian nations. Ely Parker, a Seneca sachem and engineer, became a lieutenant colonel in the Union army, serving with General Ulysses S. Grant.

Indians played crucial roles in a number of important early battles, particularly on the Confederate side. Cherokee and Seminole warriors fought valiantly with Confederates at the Battle of Pea Ridge in Tennessee in March 1862, but were defeated by a smaller but better supplied Union force. In August 1862 Indians contributed to the Confederate victory at the Second Battle of Bull Run and the following month participated in the bloodiest single day of battle in U.S. history at Antietam (Sharpsburg). The Confederate army recruited Mexican-American soldiers as well, hoping to gain control of the West's gold and silver mines. But a Union victory gained by a troop of Colorado miners at Glorieta Pass near Sante Fe, New Mexico ended that Confederate dream.

While both Union and Confederate armies recruited Indian regiments, African Americans were barred from enlisting as soldiers on either side. However, a series of Union military defeats helped transform the attitudes of northern whites. In the spring of 1862, Confederate general Stonewall Jackson won a series of stunning victories against three Union armies in Virginia's Shenandoah Valley. That June and July, General Robert E. Lee fought Union forces under General George B. McClellan to a standstill in the Seven Days Battle near Richmond. Then in August, Lee, Jackson, and General James Longstreet joined together to defeat Union troops at the Second Battle of Bull Run (Map 13.1).

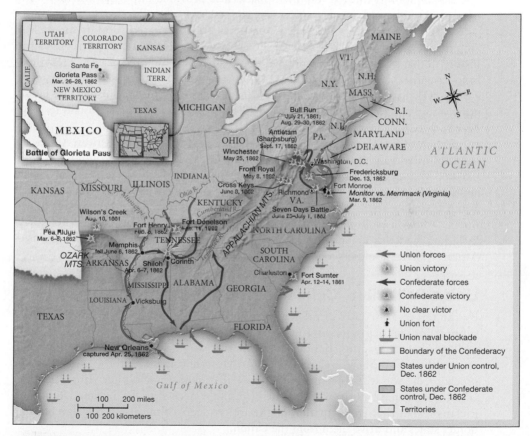

MAP 13.1

Early Civil War Battles, 1861–1862   In 1861 and 1862, the Confederate army stunned Union forces with a series of dramatic victories in Virginia and Missouri. However, the Union army won a crucial victory at Antietam (Sharpsburg); gained control of Confederate territory in Tennessee, Arkansas, and Mississippi; fended off Confederate efforts to gain New Mexico Territory; and established a successful naval blockade of Confederate ports.

As the war turned against the North, the North turned against slavery. In April 1862 Congress had approved a measure to abolish slavery in the District of Columbia, symbolizing a significant shift in Union sentiment. During that bloody summer, Congress passed a second confiscation act, declaring that the slaves of anyone who supported the Confederacy should be "forever free of their servitude, and not again held as slaves." In July Congress also approved a militia act that allowed African Americans to serve in "any military or naval service for which they may be found competent."

Support for the 1862 militia act built on Union victories as well as defeats. In April 1862 a Union blockade led to the capture of New Orleans, while the **Battle of Shiloh** in Tennessee provided the army entrée to the Mississippi valley. There Union troops came face-to-face with slavery. Few of these soldiers were abolitionists, but many were shocked by what they saw, including instruments used to torture slaves. One Union soldier reported he had seen "enough of the horror of slavery to make one an Abolitionist forever." Southern blacks also provided important intelligence to northern officers, making clear their value to the Union war effort.

Whether in victory or defeat, rising death tolls increased support for African American enlistment. The Battle of Shiloh was the bloodiest battle in American history to that point. Earlier battles had resulted in a few hundred or even a few thousand casualties, but with more than 23,000 casualties, Shiloh raised the carnage to a new level. As the war continued, such brutal battles became routine. The Union army would need every available man—white, black, and Indian—to sustain its effort against the Confederates.

Indian regiments had already proven themselves in battle, and African Americans soon followed suit. In October 1862 a group of black soldiers in the First Kansas Colored Volunteers repulsed Confederates at a battle in Missouri. In the South, white abolitionists serving as Union officers organized former slaves into units like the First South Carolina Volunteers in January 1863. A few months later, another black regiment—the Massachusetts Fifty-fourth—attracted recruits from across the North, including Frederick Douglass's three sons. For the next two years, tens of thousands of African American soldiers fought valiantly in dozens of battles.

Union Politicians Consider Emancipation

By the fall of 1862, African Americans and abolitionists had gained widespread support for emancipation as a necessary goal of the war. Lincoln and his cabinet realized that embracing abolition as a war aim would likely prevent international recognition of southern independence. As Massachusetts senator Charles Sumner proclaimed, "You will observe that I propose no crusade for abolition. [Emancipation] is to be presented strictly as a measure of military necessity." Still, some Union politicians feared that emancipation might arouse deep animosity in the slaveholding border states and drive them from the Union.

From the Confederate perspective, international recognition was critical. Support from European nations might persuade the North to accept southern independence. More immediately, recognition would ensure markets for southern agriculture and access to manufactured goods and war materiel. Confederate officials were especially focused on Britain, the leading market for cotton and a leading producer of industrial products. President Davis considered sending Rose Greenhow to England to promote the Confederate cause.

Fearing that the British might capitulate to Confederate pressure, abolitionist lecturers toured Britain, reminding residents of their early leadership in the antislavery cause. The Union's formal commitment to emancipation would certainly increase British support for its position and prevent diplomatic recognition of the Confederacy. By the summer of 1862, Lincoln was convinced, but he wanted to wait for a military victory before making a formal announcement regarding emancipation.

Instead, the Union suffered a series of defeats that summer, and Lee marched his army into Union territory in Maryland. On September 17, Longstreet joined Lee in a fierce battle along Antietam Creek as Union troops brought the Confederate advance to a standstill near the town of Sharpsburg. Union forces suffered more than 12,000 casualties and the Confederates more than 10,000, the bloodiest single day of battle in U.S. history. Yet because Lee and his army were forced to retreat, Lincoln claimed the **Battle of Antietam** as a great victory. Five days later, the president announced his preliminary **Emancipation Proclamation** to the assembled cabinet, promising to free slaves in all seceding states.

On January 1, 1863, Lincoln signed the final edict, proclaiming that slaves in areas still in rebellion were "forever free" and inviting them to enlist in the Union army. Over the next two years, tens of thousands of enslaved men fled southern plantations and fought in the Union Army alongside equal numbers of free blacks who volunteered to ensure the Confederacy's defeat. Still, the proclamation was a moderate document in many ways. Its provisions exempted from emancipation the 450,000 slaves in the loyal border states, as well as more than 300,000 slaves in Union-occupied areas of Tennessee, Louisiana, and Virginia. The proclamation also justified the abolition of southern slavery on military, not moral, grounds. Despite its limits, the Emancipation Proclamation inspired joyous celebrations among free blacks and white abolitionists, who viewed it as the first step toward slavery's final eradication.

REVIEW & RELATE	• How and why did the Union and the Confederacy treat American Indian and African American participation in the war differently? • What events occurred to make the Civil War become a war to end slavery?

War Transforms the North and the South

For soldiers and civilians seeking to survive the upheaval of war, political pronouncements rarely alleviated the dangers they faced. The war's extraordinary death tolls shocked Americans on both sides. On the home front, the prolonged conflict created labor shortages and severe inflation in both North and South. The war initially disrupted industrial and agricultural production as men were called to service, but the North recovered quickly by building on its prewar industrial base and technological know-how. In the South, manufacturing increased, with enslaved laborers pressed into service as industrial workers, but this created shortages on plantations. The changed circumstances of the war required women to take on new responsibilities as well. Yet these dramatic transformations also inspired dissent and protest as rising death tolls and rising prices made the costs of war ever clearer.

Life and Death on the Battlefield

Few soldiers entered the conflict knowing what to expect. A young private wrote that his idea of combat had been that the soldiers "would all be in line, all standing in a nice level field fighting, a number of ladies taking care of the wounded, etc., etc., but it isn't so." Improved weaponry turned battles into scenes of bloody carnage. The shift from smoothbore muskets to rifles, which had grooves that spun the bullet, made weapons far more effective at longer distances. The use of minié balls—small bullets with a deep cavity that expanded upon firing—increased fatalities as well. By 1863 Union army sharpshooters acquired new repeating rifles with metal cartridges. With more accurate rifles and deadlier bullets, the rival armies increasingly relied on heavy fortifications, elaborate trenches, and distant mortar and artillery fire when they could. Still, casualties continued to rise, especially since the trenches served as breeding grounds for disease.

The hardships and discomforts of war extended beyond combat itself. As General Lee complained before Antietam, many soldiers fought in ragged uniforms and without shoes. Rations, too, ran short. Food was dispensed sporadically and was often spoiled. Many Union troops survived primarily on an unleavened biscuit called hardtack as well as small amounts of meat and beans and enormous quantities of coffee. Their diet improved over the course of the war, however, as the Union supply system grew more efficient while Confederate troops subsisted increasingly on cornmeal and fatty meat. As early as 1862, Confederate soldiers began gathering food from the haversacks of Union dead.

For every soldier who died as a result of combat, three died of disease. Measles, dysentery, typhoid, and malaria killed thousands who drank contaminated water, ate tainted food, and were exposed to the elements. And infected soldiers on both sides carried yellow fever and malaria into towns where they built fortifications. Prisoner-of-war camps were especially deadly locales. Debilitating fevers in a camp near Danville, Virginia spread to the town, killing civilians as well as soldiers.

The sufferings of African American troops were particularly severe. The death rate from disease for black Union soldiers was nearly three times greater than that for white Union soldiers, reflecting their poorer health upon enlistment, the hard labor they performed, and the minimal medical care they received in the field. Southern blacks who began their army careers in contraband camps fared even worse, with a camp near Nashville losing a quarter of its residents to death in just three months in 1864.

For all soldiers, medical assistance was primitive. Antibiotics did not exist, antiseptics were still unknown, and anesthetics were scarce. Union medical care improved with the **U.S. Sanitary Commission**, which was established by the federal government in June 1861 to promote and coordinate better medical treatment for soldiers. Nonetheless, a commentator accurately described most field hospitals as "dirty dens of butchery and horror," where amputations often occurred with whiskey as the only anesthetic.

As the horrors of war sank in, large numbers of soldiers deserted or refused to reenlist. As volunteers declined and deserters increased, both the Confederate and the Union governments were forced to institute conscription laws to draft men into service.

The Northern Economy Expands

As the war dragged on, the North's economic advantages became more apparent. Initially, the effects of the war on northern industry had been little short of disastrous. Raw cotton for textiles disappeared, southern planters stopped ordering shoes, and trade fell off precipitously. By 1863, however, the northern economy was in high gear and could provide more arms, food, shoes, and clothing to its troops as well as for those back home. As cotton production declined, woolen manufacturing doubled; and northern iron and coal production increased 25 to 30 percent during the war. Northern factories turned out weapons and ammunition while shipyards built the fleets that blockaded southern ports.

These economic improvements were linked to a vast expansion in the federal government's activities. War Department orders fueled the industrial surge. It also created the U.S. Military Railroads unit to construct tracks in newly occupied southern territories and granted large contracts to northern railroads to carry troops and supplies. With southern Democrats out of federal office, Congress also raised tariffs on imported goods to protect northern industries. In addition, the government hired thousands of "sewing women," who were contracted to make uniforms for Union soldiers. Other women joined the federal labor force as clerical workers to sustain the expanding bureaucracy and the voluminous amounts of government-generated paperwork.

That paperwork multiplied exponentially when the federal government created a national currency and a national banking system. Before the Civil War, private banks (chartered by the states) issued their own banknotes, which were used in most economic transactions. During the war, Congress revolutionized this system, giving the federal government the power to create currency, issue federal charters to banks, and take on national debt. The government then flooded the nation with treasury bills, commonly called greenbacks. The federal budget mushroomed as well—from $63 million in 1860 to nearly $1.3 billion in 1865. By the end of the war, the federal bureaucracy had become the nation's largest single employer.

Northern manufacturers faced one daunting problem: a shortage of labor. Over half a million workers left their jobs to serve in the Union army, and others were hired by the expanding federal bureaucracy. Manufacturers dealt with the problem primarily by mechanizing more tasks and by hiring more women and children, native-born and immigrant. Combining the lower wages paid to these workers with production speedups, manufacturers improved their profits while advancing the Union cause.

Urbanization and Industrialization in the South

Although Southerners had gone to war to protect an essentially rural lifestyle, the war encouraged the growth of cities and industry. The creation of a large governmental and military bureaucracy brought thousands of Southerners to the Confederate capital of Richmond. As the war expanded, refugees also flooded into Atlanta, Savannah, Columbia, and Mobile.

Industrialization contributed to urban growth as well. With the South unable to buy industrial goods from the North and limited in its trade with Europe, military necessity spurred southern industry. Clothing and shoe factories had "sprung up almost like magic" in Natchez and Jackson, Mississippi. The Tredegar Iron Works in Richmond expanded significantly as well, employing more than 2,500 men, black and white. More than 10,000 people labored in war industries in Selma, Alabama, where one factory produced cannons. With labor in short supply, widows and orphans, enslaved blacks, and white men too old or injured to fight were recruited for industrial work in many cities.

Women Aid the War Effort

Women of all classes contributed to the war effort, North and South. Thousands filled jobs in agriculture, industry, and the government that were traditionally held by men while others assisted the military effort more directly. Most Union and Confederate officials initially opposed women's direct engagement in the war. Yet it was women's voluntary organization of relief efforts that inspired the federal government to establish the U.S. Sanitary Commission. By 1862 tens of thousands of women volunteered funds and assistance through hundreds of local chapters across the North. They hosted fund-raising fairs, coordinated sewing and knitting circles, rolled bandages, and sent supplies to the front lines. With critical shortages of medical staff, some female nurses and doctors eventually gained acceptance in northern hospitals and field camps. Led by such memorable figures as Clara Barton, Mary Ann "Mother" Bickerdyke, and Dr. Mary Walker, northern women almost entirely replaced men as military nurses by the end of the war.

In the South, too, much of the medical care was performed by women. But without government support, nursing was never recognized as a legitimate profession for women, and most nurses worked out of their own homes. As a result, a Confederate soldier's chances of dying from wounds or disease were greater than those of his Union counterpart. Southern women also worked tirelessly to supply soldiers with clothes, blankets, munitions, and food. But this work, too, was often performed locally and by individuals rather than as part of a coordinated Confederate effort.

Some Union and Confederate women played more unusual roles in the war. A few dozen women joined Rose Greenhow in gathering information for military and political leaders. One of the most effective spies on the Union side was the former fugitive Harriet Tubman, who gathered intelligence in South Carolina, including from many slaves, between 1862 and 1864. Even more women served as couriers, carrying messages across battle lines to alert officers of critical changes in military orders or in the opponent's position. In addition, at least four hundred women disguised themselves as men and fought as soldiers.

Union women also sought to influence wartime policies. Following the Emancipation Proclamation, Elizabeth Cady Stanton, Susan B. Anthony, and Lucy Stone founded the **Women's National Loyal League** and launched a massive petition drive to broaden Lincoln's policy. Collecting 260,000 signatures, two-thirds of them from women, the League demanded a congressional act "emancipating all persons of African descent" everywhere in the nation.

Dr. Mary E. Walker
Dr. Mary E. Walker received her medical degree from Syracuse Medical College and became the first female army surgeon. Wearing bloomers (pants under a skirt), she assisted soldiers and civilians in numerous battlefield areas. Captured by Confederate troops in 1864, Walker soon returned to Union ranks. She was the first woman awarded the Medal of Honor for military service. Library of Congress, LC-DIG-ppmsca-19911

Dissent and Protest in the Midst of War

Dissent roiled some border states from the start of the war. In 1863 and 1864, frustration spread across the North and the South generally with increasing casualties, declining numbers of volunteers, and rising inflation. As the war dragged on, many white Northerners began to wonder whether defeating the Confederacy was worth the cost, and many white Southerners whether saving it was.

From 1861 on, battles raged among residents in the border state of Missouri, with Confederate sympathizers refusing to accept living in a Union state. Pro-southern residents formed militias and staged guerrilla attacks on Union supporters. The militias, with the tacit support of Confederate officials, claimed thousands of lives during the war and forced the Union army to station troops in the area.

By 1863, dissent broadened to include Northerners who earlier embraced the Union cause. Some white Northerners had always opposed emancipation, based on racial prejudice or fear that a flood of black migrants would increase competition for jobs. Then, just two months after the Emancipation Proclamation went into effect, a new law deepened concerns among many working-class Northerners. The **Enrollment Act**, passed by Congress in March 1863, established a draft system to ensure sufficient soldiers for the Union army. While draftees were to be selected by an impartial lottery, the law allowed a person with $300 to pay the government in place of serving or to hire another man as a substitute. Many workers deeply resented the draft's profound inequality.

Dissent turned to violence in July 1863 when the new law went into effect. Riots broke out in cities across the North. In New York City, where inflation caused tremendous suffering and a large immigrant population solidly supported the Democratic Party, implementation of the draft triggered four days of the worst rioting Americans had ever seen. Women and men—including many Irish and German immigrants—attacked Republican draft officials, wealthy businessmen, and the free black community. Between July 13 and 16, rioters lynched at least a dozen African Americans and looted and burned the city's Colored Orphan Asylum. The violence ended only when Union troops put down the riots by force. By then, more than one hundred New Yorkers, most of them black, lay dead.

By 1864 inflation also fueled protests in the North as it eroded the earnings of rural and urban residents. Women, children, and old men took over much of the field labor in the Midwest, trying to feed their families and the army while struggling to pay their bills. Factory workers, servants, and day laborers felt the pinch as well. With federal greenbacks flooding the market and military production a priority, the price of consumer goods climbed about 20 percent faster than wages. Although industrialists garnered huge profits, workers suffered. A group of Cincinnati seamstresses complained to President Lincoln in 1864 about employers "who fatten on their contracts by grinding immense profits out of the labor of their operatives." At the same time, employers persuaded some state legislatures to prohibit strikes in wartime. The federal government, too, supported business over labor. When workers at the Parrott arms factory in Cold Spring, New York struck for higher wages in 1864, the government declared martial law and arrested the strike leaders.

Northern Democrats saw the widening unrest as a political opportunity. Although some Democratic leaders supported the war effort, many others—whom opponents called **Copperheads**, after the poisonous snake—rallied behind Ohio politician Clement L. Vallandigham in opposing the war. Presenting themselves as the "peace party," these Democrats enjoyed considerable success in eastern cities where inflation was rampant and immigrant workers were caught between low wages and military service. The party was also strong in parts of the Midwest, like Missouri, where sympathy for the southern cause and antipathy to African Americans ran deep.

In the South, too, some whites expressed growing dissatisfaction with the war. Jefferson Davis signed a conscription act in April 1862, a year before Lincoln did so, inciting widespread opposition. Here, too, men could hire a substitute if they had enough money, and an October 1862 law exempted men owning twenty or more slaves from military service. Thus, large planters, many of whom served in the Confederate legislature, had effectively exempted themselves from fighting. As one Alabama farmer fumed, "All they want is to get you pumpt up and go to fight for their infernal negroes, and after you do their fighting you may kiss their hine parts for all they care."

Small farmers were also hard hit by policies that allowed the Confederate army to take whatever supplies it needed. The army's forced acquisition of farm produce intensified food shortages that had been building since early in the war. Moreover, the lack of an extensive railroad or canal system in the South limited the distribution of what food was available.

Food shortages drove up prices on basic items like bread and corn, while the Union blockade and the focus on military needs dramatically increased prices on other consumer goods. As the Confederate government issued ever more treasury notes to finance the war, inflation soared 2,600 percent in less than three years. In spring 1863 food riots led by working-class women erupted in cities across the South, including the Confederate capital of Richmond.

Some state legislatures then tried to control food prices, but Richmond workers continued to voice their resentment. In fall 1863 a group proclaimed, "From the fact that he consumes all and produces nothing, we know that without [our] labor and production the man with money could not exist."

The devastation of the war added to all these grievances. Since most battles were fought in the Upper South or along the Confederacy's western frontier, small farmers in these regions saw their crops, animals, and fields devastated. A phrase that had seemed cynical in 1862—"A rich man's war and a poor man's fight"—became the rallying cry of the southern peace movement in 1864. Secret peace societies flourished mainly among small farmers and in regions, like the western mountains, where plantation slavery did not develop. A secret organization centered in North Carolina provided Union forces with information on southern troop movements and encouraged desertion by Confederates. In mountainous areas, draft evaders and deserters formed guerrilla groups that attacked draft officials and actively impeded the war effort. Women joined these efforts, hiding deserters, raiding grain depots, and burning the property of Confederate officials.

When slaveholders led the South out of the Union in 1861, they had assumed the loyalty of yeomen farmers, the deference of southern ladies, and the privileges of the southern way of life. Far from preserving social harmony and social order, however, the war undermined ties between elite and poor Southerners, between planters and small farmers, and between women and men. Although most white Southerners still supported the Confederacy in 1864 and internal dissent alone did not lead to defeat, it did weaken the ties that bound soldiers to their posts in the final two years of the war.

REVIEW & RELATE	• What were the economic effects of the war on the North and the South? • How did social conflicts created or heightened by the war fuel dissent and protest in the North and the South?

The Tide of War Turns, 1863–1865

In spring 1863, amid turmoil on the home front, General Robert E. Lee's army defeated a Union force twice its size at Chancellorsville, Virginia. The victory set the stage for a Confederate thrust into Pennsylvania, but Lee's decision to go on the offensive proved the Confederacy's undoing. In July 1863 the Union won two decisive military victories: at Gettysburg, Pennsylvania and Vicksburg, Mississippi. At the same time, the flood of African Americans, including former slaves, into the Union army transformed the very meaning of the war. By 1864, with the momentum favoring the Union, General Ulysses S. Grant implemented policies of hard war that forced the Confederacy to consider surrender.

Key Victories for the Union

In mid-1863 Confederate commanders believed the tide was turning in their favor. Following victories at Fredericksburg and Chancellorsville, General Lee launched an invasion of northern territory. While the Union army maneuvered to protect Washington, D.C., General Joseph Hooker resigned as head of the Union Army of the Potomac. On June 28, Lincoln appointed George A. Meade as the new Union commander, and the general immediately faced a major engagement at the **Battle of Gettysburg** in Pennsylvania. If Confederates won a victory there, European countries might finally recognize the southern nation and force the North to accept peace.

Neither Lee nor Meade set out to launch a battle in this small Pennsylvania town. But Lee was afraid of outrunning his supply lines, and Meade wanted to keep Confederates from gaining control of the roads that crossed at Gettysburg. So between July 1 and July 3, the opposing armies fought a desperate battle with Union troops occupying the high ground and Confederate forces launching deadly assaults from below (Map 13.2). Ultimately, Gettysburg proved a disaster for the South: More than 4,700 Confederates were killed, including a large number of officers; another 18,000 were wounded, captured, or missing. Although the Union suffered similar casualties, it had more men to lose, and it could claim victory.

As Lee retreated to Virginia, the South suffered another devastating defeat. Troops under General Grant had been pounding Vicksburg, Mississippi since May 1863. The **siege of Vicksburg** ended with the surrender of Confederate forces on July 4. This victory was even more important strategically than Gettysburg (Map 13.2). Combined with a victory five days later at Port Hudson, Louisiana, the Union army controlled the entire Mississippi valley, the richest plantation region in the South. This series of victories also effectively cut Louisiana, Arkansas, and Texas off from the rest of the Confederacy, ensuring Union control of the West. In November 1863 Grant's troops achieved another major victory at Chattanooga, opening up much of the South's remaining territory to invasion. Thousands of slaves deserted their plantations, and many joined the Union war effort.

That same month, November 1863, President Lincoln spoke at the official dedication ceremony for the National Cemetery at Gettysburg, Pennsylvania. In his **Gettysburg Address**, Lincoln tied the war against slavery to the fulfillment of the nation's founding ideal "that all men are created equal." He insisted that the United States "shall have a new birth of freedom—and that government of the people, by the people, and for the people, shall not perish from the earth." Only in this way, he declared, could Americans ensure that the "honored dead" had not "died in vain."

As 1864 dawned, the Union had twice as many forces in the field as the Confederacy, whose soldiers were suffering from low morale, high mortality, and

Battle of Gettysburg

PENNSYLVANIA

Gettysburg

SEMINARY RIDGE

Pickett's Charge July 3

CEMETERY RIDGE

Marsh Cr.

Rock Cr.

Union
•••• Position July 1
—— Position July 2
◄– Retreat

Confederate
•••• Position July 1
—— Position July 2
◄— Advance

Vicksburg Campaign

MISSISSIPPI

LA.

Big Black R.

Yazoo R.

Mississippi R.

Grant

Siege of Vicksburg
May 22–July 4

Champion's Hill
May 16

J. E. Johnston

Pemberton

Jackson
May 14

Grant

Grand Gulf

Port Gibson
May 1

Pearl R.

◄— Union advance
◄— Confederate advance
◄•• Confederate retreat
✷ Union victory

MAP 13.2
Battles of Gettysburg and Vicksburg, 1863   The three-day Battle of Gettysburg and the six-week siege of Vicksburg led to critical victories for the Union. Together, these victories forced General Lee's troops back into Confederate territory and gave the Union control of the Mississippi River. Still, the war was far from over. Confederate troops controlled the southern heartland, and Northerners wearied of the ever-increasing casualties.

dwindling supplies. Although some difficult battles lay ahead, the war of attrition (in which the larger, better-supplied Union forces slowly wore down their Confederate opponents) had begun to pay dividends.

The changing Union fortunes increased support for Lincoln and his congressional allies. Union victories and the Emancipation Proclamation also convinced Great Britain not to recognize the Confederacy as an independent nation. And the heroics of African American soldiers, who engaged in direct and often brutal combat against southern troops, expanded support for emancipation. Republicans, who now fully embraced abolition as a war aim, were nearly assured the presidency and a congressional majority in the 1864 elections.

Northern Democrats still campaigned for peace and the readmission of Confederate states with slavery intact. They nominated George B. McClellan, the onetime Union commander, for president. McClellan attracted working-class and immigrant voters who traditionally supported the Democrats and bore the heaviest burdens of the war. But Democratic hopes for victory in November were crushed when Union general William Tecumseh Sherman captured Atlanta, Georgia just two months before the election. Lincoln and the Republicans won easily, giving the party a clear mandate to continue the war to its conclusion.

African Americans Contribute to Victory

Lincoln's election secured the eventual downfall of slavery. Yet the president and Congress did not eradicate human bondage on their own. From the fall of 1862 on, African Americans enlisted in the Union army and helped ensure that nothing short of universal emancipation would be the outcome of the war. As Private Thomas Long, a former slave serving with the First South Carolina Volunteers, explained: "If we hadn't become sojers, all might have gone back as it was before. . . . But now tings can neber go back, because we have showed our energy and our courage and our naturally manhood."

In the border states, which were exempt from the Emancipation Proclamation, enslaved men were adamant about enlisting since those who served in the Union army were granted their freedom. Because of this provision, slaveholders in these states did everything in their power to prevent their slaves from joining the army. Despite these efforts, between 25 and 60 percent of military-age enslaved men in the four border states stole away and joined the Union army. By the end of the war, nearly 200,000 black men had served officially in the army and navy, and some 37,000 blacks had given their lives for the Union.

Yet despite their courage and commitment, black soldiers felt the sting of racism. They were segregated in camps, given the most menial jobs, and often treated as inferiors by white soldiers and officers. Particularly galling was the Union policy of paying black soldiers less than whites. African American soldiers openly protested this discrimination even after a black sergeant who voiced his views was charged with mutiny and executed by firing squad in February 1864. The War Department finally equalized wages four months later.

One primary concern of African American soldiers was to liberate slaves as Union armies moved deeper into the South. At the same time, thousands of southern slaves headed for Union lines. Even those forced to remain on plantations learned when Union troops were nearby and talked openly of emancipation. "Now they gradually threw off the mask," a slave remembered, "and were not afraid to let it be known that the 'freedom' in their songs meant freedom of the body in this world."

The Final Battles of a Hard War

In the spring of 1864, the war in the East entered its final stage. That March, Lincoln placed General Grant in charge of all Union forces. Grant embarked on a strategy of **hard war**, in which soldiers not only attacked military targets but also destroyed civilian crops, livestock, fields, and property to undermine morale and supply chains. Grant was also willing to accept huge casualties to achieve victory. Over the next year, he led his troops overland through western Virginia in an effort to take Richmond. Meanwhile, General Philip Sheridan devastated "The Breadbasket of the Confederacy" in Virginia's Shenandoah Valley, and General Sherman laid waste to the remnants of the plantation system in Georgia and the Carolinas.

Portrait of a Black Union Soldier and Family, c. 1863–1865 Taken after African Americans were allowed to join the Union Army, this daguerreotype captures a Union soldier with his wife and two daughters. He was likely a member of one of the seven Union regiments raised in Maryland, where the picture was discovered. The dresses and hats worn by the wife and daughters suggest the family was free. Library of Congress LC-DIG-ppmsca-36454

Grant's troops headed toward Richmond, where Lee's army controlled strong defensive positions. The Confederates won a series of narrow, bloody victories, but Grant continued to push forward. Although Lee lost fewer men, they were losses he could not afford given the Confederacy's much smaller population. Combining high casualties with deserters, Lee's army was melting away with each engagement. Although soldiers and civilians—North and South—called Grant "the butcher" for his seeming lack of regard for human life, the Union general was not deterred.

In the fall of 1864, implementing hard war tactics, Sheridan rendered the Shenandoah Valley a "barren waste." Called "the burning" by local residents, Sheridan's soldiers torched fields, barns, and homes and destroyed thousands of bushels of grain along with livestock, shops, and mills. His campaign demoralized civilians in the region and denied Confederate troops crucial supplies.

In the preceding months, Sherman had laid siege to Atlanta, but on September 2 his forces swept around the city and destroyed the roads and rails that connected it to the rest of the Confederacy. When General John B. Hood and his Confederate troops abandoned their posts, Sherman telegraphed Lincoln: "Atlanta is ours, and fairly won."

That victory cut the South in two, but Sherman continued on. **Sherman's March to the Sea** introduced hard war tactics to Southerners along the three-hundred-mile route from the Atlantic coast north through the Carolinas. His troops cut a path of destruction fifty to sixty miles wide. They confiscated or destroyed millions of pounds of cotton, corn, wheat, and other agricultural items; tore up thousands of miles of railroad tracks; and burned Columbia, the South Carolina capital. As Eleanor Cohen Seixas, whose family had earlier fled to Columbia for safety, recorded in her journal, "The fires raged fearfully all night" and the "vile Yankees took from us clothing, food, jewels, all our cows, horses, carriages, etc." Despite later claims that Sherman's men ravaged white women, instances of such behavior were rare, although Union soldiers did ransack homes and confiscate food and clothing.

Enslaved blacks hoped that Sherman's arrival marked their emancipation. During his victorious march, nearly 18,000 enslaved men, women, and children fled ruined plantations and sought to join the victorious troops. To their dismay, soldiers refused to take them along. Union soldiers realized that they could not care for this vast number of people and carry out their military operations. Some Union soldiers went further, abusing African American men, raping black women, or stealing their few possessions. Angry Confederates captured many blacks who were turned away, killing some and reenslaving others.

These actions caused a scandal in Washington. In January 1865, Lincoln dispatched Secretary of War Edwin Stanton to Georgia to investigate the charges. At an extraordinary meeting in Savannah, Stanton and Sherman met with black ministers to hear their complaints and hopes. The ministers spoke movingly of the war lifting "the yoke of bondage." Freed blacks, they argued, "could reap the fruit of their own labor" and, if given land, "take care of ourselves, and assist the Government in maintaining our freedom." In response, Sherman issued **Field Order Number 15**, setting aside more than 400,000 acres of captured Confederate land to be divided into small plots for former slaves. The order proved highly controversial, but it offered blacks some hope of significant change.

If many African Americans were disappointed by the actions of Union soldiers in the East, American Indians were even more devastated by developments in the West. Despite Indian nations' substantial aid to Union armies, any hope of being rewarded for their efforts vanished by 1864. Tens of thousands of whites migrated west of the Mississippi during the Civil War, and congressional passage of the Homestead Act in 1864 increased the numbers. At the same time, the U.S. army grew exponentially during the war, using its increased power to assault western Indian nations.

Attacks on Indians were not an extension of hard war policies, but rather a government-sanctioned effort to terrorize native communities. Beginning in 1862, Dakota Sioux went to war with the United States over broken treaties. After being defeated, four hundred warriors were arrested by military officials and thirty-eight executed. In 1863 California Volunteers slaughtered more than two hundred men, women, and children in a Shoshone-Bannock village in Idaho. Meanwhile thousands of white settlers had been flooding into Colorado after gold was discovered in 1858, forcing Cheyenne and Arapaho Indians off their land. In 1864 these Indians were promised refuge at Sand Creek by officers at nearby Fort Lyon. Instead, Colonel John M. Chivington led his Third Colorado Calvary in a rampage that left 125 to 160

Indian men, women, and children dead. The Sand Creek Massacre ensured that white migrants traveling in the region would be subject to Indian attacks for years to come. At the same time, in the Southwest, the Navajo were defeated by U.S. troops and their Ute allies and forced into a four-hundred-mile trek to a reservation in New Mexico.

U.S. army officers considered "winning the West" one way to restore national unity once the Civil War ended. For Indian nations, the increased migration, expanded military presence, and sheer brutality they experienced in 1863 and 1864 boded ill for their future, whichever side won the Civil War.

The War Comes to an End

As the defeat of the Confederacy loomed, the U.S. Congress finally considered abolishing slavery throughout the nation. With intense lobbying by abolitionists, petitioning by the Women's National Loyal League, the valiant efforts of Ohio Congressman James Ashley, and President Lincoln's lobbying of wavering senators, Congress passed the **Thirteenth Amendment** to the U.S. Constitution on January 31, 1865. It prohibited slavery and involuntary servitude anywhere in the United States. Some northern and western states had already enacted laws to ease racial inequities. Ohio, California, and Illinois repealed statutes barring blacks from testifying in court and serving on juries. Then, in May 1865, Massachusetts passed the first comprehensive public-accommodations law in U.S. history, ensuring equal treatment in stores, schools, theaters, and other social spaces. Cities from San Francisco to Cincinnati and New York also desegregated their streetcars.

Still hoping to stave off defeat, southern leaders also began rethinking their racial policies. The Confederate House passed a law to recruit slaves into the army in February 1865, but the Senate defeated the measure. It was too late to make a difference anyway.

In early April 1865, with Sherman heading toward Raleigh, North Carolina, Grant captured Petersburg, Virginia and then drove Lee and his forces out of Richmond. Seasoned African American troops led the final assault on the city and were among the first Union soldiers to enter the Confederate capital. On April 9, after a brief engagement at Appomattox Court House, Virginia, Lee surrendered to Grant. Within hours, Lee's troops began heading home. While sporadic fighting continued— Cherokee Stand Watie was the last Confederate general to surrender in June 1865—the back of the Confederate army had been broken.

With Lee's surrender, many Northerners hoped that the reunited nation would be stronger and more just. Jubilation in the North was short-lived, however. On April 14, Abraham Lincoln was shot at Ford's Theatre by a Confederate fanatic named John Wilkes Booth. The president died the next day, leading to great uncertainty about how peace and national unity would be achieved.

REVIEW & RELATE	• What role did African Americans play in the defeat of the South? How did attitudes toward African Americans change in the final year of the war? • How did the Union win the war against the Confederacy while defeating Indians in the West?

Conclusion: An Uncertain Future

The Civil War devastated and transformed the nation. The deadliest conflict in American history—some 600,000 to 750,000 Americans died in the war—the Civil War freed nearly 4 million Americans who had been enslaved. Soldiers who survived brought new experiences and knowledge back to their families and communities, but many were also marked—like former slaves—by deep physical and emotional wounds. The war transformed the home front as well. Northern and southern women entered the labor force and the public arena in numbers never before imagined. The northern economy flourished and the South became more urbanized, but the Confederacy was left economically ruined. Meanwhile the federal government significantly expanded during the war. It also initiated programs, like the Homestead Act, that fueled migration, intensifying conflicts in the West and devastating numerous Indian nations. Altogether, the Civil War dramatically accelerated the pace of economic, political, and social change, transforming American society both during the war and for decades afterward.

Still, the legacies of the war were far from certain in 1865. Protests during the war reflected a growing sense of class inequalities while the abolition of slavery highlighted ongoing racial disparities. Moreover, even in defeat, white Southerners honored Lee and other "heroes" of the "Lost Cause" with portraits, parades, and statues. Confederate women also worked tirelessly to preserve the memory of ordinary Confederate soldiers and of heroines like Rose O'Neal Greenhow, who had drowned in 1864 while returning from a mission to gain support in Europe.

Victorious Northerners celebrated wartime heroes as well but recognized that much still needed to be done. Frederick Douglass joined other former abolitionists in seeking to enfranchise African American men to secure their rights as freedpeople. He and his colleagues had no illusions about the lengths to which many whites would go to protect their traditional privileges. Yet many northern whites, exhausted by four years of war, hoped to leave the problems of slavery and secession behind. Others sought to rebuild the South quickly to ensure the nation's economic stability. These competing visions—between Northerners and Southerners and within each group—would shape the uncertainties of peace in ways few could imagine at the end of the war.

Chapter 13 Review

KEY TERMS

Fort Sumter (p. 310)
Battle of Bull Run (Manassas) (p. 313)
contraband (p. 314)
Battle of Shiloh (p. 316)
Battle of Antietam (p. 317)
Emancipation Proclamation (p. 317)
U.S. Sanitary Commission (p. 318)
Women's National Loyal League
   (p. 320)

Enrollment Act (p. 322)
Copperheads (p. 322)
Battle of Gettysburg (p. 324)
siege of Vicksburg (p. 324)
Gettysburg Address (p. 324)
hard war (p. 326)
Sherman's March to the Sea (p. 328)
Field Order Number 15 (p. 328)
Thirteenth Amendment (p. 329)

REVIEW & RELATE

1. What led four more states to join the Confederacy in 1861 and four other slave states to remain in the Union?
2. What advantages and disadvantages did each side have at the onset of the war?
3. How and why did the Union and the Confederacy treat American Indian and African American participation in the war differently?
4. What events occurred to make the Civil War become a war to end slavery?
5. What were the economic effects of the war on the North and the South?
6. How did social conflicts created or heightened by the war fuel dissent and protest in the North and the South?
7. What role did African Americans play in the defeat of the South? How did attitudes toward African Americans change in the final year of the war?
8. How did the Union win the war against the Confederacy while defeating Indians in the West?

TIMELINE OF EVENTS

1861
- Fort Sumter attacked
- Slaves declared "contraband"
- U.S. Sanitary Commission established
- Battle of Bull Run (Manassas)
- Confiscation Act passed

1862
- Battle of Shiloh
- Conscription act signed in South
- Battle of Antietam

1863
- Emancipation Proclamation signed
- Enrollment Act passed in North
- New York City draft riots

- Battle of Gettysburg
- Siege of Vicksburg
- Gettysburg Address

1864
- Atlanta falls
- Sand Creek Massacre
- Sherman's "March to the Sea"

1865
- More than 200,000 African Americans serve in the Union army and navy
- Field Order Number 15
- Thirteenth Amendment passed
- Lee surrenders to Grant
- Lincoln assassinated

14

Emancipation and Reconstruction

1863–1877

LEARNING OBJECTIVES

After reading this chapter you should be able to:

- Describe the challenges newly freed African Americans faced and how they responded to them.
- Analyze the influence of the president and Congress on Reconstruction policy and evaluate the successes and shortcomings of the policies they enacted.
- Evaluate the changes that took place in the society and economy of the South during Reconstruction.
- Explain how and why Reconstruction came to an end by the mid-1870s.

COMPARING AMERICAN HISTORIES

Jefferson Franklin Long spent his life improving himself and the lives of others of his race. Born a slave in Alabama in 1836, Long showed great resourcefulness in profiting from the limited opportunities available to him under slavery. His master, a tailor who moved his family to Georgia, taught him the trade, but Long taught himself to read and write. When the Civil War ended, he opened a tailor shop in Macon, Georgia. His business success allowed him to venture into Republican Party politics. Elected as Georgia's first black congressman in 1870, Long fought for the political rights of freed slaves. In his first appearance on the House floor, he opposed a bill that would allow former Confederate officials to return to Congress, noting that many belonged to secret societies, such as the Ku Klux Klan, that intimidated black citizens. Despite his pleas, the measure passed, and Long decided not to run for reelection.

333

By the mid-1880s, Long had become disillusioned with the ability of black Georgians to achieve their objectives via electoral politics. Instead, he counseled African Americans to turn to institution building as the best hope for social and economic advancement. Long helped found the Union Brotherhood Lodge, a black mutual aid society with branches throughout central Georgia, which provided social and economic services for its members. He died in 1901, as political disfranchisement and racial segregation swept through Georgia and the rest of the South.

Jefferson Long and Andrew Johnson shared many characteristics, but their views on race could not have been more different. Whereas Long fought for the right of self-determination for African Americans, Johnson believed that whites alone should govern. Born in 1808 in Raleigh, North Carolina, Johnson grew up in poverty. At the age of thirteen or fourteen, he became a tailor's apprentice and, after moving to Tennessee in 1826, like Long, opened a tailor shop. The following year, Johnson married and began to prosper, purchasing a farm and a small number of slaves.

As he made his mark in Greenville, Tennessee, Johnson became active in Democratic Party politics. A social and political outsider, Johnson gained support by championing the rights of workers and small farmers against the power of the southern aristocracy. Political success followed, and by the time the Civil War broke out, he was a U.S. senator.

When the Civil War erupted, Johnson remained loyal to the Union even after Tennessee seceded in 1861. President Abraham Lincoln rewarded Johnson by appointing him as military governor of Tennessee. In 1864 the Republican Lincoln chose the Democrat Johnson to run with him as vice president. Less than six weeks after their inauguration in March 1865, Johnson became president upon Lincoln's assassination.

Fate placed Reconstruction in the hands of Andrew Johnson. After four years, the brutal Civil War had come to a close. Yet the hard work of reunion remained. Toward this end, President Johnson oversaw the reestablishment of state governments in the former Confederate states. He considered the southern states as having fulfilled their obligations for rejoining the Union, even as they passed measures that restricted black civil and political rights. Most Northerners reached a different conclusion. Having won the bloody war, they feared losing the peace to Johnson and the defeated South.

COMPARING THE AMERICAN HISTORIES of Andrew Johnson and Jefferson Long highlights hard-fought battles to determine the fate of the postwar South and the meaning of freedom for newly emancipated African Americans. Former slaves sought to reunite their families, obtain land, and seek an education.

President Johnson rejected their pleas for assistance to fulfill these aims. However, Congress passed laws to ensure civil rights and extend the vote to African American men, although African American women, like white women, remained disfranchised. In the South, whites attempted to restore their economic and political power over African Americans by resorting to intimidation and violence. By 1877, they succeeded in bringing Reconstruction to an end with the consent of the federal government.

Emancipation

Even before the war came to a close, Reconstruction had begun on a small scale. During the Civil War, blacks remaining in Union-occupied areas, such as the South Carolina Sea Islands, gained some experience with freedom. When Union troops arrived, most southern whites fled, but enslaved workers chose to stay on the land. Some farmed for themselves, but most worked for northern whites who moved south to demonstrate the profitability of free black labor. After the war, however, former plantation owners returned. Rather than work for these whites, freedpeople preferred to establish their own farms. If forced to hire themselves out, they insisted on negotiating the terms of their employment. Wives and mothers often refused to labor for whites at all in favor of caring for their own families. These conflicts reflected the priorities that would shape the actions of freedpeople across the South in the immediate aftermath of the war. For freedom to be meaningful, it had to include economic independence, the power to make family decisions, and the right to control some community decisions.

African Americans Embrace Freedom

When U.S. troops arrived in Richmond, Virginia in April 1865, the city's enslaved population knew that freedom was, finally, theirs. Four days after Union troops arrived, 1,500 African Americans, including a large number of soldiers, packed First African Baptist, the largest of the city's black churches. During the singing of the hymn "Jesus My All to Heaven Is Gone," they raised their voices at the line "This is the way I long have sought." As news of the Confederacy's defeat spread, newly freed African Americans across the South experienced similar emotions. Many years later, Houston H. Holloway, a Georgia slave who had been sold three times before he was twenty years old, recalled the day of emancipation: "I felt like a bird out a cage. Amen. Amen, Amen. I could hardly ask to feel any better than I did that day."

For southern whites, however, the end of the war brought fear, humiliation, and uncertainty. From their perspective, the jubilation of former slaves poured salt in their wounds. In many areas, blacks celebrated their freedom under the protection of Union soldiers. When the army moved out, freedpeople suffered deeply for their enthusiasm. Whites beat, whipped, raped, and shot blacks who they felt had been too joyous in their celebration or too helpful to the Yankee invaders. As one North Carolina freedman testified, the Yankees "tol' us we were free," but once the army left, the planters "would get cruel to the slaves if they acted like they were free."

Newly freed blacks also faced less visible dangers. During the 1860s, disease swept through the South and through the contraband camps that housed many former slaves; widespread malnutrition and poor housing heightened the problem. A smallpox epidemic that spread south from Washington, D.C. killed more than sixty thousand freedpeople.

Despite the dangers, southern blacks eagerly pursued emancipation. They moved; they married; they attended school; they demanded wages; they refused to work for whites; they gathered together their families; they created black churches and civic associations; they held political meetings. Sometimes, black women and men acted on their own, pooling their resources to advance their freedom. At other times, they received help from private organizations—particularly northern missionary and educational associations—staffed mostly by former abolitionists, free blacks, and evangelical Christians.

Emancipated slaves also called on federal agencies for assistance and support. The most important of these agencies was the newly formed Bureau of Refugees, Freedmen, and Abandoned Lands, popularly known as the **Freedmen's Bureau**. Created by Congress in 1865 and signed into law by President Lincoln, the bureau provided ex-slaves with economic and legal resources. The Freedmen's Bureau also aided many former slaves in achieving one of their primary goals: obtaining land. A South Carolina freedman summed up the feeling of the newly emancipated. "Give us our own land and we take care of ourselves," he remarked. "But without land, the old masters can hire or starve us, as they please." During the last years of the war, the federal government had distributed to the freedpeople around 400,000 acres of abandoned land from the South Carolina Sea Islands to Florida. Immediately after hostilities ceased, the Freedmen's Bureau made available hundreds of thousands of additional acres to recently emancipated slaves.

Reuniting Families Torn Apart by Slavery

The first priority for many newly freed blacks was to reunite families torn apart by slavery. Men and women traveled across the South to find family members. Well into the 1870s and 1880s, parents ran advertisements in newly established black newspapers, providing what information they knew about their children's whereabouts and asking for assistance in finding them. Milly Johnson wrote to the Freedmen's Bureau in March 1867, after failing to locate the five children she had lost under slavery. She finally located three of them, but any chance of discovering the whereabouts of the other two disappeared because the records of the slave trader who purchased them burned during the war. Despite such obstacles, thousands of slave children were reunited with their parents in the 1870s.

Husbands and wives, or those who considered themselves as such despite the absence of legal marriage under slavery, also searched for each other. Those who lived on nearby plantations could now live together for the first time. Those whose spouse had been sold to distant plantations had a more difficult time. They wrote (or had letters written on their behalf) to relatives and friends who had been sold with their mate; sought assistance from government officials, churches, and even their former masters; and traveled to areas where they thought their spouse might reside.

These searches were complicated by long years of separation and the lack of any legal standing for slave marriages. In 1866 Philip Grey, a Virginia freedman, located his wife, Willie Ann, and their daughter Maria, who had been sold away to Kentucky years before. Willie Ann was eager to reunite with her husband, but in the years since being sold, she had remarried and borne three children. Her second husband had joined the Union army and was killed in battle. When Willie Ann wrote to Philip in

Winslow Homer, *A Visit from the Old Mistress*, 1876   Civil War correspondent and artist Winslow Homer visited Virginia in the mid-1870s and visually captured the tensions existing between freedpeople and former owners. Here, a former mistress visits the home of three black women. Although the house is humble, one woman refuses to stand for the "old mistress" and the other two, one holding a free-born child, eye her warily.   Smithsonian American Art Museum, Washington, D.C./ Art Resource, NY

April 1866, she explained her new circumstances, concluding: "If you love me you will love my children and you will have to promise me that you will provide for them all as well as if they were your own. . . . I know that I have lived with you and loved you then and love you still."

Most black spouses who found each other sought to legalize their relationship. A superintendent for marriages for the Freedmen's Bureau in northern Virginia reported that he gave out seventy-nine marriage certificates on a single day in May 1866. In another case, four couples went right from the fields to a local schoolhouse, still dressed in their work clothes, where the parson married them.

Of course, some former slaves hoped that freedom would allow them to leave unhappy relationships. Having never been married under the law, couples could simply separate and move on. Complications arose, however, if they had children. In Lake City, Florida in 1866, a Freedmen's Bureau agent asked his superiors for advice on how to deal with Madison Day and Maria Richards. They refused to legalize the relationship forced on them under slavery, but both sought custody of their three children. As with white couples in the mid-nineteenth century, the father was granted custody on the assumption that he had the best chance of providing for the children financially.

Freedom to Learn

Seeking land and reuniting families were only two of the many ways that southern blacks proclaimed their freedom. Learning to read and write was another. The desire to learn was all but universal. Slaves had been forbidden to read and write, and with emancipation they pursued what had been denied them. A newly liberated father in Mississippi proclaimed, "If I nebber does nothing more while I live, I shall give my children a chance to go to school, for I considers education [the] next best ting to liberty."

A variety of organizations opened schools for former slaves during the 1860s and 1870s. By 1870 nearly a quarter million blacks were attending one of the 4,300 schools established by the Freedmen's Bureau. Black and white churches and missionary societies sent hundreds of teachers, black and white, into the South to establish schools in former plantation areas. Their attitudes were often paternalistic and the schools were segregated, but the institutions they founded offered important educational resources for African Americans.

Parents worked hard to keep their children in school during the day. As children gained the rudiments of education, they passed on their knowledge to parents and older siblings whose jobs prevented them from attending school. Still, many adult freedpeople insisted on getting a bit of education for themselves. In New Bern, North Carolina, where many blacks labored until eight o'clock at night, a teacher reported that they then spent at least an hour "in earnest application to study."

Freedmen and freedwomen sought education for a variety of reasons. Some viewed it as a sign of liberation. Others knew that they must be able to read the labor contracts they signed if they were ever to challenge exploitation by whites. Some freedpeople were eager to correspond with relatives, others to read the Bible. Growing numbers hoped to participate in politics, particularly the public meetings organized by blacks in cities across the South. When such gatherings set priorities for the future, the establishment of public schools was high on the list.

Despite the enthusiasm of blacks and the efforts of the federal government and private agencies, schooling remained severely limited throughout the South. A shortage of teachers and of funding kept enrollments low among blacks and whites alike. The isolation of black farm families and the difficulties in eking out a living limited the resources available for education. By 1880, only about a quarter of African Americans were literate.

Freedom to Worship and the Leadership Role of Black Churches

One of the constant concerns freedpeople expressed was the desire to read the Bible and interpret it for themselves. A few black congregations had existed under slavery, but most slaves were forced to listen to white preachers who claimed that God created slavery.

From the moment of emancipation, freedpeople gathered at churches to celebrate community events. Black Methodist and Baptist congregations spread rapidly across the South following the Civil War. In these churches, African Americans were no longer forced to sit in the back benches or punished for moral infractions defined by white masters. Now blacks invested community resources in their own religious institutions where they filled the pews, hired the preachers, and selected boards of deacons and elders. Churches were the largest structures available to freedpeople in many communities and thus were used by a variety of community organizations. They often served as schools and hosted picnics, dances, weddings, funerals, festivals, and other events that brought blacks together. Church leaders also often served as arbiters of community standards of morality.

In the early years of emancipation black churches also served as important sites for political organizing. Some black ministers worried that political concerns would overwhelm spiritual devotions. Others agreed with the Reverend Charles H. Pearce of Florida, who declared, "A man in this State cannot do his whole duty as a minister except he looks out for the political interests of his people." Whatever the views of ministers, black churches were among the few places where African Americans could express their political views free from white interference.

REVIEW & RELATE

• What were freedpeople's highest priorities in the years immediately following the Civil War? Why?

• How did freedpeople define freedom? What steps did they take to make freedom real for themselves and their children?

National Reconstruction

Presidents Abraham Lincoln and Andrew Johnson viewed Reconstruction as a process of national reconciliation. They sketched out terms by which the former Confederate states could reclaim their political representation in the nation without serious penalties. Congressional Republicans, however, had a more thoroughgoing reconstruction in mind. Like many African Americans, Republican congressional leaders expected the South to extend constitutional rights to the freedmen and to provide them with the political and economic resources to sustain their freedom. Over the next decade, these competing visions of Reconstruction played out in a hard-fought and tumultuous battle over the meaning of the South's defeat and the emancipation of blacks.

Abraham Lincoln Plans for Reunification

In December 1863, President Lincoln issued the **Proclamation of Amnesty and Reconstruction**, which asked relatively little of the southern states. Lincoln declared that defeated states would have to accept the abolition of slavery, but then new governments could be formed when 10 percent of those eligible to vote in 1860 (which in practice meant white southern men but not blacks) swore an oath of allegiance to the United States. Lincoln's plan granted amnesty to all but the highest-ranking Confederate officials, and the restored voters in each state would elect members to a constitutional convention and representatives to take their seats in Congress. In the next year and a half, Arkansas, Louisiana, and Tennessee reestablished their governments under Lincoln's "Ten Percent Plan."

Republicans in Congress had other ideas. Radical Republicans argued that the Confederate states should be treated as "conquered provinces" subject to congressional supervision. In 1864 Congress passed the Wade-Davis bill, which established much higher barriers for readmission to the Union than did Lincoln's plan. For instance, the Wade-Davis bill substituted 50 percent of voters for the president's 10 percent requirement. Lincoln put a stop to this harsher proposal by using a pocket veto—refusing to sign it within ten days of Congress's adjournment.

Although Lincoln and congressional Republicans disagreed about many aspects of postwar policy, Lincoln was flexible, and his actions mirrored his desire both to heal the Union and to help southern blacks. For example, the president supported the **Thirteenth Amendment**, abolishing slavery, which passed Congress in January 1865 and was sent to the states for ratification. In March 1865, Lincoln signed the law to create the Freedmen's Bureau. That same month, the president expressed his sincere wish for reconciliation between the North and the South. "With malice toward none, with charity for all," Lincoln declared in his second inaugural address, "let us strive on to finish the work . . . to bind up the nation's wounds." Lincoln would not, however, have the opportunity to implement his balanced approach to Reconstruction. When he was assassinated in April 1865, it fell to Andrew Johnson, a very different sort of politician, to lead the country through the process of reintegration.

Andrew Johnson and Presidential Reconstruction

The nation needed a president who could transmit northern desires to the South with clarity and conviction and ensure that they were carried out. Instead, the nation got a president who substituted his own aims for those of the North, refused to engage in meaningful compromise, and misled the South into believing that he could achieve restoration quickly. In the 1864 election, Lincoln chose Johnson, a southern Democrat, as his running mate in a thinly veiled effort to attract border-state voters. The vice presidency was normally an inconsequential role, so it mattered little to Lincoln that Johnson was out of step with many Republican Party positions.

As president, however, Johnson's views took on profound importance. Born into rural poverty, Johnson had no sympathy for the southern aristocracy. Yet he had been a slave owner, so his political opposition to slavery was not rooted in moral convictions. Instead, it sprang from the belief that slavery gave plantation owners inordinate power and wealth, which came at the expense of the majority of white Southerners, who owned no slaves. Johnson saw emancipation as a means to "break down an odious and dangerous [planter] aristocracy," not to empower blacks. Consequently, he was unconcerned with the fate of African Americans in the postwar South. Six months after taking office, President Johnson rescinded the wartime order to distribute confiscated land to freedpeople in the Sea Islands. He saw no reason to punish the Confederacy's leaders, because he believed that the end of slavery would doom the southern aristocracy. He hoped to bring the South back into the Union as quickly as possible and then let Southerners take care of their own affairs.

Johnson's views, combined with a lack of political savvy and skill, ensured his inability to work constructively with congressional Republicans, even the moderates who constituted the majority. Moderate Republicans shared the prevalent belief of their time that blacks were inferior to whites, but they argued that the federal government needed to protect newly emancipated slaves. Senator Lyman Trumbull of Illinois, for example, warned that without national legislation, ex-slaves would "be tyrannized over, abused, and virtually reenslaved." The moderates expected southern states, where 90 percent of African Americans lived, to extend basic civil rights to the freedpeople, including equal protection, due process of law, and the right to work and hold property.

Nearly all Republicans shared these positions, but the Radical wing of the party wanted to go further. Led by Senator Charles Sumner of Massachusetts and Congressman Thaddeus Stevens of Pennsylvania, this small but influential group advocated suffrage, or voting rights, for African American men as well as the redistribution of southern plantation lands to freed slaves. Stevens called on the federal government to provide freedpeople "a homestead of forty acres of land," which would give them some measure of autonomy. These efforts failed, and the Republican Party proved unable to pass a comprehensive land distribution program that enabled freed blacks to gain economic independence. Nonetheless, whatever disagreements between Radicals and moderates, all Republicans believed that Congress should have a strong voice in determining the fate of the former Confederate states. From May to December 1865, with Congress out of session, they waited to see what Johnson's restoration plan would produce, ready to assert themselves if his policies deviated too much from their own.

At first, it seemed as if Johnson would proceed as they hoped. He appointed provisional governors to convene new state constitutional conventions and urged these

Mourning at Stonewall Jackson's Gravesite, 1866 Many Northerners were concerned that the defeat of the Confederacy did not lessen white Southerners' devotion to the "Lost Cause" or the heroism of soldiers who fought to maintain a society based on the domination of African Americans. Women, who led the efforts to memorialize Confederate soldiers, are shown at the gravesite of General Stonewall Jackson in Lexington, Virginia. Virginia Military Institute Archives conventions to ratify the Thirteenth Amendment, abolishing slavery, and revoke the states' ordinances of secession. He also allowed the majority of white Southerners to obtain amnesty and a pardon by swearing their loyalty to the U.S. Constitution, but he required those who had held more than $20,000 of taxable property—the members of the southern aristocracy—to petition him for a special pardon to restore their rights. Republicans expected him to be harsh in dealing with his former political foes. Instead, Johnson relished the reversal of roles that put members of the southern elite at his mercy. As the once prominent petitioners paraded before him, the president granted almost all of their requests for pardons.

By the time Congress convened in December 1865, Johnson was satisfied that the southern states had fulfilled his requirements for restoration. Moderate and Radical Republicans disagreed, seeing few signs of change or contrition in the South. Mississippi, for example, rejected ratification of the Thirteenth Amendment. As a result of Johnson's liberal pardon policy, many former leaders of the Confederacy won election to state constitutional conventions and to Congress. Indeed, Georgians elected Confederate vice president Alexander H. Stephens to the U.S. Senate.

Far from providing freedpeople with basic civil rights, the southern states passed a variety of **black codes** intended to reduce African Americans to a condition as close to slavery as possible. Some laws prohibited blacks from bearing arms; others outlawed intermarriage and excluded blacks from serving on juries. The codes also made it difficult for blacks to leave plantations unless they proved they could support themselves. Laws like this were designed to ensure that white landowners had a supply of cheap black labor despite slavery's abolition.

Northerners viewed this situation with alarm. In their eyes, the postwar South looked very similar to the Old South, with a few cosmetic adjustments. If the black codes prevailed, one Republican proclaimed, "then I demand to know of what practical value is the amendment abolishing slavery?" Others wondered what their wartime sacrifices meant if the South admitted no mistakes, was led by the same people, and continued to oppress its black inhabitants.

Johnson and Congressional Resistance

Faced with growing opposition in the North, Johnson stubbornly held his ground. He insisted that the southern states had followed his plan and were entitled to resume their representation in Congress. Republicans objected, and in December 1865 they barred the admission of southern lawmakers. But Johnson refused to compromise. In January 1866, the president rejected a bill passed by Congress to extend the life of the Freedmen's Bureau for two years. A few months later, he vetoed the Civil Rights Act, which Congress had passed to protect freedpeople from the restrictions placed on them by the black codes. These bills represented a consensus among moderate and Radical Republicans on the federal government's responsibility toward former slaves.

Johnson justified his vetoes on both constitutional and personal grounds. He and other Democrats contended that so long as Congress refused to admit southern representatives, it could not legally pass laws affecting the South. The president also condemned the Freedmen's Bureau bill because it infringed on the right of states to handle internal affairs such as education and economic policies. Johnson's vetoes exposed his racism and his lifelong belief that the evil of slavery lay in the harm it did to poor whites, not to enslaved blacks. Johnson argued that the bills he vetoed discriminated against whites, who would receive no benefits under them, and thus put whites at a disadvantage with blacks who received government assistance. Johnson's private secretary reported in his diary, "The president has at times exhibited a morbid distress and feeling against the Negroes."

Johnson's actions united moderates and Radicals against him. In April 1866, Congress repassed both the Freedmen's Bureau extension and Civil Rights Act over the president's vetoes. In June, lawmakers adopted the **Fourteenth Amendment**, which incorporated many of the provisions of the Civil Rights Act, and submitted it to the states for ratification (see Appendix). Reflecting its confrontational dealings with the president, Congress wanted to ensure more permanent protection for African Americans than simple legislation could provide. Lawmakers also wanted to act quickly, as the situation in the South seemed to be deteriorating rapidly. In May 1866, a race riot had broken out in Memphis, Tennessee. For a day and a half, white mobs, egged on by local police, went on a rampage, during which they terrorized blacks and burned their homes and churches. "The late riots in our city," the white editor of a Memphis newspaper asserted, "have satisfied all of one thing, that the *southern man* will not be ruled by the *negro*."

The Fourteenth Amendment defined citizenship to include African Americans, thereby nullifying the ruling in the *Dred Scott* case of 1857, which declared that blacks were not citizens. It extended equal protection and due process of law to all persons, not only citizens. The amendment repudiated Confederate debts, which some state governments had refused to do, and it barred Confederate officeholders from holding elective office unless Congress removed this provision by a two-thirds vote. Although most Republicans were upset with Johnson's behavior, at this point they were not willing to embrace the Radical position entirely. Rather than granting the right to vote to black males at least twenty-one years of age, the Fourteenth Amendment gave the states the option of excluding blacks and accepting a reduction in congressional representation if they did so.

Johnson remained inflexible. Instead of counseling the southern states to accept the Fourteenth Amendment, which would have sped up their readmission to the Union, he encouraged them to reject it. In the fall of 1866, Johnson decided to take his case directly to northern voters before the midterm congressional elections. Campaigning for candidates who shared his views, he embarked on a swing through the Midwest. Out of touch with northern opinion, Johnson attacked Republican lawmakers and engaged in shouting matches with audiences. On election day, Republicans increased their majorities in Congress and now controlled two-thirds of the seats, providing them with greater power to override presidential vetoes.

Congressional Reconstruction

When the Fortieth Congress convened in 1867, Republican lawmakers charted a new course for Reconstruction. With moderates and Radicals united against the president, Congress intended to force the former Confederate states not only to protect the basic civil rights of African Americans but also to grant them the vote. Moderates now agreed with Radicals that unless blacks had access to the ballot, they would not be able to sustain their freedom. Extending the suffrage to African Americans also aided the fortunes of the Republican Party in the South by adding significant numbers of

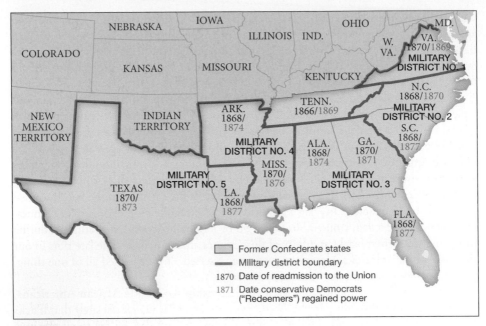

MAP 14.1

Reconstruction in the South   In 1867 Congress enacted legislation dividing the former Confederate states into five military districts. All the states were readmitted to the Union by 1870, and white conservative Democrats (Redeemers) had replaced Republicans in most states by 1875. Only in Florida, Louisiana, and South Carolina did federal troops remain until 1877.

new voters. By the end of March, Congress enacted three Military Reconstruction Acts. Together they divided ten southern states into five military districts, each under the supervision of a Union general (Map 14.1). The male voters of each state, regardless of race, were to elect delegates to a constitutional convention; only former Confederate officials were disfranchised. The conventions were required to draft constitutions that guaranteed black suffrage and ratified the Fourteenth Amendment. Within a year, North Carolina, South Carolina, Florida, Alabama, Louisiana, and Arkansas had fulfilled these obligations and reentered the Union.

Having ensured congressional Reconstruction in the South, Republican lawmakers turned their attention to disciplining the president. Johnson continued to resist their policies and used his power as commander in chief to order generals in the military districts to soften the intent of congressional Reconstruction. In response, Congress passed the Command of the Army Act in 1867, which required the president to issue all orders to army commanders in the field through the General of the Army in Washington, D.C., Ulysses S. Grant. The Radicals knew they could count on Grant to carry out their policies. Even more threatening to presidential power, Congress passed the **Tenure of Office Act**, which prevented Johnson from firing cabinet officers sympathetic to congressional Reconstruction. This measure barred the chief executive from removing from office any appointee that the Senate had ratified previously without returning to the Senate for approval.

Convinced that the new law was unconstitutional and outraged at the effort to limit his power, the quick-tempered Johnson chose to confront the Radical Republicans directly rather than seek a way around a congressional showdown. In February 1868, Johnson fired Secretary of War Edwin Stanton, a Lincoln appointee and a Radical sympathizer, without Senate approval. In response, congressional Radicals prepared articles of impeachment.

In late February, the House voted 126 to 47 to impeach Johnson, the first president ever to be impeached, or charged with unlawful activity. The case then went to trial in the Senate, where the chief justice of the United States presided and a two-thirds vote was necessary for conviction and removal from office. After a six-week hearing, the Senate fell one vote short of convicting Johnson. Most crucial for Johnson's fate were the votes of seven moderate Republicans who refused to find the president guilty of violating his oath to uphold the Constitution. They were convinced that Johnson's actions were insufficient to merit the enormous step of removing a president from office. Although Johnson remained in office, Congress effectively ended his power to shape Reconstruction policy.

The Republicans had restrained Johnson, and in 1868 they won back the presidency. Ulysses S. Grant, the popular Civil War general, ran against Horatio Seymour, the Democratic governor of New York. Although an ally of the Radical Republicans, Grant called for reconciliation with the South. He easily defeated Seymour, winning nearly 53 percent of the popular vote and 73 percent of the electoral vote.

The Struggle for Universal Suffrage

In February 1869, Congress passed the **Fifteenth Amendment** to protect black male suffrage, which had initially been guaranteed by the Military Reconstruction Acts. A compromise between moderate and Radical Republicans, the amendment prohibited voting discrimination based on race, but it did not deny states the power to impose qualifications based on literacy, payment of taxes, moral character, or any other standard that did not directly relate to race. Subsequently, the wording of the amendment provided loopholes for white leaders to disfranchise African Americans. The amendment did, however, cover the entire nation, including the North, where states like Connecticut, Kansas, Michigan, New York, Ohio, and Wisconsin still excluded blacks from voting.

The Fifteenth Amendment sparked serious conflicts not only within the South but also among old abolitionist allies. The American Anti-Slavery Society disbanded with emancipation, but many members believed that important work remained to be done to guarantee the rights of freedpeople. They formed the **American Equal Rights Association** immediately following the war, but members divided over the Fifteenth Amendment.

Some women's rights advocates, including Elizabeth Cady Stanton and Susan B. Anthony, had earlier objected to the Fourteenth Amendment because it inserted the word *male* into the Constitution for the first time when describing citizens. Although they had supported abolition before the war, Stanton and Anthony worried that postwar policies intended to enhance the rights of southern black men would further limit the rights of women. While most African American activists embraced the Fifteenth Amendment, a few voiced concern. At a meeting of the Equal Rights Association in

Frances Ellen Watkins Harper Born a free person of color in Baltimore, Frances Ellen Watkins Harper distinguished herself as a poet, a teacher, and an abolitionist. After the Civil War, she became a staunch advocate of women's suffrage and a supporter of the Fifteenth Amendment, which set her at odds with the suffragists Susan B. Anthony and Elizabeth Cady Stanton. Documenting the American South, The University of North Carolina at Chapel Hill http://docsouth.unc.edu/neh/brownhal/ill22.html

1867, Sojourner Truth noted, "There is quite a stir about colored men getting their rights, but not a word about colored women."

At the 1869 meeting of the Equal Rights Association, differences over the measure erupted into open conflict. Stanton and Anthony denounced suffrage for black men only, and Stanton now supported her position on racial grounds. She claimed that the "dregs of China, Germany, England, Ireland, and Africa" were degrading the U.S. polity and argued that white, educated women should certainly have the same rights as immigrant and African American men. Black and white supporters of the Fifteenth Amendment, including Frances Ellen Watkins Harper, Wendell Phillips, Abby Kelley, and Frederick Douglass, denounced Stanton's bigotry. Believing that southern black men urgently needed suffrage to protect their newly won freedom, they argued that ratification of the Fifteenth Amendment would speed progress toward the enfranchisement of women, black and white.

This conflict led to the formation of competing organizations committed to women's suffrage. The National Woman Suffrage Association, established by Stanton and Anthony, allowed only women as members and opposed ratification of the Fifteenth Amendment. The American Woman Suffrage Association, which attracted the support of women and men, white and black, supported ratification. Less than a year later, in the spring of 1870, the Fifteenth Amendment was ratified and went into effect.

Since the amendment did not grant the vote to either white or black women, women suffragists attempted to use the Fourteenth Amendment to achieve their goal. In 1875 Virginia Minor, who had been denied the ballot in Missouri, argued that the right to vote was one of the "privileges and immunities" granted to all citizens under the Fourteenth Amendment. In *Minor v. Happersatt*, the Supreme Court ruled against her, and most women were denied national suffrage for decades thereafter.

REVIEW & RELATE	• What was President Johnson's plan for reconstruction? How were his views out of step with those of most Republicans? • What characterized congressional Reconstruction? What priorities were reflected in congressional Reconstruction legislation?

Remaking the South

With President Johnson's power effectively curtailed, reconstruction of the South moved quickly. New state legislatures, ruled by a coalition of southern whites and blacks and white northern migrants, enacted political, economic, and social reforms that improved the overall quality of life in the South. Despite these changes, many black and white Southerners barely eked out a living under the planter-dominated sharecropping system. Moreover, the biracial Reconstruction governments lasted a relatively short time, as conservative whites used a variety of tactics, including terror and race baiting, to defeat their opponents at the polls.

Whites Reconstruct the South

During the first years of congressional Reconstruction, two groups of whites occupied the majority of elective offices in the South. A significant number of native-born Southerners joined Republicans in forging postwar constitutions and governments. Before the war, some had belonged to the Whig Party and opposed secession from the Union. Western sections of Alabama, Georgia, North Carolina, and Tennessee had demonstrated a fiercely independent strain, and many residents had remained loyal to the Union. Small merchants and farmers who detested large plantation owners also threw in their lot with the Republicans. Even a few ex-Confederates, such as General James A. Longstreet, decided that the South must change and allied with the Republicans. The majority of whites who continued to support the Democratic Party viewed these whites as traitors. They showed their distaste by calling them **scalawags**, an unflattering term meaning "scoundrels."

At the same time, Northerners came south to support Republican Reconstruction. They had varied reasons for making the journey, but most considered the South a new frontier to be conquered culturally, politically, and economically. Some—white and black—had served in the Union army during the war, liked what they saw of the region, and decided to settle there. Some of both races came to provide education and assist the freedpeople in adjusting to their new lives. As a relatively underdeveloped area, the South also beckoned fortune seekers and adventurers who saw opportunities to get rich. Southern Democrats denounced such northern interlopers, particularly whites, as **carpetbaggers**, suggesting that they invaded the region with all their possessions in a satchel, seeking to plunder it and then leave. While Northerners did seek economic opportunity, they were acting as Americans always had in settling new frontiers and pursuing dreams of success. In fact, much of the animosity directed toward them resulted primarily not from their mere presence, but from their efforts to ally with African Americans in reshaping the South.

Black Political Participation and Economic Opportunities

Still, the primary targets of southern white hostility were African Americans who attempted to exercise their hard-won freedom. Blacks constituted a majority of voters in five states—Alabama, Florida, South Carolina, Mississippi, and Louisiana—while in Georgia, North Carolina, Texas, and Virginia they fell short of a majority. They did not use their ballots to impose black rule on the South, as many white Southerners feared. Only in South Carolina did African Americans control the state legislature, and in no state did they manage to elect a governor. Nevertheless, for the first time in American history, blacks won a wide variety of elected positions. More than six hundred blacks served in state legislatures; another sixteen, including Jefferson Long, held seats in the U.S. House of Representatives; and two from Mississippi were chosen to serve in the U.S. Senate.

Former slaves showed enthusiasm for politics in other ways, too. African Americans considered politics a community responsibility, and in addition to casting ballots, they held rallies and mass meetings to discuss issues and choose candidates. Although they could not vote, women attended these gatherings and helped influence their outcome. Covering a Republican convention in Richmond in October 1867, held in the First African Baptist Church, the *New York Times* reported that "the entire colored population of Richmond" attended. In addition, freedpeople formed mutual aid associations to promote education, economic advancement, and social welfare programs, all of which they saw as deeply intertwined with politics.

Southern blacks also bolstered their freedom by building alliances with sympathetic whites. These interracial political coalitions produced considerable reform in the South. They created the first public school systems; provided funds for social services, such as poor relief and state hospitals; upgraded prisons; and rebuilt the South's transportation system. Moreover, the state constitutions that the Republicans wrote brought a greater measure of political democracy and equality to the South by extending suffrage to poor white men as well as black men. Some states allowed married women greater control over their property and liberalized the criminal justice system. In effect, these Reconstruction governments brought the South into the nineteenth century.

Obtaining political representation was one way in which African Americans defined freedom. Economic independence constituted a second. Without government-sponsored land redistribution, however, the options for southern blacks remained limited. Lacking capital to purchase farms, most entered into various forms of tenant contracts with large landowners. **Sharecropping** proved the most common arrangement. Blacks and poor whites became sharecroppers for much the same reasons. They received tools and supplies from landowners and farmed their own plots of land on the plantation. In exchange, sharecroppers turned over a portion of their harvest to the owner and kept the rest for themselves.

The benefits of sharecropping proved less valuable to black farmers in practice than in theory. To tide them over during the growing season, croppers had to purchase household provisions on credit from a local merchant, who was often also their landlord. At the mercy of store owners who kept the books and charged high interest rates, tenants usually found themselves in considerable debt at the end of the year. To satisfy the debt, merchants devised a crop lien system in which tenants pledged a portion of their yearly crop to satisfy what they owed. Falling prices for agricultural crops in this period ensured that most indebted tenants did not receive sufficient return on their produce to get out of debt and thus remained bound to their landlords. For many African Americans, sharecropping turned into a form of virtual slavery.

The picture for black farmers was not all bleak, however. About 20 percent of black farmers managed to buy their own land. Through careful management and extremely hard work, black families planted gardens for household consumption and raised chickens for eggs and meat. Despite its pitfalls, sharecropping provided a limited measure of labor independence and allowed some blacks to accumulate small amounts of cash.

Following the war's devastation, many of the South's white small farmers, known as yeomen, also fell into sharecropping. Meanwhile, many planters' sons abandoned farming and became lawyers, bankers, and merchants. Despite these changes, one thing remained the same: White elites ruled over blacks and poor whites, and they kept these two economically exploited groups from uniting by fanning the flames of racial prejudice.

Economic hardship and racial bigotry drove many blacks to leave the South. In 1879 former slaves, known as **Exodusters**, pooled their resources to create land companies and purchase property in Kansas on which to settle. They encouraged an exodus of some 25,000 African Americans from the South. Kansas was ruled by the Republican Party and had been home to the great antislavery martyr John Brown. As one hopeful freedman from Louisiana wrote to the Kansas governor in 1879, "I am anxious to reach your state . . . because of the sacredness of her soil washed in the blood of humanitarians for the cause of black freedom." Poor-quality land and unpredictable weather often made farming on the Great Plains hard and unrewarding. Nevertheless, for many black migrants, the chance to own their own land and escape the oppression of the South was worth the hardships. In 1880 the census counted 40,000 blacks living in Kansas.

White Resistance to Congressional Reconstruction

Despite the Republican record of accomplishment during Reconstruction, white Southerners did not accept its legitimacy. They accused interracial governments of conducting a spending spree that raised taxes and encouraged corruption. Indeed, taxes did rise significantly, but mainly because legislatures funded much-needed educational and social services. Corruption on building projects and railroad construction was common during this time. Still, it is unfair to single out Reconstruction governments and especially black legislators as inherently depraved, as their Democratic opponents acted the same way when given the opportunity. Economic scandals were part of American life after the Civil War. As enormous business opportunities arose in the postwar years, many economic and political leaders made unlawful deals to enrich themselves. Furthermore, southern opponents of Reconstruction exaggerated its harshness. In contrast to revolutions and civil wars in other countries, only one rebel was executed for war crimes (the commandant of Andersonville Prison in Georgia); only one high-ranking official went to prison (Jefferson Davis); no official was forced into exile, though some fled voluntarily; and most rebels regained voting rights and the ability to hold office within seven years after the end of the rebellion.

Most important, these Reconstruction governments had only limited opportunities to transform the South. By the end of 1870, civilian rule had returned to all of the former Confederate states, and they had reentered the Union. Republican rule did not continue past 1870 in Virginia, North Carolina, and Tennessee and did not extend beyond 1871 in Georgia and 1873 in Texas. In 1874 Democrats deposed Republicans in Arkansas and Alabama; two years later, Democrats triumphed in Mississippi. In only three states—Louisiana, Florida, and South Carolina—did Reconstruction last until 1877.

The Democrats who replaced Republicans trumpeted their victories as bringing "redemption" to the South. Of course, these so-called **Redeemers** were referring to the white South. For black Republicans and their white allies, redemption meant defeat. Democratic victories came at the ballot boxes, but violence, intimidation, and fraud paved the way. In 1865 in Pulaski, Tennessee General Nathan Bedford Forrest organized Confederate veterans into a social club called the **Knights of the Ku Klux Klan (KKK)**. Spreading throughout the South, its followers donned robes and masks to hide their identities and terrify their victims. Gun-wielding Ku Kluxers rode on horseback to the homes and churches of black and white Republicans to keep them from voting. When threats did not work, they beat and murdered their victims. In 1871, for example, 150 African Americans were killed in Jackson County in the Florida Panhandle. A black clergyman lamented, "That is where Satan has his seat." There and elsewhere, many of the individuals targeted had managed to buy property, gain political leadership, or in other ways defy white stereotypes of African American inferiority. Other white supremacist organizations joined the Klan in waging a reign of terror. During the 1875 election in Mississippi, which toppled the Republican government, armed terrorists killed hundreds of Republicans and scared many more away from the polls.

To combat the terror unleashed by the Klan and its allies, Congress passed three **Force Acts** in 1870 and 1871. These measures empowered the president to dispatch officials into the South to supervise elections and prevent voting interference. Directed specifically at the KKK, one law barred secret organizations from using force to violate equal protection of the laws. In 1872 Congress established a joint committee to probe Klan tactics, and its investigations produced thirteen volumes of gripping testimony about the horrors perpetrated by the Klan. Elias Hill, a freedman from South Carolina who had become a Baptist preacher and teacher, was one of those who appeared before Congress. He and his brother lived next door to each other. The Klansmen went first to his brother's house, where, as Hill testified, they "broke open the door and attacked his wife, and I heard her screaming and mourning [moaning]. . . . At last I heard them have [rape] her in the yard." When the Klansmen discovered Elias Hill, they dragged him out of his house and beat, whipped, and threatened to kill him. On the basis of such testimony, the federal government prosecuted some 3,000 Klansmen. Only 600 were convicted, however. As the Klan disbanded in the wake of federal prosecutions, other vigilante organizations arose to take its place.

REVIEW & RELATE

- What role did black people play in remaking southern society during Reconstruction?
- How did southern whites fight back against Reconstruction? What role did terrorism and political violence play in this effort?

The Unraveling of Reconstruction

The violence, intimidation, and fraud perpetrated by Redeemers does not fully explain the unraveling of Reconstruction. By the early 1870s most white Northerners had come to believe that they had done more than enough for black Southerners, and it was time to focus on other issues. Growing economic problems intensified this feeling. Still reeling from the amount of blood shed during the war, white Americans, north and south, turned their attention toward burying and memorializing the Civil War dead. White America was once again united, if only in the shared belief that it was time to move on, consigning the issues of slavery and civil rights to history.

The Republican Retreat

Most northern whites shared the racial prejudices of their counterparts in the South. Although they had supported protection of black civil rights and suffrage, they still believed that African Americans were inferior to whites and were horrified by the idea of social integration. They began to sympathize with Southern whites' racist complaints that blacks were not capable of governing honestly and effectively.

In 1872 a group calling themselves Liberal Republicans challenged the reelection of President Grant. Financial scandals had racked the Grant administration. This high level corruption reflected other get-rich-quick schemes connected to economic speculation and development following the Civil War. Outraged by the rising level of immoral behavior in government and business, Liberal Republicans nominated Horace Greeley, editor of the *New York Tribune*, to run against Grant. They linked government corruption to the expansion of federal power that accompanied Reconstruction and called for the removal of troops from the South and amnesty for all former Confederates. They also campaigned for civil service reform, which would base government employment on a merit system and abolish the "spoils system"—in which the party in power rewarded loyal supporters with political appointments—that had been introduced by Andrew Jackson in the 1820s.

The Democratic Party believed that Liberal Republicans offered the best chance to defeat Grant, and it endorsed Greeley. Despite the scandals that surrounded him, Grant remained popular. Moreover, the main body of Republicans "waved the bloody shirt," reminding northern voters that a ballot cast for the opposition tarnished the memory of brave Union soldiers killed during the war. The president won reelection with an even greater margin than he had four years earlier. Nevertheless, the attacks against Grant foreshadowed the Republican retreat on Reconstruction. Among the Democrats sniping at Grant was Andrew Johnson. Johnson had returned to Tennessee, and in 1874 the state legislature chose the former president to serve in the U.S. Senate. He continued to speak out against the presence of federal troops in the South until his death in 1875.

Congressional and Judicial Retreat

By the time Grant began his second term, Congress was already considering bills to restore officeholding rights to former Confederates who had not yet sworn allegiance to the Union. Black representatives, including Georgia congressman Jefferson Long, as well as some white lawmakers, remained opposed to such measures, but in 1872 Congress removed the penalties placed on former Confederates by the Fourteenth Amendment and permitted nearly all rebel leaders the right to vote and hold office. Two years later, for the first time since the start of the Civil War, the Democrats gained a majority in the House of Representatives and prepared to remove the remaining troops from the South.

Republican leaders also rethought their top priority with economic concerns increasingly replacing racial considerations. In 1873 a financial panic resulting from the collapse of the Northern Pacific Railroad triggered a severe economic depression lasting late into the decade. Tens of thousands of unemployed workers across the country worried more about finding jobs than they did about black civil rights. Businessmen, too, were plagued with widespread bankruptcy. When strikes erupted across the country in 1877, most notably the Great Railway Strike, in which more than half a million workers walked off the job, employers asked the U.S. government to remove troops from the South and dispatch them against strikers in the North and West.

While white Northerners sought ways to extricate themselves from Reconstruction, the Supreme Court weakened enforcement of the civil rights acts. In 1873 the *Slaughterhouse* cases defined the rights that African Americans were entitled to under the Fourteenth Amendment very narrowly. Reflecting the shift from moral to economic concerns, the justices interpreted the amendment as extending greater protection to corporations in conducting business than to blacks. As a result, blacks had to depend on southern state governments to protect their civil rights, the same state authorities that had deprived them of their rights in the first place. In *United States v. Cruikshank* (1876), the high court narrowed the Fourteenth Amendment further, ruling that it protected blacks against abuses only by state officials and agencies, not by private groups such as the Ku Klux Klan. Seven years later, the Court struck down the Civil Rights Act of 1875, which had extended "full and equal treatment" in public accommodations for persons of all races.

The Presidential Compromise of 1876

The presidential election of 1876 set in motion events that officially brought Reconstruction to an end. The Republicans nominated the governor of Ohio, Rutherford B. Hayes, who was chosen partly because he was untainted by the corruption that plagued the Grant administration. The Democrats selected their own anticorruption crusader, Governor Samuel J. Tilden of New York.

The outcome of the election depended on twenty disputed electoral votes, nineteen from the South and one from Oregon. Tilden won 51 percent of the popular vote, but Reconstruction political battles in Florida, Louisiana, and South Carolina put the election up for grabs. In each of these states, the outgoing Republican administration certified Hayes as the winner, while the incoming Democratic regime declared for Tilden.

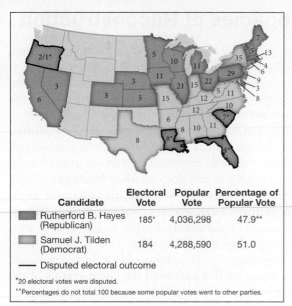

MAP 14.2
The Election of 1876 The presidential election of 1876 got swept up in Reconstruction politics. Democrats defeated Republicans in Florida, Louisiana, and South Carolina, but both parties claimed the electoral votes for their candidates. A federal electoral commission set up to investigate the twenty disputed votes, including one from Oregon, awarded the votes and the election to the Republican, Rutherford B. Hayes.

Candidate	Electoral Vote	Popular Vote	Percentage of Popular Vote
Rutherford B. Hayes (Republican)	185*	4,036,298	47.9**
Samuel J. Tilden (Democrat)	184	4,288,590	51.0
— Disputed electoral outcome			

*20 electoral votes were disputed.
**Percentages do not total 100 because some popular votes went to other parties.

The Constitution assigns Congress the task of counting and certifying the electoral votes submitted by the states. Normally, this is a mere formality, but 1876 was different. Democrats controlled the House, Republicans controlled the Senate, and neither branch would budge on which votes to count. Hayes needed all twenty for victory; Tilden needed only one. To break the logjam, Congress created a fifteen-member Joint Electoral Commission, composed of seven Democrats, seven Republicans, and one independent. Ultimately, a majority voted to count all twenty votes for the Republican Hayes, making him president (Map 14.2).

Still, Congress had to ratify this count, and disgruntled southern Democrats in the Senate threatened a filibuster—unlimited debate—to block certification of Hayes. With the March 4, 1877 date for the presidential inauguration creeping perilously close and no winner officially declared, behind-the-scenes negotiations finally settled the controversy. A series of meetings between Hayes supporters and southern Democrats led to a bargain. According to the agreement, Democrats would support Hayes in exchange for the president appointing a Southerner to his cabinet, withdrawing the last federal troops from the South, and endorsing construction of a transcontinental railroad through the South. This **compromise of 1877** averted a crisis over presidential succession, underscored increased southern Democratic influence within Congress, and marked the end of strong federal protections for African Americans in the South.

REVIEW & RELATE

- Why did northern interest in Reconstruction wane in the 1870s?
- What common values and beliefs among white Americans were reflected in the compromise of 1877?

Conclusion: The Legacies of Reconstruction

Reconstruction was, in many ways, profoundly limited. Notwithstanding the efforts of the Freedmen's Bureau, African Americans did not receive the landownership that would have provided them with economic independence and bolstered their freedom from the racist assaults of white Southerners. The civil and political rights that the federal government conferred did not withstand the efforts of former Confederates to disfranchise and deprive the freedpeople of equal rights. The Republican Party shifted its priorities, and Democrats gained enough political power nationally to short-circuit federal intervention, even as numerous problems remained unresolved in the South. Northern support for racial equality did not run very deep, so white Northerners, who shared many of the prejudices of white Southerners, were happy to extricate themselves from further intervention in southern racial matters. Nor was there sufficient support to give women, white or black, the right to vote. Finally, federal courts, with growing concerns over economic rather than social issues, sanctioned Northerners' retreat by providing constitutional legitimacy for abandoning black Southerners and rejecting women's suffrage in court decisions that narrowed the interpretation of the Fourteenth and Fifteenth Amendments.

Despite all of this, Reconstruction did transform the country. As a result of Reconstruction, slavery was abolished and the legal basis for freedom was enshrined in the Constitution. Indeed, blacks exercised a measure of political and economic freedom during Reconstruction that never entirely disappeared over the decades to come. In many areas, freedpeople, exemplified by Congressman Jefferson Franklin Long and many others, asserted what they never could have during slavery—control over their lives, their churches, their labor, their education, and their families. What they could not practice during their own time, their descendants would one day revive through the promises codified in the Fourteenth and Fifteenth Amendments.

African Americans transformed not only themselves; they transformed the nation. The Constitution became much more democratic and egalitarian through inclusion of the Reconstruction amendments. Reconstruction lawmakers took an important step toward making the United States the "more perfect union" that the nation's Founders had pledged to create. Reconstruction established a model for expanding the power of the federal government to resolve domestic crises that lay beyond the abilities of states and ordinary citizens. It remained a powerful legacy for elected officials who dared to invoke it. And Reconstruction transformed the South to its everlasting benefit. It modernized state constitutions, expanded educational and social welfare systems, and unleashed the repressed potential for industrialization and economic development that the preservation of slavery had restrained. Ironically, Reconstruction did as much for white Southerners as it did for black Southerners in liberating them from the past.

Chapter 14 Review

KEY TERMS

Freedmen's Bureau (p. 336)
Proclamation of Amnesty and
  Reconstruction (p. 339)
Thirteenth Amendment (p. 340)
black codes (p. 342)
Fourteenth Amendment (p. 343)
Tenure of Office Act (p. 344)
Fifteenth Amendment (p. 345)
American Equal Rights Association
  (p. 345)

scalawags (p. 347)
carpetbaggers (p. 348)
sharecropping (p. 348)
Exodusters (p. 349)
Redeemers (p. 350)
Knights of the Ku Klux
  Klan (p. 350)
Force Acts (p. 350)
compromise of 1877
  (p. 353)

REVIEW & RELATE

1. What were freedpeople's highest priorities in the years immediately following the Civil War? Why?

2. How did freedpeople define freedom? What steps did they take to make freedom real for themselves and their children?

3. What was President Johnson's plan for reconstruction? How were his views out of step with those of most Republicans?

4. What characterized congressional Reconstruction? What priorities were reflected in congressional Reconstruction legislation?

5. What role did black people play in remaking southern society during Reconstruction?

6. How did southern whites fight back against Reconstruction? What role did terrorism and political violence play in this effort?

7. Why did northern interest in Reconstruction wane in the 1870s?

8. What common values and beliefs among white Americans were reflected in the compromise of 1877?

TIMELINE OF EVENTS

1863
- Lincoln issues Proclamation of Amnesty and Reconstruction

1865
- Ku Klux Klan formed
- Freedmen's Bureau established
- Thirteenth Amendment passed
- Lincoln assassinated; Andrew Johnson becomes president

1866
- Freedmen's Bureau and Civil Rights Act extended over Johnson's presidential veto
- Fourteenth Amendment passed

1867
- Military Reconstruction Acts
- Command of the Army and Tenure of Office Acts passed

1868
- Andrew Johnson impeached

1869
- Fifteenth Amendment passed
- Women's suffrage movement splits over support of Fifteenth Amendment

1870
- 250,000 blacks attend schools established by the Freedmen's Bureau
- Civilian rule returns to the South

1870–1872
- Congress takes steps to curb Ku Klux Klan violence in the South

1873
- Financial panic sparks depression

1873–1883
- Supreme Court limits rights of African Americans

1875
- Civil Rights Act passed

1877
- Rutherford B. Hayes becomes president
- Reconstruction ends

1879
- Black Exodusters migrate from South to Kansas

Appendix

THE DECLARATION OF INDEPENDENCE

In Congress, July 4, 1776.

The unanimous Declaration of the thirteen United States of America

When in the course of human events, it becomes necessary for one people to dissolve the political bands which have connected them with another, and to assume, among the powers of the earth, the separate and equal station to which the laws of nature and of nature's God entitle them, a decent respect to the opinions of mankind requires that they should declare the causes which impel them to the separation.

We hold these truths to be self-evident, that all men are created equal; that they are endowed by their Creator with certain unalienable rights; that among these, are life, liberty, and the pursuit of happiness. That, to secure these rights, governments are instituted among men, deriving their just powers from the consent of the governed; that, whenever any form of government becomes destructive of these ends, it is the right of the people to alter or to abolish it, and to institute a new government, laying its foundation on such principles, and organizing its powers in such form, as to them shall seem most likely to effect their safety and happiness. Prudence, indeed, will dictate that governments long established, should not be changed for light and transient causes; and, accordingly, all experience hath shown, that mankind are more disposed to suffer, while evils are sufferable, than to right themselves by abolishing the forms to which they are accustomed. But, when a long train of abuses and usurpations, pursuing invariably the same object, evinces a design to reduce them under absolute despotism, it is their right, it is their duty, to throw off such government and to provide new guards for their future security. Such has been the patient sufferance of these colonies, and such is now the necessity which constrains them to alter their former systems of government. The history of the present King of Great Britain is a history of repeated injuries and usurpations, all having, in direct object, the establishment of an absolute tyranny over these States. To prove this, let facts be submitted to a candid world: He has refused his assent to laws the most wholesome and necessary for the public good.

He has forbidden his governors to pass laws of immediate and pressing importance, unless suspended in their operation till his assent should be obtained; and, when so suspended, he has utterly neglected to attend to them.

He has refused to pass other laws for the accommodation of large districts of people, unless those people would relinquish the right of representation in the legislature; a right inestimable to them, and formidable to tyrants only.

He has called together legislative bodies at places unusual, uncomfortable, and distant from the depository of their public records, for the sole purpose of fatiguing them into compliance with his measures.

He has dissolved representative houses repeatedly for opposing, with manly firmness, his invasions on the rights of the people.

He has refused, for a long time after such dissolutions, to cause others to be elected; whereby the legislative powers, incapable of annihilation, have returned to the people at large for their exercise; the state remaining in the mean-time exposed to all the danger of invasion from without, and convulsions within.

He has endeavoured to prevent the population of these States; for that purpose, obstructing the laws for naturalization of foreigners, refusing to pass others to encourage their migration hither, and raising the conditions of new appropriations of lands.

He has obstructed the administration of justice, by refusing his assent to laws for establishing judiciary powers.

He has made judges dependent on his will alone, for the tenure of their offices, and the amount and payment of their salaries.

He has erected a multitude of new offices, and sent hither swarms of officers to harass our people, and eat out their substance.

He has kept among us, in times of peace, standing armies, without the consent of our legislature.

He has affected to render the military independent of, and superior to, the civil power.

He has combined, with others, to subject us to a jurisdiction foreign to our Constitution, and unacknowledged by our laws; giving his assent to their acts of pretended legislation:

For quartering large bodies of armed troops among us:

For protecting them by a mock trial, from punishment, for any murders which they should commit on the inhabitants of these States:

For cutting off our trade with all parts of the world:

For imposing taxes on us without our consent:

For depriving us, in many cases, of the benefit of trial by jury:

For transporting us beyond seas to be tried for pretended offences:

For abolishing the free system of English laws in a neighboring province, establishing therein an arbitrary government, and enlarging its boundaries, so as to render it at once an example and fit instrument for introducing the same absolute rule into these colonies:

For taking away our charters, abolishing our most valuable laws, and altering, fundamentally, the powers of our governments:

For suspending our own legislatures, and declaring themselves invested with power to legislate for us in all cases whatsoever.

He has abdicated government here, by declaring us out of his protection, and waging war against us.

He has plundered our seas, ravaged our coasts, burnt our towns, and destroyed the lives of our people.

He is, at this time, transporting large armies of foreign mercenaries to complete the works of death, desolation, and tyranny, already begun, with circumstances of cruelty and perfidy scarcely paralleled in the most barbarous ages, and totally unworthy the head of a civilized nation.

He has constrained our fellow citizens, taken captive on the high seas, to bear arms against their country, to become the executioners of their friends, and brethren, or to fall themselves by their hands.

He has excited domestic insurrections amongst us, and has endeavored to bring on the inhabitants of our frontiers, the merciless Indian savages, whose known rule of warfare is an undistinguished destruction of all ages, sexes, and conditions.

In every stage of these oppressions, we have petitioned for redress; in the most humble terms; our repeated petitions have been answered only by repeated injury. A prince, whose character is thus marked by every act which may define a tyrant, is unfit to be the ruler of a free people.

Nor have we been wanting in attention to our British brethren. We have warned them, from time to time, of attempts made by their legislature to extend an unwarrantable jurisdiction over us. We have reminded them of the circumstances of our emigration and settlement here. We have appealed to their native justice and magnanimity, and we have conjured them, by the ties of our common kindred, to disavow these usurpations, which would inevitably interrupt our connections and correspondence. They, too, have been deaf to the voice of justice and consanguinity. We must, therefore, acquiesce in the necessity which denounces our separation, and hold them as we hold the rest of mankind, enemies in war, in peace, friends.

We, therefore, the representatives of the United States of America, in general Congress assembled, appealing to the Supreme Judge of the world for the rectitude of our intentions, do, in the name, and by authority of the good people of these colonies, solemnly publish and declare, that these united colonies are, and of right ought to be, free and independent states: that they are absolved from all allegiance to the British Crown, and that all political connection between them and the state of Great Britain is, and ought to be, totally dissolved; and that, as free and independent states, they have full power to levy war, conclude peace, contract alliances, establish commerce, and to do all other acts and things which independent states may of right do. And, for the support of this declaration, with a firm reliance on the protection of Divine Providence, we mutually pledge to each other our lives, our fortunes, and our sacred honor.

The foregoing Declaration was, by order of Congress, engrossed, and signed by the following members:

JOHN HANCOCK

New Hampshire
Josiah Bartlett
William Whipple
Matthew Thornton

Massachusetts Bay
Samuel Adams
John Adams
Robert Treat Paine
Elbridge Gerry

Rhode Island
Stephen Hopkins
William Ellery

Connecticut
Roger Sherman
Samuel Huntington
William Williams
Oliver Wolcott

New York
William Floyd
Phillip Livingston
Francis Lewis
Lewis Morris

New Jersey
Richard Stockton
John Witherspoon
Francis Hopkinson
John Hart
Abraham Clark

Pennsylvania
Robert Morris
Benjamin Rush
Benjamin Franklin
John Morton
George Clymer
James Smith
George Taylor
James Wilson
George Ross
Caesar Rodney
George Read
Thomas M'Kean

Maryland
Samuel Chase
William Paca
Thomas Stone
Charles Carroll, of Carrollton

North Carolina
William Hooper
Joseph Hewes
John Penn

South Carolina
Edward Rutledge
Thomas Heyward, Jr.
Thomas Lynch, Jr.
Arthur Middleton

Virginia
George Wythe
Richard Henry Lee
Thomas Jefferson
Benjamin Harrison
Thomas Nelson, Jr.
Francis Lightfoot Lee
Carter Braxton

Georgia
Button Gwinnett
Lyman Hall
George Walton

Resolved, That copies of the Declaration be sent to the several assemblies, conventions, and committees, or councils of safety, and to the several commanding officers of the continental troops; that it be proclaimed in each of the United States, at the head of the army.

THE ARTICLES OF CONFEDERATION AND PERPETUAL UNION

Agreed to in Congress, November 15, 1777.
Ratified March 1781.

Between the states of New Hampshire, Massachusetts Bay, Rhode Island and Providence Plantations, Connecticut, New York, New Jersey, Pennsylvania, Delaware, Maryland, Virginia, North Carolina, South Carolina, Georgia.*

Article 1

The stile of this confederacy shall be "The United States of America."

Article 2

Each State retains its sovereignty, freedom and independence, and every power, jurisdiction, and right, which is not by this confederation expressly delegated to the United States, in Congress assembled.

Article 3

The said states hereby severally enter into a firm league of friendship with each other for their common defence, the security of their liberties and their mutual and general welfare; binding themselves to assist each other against all force offered to, or attacks made upon them, or any of them, on account of religion, sovereignty, trade, or any other pretence whatever.

Article 4

The better to secure and perpetuate mutual friendship and intercourse among the people of the different states in this union, the free inhabitants of each of these states, paupers, vagabonds, and fugitives from justice excepted, shall be entitled to all privileges and immunities of free citizens in the several states; and the people of each State shall have free ingress and regress to and from any other State, and shall enjoy therein all the privileges of trade and commerce, subject to the same duties, impositions, and restrictions, as the inhabitants thereof respectively; provided, that such restrictions shall not extend so far as to prevent the removal of property, imported into any State, to any other State of which the owner is an inhabitant; provided also, that no imposition, duties, or restriction, shall be laid by any State on the property of the United States, or either of them. If any person guilty of, or charged with treason, felony, or other high misdemeanor in any State, shall flee from justice and be found in any of the United States, he shall, upon demand of the governor or executive power of the State from which he fled, be delivered up and removed to the State having jurisdiction of his offence. Full faith and credit shall be given in each of these states to the records, acts, and judicial proceedings of the courts and magistrates of every other State.

Article 5

For the more convenient management of the general interests of the United States, delegates shall be annually appointed, in such manner as the legislature of each State shall direct, to meet

---

*This copy of the final draft of the Articles of Confederation to taken from the Journals, 9:907–925, November 15, 1777.

in Congress, on the 1st Monday in November in every year, with a power reserved to each State to recall its delegates, or any of them, at any time within the year, and to send others in their stead for the remainder of the year.

No State shall be represented in Congress by less than two, nor by more than seven members; and no person shall be capable of being a delegate for more than three years in any term of six years; nor shall any person, being a delegate, be capable of holding any office under the United States, for which he, or any other for his benefit, receives any salary, fees, or emolument of any kind.

Each State shall maintain its own delegates in a meeting of the states, and while they act as members of the committee of the states.

In determining questions in the United States, in Congress assembled, each State shall have one vote.

Freedom of speech and debate in Congress shall not be impeached or questioned in any court or place out of Congress: and the members of Congress shall be protected in their persons from arrests and imprisonments, during the time of their going to and from, and attendance on Congress, except for treason, felony, or breach of the peace.

Article 6

No State, without the consent of the United States, in Congress assembled, shall send any embassy to, or receive any embassy from, or enter into any conference, agreement, alliance, or treaty with any king, prince, or state; nor shall any person, holding any office of profit or trust under the United States, or any of them, accept of any present, emolument, office or title, of any kind whatever, from any king, prince, or foreign state; nor shall the United States, in Congress assembled, or any of them, grant any title of nobility.

No two or more states shall enter into any treaty, confederation, or alliance, whatever, between them, without the consent of the United States, in Congress assembled, specifying accurately the purposes for which the same is to be entered into, and how long it shall continue.

No state shall lay any imposts or duties which may interfere with any stipulations in treaties entered into by the United States, in Congress assembled, with any king, prince, or state, in pursuance of any treaties already proposed by Congress to the courts of France and Spain.

No vessels of war shall be kept up in time of peace by any State, except such number only as shall be deemed necessary by the United States, in Congress assembled, for the defence of such State or its trade; nor shall any body of forces be kept up by any State, in time of peace, except such number only as, in the judgment of the United States, in Congress assembled, shall be deemed requisite to garrison the forts necessary for the defence of such State; but every State shall always keep up a well regulated and disciplined militia, sufficiently armed and accoutred, and shall provide, and constantly have ready for use, in public stores, a due number of field pieces and tents, and a proper quantity of arms, ammunition and camp equipage.

No State shall engage in any war without the consent of the United States, in Congress assembled, unless such State be actually invaded by enemies, or shall have received certain advice of a resolution being formed by some nation of Indians to invade such State, and the danger is so imminent as not to admit of a delay till the United States, in Congress assembled, can be consulted; nor shall any State grant commissions to any ships or vessels of war, nor letters of marque or reprisal, except it be after a declaration of war by the United States, in Congress assembled, and then only against the kingdom or state, and the subjects thereof, against which war has been so declared, and under such regulations as shall be established by the United States, in Congress assembled, unless such State be infested by pirates, in which case vessels of war may be fitted out for that occasion, and kept so long as the danger shall continue, or until the United States, in Congress assembled, shall determine otherwise.

Article 7

When land forces are raised by any State for the common defence, all officers of or under the rank of colonel, shall be appointed by the legislature of each State respectively, by whom such forces shall be raised, or in such manner as such State shall direct; and all vacancies shall be filled up by the State which first made the appointment.

Article 8

All charges of war and all other expences, that shall be incurred for the common defence or general welfare, and allowed by the United States, in Congress assembled, shall be defrayed out of a common treasury, which shall be supplied by the several states, in proportion to the value of all land within each State, granted to or surveyed for any person, as such land and the buildings and improvements thereon shall be estimated according to such mode as the United States, in Congress assembled, shall, from time to time, direct and appoint.

The taxes for paying that proportion shall be laid and levied by the authority and direction of the legislatures of the several states, within the time agreed upon by the United States, in Congress assembled.

Article 9

The United States, in Congress assembled, shall have the sole and exclusive right and power of determining on peace and war, except in the cases mentioned in the 6th article; of sending and receiving ambassadors; entering into treaties and alliances, provided that no treaty of commerce shall be made, whereby the legislative power of the respective states shall be restrained from imposing such imposts and duties on foreigners as their own people are subjected to, or from prohibiting the exportation or importation of any species of goods or commodities whatsoever; of establishing rules for deciding, in all cases, what captures on land or water shall be legal, and in what manner prizes, taken by land or naval forces in the service of the United States, shall be divided or appropriated; of granting letters of marque and reprisal in times of peace; appointing courts for the trial of piracies and felonies committed on the high seas, and establishing courts for receiving and determining, finally, appeals in all cases of captures; provided, that no member of Congress shall be appointed a judge of any of the said courts.

The United States, in Congress assembled, shall also be the last resort on appeal in all disputes and differences now subsisting, or that hereafter may arise between two or more states concerning boundary, jurisdiction or any other cause whatever; which authority shall always be exercised in the manner following: whenever the legislative or executive authority, or lawful agent of any State, in controversy with another, shall present a petition to Congress, stating the matter in question, and praying for a hearing, notice thereof shall be given, by order of Congress, to the legislative or executive authority of the other State in controversy, and a day assigned for the appearance of the parties by their lawful agents, who shall then be directed to appoint, by joint consent, commissioners or judges to constitute a court for hearing and determining the matter in question; but, if they cannot agree, Congress shall name three persons out of each of the United States, and from the list of such persons each party shall alternately strike out one, the petitioners beginning, until the number shall be reduced to thirteen; and from that number not less than seven, nor more than nine names, as Congress shall direct, shall, in the presence of Congress, be drawn out by lot; and the persons whose names shall be so drawn, or any five of them, shall be commissioners or judges to hear and finally determine the controversy, so always as a major part of the judges who shall hear the cause shall agree in the determination; and if either party shall neglect to attend at the day appointed, without shewing reasons which Congress shall judge sufficient, or, being present, shall refuse to strike, the Congress shall proceed to nominate three persons out of each State, and the secretary of Congress shall strike in behalf of such party absent or refusing; and the judgment and sentence of the court to be appointed, in the manner before prescribed, shall be final and conclusive; and if any of the parties shall refuse to submit to the authority of such court, or to appear or defend their claim or cause, the court shall nevertheless proceed to pronounce sentence or judgment, which shall, in like manner, be final and decisive, the judgment or sentence and other proceedings begin, in either case, transmitted to Congress, and lodged among the acts of Congress for the security of the parties concerned: provided, that every commissioner, before he sits in judgment, shall take an oath, to be administered by one of the judges of the supreme or superior court of the State where the cause shall be tried, "well and truly to hear and determine the matter in question, according to the best of his judgment, without favour, affection, or hope of reward:" provided, also, that no State shall be deprived of territory for the benefit of the United States.

All controversies concerning the private right of soil, claimed under different grants of two or more states, whose jurisdictions, as they may respect such lands and the states which passed such grants, are adjusted, the said grants, or either of them, being at the same time claimed to have originated antecedent to such settlement of jurisdiction, shall, on the petition of either party to the Congress of the United States, be finally determined, as near as may be, in the same manner as is before prescribed for deciding disputes respecting territorial jurisdiction between different states.

The United States, in Congress assembled, shall also have the sole and exclusive right and power of regulating the alloy and value of coin struck by their own authority, or by that of the respective states; fixing the standard of weights and measures throughout the United States; regulating the trade and managing all affairs with the Indians not members of any of the states; provided that the legislative right of any State within its own limits be not infringed or violated; establishing and regulating post offices from one State to another throughout all the United States, and exacting such postage on the papers passing through the same as may be requisite to defray the expences of the said office; appointing all officers of the land forces in the service of the United States, excepting regimental officers; appointing all the officers of the naval forces, and commissioning all officers whatever in the service of the United States; making rules for the government and regulation of the said land and naval forces, and directing their operations.

The United States, in Congress assembled, shall have authority to appoint a committee to sit in the recess of Congress, to be denominated "a Committee of the States," and to consist of one delegate from each State, and to appoint such other committees and civil officers as may be necessary for managing the general affairs of the United States, under their direction; to appoint one of their number to preside; provided that no person be allowed to serve in the office of president more than one year in any term of three years; to ascertain the necessary sums of money to be raised for the service of the United States, and to appropriate and apply the same for defraying the public expences; to borrow money or emit bills on the credit of the United States, transmitting, every half year, to the respective states, an account of the sums of money so borrowed or emitted; to build and equip a navy; to agree upon the number of land forces, and to make requisitions from each State for its quota, in proportion to the number of white inhabitants in such State; which requisitions shall be binding; and thereupon, the legislature of each State shall appoint the regimental officers, raise the men, and cloathe, arm, and equip them in a soldier-like manner, at the expence of the United States; and the officers and men so cloathed, armed, and equipped, shall march to the place appointed and within the time agreed on by the United States, in Congress assembled; but if the United States, in Congress assembled, shall, on consideration of circumstances, judge proper that any State should not raise men, or should raise a smaller number than its quota, and that any other State should raise a greater number of men than the quota thereof, such extra number shall be raised, officered, cloathed, armed, and equipped in the same manner as the quota of such State, unless the legislature of such State shall judge that such extra number cannot be safely spared out of the same, in which case they shall raise, officer, cloathe, arm, and equip as many of such extra number as they judge can be safely spared. And the officers and men so cloathed, armed, and equipped, shall march to the place appointed and within the time agreed on by the United States, in Congress assembled.

The United States, in Congress assembled, shall never engage in a war, nor grant letters of marque and reprisal in time of peace, nor enter into any treaties or alliances, nor coin money, nor regulate the value thereof, nor ascertain the sums and expences necessary for the defence and welfare of the United States, or any of them: nor emit bills, nor borrow money on the credit of the United States, nor appropriate money, nor agree upon the number of vessels of war to be built or purchased, or the number of land or sea forces to be raised, nor appoint a commander in chief of the army or navy, unless nine states assent to the same; nor shall a question on any other point, except for adjourning from day to day, be determined, unless by the votes of a majority of the United States, in Congress assembled.

The Congress of the United States shall have power to adjourn to any time within the year, and to any place within the United States, so that no period of adjournment be for a longer duration than the space of six months, and shall publish the journal of their proceedings monthly, except such parts thereof, relating to treaties, alliances or military operations, as, in their judgment, require secrecy; and the yeas and nays of the delegates of each State on any question shall be entered on the journal, when it is desired by any delegate; and the delegates of a State, or any of them, at his, or their request, shall be furnished with a transcript of the said journal, except such parts as are above excepted, to lay before the legislatures of the several states.

Article 10

The committee of the states, or any nine of them, shall be authorized to execute, in the recess of Congress, such of the powers of Congress as the United States, in Congress assembled, by the consent of nine states, shall, from time to time, think expedient to vest them with; provided, that no power be delegated to the said committee, for the exercise of which, by the articles of confederation, the voice of nine states, in the Congress of the United States assembled, is requisite.

Article 11

Canada acceding to this confederation, and joining in the measures of the United States, shall be admitted into and entitled to all the advantages of this union; but no other colony shall be admitted into the same, unless such admission be agreed to by nine states.

Article 12

All bills of credit emitted, monies borrowed and debts contracted by, or under the authority of Congress before the assembling of the United States, in pursuance of the present confederation, shall be deemed and considered as a charge against the United States, for payment and satisfaction whereof the said United States and the public faith are hereby solemnly pledged.

Article 13

Every State shall abide by the determinations of the United States, in Congress assembled, on all questions which, by this confederation, are submitted to them. And the articles of this confederation shall be inviolably observed by every State, and the union shall be perpetual; nor shall any alteration at any time hereafter be made in any of them, unless such alteration be agreed to in a Congress of the United States, and be afterwards confirmed by the legislatures of every State.

These articles shall be proposed to the legislatures of all the United States, to be considered, and if approved of by them, they are advised to authorize their delegates to ratify the same in the Congress of the United States; which being done, the same shall become conclusive.

THE CONSTITUTION OF THE UNITED STATES*

Agreed to by Philadelphia Convention, September 17, 1787.
Implemented March 4, 1789.

Preamble

We the people of the United States, in order to form a more perfect union, establish justice, insure domestic tranquility, provide for the common defense, promote the general welfare, and secure the blessings of liberty to ourselves and our posterity, do ordain and establish this Constitution for the United States of America.

Article I

Section 1. All legislative powers herein granted shall be vested in a Congress of the United States, which shall consist of a Senate and a House of Representatives.

Section 2. The House of Representatives shall be composed of members chosen every second year by the people of the several States, and the electors in each State shall have the qualifications requisite for electors of the most numerous branch of the State Legislature.

No person shall be a Representative who shall not have attained to the age of twenty-five years, and been seven years a citizen of the United States, and who shall not, when elected, be an inhabitant of that State in which he shall be chosen.

Representatives and direct taxes shall be apportioned among the several States which may be included within this Union, according to their respective numbers, *which shall be determined by adding to the whole number of free persons, including those bound to service for a term of years and excluding Indians not taxed, three fifths of all other persons.* The actual enumeration shall be made within three years after the first meeting of the Congress of the United States, and within every subsequent term of ten years, in such manner as they shall by law direct. The number of Representatives shall not exceed one for every thirty thousand, but each State shall have at least one Representative; and until such enumeration shall be made, *the State of New Hampshire shall be entitled to choose three, Massachusetts eight, Rhode Island and Providence Plantations one, Connecticut five, New York six, New Jersey four, Pennsylvania eight, Delaware one, Maryland six, Virginia ten, North Carolina five, South Carolina five, and Georgia three.*

When vacancies happen in the representation from any State, the Executive authority thereof shall issue writs of election to fill such vacancies.

The House of Representatives shall choose their Speaker and other officers; and shall have the sole power of impeachment.

Section 3. The Senate of the United States shall be composed of two Senators from each State, *chosen by the legislature thereof,* for six years; and each Senator shall have one vote.

Immediately after they shall be assembled in consequence of the first election, they shall be divided as equally as may be into three classes. The seats of the Senators of the first class shall be vacated at the expiration of the second year, of the second class at the expiration of the fourth year, and of the third class at the expiration of the sixth year, so that one-third may be chosen every second year; and if vacancies happen by resignation or otherwise, during the recess of the legislature of any State, the Executive thereof may make temporary appointments until the next meeting of the legislature, which shall then fill such vacancies.

No person shall be a Senator who shall not have attained to the age of thirty years, and been nine years a citizen of the United States, and who shall not, when elected, be an inhabitant of that State for which he shall be chosen.

*Passages no longer in effect are in italic type.

The Vice-President of the United States shall be President of the Senate, but shall have no vote, unless they be equally divided.

The Senate shall choose their other officers, and also a President pro tempore, in the absence of the Vice-President, or when he shall exercise the office of President of the United States.

The Senate shall have the sole power to try all impeachments. When sitting for that purpose, they shall be on oath or affirmation. When the President of the United States is tried, the Chief Justice shall preside: and no person shall be convicted without the concurrence of two-thirds of the members present.

Judgment in cases of impeachment shall not extend further than to removal from the office, and disqualification to hold and enjoy any office of honor, trust or profit under the United States: but the party convicted shall nevertheless be liable and subject to indictment, trial, judgment and punishment, according to law.

Section 4. The times, places and manner of holding elections for Senators and Representatives shall be prescribed in each State by the legislature thereof; but the Congress may at any time by law make or alter such regulations, except as to the places of choosing Senators.

The Congress shall assemble at least once in every year, and such meeting *shall be on the first Monday in December, unless they shall by law appoint a different day.*

Section 5. Each house shall be the judge of the elections, returns and qualifications of its own members, and a majority of each shall constitute a quorum to do business; but a smaller number may adjourn from day to day, and may be authorized to compel the attendance of absent members, in such manner, and under such penalties, as each house may provide.

Each house may determine the rules of its proceedings, punish its members for disorderly behavior, and with the concurrence of two-thirds, expel a member.

Each house shall keep a journal of its proceedings, and from time to time publish the same, excepting such parts as may in their judgment require secrecy; and the yeas and nays of the members of either house on any question shall, at the desire of one fifth of those present, be entered on the journal.

Neither house, during the session of Congress, shall, without the consent of the other, adjourn for more than three days, nor to any other place than that in which the two houses shall be sitting.

Section 6. The Senators and Representatives shall receive a compensation for their services, to be ascertained by law and paid out of the treasury of the United States. They shall in all cases except treason, felony and breach of the peace, be privileged from arrest during their attendance at the session of their respective houses, and in going to and returning from the same; and for any speech or debate in either house, they shall not be questioned in any other place.

No Senator or Representative shall, during the time for which he was elected, be appointed to any civil office under the authority of the United States, which shall have been created, or the emoluments whereof shall have been increased, during such time; and no person holding any office under the United States shall be a member of either house during his continuance in office.

Section 7. All bills for raising revenue shall originate in the House of Representatives; but the Senate may propose or concur with amendments as on other bills.

Every bill which shall have passed the House of Representatives and the Senate, shall, before it become a law, be presented to the President of the United States; if he approve he shall sign it, but if not he shall return it with objections to that house in which it shall have originated, who shall enter the objections at large on their journal, and proceed to reconsider it. If after such reconsideration two-thirds of that house shall agree to pass the bill, it shall be sent, together with the objections, to the other house, by which it shall likewise be reconsidered, and, if approved by two-thirds of that house, it shall become a law. But in all such cases the votes of both houses shall be determined by yeas and nays, and the names of the persons voting for and against the bill shall be entered on the journal of each house respectively. If any bill shall not be returned by the President within ten days (Sundays excepted) after it shall have been presented to him, the same shall be a law, in like manner as if he had signed it, unless the Congress by their adjournment prevent its return, in which case it shall not be a law.

Every order, resolution, or vote to which the concurrence of the Senate and House of Representatives may be necessary (except on a question of adjournment) shall be presented to the President of the United States; and before the same shall take effect, shall be approved by him, or being disapproved by him, shall be repassed by two-thirds of the Senate and House of Representatives, according to the rules and limitations prescribed in the case of a bill.

Section 8. The Congress shall have power

To lay and collect taxes, duties, imposts, and excises, to pay the debts and provide for the common defense and general welfare of the United States; but all duties, imposts and excises shall be uniform throughout the United States;

To borrow money on the credit of the United States;

To regulate commerce with foreign nations, and among the several States, and with the Indian tribes;

To establish an uniform rule of naturalization, and uniform laws on the subject of bankruptcies throughout the United States;

To coin money, regulate the value thereof, and of foreign coin, and fix the standard of weights and measures;

To provide for the punishment of counterfeiting the securities and current coin of the United States;

establish post offices and post roads;

To promote the progress of science and useful arts by securing for limited times to authors and inventors the exclusive right to their respective writings and discoveries;

To constitute tribunals inferior to the Supreme Court;

To define and punish piracies and felonies committed on the high seas and offences against the law of nations;

To declare war, grant letters of marque and reprisal, and make rules concerning captures on land and water;

To raise and support armies, but no appropriation of money to that use shall be for a longer term than two years;

To provide and maintain a navy;

To make rules for the government and regulation of the land and naval forces;

To provide for calling forth the militia to execute the laws of the Union, suppress insurrections and repel invasions;

To provide for organizing, arming, and disciplining the militia, and for governing such part of them as may be employed in the service of the United States, reserving to the States respectively the appointment of the officers, and the authority of training the militia according to the discipline prescribed by Congress;

To exercise exclusive legislation in all cases whatsoever, over such district (not exceeding ten miles square) as may, by cession of particular States, and the acceptance of Congress, become the seat of the government of the United States, and to exercise like authority over all places purchased by the consent of the legislature of the State, in which the same shall be, for erection of forts, magazines, arsenals, dock-yards, and other needful buildings;—and

To make all laws which shall be necessary and proper for carrying into execution the foregoing powers, and all other powers vested by this Constitution in the government of the United States, or in any department or officer thereof.

Section 9. *The migration or importation of such persons as any of the States now existing shall think proper to admit shall not be prohibited by the Congress prior to the year one thousand eight*

hundred and eight; but a tax or duty may be imposed on such importation, not exceeding ten dollars for each person.

The privilege of the writ of habeas corpus shall not be suspended, unless when in cases of rebellion or invasion the public safety may require it.

No bill of attainder or ex post facto law shall be passed.

No capitation, or other direct, tax shall be laid, unless in proportion to the census or enumeration herein before directed to be taken.

No tax or duty shall be laid on articles exported from any State.

No preference shall be given by any regulation of commerce or revenue to the ports of one State over those of another; nor shall vessels bound to, or from, one State be obliged to enter, clear, or pay duties in another.

No money shall be drawn from the treasury, but in consequence of appropriations made by law; and a regular statement and account of the receipts and expenditures of all public money shall be published from time to time.

No title of nobility shall be granted by the United States: and no person holding any office of profit or trust under them, shall, without the consent of the Congress, accept of any present, emolument, office, or title, of any kind whatever, from any king, prince, or foreign state.

Section 10. No State shall enter into any treaty, alliance, or confederation; grant letters of marque and reprisal; coin money; emit bills of credit; make anything but gold and silver coin a tender in payment of debts; pass any bill of attainder, ex post facto law, or law impairing the obligation of contracts, or grant any title of nobility.

No State shall, without the consent of Congress, lay any imposts or duties on imports or exports, except what may be absolutely necessary for executing its inspection laws: and the net produce of all duties and imposts, laid by any State on imports or exports, shall be for the use of the treasury of the United States; and all such laws shall be subject to the revision and control of the Congress.

No State shall, without the consent of Congress, lay any duty of tonnage, keep troops, or ships of war in time of peace, enter into any agreement or compact with another State, or with a foreign power, or engage in war, unless actually invaded, or in such imminent danger as will not admit of delay.

Article II

Section 1. The executive power shall be vested in a President of the United States of America. He shall hold his office during the term of four years, and, together with the Vice-President, chosen for the same term, be elected as follows:

Each State shall appoint, in such manner as the legislature thereof may direct, a number of electors, equal to the whole number of Senators and Representatives to which the State may be entitled in the Congress; but no Senator or Representative, or person holding an office of trust or profit under the United States, shall be appointed an elector.

The electors shall meet in their respective States, and vote by ballot for two persons, of whom one at least shall not be an inhabitant of the same State with themselves. And they shall make a list of all the persons voted for, and of the number of votes for each; which list they shall sign and certify, and transmit sealed to the seat of government of the United States, directed to the President of the Senate. The President of the Senate shall, in the presence of the Senate and House of Representatives, open all the certificates, and the votes shall then be counted. The person having the greatest number of votes shall be the President, if such number be a majority of the whole number of electors appointed; and if there be more than one who have such majority, and have an equal number of votes, then the House of Representatives shall immediately choose by ballot one of them for President; and if no person have a majority, then from the five highest on the list said house shall in like manner choose the President. But in choosing the President the votes shall be taken by States, the representation from each State having one vote; a quorum for this purpose shall consist of a member or members from two-thirds of the States, and a majority of all the States shall be necessary to a choice. In every case, after the choice of the President, the person having the greatest number of votes of the electors shall be the Vice-President. But if there should remain two or more who have equal votes, the Senate shall choose from them by ballot the Vice-President.

The Congress may determine the time of choosing the electors, and the day on which they shall give their votes; which day shall be the same throughout the United States.

No person except a natural-born citizen, *or a citizen of the United States at the time of the adoption of this Constitution,* shall be eligible to the office of President; neither shall any person be eligible to that office who shall not have attained to the age of thirty-five years, and been fourteen years a resident within the United States.

In cases of the removal of the President from office or of his death, resignation, or inability to discharge the powers and duties of the said office, the same shall devolve on the Vice-President, and the Congress may by law provide for the case of removal, death, resignation, or inability, both of the President and Vice-President, declaring what officer shall then act as President, and such officer shall act accordingly, until the disability be removed, or a President shall be elected.

The President shall, at stated times, receive for his services a compensation, which shall neither be increased nor diminished during the period for which he shall have been elected, and he shall not receive within that period any other emolument from the United States, or any of them.

Before he enter on the execution of his office, he shall take the following oath or affirmation:—"I do solemnly swear (or affirm) that I will faithfully execute the office of the President of the United States, and will to the best of my ability preserve, protect and defend the Constitution of the United States."

Section 2. The President shall be commander in chief of the army and navy of the United States, and of the militia of the several States, when called into the actual service of the United States; he may require the opinion, in writing, of the principal officer in each of the executive departments, upon any subject relating to the duties of their respective offices, and he shall have power to grant reprieves and pardons for offenses against the United States, except in cases of impeachment.

He shall have power, by and with the advice and consent of the Senate, to make treaties, provided two-thirds of the Senators present concur; and he shall nominate, and by and with the advice and consent of the Senate, shall appoint ambassadors, other public ministers and consuls, judges of the Supreme Court, and all other officers of the United States, whose appointments are not herein otherwise provided for, and which shall be established by law: but Congress may by law vest the appointment of such inferior officers, as they think proper, in the President alone, in the courts of law, or in the heads of departments.

The President shall have power to fill up all vacancies that may happen during the recess of the Senate, by granting commissions which shall expire at the end of their next session.

Section 3. He shall from time to time give to the Congress information of the state of the Union, and recommend to their consideration such measures as he shall judge necessary and expedient; he may, on extraordinary occasions, convene both houses, or either of them, and in case of disagreement between them, with respect to the time of adjournment, he may adjourn them to such time as he shall think proper; he shall receive ambassadors and other public ministers; he shall take care that the laws be faithfully executed, and shall commission all the officers of the United States.

Section 4. The President, Vice-President and all civil officers of the United States shall be removed from office on impeachment for, and on conviction of, treason, bribery, or other high crimes and misdemeanors.

Article III

Section 1. The judicial power of the United States shall be vested in one Supreme Court, and in such inferior courts as the Congress may from time to time ordain and establish. The judges, both of the Supreme and inferior courts, shall hold their offices during good behavior, and shall, at stated times, receive for their services a compensation which shall not be diminished during their continuance in office.

Section 2. The judicial power shall extend to all cases, in law and equity, arising under this Constitution, the laws of the United States, and treaties made, or which shall be made, under their authority;—to all cases affecting ambassadors, other public ministers and consuls;—to all cases of admiralty and maritime jurisdiction;—to controversies to which the United States shall be a party;—to controversies between two or more States;—between a State and citizens of another State;—between citizens of different States;—between citizens of the same State claiming lands under grants of different States, and between a State, or the citizens thereof, and foreign states, citizens or subjects.

In all cases affecting ambassadors, other public ministers and consuls, and those in which a State shall be party, the Supreme Court shall have original jurisdiction. In all the other cases before mentioned, the Supreme Court shall have appellate jurisdiction, both as to law and fact, with such exceptions, and under such regulations, as the Congress shall make.

The trial of all crimes, except in cases of impeachment, shall be by jury; and such trial shall be held in the State where said crimes shall have been committed; but when not committed within any State, the trial shall be at such place or places as the Congress may by Law have directed.

Section 3. Treason against the United States shall consist only in levying war against them, or in adhering to their enemies, giving them aid and comfort. No person shall be convicted of treason unless on the testimony of two witnesses to the same overt act, or on confession in open court.

The Congress shall have power to declare the punishment of treason, but no attainder of treason shall work corruption of blood, or forfeiture except during the life of the person attainted.

Article IV

Section 1. Full faith and credit shall be given in each State to the public acts, records, and judicial proceedings of every other State. And the Congress may by general laws prescribe the manner in which such acts, records, and proceedings shall be proved, and the effect thereof.

Section 2. The citizens of each State shall be entitled to all privileges and immunities of citizens in the several States.

A person charged in any State with treason, felony, or other crime, who shall flee from justice, and be found in another State, shall on demand of the executive authority of the State from which he fled, be delivered up, to be removed to the State having jurisdiction of the crime.

No Person held to service or labor in one State, under the laws thereof, escaping into another, shall, in consequence of any law or regulation therein, be discharged from such service or labor, but shall be delivered up on claim of the party to whom such service or labor may be due.

Section 3. New States may be admitted by the Congress into this Union; but no new State shall be formed or erected within the jurisdiction of any other State; nor any State be formed by the junction of two or more States, or parts of States, without the consent of the legislatures of the States concerned as well as of the Congress.

The Congress shall have power to dispose of and make all needful rules and regulations respecting the territory or other property belonging to the United States; and nothing in this Constitution shall be so construed as to prejudice any claims of the United States, or of any particular State.

Section 4. The United States shall guarantee to every State in this Union a republican form of government, and shall protect each of them against invasion; and on application of the legislature, or of the executive (when the legislature cannot be convened), against domestic violence.

Article V

The Congress, whenever two-thirds of both houses shall deem it necessary, shall propose amendments to this Constitution, or, on the application of the legislatures of two-thirds of the several States, shall call a convention for proposing amendments, which, in either case, shall be valid to all intents and purposes, as part of this Constitution, when ratified by the legislatures of three-fourths of the several States, or by conventions in three-fourths thereof, as the one or the other mode of ratification may be proposed by the Congress; *provided that no amendments which may be made prior to the year one thousand eight hundred and eight shall in any manner affect the first and fourth clauses in the ninth section of the first article;* and that no State, without its consent, shall be deprived of its equal suffrage in the Senate.

Article VI

All debts contracted and engagements entered into, before the adoption of this Constitution, shall be as valid against the United States under this Constitution, as under the Confederation.

This Constitution, and the laws of the United States which shall be made in pursuance thereof; and all treaties made, or which shall be made, under the authority of the United States, shall be the supreme law of the land; and the judges in every State shall be bound thereby, anything in the Constitution or laws of any State to the contrary notwithstanding.

The Senators and Representatives before mentioned, and the members of the several State legislatures, and all executive and judicial officers, both of the United States and of the several States, shall be bound by oath or affirmation to support this Constitution; but no religious test shall ever be required as a qualification to any office or public trust under the United States.

Article VII

The ratification of the conventions of nine States shall be sufficient for the establishment of this Constitution between the States so ratifying the same.

Done in convention by the unanimous consent of the States present, the seventeenth day of September in the year of our Lord one thousand seven hundred and eighty-seven and of the Independence of the United States of America the twelfth. In witness whereof we have hereunto subscribed our names.

GEORGE WASHINGTON, President and Deputy from Virginia

New Hampshire
John Langdon
Nicholas Gilman

Massachusetts
Nathaniel Gorham
Rufus King

Connecticut
William Samuel
 Johnson
Roger Sherman

New York
Alexander Hamilton

New Jersey
William Livingston
David Brearley
William Paterson
Jonathan Dayton

Pennsylvania
Benjamin Franklin
Thomas Mifflin
Robert Morris

George Clymer
Thomas FitzSimons
Jared Ingersoll
James Wilson
Gouverneur Morris

Delaware
George Read
Gunning Bedford, Jr.
John Dickinson
Richard Bassett
Jacob Broom

Maryland	**North Carolina**	Charles Pinckney
James McHenry	William Blount	Pierce Butler
Daniel of St. Thomas Jenifer	Richard Dobbs Spaight	
Daniel Carroll	Hugh Williamson	**Georgia**
		William Few
Virginia	**South Carolina**	Abraham Baldwin
John Blair	John Rutledge	
James Madison, Jr.	Charles Cotesworth Pinckney	

AMENDMENTS TO THE CONSTITUTION
(including six unratified amendments)

Amendment I
[RATIFIED **1791**]

Congress shall make no law respecting an establishment of religion, or prohibiting the free exercise thereof; or abridging the freedom of speech, or of the press; or the right of the people peaceably to assemble, and to petition the government for a redress of grievances.

Amendment II
[RATIFIED **1791**]

A well-regulated militia being necessary to the security of a free State, the right of the people to keep and bear arms shall not be infringed.

Amendment III
[RATIFIED **1791**]

No soldier shall, in time of peace, be quartered in any house without the consent of the owner, nor in time of war, but in a manner to be prescribed by law.

Amendment IV
[RATIFIED **1791**]

The right of the people to be secure in their persons, houses, papers, and effects, against unreasonable searches and seizures, shall not be violated, and no warrants shall issue but upon probable cause, supported by oath or affirmation, and particularly describing the place to be searched, and the persons or things to be seized.

Amendment V
[RATIFIED **1791**]

No person shall be held to answer for a capital, or otherwise infamous crime, unless on a presentment or indictment of a grand jury, except in cases arising in the land or naval forces, or in the militia, when in actual service in time of war or public danger; nor shall any person be subject for the same offence to be twice put in jeopardy of life or limb; nor shall be compelled in any criminal case to be a witness against himself, nor be deprived of life, liberty, or property, without due process of law; nor shall private property be taken for public use without just compensation.

Amendment VI

[RATIFIED **1791**]

In all criminal prosecutions, the accused shall enjoy the right to a speedy and public trial, by an impartial jury of the State and district wherein the crime shall have been committed, which district shall have been previously ascertained by law, and to be informed of the nature and cause of the accusation; to be confronted with the witnesses against him; to have compulsory process for obtaining witnesses in his favor, and to have the assistance of counsel for his defence.

Amendment VII

[RATIFIED **1791**]

In suits at common law, where the value in controversy shall exceed twenty dollars, the right of trial by jury shall be preserved, and no fact tried by a jury shall be otherwise reexamined in any court of the United States, than according to the rules of the common law.

Amendment VIII

[RATIFIED **1791**]

Excessive bail shall not be required, nor excessive fines imposed, nor cruel and unusual punishments inflicted.

Amendment IX

[RATIFIED **1791**]

The enumeration in the Constitution, of certain rights, shall not be construed to deny or disparage others retained by the people.

Amendment X

[RATIFIED **1791**]

The powers not delegated to the United States by the Constitution, nor prohibited by it to the States, are reserved to the States respectively, or to the people.

Unratified Amendment

[REAPPORTIONMENT AMENDMENT (PROPOSED BY CONGRESS SEPTEMBER **25, 1789,** ALONG WITH THE BILL OF RIGHTS)]

After the first enumeration required by the first article of the Constitution, there shall be one Representative for every thirty thousand, until the number shall amount to one hundred, after which the proportion shall be so regulated by Congress, that there shall be not less than one hundred Representatives, nor less than one Representative for every forty thousand persons, until the number of Representatives shall amount to two hundred; after which the proportion shall be so regulated by Congress, that there shall not be less than two hundred Representatives, nor more than one Representative for every fifty thousand persons.

Amendment XI

[RATIFIED **1798**]

The judicial power of the United States shall not be construed to extend to any suit in law or equity, commenced or prosecuted against one of the United States by citizens of another State, or by citizens or subjects of any foreign state.

Amendment XII

[RATIFIED **1804**]

The electors shall meet in their respective States, and vote by ballot for President and Vice-President, one of whom, at least, shall not be an inhabitant of the same State with themselves; they shall name in their ballots the person voted for as President, and in distinct ballots the person voted for as Vice-President, and they shall make distinct lists of all persons voted for as President, and of all persons voted for as Vice-President, and of the number of votes for each, which lists they shall sign and certify, and transmit sealed to the seat of government of the United States, directed to the President of the Senate;—the President of the Senate shall, in the presence of the Senate and House of Representatives, open all the certificates and the votes shall then be counted;—the person having the greatest number of votes for President shall be the President, if such number be a majority of the whole number of electors appointed; and if no person have such majority, then from the persons having the highest numbers not exceeding three on the list of those voted for as President, the House of Representatives shall choose immediately, by ballot, the President. But in choosing the President, the votes shall be taken by States, the representation from each State having one vote; a quorum for this purpose shall consist of a member or members from two-thirds of the States, and a majority of all the States shall be necessary to a choice. And if the House of Representatives shall not choose a President whenever the right of choice shall devolve upon them, before *the fourth day of March* next following, then the Vice-President shall act as President, as in the case of the death or other constitutional disability of the President.

The person having the greatest number of votes as Vice-President shall be the Vice-President, if such number be a majority of the whole number of electors appointed; and if no person have a majority, then from the two highest numbers on the list the Senate shall choose the Vice-President; a quorum for the purpose shall consist of two-thirds of the whole number of Senators, and a majority of the whole number shall be necessary to a choice. But no person constitutionally ineligible to the office of President shall be eligible to that of Vice-President of the United States.

Unratified Amendment

[TITLES OF NOBILITY AMENDMENT (PROPOSED BY CONGRESS MAY **1, 1810**)]

If any citizen of the United States shall accept, claim, receive or retain any title of nobility or honor or shall, without the consent of Congress, accept and retain any present, pension, office or emolument of any kind whatever, from any emperor, king, prince or foreign power, such person shall cease to be a citizen of the United States, and shall be incapable of holding any office of trust or profit under them or either of them.

Unratified Amendment

[CORWIN AMENDMENT (PROPOSED BY CONGRESS MARCH **2, 1861**)]

No amendment shall be made to the Constitution which will authorize or give to Congress the power to abolish or interfere, within any State, with the domestic institutions thereof, including that of persons held to labor or service by the laws of said State.

Amendment XIII

[RATIFIED **1865**]

Section 1. Neither slavery nor involuntary servitude, except as a punishment for crime whereof the party shall have been duly convicted, shall exist within the United States, or any place subject to their jurisdiction.

Section 2. Congress shall have power to enforce this article by appropriate legislation.

Amendment XIV

[RATIFIED 1868]

Section 1. All persons born or naturalized in the United States, and subject to the jurisdiction thereof, are citizens of the United States and of the State wherein they reside. No State shall make or enforce any law which shall abridge the privileges or immunities of citizens of the United States; nor shall any State deprive any person of life, liberty, or property, without due process of law; nor deny to any person within its jurisdiction the equal protection of the laws.

Section 2. Representatives shall be appointed among the several States according to their respective numbers, counting the whole number of persons in each State, excluding Indians not taxed. But when the right to vote at any election for the choice of Electors for President and Vice-President of the United States, Representatives in Congress, the executive and judicial officers of a State, or the members of the legislature thereof, is denied to any of the *male* inhabitants of such State, being *twenty-one* years of age and citizens of the United States, or in any way abridged, except for participation in rebellion, or other crime, the basis of representation therein shall be reduced in the proportion which the number of such male citizens shall bear to the whole number of *male* citizens *twenty-one* years of age in such State.

Section 3. No person shall be a Senator or Representative in Congress, or Elector of President and Vice-President, or hold any office, civil or military, under the United States, or under any State, who, having previously taken an oath, as a member of Congress, or as an officer of the United States, or as a member of any State legislature, or as an executive or judicial officer of any State, to support the Constitution of the United States, shall have engaged in insurrection or rebellion against the same, or given aid or comfort to the enemies thereof. Congress may, by a vote of two-thirds of each house, remove such disability.

Section 4. The validity of the public debt of the United States, authorized by law, including debts incurred for payment of pensions and bounties for services in suppressing insurrection or rebellion, shall not be questioned. But neither the United States nor any State shall assume or pay any debt or obligation incurred in aid of insurrection or rebellion against the United States, or any claim for the loss or emancipation of any slave; but all such debts, obligations, and claims shall be held illegal and void.

Section 5. The Congress shall have power to enforce, by appropriate legislation, the provisions of this article.

Amendment XV

[RATIFIED 1870]

Section 1. The right of citizens of the United States to vote shall not be denied or abridged by the United States or by any State on account of race, color, or previous condition of servitude.

Section 2. The Congress shall have power to enforce this article by appropriate legislation.

Amendment XVI

[RATIFIED 1913]

The Congress shall have power to lay and collect taxes on incomes, from whatever source derived, without apportionment among the several States, and without regard to any census or enumeration.

Amendment XVII

[RATIFIED 1913]

Section 1. The Senate of the United States shall be composed of two Senators from each State, elected by the people thereof, for six years; and each Senator shall have one vote. The electors in each State shall have the qualifications requisite for electors of [voters for] the most numerous branch of the State legislatures.

Section 2. When vacancies happen in the representation of any State in the Senate, the executive authority of such State shall issue writs of election to fill such vacancies: Provided, that the Legislature of any State may empower the executive thereof to make temporary appointments until the people fill the vacancies by election as the Legislature may direct.

Section 3. *This amendment shall not be so construed as to affect the election or term of any Senator chosen before it becomes valid as part of the Constitution.*

Amendment XVIII

[RATIFIED 1919; REPEALED 1933 BY AMENDMENT XXI]

Section 1. *After one year from the ratification of this article the manufacture, sale, or transportation of intoxicating liquors within, the importation thereof into, or the exportation thereof from the United States and all territory subject to the jurisdiction thereof, for beverage purposes, is hereby prohibited.*

Section 2. *The Congress and the several States shall have concurrent power to enforce this article by appropriate legislation.*

Section 3. *This article shall be inoperative unless it shall have been ratified as an amendment to the Constitution by the legislatures of the several States, as provided by the Constitution, within seven years from the date of the submission thereof to the States by the Congress.*

Amendment XIX

[RATIFIED 1920]

Section 1. The right of citizens of the United States to vote shall not be denied or abridged by the United States or by any State on account of sex.

Section 2. Congress shall have the power to enforce this article by appropriate legislation.

Unratified Amendment

[CHILD LABOR AMENDMENT (PROPOSED BY CONGRESS JUNE 2, 1924)]

Section 1. *The Congress shall have power to limit, regulate, and prohibit the labor of persons under eighteen years of age.*

Section 2. *The power of the several States is unimpaired by this article except that the operation of State laws shall be suspended to the extent necessary to give effect to legislation enacted by Congress.*

Amendment XX

[RATIFIED 1933]

Section 1. The terms of the President and Vice-President shall end at noon on the 20th day of January, and the terms of Senators and Representatives at noon on the 3rd day of January, of the years in which such terms would have ended if this article had not been ratified; and the terms of their successors shall then begin.

Section 2. The Congress shall assemble at least once in every year, and such meeting shall begin at noon on the 3rd day of January, unless they shall by law appoint a different day.

Section 3. If, at the time fixed for the beginning of the term of the President, the President-elect shall have died, the Vice-President-elect shall become President. If a President shall not have been chosen before the time fixed for the beginning of his term, or if the President-elect shall have failed to qualify, then the Vice-President-elect shall act as President until a President shall have qualified; and the Congress may by law provide for the case wherein neither a President-elect nor a Vice-President-elect shall have qualified, declaring who shall then act as President, or the manner in which one who is to act shall be selected, and such person shall act accordingly until a President or Vice-President shall have qualified.

Section 4. The Congress may by law provide for the case of the death of any of the persons from whom the House of Representatives may choose a President whenever the right of choice shall have devolved upon them, and for the case of the death of any of the persons from whom the Senate may choose a Vice-President whenever the right of choice shall have devolved upon them.

Section 5. Sections 1 and 2 shall take effect on the 15th day of October following the ratification of this article.

Section 6. This article shall be inoperative unless it shall have been ratified as an amendment to the Constitution by the Legislatures of three-fourths of the several States within seven years from the date of its submission.

Amendment XXI

[RATIFIED 1933]

Section 1. The eighteenth article of amendment to the Constitution of the United States is hereby repealed.

Section 2. The transportation or importation into any State, Territory, or Possession of the United States for delivery or use therein of intoxicating liquors, in violation of the laws thereof, is hereby prohibited.

Section 3. This article shall be inoperative unless it shall have been ratified as an amendment to the Constitution by conventions in the several States, as provided in the Constitution, within seven years from the date of the submission thereof to the States by the Congress.

Amendment XXII

[RATIFIED 1951]

Section 1. No person shall be elected to the office of the President more than twice, and no person who has held the office of President, or acted as President, for more than two years of a term to which some other person was elected President shall be elected to the office of President more than once. But this article shall not apply to any person holding the office of President when this Article was proposed by the Congress, and shall not prevent any person who may be holding the office of President, or acting as President, during the term within which this Article becomes operative from holding the office of President or acting as President during the remainder of such term.

Section 2. This article shall be inoperative unless it shall have been ratified as an amendment to the Constitution by the legislatures of three-fourths of the several States within seven years from the date of its submission to the States by the Congress.

Amendment XXIII

[RATIFIED 1961]

Section 1. The District constituting the seat of Government of the United States shall appoint in such manner as the Congress may direct: A number of electors of President and Vice-President equal to the whole number of Senators and Representatives in Congress to which the District would be entitled if it were a State, but in no event more than the least populous State; they shall be in addition to those appointed by the States, but they shall be considered for the purposes of the election of President and Vice-President, to be electors appointed by a State; and they shall meet in the District and perform such duties as provided by the twelfth article of amendment.

Section 2. The Congress shall have the power to enforce this article by appropriate legislation.

Amendment XXIV

[RATIFIED 1964]

Section 1. The right of citizens of the United States to vote in any primary or other election for President or Vice-President, for electors for President or Vice-President, or for Senator or Representative in Congress, shall not be denied or abridged by the United States or any State by reason of failure to pay any poll tax or other tax.

Section 2. The Congress shall have the power to enforce this article by appropriate legislation.

Amendment XXV

[RATIFIED 1967]

Section 1. In case of the removal of the President from office or of his death or resignation, the Vice-President shall become President.

Section 2. Whenever there is a vacancy in the office of the Vice-President, the President shall nominate a Vice-President who shall take office upon confirmation by a majority vote of both Houses of Congress.

Section 3. Whenever the President transmits to the President pro tempore of the Senate and the Speaker of the House of Representatives his written declaration that he is unable to discharge the powers and duties of his office, and until he transmits to them a written declaration to the contrary, such powers and duties shall be discharged by the Vice-President as Acting President.

Section 4. Whenever the Vice-President and a majority of either the principal officers of the executive departments or of such other body as Congress may by law provide, transmit to the President pro tempore of the Senate and the Speaker of the House of Representatives their written declaration that the President is unable to discharge the powers and duties of his office, the Vice-President shall immediately assume the powers and duties of the office as Acting President.

Thereafter, when the President transmits to the President pro tempore of the Senate and the Speaker of the House of Representatives his written declaration that no inability exists, he shall resume the powers and duties of his office unless the Vice-President and a majority of either the principal officers of the executive department[s] or of such other body as Congress may by law provide, transmit within four days to the President pro tempore of the Senate and the Speaker of the House of Representatives their written declaration that the President is unable to discharge the powers and duties of his office. Thereupon Congress shall decide the issue, assembling within forty-eight hours for that purpose if not in session. If the Congress, within twenty-one days after receipt of the latter written declaration, or, if Congress is not in session, within twenty-one days after Congress is required to assemble, determines by two-thirds vote of both Houses that the President is unable to discharge the powers and duties of his office, the Vice-President shall continue to discharge the same as Acting President; otherwise, the President shall resume the powers and duties of his office.

Amendment XXVI

[RATIFIED 1971]

Section 1. The right of citizens of the United States, who are eighteen years of age or older, to vote shall not be denied or abridged by the United States or by any State on account of age.

Section 2. The Congress shall have power to enforce this article by appropriate legislation.

Unratified Amendment

[EQUAL RIGHTS AMENDMENT (PROPOSED BY CONGRESS MARCH 22, 1972; SEVEN-YEAR DEADLINE FOR RATIFICATION EXTENDED TO JUNE 30, 1982)]

Section 1. *Equality of rights under the law shall not be denied or abridged by the United States or by any State on account of sex.*

Section 2. *The Congress shall have the power to enforce, by appropriate legislation, the provisions of this article.*

Section 3. *This amendment shall take effect two years after the date of ratification.*

Unratified Amendment

[D.C. STATEHOOD AMENDMENT (PROPOSED BY CONGRESS AUGUST 22, 1978)]

Section 1. *For purposes of representation in the Congress, election of the President and Vice-President, and article V of this Constitution, the District constituting the seat of government of the United States shall be treated as though it were a State.*

Section 2. *The exercise of the rights and powers conferred under this article shall be by the people of the District constituting the seat of government, and as shall be provided by Congress.*

Section 3. *The twenty-third article of amendment to the Constitution of the United States is hereby repealed.*

Section 4. *This article shall be inoperative, unless it shall have been ratified as an amendment to the Constitution by the legislatures of three-fourths of the several states within seven years from the date of its submission.*

Amendment XXVII

[RATIFIED 1992]

No law, varying the compensation for the services of the Senators and Representatives, shall take effect, until an election of Representatives shall have intervened.

Admission of States to the Union

State	Year of Admission	State	Year of Admission
Delaware	1787	Michigan	1837
Pennsylvania	1787	Florida	1845
New Jersey	1787	Texas	1845
Georgia	1788	Iowa	1846
Connecticut	1788	Wisconsin	1848
Massachusetts	1788	California	1850
Maryland	1788	Minnesota	1858
South Carolina	1788	Oregon	1859
New Hampshire	1788	Kansas	1861
Virginia	1788	West Virginia	1863
New York	1788	Nevada	1864
North Carolina	1789	Nebraska	1867
Rhode Island	1790	Colorado	1876
Vermont	1791	North Dakota	1889
Kentucky	1792	South Dakota	1889
Tennessee	1796	Montana	1889
Ohio	1803	Washington	1889
Louisiana	1812	Idaho	1890
Indiana	1816	Wyoming	1890
Mississippi	1817	Utah	1896
Illinois	1818	Oklahoma	1907
Alabama	1819	New Mexico	1912
Maine	1820	Arizona	1912
Missouri	1821	Alaska	1959
Arkansas	1836	Hawaii	1959

Presidents of the United States

President	Term	President	Term
George Washington	1789–1797	Grover Cleveland	1893–1897
John Adams	1797–1801	William McKinley	1897–1901
Thomas Jefferson	1801–1809	Theodore Roosevelt	1901–1909
James Madison	1809–1817	William H. Taft	1909–1913
James Monroe	1817–1825	Woodrow Wilson	1913–1921
John Quincy Adams	1825–1829	Warren G. Harding	1921–1923
Andrew Jackson	1829–1837	Calvin Coolidge	1923–1929
Martin Van Buren	1837–1841	Herbert Hoover	1929–1933
William H. Harrison	1841	Franklin D. Roosevelt	1933–1945
John Tyler	1841–1845	Harry S. Truman	1945–1953
James K. Polk	1845–1849	Dwight D. Eisenhower	1953–1961
Zachary Taylor	1849–1850	John F. Kennedy	1961–1963
Millard Fillmore	1850–1853	Lyndon B. Johnson	1963–1969
Franklin Pierce	1853–1857	Richard M. Nixon	1969–1974
James Buchanan	1857–1861	Gerald R. Ford	1974–1977
Abraham Lincoln	1861–1865	Jimmy Carter	1977–1981
Andrew Johnson	1865–1869	Ronald Reagan	1981–1989
Ulysses S. Grant	1869–1877	George H. W. Bush	1989–1993
Rutherford B. Hayes	1877–1881	Bill Clinton	1993–2001
James A. Garfield	1881	George W. Bush	2001–2009
Chester A. Arthur	1881–1885	Barack Obama	2009–2017
Grover Cleveland	1885–1889	Donald J. Trump	2017–Present
Benjamin Harrison	1889–1893		

Glossary of Key Terms

Adams-Onís Treaty Treaty negotiated by John Quincy Adams and signed in 1819 by which Spain ceded all of its lands east of the Mississippi River to the United States.

Alamo Texas fort captured by General Santa Anna on March 6, 1836, from rebel defenders. Sensationalist accounts of the siege of the Alamo increased popular support in the United States for Texas independence.

Albany Congress June 1754 meeting in Albany, New York, of Iroquois and colonial representatives meant to facilitate better relations between Britain and the Iroquois Confederacy. Benjamin Franklin also put forward a plan for colonial union that was never implemented.

Alien and Sedition Acts 1798 security acts passed by the Federalist-controlled Congress. The Alien Act allowed the president to imprison or deport noncitizens; the Sedition Act placed significant restrictions on political speech.

American Anti-Slavery Society (AASS) Abolitionist society founded by William Lloyd Garrison in 1833 that became the most important northern abolitionist organization of the period.

American Colonization Society (ACS) Organization formed in 1817 to establish colonies of freed slaves and freeborn blacks in Africa. The ACS was led by a group of white elites whose primary goal was to rid the nation of African Americans.

American Equal Rights Association Group of black and white women and men formed in 1866 to promote gender and racial equality. The organization split in 1869 over support for the Fifteenth Amendment.

American System Plan proposed by Henry Clay to promote the U.S. economy by combining federally funded internal improvements to aid farmers with federal tariffs to protect U.S. manufacturing and a national bank to oversee economic development.

American system of manufacturing Production system focused on water-powered machinery, division of labor, and the use of interchangeable parts. The introduction of the American system in the early nineteenth century greatly increased the productivity of American manufacturing.

Antifederalists Opponents of ratification of the Constitution. Antifederalists were generally more rural and less wealthy than the Federalists.

Appeal . . . to the Colored Citizens of the World Radical abolitionist pamphlet published by David Walker in 1829. Walker's work inspired some white abolitionists to take a more radical stance on slavery.

Articles of Confederation Plan for national government proposed by the Continental Congress in 1777 and ratified in March 1781. The Articles of Confederation gave the national government limited powers, reflecting widespread fear of centralized authority.

Aztecs Spanish term for the Mexica, an indigenous people who built an empire in present-day Mexico in the centuries before the arrival of the Spaniards. The Aztecs built their empire through conquest.

Bacon's Rebellion 1676 uprising in Virginia led by Nathaniel Bacon. Bacon and his followers, many of whom were former servants, were upset by the Virginia governor's unwillingness to send troops to intervene in conflicts between settlers and Indians and by the lack of representation of western settlers in the House of Burgesses.

Battle of Antietam Fought in September 1862, this Civil War battle was the bloodiest single day in U.S. military history, but it gave Abraham Lincoln the victory he sought before announcing the Emancipation Proclamation.

Battle of Bull Run (Manassas) First major battle of the Civil War at which Confederate troops routed Union forces in July 1861.

Battle of Bunker Hill Early Revolutionary War battle in which British troops narrowly defeated patriot militias, emboldening patriot forces.

Battle of Fallen Timbers Battle at which U.S. General Anthony Wayne won a major victory over a multi-tribe coalition of American Indians in the Northwest Territory in 1794.

Battle of Gettysburg Key July 1863 battle that helped turn the tide for the Union. The Union victory at Gettysburg, combined with a victory at Vicksburg that same month, positioned the Union to push farther into the South.

Battle of Horseshoe Bend In 1814, Tennessee militia led by Andrew Jackson fought alongside Cherokee warriors to defeat Creek forces allied with Britain during the War of 1812.

Battle of Oriskany In one of the bloodiest Revolutionary War battles, a force of German-American farmers and Oneida Indians deterred British troops and their Indian allies in central New York State, leaving British forces further east vulnerable to attack by the Continental Army.

Battle of Saratoga Key Revolutionary War battle fought at Saratoga, New York. The patriot victory there in October 1777 provided hope that the colonists could prevail and increased the chances that the French would formally join the patriot side.

Battle of Shiloh April 1862 battle in Tennessee that provided the Union entrance to the Mississippi valley. Shiloh was the bloodiest battle in American history to that point.

Battle of Yorktown Decisive battle in which the surrender of British forces on October 19, 1781, at Yorktown, Virginia, effectively sealed the patriot victory in the Revolutionary War.

benign neglect British colonial policy from about 1700 to 1760 that relaxed supervision of internal colonial affairs as long as the North American colonies produced sufficient raw materials and revenue; also known as *salutary neglect*.

Beringia Land bridge that linked Siberia and Alaska during the Wisconsin period. Migrants from northeast Asia used this bridge to travel to North America.

Bill of Rights The first ten amendments to the Constitution. These ten amendments helped reassure Americans who feared that the federal government established under the Constitution would infringe on the rights of individuals and states.

black codes Racial laws passed in the immediate aftermath of the Civil War by southern legislatures. The black codes were intended to reduce free African Americans to a condition as close to slavery as possible.

Black Death The epidemic of bubonic plague that swept through Europe beginning in the mid-fourteenth century and wiped out roughly half of Europe's population.

Bleeding Kansas The Kansas Territory during a period of violent conflicts over the fate of slavery in the mid-1850s. The violence in Kansas intensified the sectional division over slavery.

Boston Massacre 1770 clash between colonial protesters and British soldiers in Boston that led to the death of five colonists. The bloody conflict was used to promote the patriot cause.

carpetbaggers Derogatory term for white Northerners who moved to the South in the years following the Civil War. Many white Southerners believed that such migrants were intent on exploiting their suffering.

Church of England National church established by Henry VIII after he split with the Catholic Church.

Coercive Acts (Intolerable Acts) 1774 act of Parliament passed in response to the Boston Tea Party. The Coercive Acts were meant to force the colonists into submission, but they only resulted in increased resistance. Colonial patriots called them the Intolerable Acts.

Columbian exchange The biological exchange between the Americas and the rest of the world. Although the initial impact of the Columbian exchange was strongest in the Americas and Europe, it was soon felt all over the world.

committee of correspondence Type of committee first established in Massachusetts to circulate concerns and reports of protests and other events to leaders in other colonies in the aftermath of the Sugar Act.

Common Sense Pamphlet arguing in favor of independence written by Thomas Paine and published in 1776. *Common Sense* was widely read and had an important impact on the debate over declaring independence from Britain.

Compromise of 1850 Series of acts following California's application for admission as a free state. Meant to quell sectional tensions over slavery, the act was intended to provide something for all sides but ended up fueling more conflicts.

Compromise of 1877 Compromise between Republicans and southern Democrats that resulted in the election of Rutherford B. Hayes. Southern Democrats agreed to support Hayes in the disputed presidential election in exchange for his promise to end Reconstruction.

Confederate States of America Nation established in 1861 by the eleven slave states that seceded between December 1860 and April 1861.

conquistadors Spanish soldiers who were central to the conquest of the civilizations of the Americas. Once conquest was complete, conquistadors often extracted wealth from the people and lands they now ruled.

Continental Congress Congress convened in Philadelphia in 1774 in response to the Coercive Acts. The delegates hoped to reestablish the freedoms colonists had enjoyed in earlier times.

contraband Designation assigned to escaped slaves by Union general Benjamin Butler in May 1861. By designating slaves as property forfeited by the act of rebellion, the Union was able to strike at slavery without proclaiming a general emancipation.

Copperheads Northern Democrats who did not support the Union war effort. Such Democrats enjoyed considerable support in eastern cities and parts of the Midwest.

Corps of Discovery Expedition organized by the U.S. government to explore the Louisiana Territory. Led by Meriwether Lewis and William Clark, the expedition set out in May 1804 and journeyed to the Pacific coast and back by 1806 with the aid of interpreters like Sacagawea.

cotton gin Machine invented by Eli Whitney in 1793 to deseed short-staple cotton. The cotton gin dramatically reduced the time and labor involved in deseeding, facilitating the expansion of cotton production in the South and West.

Crittenden plan A political compromise over slavery which failed after seven southern states seceded from the Union in early 1861. It would have protected slavery from federal interference where it already existed and extended the Missouri Compromise line to California.

Crusades Eleventh- and twelfth-century campaigns to reclaim the Holy Land for the Roman Catholic Church. The Crusades were, on the whole, a military failure, but they did stimulate trade and inspire Europeans to seek better connections with the larger world.

cult of domesticity New ideals of womanhood that emerged alongside the middle class in the 1830s and 1840s that advocated women's relegation to the domestic sphere where they could devote themselves to the care of children, the home, and hard-working husbands.

Declaration of Independence Document declaring the independence of the colonies from Great Britain. Drafted by Thomas Jefferson and then debated and revised by the Continental Congress, the Declaration was made public on July 4, 1776.

Declaration of Sentiments Call for women's rights in marriage, family, religion, politics, and law issued at the 1848 Seneca Falls convention. It was signed by 100 of the 300 participants.

Democratic-Republicans Political party that emerged out of opposition to Federalist policies in the 1790s. The Democratic-Republicans chose Thomas Jefferson as their presidential candidate in 1796, 1800, and 1804.

Democrats and National Republicans Two parties that resulted from the split of the Democratic-Republicans in the early 1820s. Andrew Jackson emerged as the leader of the Democrats.

deskilling The replacement of skilled labor with unskilled labor and machines.

***Dred Scott* decision** 1857 Supreme Court case centered on the status of Dred Scott and his family. In its ruling, the Court denied the claim that black men had any rights and blocked Congress from excluding slavery from any territory.

Dunmore's Proclamation 1775 proclamation issued by the British commander Lord Dunmore that offered freedom to all enslaved African Americans who joined the British army. The proclamation heightened concerns among some patriots about the consequences of independence.

Emancipation Proclamation January 1, 1863, proclamation that declared all slaves in areas still in rebellion "forever free." While stopping short of abolishing slavery, the Emancipation Proclamation was, nonetheless, seen by blacks and abolitionists as a great victory.

Embargo Act 1807 act that prohibited American ships from leaving their home ports until Britain and France repealed restrictions on U.S. trade. The act had a devastating impact on American commerce.

encomienda System first established by Christopher Columbus by which Spanish leaders in the Americas received land and the labor of all Indians residing on it. From the Indian point of view, the encomienda system amounted to little more than enslavement.

Enlightenment European cultural movement that emphasized rational and scientific thinking over traditional religion and superstition. Enlightenment thought appealed to many colonial elites.

Enrollment Act March 1863 Union draft law that provided for draftees to be selected by an impartial lottery. A loophole in the law that allowed wealthy Americans to escape service by paying $300 or hiring a substitute created widespread resentment.

Enterprise of the Indies Christopher Columbus's proposal to sail west across the Atlantic to Japan and China. In 1492 Columbus gained support for the venture from Ferdinand and Isabella of Spain.

Erie Canal Canal built in the early 1820s that made water transport from the Great Lakes to New York City possible. The success of the Erie Canal inspired many similar projects and ensured New York City's place as the premier international port in the United States.

Exodusters Blacks who migrated from the South to Kansas in 1879 seeking land and a better way of life.

Federalists Supporters of ratification of the Constitution, many of whom came from urban and commercial backgrounds.

Field Order Number 15 Order issued by General William Sherman in January 1865 setting aside more than 400,000 acres of Confederate land to be divided into plots for former slaves. Sherman's order came in response to pressure from African American leaders.

Fifteenth Amendment Amendment to the Constitution prohibiting the abridgment of a citizen's right to vote on the basis of "race, color, or previous condition of servitude." From the 1870s on, southern states devised numerous strategies for circumventing the Fifteenth Amendment.

filibusters Unauthorized military expeditions launched by U.S. adventurers to gain control of Cuba, Nicaragua, and other Spanish territories in the 1850s.

Force Acts Three acts passed by the U.S. Congress in 1870 and 1871 in response to vigilante attacks on southern blacks. The acts were designed to protect black political rights and end violence by the Ku Klux Klan and similar organizations.

Fort Sumter Union fort that guarded the harbor in Charleston, South Carolina. The Confederacy's decision to fire on the fort and block resupply in April 1861 marked the beginning of the Civil War.

Fourteenth Amendment Amendment to the Constitution defining citizenship and protecting individual civil and political rights from abridgment by the states. Adopted during Reconstruction, the Fourteenth Amendment overturned the *Dred Scott* decision.

Freedmen's Bureau Federal agency created in 1865 to provide ex-slaves with economic and legal resources. The Freedmen's Bureau played an active role in shaping black life in the postwar South.

Free-Soil Party Party founded by political abolitionists in 1848 to expand the appeal of the Liberty Party by focusing less on the moral wrongs of slavery and more on the benefits of providing economic opportunities for northern whites in western territories.

Fugitive Slave Act of 1850 Act strengthening earlier fugitive slave laws, passed as part of the Compromise of 1850. The Fugitive Slave Act provoked widespread anger in the North and intensified sectional tensions.

gag rule Rule passed by the House of Representatives in 1836 to table, or postpone action on, all antislavery petitions without hearing them read to stifle debate over slavery. It was renewed annually until it was rescinded in 1844.

Glorious Revolution 1688 rebellion that forced James II from the English throne and replaced him with William and Mary. The Glorious Revolution led to greater political and commercial autonomy for the British colonies.

gold rush The rapid influx of migrants into California after the discovery of gold in 1848. Migrants came from all over the world seeking riches.

Great Awakening Series of religious revivals in colonial America that began in 1720 and lasted to about 1750.

Haitian Revolution Revolt against French rule by free and enslaved blacks in the 1790s on the island of Saint Domingue. The revolution led in 1803 to the establishment of Haiti, the first independent black-led nation in the Americas.

hard war The strategy promoted by General Ulysses S. Grant in which Union forces destroyed civilian crops, livestock, fields, and property to undermine Confederate morale and supply chains.

Hartford Convention 1814 convention of Federalists opposed to the War of 1812. Delegates to the convention considered a number of constitutional amendments, as well as the possibility of secession.

Hopewell people Indian people who established a thriving culture near the Mississippi River in the early centuries C.E.

horticulture A form of agriculture in which people work small plots of land with simple tools.

House of Burgesses Local governing body in Virginia established by the English crown in 1619.

import duty Tax imposed on goods imported into the colonies, paid by the importer rather than directly by the consumer; also known as a *tariff*.

impressment The forced enlistment of civilians into the army or navy. The impressment of residents of colonial seaports into the British navy was a major source of complaint in the eighteenth century.

Incas Andean people who built an empire in the centuries before the arrival of the Spaniards. At the height of their power in the fifteenth century, the Incas controlled some sixteen million people.

indentured servants Servants contracted to work for a set period of time without pay. Many early migrants to the English colonies indentured themselves in exchange for the price of passage to North America.

Indian Removal Act 1830 act by which Indian peoples in the East were forced to exchange their lands for territory west of the Mississippi River. Andrew Jackson was an ardent supporter of Indian removal.

Intolerable Acts *See* Coercive Acts.

Jamestown The first successful English colony in North America. Settled in 1607, Jamestown was founded by soldiers and adventurers under the leadership of Captain John Smith.

Jay Treaty 1796 treaty that required British forces to withdraw from U.S. soil, required American repayment of debts to British firms, and limited U.S. trade with the British West Indies.

Judiciary Act Act passed in 1801 by the Federalist-controlled Congress to expand the federal court system by creating sixteen circuit (regional) courts, with new judges appointed for each, just before Democratic-Republicans took control of the presidency and Congress.

Kansas-Nebraska Act 1854 act creating the territories of Kansas and Nebraska out of what was then Indian land. The act stipulated that the issue of slavery would be settled by a popular referendum in each territory.

King William's War 1689–1697 war that began as a conflict over competing French and English interests on the European continent but soon spread to the American frontier. Both sides pulled Indian allies into the war.

Knights of the Ku Klux Klan (KKK) Organization formed in 1865 by General Nathan Bedford Forrest to enforce prewar racial norms. Members of the KKK used threats and violence to intimidate blacks and white Republicans.

Liberator Radical abolitionist newspaper launched by William Lloyd Garrison in 1831. Through the *Liberator*, Garrison called for immediate, uncompensated emancipation of slaves.

Liberty Party Antislavery political party formed in 1840. The Liberty Party, along with the Free-Soil Party, helped place slavery at the center of national political debates.

Louisiana Purchase U.S. government's 1803 purchase from France of the vast territory stretching from the Mississippi River to the Rocky Mountains and from New Orleans to present-day Montana, doubling the size of the nation.

loyalist A colonial supporter of the British during the Revolutionary War. Loyalists came from all economic backgrounds and had a variety of motives for siding with the British.

manifest destiny Term coined by John L. O'Sullivan in 1845 to describe what he saw as the nation's God-given right to expand its borders. Throughout the nineteenth century, the concept of manifest destiny was used to justify U.S. expansion.

Marbury v. Madison 1803 Supreme Court decision that established the authority of the Supreme Court to rule on the constitutionality of federal laws.

market revolution Innovations in agriculture, industry, communication, and transportation in the early 1800s fueled increased efficiency and productivity and linked northern industry with western farms and southern plantations.

Maya People who established large cities in the Yucatán peninsula. Mayan civilization was strongest between 300 and 800 C.E.

Mayflower Compact Written constitution created by the Pilgrims upon their arrival in Plymouth. The Mayflower Compact was the first written constitution adopted in North America.

McCulloch v. Maryland 1819 Supreme Court decision that reinforced the federal government's ability to employ an expansive understanding of the implied powers clause of the Constitution.

mercantilism Economic system centered on the maintenance of a favorable balance of trade for the home country, with more gold and silver flowing into that country than flowed out. Seventeenth- and eighteenth-century British colonial policy was heavily shaped by mercantilism.

Metacom's War 1675–1676 conflict between New England settlers and the region's Indians. The settlers were the eventual victors, but fighting was fierce and casualties on both sides were high.

Middle Passage The brutal voyage of slave ships laden with human cargo from Africa to the Americas. The voyage was the middle segment in a triangular journey that began in Europe, went first to Africa, then to the Americas, and finally back to Europe.

Missouri Compromise 1820 act that allowed Missouri to enter the Union as a slave state and Maine to enter as a free state and established the southern border of Missouri as the boundary between slave and free states throughout the Louisiana Territory.

Monroe Doctrine Assertion by President James Monroe in 1823 that the Western Hemisphere was part of the U.S. sphere of influence. Although the United States lacked the power to back up this claim, it signaled an intention to challenge Europeans for authority in the Atlantic world.

multiplier effect The diverse changes spurred by a single invention, including other inventions it spawns and the broader economic, social, and political transformations it fuels.

Nat Turner's rebellion 1831 slave uprising in Virginia led by Nat Turner. Turner's rebellion instilled panic among white Southerners, leading to tighter control of African Americans and reconsideration of the institution of slavery.

National Republicans *See* Democrats and National Republicans.

National Road Road constructed using federal funds that ran from western Maryland through southwestern Pennsylvania to Wheeling, West Virginia; also called the Cumberland Road. Completed in 1818, the road was part of a larger push to improve the nation's infrastructure.

nativists Anti-immigrant Americans who launched public campaigns against foreigners in the 1840s. Nativism emerged as a response to increased immigration to the United States in the 1830s and 1840s, particularly the large influx of Catholic immigrants.

Navigation Acts Acts passed by Parliament in the 1650s and 1660s that prohibited smuggling, established guidelines for legal commerce, and set duties on trade items. In the 1760s, British authorities sought to fully enforce these laws, leading to resistance by colonists.

New Jersey Plan A proposal to the 1787 Constitutional Convention that highlighted the needs of small states by creating one legislative house in the federal government and granting each state equal representation in it.

New Light clergy Colonial clergy who called for religious revivals and emphasized the emotional aspects of spiritual commitment. The New Lights were leaders in the Great Awakening.

Non-Intercourse Act Act passed by Congress in 1809 allowing Americans to trade with every nation except France and Britain. The act failed to stop the seizure of American ships or improve the economy.

Northwest Ordinance Act of the confederation congress that provided for the survey, sale, and eventual division into states of the Northwest Territory. The 1787 act clarified the process by which territories could become states.

nullification The doctrine that individual states have the right to declare federal laws unconstitutional and, therefore, void within their borders. South Carolina attempted to invoke the doctrine of nullification in response to the tariff of 1832.

Old Light clergy Colonial clergy from established churches who supported the religious status quo in the early eighteenth century.

Oregon Trail The route west from the Missouri River to the Oregon Territory. By 1860, some 350,000 Americans had made the three- to six-month journey along the trail.

Ostend Manifesto This 1854 letter from U.S. ambassadors and the Secretary of State to President Franklin Pierce urged him to conquer Cuba. When it was leaked to the press, Northerners voiced outrage at what they saw as a plot to expand slave territories.

panic of 1819 The nation's first severe recession. The panic of 1819 lasted four years and resulted from irresponsible banking practices and the declining demand abroad for American goods, including cotton.

panic of 1837 Severe economic recession that began shortly after Martin Van Buren's presidential inauguration. The panic of 1837 started in the South and was rooted in the changing fortunes of American cotton in Great Britain.

patriarchal family Model of the family in which fathers have absolute authority over wives, children, and servants. Most colonial Americans accepted the patriarchal model of the family, at least as an ideal.

Peace of Paris 1763 peace treaty that brought the Seven Years' War to a close. Under the terms of the treaty, Britain gained control of North America east of the Mississippi River and of present-day Canada.

Pendleton Civil Service Reform Act 1883 act that required federal jobs to be awarded on the basis of merit through competitive exams rather than through political connections.

Pequot War 1636–1637 conflict between New England settlers, their Narragansett allies, and the Pequots. The English saw the Pequots as both a threat and an obstacle to further English expansion.

Petticoat Affair 1829 political conflict over Andrew Jackson's appointment of John Eaton as secretary of war. Eaton was married to a woman of allegedly questionable character, and the wives of many prominent Washington politicians organized a campaign to snub her.

Pietists German Protestants who decried the power of established churches and urged individuals to follow their hearts rather than their heads in spiritual matters. Pietism had a profound influence on the leaders of the Great Awakening.

Pilgrims Group of English religious dissenters who established a settlement at Plymouth, Massachusetts, in 1620. Unlike more mainstream Protestants, the Pilgrims were separatists who aimed to sever all connections with the Church of England.

Pinckney Treaty 1796 treaty that defined the boundary between U.S. and Spanish territory in the South and opened the Mississippi River and New Orleans to U.S. shipping.

Planters Southern whites who owned the largest plantations and forged a distinct culture and economy around the institution of slavery.

Powhatan Confederacy Large and powerful Indian confederation in Virginia. The Jamestown settlers had a complicated and contentious relationship with the leaders of the Powhatan Confederacy.

Proclamation Line of 1763 Act of Parliament that restricted colonial settlement west of the Appalachian Mountains. The Proclamation Line sparked protests from rich and poor colonists alike.

Proclamation of Amnesty and Reconstruction 1863 proclamation that established the basic parameters of President Abraham Lincoln's approach to Reconstruction. Lincoln's plan would have readmitted the South to the Union on relatively lenient terms.

proprietary colonies Colonies granted to individuals, rather than held directly by the crown or given to chartered companies. Proprietors of such colonies, such as William Penn of Pennsylvania, had considerable leeway to distribute land and govern as they pleased.

Protestantism Religious movement initiated in the early sixteenth century that resulted in a permanent division within European Christianity. Protestants differed with Catholics over the nature of salvation, the role of priests, and the organization of the church.

Pueblo revolt 1680 uprising of Pueblo Indians against Spanish forces in New Mexico that led to the Spaniards' temporary retreat from the area. The uprising was sparked by mistreatment and the suppression of Indian culture and religion.

Puritans Radical English Protestants who hoped to reform the Church of England. The first Puritan settlers in the Americas arrived in Massachusetts in 1630.

Redeemers White, conservative Democrats who challenged and overthrew Republican rule in the South during Reconstruction.

redemptioners Immigrants who borrowed money from shipping agents to cover the costs of transport to America, loans that were repaid, or "redeemed," by colonial employers. Redemptioners worked for their "redeemers" for a set number of years.

Regulators Local organizations formed in North and South Carolina to protest and resist unpopular policies. After first seeking redress through official institutions, Regulators went on to establish militias and other institutions of self-governance.

Renaissance The cultural and intellectual flowering that began in Italy in the fifteenth century and then spread north. The Renaissance occurred at the same time that European rulers were pushing for greater political unification of their states.

republican motherhood In the 1790s, some leaders supported women's education so that they could instruct their sons in principles of republican government.

Republican Party Party formed in 1854 that was committed to stopping the expansion of slavery and advocated economic development and internal improvements. Although their appeal was limited to the North, the Republicans quickly became a major political force.

scalawags Derisive term for white Southerners who supported Reconstruction.

Second Continental Congress Assembly of colonial representatives that served as a national government during the Revolutionary War. Despite limited formal powers, the Continental Congress coordinated the war effort and conducted negotiations with outside powers.

Second Great Awakening Evangelical revival movement that began in the South in the early nineteenth century and then spread to the North. The social and economic changes of the first half of the nineteenth century were a major spur to religious revivals, which in turn spurred social reform movements.

Second Party System When the Whig Party formed in 1834, they posed the first significant challenge to Democratic Party control in two decades.

Second Seminole War 1835–1842 war between the Seminoles, including fugitive slaves who had joined the tribe, and the U.S. government over whether the Seminoles would be forced to leave Florida and settle west of the Mississippi River. Despite substantial investments of men, money, and resources, it took seven years for the United States to achieve victory.

sharecropping A system that emerged as the dominant mode of agricultural production in the South in the years after the Civil War. Under the sharecropping system, sharecroppers received tools and supplies from landowners in exchange for a share of the eventual harvest.

Shays's Rebellion 1786 rebellion by western Massachusetts farmers caused primarily by economic turmoil in the aftermath of the Revolutionary War.

Sherman's March to the Sea Hard war tactics employed by General William Tecumseh Sherman to capture Atlanta and huge swaths of Georgia and the Carolinas, devastating this crucial region of the Confederacy in 1864.

siege of Vicksburg After a prolonged siege, Union troops forced Confederate forces to surrender at Vicksburg, Mississippi, leading to Union control of the rich Mississippi River valley.

slave laws A series of laws that defined slavery as a distinct status based on racial identity and which passed that status on through future generations.

Sons of Liberty Boston organization first formed to protest the Stamp Act. The Sons of Liberty spread to other colonies and played an important role in the unrest leading to the American Revolution.

spectral evidence Evidence given by spirits acting through possessed individuals. A number of the accused in the 1692 Salem witch trials were convicted on the basis of spectral evidence.

spoils system Patronage system introduced by Andrew Jackson in which federal offices were awarded on the basis of political loyalty. The system remained in place until the late nineteenth century.

Stono rebellion 1739 uprising by African and African American slaves in South Carolina. In the aftermath of the uprising, white fear of slave revolts intensified.

Sugar Act 1764 act of Parliament that imposed an import tax on sugar, coffee, wines, and other luxury items. The Sugar Act sparked colonial protests that would escalate over time as new revenue measures were enacted.

Tariff of Abominations White Southerners' name for the 1828 Congressional tariff act that benefited northern manufacturers and merchants at the expense of agriculture, especially southern plantations.

Tejanos Mexican residents of Texas. Although some Tejano elites allied themselves with American settlers, most American settlers resisted the adoption of Tejano culture.

temperance The movement to moderate and then ban the sale and consumption of alcohol. The American temperance movement emerged in the early nineteenth century as part of the larger push for improving society from the 1820s to the 1850s.

Tenure of Office Act Law passed by Congress in 1867 to prevent President Andrew Johnson from removing cabinet members sympathetic to the Republican Party's approach to congressional Reconstruction without Senate approval. Johnson was impeached, but not convicted, for violating the act.

Thirteenth Amendment Amendment to the Constitution abolishing slavery. The Thirteenth Amendment was passed in January 1865 and sent to the states for ratification.

three-fifths compromise Compromise between northern and southern delegates to the 1787 Constitutional Convention to count enslaved persons as three-fifths of a free person in apportioning representation in the House of Representatives and taxation by the federal government.

Townshend Act 1767 act of Parliament that instituted an import tax on a range of items including glass, lead, paint, paper, and tea. The Townshend Act prompted a boycott of British goods and contributed to violence between British soldiers and colonists.

Trail of Tears The forced march of some 15,000 Cherokees from Georgia to Indian Territory. Inadequate planning, food, water, sanitation, and medicine led to the deaths of thousands of Cherokees.

transcendentalism A movement founded by Ralph Waldo Emerson in the 1830s that proposed that individuals look inside themselves and to nature for spiritual and moral guidance rather than to the dogmas of formal religion. Transcendentalism attracted a number of important American writers and artists to its vision.

Treaty of Fort Stanwix 1784 treaty in which U.S. commissioners coerced Iroquois delegates into ceding vast tracts of land in western New York and the Ohio River Valley to the United States.

Treaty of Ghent Accord signed in December 1814 ending the War of 1812 and returning to U.S. and Britain the lands each controlled before the war.

Treaty of Greenville 1795 treaty signed following the Battle of Fallen Timbers through which Indians in the Northwest Territory were forced to ceded vast tracts of land to the United States.

Treaty of Guadalupe Hidalgo 1848 treaty ending the Mexican-American War. By the terms of the treaty, the United States acquired control over Texas north and east of the Rio Grande plus the

New Mexico territory, which included present-day Arizona and New Mexico and parts of Utah, Nevada, and Colorado. The treaty also ceded Alta California, which had declared itself an independent republic during the war, to the United States.

Treaty of New Echota 1836 treaty in which a group of Cherokee men agreed to exchange their land in the Southeast for money and land in Indian Territory. Despite the fact that the treaty was obtained without tribal sanction, it was approved by the U.S. Congress.

Treaty (Peace) of Paris 1783 treaty that formally ended the conflict between Britain and its North American colonies. The newly established United States gained benefits from the treaty.

Tuscarora War War launched by Tuscarora Indians from 1711 to 1715 against European settlers in North Carolina and their allies from the Yamasee, Catawba, and Cherokee nations. The Tuscaroras forfeited their lands when they signed the peace treaty and many then joined the Iroquois Confederacy to the north.

U.S. Sanitary Commission Federal organization established in June 1861 to improve and coordinate the medical care of Union soldiers. Northern women played a key role in the work of the commission.

Uncle Tom's Cabin Novel published in 1852 by Harriet Beecher Stowe. Meant to publicize the evils of slavery, the novel struck an emotional chord in the North and was an international best seller.

underground railroad A series of routes from southern plantation areas to northern free states and Canada along which abolitionist supporters, known as conductors, provided hiding places and transportation for runaway slaves seeking freedom.

utopian societies Communities formed in the first half of the nineteenth century to embody alternative social and economic visions and to create models for society at large to follow.

Valley Forge Site of Continental Army winter encampment in 1777–1778. Despite the harsh conditions, the Continental Army emerged from its encampment at Valley Forge as a more effective fighting force.

Virginia and Kentucky Resolutions Resolutions passed by legislatures in Virginia and Kentucky that declared the Alien and Sedition Acts (1798) "void and of no force" in their states.

Virginia Plan Plan put forth at the beginning of the 1787 Constitutional Convention that introduced the ideas of a strong central government, a bicameral legislature, and a system of representation based on population.

Walking Purchase 1737 treaty that allowed Pennsylvania to expand its boundaries at the expense of the Delaware Indians. The treaty, quite possibly a forgery, allowed the British to add territory that could be walked off in a day and a half.

War of the Spanish Succession 1702–1713 war over control of Spain and its colonies; also called Queen Anne's War. Although the Treaty of Utrecht that ended the war in 1713 was intended to bring peace through the establishment of a balance of power, imperial conflict continued to escalate.

Whig Party Political party formed in the 1830s to challenge the power of the Democratic Party. The Whigs attempted to forge a diverse coalition from around the country by promoting commercial interests and moral reforms.

Whiskey Rebellion Uprising by western Pennsylvania farmers who led protests against the excise tax on whiskey in the early 1790s.

white supremacy An ideology promoted by southern planters and intellectuals that maintained that all whites, regardless of class or education, were superior to all blacks.

Wilmot Proviso 1846 proposal by Democratic congressman David Wilmot of Pennsylvania to outlaw slavery in all territory acquired from Mexico. The proposal was defeated, but the fight over its adoption foreshadowed the sectional conflicts of the 1850s.

Women's National Loyal League Organization founded by abolitionist women during the Civil War to press Lincoln and Congress to enact universal emancipation.

XYZ affair 1798 incident in which French agents demanded bribes before meeting with American diplomatic representatives.

Yamasee War A pan-Indian war from 1715 to 1717 led by the Yamasee who intended, but failed, to oust the British from South Carolina.

yeomen farmers Southern independent landowners who did not own slaves. Although yeomen farmers had connections to the South's plantation economy, many realized that their interests were not always identical to those of the planter elite.

Index